MW01256338

ATTACHMENT IN RELIGION AND SPIRITUALITY

ATTACHMENT IN RELIGION AND SPIRITUALITY
A Wider View

Pehr Granqvist

Foreword by Phillip R. Shaver

THE GUILFORD PRESS
New York   London

Copyright © 2020 The Guilford Press
A Division of Guilford Publications, Inc.
370 Seventh Avenue, Suite 1200, New York, NY 10001
www.guilford.com

Printed in the United States of America

This book is printed on acid-free paper.

Last digit is print number: 9 8 7 6 5 4 3 2 1

Library of Congress Cataloging-in-Publication Data

Names: Granqvist, Pehr, author.
Title: Attachment in religion and spirituality : a wider view / Pehr Granqvist.
Description: New York : The Guilford Press, [2020] | Includes bibliographical
    references and index. |
Identifiers: LCCN 2019040011 | ISBN 9781462542680 (hardcover)
Subjects: LCSH: Attachment behavior. | Developmental psychology. |
    Spirituality. | Religion.
Classification: LCC BF575.A86 .G725 2020 | DDC 204/.2—dc23
LC record available at https://lccn.loc.gov/2019040011

For Emma, the White Dawn Star, and the River

About the Author

Pehr Granqvist, PhD, is Professor of Developmental Psychology at Stockholm University, Sweden. He has studied the attachment–religion connection since the mid-1990s, originally as part of his doctoral studies at Uppsala University, Sweden. His research in this area—as well as in the psychology of religion and the field of attachment more generally— is widely cited and recognized internationally. Dr. Granqvist is a recipient of the Margaret Gorman Early Career Award from Division 36 (Psychology of Religion and Spirituality) of the American Psychological Association and the Godin Prize from the International Association for the Psychology of Religion, among others. In 2018, he was a visiting scholar at the University of California, Berkeley.

Foreword

Never in my wildest dreams did I imagine, back in 1990, when then doctoral student Lee Kirkpatrick and I published a preliminary article on "attachment and religion," that we were taking the first baby steps into what has since become a huge, complex, and multinational research area. By 2005, enough work had been published on attachment and religion to allow Kirkpatrick to create a pioneering book: *Attachment, Evolution, and the Psychology of Religion*. Since then, much important new theorizing and creative research on religion has been done in psychology and related fields, inspiring Pehr Granqvist to write this important and fascinating new work, *Attachment in Religion and Spirituality: A Wider View*. Fortunately for anyone interested in attachment theory, religion, and their interconnections, the book is a gem!

It is very broad ranging (hence the subtitle's "wider view"), impressively multidisciplinary, and beautifully organized and argued. It is lucidly and gracefully written, with a pleasing mixture of careful, accurate scholarly writing; vivid, compelling case studies; quirky quotations from some of Granqvist's favorite songs; and wry, mildly self-deprecating Swedish humor. Granqvist is both appropriately, and sometimes sharply, critical of other authors and researchers, and yet at the same time generous and comprehensive in his coverage of the many different literatures related to the "attachment–religion connection."

Granqvist is uniquely qualified to write this book because of his extensive reading and training in multiple areas of psychology (cognitive, developmental, social, clinical, cultural, and evolutionary); his mastery of the two main traditions in attachment research, one stemming from Ainsworth and Main's observational and interview methods, the other stemming from questionnaire and laboratory-experimental work by personality–social psychologists; his integrative writing with Kirkpatrick on attachment and religion (e.g., in the *Handbook of Attachment*); his extension of attachment–religion research from monotheistic, institutionally organized religions (especially Christianity) to personal mysticism and "New Age" spirituality; and his familiarity with both North American and European cultures.

Religion is important to both scientists and the general public for many reasons. It is a primary source of meaning and comfort for literally billions of people; it provides convenient access to community involvement and social support for many; it is the inspiration for works of music, art, and architecture that are among human beings' most impressive and beautiful creations; it is the most common way to cope with death—one's own and that of close others. At the same time, religion has sometimes been a barrier to scientific progress (e.g., the Catholic Church's objections to Galileo's telescopic observations; fundamentalists' attempts to squelch Darwin's theory of evolution). Moreover, religion has been involved in countless bloody wars in which one group's theology and morality are perceived as threatened by the theology and morality of another group (e.g., witness today's fear, in the United States, of Islamic Sharia Law).

Although all theologies are challenged by scientific theories and data (e.g., Freud's classic *The Future of an Illusion* and Dawkins's recent *The God Delusion*), and although involvement in organized religion has been dramatically declining in both Europe and North America, religious and spiritual experiences are still extremely common and viewed as supremely important everywhere in the world. The growth of interest in various forms of spirituality suggests that the decline of organized religion does not imply a decline in interest in spiritual practices and experiences.

As scientists and as curious laypeople, many of us want to know how to explain the apparently universal tendency for humans to believe in and appeal for help to gods, spirits, and mystical forces, despite their invisibility and, to use Granqvist's term, their noncorporality. Although some authors have postulated single instinctual, neural bases of religion (e.g., a religion or faith "instinct"), it is now more common to believe that religiosity relies on several different processes and mechanisms that combine to make the existence of God or other spiritual forces seem plausible, if not obvious. Children naturally develop "mind-reading" (mentalization) skills as part of early (preschool) development. They realize that people (and animals) have motives, goals, and intentions, and they tend to apply their "theory of mind" (as researchers call it) to a variety of moving objects, such as dolls, the moon, and the wind. The ubiquity of their application of mentalization and theory of mind to various phenomena in addition to people makes it easy for them to believe that there are invisible, noncorporeal actors such as gods and ghosts behind natural phenomena. This imagination is often directed in culturally approved directions by a local religion, usually communicated to the children by parents, clergy, and neighbors.

Another factor making religious beliefs attractive to both children and adults is fear of death or serious injury. As made salient by "terror management" theorists in psychology, humans are the only animals that realize they are vulnerable to death and destruction. They are therefore eager to learn that if they follow the locally approved religious guidelines, they can attain eternal life. Cultures take advantage of this death-defying imaginative leap by shaping their members' beliefs and behavior in ways that promote social organization, community survival, and social cohesion in times of threats and war.

Although Granqvist discusses these and other underpinnings of religion, he devotes most of his attention to what John Bowlby and his theoretical successors have called the "attachment behavioral system." Humans (and other primates) are born with a natural tendency to seek protection and support from an "attachment figure" (often a parent) when they feel threatened or in need. This attachment behavior is a human universal that can be coopted for religious purposes because once a child experiences fear and relief from fear in the arms of a human attachment figure, it becomes easy to imagine that there is an even "bigger and wiser" figure, God, who can be called upon anywhere, at any time, as a safe haven and secure base. This natural process, augmented by cognitive universals such as mentalization, can be channeled ("sculpted," to use Granqvist's term) by religious socialization, and this socialization is clearly important. No one, when experiencing intense threat and fear, would specifically imagine Jehovah or Allah or Ahura Mazda, or any of humans' countless other specific gods, without cultural input. One valuable feature of Granqvist's analysis is his careful consideration of the interplay of innate and social-developmental contributions to religiosity.

One advantage of attachment theory as an approach to understanding and empirically studying religion is that, from the beginning, it has stressed both normative (general) processes (attachment to a stronger and wiser figure) and individual differences. Mary Ainsworth, Bowlby's main partner in developing and testing attachment theory, noticed systematic individual differences in both an African and an American research sample of mothers and infants and developed a way to reliably identify these differences in the laboratory. Eventually, various measures of the adult analogues of these differences were developed, one of which

Kirkpatrick and I used in our early studies of both "romantic" and religious attachment. (Granqvist has used these and other, more intensive, interview measures in his own studies, many of which are discussed in this book.)

Individual differences in religiosity and religious experiences were intuitively and brilliantly analyzed by William James in his classic book *The Varieties of Religious Experience.* Granqvist shows how James's "healthy-minded" religion relates to secure attachment, which is one of many ways that parental treatment can affect a child's later religiosity. Children who are treated sensitively and responsively by parents tend to be more cooperative with parents and more likely to comfortably accept socialization by them, including socialization into the parents' religion. In addition, secure children's image of God bears strong resemblance to their positive "internal working models" of parents. Just as attachment researchers, following Ainsworth, have identified and described insecure as well as secure attachments, James discussed forms of religiosity that were not so healthy-minded, forms associated with "sick souls" and "dark nights of the soul." Because attachment researchers had developed measures of different kinds of insecure attachment (e.g., anxious, avoidant, disorganized), it was possible for Granqvist and others to show how various forms of "unhealthy" religiosity relate to specific insecure forms of attachment. This work then allowed research on possible "compensatory" or remedial paths to more secure forms of attachment and religion.

Attachment theory places enormous weight on the concept of security in the two forms delineated by Ainsworth: *safe haven* and *secure base.* The notion of security rooted in a safe haven (providing protection from threats and stressors) fits well with the notion of God and religion (e.g., patron saints, guardian angels, sacred songs and scriptures) as a safe haven. The concept of having a "secure base for exploration" is perhaps less evident in most people's conception of God and religion, but there are many stories and hymns that stress being able to tackle difficult tasks and projects with God's almighty support.

Once the theoretical importance of "felt security" is recognized, our scientific interest is aroused in other ways that felt security might be obtained. One of the most important and unusual chapters in this book (Chapter 11) deals with the possibility that tangible sources of security provided by government welfare (e.g., education, housing, unemployment insurance, health care, child care) make religion less necessary and less attractive. Granqvist cites impressive evidence that when a society—through a welfare state—provides more sources of social and economic security, religiosity declines. This fact inspired him to conduct preliminary studies to determine whether the welfare state can serve psychologically as a safe haven and secure base in the same way that a parent, a romantic partner, or God can, and the answer appears to be no. This suggests that the human brain is constructed to expect a human or human-like attachment figure, and the place of that figure in the mind cannot be occupied by something as abstract or impersonal as a welfare state.

This line of work raises questions about how well a person and a society can prosper without organized religion, a challenge that may be in store for most Western societies. One possibility is that people who have most of their material needs securely provided by their government will seek religious or spiritual experiences, if at all, outside the bounds of traditional, especially monotheistic, religions. This seems to be the path being pursued, for example, by the many people who get involved in meditation, yoga, body work, and experimentation with psychedelic drugs. At present, these seem to be mainly forms of exploration (in the attachment-theory sense), not attachment. There are many research possibilities in the emerging field of the psychology of secularism, and Granqvist provides pioneering examples.

Another avenue for further research concerns religion at the group level (churches, denominations, synagogues, sects). In thinking about the role of in-group conformity and out-group hostility in the history of religious conflict, I realize that the attachment-theoretical approach to religion pursued by Granqvist focuses mainly on religiosity at the level of the individual, as was also the case with James's *Varieties*. This is a crucial level, of course, especially for us as individual "seekers." But it ignores the group-level processes and functions that make religion problematic when it compels strict conformity, combines religious with political imagery and language, violently attacks rival groups, and sacrifices thousands of individuals in the service of group goals during warfare.

Granqvist has done an excellent job of combining modern evolutionary, cognitive, and developmental theories and research to provide a wider view of the connections between attachment and religion, mostly at the level of individuals and families. That in itself is a huge job. But we are left needing an integration of Granqvist's many insights with an analysis of religion at the group level. Perhaps Granqvist will turn his considerable talents to that task next. I hope so. Meanwhile, I congratulate him on this brilliant study of attachment and religion. The book is destined to become a classic.

PHILLIP R. SHAVER, PHD

Acknowledgments

In a just world, every author would have an editor like Phillip Shaver—skilled, wise, direct, efficient, knowledgeable, and unbelievably perseverant. Apart from text editing, Phil guided me throughout the thick and thin of writing, helped me aspire higher when inspiration was dissipating, picked me up out of unnecessary holes that I had dug myself into, and taught me many additional lessons along the way. In short, his generosity has been enormous and my gratitude to him is infinite. The book would not have been nearly as good without him, and I would have had much less fun writing it. Any remaining mistakes are of course mine and mine alone.

Undying thanks to family and friends! The "all work–no play" situation associated with my work on this book surely made me unavailable and inaccessible at times. I am especially grateful to Emma, my beloved partner in crime, and our four children. Not only did you allow me to retreat into the cave—playing on my own instead of with you, and while busy life surrounded—you also came along to California for 7 months, despite the many, many practical challenges and efforts involved. The importance of the joy and support you bring to my life cannot be overestimated.

Thanks to the team at The Guilford Press for taking on this book and for working hard with its production, promotion, and distribution: Seymour Weingarten, Carolyn Graham, Paul Gordon, Carly DaSilva, Judith Grauman, Juliet Simon, and Laura Specht Patchkofsky.

Science is a highly communal undertaking, and I have been unusually fortunate with the company I keep. I am especially indebted to Lee Kirkpatrick. Lee (together with Phil Shaver) not only pioneered the attachment–religion connection as a research framework, thus providing much of the foundation for my own work, but he has also been an indispensable coauthor on several key papers covered herein. Lee and I have had some specific theoretical disagreements over the years, but we have been able to talk about them in an open and respectful manner. He has challenged me in ways that have been very fruitful, forcing me to sharpen my own thinking. On top of this, he has always generously promoted my work throughout the years. Finally, Lee graciously reviewed my initial book proposal, as did Ray Paloutzian, Ralph Hood, and an anonymous reviewer; thanks to you all! Likewise, in her capacity as PhD advisor and mentor, Berit Hagekull played a key role in enabling the research covered in this book; thank you for your support and wisdom. Also, my dear friends Mary Main and Erik Hesse have been generous beyond words throughout the years. Not only did they initially host me as a visiting PhD student in Berkeley and then mentor me as a post-doc, but they also taught me more about attachment than anyone could justifiably ask for. They provided a sunny refuge on many occasions and for many years, when the great darkness took its toll on Sweden and me in the fall and winter seasons. As if they had not done enough, they hosted me on my sabbatical as a visiting scholar at UC Berkeley, where the lion's share of this book was drafted. In addition, thanks to many other dear friends who have passed through the Bay Area throughout the years— you know who you are!

I am grateful to several additional colleagues who have worked on the attachment–religion connection with me: Andreas Birgegård, Anders Broberg, Rosalinda Cassibba & Co., Aaron Cherniak, Ward Davis & Co., Jessie Dezutter & Co., Jane Dickie, Mari Fransson, Peter Hill, Tord Ivarsson, Kristin Laurin, Mario Mikulincer & Co., Frances Nkara, Phil Shaver (again!), and many, many students. I am also indebted to a long list of additional coworkers for other strands of cooperative work covered in this book, including Anna Blomkvist, Gunilla Bohlin, Diana Cortes, Robbie Duschinsky, Liliann Döllinger, Miguel Farias, Tommie Forslund, Mats Fredrikson, Catarina Furmark, Wolfgang Friedlmeier, Kari Halstensen, Mårten Hammarlund, Dan Larhammar, Marcus Larsson, Lene Lindberg, Marco Tullio-Liuzza, Rebekah Richert, Ingela Visuri, Camilla von Below, Marinus van IJzendoorn, and the "disorganized attachment consortium," along with many others.

My gratitude to Ralph Hood, Ward Davis, and Robbie Duschinsky, who read a draft of the full book and provided many useful suggestions for improvements. Thank you also to Lars Alberyd, Etzel Cardeña, Joel Gruneau Brulin, Tommie Forslund, Frances Nkara, Marcus Larsson, and Marinus van IJzendoorn for useful feedback on selected parts and chapters.

Thanks to the multiple funders who have supported the writing of this book and associated research: Stockholm University and its sabbatical program, the John Templeton Foundation (Grant No. 51897), the Swedish Research Council, the Bank of Sweden Tercentenary Foundation, and the Sasakawa Young Leaders' Fellowship Fund.

Finally, I am grateful to those who have participated in our research over the years, especially in the in-depth interview studies. Thank you for sharing some of your most private thoughts and experiences with us and for chipping in to science! Without you, this book and its associated research could not have seen the light of day.

Contents

Prologue

Setting the Stage

"**W**hy do you study religion and spirituality?" I have been asked this question about my research more frequently than any other. It has been posed to me by friend and foe alike, especially by my fellow psychology colleagues. The honest answer, which I incidentally never divulge, is that I have experienced a personal longing for and occasionally even a sense of connection with something I cannot articulate. Furthermore, I strongly suspect that the same applies to many other individuals and that this longing and sense of connection are key psychological underpinnings of religion and spirituality. In fact, understanding why humans are so disposed has the potential to yield profound insight into human nature.

The sheer frequency of the question—why study religion and spirituality?—initially puzzled me, but it just kept coming. Shying away from personal confession (which is somewhat frowned upon among us Swedes), I usually answer it defensively—Is it not obvious why religion and spirituality are of key interest to psychological science?—and I then move on to give scientific answers. First, religion and spirituality are cross-cultural and historical *universals,* present in all cultures and historical periods studied (e.g., Brown, 1991). Second, they are *unique* to our species; despite being functionally similar to us in so many ways, both genetically and behaviorally, other primates and animals do not display the characteristic behavioral and (as far as we know) cognitive attributes that serve as foundations for religion and spirituality. Third, religion and spirituality concern something *unobservable* (god[s], spirits). Fourth, in spite of—or perhaps because of—their unobservable nature, gods and spirits are nonetheless of central *importance* to cultures, societies, and individuals. Finally, this is especially so in times of *crisis*. No wonder then that anthropologists, sociologists, and historians have always had a natural interest in humans' religious and spiritual experiences and expressions, across different cultures, societies, and historical periods.

One might think that religion and spirituality would also be a primary topic for research psychologists, but this has not always been the case. During the period between 1940 and the 1990s, research psychologists and psychology departments exhibited a peculiar disinterest in religion and spirituality. And these topics still lie outside the psychological mainstream. Indeed, the psychology of religion and spirituality has been viewed as a fringe field, garnering almost no academic positions and very limited research funding opportunities. As a consequence, wide intellectual terrains have remained open for anyone willing to explore them, with the potential for making important and original contributions.

In fact, so marked has psychologists' disinterest in religion been that their most prestigious and long-standing organization—the American Psychological Association—felt compelled to issue a critical resolution concerning psychology's bias against religion, including the psychological study of it (American Psychological Association Council of Representatives, 2007). This bias has made most research psychologists deaf and blind to the many fascinating and socially relevant aspects of religion. One goal of this book is to open psychologists' eyes and ears to issues related to religion and spirituality and move those topics further into the psychological mainstream, where they belong. I return, in the Epilogue, to the stumbling blocks that I hope this book helps to remove.

THE PENDULUM SWINGS—AND THEN SWINGS AGAIN

In startling contrast to decades' neglect of religion and spirituality in psychology, the key pioneers of psychology—Wilhelm Wundt, William James, Stanley Hall, Sigmund Freud, and Carl Gustav Jung, among many others—were profoundly interested in the psychological study of religion and spirituality. The early interest in religion waned for half a century or so during the reigns of behaviorism and the subsequent "cognitive revolution" in psychology. Beliefs and subjective experiences had fallen out of favor in psychology, and with them went much of religion and spirituality (e.g., Paloutzian & Park, 2013).

In my view, the bias against religion and spirituality during much of the 20th century is quite understandable for other, more specific reasons. During those decades, psychologists of religion were somewhat obsessed with what has been described as a "measurement paradigm" (e.g., Gorsuch, 1984; Hill, 2005). This emphasis on measurement came at the expense of both rigorous theory development and "thick descriptions" of religious thought, experience, and behavior. Moreover, psychologists of religion typically created self-report measures, at the expense of other modes of assessment, to tap what they viewed as healthy, moral, and humanitarian forms of religiousness. This yielded an unfortunate form of psychological apologetics—or a psychology *by* religion (Batson, 1997)—which may help to explain why studying religion or spirituality sometimes came to be perceived as synonymous with being religious or spiritual. (It seems likely that many of the researchers who persisted with research on religion were fairly religious themselves.)

Following these less productive decades for the psychology of religion, religion and spirituality are now again becoming more legitimate topics of study (Paloutzian & Park, 2013). For example, the American Psychological Association has established a new journal devoted to the topic (*The Psychology of Religion and Spirituality,* established in 2012); religion and spirituality are increasingly covered in general psychology textbooks; funding options have become more widely available (partly due to the John Templeton Foundation); and substantial theoretical and methodological advancements have been made in the psychology of religion. I discuss these developments throughout this book.

MORE ABOUT THIS BOOK

The primary aim of this book is to examine the ways in which aspects of religion and spirituality are linked to emotional attachment processes and close relationships. My approach is heavily influenced by John Bowlby's (1969/1982) attachment theory and the enormous amount of research it has generated in developmental, social, and clinical psychology (reviewed extensively in Cassidy & Shaver, 2016). The religion-as-attachment research presented here is one approach (among others) that is helping to pull the study of religion and spirituality back into mainstream psychology. Still, much of the frontline psychological study of religion is performed in the outskirts of psychological science—particularly in cognitive and evolutionary science. A major aim of this book is to demonstrate the utility of approaching religion and spirituality from the perspective of a mainstream theory in developmental, social, and clinical psychology. This book educates readers who are not yet familiar with attachment theory and the attachment-theoretical approach to religion and spirituality. In addition, it greatly benefits attachment researchers and clinicians who apply attachment theory and research, especially those who have not kept up with the large body of research and theorizing that not only applies insights from previous attachment research to religion and spirituality but that also contributes to attachment theory itself.

The central concepts in this book are "attachment," "religion," "spirituality," and "a wider view." I introduce the concept of attachment in some detail in the next chapter. I do not attempt to provide precise definitions of "religion" and "spirituality," for reasons that will become increasingly apparent to readers as they proceed through the book. Suffice to say here that the etymological root of religion ("being bound") is almost synonymous with the core of what attachment entails (i.e., an "affectional bond"). However, in practice, religion is often understood as a collective, organized enterprise comprising many different facets of being bound, and not just to God but also to a particular group (a religious community) and a set of traditions (beliefs, norms, rituals). It is in this sense that I use the term "religion" in this book. In contrast, I use "spirituality" as a related but narrower term, referring to the experiential components that "bind" a particular individual to what is perceived as sacred or transcendent—often, but by no means always a deity, or deities. Furthermore, I assign equal weight to understanding religion (i.e., collective and organized components) and spirituality (i.e., private, experiential components).

One reason for my refusal to give fixed, formal definitions of religion and spirituality is that neither religion nor spirituality is a natural kind, or an inherent property of nature, unlike, say, molecules in chemistry, viruses in medicine, or species in biology. In fact, natural kinds are difficult enough to define, at least in classical terms of necessary and sufficient conditions (i.e., essentialism in philosophy). Although the human mind appears naturally predisposed to produce what may be described as religious and spiritual "output," I will argue that the particularities that make us label such output "religious" and "spiritual" are by no means inevitable products of the human mind. That religion and spirituality are not natural kinds is important because it means that any attempt to draw a tight boundary around them through formal definitions is to some extent arbitrary and thus doomed to fail. Better, then, to have a pragmatic and provisional point of departure.

Regarding the demarcation of religion and spirituality from what would appear as their closest conceptual opposite—"the secular"— religion and spirituality typically center on some metaphysical unobservable (i.e., gods, spirits), whereas "the secular" supposedly does not.

However, on closer examination, such a distinction is more apparent than real, and it may be restricted largely to content (e.g., God vs. not) rather than functional considerations. This is because much of communal life, deriving from humans' unique capacity for cooperation organized around abstract, symbolic ideas, involves concepts such as ideologies, values, corporations, and social contracts, which in some ways are not much different from religious concepts. Indeed, Harari (2014) refers to them all as "fictions" or "mythologies." Rather than making firm demarcations from the secular by means of unobservable, symbolic, or abstract referents, throughout this book I argue that psychological processes that apply to religion and spirituality also tend to apply to many of the things we usually consider secular. Thus, it may be more than a historical coincidence that, ironically, the very notion of "the secular" is an inherently Christian idea (e.g., Taylor, 2007).

As for "a wider view," this book tackles both normative (species-typical) processes (Part I, Chapters 1–3) and individual differences (Part II, Chapters 4–6). And it does so with reference both to the general, normal population and to clinical populations (Parts II and III, Chapters 6–9). Similarly, in addition to reviewing group-level (general, nomothetic) psychological research, I include clinical case studies (the idiographic approach), which have not been previously presented (Chapters 5, 6, and 8). I also explore how the conception of religion/spirituality as attachment converges with and diverges from other influential concepts and theories in the psychological science of religion (Part IV, Chapters 9 and 10).

On the whole, I cast a wider net regarding connections between attachment and religion/spirituality than that proposed in a previous book published by The Guilford Press (Kirkpatrick, 2005). Kirkpatrick argued that the attachment–religion connection should be understood within a larger, specific kind of evolutionary psychological framework. In so doing, he drew heavily on a reinterpretation of attachment as a reproductive (rather than survival) strategy. As an integral part of his evolutionary psychological approach (emphasizing domain specificity and gene-level selection), he expressed discontent with what he viewed as "tabula rasa" ideas, such as social and cultural learning processes being involved in the attachment–religion connection.

In contrast, in this book I do not stand on the shoulders of a single kind of evolutionary psychology. Instead, I stand on the shoulders of a variety of evolutionary perspectives, including ethology, "evo devo" biology, gene–culture coevolution, cultural evolution, behavioral ecology, and even (modern-day) sociobiology. Thus, I argue in favor of fewer restrictions in our understanding of evolution and attachment, and of how evolution and attachment are expressed in the context of religion and spirituality. For example, I delineate an understanding of what Bowlby (1969/1982) called the attachment behavioral system as a system that is open to "calibrating" feedback, not just pertaining to a caregiver's responses to oneself, but also to more general cultural and social learning. In addition, I examine attachment not just in relation to beliefs in a personal God (i.e., theistic religion), but also in relation to nontheistic expressions of spirituality, such as New Age spirituality and mystical experiences (Chapter 8), and strands of Buddhism (Chapter 2). Similarly, I investigate not only how attachment is expressed in religion/ spirituality, but also how aspects of culture and related social learning processes—in part via their influences on attachment—may shape our ways of expressing religion and spirituality, especially after the early years of life (see especially Chapters 3 and 11).

In so doing, I attend not only to attachment-related cultural expressions of religion and spirituality, but also to what we usually term "secularism." With large parts of contemporary Western Europe as a case in point, I argue that national welfare systems, which constitute the core of many European societies, have paved the way for people's largely "secular" outlooks on life, and I explore the implications of this cultural transition for adult attachment more generally. Thus, literatures in the fields of political science and international economics are brought to the psychology of religion and spirituality (Part V, Chapter 11).

In choosing overarching frameworks that hold these conceptual pieces together, I depart from a general nature–nurture interaction model to understand human development, in which underspecified genetic predispositions (i.e., nature) are understood to be co-sculpted by the environment (i.e., nurture). I also draw on Bronfenbrenner's (1979; Bronfenbrenner & Ceci, 1994) bioecological systems perspective, highlighting the need to consider how the developing person is affected not just by the microsystem (e.g., genes and the proximal calibration of the attachment system in close family relationships) but also by the macrosystem (culture, society). In fact, in this book I argue that parameters of the macrosystem ultimately contribute to shaping the expression of attachment, again especially after the early years of life (Chapters 3 and 11). In some contexts, this system may produce religious/spiritual outcomes with great frequency, but in others it will more often produce what we usually view as secular outcomes.

GUIDING PRINCIPLES

There are a few underlying principles of central importance for the arguments in this book. These principles are often latent, hidden behind the explicit text but actually central to my analysis. These principles deserve to be explicitly mentioned here, at the outset.

Interactionism

Nature–nurture interaction is pivotal for understanding human development in general and religious and spiritual development in particular. Thus, we should not ask whether genes (including genetic predispositions) or environments (including culture) shape religious and spiritual development, let alone how much genes or environments account for variation in religiosity and spirituality. Both genes and environments contribute, of course, but it is important to realize that they do not exert additive influences. Hence, it's not as though nature produces our brains/ minds, and then culture just provides the religious content (cf. Kelemen, 2004). Human development is much more intricate. As elaborated elsewhere (Granqvist & Nkara, 2017), the nature–nurture interaction framework employed in this book should not be understood as "nature + nurture," where core cognitions (or intuitive ontologies) are understood as "naturally" unfolding according to some preset developmental plan, independently of experience, and then cultural/social learning merely fills in the content details (e.g., God vs. not, Christ vs. Krishna). Rather, I hold that relational and observational experience co-sculpts our core cognitive *dispositions* from the very onset of development in a truly interactive fashion (thus, "nature × nurture"). As an analogy,[1] development can be said to result in very different kinds of sculptures, reflecting the particular interactions that have taken place between clay (nature) and sculptor (nurture). Development is not, however, analogous to the unfolding (triggered by nurture) of a piece of ready-made cloth (nature). As illustrated in much "evo devo" biology research on embryonic and brain development, genes considerably underspecify the development even of very basic systems, relying on context to sculpt them into networks that are functional in the local environments facing the developing organism. Hence, in this book we are concerned with how our genetic predispositions (most notably the attachment system) are sculpted by our environments to produce certain religious and spiritual, as well as secular, developmental outcomes.

Relationalism

The human mind is inherently relational. Not only is it fundamentally sculpted by relational experiences, but it also—and almost unceasingly—keeps searching for relational partners, and it does so even when none appears to be visibly (audibly, olfactorily, etc.) present. The human mind is particularly prone to "invent" relational partners in situations of marked need, whether the need in a specific situation is of a largely cognitive or affective nature. In fact, and as is often highlighted in cognitive science, so relational is the human mind that it has a strong proclivity to relate to nature (the moon, the wind), artifacts (such as robots), and unobservables as though they had human-like properties, a phenomenon known as "anthropomorphism" (e.g., Epley, Waytz, & Cacioppo, 2007; see also Bartz, Tchalova, & Fenerci, 2016). In other words, the relational partners sought by the mind are assumed to have agency, intentions, and other human mental properties.

Domain-General and Abstract Thought

Accounts of the human mind in much of evolutionary and cognitive science have favored "modular" or "domain-specific" approaches. In these approaches, the mind is not an all-purpose information processor, but contains specialized psychological mechanisms designed to solve recurrent adaptive problems (e.g., Tooby & Cosmides, 1990). Yet there should be no doubt that the human mind also has features and modes of information processing that are common across modules and evolutionary domains. Thus, although we may be inclined to rapidly process stimuli (such as snakes and spiders) that have conceivably been directly associated with survival and reproduction, with some effort we can also process stimuli that have presumably been less directly associated with survival and reproduction in ancestral environments (such as random strings of digits).

To fully understand the defining elements of religion and spirituality, it is necessary to give due attention to one such domain-general feature of the human mind, namely, its capacity to engage in abstract thought. Even unobservables may be real. For example, human children often spontaneously engage with what adults call "imaginary companions." For the most part, children also realize that imaginary companions are fictional playmates, but some children in some contexts treat these companions as if they were "real" (see Chapters 1 and 3).

Notably, from combining the themes of relationalism, anthropomorphism, and our capacity for abstract thought, religion/spirituality might seem to be an almost inevitable product of the human mind. Not surprisingly, therefore, in recent decades many scholars have emphasized the cognitive "naturalness" of religion, just as previous generations of intellectuals spoke of "Homo religiosus"—of humans as inherently religious and spiritual. As intuitively appealing as these "religion-as-natural" conclusions may be, at least for scholars residing in contexts where religion and spirituality are culturally normative, I argue that they are nonetheless flawed. In keeping with the nature–nurture interactionist framework adopted in this book, I believe that certain contextual conditions (nurture) are also required for the underlying systems of the mind to develop in such a way as to produce religious and spiritual "output." In much of this book, I examine what those contextual conditions are and how they may sculpt our evolved psychological systems into producing certain religious, spiritual, and secular output.

Methodological Pluralism

Open minds learn more rigorously from their surroundings than do closed minds. As in child development, so in science. Perhaps that is in part because open minds implicitly embrace methodological pluralism. They operate with a variety of nondefensive strategies and undistorted curiosity to explore their surroundings. Open minds manipulate physical objects, observe their natural properties—by touching, smelling, looking, and tasting them—and discern how those objects interact with other features of the environment. Open minds are hesitant to pass judgment; they first seek to grasp, predict, and explain.

Any topic in science may be approached from different angles and via differing methodologies. This is the case even when the overarching framework (e.g., attachment theory) is the same. If the resultant knowledge converges, we can have stronger confidence in its robustness and generality. If it does not converge, we are forced to make distinctions and revisions, which then open up the field to new endeavors and serve important heuristic functions for science in the future.

This book reflects a strong advocacy for methodological pluralism, a position that should be understood as paying tribute to William James (1902), but also to Bowlby (see Chapter 1). Although certain methodologies, most notably the experimental method, have a privileged position in much of psychological science—largely because of its capacity to tease apart cause–effect relations and to rule out extraneous influences—no one particular methodology is or should be regarded as the be-all and end-all of psychological science. One of the reasons why psychological science is so vibrant is that it encompasses the full academic range of approaches: from the natural sciences, via the social sciences, to the humanities; from the reductive to the holistic; from the quantitative to the qualitative; from the nomothetic to the idiographic; from the explanatory, via the exploratory, to the emancipatory; from the objective to the subjective; from the cultural, via the societal, to the individual; from the individual, via evolved systems, to genes and biochemistry; and so on. In this book, I try to do justice to all of these approaches, insofar as they have a bearing on the attachment–religion connection.

The attachment–religion research that my colleagues and I have conducted and that is covered in this book has involved diverse age groups (children, adolescents, young to middle-aged adults, elders) and research designs (cross-sectional, longitudinal, experimental, quasi-experimental, case studies). We have studied samples drawn from a variety of nations (e.g., Sweden, the United States, Israel, Italy), religious/spiritual denominations (e.g., Lutherans, Pentecostals, New Agers, Baptists, devout Catholics, Orthodox Jews), and secular contexts (Sweden). And we have used very different kinds of data collection methods (e.g., qualitative/open participant descriptions, standardized questionnaires, coded semistructured interviews, semiprojective tests, lexical decision tasks, and other implicit tasks). Readers who prefer one approach—*the* approach—may find that one represented somewhere in this book. But readers who are willing to digest a plurality of approaches will be more amply rewarded.

Ontological Agnosticism

I wish it went without saying, but as it doesn't, so here it comes: No argument made in this book should be interpreted as implying that God or other religious/spiritual entities exist in the real world of events, or that they do *not* exist in the real world of events. In other words, the intellectual undertaking that we have ahead of us does not lend itself to ontological inferences regarding the actual existence of deities; deities are not embraced, nor are they ruled out (or "reduced"). Readers looking for advice on God's existence may want to seek out some other book. The author of the book in your hands simply has no clue.

PART I

NORMATIVE ASPECTS OF ATTACHMENT, RELIGION, AND SPIRITUALITY

Attachment theory and research form an unusual research program in the psychological sciences by focusing *both* on species-typical processes (or "normative" attachment considerations) and on individual differences (in attachment organization). The attachment framework accommodates both in an apparently seamless fashion. To use experimental terminology, attachment theory speaks both to main effects (normative considerations) and to moderators (individual differences). That the theory accounts for both commonalities and variations among humans may be one important reason why it has withstood the test of time, as it has for more than half a century. Indeed, attachment theory has emerged and maintained the role of a leading relationship-oriented framework within large areas of the psychological sciences, including the developmental, social, personality, clinical, and biological subfields of psychology.

Naturally, religion and spirituality are also species-typical phenomena—again, humanity is supposedly "Homo religiosus"—that simultaneously contain marked variations within the human species. Such variations are present among individuals, societies, cultures, and historical periods. It follows that a deep psychological analysis of religion and spirituality should be informative concerning both the commonalities and the variations observed in their occurrences. I argue that the attachment framework, unlike almost all other frameworks offered in the psychological sciences, is well suited to accomplish this double feat.

In this first part of the book (comprising Chapters 1–3), I deal with the species-typical (normative) components of attachment (Chapter 1) and the attachment–religion/spirituality connection (Chapter 2). In the third and final chapter, I examine why and how the attachment–religion/spirituality connection characteristically emerges and transforms over the course of human development (i.e., in ontogeny). In this first part of the book, I largely cast a blind eye on individual differences as well as other sources of variation (such as cultural, societal, and historical) both in attachment and in the attachment–religion/spirituality connection. Individual differences are the topic of the next major part of the book, Part II. The last parts of the book deal with cultural, societal, and historical sources of variation (see especially Part V). In other words, our intellectual journey will move from foundational commonalities to important particulars.

CHAPTER 1

Normative Features of Attachment

This chapter is divided into five main sections. In the first, the historical development of attachment theory is described. Second, the theory's principal concepts are defined and its evolutionary and psychobiological assumptions are delineated. In that second section, I also revisit and reevaluate the central assumptions of attachment theory in light of contemporary evolutionary considerations. The third main section delineates the basic representational aspects and associated psychological defenses addressed in the theory. In the fourth section, I examine, developmentally, how the attachment system matures during the first years of life. Fifth and finally, the notion of surrogate attachment "figures"—which most attachment scholars have overlooked to date—is briefly examined in light of a developmental perspective.

THE HISTORICAL DEVELOPMENT OF ATTACHMENT THEORY

John Bowlby (1907–1990), a British child psychiatrist and psychoanalyst, was the founding father of attachment theory. Like so many developments in the history of science, attachment theory was spawned by certain practical needs. Most notably, in the post–World War II era, there was a great need to understand what effects the loss of and separation from caregivers had on child development. Bowlby was determined to find a valid conceptual framework suitable to respond to those needs. Since no such platform existed at the time—at least not in Bowlby's view—he had to develop one himself. To accomplish this, he set out upon a wide intellectually exploratory path. Attachment theory is the product of Bowlby's creative integration of such diverse fields as ethology, psychoanalysis, cybernetics, and cognitive science (for an excellent scholarly source on the historical development of attachment theory, see Duschinsky, 2020).

Based on his clinical work as a child psychiatrist, Bowlby published an early paper ("Forty-Four Juvenile Thieves," 1944) in which he argued that losses of and repeated separations from caregivers in childhood were etiologically significant background factors leading these juvenile thieves to develop their characteristically "affectionless characters" and antisocial behavior problems. This assumption was based on noticing that separations and losses were substantially overrepresented in this particular clinical group compared to the other clinical groups available to Bowlby.

Bowlby's early conclusions about the adverse effects of disrupted relationships with caregivers received additional nourishment from some of Anna Freud and Dorothy Burlingham's (1943) findings. They learned that children who remained in the bomb shelters with their caregivers while London was being bombed during World War II fared much better than children who were separated from their caregivers and sent to families in the more peaceful British countryside. The conclusion seemed clear: Separations speak even louder than bombs in child development.

Some years later, the World Health Organization asked Bowlby to compile available knowledge on homeless children and on how their situations could be improved. That work resulted in Bowlby's book, *Maternal Care and Mental Health* (1951; later released as *Child Care and the Growth of Love,* 1953). In this book, Bowlby continued to argue for the vital importance of unbroken affectional bonds for healthy child development. His report was translated into many languages and was distributed in more copies than any prior World Health Organization report. Bowlby had gained fame.

An important reason why Bowlby's message was so widely spread was that children's experiences of separation were common at the time throughout much of the Western world. Apart from war-related separations, children were being sent to institutional care because of (alleged) maltreatment in their original homes; children were sent to boarding schools to attain proper education, while their parents could work unlimited hours; and children were separated from their parents in conjunction with hospital stays—caregivers weren't allowed at the hospitals out of fear that viruses would spread.

To extend the largely clinical and anecdotal sources of evidence for the adverse effects of separation and loss, Bowlby initiated a systematic empirical study of children's reactions to separation, conducted in hospitals and institutions. Together with two social workers—a husband and wife named James and Joyce Robertson—Bowlby filmed 1- to 4-year-old children's reactions to those separations (see Robertson, 1963). Some of the films, most notably *John, 17 Months,* became immediate classics, presumably because of the children's dramatic reactions to separation.

This study, more than any other source, inspired Bowlby to delineate his famous separation phases—the sequence of *protest* (anxiety, searching, hypervigilance, refusal to be soothed by substitutes) and *despair* (depression, lethargy, disturbed eating and sleeping patterns), ultimately giving way to *detachment* (a defensive "shutting-down" of attachment behaviors). Although detachment may be greeted as welcome (e.g., by child nurses or boarding school staff), because the child then starts accepting care and consolation from others, it is highly defensive. When the child is reunited with his or her attachment figures, he or she typically ignores or rebuffs them and often protests against bids for closeness with them. Genuine *reorganization* requires that the defenses underlying detachment have been relaxed and it usually takes considerable time; the child has then mourned sufficiently and can develop new attachments without defensive interference. As a response to this work, the routines for hospital and extraparental care changed dramatically throughout the Western world from the late 1950s onward. For example, separations came to be avoided as part of normal hospital care. Also, placement of children in large institutions was avoided by means of supportive social work in the child's original families (see Granqvist, 2016b, for indications that such work is regrettably being reduced or eliminated at present). When supportive work failed, children were instead placed in foster care or in adoptive families where new attachment bonds could develop.

In hindsight, it is tempting to ask why mental health and child experts sanctioned children's repeated and prolonged separations from caregivers in the first place. The answer is simple: Informed by influential behaviorist learning principles and psychoanalytic drive theories, the child's emotional bond to its primary caregiver was widely believed to be merely secondary in importance to nutrition. The mother, and in particular her breast, was believed to be a conditioned stimulus (classical behaviorism) or source of drive gratification (psychoanalysis); alternately, nutrition was viewed as a primary reinforcer of clinging (radical behaviorism) (e.g., Sears, Maccoby, & Levin, 1957/1976). In any event, as long as the child got nutrition and physical care from someone—anyone—he or she was widely believed to suffer no serious harm from maternal separation. It is safe to conclude that these "secondary drive" ideas provided an exceptionally poor fit with the data.

Harry Harlow's (e.g., 1958) research similarly threw the secondary drive ideas overboard based on a different primate species, rhesus monkeys. His studies clearly showed that infant monkeys separated from their mothers soon after birth preferentially clung to and sought protection from surrogate wire mothers who displayed certain species-typical traits (e.g., a certain temperature, soft cloth covering, monkey-like face) rather than from surrogate wire mothers who did not display those traits but who nevertheless provided the infants' nutrition. So strong were the rhesus infants' preferences for the more species-typical surrogate mothers that the infants continued to cling to them even when the surrogate mothers subjected the infants to physical abuse (e.g., metal prods intermittently punching the infants while they were clinging).[1] This latter observation, along with many findings from naturalistic research on humans and other animals, indicates that "attachment" behavior is very difficult to extinguish, again demonstrating that behaviorist learning theory provides a poor fit with the data. It is no wonder, then, that Bowlby felt compelled to develop a theory of his own that could provide a more valid explanation for why affectional bonds develop and endure. Based on his emerging attachment theory, Bowlby argued that it was logical for infants to display attachment behaviors even to abusive caregivers. As we shall see, if the function of the attachment behavioral system is protection of the infant, via seeking and maintaining proximity to caregiver(s), particularly in situations signaling potential danger, infants should "instinctually" seek proximity when frightened.

Though a form of rapprochement between psychoanalysis and attachment theory has since taken place (see Chapter 9), psychoanalysts of his time treated Bowlby as nothing short of heretical. Indeed, even though Bowlby sought to reform psychoanalysis from within, he was virtually expelled from the psychoanalytic community, but he nonetheless remained a (passive) member of the British Psychoanalytic Association until his death (e.g., Karen, 1994). Not only was Bowlby criticized for overestimating the importance of separation at the expense of other psychoanalytic ideas, but he disputed the validity of the foundational drive theory itself and replaced it with what appeared to his psychoanalytic colleagues to be overly mechanical principles from control system theories, which had been developed in distant disciplines such as engineering and ethology.

To find an alternative explanation to those provided by secondary drive theories, Bowlby invited researchers and theorists from a number of different sciences (e.g., ethology, psychiatry, cognitive psychology, sociology, social anthropology) to a series of seminars in London (at the Tavistock) that continued for years and had a profound influence on the development of attachment theory. Ethologist Robert Hinde, who developed control systems principles for understanding animal behavior (see, e.g., 1966), was particularly important for Bowlby's thinking (and vice versa). They had been personal friends since the 1950s.

Influenced and supported by Bowlby, Hinde shifted his own research interest toward mother–infant interactions in rhesus monkeys. Hinde's naturalistic research indicated that infant rhesus monkeys showed a pattern of behaviors in relation to their mothers that was highly similar to that shown by human infants (van der Horst, van der Veer, & van IJzendoorn, 2007). Bowlby became increasingly convinced of the great potential of explaining human attachment behaviors using evolutionary and ethological theory. Not only was ethology concerned with the development of close social bonds between animal offspring and their parents, but it was firmly anchored in the usage of empirically grounded methods, such as naturalistic observations, which fit with Bowlby's scientific ideals.

Another researcher who had a profound influence on the development of attachment theory was Mary Ainsworth. In her book *Infancy in Uganda* (Ainsworth, 1967), she provided the first systematic naturalistic observations of attachment behaviors in human infants based on Bowlby's emerging theory. She also contributed central theoretical concepts such as *secure base* and *maternal sensitivity*. Last but not least, she designed the *Strange Situation* procedure (Ainsworth & Bell, 1970; Ainsworth, Blehar, Waters, & Wall, 1978), which thenceforward became the gold standard among infant–attachment assessment methods. That contribution also extended the theory into a consideration of dyadic, and eventually individual, differences in attachment organization (see Chapter 4).

Bowlby formally presented attachment theory in a three-volume book, *Attachment and Loss* (1969/1982, 1973, 1980). Toward the end of his life, he came full circle with a book (1988) on the clinical and therapeutic implications of the theory (discussed here in Chapter 7). As a testimony to his methodological pluralism, Bowlby's very last book— released posthumously—was a psychobiography of an intellectual hero, Charles Darwin (Bowlby, 1992).

CENTRAL CONCEPTS AND ASSUMPTIONS OF ATTACHMENT THEORY

This section concerns the evolutionary foundations of the attachment system and its functions (see Forslund & Granqvist, 2016b). Bowlby understood the phenomenon of attachment in terms of a primary motivational system—the *attachment behavioral system*—and not as secondary to any other processes, such as psychical energies or the caregiver's provision of nourishment. Universally, human infants form strong emotional bonds—*attachments*—to their caregivers (i.e., *attachment figures*). Children who have formed attachments protest separations from, mourn losses of, and seek to obtain or maintain proximity to their attachment figures. They do so by means of *attachment behaviors*— any behavior designed to obtain/maintain proximity to the attachment figure. Such behaviors include positive (e.g., smiling, vocalizing) and aversive (e.g., crying, screaming) signaling behaviors as well as directed actions such as approach and reaching.

Children's proximity seeking is particularly evident in situations that provide natural clues to danger, when the attachment figure functions as a *safe haven* for the child. However, infants and young children monitor their attachment figure's whereabouts even in the absence of threat signals, using the attachment figure as a reference point, or a *secure base*, for exploration of the environment. When the child uses the attachment figure in these ways, it is important to note that he or she implicitly assesses the attachment figure as *stronger and wiser* than the self. Thus, there is an asymmetry embedded in attachment relationships; the perceptibly weaker and less knowledgeable participant "attaches," whereas the perceptibly stronger and more knowledgeable participant provides care. Hence—and common misconceptions to the contrary—caregivers do not, in terms of this theory, develop attachments to their infants and children (at least not until the children are much older), except in very rare and dysfunctional situations (i.e., when roles are reversed and young children care for a depressed or alcohol-addicted parent). The affectional ties that caregivers develop to their infants and young children are instead labeled, in the attachment literature, emotional or affectional *bonding*. Bonding or caregiving behaviors are instead believed to be organized by an evolved caregiving system, which complements and responds to the child's attachment system in important ways (as discussed further below).

Evolution of Behavioral Systems

Bowlby's theoretical starting point was evolutionary theory, based on Darwin's (1859) theory of natural selection. In fact, Bowlby (1969/1982, p. 172) explicitly stated that attachment theory is "a direct descendant of the theory outlined by Darwin in *The Origin of Species*." Moreover, Bowlby thought that ethology (the study of animal behavior) was the best application of Darwin's theory to behavioral systems, and he drew heavily from the ethological research available at the time. Indeed, it has been said that Bowlby was a psychoanalyst by trade but an ethologist at heart (Suomi, 1995). Besides being influenced by Hinde and Harlow, Bowlby was markedly influenced by Konrad Lorenz (e.g., 1937) and Niko Tinbergen (e.g., 1951, 1963).

Accordingly, Bowlby argued that insights into human behavioral systems may be gained from knowledge about the behavioral systems of other species and that our behavioral systems, although they may seem unique to us, should be seen as modifications of prototypes and predecessors found in other species. In Bowlby's own words (1969/1982, p. 7): "we share anatomical and physiological features with lower species, and it would be odd were we not to share none of the behavioral features that go with them."

Bowlby considered Lorenz's (1937) research on birds' *imprinting* as the first findings to seriously question the behaviorists' secondary drive hypothesis. Bird offspring, who themselves had the ability to find food and thus were not reliant on their parents for nutrition, nonetheless formed strong bonds to and followed the parent wherever it went. Hence, Bowlby reasoned that proximity to the parent must have evolved because of some function other than provision of nourishment. He therefore accepted the phenomenon of imprinting in a general sense, as implying the development of a clear preference for a specific other, a preference that develops rather quickly and during a limited phase of life (i.e., *sensitive period*), and that once formed remains relatively fixed. However, and as Bowlby (1969/1982) acknowledged, drawing conclusions about behavioral systems in humans from behavioral systems in birds is problematic, as the phylogenetic lines of birds and mammals parted company early in evolution. Therefore, Harlow's and Hinde's studies of rhesus monkeys became important for Bowlby in bridging this phylogenetic gap. Indeed, Bowlby tailored attachment theory to account not only for the behaviors shown by human infants, but also those behaviors shown by our closest evolutionary relatives (Suomi, 2008).

More specifically, Bowlby (1969/1982) argued that humans, like all other species, became endowed with behavioral systems that, once evolved, were retained because they served adaptive functions in humans' ancestral, species-typical environments, which Bowlby labeled—in the singular—as the *environment of evolutionary adaptedness (EEA)*. More specifically, individuals who became endowed with certain behavioral systems presumably had increased rates of survival (i.e., natural selection) and ultimately reproduction (i.e., sexual selection). Thus, the genes of these individuals were differentially passed on to future generations, and such behavioral systems became relatively stable characteristics of our species.

Predictable Outcomes and Functional Consequences of Behavioral Systems

Bowlby (1969/1982) used the term *predictable outcome* to denote the species-typical functional consequence of the activation of a behavioral system. Regarding activation of the attachment system, Bowlby argued that proximity to caregivers is its predictable outcome and that increased survival via protection from dangers is its functional consequence. Thus, the attachment behaviors that children show when the attachment system is triggered by internal signals (e.g., pain, illness) or external signals (e.g., predators approaching, separation from the caregiver) typically result in increasing proximity to caregivers, and proximity in turn typically promotes protection and thereby survival. Bowlby was careful to differentiate between predictable outcome and functional consequence because they do not always correspond at the individual level. In any given individual, the functional consequence (e.g., protection) may only sometimes follow from activation of a particular behavioral system (e.g., the attachment system).

In any given individual, a behavioral system becomes active, reaches a predictable outcome, and then becomes inactive, all without reference to the system's function. Bowlby (1969/1982) exemplified this sequence with infants' sucking on pacifiers, which does not result in nutrition. Another example might be sexual behaviors (e.g., oral sex, masturbation) that do not result in insemination, let alone reproduction. Regarding the attachment system, some children's proximity seeking is met by rebuff/rejection or even by potentially harmful responses (cf. Harlow's rhesus monkeys), and still proximity seeking may ensue. Bowlby therefore argued that understanding any behavioral system's function is impossible from studying only a single individual; instead, it necessitates studying a larger population.

The Environment of Evolutionary Adaptedness

In tracing the functions of behavioral systems, and the attachment system in particular, Bowlby argued that their functions must be sought in the environment in which a species has historically evolved (i.e., EEA), which has provided the pertinent selection pressures. This assumption and associated terminology was later picked up as an important guiding principle in evolutionary psychology and its emphasis on the "adapted" mind (see Laland & Brown, 2011; Tooby & Cosmides, 1990). Bowlby argued that in our species' ancestral environment, humans were living as nomads in small hunter-gatherer societies, in environments comparable to those of other large ground-living species of primates. A key threat in our ancestral environments, according to Bowlby, was the risk of falling prey to predators. Thus, a behavioral system that helped to increase and maintain proximity to expectably protective caregiver(s) should have served an important function that increased the offspring's chances of survival (and ultimately reproduction) in view of this threat.

Human neonates are indeed very vulnerable and thus dependent on their caregiver's support for an extended period of time largely unparalleled in other species. Bowlby (1969/1982, p. 143) noted that "because immature organisms are usually very vulnerable they are commonly endowed with behavioral equipment that produces behaviors specifically likely to minimize risk, e.g. behavior that maintains proximity to a parent." Thus, Bowlby argued that proximity to caregivers is the singular predictable outcome of the attachment system, as proximity to caregivers has specifically reduced the risk of predation and other dangers , via protection of the infant. In other words, Bowlby argued for a narrow definition of the functional consequence of proximity, and he explicitly argued against alternative explanations, such as proximity to caregivers also facilitating the function of learning fitness-related skills from caregivers. We return to this point later in this chapter when we revisit attachment theory from the perspective of contemporary evolutionary science.

Bowlby also offered adaptationist interpretations of the characteristic sequence of children's reactions to separation from their caregivers, referenced above. Protest, shown by aversive signaling behaviors, presumably aids in pulling the caregiver's attention back to the offspring and may prevent further separation (i.e., proximity maintenance). Evolutionarily, children left unattended in our EEA were likely more susceptible to predators. In times of despair, children's motor activity typically declines and they become quieter. Evolutionarily, this may have been an adaptive "secondary" strategy, as excess movement and loud protests could increase the risk of predation, especially when the attachment figure is not available. During detachment, infants become more receptive toward other individuals, which may facilitate the formation of new and potentially protective attachment bonds.

Furthermore, Bowlby referred to attachment behaviors as "instinctual" in a descriptive sense, pertaining to behaviors that show marked regularities within a species; are not a simple response to a stimulus but a sequence of behaviors; have had obvious adaptive value; and typically develop even when most opportunities for learning are absent. Bowlby also argued that the similarities between humans and other animals was likely due to convergent evolution since many species have shared the same EEA, including a risk of predation.

Interestingly, attachment theory, as outlined by Bowlby, has been successfully applied to ethological research on rhesus monkeys. As reviewed by Suomi (2008), infant rhesus monkeys show some patterns of relationships with their mothers that parallel the attachment patterns observed in human infants. Just as with humans, monkeys' attachment patterns depend on their caregivers' patterns of responding to infant bids for proximity and protection. Similarly, the "secure base" phenomenon (exploring the environment more confidently when in the presence of an attachment figure) has also been observed in infant rhesus monkeys. Furthermore, rhesus infants' inability to use the mother as a secure base is related to troubled socioemotional development. Not surprisingly, similar observations have been made of infant chimpanzees adopted by human caregivers (van IJzendoorn, Bard, Bakermans-Kranenburg, & Ivan, 2008). Thus, among other developments, attachment theory has come full circle, via human psychology, from the ethological animal research that inspired it back to animal research.

Nature versus Nurture and Behavioral Systems

Bowlby sought to avoid a misleading debate as to whether the attachment behavioral system was innate *or* learned—the old and dated nature *versus* nurture issue. In line with Bowlby's position, most developmental scholars no longer take that dichotomy seriously, nor its corollary of *how much* of a trait (or of variance in a trait) is explained by nature (genes) or nurture (environments), respectively. Instead, and in keeping with the nature–nurture interactionist framework adopted in this book, contemporary developmental scholars typically seek to understand how nature and nurture jointly shape development, in this case of behavioral systems (e.g., Granqvist & Nkara, 2017; Overton, 2013). Incidentally, Bowlby did the same, in advance of the field more generally.

Drawing on Hinde (1966), Bowlby thought of behavioral systems on a continuum of more or less "environmentally stable or labile," with marked environmental effects and learning most pertinent to more labile systems. Bowlby (1969/1982, p. 46) also argued that what is inherited is not an instinct per se, but a *potential to develop* certain sorts of behavioral systems, and that "the forms . . . differ in some measure according to the particular environment in which development takes place." Furthermore, Bowlby claimed that the human attachment system is a moderately stable system. The system's stability does not stem from genes alone, however, but also from the fact that its surrounding environment remains in the range of species-typical environments (cf. "experience expectancy"; Greenough, Black, & Wallace, 1987). Importantly, the species-typical environment of mammalian offspring includes caregivers who respond to infants' signals. If not for them, attachment would presumably not develop.

Indeed, Bowlby (1969/1982) argued that the attachment system is complemented by a caregiving system in adults, which makes (most) caregivers responsive to their children's signals. Thus, child attachment develops through a collaborative and synchronized process, with children being socially biased and prepared to attach to their caregivers by actively drawing their attention through signaling behaviors, and with caregivers being biased to respond to their children's signals by providing a safe haven and secure base (Simpson & Belsky, 2016). Thus, children are both active evokers *and* recipients of care.

Moderate stability implies that the attachment system can also be described as moderately labile. Although labile systems typically have a disadvantage of taking time to mature and become functional, Bowlby (1969/1982) argued that the advantage of such systems, which are highly open to learning, is that they permit modifications to suit the particular local environment. However, no system can be suited to work in all environments, and if a system is "programmed" for a particular environment, it may not work well in radically different environments. Regarding attachment, openness to learning is most notably seen in the relation between the quality of caregiving (e.g., sensitivity) that children receive and the different patterns of attachment they develop as a consequence (see Chapter 4). In sum, Bowlby's attachment theory represents a nature–nurture interaction framework. The attachment system, though designed by selection pressures in ancestral environments, is co-sculpted by the environments encountered by the developing person.

A "Control" Systems Approach to Behavioral Systems

As noted, Bowlby (1969/1982)—again inspired by Hinde (1966)—drew from control systems theory for understanding the basic structure of the attachment system. Any system serves a particular function (i.e., has an instruction/plan), a "set goal" that it is preprogrammed to achieve. Bowlby argued that the set goal of the attachment system is continuous rather than time-limited, as the task of the system is to control an ongoing relationship (i.e., continuous maintenance of spatial relations with reference to the attachment figure over time).

Apart from having a set goal, *feedback* is an important part of more complex control systems—the attachment system included—that distinguishes such systems from simpler ones, such as reflexes and fixed action patterns (which govern, e.g., nest-building among birds and the collection of pollen by bees; Bateson & Hinde, 1976). With feedback, and using machines (e.g., thermostats, guided missiles) as an analogy, Bowlby (1969/1982, p. 42) referred to processes "whereby the actual effects of performance are continuously reported back to a central regulating apparatus whereby they are compared with whatever instruction the machine was given; the machine's further action is then determined by the result of this comparison and the effects of its performance are thus brought ever closer to the initial instruction."

The attachment system's degree of activation varies depending on sensory input. In Bowlby's view, natural clues to danger (e.g., a predator approaching) provide activating signals for the attachment system, and natural clues to safety (most notably physical proximity to an attachment figure) provide terminating signals. In other words, and unlike fixed action patterns, which are often rigidly organized as chains of behaviors in a specific order, Bowlby (1969/1982) argued that complex systems like the attachment system are "goal-corrected." Such goal-corrected systems are typically organized by means of plans in plan hierarchies (in today's cognitive neuroscience, often called executive functions). Bowlby drew from Tinbergen (1951) and Miller, Galanter, and Pribram (1960) in suggesting that goal-corrected systems can make use of varying behaviors depending on situational constraints, and that they can perform behaviors in different orders. For example, following activation of the attachment system, a child can cry in one situation, approach in another, and cling to the caregiver in a third. The advantage of such systems is that the predictable outcome can be achieved by various means and in a variety of situations. In line with humans' renowned flexibility, many human behavioral systems are complex and goal-corrected, although some are simpler (e.g., reflexes; Bowlby, 1969/1982).

Bowlby also maintained that behavioral systems operate not in isolation from, but in close interaction with, one another. For example, expressions of the infant's attachment system activate the caregiver's caregiving system. Such interaction occurs not only between individuals but also within them. For example, activation of the infant's attachment system deactivates the infant's exploratory system. We return to this idea in Chapter 4.

Attachment Theory Vis-à-Vis Contemporary Evolutionary Sciences

Many of Bowlby's core ideas regarding attachment have proved sustainable. For example, there is wide consensus that attachment is a universal feature of primate species; that it may profitably be viewed as governed by an evolved and adaptive behavioral control system (i.e., the attachment system); and that this system is co-sculpted by the developing individual's relational experiences. In view of how quickly most tables turn in science, Bowlby has made an exceptionally enduring scientific contribution, especially considering the vibrant research and theory developments that have since taken place in the evolutionary sciences. Nonetheless, and as Cassidy (2016, p. 18) has recently pointed out, "because attachment theory is so firmly based in evolutionary theory, continuous revision of evolutionary theory brings with it a need to rethink some components of attachment theory." When rethinking the components of attachment theory, later developments in evolutionary science do suggest some important modifications. I argue throughout this book that a common denominator among these needed modifications—and in line with the "wider view" adopted here—is that Bowlby's evolutionary reasoning was unnecessarily narrow.

Inclusive fitness theory may now be regarded as the current superordinate theory of evolution (Simpson & Belsky, 2008), encompassing Darwin's notion of fitness according to one's own survival and reproduction, as well as Hamilton's (1964) notion of kin selection (i.e., fitness also includes successful reproduction by genetic relatives). Theories addressing specific adaptive problems (or domains) that humans have faced are placed one level below and called "middle-level theories." Today attachment theory is generally seen as one such middle-level evolutionary theory.

Based on sociobiological "gene's-eye view" reasoning, it can be argued that Bowlby's attachment theory fails to distinguish between the different genetic interests of parents and offspring (see Trivers, 1974). In Robert Trivers's view, there is an inherent genetic conflict of interest between them, which can be understood as a simple derivative of the facts that a given offspring carries merely 50% of a given parent's genes but 100% of the self's genes, and yet this offspring requires plenty of parental resources (i.e., investment) to survive and reproduce. Thus, from a given offspring's "gene's-eye view," the parents' investment should be maximized to the self, insofar as siblings and other related gene carriers merely survive and reproduce. Yet parents must distribute their limited resources across tasks and (often) multiple offspring, thus yielding the parent–offspring conflict. In contrast, in Bowlby's view, there generally was (in evolutionary history) and still is harmony between the child's attachment system and the caregiver's caregiving system insofar as these systems share the same predictable outcome and evolutionary function: physical proximity and protection of offspring (see George & Solomon, 2008). In the second edition of *Attachment* (1969/1982), Bowlby addressed this seeming incompatibility between his and Trivers's perspectives. While crediting Trivers's (1974) contribution (e.g., for understanding sibling rivalry), Bowlby concluded that his own theory could be left basically unadjusted, side by side with that of Trivers.

Nonetheless, Trivers's perspective—more so than Bowlby's (and later Ainsworth's) more "idealistic" portrayals—may serve as a sobering reminder that protection of a given offspring is by no means the be-all and end-all of caregiving relationships. Moreover, Trivers's perspective should strike a chord for every parent who has had to juggle the demands posed not just by one infant but by several children of different

ages, along with work, domestic chores, and the time needed for reha-
bilitation.

However, in support of Bowlby's behavioral systems approach to
caregiving and quite contrary to Trivers's principles, humans and other
animals sometimes develop strong emotional bonds not just to their own
biological offspring but also to genetically unrelated infants and children—indeed, even to offspring of other species (for charming examples,
see Holland, 2013). If they did not do so, adoption would be a very bad
idea, which it evidently is not (e.g., van IJzendoorn & Juffer, 2006).
Thus, in the end, the validity of Bowlby's behavioral systems approach
remains unchallenged, which by no means implies that it provides a
comprehensive model of caregiving or relationships from an evolutionary perspective.

In view of inclusive fitness considerations, it has also been argued
that Bowlby focused too much on the survival function (i.e., natural selection) of attachment in early offspring development and that he did not
sufficiently address its role in differential reproduction (i.e., sexual selection; e.g., Kirkpatrick, 2005; Simpson & Belsky, 2016). Consequently,
and drawing on a behavioral ecology framework (e.g., Davies, Krebs, &
West, 2012), researchers have reported that childhood attachment and
associated environmental variability are related to different reproductive
strategies later in development (e.g., Belsky, 2007). For example, Belsky,
Houts, and Fearon (2010) found that insecure attachment among toddler girls is predictive of early pubertal maturation, over and above the
heritability of such maturation, perhaps encouraging earlier menarche
and reproduction, which might have once been adaptive in dangerous or
scarce environments. Findings like these are important in further illustrating that attachment is not merely about the "adapted mind" (e.g.,
Barkow, Cosmides, & Tooby, 1992)—that is, a mind adapted to selection pressures in past environments (cf. Bowlby's EEA). It is also about
the "adapting" mind: The developing person adapts to his or her current,
local relational environment, which in turn forecasts his or her future
reproductive bets. If anyone had the impression that attachment theory
merely reflects a "Stone Age mind" idea (cf. Buller, 2005), then that
person failed to read Bowlby properly. The recent attachment-related
developments in evolutionary thinking represent a further move away
from such an idea.

Bowlby has also been criticized for advocating a notion of EEA in
the singular (Simpson & Belsky, 2016), despite human evolution having
taken place—and continuing to take place (e.g., Laland, 2017)—in very
different ecological niches, spanning from the arctic to the desert, and in
the context of very different caregiving arrangements (e.g., Hrdy, 2011).
For these reasons, Bowlby may have underestimated the developing

person's degree of plasticity and consequent behavioral flexibility in adapting to variable local conditions. This flexibility may in turn be a direct reflection of the marked variation in humans' environments—in the plural—of evolutionary adaptation. I return to this topic in Chapter 4 and elsewhere in this book.

By the same token, Bowlby probably had an unnecessarily narrow understanding of both the selection pressure(s) underlying the evolution of the attachment system and this system's functional consequence(s). In the former case, primate neonates and infants—human ones in particular—have not only risked falling prey to predators, which Bowlby (1969/1982) claimed was the selection pressure par excellence in the evolution of the attachment system. As Bowlby (e.g., 1991) was well aware, human neonates and infants have been vulnerable to a host of additional natural dangers, including starvation, sudden temperature changes, strangers (i.e., conspecific kidnappers), infections, hazardous falls, suffocation, poisoning, and other kinds of injuries (see also Hesse & Main, 2006). All of these dangers may have figured in the selection pressures to which the *hominin* version of the attachment system provided an answer. Indeed, all of these threats and dangers tend to yield attachment behaviors in human infants, such as crying (e.g., James-Roberts & Halil, 1991). Notably, that selection pressures for attachment were likely in the plural, not in the singular, implies that the attachment system may have been an even more important solution than Bowlby realized. Just as infant crying serves the all-purpose function of alerting caregivers that something—anything—is wrong, the attachment system in human infants appears to function as a "domain-general" system for keeping infants safe and sound.

Regarding the attachment system's functional consequence(s), I contend that Bowlby restricted his attention unnecessarily to (merely) protection at the expense of other vital functions, a position he came to significantly qualify toward the end of his life (Bowlby, 1991). Yet he restricted his attention for what was a good reason at the time: distinguishing attachment theory from behaviorism. This narrowing of attention also increased the specificity of attachment theory. Besides providing protection, however, proximity to the caregiver is an important platform for the child's exploration and learning—including social learning from the caregiver. That the attachment system yields—and has presumably always yielded—more than one functional consequence increases the system's importance. For example, learning from caregivers and other attachment figures in the child's local environment or culture is vital not only for survival (e.g., aiding in the identification of "unnatural" clues to danger), but it can also promote the developing person's adaptation to local pressures resulting from cultural circumstances and demands.

Consequently, understanding social and cultural learning has become important in evolutionary science, especially since the introduction of behavioral ecology (Davies et al., 2012), cultural evolution (Cavalli-Sforza & Feldman, 1981), and gene–culture coevolution (Boyd & Richerson, 2008) models. Social learning is thus no longer the province of behaviorist psychology, as it was when Bowlby formulated attachment theory. In line with the "wider view" adopted in this book, I argue that attachment has facilitated important aspects of cultural learning and evolution (in particular, see Chapters 5 and 10). This potential of attachment theory has remained hidden largely because of Bowlby's position on protection as the singular functional consequence of the attachment system.

Finally, attachment theory has been criticized for placing too much emphasis on mothers as the "principal" attachment figures (e.g., Hrdy, 2011). Bowlby did clarify that a particular biological sex was not a necessary condition for an attachment figure, but he also asserted a monotropy principle (i.e., one attachment figure is principal in importance for the child, others secondary, tertiary, etc., in importance; Bowlby, 1969/1982). Although the empirical jury on that matter is still out, Sarah Hrdy's (e.g., 2011) cooperative breeding theory emphasizes that cooperative parenting, involving other adults and older siblings (alloparents) beyond mothers, has likely been the norm throughout our ancestral history.

The widespread practice of alloparenting serves as my final example that Bowlby was unnecessarily narrow in some of his foundational assumptions. Ironically, this shortcoming was probably intimately linked to Bowlby's strengths as a theorist: his ability to cut nature at its joints while carving out theoretical principles that freed his theory from the shackles of psychoanalytic drive theory and behaviorist psychology. Without the specificity that Bowlby sought with his theory, he could have left us with just another vaguely formulated object-relations theory or, perhaps, some version of "Stone Age mind" nativism. Thus, in the end, Bowlby may have been wise—considering what was available and at stake at the time—to restrict his attention from the plural possibilities to the singular definitives.

REPRESENTATIONAL ASPECTS
AND ASSOCIATED PSYCHOLOGICAL DEFENSES

In this section, I elaborate on the representational and defensive processes that, in Bowlby's and other attachment theorists' views, are associated with the hominin version of the attachment system and with attachment relationships more generally. These representational and defensive components add more layers of complexity to the attachment system on top of the general psychobiological principles outlined in the preceding sections. Moreover, Bowlby's portrayal of the occasionally defensive nature of attachment-related mental representations implies that his analogies to simple mechanical systems, and to principles of cognitive science more generally, can be taken only so far. This portrayal also indicates that Bowlby was indeed not only an ethologist at heart but also a psychodynamic theorist after all.

Internal Working Models

For goal-corrected systems to be serviceable, organisms must be able to organize pertinent sensory input ("feedback") and store such input in memory. In other words, they need to be able to form relevant representations of the world. As was typical for Bowlby, he did not make do with the most widely used concepts available at the time to denote such representations, whether it be "schema" from cognitive psychology or "object representation" from psychoanalysis. In Bowlby's view, those concepts were too static and passive. Instead, he borrowed the term "internal working models" (IWMs) from early artificial intelligence theory (Craik, 1943; Young, 1964) to denote the active, predictive, and prescriptive nature of mental representations. Part of our flexibility, adaptability, and complexity as a species is contingent on our ability to conduct small-scale mental experiments (i.e., based on our IWMs) to guide our behavior in future situations that are to varying degrees similar to ones that have already been encountered. Bowlby argued that we construct an organismic model (a model of ourselves, our worth, and our abilities) and an environmental model (including a model of others and what to expect from them). These models, which are often referred to as models of "self" and "others" in attachment theory, are thought to be complementary. In order to function adaptively and not become too rigid, these models must be open to learning so that they can be continuously updated; hence the idea of *working* models.

Importantly, IWMs not only involve models of self and others in strictly interpersonal situations. In early artificial intelligence theorizing (Craik, 1943; Young, 1964), as well as in Bowlby's (1973, 1980) theory, IWMs were used to denote all sorts of functionally important mental representations that complex organisms—and other conceivable intelligences—form of the world. Thus, IWMs apply to our general models of how the world works. Although this has understandably received far less attention in the attachment literature than models of self and others, one of Bowlby's core insights was that attachment-related experiences affect people's broader view of the world as well. Accordingly, Bowlby wrote about "the working model of the world" (1973, p. 203) and even claimed that "every situation we meet with in life is construed in terms of the representational models we have of the world about us and of ourselves" (Bowlby, 1980, p. 229).

Drawing from Piaget (e.g., 1954/2013), Bowlby argued that we typically make only slight corrections to our models, and that IWMs gain increasing stability in large part owing to (1) information *assimilation* into the current models and (2) increasing *automaticity* of processing and behavior. One consequence of the child bringing his or her increasingly corroborated predictions into the world and into later relationships is that these expectations will often be perceived as verified. For example, a child expecting others to be controlling or punishing will often learn to conceal what he or she is doing, paradoxically increasing the likelihood of being punished for both misbehaving and concealing it. In a very real sense, relational life is in part a self-fulfilling prophecy. Naturally, environmental stability—as in the caregiver's sensitivity over time and situations—contributes even further to the stability of IWMs.

Given sufficiently strong new or disconfirming input, however, substantial change in IWMs may occur through a process of *accommodation* (Piaget, 1954/2013). That would be predicted, for example, if a child's caregiver changes markedly and permanently from having been characteristically highly sensitive to being highly insensitive, or vice versa. In Bowlby's (1973) view, IWMs are thus in principle always open to modification, especially in transitional periods (e.g., shifting of caregivers, adolescence), although their plasticity naturally diminishes with increasing age. Bowlby's stance with regard to the stability versus lability of IWMs can hence be summarized as an expectation of *general continuity* and *lawful* (i.e., predictable or interpretable) *discontinuity*.

Furthermore, Bowlby (1969/1982) argued that IWMs are hierarchically organized, with the top level comprising highly general models of self, others, and the world. In line with his monotropy idea, the child's real, early interaction history with its principal (usually its primary) attachment figure will have unparalleled influence on these general-level models. The child will typically try out these models in relation to other (later) relationship partners and situations, but will ultimately form new models of them based on the real characteristics of those relationships and situations (see also Ainsworth & Marvin, 1995). This is how the child comes to develop distinct IWMs related to his or her relationships with mother, father, and other caregivers, and then to other attachment figures later in development. The general, top-level IWMs of self, other, and the world will ultimately reflect the sum total of an individual's attachment-related experiences, though with unparalleled weight assigned to early experience (cf. the "prototype" hypothesis; e.g., Ainsworth & Marvin, 1995; Fraley, 2002; Fraley, Vicary, Brumbaugh, & Roisman, 2011).

Although the level at which IWMs operate is largely a matter of speculation, it seems likely, as a minimum, that people maintain both (1) IWMs of attachment figures in general and (2) IWMs specific to particular relationships. Collins and Read (1994) have suggested that one level below the highly generalized models of self, other, and the world, there is a second level comprising models of parent–child relationships as distinct from peer relationships, and so on (cf. Overall, Fletcher, & Friesen, 2003). Whether or not various levels of attachment-relevant mental representations are arranged in this precise hierarchical structure—they can also be thought of as nodes in an attachment-related neural network (e.g., Mikulincer & Shaver, 2016)—it seems certain that IWMs of various levels of generality are interconnected to some degree (e.g., Fraley, Roisman, Booth-LaForce, Owen, & Holland, 2013; Overall et al., 2003; Roisman, Sroufe, Madsen, & Collins, 2001). In later chapters, we examine how working models may extend or generalize to people's representations of God (and other religious personages) in relation to themselves (in particular, see Chapter 5).

Psychological Defenses

Bowlby, like Freud and subsequent psychoanalysts, was convinced that humans possess psychological defenses that protect them against anxiety and contextually maladaptive behaviors. Such defenses were in Bowlby's view intimately tied to IWMs. Again characteristically, Bowlby did not merely accept the classically named psychoanalytic defenses (e.g., denial, projection, splitting, repression), but instead formulated attachment-related defenses in terms of information processing and memory functions, following Dixon (1971) and Norman (1976). He suggested that attachment-related defenses should be understood in terms of the development of certain cognitive–affective strategies that deal with threatening information regarding attachment (Bowlby, 1980).

Specifically, Bowlby (1973, 1980) argued for two mutually dependent strategies: *defensive exclusion* and *shifting of attention*. The idea of defensive exclusion was based on the well-established principle of selective exclusion in cognitive psychology; organisms exclude irrelevant information to liberate processing capacity for dealing with task-central information. "Defensive" exclusion is based on similar processes, but with the goal of shielding the organism from thoughts and feelings that would cause overwhelming anxiety and suffering at the experiential level and maladaptive functioning at the behavioral level. Thus, attachment-related information (e.g., about a separation) might be excluded in the service of (defensive) exploration. Alternatively, exploration-related information (e.g., about novel toys) might be excluded in the service of attachment (i.e., remaining hypervigilant about the caregiver's accessibility even when there are no signs of danger).

Defensive shifting of attention is intimately connected to defensive exclusion. It is seen, for example, when a child—in spite of attachment–system activation—shifts his or her attention away from attachment and instead focuses attention on other aspects of a situation (e.g., toys) or on persons other than the attachment figure (e.g., Main, 1990). While such attentional shifting is an observable aspect of child behavior in specific situations (such as in the Strange Situation procedure; see Chapter 4), over time and maturation, it can become a habitual strategy for approaching attachment-related information (cf. Main, Goldwyn, & Hesse's [2003] concept, "state of mind" regarding attachment).

Bowlby (e.g., 1973, 1980) and others (e.g., Main, 1990) have suggested that the development of psychological defenses stems from untoward early relational experiences with caregivers. Memories of these interactions become organized as part of the person's (implicit) IWMs of self and others. Relatedly, Bowlby and other attachment theorists have assumed that repeated experiences with insensitive caregiving leads to the development of structurally incoherent (or multiple) IWMs. This is seen, for example, when a person says one thing but does the opposite. Technically, the later emerging explicit (or declarative, semantic, conscious) components of IWMs differ from the implicit (procedural, episodic, unconscious) components. The young child (approximately 0–3 years) is particularly vulnerable to developing structurally incoherent models because the child has not yet mastered appearance–reality distinctions (Main, 1991). Thus, if the caregiver says "I love you" but consistently acts in a rejecting manner toward the child when the child is afraid or sad, the child will receive two incompatible messages and will treat both as true (i.e., "I am loved," conscious processing; "When distressed, I should avoid my caregiver and distract myself," unconscious processing). When asked about such a caregiver later, the person may well declare that the caregiver was loving and sensitive (explicit/semantic processing) and yet will fail to provide convincingly converging examples from lived experience (implicit/episodic processing).

Bowlby (1973) and Main (1981, 1990) further argued that these defenses may be adaptive in the short run, for example, in allowing the child a conditional form of proximity to a rejecting caregiver—being in sufficient physical proximity that the attachment figure may come to the child's aid in the case of real alarm. Also, the continued display of attachment behaviors would run the risk of causing further frustration to the already rejecting attachment figure. By the child inhibiting those displays (i.e., deactivating the attachment system), the risk that the attachment figure would permanently abandon, maltreat, or even kill the child (see Hrdy, 1999) should decrease (cf. Main, 1981).

However, these defenses risk being maladaptive in the long run, as the attachment system may become more or less chronically deactivated or hyperactivated (Mikulincer & Shaver, 2016). In the former case the child might miss real signs of danger, and in the latter the child might miss many opportunities to explore and learn from the environment.

Bowlby (1980) briefly elaborated on a third process yielding structural incoherence in IWMs, which had some overlap with defensive exclusion but was discussed particularly in the context of traumatic events, such as loss of an attachment figure, namely, *segregated systems.* The underlying idea was that if a stressor is sufficiently severe, and especially if it originates in one's relationship with an attachment figure, the individual may be unable to process that event in an integrated fashion. The phenomenon bears a striking resemblance to what psychoanalytic theory identifies as "dissociation." However, true to his character, Bowlby instead picked his preferred "segregated systems" term from systems theory as employed in ethology. Hinde (1966) had described numerous examples of conflict behavior in other animals, thought to result from simultaneous or sequential activation of competing behavioral systems (e.g., fight–flight conflict).

One attachment-related traumatic event that readily yields segregated processes is the loss of an attachment figure. This event is not only highly stressful in its own right, thus yielding protest and despair, but it also eliminates the availability of the very person from whom the individual would usually seek support when distressed. Hence, this is a "double blow" to the attachment system. Consequently, acute bereavement often manifests itself in the form of behavioral and cognitive disorganization or disorientation. For example, the bereaved individual may continue to display searching behaviors for the lost person, which implies that this person is still represented as (somehow) alive. Segregation is thus expressed in the form of incompatible representations; in this case, the deceased person is simultaneously represented as both dead and not dead. According to Bowlby (1980), reorganization following loss requires that the bereaved individual eventually accommodates information regarding the lost person's permanent inaccessibility, which can take months, sometimes years, post-bereavement (see also Fraley & Shaver, 2016).

Experiences of being physically abused by an attachment figure, such as a parent or a spouse, is another example that readily yields segregated processes (Bowlby, 1980). Like loss, abuse is itself distressing, indeed highly frightening, which potently activates the attachment system. What creates segregation here is that the individual also represents the abusive partner as an attachment figure, that is, someone to turn to when distressed and frightened. Perhaps this happens for good reasons; the attachment figure is not just a target for the individual's attachment system but may also have displayed comforting behaviors on numerous occasions in the past. Most perpetrators are not abusive 24 hours a day, 7 days a week. The dilemma, however, is that the attachment figure will come to be represented in a fundamentally incompatible fashion: as perpetrator to flee from and as attachment figure to approach (cf. some of Harlow's rhesus infants, referenced above). In later chapters (particularly Chapter 8), we see how such segregated processes may be expressed in people's religious and spiritual experiences.

Importantly, like other ethologists—and unlike many psychoanalysts who view dissociation as a defense mechanism (e.g., a mental "escape" from threat)—Bowlby did not necessarily imply that segregation should be viewed as defensive, let alone adaptive. Segregation may be defensive and adaptive, of course, but it may just as well express or contribute to system breakdown (Liotti, 2009), and perhaps in some instances indicates temporary confusion before the organism has settled on an organized course of action (i.e., one behavioral system has trumped a competing one; see Reisz, Duschinsky, & Siegel, 2018).

More on Internal Working Models and Psychological Defenses Vis-à-Vis Psychoanalysis and Cognitive Science

Although Bowlby evidently distanced his theorizing on IWMs and defenses in many ways from psychoanalysis, he was also careful to point out that IWMs were "none other than the internal worlds of psychoanalysis seen in a new perspective" (1969/1982, p. 82). As a further point of convergence with psychoanalysis, Bowlby regarded psychopathology (cf. neurosis) as due in no small part to rigid, inaccurate, and contextually maladaptive IWMs, which were originally based on real, lived experiences in which they may have been contextually adaptive.

Bowlby's approach to IWMs and defenses may profitably be viewed as an attempted rapprochement between psychoanalysis and cognitive science. While Bowlby obviously drew heavily on cognitive principles and employed terminology borrowed from the cognitive sciences, he also brought psychoanalytic ideas of defenses and affect—both of which have been notoriously overlooked in cognitive science—to bear upon his understanding of the nature and workings of attachment-related mental representations. Regrettably, in my view, cognitive scientists have not paid sufficient attention to the wisdom of Bowlby's move regarding affects and defenses (see Chapter 10 for the consequences this neglect has had for the cognitive science of religion).

Perhaps equally unsurprisingly, psychoanalysts were largely dumbfounded by Bowlby's seemingly schematic and mechanistic understanding of mental representations and associated defenses, which seemed to offer no place for ideas about fantasy and imagination (e.g., Karen, 1994). Although many psychoanalysts have since become much more compelled by attachment theory—and in no small part due to Mary Main's contributions (e.g., Main, Kaplan, & Cassidy, 1985; Main & Solomon, 1990; though see also Bowlby, 1988)—the defenses postulated within attachment theory and research still appear somewhat schematic and mechanistic, especially if viewed from the vantage point of psychoanalysis, in which the plethora of postulated defenses is quite intricate indeed.

As a specific case in point reflecting the poverty of suggested defenses within attachment theory, attachment theorists have not been compelled to theorize about possible defense mechanisms operating among children who are "securely" attached (an issue further dealt with in Chapter 4). It is as if the interaction histories leading to secure attachment have been understood in such rosy colors that no defense would be called for. In view of psychoanalytic and parent–offspring conflict theories, both of which portray relationships as inherently conflictual, attachment theorists surely paint an overly positive portrayal of "secure" relationships and, consequently, of how the mind works in such relationships (cf. Gullestad, 2001; Wulff, 2006). After all, even characteristically sensitive caregivers may occasionally get the blues, becoming frustrated, spanking their children, yelling at them, and the like. Accordingly, securely attached offspring should also have to erect defenses when such occasions arise.

Notably, however, Bowlby was again trying to cut nature at its joints rather than to engage with all particularities of nature. And he did so rather successfully. For example, there should be no doubt that receiving sensitive and responsive caregiving (i.e., the pathway par excellence to secure attachment) calls for relatively less defensive processes—and less *rigid* defenses—than does insensitive and unresponsive caregiving. Similarly, sensitive and responsive caregiving facilitates reparative opportunities for children to resolve conflict with their caregivers, which also attenuates the need for rigidly organized defenses.

Furthermore, it is important to note that Bowlby did not make his own principal task that of theorizing about specific attachment types—whether secure or insecure—as did many later attachment theorists and researchers. Thus, it was not Bowlby who pinned particular defenses to particular insecure forms of attachment (again, see Chapter 4). Finally, unlike psychoanalysis, attachment theory was not offered as a comprehensive theory of the mind but, rather, as a considerably more narrow and precise theory specifically about attachment (cf. Wulff, 2006). Hence, the fact that attachment theory postulates a certain few defensive processes in the attachment domain does not imply that there are no other defenses besides those discussed by Bowlby that are operative in other domains of mental life, including domains of relationships other than attachment.

HOW ATTACHMENT UNFOLDS
AND TRANSFORMS IN EARLY DEVELOPMENT

In this section, I provide a brief outline of how attachment develops in humans during the first few years of life and discuss the general principles Bowlby believed to underlie this development. In later chapters (especially Chapter 3), this outline will be supplemented with an overview of how attachment develops beyond the early years.

General Principles

Bowlby (1969/1982) introduced a useful, general way of thinking about development in which development is understood as resulting from increases in the *differentiation, integration,* and *complexity* of evolved neural systems, one of which is the attachment system. Due to the marked immaturity and plasticity of the human newborn's brain, many of these increases take place during the first few years of life. Importantly, maturation is understood as accomplished in no small part by environmental co-sculpting of the evolved systems. In other words, the maturation of attachment emerges partly from life experiences, as well as from concomitant motoric and cognitive developments. Thus, although attachment theory is a maturational theory of the development of a neural system, it should not be confused with any form of "nativism" in which heredity is portrayed as providing the bread and butter of development while environmental factors merely fill in some (less important) content details.

   After reviewing a number of observations of human and other mammalian infants, Bowlby (1969/1982, p. 222) concluded that "the development of attachment behavior in human infants, though much slower, is of a piece with that seen in non-human mammals. Much evidence supports that conclusion and none contradicts it." He noted, for example, that once an attachment has formed, infants prefer the attachment figure to other individuals; this preference typically persists even in the face of separations. Like other mammals, human infants are also born with the capacity to cling and show a narrowing of responsiveness to relationship partners (i.e., increased differentiation), which with development becomes more directed toward a few partners, especially their caregivers. Human infants also show a marked bias toward responding to particular stimuli (such as human faces), and the more experience with a particular person the infant has, the stronger the infant's preference for that person.

As noted, Bowlby argued for a maturational developmental perspective on goal-corrected systems. But the attachment system, he argued, is not a functional goal-corrected system at birth; rather, it develops into one with maturation. The reason is that the operation of goal-directed systems is mediated by various other systems and is thus dependent on how those other systems develop (i.e., increased integration). Therefore, Bowlby (1969/1982) maintained that behavioral control systems tend to be simple and rigidly organized as simple chains among neonates but that they become more complex and goal-corrected (i.e., increased in complexity) over time as simpler systems become integrated under higher-order systems.

For example, reliance on sensory feedback makes the attachment system dependent on the development of the sensory organs. Behaviors also need to be oriented, and effector equipment such as locomotor ability is therefore important for goal-corrected behavior. A child who has acquired the abilities required to crawl or walk is more able to independently regulate proximity to the caregiver in a goal-directed manner than is a child who has not acquired such abilities.

The Maturation of Attachment during the First Few Years of Life

In the process of developing selective attachments to caregivers, the infant moves from a kind of socially "promiscuous" responsiveness (e.g., smiling) to whomever happens to interact with the infant during his or her first few months of life. Bowlby (1969/1982) described this phase as the "preattachment" phase. Although much research on neonates has since shown that they have a clearer preference for their familiar caregivers (e.g., those individuals' voices, their smell) over unfamiliar interaction partners than Bowlby realized, it usually takes more than 6–7 months before a full-fledged attachment relationship with caregivers has been established ("prototypical attachment," in Bowlby's [1969/1982] words).

The maturation of attachment during the second half of the first year of life is seen in an increasingly salient preference for the familiar caregivers, coupled with separation anxiety when parted from those caregivers and wariness of interacting with strangers. Although the intensity of expressions of separation anxiety and stranger wariness is notably variable across children and cultures—in part due to temperamental factors and cultural caregiving practices—both phenomena are strongly normative (i.e., species-typical), indeed probably universal (Bowlby, 1973). Attachment formation also coalesces with infants' increased physical mobility (as evident in crawling and walking) and cognitive developments, most notably object permanence (i.e., the understanding that an object, such as the attachment figure, will continue to exist even when not perceptibly present). Jointly, these developing motoric and cognitive abilities enable infants not just to actively seek proximity to their caregivers and to search for them when they are absent (such as during a brief separation), but also to venture off into potentially dangerous territories. At this age, the attachment system kicks into high gear and becomes visibly functional. Much of the infant–toddler's life—at roughly 9–18 months of age—is thenceforward organized around the principal task of establishing and maintaining reasonable proximity to attachment figures while also exploring the surrounding world with all its appealing objects and settings.

Thus, the infant–toddler actively turns to attachment figures as safe havens when alarmed (e.g., frightened) by danger cues. Even more tellingly, the infant–toddler increasingly uses attachment figures as secure bases for exploration, which is particularly important in situations of uncertainty. By means of social referencing—using the attachment figure's emotional and gestural expressions as a cue—the infant–toddler puts his or her newly acquired gross motor abilities to use and is especially open to treading new exploratory terrain when in the presence of a secure base (e.g., Sorce, Emde, Campos, & Klinnert, 1985).

At roughly the ages of 3–5 years, the preschooler's relationships with attachment figures gain further flexibility and depth. This is presumably a function not just of repeated interaction sequences corroborating the child's working models of self and other but also of increased language abilities and further cognitive developments. The child's ability to "mentalize" (e.g., Fonagy, Gergely, & Jurist, 2004), that is, to represent the minds of others ("mind reading") and to distinguish others' minds from that of one's own, is an especially important developmental achievement in this regard (e.g., Fonagy & Target, 1997). Regarding flexibility, the child can now understand that in most situations, such as during separations in familiar settings, there is no need to resort to overt attachment behaviors (such as crying or following) because of an internalized representation of the attachment figure as someone who, for example, "plans" or "intends" to come back or who "cares about" how the self is feeling (Bowlby's [1988] "internalized secure base"). Consequently, the child can now endure somewhat longer separations from caregivers—say, a full day at preschool—in a manner that is less resource-taxing than during the first and second years of life (Bowlby, 1973).

Regarding depth, the preschooler can engage in mind-related conversations with his or her caregivers (and others), which, when not deceptive, has the potential to considerably expand the child's understanding of self and others and to facilitate relational repair when things have temporarily gone sour. A caregiver of a terrified 3-year-old who has been lost in the supermarket may tenderly declare, upon reunion, that "I am SO sorry, honey; I didn't *mean* to walk away on you! I *thought* you *noticed* where I was going and that you *planned* to follow me." Along with comforting hugs, mentalizing utterances (*italicized*) like these can effectively restore the child's sense of confidence, not just in the parent's accessibility and the self's continued worthiness of care but also in the good intentions of the parent's mind. The child of preschool age may also realize that the parent's mind is the "real deal" and is what's driving the parent's behaviors, so even if the behaviors happen to fall short of perfection from time to time, the parent's mind may still be represented as reliable and loving. Because of the increased flexibility of the relationship that ensues, Bowlby (1969/1982) referred to this final phase of attachment relationship development as the "goal-corrected partnership."

SURROGATE OBJECTS OF ATTACHMENT

Of special interest for the application of attachment theory to religion and spirituality is the observation that attachment behaviors may be directed not just to an individual's regular, "animate" attachment figures—most notably caregivers and, later in life, spouses and close friends—but also to a host of other surrogate relationship partners. The founders of attachment theory briefly discussed the possibility that individuals who have been inadequately cared for or whose regular attachment figures are currently unavailable for one reason or another may select certain other persons or person-substitutes as surrogate targets for their attachment systems (Ainsworth, 1985; Bowlby, 1969/1982). However, subsequent attachment researchers largely neglected to pursue the use of attachment surrogates in their research. Instead they focused primarily on principal attachments and their socioemotional correlates in later development (often via presumed continuity and generalization of working models). This left a major gap in the literature on people's use of attachment surrogates. This gap is an important part of what has inspired my colleagues and me to engage in attachment research on religion.

Bowlby wrote, on the use of attachment figures, that

> whenever the "natural" object of attachment behaviour is unavail-
> able, the behaviour can become directed towards some substitute
> object. Even though it is inanimate, such an object frequently appears
> capable of filling the role of an important, though subsidiary, attach-
> ment "figure." Like the principal attachment figure, the inanimate
> substitute is sought especially when a child is tired, ill, or distressed.
> (1969/1982, p. 313)

Bowlby then went on to exemplify such substitute objects with teddy
bears, pacifiers, and comforting blankets. Such objects have been termed
"transitional" objects by psychoanalysts (Winnicott, 1953) because they
may aid a child in temporarily transitioning from his or her primary
objects of attachment to other situations and persons, say, to a day at
day care and to the day care staff. Understood in this way, such objects
may indeed correctly be understood as transitional.

However, and presumably because of the effectively soothing effects
of these objects, children may develop surprisingly strong—indeed
rigid—ties to them. For example, young children commonly refuse
to have their blankets and teddy bears washed, as it may change the
objects' appearance, and they often react with intense protest when the
object is misplaced or, even worse, lost. Should the latter happen, it is
common for parents to go out of their way to replace the lost object. If
it is out of stock in the local store, the parent may drive a long way to
find a replacement and then "rough it up" to make it look more like the
old one. Even then, the child may say, "It doesn't smell right" and reject
the hard-won replacement. Similar stories about difficulties involved in
getting children to stop using their pacifiers are commonly heard among
parents.

Young children may become so dependent on their surrogate objects
that those objects may trump or supersede the significance of children's
actual caregivers in certain situations. Such "idolatry," to use a religious
term, is known to make attachment assessments (described in Chapter 4)
somewhat challenging, as when a child fails to calm down after a separation–reunion sequence with a parent until the child is finally reunited
with his or her true object of affection: the pacifier!

My point here is not to say that such a child has an attachment to
the pacifier but not to its parent, let alone a "stronger" or more secure
attachment to the pacifier (cf. Hong & Townes, 1976; van IJzendoorn
et al., 1983). Rather, I wish to indicate that attachment behavior may
be directed to convenient targets that we usually do not—and for good
reason (see Chapter 2)—think of as attachment figures proper. Thus,

Bowlby was probably right to term such objects attachment "figures" in quotation marks (see the quotation above). A related point is that such surrogate objects may be much more than transitional (from parent to surrounding) for an individual child. Indeed, they may actively interfere with the child's display of attachment behavior to his or her regular attachment figures.

Although infants' and toddlers' use of attachment surrogates is typically directed to concrete objects, from preschool age onward—and via the cognitive developments described in the preceding section—the child's cast of surrogate objects may come to include a whole new set of abstract, invisible, and noncorporeal characters. Thus, as children experience themselves thinking and planning, and imagine the intentions of their social interaction partners, they may begin to apply their mentalizing ideas to abstract, symbolic—yet typically highly anthropomorphized—others.

For example, the child starts to elaborate and interact with "imaginary"—to use adults' terminology—companions (e.g., Taylor, 2001). Although not the typical scenario, in some children's minds, especially children experiencing low levels of psychological well-being (Bonne, Canetti, Bachar, De-Nour, & Shalev, 1999; Hoff, 2005), these imaginary companions take on a "real" existence and may be viewed as some of the principal relationship partners in the child's mind. It seems reasonable to conjecture that this is particularly likely when the child's primary attachment figures are unavailable, for whatever reason (cf. Hong & Townes, 1976).

Such imaginary figures often exit from children's minds as suddenly as they entered them, and most have exited by middle childhood. At least that is the way it seems among children from the white, educated, industrialized, rich, and democratic parts of the world (WEIRD; e.g., Henrich, Heine, & Norenzayan, 2010). Piaget (1954/2013) attributed their exit from children's minds to cognitive maturation; as children outgrow "preoperational egocentrism," they also say farewell to "animistic thinking" in general and to imaginary figures in particular. However, as I have pointed out elsewhere (Granqvist, 2014b), this analysis is problematic for two reasons. First, preschool children's somewhat elevated tendencies for animistic (or "magical") thinking is partially due to incomplete object knowledge and not to animistic thinking per se (e.g., Jipson & Gelman, 2007). Second, as illustrated by the widespread historical and global presence of religion, mythologies, and folk beliefs, animistic (or magical) thinking is rarely fully outgrown. Rather, such thinking usually becomes focused on other entities that, for one reason or the other, have found acceptance in the cultural milieu and historical era surrounding the individual (cf. Boyatzis, 2005, 2017). With those final remarks, we are ready to start addressing matters of religion and spirituality from an attachment viewpoint.

CHAPTER SUMMARY

In this chapter, I have outlined the historical development of attachment theory, from Bowlby's early work as a child psychoanalyst to the extended work required to formalize his ethological attachment theory. Next, the theory's principal concepts were defined and its evolutionary and psychobiological assumptions delineated. We revisited the central assumptions of attachment theory in the light of contemporary evolutionary considerations, and I concluded that, although attachment theory has by all reasonable criteria been a remarkable scientific contribution, Bowlby was unnecessarily narrow—or singular—in some of his central assumptions. In particular, I contend that attachment has always had functional consequences beyond protection and survival. Key among these consequences, at least for the present book, is social or cultural learning: Attachment is an effective platform for cultural transmission, and thereby facilitates the child's incorporation into a given culture. I also delineated the basic representational aspects and psychological defenses addressed in the theory, and I drew evaluative parallels to cognitive science and psychoanalysis. In the developmental section of the chapter, I described how attachment matures during the first few years of life and according to what principles. Finally, "surrogate" attachment objects were discussed from a developmental perspective.

CHAPTER 2

God as a Noncorporeal Attachment Figure

In this chapter, I consider the nature of God as conceived within the world's major faith traditions, with particular emphasis on theistic traditions, especially Christianity. The central argument of the chapter is that God[1] is conceptualized or constructed and perceived as, among other things, a noncorporeal attachment figure.

Almost three decades ago, Lee Kirkpatrick and Phillip Shaver (1990) pioneered this area of theorizing and research. Since then, the religion-as-attachment idea has become one of the most central notions in the contemporary psychology of religion and spirituality (e.g., Paloutzian & Park, 2013). Besides acknowledging the importance of Kirkpatrick and Shaver's creative and integrative work, I believe that this achievement flows naturally from the heuristic potential of attachment theory itself. In hindsight, the idea to approach the psychology of religion and spirituality from an attachment viewpoint seems like a "no brainer." Yet the idea could have been outlined in so many other ways that would have limited its heuristic potential, so the work performed by Kirkpatrick and Shaver definitively deserves recognition.

There are two additional reasons, I believe, that the religion-as-attachment approach "has flown" in the psychology of religion and spirituality. First, considered as a whole, empirical research on the attachment–religion connection has benefited from a combination of both methodological rigor *and* methodological pluralism. Without pointing any fingers, this combination of assests does not characterize most other approaches to the psychology of religion and spirituality. Much of the pertinent attachment research will be covered in this part and Part II of the book. Second, I argue that, ironically, a major strength of the attachment approach to religion is that attachment theory was not founded specifically to understand religion. Quite the contrary, and—as we saw in the previous chapter—attachment theory was created to make sense of a basic but fundamental aspect of mammalian and primate functioning, namely, our strong proclivity to form affectional relational bonds. Incidentally, or so it may seem, this is also at the core of religion and spirituality. In that sense, we can say that attachment theory is truly a "load-bearing" (Batson, 1997) framework for understanding some central components of religion and spirituality. For the same reason, the attachment approach has also proved helpful in pulling the psychology of religion and spirituality into the mainstream of psychological science.

In this chapter, I review evidence that God is constructed, perceived, and used as an attachment figure. In fact, I argue that believers' perceived personal relationship with God actually functions, psychologically, much like other attachment relationships do. The arguments in the lion's share of the chapter build up a simple, straightforward story, one that implicitly rests on what philosophers refer to as "essentialist" considerations regarding categories: Something belongs to a particular category if it meets the necessary and sufficient conditions (or criteria) for category membership. However, I also discuss the obvious differences between God and other attachment figures, which has caused some critics to question whether a relationship with God can really be an attachment relationship. Via a detour into consideration of Wittgenstein's (1953/1999) notion of family resemblances among members of a category, I conclude that "attachment to God" belongs in the family of attachment relationships, but that this particular attachment relationship forms a special subclass of "noncorporeal" attachments. Finally, I briefly discuss nontheistic religions (such as some forms of Buddhism) vis-à-vis attachment.

GOD AS ATTACHMENT FIGURE

As we saw in the previous chapter, Bowlby (1969/1982)—and later Ainsworth (1985)—discussed the constituents of attachment relationships in terms of an *affectional bond* between *two individuals*. Furthermore, the attached person selectively maintains *physical proximity* to his or her attachment figure(s). Upon involuntary separation (or threat thereof) from an attachment figure, the attached person typically *protests* and experiences *separation anxiety* (e.g., cries and searches for the attachment figure). Following permanent loss of an attachment figure, *grief* occurs and a *mourning* process is typically initiated, proceeding in accordance with the protest–despair–detachment–reorganization cycle. Furthermore, the attached person typically uses the attachment figure as a *safe haven* when distressed and as a *secure base* when exploring other aspects of the surroundings. Finally, in using the attachment figure in these ways, the attached person implicitly assesses the attachment figure as *stronger and wiser* than the self. Any relationship that meets the italicized components (or criteria) would clearly qualify as an attachment relationship (i.e., would meet the essential conditions for category membership).

As a corollary, relationships that do not meet these criteria may not qualify for category membership. Although in science we generally attempt to define categories in this clear-cut way, developmental science often forces us to be a bit more flexible because psychological phenomena change as a function of development. Even the typical preschooler's relationship with his or her principal attachment figure will deviate substantially from the conditions for attachment relationships noted above. As we saw in the previous chapter, the preschooler typically does not seek to maintain physical proximity to his or her attachment figure at all times, nor does he or she necessarily protest against separations, despite the very likely prospect of a full day at preschool away from the attachment figure. Instead, the child carries with him or her an internalized representation of the attachment figure as a secure base, and when reliance on that representation does not suffice, the child may also turn to attachment surrogates (e.g., blankets, preschool staff). Rather than concluding that the preschooler no longer has an attachment relationship with his or her principal attachment figure, some four decades ago influential attachment researchers Alan Sroufe and Everett Waters (1977) concluded that "felt security" is a more viable set goal, rather than physical proximity, to consider when studying children beyond infancy and toddlerhood. And felt security—or the psychological sense of being safe and secure—may be attained by a variety of attachment-related means besides proximity seeking, as we saw in the previous chapter. The conclusion seems clear: Maturational changes should be taken into account, and definitional criteria should be adjusted accordingly, to settle issues of membership in the attachment relationship category. This conclusion should not come as a surprise, considering that attachment theory is a developmental theory about a phenomenon that develops and is transformed throughout the lifespan.

In the sections that follow, building on previous work by Kirkpatrick (2005) and Granqvist and Kirkpatrick (2016), I first note the general considerations—points of departure—for launching the idea of an attachment–religion connection. Next, I discuss how God, and people's perceived relationships with God, fit the specific definitional criteria of attachment figures and relationships noted above, dividing the section by type of attachment criteria. This will conclude the "straightforward story" of God as an attachment figure.

In the review, I draw on two general sources of evidence. The first source predates religion-as-attachment theory and research, and includes evidence from religious texts, religious phenomenology, and a century of prior literature in the psychology of religion. Although this evidence might seem to suffice for the arguments offered, it could also reflect little more than confirmation (or verification) biases (e.g., Nickerson, 1998) stemming from a post-hoc, selective reading of huge and divergent chunks of literature, in which theory-suitable publications are cited whereas others are discarded. After all, we know that this is how people's minds often work, and the minds of scientists are not necessarily much different. Thus, the second source of evidence stems directly from religion-as-attachment research—in other words, from research designed a priori to test predictions based on the application of attachment theory to religion and spirituality. As we will see, pertinent research includes studies based on experimental and quasi-experimental designs (e.g., subliminal priming methodology, lexical decisions) as well as correlational (cross-sectional and prospective) designs and qualitative methodologies.

Throughout the chapter, I review literature pertaining mostly to adults. The next, developmental chapter (Chapter 3) covers literature that also includes children and adolescents, and then specifically from an attachment-maturational point of view.

Points of Departure

The most obvious starting point for the attachment–religion connection is that of *relationality*. Monotheistic religions, particularly Protestant Christianity, have at their core a belief in a personal God with whom believers have some kind of personal, interactive relationship. Indeed, the very word "religion," stemming from the Latin "religare" or "relegere," means "being bound" (Ferm, 1945). This relationship connotation corresponds with how people evaluate their own faith. For example, when asked to make a forced choice about what is most central to their own view of "faith"—a set of beliefs, membership in a church or synagogue, finding meaning in life, or a relationship with God—a slight majority (51%) of an American Gallup sample chose a relationship with God, compared to considerably lower percentages for each of the other alternatives (Gallup & Jones, 1989). According to Greeley (1981, p. 18),

"Just as the story of anyone's life is the story of relationships—so each person's religious story is a story of relationships."

A second, central and related point for the attachment–religion connection is the centrality of *love* in religious belief systems, and perhaps even more so in people's actual perceived relationships with God. (I hasten to add here that the centrality of the emotion of love does not negate the occasional presence of other, negative emotions; see Chapters 5–8). As concluded in an early text in the psychology of religion (Thouless, 1923, p. 132), the powerful emotional experiences associated with religion are often expressed "in the language of human love." Consequently, the process of sudden religious conversion has frequently been likened to falling in love (James, 1902; Thouless, 1923). Based on one of the best religious conversion studies yet conducted, Ullman (1989, p. xvi) concluded from her in-depth interviews with converts, that

> what I initially considered primarily a change of ideology turned out to be more akin to a falling in love. . . . [C]onversion pivots around a sudden attachment, an infatuation with a real or imagined figure which occurs on a background of great emotional turmoil. The typical convert was transformed not by a religion, but by a person. The discovery of a new truth was indistinguishable from a discovery of a new relationship, which relieved, temporarily, the upheaval of the previous life. This intense and omnipresent attachment discovered in the religious experience promised the convert everlasting guidance and love, for the object of the convert's infatuation was perceived as infallible.

A third—and again related—starting point for the attachment–religion connection pertains to believers' *representations of God*. God is represented, psychologically, as a kind of parental figure. This idea is, of course, hardly new. The most familiar version is probably Freud's (e.g., 1961b) characterization of God as a projected (or exalted) father figure (see Chapter 9). As other scholars have noted, however, the deities of the oldest known religions were often maternal figures, and modern Protestantism is in fact unusual in its lack of female deities (e.g., Wenegrat, 1989).

Whether representations of God more closely resemble maternal or paternal images has been an important issue for research in the psychology of religion and spirituality, with mixed results. Some early studies seemed to suggest that God images are more closely related to maternal than to paternal images (Godin & Hallez, 1965; Nelson, 1971; Strunk, 1959), whereas other studies suggested that God is perceived as more similar to one's preferred parent (Nelson & Jones, 1957). Whatever the average case may be, a particular individual's God representation is likely to be affected both by his or her unique relational experiences with earthly mother and father figures and by the particular content messages (e.g., regarding God's gender) the person encounters in his or her religious (sub-)culture. In general, though, people's representations of God reflect a combination of both stereotypically maternal and paternal qualities (Vergote & Tamayo, 1981). This observation ties in with the fact that most children develop multiple attachment relationships—with mothers, fathers, and others (cf. Hrdy, 2011). Accordingly, God is probably best viewed neither as an exalted father figure nor as an exalted mother figure, but rather as an exalted attachment figure.

There is considerable evidence to support the idea that believers represent God as an exalted attachment figure. One line of suggestive evidence comes from religious writings and songs. Wenegrat (1989) noted, for example, a remarkable degree of attachment imagery in the Psalms (see also Bosworth, 2015a). For merely one example, consider Psalm 27: "The Lord is my light and my salvation; whom shall I fear? The Lord is the stronghold of my life; of whom shall I be afraid?" And from the world of hymns, consider: "Children of the heavenly Father, safely in His bosom gather" (Sandell, 1855, as cited in Walter, 2013). A central theme of Protestant hymns is indeed the "infantile return to a powerful and loving protector who shields humankind from all harm" (Wulff, 1991, p. 304; cf. Bosworth, 2015a). For more recent examples, from the world of song in popular music, consider: "In my hour of darkness, in my time of need, oh Lord grant me wisdom, oh Lord grant me speed" (Gram Parsons, from *Grievous Angel,* 1974), and "Lord it's hard to be alone, help me make it through the night" (Kris Kristofferson, from *Kristofferson,* 1970).

Within the psychology of religion, factor-analytic studies of God images consistently find a large first factor laden with attachment-related descriptors (see Hood, Hill, & Spilka, 2009). For example, Gorsuch's (1968) first factor ("benevolent deity") included descriptors such as "comforting," "loving," and "protective," as well as the reverse of "distant" and "inaccessible." Similarly, Spilka, Armatas, and Nussbaum (1964) found a large general factor that included the items "comforting," "supporting," "protective," "strong," and "helpful." Tamayo and Desjardins (1976) found a first factor (labeled "availability") containing items such as "who gives comfort," "a warm-hearted refuge," "always ready with open arms," "who will take loving care of me," and "who is always waiting for me." In a factor analysis of religious attitudes and beliefs, the largest factor was "nearness to God" (Broen, 1957). The author concluded, "Persons with high loadings on this factor would tend to feel that God was very real and constantly near and accessible. These persons feel they commune with God—'walk and talk' with Him" (p. 177). To sum up, God seems clearly to capture the essence of the protective other that most parents represent to a child. As American theologian Gordon Kaufman (1981, p. 67) concluded a decade prior to Kirkpatrick and Shaver's (1990) pioneering work: "The idea of God is the idea of an absolutely adequate attachment-figure. . . . God is thought of as a protective and caring parent who is always reliable and always available to its children when they are in need."

Jointly, these themes of *relationality, love,* and *parent–child-like representations of God* in *relation to self* suggest a striking analogy between religious beliefs and experiences on the one hand and attachment relationships on the other. However, these analogies will take us only so far. For example, they demonstrate that some believers tend to establish an affectional bond with a God perceived as stronger and wiser than themselves. However, they do not suffice to demonstrate that believers' actual, perceived relationships with God typically function fully as attachment relationships. Such a demonstration requires that we pay careful attention to whether believers' perceived relationships with God meet all of the defining criteria for attachment relationships (see Kimball, Cook, Boyatzis, & Leonard, 2013, for how this can be profitably done in research). This is what I will do next. Notably, I will for the moment set aside the issue of whether God can be understood as an individual ("affectional bonds between *two individuals*"), and return to that later.

Seeking and Maintaining Proximity to God

The biological function of the attachment system, as described by Bowlby (1969/1982), is the maintenance of proximity between an infant and an expectably protective attachment figure. To achieve this objective, infants engage in a variety of behaviors such as crying, raising arms (to be picked up), clinging, crawling, or walking to and following. As we have seen, somewhat older children may accomplish "felt security" (Sroufe & Waters, 1977a) via other, nonphysical means.

Although we cannot ascertain with any certainty that religious believers obtain or maintain actual proximity to God (i.e., because God is invisible), religious life is replete with examples demonstrating that they certainly try to and do, in some cases, *experience* closeness to God. Religions provide a variety of ways of enhancing such experiences. Central to most theistic religions is the idea that God is omnipresent; thus, one is always "in proximity" to God. Religious literature frequently portrays God as always being by one's side, watching over one, and carrying one through life. These expressions are interpreted quite literally by believers with some fundamentalist persuasions but are viewed as more symbolic (or metaphorical) by believers with more liberal theological persuasions. Yet it is hard to determine with any certainty whether God is actually present in a given situation, and metaphors can do only so much to carry one through some of life's ordeals. Thus, cues that are more concrete may be valuable in enhancing perceptions of proximity to God. Consequently, religions typically provide places of worship where believers can go to be closer to God, or at least to facilitate the experience of closeness. In addition, a variety of idols and symbols—such as the Torah scroll in Judaism, the cross in Christianity, the star and crescent in Islam—may continually remind the believer of God's presence.

Prayer is probably the most important form of proximity-maintaining attachment behavior directed toward God (Reed, 1978). This is not to say that prayer merely fills an attachment-related function (for a comprehensive treatise on the psychology of prayer, see Spilka & Ladd, 2012). Indeed, it would be surprising if it merely filled one function, considering that prayer is "the most often practiced form of religiosity" (Trier & Shupe, 1991, p. 354). Consequently, Foster (1992) conceptually identified as many as 21 different kinds of prayers. Nonetheless, I maintain that its capacity to yield a sense of connection with the divine is central to many forms of prayer and that this is probably one reason for prayer permeating religious life across the world's many religious traditions.

Accordingly, Heiler (1932, p. 356), in his classic study of prayer, concluded that a devout person who prays "believes that he speaks with a God, immediately present and personal," and that "the man who prays feels himself very close to this personal God." Among the major forms of prayer reviewed in a psychology of religion textbook (Hood, Spilka, Hunsberger, & Gorsuch, 1996, p. 467), two in particular seem to be clearly related to proximity maintenance: "contemplative" prayer ("attempts to relate deeply to one's God") and "meditational" prayer (prayer "concerned with one's relationship to God"). To those we can add "petitionary," or help-seeking, requesting forms of prayer, which are believed to be the oldest form of prayer practiced (Hood et al., 2009). These forms could all be placed into Spilka and Ladd's (2012) larger category of "upward" prayer (i.e., human–divine connection), as distinguished from "outward" (human–human connection) or "inward" (self-connection) prayer. Prayer, in some of these "upward" forms, seems largely analogous to social referencing and secure base behaviors in young children—an intermittent checking back to make sure the attachment figure is attentive and accessible (e.g., Campos & Stenberg, 1981)—although petitionary prayers have more in common with the safe haven function of attachment.

In summary, although God's invisibility and presumed omnipresence are complicating matters, religious people do seek closeness to God and often via prayer. In addition, religions provide resources to help people attain a sense of closeness to God.

Separation and Loss Responses

As outlined by Ainsworth (1985; see also Bowlby, 1973, 1980), involuntary separation from an attachment figure—indeed the mere threat thereof—causes anxiety in the attached person at the experiential level as well as protest at the behavioral level. Similarly, permanent loss of an attachment figure causes grief, and a mourning process is initiated, which then typically unfolds in accordance with the protest–despair–detachment–reorganization cycle.

Determining whether people's perceived relationship with God meets these criteria is a thorny matter because one does not become separated from, or lose a relationship with, God in the same way as one might lose a human relationship partner. For example, God does not drop you off at the office for a full day at work while God is away attending to other matters, nor does God file for divorce, let alone sail off to fight wars. Accordingly, feeling entirely separated from God appears to be fairly uncommon, even among believers who—like Job of the Old Testament—have faced unjust hardships such as natural disasters (e.g., Davis, Kimball, Aten, Hamilton, et al., 2019). In line with much theological doctrine, most believers probably see the risk of true separation from God as coming only in the hereafter, at which point one spends eternity either with God or separated from God; as it were, you're either "in" or you're "out." Notably, in much of contemporary Christian theology, separation from God is the essence of hell (e.g., Hall, 2017).

Before the hereafter, the most obvious approximation to separation from or loss of God is apostasy (or deconversion)—giving up or losing one's religion. It is not clear, however, whether "losing" one's religion, presumably including one's relationship with God, can be expected to cause grief because it is the ex-believer rather than God who abandons the relationship. Even so, and presuming that apostasy signals detachment from God and religion, the apostate will ultimately still have to reorganize to a life without God and religion. In reality, apostasy is not arbitrary, and apostates may well feel that it was God, or perhaps their religious community, who abandoned them rather than the other way around (e.g., Streib, Silver, Csöff, Keller, & Hood, 2011). In either case, there are clearly instances in some believers' religious lives when they are unable to experience a previously felt communion with God. This may well occur in situations where the urge to feel such communion is experienced as acute. In much religious and mystical literature, such states are often referred to as a "wilderness experience" (e.g., James, 1902), a "dark night of the soul" (St. John of the Cross, 1990), or perhaps a "paradise lost." The best-known example of such an experience is probably when Christ himself—betrayed by his disciples, tortured by the Romans, and nailed on the cross—cried out, "My God, My God, why hast Thou forsaken me?"

A PhD student friend of mine from Uppsala University (where I studied at the time) and I conducted an experimental paraphrase of Christ's situation (Birgegard & Granqvist, 2004). More specifically, we subliminally exposed (5 milliseconds each, for 10 exposures) 113 adult theistic (mostly Christian) believers either with a separation prime targeting their perceived relationship with God ("God has abandoned me") or with attachment-neutral control primes ("People are walking," "God has many names"). The reason for doing this subliminally (below the threshold of subjective awareness) rather than supraliminally (above the threshold of subjective awareness) is that we wanted to prevent participants from engaging in controlled, deliberate, or effortful processing, thus preventing them from producing defensive or "theologically correct" (e.g., Barrett, 1999) responses. Instead, we were interested in the habitual workings of their minds, when they were not maintaining conscious control. We then examined whether their wish to be close to God had increased, as expected, from pre- to postexposure as a result of the separation-from-God priming. In other words, we sought to create a conceptually analogous situation for adult theistic believers to the separation situation in which infants find themselves when infant attachment to a caregiver is assessed (see Chapter 4). Although modest support was obtained for the prediction of an increased wish to be close to God following separation-from-God priming (effect sizes [d] = 0.35 and 0.34; see Study 3, Birgegard & Granqvist, 2004), results between specific experimental and control conditions were not statistically significant. Notably, however, there were individual differences, similar to the ones seen in infant attachment assessments, that strongly moderated (or qualified) the effects of attachment activation on religious outcomes, as I discuss later (see Chapter 5).

In a series of noteworthy papers, Bosworth (2013a, 2013b, 2015b) has made the case that the common biblical theme of weeping expresses a clear attachment-related function of the protagonist trying to restore contact with and help from God in order to alleviate pain and suffering. This is quite akin to crying (or engaging in other protest behavior) in children who seek to obtain contact with their caregivers. This theme is particularly common in the psalms, though Bosworth (2013a, 2015b) also discusses passages in Genesis and the case of the "weeping prophet"

(Jeremiah) and his "weeping God." Tellingly, weeping episodes in the psalms tend to end with restored contact with and praise of God, so they are organized as a separation–reunion (or crisis–resolution) sequence. Consider, for example, Psalm 42, which begins as follows:

> As the deer pants for streams of water,
> so my soul pants for you, my God.
> My soul thirsts for God, for the living God.
> When can I go and meet with God?
> My tears have been my food
> day and night,
> while people say to me all day long,
> "Where is your God?"
> These things I remember
> as I pour out my soul

Toward the end of the psalm, the protagonist's suffering suddenly abates:

> Why, my soul, are you downcast?
> Why so disturbed within me?
> Put your hope in God,
> for I will yet praise him,
> my Savior and my God.

This consideration of weeping naturally leads to considering the attachment components of grief and mourning, which would be instigated if the lost object of attachment were nowhere to be found. Pargament (1997) discusses several examples of atrocity-stricken soldiers and Holocaust survivors who, despite initially believing that God was on their side, ultimately came to the "realization" that God is, after all, dead (see also post–World War II "death of God" theology, e.g., Altizer, Hamilton, & Hamilton, 1966). This realization is not first and foremost an intellectual or cognitively driven conclusion (as it might have been for a deistic Enlightenment philosopher like Voltaire), but rather it is a highly emotionally charged and painful one. The "God is dead" experience probably resembles the "postdivorce" predicament of former cult members who have opted out of their cults and have not yet accommodated to a life outside of it (e.g., Wright, 1987): life in a spinning void with no foundation. As noted, reorganization usually requires plenty of time following loss. However, whether these experiences are ones specifically of grief and whether a protest–despair–detachment–reorganization cycle unfolds remains for future research to determine. Whatever the case may be, it appears fairly uncommon for religious believers to experience the complete loss of God, even following natural disasters (Davis, Kimball,

Aten, Hamilton, et al., 2019). Loss of God, though a prominent theme in some of Swedish filmmaker Ingmar Bergman's foremost masterpieces (e.g., *The Seventh Seal, The Virgin Spring, Winter Light, The Silence*), thus provides a somewhat poor fit with the data.

To summarize, although there are intriguing parallels suggesting that religious believers may react with separation protest and anxiety when confronted with (threat of) separation from God, and possibly with mourning following the experiential loss of God, we do not yet have unequivocal evidence in support of this conclusion. Granted, this lack of unequivocal evidence is likely to stem, in part, from God's unique characteristics (noted above) but also, in part, from the scant and inconclusive empirical research conducted thus far on the matter.

God as a Safe Haven

Another defining component of attachment is that it includes an attachment figure serving as a haven of safety in times of danger or threat. Bowlby (1969/1982) discussed three kinds of situations that activate the attachment system and thus elicit attachment behavior: (1) frightening or alarming environmental events; (2) illness, injury, or fatigue; and (3) separation or threat of separation from attachment figures. Regarding separation, we have already discussed responses to separation from and loss of God, so in this section I discuss religious responses to separation from and loss of one's regular, "earthly" attachment figures.

Although misleading if understood as a comprehensive conclusion regarding all functions of religion and spirituality, religion does appear to be rooted at least partly in various needs for protection and felt security, as Feuerbach (1854/2004), Freud (1961b), Marx (1844/1977), and many others have long speculated. As a common adage has it: There are no atheists in foxholes (although see Chapter 11 and Granqvist & Moström, 2014). Accordingly, Hood and colleagues (1996, pp. 386–387) concluded that people are most likely to "turn to their gods in times of trouble and crisis." They listed three general classes of potential triggers: "illness, disability, and other negative life events that cause both mental and physical distress; the anticipated or actual death of friends and relatives; and dealing with an adverse life situation." This list, in turn, closely resembles Bowlby's (1969/1982) discussion of factors thought to activate the attachment system.

A large body of empirical evidence supports the view that people often turn to religion particularly when they find themselves in the dark alleys of their lives (although, as seen in a burgeoning literature, people may also turn to religion when they find themselves on the sunny side of the street, e.g., Hood et al., 2009; see also Chapter 5). Moreover, the more serious a situation is, and thus the less able the individual is to deal with it on his or her own, the more likely it is to provoke a religious response (Pargament, 1997). For example, being personally affected by an earthquake scoring 3 or 4 on the Richter scale, which merely causes some minor tremors, will not necessarily do the trick, but being personally affected by an earthquake scoring 7, which causes a disaster, very well might (see Sibley & Bulbulia, 2012). It is noteworthy that at such times people primarily turn to faith and prayer (i.e., akin to attachment behavior) rather than to church (i.e., a proxy for social support; Argyle & Beit-Hallahmi, 1975).

When applying coping theory and research from mainstream psychology to the psychology of religion and spirituality, Pargament (1997) outlined various religious coping strategies that people employ when faced with stress. Those strategies include such attachment-related responses as "experienced God's love and care," "realized God was trying to strengthen me," and "let God solve my problems for me." Furthermore, research undertaken within a coping framework has documented that religious individuals tend to turn to God particularly when faced with threats (e.g., danger) and loss (e.g., death of a loved one) (Bjorck & Cohen, 1993; McCrae, 1984).

Frightening, Alarming Events and Crises

With respect to environmental stressors, empirical research suggests that there are indeed few atheists in foxholes (at least in some parts of the world; see Chapter 11): Combat soldiers do pray frequently (Stouffer, 1949). As Allport concluded from his interviews with war veterans (1950, p. 57): "The individual in distress craves affection and security. Sometimes a human bond will suffice, more often it will not." Granted, soldiers may develop strong attachments to their war buddies under combat conditions, and attachments to individuals back home may continue to provide a source of strength (as internalized secure bases), perhaps decreasing the probability of turning to God for protection. As a veteran reported to Allport (1950, p. 56), "There were atheists in foxholes, but most of them were in love." Nonetheless, it may take an omnipotent deity to provide an adequate safe haven when the bullets start flying.

Other severe stressors—beyond earthquakes and warfare—can lead to crises in which other attachment figures may be perceived as insufficient. For example, in a recent prospective study of Louisiana flood survivors, Davis and colleagues (Davis, Kimball, Aten, Andrews, et al., 2019; Davis, Kimball, Aten, Hamilton, et al., 2019), using Kimball and colleagues' (2013) attachment-to-God coding scheme, reported that survivors who were directly and personally affected by the flooding were especially prone to describe their personal relationships with God using safe haven language (e.g., God as a source of protection, comfort, or nurturance). As compared to predisaster (when 36% emphasized God as a safe haven), this proclivity was particularly notable one month postdisaster (82%). (Interestingly, depiction of God as a secure base showed the reverse pattern; see Davis, Kimball, Aten, Hamilton, et al., 2019.)

Also, more than a century of research supports the claim that sudden religious conversions are most likely during times of severe emotional distress and crisis (Clark, 1929; Galanter, 1979; James, 1902; Starbuck, 1899; Ullman, 1982). According to Strickland (1924), the turning point in the sudden religious conversion process comes when one surrenders oneself to God and places one's problems in God's hands (see Chapter 5 for more gradual conversions). Hence, even individuals who did not experience a relationship with God prior to a crisis may come to do so if sufficiently stressed.

Moreover, the source of the distress precipitating religious conversions is often relationship-related; relationship problems with parents and romantic partners have been frequently cited (Granqvist, 1998; Kirkpatrick & Shaver, 1990). For example, in the first attachment–religion study that I—then an undergraduate student at Uppsala University—conducted, one respondent who had experienced a major religious change (i.e., religious beliefs had become much more important) said that she did so following a period of "relationship-problems in the family." She proceeded by saying, "My faith filled my life with something 'more' and provided a frame of reference for life events" (Granqvist, 1998, p. 360). Other common crisis-related themes in that study were divorce and bereavement (discussed below), mental or physical illness, and crises not otherwise specified.

In addition, a set of experimental studies that we have since conducted have shown that appraisal of threat does not require conscious processing to result in increased God-related cognitions (Birgegard & Granqvist, 2004; Granqvist, Mikulincer, Gewirtz, & Shaver, 2012). For example, in an experiment explicitly designed to test the religion-as-attachment model in a Jewish sample of 110 Israeli college students, participants showed increased psychological accessibility to God (or to the concept of God) in a lexical decision task specifically following subliminal exposure to threats (i.e., failure and death; Granqvist et al., 2012, Study 2; for failed replications, however, see Gruneau Brulin, Hill, Laurin, Mikulincer, & Granqvist, 2018, and Chapter 11).

Illness, Injury, Fatigue

Not surprisingly, several studies have shown prayer and other religious responses to be especially common methods of coping with many kinds of serious physical illnesses (for a comprehensive review, see Koenig, King, & Carson, 2012; see also Chapter 7). For example, O'Brien (1982) observed that many renal-failure patients saw God as providing comfort, nurturance, and a source of personal strength for getting through the ailments associated with the condition. Similarly, Gibbs and Achterberg-Lawlis (1978) found that terminally ill cancer patients depended strongly on their religious beliefs and values in coping with imminent death and in mitigating death anxiety. In a more recent example, Cassibba and colleagues (2014) observed that, among patients with a serious disease who were undergoing cancer and renal failure treatments, perceptions of God as consistently available and supportive (i.e., "secure" attachment to God) were related to a "fighting spirit," whereas perceptions of God as distant or inconsistently supportive (i.e., "insecure" attachment to God) were linked to a sense of hopelessness. Other studies have shown religion to be particularly helpful to people who cope with *chronic* rather than acute illness (e.g., Mattlin, Wethington, & Kessler, 1990).

Separation and Loss from "Earthly" Attachment Figures

Research suggests that religiousness and prayer tend to increase following the death of or (threat of) separation from loved ones and that religious beliefs are correlated positively with successful coping at these times (e.g., Cicirelli, 2004; Loveland, 1968; Parkes, 1972). Relevant research has focused mostly on the effects of spousal (i.e., the principal attachment relationship in adulthood) separation/bereavement. As noted in Chapter 1, loss of a principal attachment figure is a particularly powerful stressor in part because it eliminates the availability of the person to whom one would otherwise be likely to turn for support in a stressful situation. When a human attachment figure is lost, a perceived relationship with God may therefore become an appealing alternative.

I have already noted, in reference to Granqvist (1998), that many of the crises reported retrospectively by religious converts involved relationship-focused difficulties, including loss of or separation from attachment figures, particularly through relationship breakups and divorce (see also Kirkpatrick & Shaver, 1990). Similarly, Brown, Nesse, House, and Utz (2004) have provided converging evidence from a large-scale ($N = 1,532$), population-based prospective longitudinal study of elderly Americans. Some of the participants were destined to suffer bereavement during the course of the study, so Brown and colleagues saw a unique opportunity to test whether loss of an attachment figure would indeed lead to a stronger reliance on one's religious beliefs, as predicted by the attachment–religion model. Their study yielded three notable findings of relevance here. First, they found a prospective increase in the importance of religious beliefs for the bereaved individuals compared to a matched comparison group of nonbereaved individuals. Second, grief over the loss prospectively decreased among the bereaved who had reported increased importance of their religious beliefs versus those who had not reported increased importance of their religious beliefs. Third and finally, these effects withstood statistical control of a host of covariates (such as "Big Five" personality dimensions), and none of them were obtained when church attendance rather than importance of religious beliefs was studied. Considered jointly, Brown and colleagues' findings indicate that it may be the attachment components of the individual's religiousness that are activated following loss of an attachment figure and that these, in turn, contribute to a more favorable outcome (see also Chapter 7).

Although Brown and colleagues' (2004) study was impressive (in my view it is probably the best naturalistic study yet conducted on the attachment–religion connection), it was necessarily a correlational study. In other words, nothing was manipulated, so cause–effect relations cannot be definitively delineated. In addition, the study concerned the presumed effects of real-life losses and separations, not threats of loss or separation. However, one of our experimental studies yielded further support for the prediction (Birgegard & Granqvist, 2004, Study 2). In that experiment ($N = 61$), theistic believers showed a moderate-sized increase ($d = 0.61$) in their wish to be close to God following a subliminal separation threat ("Mother is gone") targeting their relationship with their mother (i.e., the principal attachment figure in childhood), compared to participants in an attachment-neutral control condition.

In conclusion, there is abundant evidence for the notion of God as a safe haven. Support for that idea is not only relatively consistent across empirical studies but it also comes from many sources, ranging from religious phenomenology and texts, via psychology of religion literature predating (or parallel to) the attachment–religion connection, to attachment-informed naturalistic research and hard-boiled lab experiments.

Finally, it is noteworthy that the safe haven function of religion described above is embedded in the religious individual's relationship with an institutionally sanctioned and anthropomorphic deity. However, many seemingly spontaneous occurrences of "paranormal" experiences that are not sanctioned by institutionalized religion and that do not revolve around an anthropomorphic deity—such as extrasensory perception (ESP) and out-of-body experiences—may also be precipitated by significant turmoil (e.g., Irwin, 1993, 2009). Given that such experiences may occur in the absence of attributions to a divine power or any other form of comforting presence, their occurrence does not require perceptions of the availability of a safe haven. Later (Chapters 6–8), I discuss the possibility that religious experiences occurring in relation to perceptions of a comforting safe haven may have different correlates and sequelae than paranormal experiences occurring in the absence of such perceptions.

God as a Secure Base

Another defining characteristic of an attachment relationship is that it provides a secure base for exploration and, relatedly, a sense of felt security. Religious literature is again replete with examples. Perhaps the best-known example is the 23rd Psalm: "Yea, though I walk through the valley of the shadow of death, I will fear no evil: for thou art with me; thy rod and thy staff, they comfort me." Elsewhere in the Psalms, God is described or addressed as "a shield for me" (3:3), "the Lord hears when I call to Him" (4:3), "my rock, and my fortress" (18:2), "He guides me along the right paths" (23:3) and is "the strength of my life" (27:1).

It is not difficult to fathom how an attachment figure who is simultaneously omnipresent, omniscient, *and* omnipotent—all very impressive qualities that are likely to make other attachment figures green with envy—can provide the most secure of secure bases. This is what led Kaufman (1981) to his conclusion that God represents an "absolutely adequate attachment figure." Writing about faith, Johnson (1945, p. 191) similarly concluded:

> The emotional quality of faith is indicated in a basic confidence and security that gives one assurance. In this sense faith is the opposite of fear, anxiety, and uncertainty. Without emotional security there is no relaxation, but tension, distress, and instability. Assurance is the firm emotional undertone that enables one to have steady nerves and calm poise in the face of danger or confusion.

Johnson's portrayal of faith closely resembles Bowlby's (1973, p. 202) own later descriptions of the secure base and its psychological effects: "When an individual is confident that an attachment figure will be available to him whenever he desires it, that person will be much less prone to either intense or chronic fear than will an individual who for any reason has no such confidence." In their eagerness to study religious outcomes in reaction to stressful events, researchers have unfortunately paid less attention to the question of how religious beliefs and experiences affect behavior and cognition in the absence of stressors. Thus, there is less direct evidence for a secure-base function of religion than for a safe haven function.

Nevertheless, there is also both direct and indirect support for a secure-base function. Some of the research supportive of indirect effects was reviewed in the "points of departure" section above, and some will be reviewed in Chapter 7, where I examine mental health in relation to the attachment–religion connection. Regarding direct effects, the notion of God as a secure base received support in two of our experiments with theistic Jews in Israel (Granqvist, Mikulincer, et al., 2012). In the first of these experiments (Study 3), which included 79 participants, we subliminally primed study participants with the word "God" and a neutral control ("Ton") to test whether exposure to the presumed secure base (i.e., God) does indeed facilitate psychological access to positive, secure-base-related concepts (e.g., "loving," responsive," "accepting") in a lexical decision task. Besides secure-base-related target words, we also used neutral target words (e.g., "window") and, importantly, negative words (e.g., "controlling," "harsh," "strict"). Negative target words were included because doing so enabled us to test the presumption, common among psychologists, that God first and foremost has negative connotations deep in people's minds. Our findings, however, were very clear: Subliminal exposure to "God" significantly heightened the average participant's cognitive access specifically to positive, secure-base-related concepts, and not to negative or neutral concepts.

In a follow-up experiment with a new sample ($N = 78$), we tested the additional secure-base corollary that if one's relationship with God functions as a secure base from which to explore one's immediate surroundings, then a reminder of that relationship should lead to positive affect, which then transfers to one's immediate surroundings (see also Mikulincer, Hirschberger, Nachmias, & Gillath, 2001). In line with that prediction, we found that priming with a religious symbol (a Torah scroll)—compared with a neutral symbol (a "plain" book) or no symbol at all—caused participants to have a greater liking for neutral material (Chinese ideograms).

In addition, a separate line of experiments has supported the secure-base corollary that reminders of God (compared with neutral material) make religious study participants (from the United States and Sweden) more willing to take recreational (cf. exploratory) risks, such as scuba diving (Gruneau Brulin et al., 2018; Kupor, Laurin, & Levav, 2015). The findings from Kupor and colleagues (2015) indicate that this effect may be due to reminders of God causing people to view these risks as less dangerous, via a sense of being protected by God.

In conclusion, although the secure-base component of believers' relationships with God has been subjected to considerably less research than the safe haven function, it has nonetheless been uniformly supported, by both direct and indirect sources of evidence. The case in favor of this conclusion will be further strengthened when we consider attachment to God in relation to matters of mental health (Chapter 7).

The Attachment Figure Is Perceived to Be Stronger and Wiser

To highlight the asymmetrical nature of attachment, Bowlby (1969/1982) used the term "attachment relationship" to denote the relationship that a weaker, less knowledgeable individual has with another individual perceived as stronger and wiser. The prototypical case is of course that of a mammalian offspring with its adult caregiver(s).

Concerning believers' perceived relationship with God, it almost goes without saying that believers typically do perceive God as very much stronger and wiser than themselves. In fact, according to much theological doctrine, God is supposedly omnipotent (can do anything), omniscient (knows everything), and omnipresent (is everywhere), in addition to being omnibenevolent (all good). That is not to say that every religious believer always represents God in all of these charitable ways at the same time. If they did, they would probably shrug their shoulders at the eternal and pervasive problem of theodicy—that is, the existence of suffering (or evil) in spite of God's "super traits." Instead, this problem is at least as real for religious believers as it is for nonbelievers, although believers to a larger extent than nonbelievers tend to blame suffering/evil on human ignorance or wickedness (Furnham & Brown, 1992). Although speculative, I suspect that such maneuvers aid believers in maintaining a benevolent representation of a God who is also very strong and wise, and who harmonizes with the messages they receive in their religious (sub-)cultures. When the believer is faced with adversity, God will not just know (omniscience) and will not just be able to help (omnipotence), but will also want to help the individual to overcome that adversity (benevolence). As noted, these attributes are difficult for earthly caregivers, sensitive though they may be, to compete with. Those caregivers may suffice to calm you down when the ground trembles a little, say, following a minor or moderate earthquake. Unlike God, however, they are unlikely to be of much help when the ground opens up underneath your feet in conjunction with a disastrous earthquake.

Concluding the "Straightforward Story"

To conclude this section on believers' perceived relationships with God in relation to the constituents of attachment relationships, we have seen persuasive evidence that the former might belong in the same class as the latter. God does indeed appear to *function*, psychologically, as an attachment figure in the minds of many religious believers. This conclusion holds up, I argue, at least in the theistic traditions studied to date (i.e., mostly Christianity and Judaism, although for the case of Islam, see additional evidence in Ghobary, Miner, & Proctor, 2013; Miner, Ghobary, Dowson, & Proctor, 2014). The case holds up particularly well for the safe haven function of attachment.

Granted, there was less persuasive evidence for mourning, and for the protest–despair–detachment–reorganization cycle in particular, than for the other components, but it would seem unreasonable to render the attachment–God link unsupported merely for that reason, especially as the lack of evidence stems largely from scant research. Future research may well yield support for those aspects as well. In addition, the secure-base component has been far less studied than the safe haven function, although both the direct and indirect sources of available evidence do uniformly support the notion of God as a secure base. Finally, support for some of the components was difficult to establish because of God's unique characteristics as an invisible, eternal entity who is always in proximity to people, who thus never dies and from whom one cannot really separate, at least not until the hereafter. However, rather than challenging the inclusion of "attachment to God" in the class of real attachment relationships, I believe it is more reasonable to evaluate these unique characteristics of God as providing additional support for the conclusion that God is constructed as an attachment figure, and not just as any attachment figure but indeed as the ideal one—the one "who is always there" and whose benevolence, knowledge, and power are nothing short of perfection.

Wait a Minute, Is God *Really* an Attachment Figure?

Beyond the lack of persuasive evidence for some attachment components, there are at least three interrelated problems with the straightforward conclusion that God is an attachment figure proper. The first is that this particular attachment figure is *invisible,* and thus we cannot determine with any empirical confidence that it actually exists outside the minds of religious believers. Thus, although believers may develop the sense of an attachment relationship to God—which psychologically *functions* like other attachments—can we really conclude that God *is* an attachment figure when we cannot rule out the possibility that God is merely a figment of believers' imaginations?

Second, other attachment relationships form over time as a function of a *continuous, physical, and reciprocal interaction history* between the attached person and the attachment figure (as captured in Bowlby's [1969/1982] discussion of the phases of attachment formation). The infant signals and the caregiver responds (often with physical contact) on many, many occasions during the first months of life, and an attachment forms only as a consequence of such repeated interaction sequences. Moreover, such is the case not only for children, but also for adult couple members who have formed a pair bond (e.g., Zeifman & Hazan, 2016; see also Chapter 3).

Whether religious believers actually have an interaction history with God is debatable. Many believers *think* they do (i.e., as an inherent part of their theistic beliefs and related experiences), but many nonbelievers are likely to think that believers are, in fact, delusional (i.e., as an expression of the nonbelievers' own atheistic beliefs; see Dawkins's *The God Delusion* [2006] as an example). Notably, however, even within religious people's beliefs and experiences, it is exceptional for most of them to experience their relationship with God as physically concrete on more than perhaps rare occasions (for example, in the context of a mystical experience; see Chapter 8), if indeed on any occasions at all. Consequently, religious expressions such as "being held by God" are probably understood largely as metaphorical rather than "real," in a physical sense, even by religious believers (although there are important denominational differences in this respect).

Third, it should be recalled that an attachment figure, in Ainsworth's (1985) usage of the term, has to be an *individual* (i.e., because attachment is "an affectional bond between two individuals"[2]). Above, I set aside this consideration because I think it undermines the "straightforward," implicitly essentialist story of God as attachment figure that I told there. Granted, God is mentally carved out of anthropomorphic, personalized material, but it would be a stretch to call God an individual proper. Some Christians and potentially Hindus as well might disagree, noting that the historical Jesus (and perhaps Krishna too) was in fact an individual. Although it is indeed telling from an attachment viewpoint that deities are made into personages and individuals are sometimes viewed as deities, neither Jesus nor Krishna is currently present as an individual. In addition, from a theological point of view—if I may—I think it would be a mistake to reduce God to an individual. This is because God is supposedly also, for example, ineffable, eternal, invisible, abstract, and mysterious, and individuals do not have such properties. Furthermore, well-developed and cultured religious minds tend to embrace those latter qualities at the expense of an anthropomorphic understanding of God (e.g., Fowler & Dell, 2006; Silverman, Johnson, & Cohen, 2016; Streib, 2001). They might express concerns about overanthropomorphizations of God—"the man in the clouds," for example—as relics of childish thought. Indeed, they could rightly point to extant literature on "God, the attachment figure" as a case in point (cf. Wulff, 2006).

Furthermore, if we were to remove the "individual" requisite for inclusion in the class of attachment figures, then the gate for potential attachment figures becomes—in my view—excessively open. Nonindividual entities such as blankets, teddy bears, pacifiers, smartphones, groups, nations, places, nature, cigarettes, a favorite pipe, needles (for drugs), buildings, and many more could then be included in the class of attachment figures because those things may display *some* fit to the attachment relationship criteria without qualifying for Ainsworth's (1985) requisite of a relationship with an individual.

Notably, and perhaps for these reasons, neither Bowlby nor Ainsworth ever discussed, in published writing at least,[3] the possibility that God should be included in the attachment figure category. Moreover, this is in spite of their serious considerations of other candidate attachments, such as spousal attachment, attachment to older siblings and relatives, to day care providers, teachers, mentors, and even priests and pastors (see Ainsworth, 1985).

In summary, then, should we really conclude that an invisible entity, who is not an individual (at least not a corporeal one), whose actual responsiveness remains disputable—and for the most part may be understood as metaphorical—qualifies *qua* attachment figure? This is not what Bowlby and Ainsworth had in mind, nor what later developmental psychologists have had in mind, with the concept of attachment figure. Hence, insofar as we approach "attachment" as an essentialist, criterion-based construct, the simple, straightforward conclusion would seem to be: No, God does not meet all of the "necessary conditions" for inclusion in the class of attachment figures. Yet, as a psychologist, I have to confess that I am less interested in living with the somewhat arbitrary boundary conditions of abstract concepts (such as "attachments") than with the actual workings of the human mind; and in many religious believers' minds, God definitely does seem to *function* as an attachment figure. Moreover, I argue that if we move beyond essentialism (which we should, for reasons noted below), we can legitimately categorize "attachment to God" as a functional member of the larger "family" of attachment relationships.

The Fuzzy Boundary Story

Although it is doubtful that the most fruitful approach to deciding category membership is a definition based on necessary and sufficient conditions, for reasons of scientific convention I nonetheless applied this approach in the sections above. A very different approach is suggested by taking (the late) Wittgenstein's (1953/1999) notion of "family resemblances" seriously. After finding different kinds of similarities among instances of a category (e.g., the category "games") but finding no "essence," Wittgenstein concluded, "I can think of no better expression to characterize these similarities than 'family resemblances'; for the various resemblances between members of a family: build, features, colour of eyes, gait, temperament, etc. etc. overlap and criss-cross in the same way.—And I shall say: 'games' form a family" (p. 66). Virtually all psychological constructs are fuzzy in this way, and this is because they refer to experiences, which are difficult to capture in words, and ranges of behavior whose meaning depends on contexts, cultures, and more. Therefore, when I conclude that God often functions as an attachment figure for religious believers, I do not do so with an essentialist understanding of "attachment" in mind. To the contrary, in this book, "attachment" and "attachment figure" should be understood as having somewhat fuzzy boundaries. More specifically, I accept "attachment to God" as bearing a persuasive family resemblance to a child's attachment to parents. And I believe that the value of conceptualizing God as an attachment figure has been demonstrated by the large body of research, reviewed above and in later chapters, that this approach has inspired.

Much research in cognitive psychology dealing with how people *actually* categorize things suggests that we should take Wittgenstein seriously. In general, that research has strongly supported models of categorization based on Eleanor Rosch's conception of fuzzy categories organized around prototypes, an alternative to essentialist ("necessary and sufficient conditions") models. (See, e.g., Rosch 1987, 1988; Rosch & Mervis, 1975; and many applications of Rosch's ideas in the study of emotion—e.g., Shaver, Murdaya, & Fraley, 2001; Shaver, Schwartz, Kirson, & O'Connor, 1987.) Taking Rosch's prototype approach to defining attachment, most attachment scholars would probably agree that the infant–caregiver relationship, at infant age 12–20 months, is the category prototype, and I conjecture that so would most other people if they participated in a categorization study. In order to add a new "family member" to the attachment category, it seems reasonable to request that it bear convincing resemblances to the prototype. Most attachment scholars would probably also agree that, in descending order, the typical preschooler's, school-age child's, adolescent's, and young adult's relationships with parents continue to bear sufficient resemblances to the infant–caregiver attachment prototype for continued class membership to be warranted.

This is the case in spite of the developing person's decreased "needs" for physical proximity and the availability of the parent as a safe haven and secure base. It is still likely to be an affectional bond with another individual; sufficient attachment system activation may still trigger the somewhat older individual's mental representation of the parent; and the parent's death is still likely to lead to mourning, for example. Similarly, most attachment scholars probably agree, in line with Bowlby's (1980) analysis, that adult pair bonds (e.g., the bond between marital partners) typically display sufficient resemblances to the prototype to qualify for inclusion in the attachment category, even though none of the partners is necessarily perceived as much stronger and wiser than the other. (That is, this relationship does not have the characteristic asymmetry of the infant–caregiver prototype, except in certain circumstances, when one person is troubled and seeks proximity to the other as a safe haven and secure base). Although perhaps more controversial, most attachment scholars would probably also agree that attachments—in the family resemblance sense—continue for a considerable time period after the death of an attachment figure, even when he or she cannot possibly respond physically to the attached person (see Fraley & Shaver, 2016).

My main conclusion from this discussion of category membership is that research has demonstrated that "attachment to God" bears sufficient similarities with the infant–caregiver prototype that it should be included in the family of attachment relationships. Yet, the fact remains that God is potentially nonexistent, invisible, and perhaps not *really* an individual. The fact that God is often sensed more in a metaphorical than in a physical way indicates that there are real and substantial dissimilarities with virtually all other attachment figures. In fact, so marked are these differences that we should probably use some special signifier to make clear that we are talking about a special case of the attachment category. Such a signifier may also help to prevent dilution of the attachment construct. For these reasons, I refer to God as a *noncorporeal* attachment figure and to a believer's perceived relationship with God as a *noncorporeal* attachment relationship. Although "noncorporeal" is a difficult word to say, I use it for lack of a more suitable word.[4] Readers allergic to unusual terminology should feel free to say "nonphysical" in reference to what I mean, although with the qualifier (noted above) that God may sometimes be *experienced* physically (see Chapter 8).

I wish to clarify that the "noncorporeal" (or nonphysical) adjective should not be understood to imply "less important," let alone "less real." As the reader will be aware—certainly after reading this book, if not before—for humans, nonphysical entities are often every bit as important and real as physical ones, if not more so. The proclivity to imbue the world with nonphysical entities, to view them as central in the universe, and to congregate and cooperate around them as though they were more important and real than what's physically observable is one of the most intriguing aspects of human functioning. It sets humans apart from other members of the animal kingdom (Harari, 2014). This proclivity develops fairly early in child development, as we shall see in the next chapter.

Noncorporeal Attachments in Nontheistic Religions?

In this chapter, I have mostly referred to research on theistic religions, Protestant Christianity in particular. This naturally raises the question of whether God or some other noncorporeal entity functions as an attachment figure in other religious traditions as well.

In general, even in Eastern religions—which many Westerners tend to think of as "godless" philosophies—there is a marked tendency, among common men and women in particular, to treat religious figures as though they were gods who can hear what you pray for and see what you sacrifice to them. This seems to apply to many Buddhists' ways of relating to Buddha or to some Bodhisattva within Mahayana Buddhism (such as the Dalai Lama). Both within and beyond Buddhism, it also seems to apply to how the common man and woman relates to ancestral spirits, imported from folk religions (see Kirkpatrick, 1994). In other words, attachment components such as seeking closeness with and felt security from religious figures may well be present, even though the religion itself is not theistic in the formal sense.

Beyond the possibility of attachment to nontheistic religious figures, and in line with the "wider view" adopted in this book, there are many other intriguing commonalities between attachment and Buddhist practices. Such commonalities have been reviewed in more detail elsewhere (e.g., Granqvist, Mikulincer, & Shaver, 2010; Mikulincer & Shaver, 2016). Suffice to say here that a common form of compassion meditation involves remembering what it feels like to have an attachment figure provide one with unconditional love; this love is then turned outward toward other people, at first in one's imagination but later in behavior as well (e.g., Chödrön, 2008). As though she were an attachment theorist—although she is actually a Buddhist nun—Chödrön (2008, pp. 23–24) notes that "our mind is always seeking zones of safety." She continues, "We fear losing our illusion of security—that's what makes us so anxious." Here Buddhism and attachment theory may seem to part company, as most attachment theorists hold that the zones of safety associated with actual interpersonal attachments do not just yield illusions of security but actual security. However, if we desperately "grasp for" security in another person (as do, for example, many preoccupied adults; see Chapter 6), this may both reflect and exacerbate anxiety. Furthermore, one of the most common Buddhist prayers is "I take refuge in the Buddha, the Dharma, and the Sangha." Viewed from an attachment perspective, this might translate to relying on mental representations of a loving, compassionate, and insightful teacher (the Buddha), his teachings (the Dharma), and the community of fellow Buddhist believers (Sangha), to attain a safe haven and secure base.

Naturally, not everything within every single religious tradition is best understood from an attachment viewpoint. For example, I suspect that the "theologically" well-educated elites living (faithfully) within philosophy of life traditions such as Daoism, Confucianism, and strands of Hinayana Buddhism do not develop attachments to religious figures (such as the Buddha) or to metaphysical principles (such as the Dao). Those religions—if that word applies, which is itself a thorny issue—do not profess that there is any invisible external agent beyond the self with whom "believers" can develop a personal relationship. Rather, those traditions tend to deemphasize metaphysical beliefs and instead emphasize certain "nongrasping" mindsets as well as practices and techniques used to bring them about.

If "faithful" adherents of Daoism and Confucianism did develop religious attachments, it would indicate that the attachment system finds noncorporeal targets even when the mind is trained and "socialized" *not* to do so. However, and as we have elaborated elsewhere, nature (e.g., the attachment system) for the most part acts in concert with, not in opposition to, nurture (e.g., training, socialization; Granqvist & Nkara, 2017).

Finally, I would like to make clear that in this chapter I have not sought to provide a pathway for consideration of other attachment relationships beyond attachment to God. The proposal for any new attachment candidate (attachment to place, to smartphones, to imaginary companions, etc.) should be evaluated, both conceptually and empirically, in its own right.

CHAPTER SUMMARY

In this chapter I have reviewed evidence that God is constructed, perceived, and used as an attachment figure. Believers' perceived personal relationships with God function, psychologically, much like other attachment relationships do. Not only do the themes of relationality, love, and parent–childlike representations of God in relation to self suggest a striking analogy between religious beliefs/experiences and attachment relationships, but empirical research also indicates that religious believers' perceived relationships with God often tend to meet many of the more precise aspects (criteria) thought to characterize attachment relationships. In particular, religious believers strive to achieve or maintain personal closeness to God, they use God as a safe haven when distressed, and they assess God as a stronger and wiser other, who is represented as a secure base when exploring other matters. In sum, religious believers tend to derive felt security in their perceived relationship with God, just as people do in other attachment relationships. I also attended to the real and substantial differences between God and other attachment figures; unlike most other attachment figures, God is an invisible entity, who is not a corporeal individual and whose actual responsiveness remains disputable (and may often be understood as metaphorical). However, I argued that, like most psychological constructs, "attachment" is a fuzzy category that should not be approached in an essentialist manner (in terms of necessary/sufficient conditions) after all. I concluded that "attachment to God" belongs in the family of attachment relationships but that it falls within a special subclass of noncorporeal attachments. At the end of the day, it doesn't really matter much whether one is willing to approach attachment as a fuzzy category and/or whether one is willing to include God as a noncorporeal member of that category. In either case, the value of conceptualizing God as an attachment figure has been demonstrated empirically by the large body of research reviewed in this and later chapters. Finally, I discussed nontheistic expressions of spirituality, such as in Buddhism, noting that they sometimes conform with attachments and sometimes not.

CHAPTER 3

Religious and Spiritual Development in Relation to Attachment Maturation

In the previous chapter, I got slightly ahead of myself by focusing on the attachment–religion connection in adulthood, sidestepping the story of how religious and spiritual development unfolds at younger ages. In this chapter I adopt a lifespan developmental–maturational approach, arguing that people's representations of and perceived relationships with a deity go hand in hand with—indeed are directly built upon—attachment-related maturation. The bulk of this chapter provides a developmental account of religious and spiritual development from an attachment–maturation viewpoint, divided into sections according to developmental period. But before addressing the developmental periods and transitions themselves, I briefly explain some of the underlying principles.

UNDERLYING DEVELOPMENTAL PRINCIPLES

The term "maturation" is often misunderstood to imply that development is simply a natural function of some hardwired neural program (or developmental "plan") that inevitably unfolds over time, almost regardless of environmental input. Although I have already stated (in the Prologue) that this is not the maturational model I adopt in this book, the matter deserves more attention. This is because misunderstandings of maturation interfere with a proper understanding of how and why development occurs. To give a few simple examples: The embryo doesn't develop into a healthy fetus, with a well-functioning brain, in the absence of exogenously derived nutrition, nor in the frequent presence of teratogens (i.e., toxic substances that pass through the placenta). Similarly, although neonates are genetically predisposed to detect and recognize visual patterns associated with human faces, the neural mechanism for face recognition requires actual, repeated exposure to human faces to develop appropriately (e.g., Greenough et al., 1987). More generally, although neonates and infants come equipped with a marked social responsiveness, in the absence of social stimulation (say, from a caregiver), development unfolds unfavorably.

The environmental inputs are so normative (or species-typical) that virtually all developing persons encounter them, and virtually all persons develop in species-typical ways. Although of foundational importance in development, because such environmental inputs display almost no variation, their importance is—ironically—easy to miss. This risk is especially notable for scholars who give privileged attention to individual differences (or trait variation) at the expense of species-typical development (Harris, 2011; Pinker, 2003). However, we inherit not just our ancestors' genes but also the most foundational aspects of our ancestors' environments, and we are genetically predisposed to profit from those "experience-expected" aspects of environments (Greenough et al., 1987).

Even when some genetic variation is present, species-typical environments may "canalize" (via epigenetic regulation) virtually all offspring to develop species-typical characteristics that are necessary for survival and reproduction. The notion of canalization (i.e., the ability of an organism to produce the same phenotype despite variation in genotype [or environment]) may seem new and somewhat speculative. But the idea of canalization dates back to the writings of embryologist (developmental biologist) and pioneering system theorist Conrad Waddington (e.g., 1942; see also 1957) in the late 1930s to early 1940s. Nevertheless, it took some 50 years for most scholars to appreciate epigenetics and to reveal the epigenetic mechanisms at work. The principle of canalization was central to Bowlby's (1969/1982) understanding of how nature and nurture interact in the development of attachment.

Despite my emphasis on the importance of certain environmental inputs, I do not want this stance to be mistaken for a biased focus on nurture (environmental factors) at the expense of nature (genetic predispositions). To the contrary, and in line with my advocacy of nature–nurture interactions permeating virtually everything in development, I could restate my argument to place an equally strong emphasis on genes: Without certain DNA and associated genetic predispositions, none of the aforementioned environmental factors would bring about any of those species-typical developmental acquisitions. In short, species-typical developmental maturation builds on nature–nurture interaction.

Beyond maturation, the challenges we confront in understanding religious and spiritual development require that we take Bowlby (1969/1982) seriously in his conclusion that the functional development of behavioral systems reflects increases in *differentiation, integration,* and *complexity.* To Bowlby's list, we can now add the more recent concept of *developmental plasticity* (strongly implied by Bowlby) as underlying those increases. Regarding increased differentiation, from the neonate's seemingly "promiscuous" social responsiveness, the infant and later the child will differentiate his or her responsiveness so that it becomes directed particularly to those people (i.e., attachment figures) who have responded to the developing person's signals. Concerning increased integration, from the neonate's seemingly random and uncoordinated bodily movements, the infant and later the child will have his or her bodily movements, cognitive processes, and emotional states increasingly coordinated with one another.

Bowlby (1969/1982) emphasized that the development of attachment is contingent on, indeed integrated with, other aspects of development. These include many kinds of developmental acquisitions: cognitive (e.g., object permanence, representational abilities, mentalization), motoric (e.g., increased mobility), emotional (e.g., basic emotions) and self-related (e.g., self-conscious emotions). As development unfolds beyond the early years, the attachment system becomes increasingly connected with other aspects of functioning. Finally, regarding increased complexity, from the neonate's reliance on rigidly organized reflexes, the child will increasingly take executive control of his or her actions, flexibly adjusting them to the expected demands of specific situations while considering alternative courses of action.

Such plasticity-driven increases in differentiation, integration, and complexity jointly enable diversity in development. For example, some developing persons will adopt religious and spiritual entities as targets for their attachment systems, whereas others will not. Also, as increased integration occurs, the attachment system will rarely "act on its own," as some insular neurocognitive mechanism, but will typically interact with other modalities. This is important with regard to religious and spiritual development because the pertinent literature is replete with proposed neural and cognitive mechanisms thought to underlie religious and spiritual development. In other words, the attachment system does not produce religious and spiritual development on its own, but rather in concert with other, interrelated neural and cognitive modalities. Indeed, if the attachment system yielded development on its own, we would expect to see corresponding religious and spiritual developments in other primate species, but we do not. Thus, neither the attachment system per se nor any other specific neural/cognitive modality is sufficient for understanding religious and spiritual development.

If we were to design a religious/spiritual artificial intelligence (AI) machine, closely mimicking humans, we would need to program the machine not just with the hominin version of the attachment system, but also with other interrelated systems. We would also have to ascertain that these systems communicate closely with one another rather than act in isolation. I therefore do not restrict my developmental analysis of religious and spiritual development solely to attachment considerations in the sections that follow; I also examine how the attachment system joins forces with other modalities in development.

The AI engineer would also have to create a machine whose systems are open to feedback from the surrounding environment. Such feedback must include "calibrating" the influence of the surrounding environment as it responds to the machine's attachment behaviors, enabling the machine to form generalizing working models of self and others (see Chapter 5). In addition, such feedback must include aspects of the surrounding culture from which the machine may identify and learn about (e.g., via observation) particular religious and spiritual entities. If the environment provides content messages indicating that a particular nonobservable entity deeply cares about and actually responds to attachment behavior, then the machine will be more likely to seek out and maintain that nonobservable entity as a target of its attachment system and other related systems. This means that, in understanding religious and spiritual development from an attachment perspective, we must also consider the role of social (or cultural) learning. I deal with such learning in the following sections of this chapter (and in more detail in Chapters 5 and 10).

RELIGIOUS AND SPIRITUAL DEVELOPMENT VIS-À-VIS ATTACHMENT MATURATION

This section is divided by developmental period—infancy and toddlerhood; the preschool period; middle childhood; adolescence and early adulthood; and, finally, middle adulthood and old age. Readers who have a particular interest in a specific period are referred to other sources (Granqvist, 2012, 2014b, 2016a; Granqvist & Dickie, 2006; Richert & Granqvist, 2013). Because religious and spiritual development build coherently upon attachment-related maturations that occur during these developmental periods, it is important to pay attention first to the basic attachment-related maturations from which religious and spiritual development emanate. I introduced attachment maturation from birth through the preschool period in Chapter 1, as part of my delineation of Bowlby's phases from preattachment to the goal-corrected partnership, and I do not repeat that account here. Instead, I describe developmental acquisitions beyond attachment. For the subsections dealing with middle childhood through old age, I first introduce pertinent attachment-related developments along with other important developmental acquisitions and then consider related religious and spiritual developments.

Infancy and Toddlerhood

Beyond attachment-related maturation, and due to the marked immaturity and plasticity of a human newborn's brain, much of the increases in differentiation, integration, and complexity take place during the first 2 years of life. This reflects the maturation of genetically based neural systems, part of which is accomplished by environmental input (or feedback) to those systems.

Taking cognitive development as a first illustration, Piaget (1926/1930) argued that the infant initially develops cognitive schemas from highly concrete sensorimotor exploration (i.e., by means of body movements and sensory registration). Through the acquisition of object permanence and an increasing reliance on mental representations, in the second year of life the toddler becomes capable of more complex ways of understanding and representing the world, partly due to an integration of schemas. Developmental "core" cognition theorists (e.g., Wellman & Gelman, 1992) have made a compelling case that infants also come equipped with a genetic preparedness for acquiring knowledge especially rapidly in certain core functional domains (e.g., infants have an intuitive understanding of elementary physics).

Development of the self is a second illustrative example. In the first months of life, infants possess an implicit sense of the self as distinct from surroundings (i.e., self-awareness; e.g., Rochat & Hespos, 1997), but more than a year typically elapses before they gain an explicit understanding of that self (i.e., exhibiting self-recognition; e.g., Harter, 1999). Following the development of self-recognition, the toddler's emotional repertoire also becomes increasingly complex, reflecting an integration of self-relevant information with emotional states, as expressed in the rudimentary self-conscious emotions: guilt, shame, pride, and envy. Like language for explicit social communication, emotions are an infant's principal mode of implicit social communication, and emotions need first and foremost to be understood as socially functional tools. Consequently, early emotional development enables infants to "read" others' emotional states (e.g., Stenberg, 2003).

Imitation is also important as a general tool that increases a young child's social adaptation (e.g., Bjorklund, 1997; Tomasello, Kruger, & Ratner, 1993). Shortly after birth, infants are capable of imitating not just emotional expressions (i.e., via emotional contagion; e.g., Stern, 1985) but also other forms of simple overt behaviors (such as a protruded tongue), presumably reflecting activation of the brain's mirror neuron system (Iacoboni & Dapretto, 2006). Later, the infant gains an increasing ability for delayed imitation and may also imitate more complex behavioral sequences (e.g., Barr, Muentener, & Garcia, 2007).

With regard to religious and spiritual development, the aforementioned developmental acquisitions of infancy and toddlerhood display a notably *paradoxical* relation to religious and spiritual development (Granqvist, 2014b). On one hand, infants and toddlers are absorbed in the worlds of their senses; how concrete things look, feel, taste, smell, and sound. Indeed, they are for the most part happily unaware of any invisible world. For that reason alone, I think this phase of development is best viewed as prereligious and prespiritual. Infants are ideally basking in the love provided by caregivers, and their caregivers can be seen, felt, heard, smelled, and tasted. The infant's mental representations similarly concern concrete objects, people, and situations, although he or she may become interested in (or surprised by) counterintuitive material that violates implicit expectations of how the world works (e.g., an object violating the laws of gravity; Baillargeon & DeVos, 1991; Camras et al., 2002). Also, and as noted in Chapter 1, to the extent that the infant–toddler directs attachment behaviors to surrogate objects (e.g., in periods of separation from attachment figures), those objects tend to be highly concrete (e.g., a pacifier or familiar blanket). Notably, such surrogate objects become increasingly important as a function of increased autonomy as the growing toddler makes his or her way into the outer world (e.g., full days at day care).

On the other hand, I argue that development in infancy and toddlerhood is unparalleled in importance for what, at later stages of development, becomes religious and spiritual development. Although it is difficult to empirically substantiate because of insufficient variation in children's developmental environments, I conjecture that if no caregiver has interacted with a particular infant–toddler, enabling no attachment relationship to develop during the first years of life, the child will not only be at a disadvantage for developing attachments to other humans (e.g., Zeanah, Smyke, Koga, & Carlson, 2005) but also will have difficulty directing attachment behaviors to noncorporeal attachment targets, such as God, later in development. This is because the attachment system would be chronically thwarted due to insufficient environmental feedback during a sensitive phase of development. Put differently, there would be no interaction history as a basis for working models of self and others to develop from, let alone generalize from (see Chapter 5).

Relatedly, an infant–toddler who has had no contact with an intentional being—for example, no experience of joint attention or of being "pointed" or directed toward certain stimuli—would probably not acquire mentalization skills later in development. For that reason, such a child would probably be unable to imagine or attribute mind states to divine agents. For the same reason, if the infant–toddler never had an experience of objects reappearing after being out of sight, he or she would probably not develop object permanence, and would therefore not gain an understanding that entities (again, including God) may exist even if they are not perceived. Similarly, if the infant–toddler were never to perceive an object in motion, he or she might not gain an understanding of elementary physics (e.g., gravity). Later in development, such a child would presumably not wonder about "ultimate" causation, such as whatever it is that causes the law of gravity to exist. By extension, that child would presumably not be drawn to the intuitive appeal of the cosmological (or first cause, Aristotle's prime mover) argument for God's existence. Finally, a child who is not exposed to human language would not develop linguistic comprehension and would, needless to say, not be able to make much sense of language-coded, culturally entrenched ideas about God.

These are but a few examples from a long list of developmental acquisitions in infancy and toddlerhood that are critically important for later religious and spiritual development. They are easy to overlook because of insufficient variation across individuals, but that should not blind us to their foundational importance. In other words, virtually all infants possess the "right" genetic predispositions and are exposed to harmonizing environments enabling them to acquire attachments, mentalization skills, object permanence, elementary physics, and language comprehension.

Although I have said that infancy and toddlerhood are prereligious, prespiritual phases of development, this contention is largely informed (or constrained, perhaps) by my understanding of "religious" and "spiritual" (i.e., as presuming some appreciation of noncorporeal entities such as God, the sacred, and the transcendent). If we were to adopt a more inclusive understanding of the religious and spiritual, we might come to a different conclusion (as see, e.g., Miller, 2015). For example, the neonate's and young infant's psychological states might be viewed as "all-spiritual" (or perhaps "proto-spiritual"). The newborn is ideally bathing in the love of caregivers, incapable of visual acuity, with no clear, *explicit* sense of the world's physical layout, boundaries, or time–space relations, or of his or her own distinct self, and with milk (like manna) "pouring from the sky." Then color vision and an increased sense of being "connected" to caregivers emerges for the young infant to top things off. In this respect, the newborn and young infant might experience the world somewhat "psychedelically" (cf. Freud's, 1961a, quasi-spiritual notion of the "oceanic feeling").

My understanding of "spiritual" as something beyond "oceanic feeling" converges with the way some developmental scholars have approached the construct of dissociation. Understood as "disintegration of self," dissociation is a useful idea only at ages at which most children have acquired a firmly integrated sense of self (Carlson, Yates, & Sroufe, 2009). Likewise, I think "spiritual" becomes a useful term at ages occurring after children have achieved a capacity for sensing a connection to something that cannot be perceived with their ordinary senses (i.e., a noncorporeal other, such as God). Similarly, "mystical experience" (see also Chapter 8) becomes a useful term when the individual has achieved explicit self-recognition and a clear sense of time–space relations and of the world's "linear" layout. Mystical experiences involve a sense that these basic acquisitions are being superseded. Indeed, unless such experiences contrasted with those normal acquisitions, they would probably not be perceived as special.

By the same token, with a more inclusive (less protestant and individualistic) understanding of "religious," it would be legitimate to argue (say, in anthropology or sociology) that if the infant–toddler is brought up in a religious home, surrounded by a religious community, regularly taken to church, mosque, or synagogue, then he or she is in fact religious (i.e., as culturally defined). As a developmental psychologist, however, and while acknowledging the importance of religious contexts, cultures, and institutions, my principal focus is on the developing individual's mind, including his or her beliefs, experiences, and behaviors.

The Preschool Period

Although most matters of development are solidly set in motion during the first 2 years of life, many core acquisitions underlying religious and spiritual development unfold during early childhood (roughly ages 2–5). Beyond (but related to) attachment-related maturation (again, as reviewed in Chapter 1), this is particularly the case for cognitive aspects of development. Entering what Piaget (1926/1930) labeled the preoperational period, the child is now capable of representing the world symbolically (e.g., in language and via other symbols such as pictures). The world has moved inside the mind of the child, and children are increasingly relying on their own mental representations of the world in their exploration of it. This is evident in pretend play, such as when a 2- or 3-year-old is acting out his or her representation of dinner preparations with a pretend conversationalist, setting the pretend-table with twigs and stones, perhaps the latest additions from one of many gathering expeditions. Although Piaget did note such advancements, he focused his attention mainly on the limitations of preoperational thought. As is well recognized, however, Piaget gravely underestimated the cognitive capacities of children at these ages (e.g., Gopnik, 1996).

Relatedly, evolutionary developmental psychologists (e.g., Bjorklund & Blasi, 2005) have suggested that mind-related knowledge (or a "mentalizing" capacity) is a "core" cognitive domain. This is presumably because some knowledge of others' minds has for millennia been pivotal for social communication (e.g., cooperation) and acceptance, which have in turn been essential for survival and reproduction. An important argument in favor of such an interpretation is that we never directly observe the mental operations of others; rather, we merely observe their behaviors. As we have seen, a seed for mentalizing capacities is already developing during the first year of life (e.g., joint attention) but then makes greater headway during the second to third years, when children typically start to use mind-related concepts and to appreciate that others' perspectives may differ from their own. This capacity climaxes in a full-blown "theory of mind" by roughly 4 years of age (Wellman, Cross, & Watson, 2001); the child now typically understands that others may entertain false beliefs.

Regarding religious and spiritual development, and largely via cognitive acquisitions, preschool-age children's lists of attachment–surrogate objects have extended to feature unseen, noncorporeal, and yet highly anthropomorphized others, such as imaginary companions (see Chapter 1). It should be clear that God is also potentially lurking around the corner (or behind a cloud) as an attachment surrogate because everything in development is now in place for children to "receive" God, and perhaps to ultimately part company with the other "idolatrous" surrogate objects they have engaged with. Naturally, this means that the mind of the preschooler is hyperreceptive to religious and spiritual ideas when they are presented by people in the child's immediate surroundings. Religious or spiritual parents may therefore be especially focused on this period of child development because it gives them a unique opportunity to cultivate their child's emerging relationship with God.

The seemingly "hyperactive" application of symbolic thinking and mentalizing attributions that characterizes early childhood does indeed make this a developmental period of spirituality in the making. For example, Rizzuto (1979) has suggested that this period gives birth to the "living God"; thus, God may ultimately take the throne as a living mental representation in the child's cast of unseen characters. Supportive research for this conclusion comes from cognitive science of religion studies on children's use of religious concepts as well as from studies informed by attachment theory. Because cognitive and attachment-related developments are highly interrelated, I review key findings from both threads of literature here. My review is necessarily selective and is slightly biased by a focus on findings pertaining to anthropomorphism.

Developing Religious Cognition

Much of the cognitive science of religion has focused on the relation between developing social cognition (or mentalization) and agency attributions in relation to preschool-age children's understanding of religious concepts. This focus has been driven by hypotheses about social cognition and agency detection as core cognitive mechanisms underlying humans' representations of supernatural agents (e.g., Barrett, 2004; Bering, 2006; Bloom, 2007; Boyer, 2001). Even when children are not exposed to religious thought, so the argument goes, they will be quick to invent it themselves because religious cognition is supposedly "natural" (for a strong position here, see Barrett's *Born Believers* [2012]), even "unlearned" (Bloom, 2007). Though children may of course not necessarily come up with explicit religious terms, such as God, their reasoning will nonetheless often be teleological and filled with other features of anthropomorphic thinking.

For example, and heightening their memorability, supernatural beings tend to be viewed as persons but with some minimal counterintuitive properties (e.g., Boyer, 2001). For a second example, Barrett (2004) has proposed that humans, starting in early childhood, develop a hypersensitive agency-detection device (HADD), which has supposedly increased fitness by aiding people in identifying causal agents. In the many situations of unclear causality, it may have been optimally self-protective to assume the presence of a causal agent (e.g., an unobserved predator), even when none was actually present. By extension, then, God or some other unobserved entity might be conceived as the cause of ambiguous events.

For a third example, researchers have found that around the age when children comprehend that people may have false beliefs, they do not attribute the same false beliefs to God (e.g., Barrett, Richert, & Driesenga, 2001). However, whereas most adults tend to anthropomorphize certain fictional beings (e.g., zombies, superheroes) much more than God, children at these young ages attribute as many human-like properties to God as they do to such fictional beings (e.g., Shtulman, 2008). These findings illustrate a common observation, made also in previous Piaget-inspired stage models of religious development (see Hood et al., 2009): Early childhood conceptions of God are very concrete. As another case in point, God is particularly likely to be described and drawn as a person

(Heller, 1986). However, another Piaget-influenced conceptualization of a "magical" stage—reflecting the child's presumed failure to distinguish between reality and fantasy (see Hood et al., 2009, for a review)—seems misguided. Children in early childhood are less concerned with questions of ontology or existence than are older individuals (some adults seem particularly obsessed by them), and therefore preschool-age children *may appear* incapable of distinguishing between fantasy and reality (cf. Woolley, 1997, but see also Legare, Evans, Rosengren, & Harris, 2012). However, already at these ages, God and other religious entities typically begin to part company with other fictional beings; other beings, unlike God, are typically viewed as pretend figures even in early childhood (e.g., Shtulman, 2008).

Another area of interest that illuminates the development of religious thinking concerns children's explanations of "origins." Again reflecting reliance on anthropomorphic thinking (i.e., "naive biology"; Hatano & Inagaki, 1994), preschool-age children demonstrate a preference for teleological or intentionalist explanations (explanations in terms of some purpose) over physical (i.e., quasi-scientific) explanations of the origin of biological properties. This preference seems to persist throughout most of early and into middle childhood (e.g., Kelemen, 1999). Thus, not surprisingly, preschool-age children tend to prefer creation (i.e., God's work) as an explanation for the origins of species and the earth over evolutionarily informed explanations (Evans, 2001).

The Emergence of "Attachment to God"

The anthropomorphic representation of God, emphasized in much of the cognitive science research on religious development, presumably aids children in making God viable as a noncorporeal attachment figure. In addition to their more purely "cognitive" components, however, children's representations of God also carry an affective load that is influenced by the child's interaction history with attachment figures (via generalizing working models; see Chapter 5). Regarding normative (or typical) attachment processes, empirical data from early childhood onward indicate that God is perceived as a potentially available safe haven in times of stress. For example, using a quasi-experimental and semiprojective methodology, a study of American preschool and elementary school children found that they placed a God symbol closer to a fictional child when the fictional child was in attachment-activating situations than when the fictional child was in situations that should be less clear-cut as activators of the attachment system (Eshleman, Dickie, Merasco, Shepard, & Johnson, 1999). These findings have since been conceptually replicated, with tighter experimental controls, in three additional studies of children in early to middle childhood from Italy, Sweden, and the United States (Cassibba, Granqvist, & Costantini, 2013; Dickie, Charland, & Poll, 2005; Granqvist, Ljungdahl, & Dickie, 2007). However, whether the other components of attachment discussed in Chapter 2 (e.g., secure base) apply to preschool-age children's emerging representations of God remains for future research to determine.

The Role of Culture Reiterated

The research reviewed above illustrates how certain core cognitive–affective dispositions find a clear anthropomorphized expression in children's developing understanding of religious concepts, including their representation of God as an attachment figure. However, in that review, I volitionally set aside the influence of cultural factors. Such an influence is highly visible even in some of the reviewed studies.

For example, although Evans (2001) observed a preference for creationist over evolutionary origin explanations among younger children from secular schools, she also found moderating roles of age and school context, such that children with increasing age came to mirror the explanations favored by their parents and other authority figures in their particular (sub-)cultures. Moreover, later research with Chinese school children indicated that any presumed cognitive disposition for anthropomorphism does not universally yield creationist accounts of origins. Regardless of age (ages spanning 6–14 years), Chinese children overwhelmingly endorsed evolutionary explanations for the origins of humans and other animals (Smith & Richert, 2011).

Swedish children from secular homes placed a God symbol closer to a fictional child in attachment-activating situations as compared with attachment–neutral situations, suggesting that a religious background is not a necessary condition for children to represent God as a safe haven (Granqvist, Ivarsson, Broberg, & Hagekull, 2007). However, children from religious homes placed the God symbol closer than did children from secular homes across both types of situations. Not surprisingly, these latter findings indicate that being raised in a religious home also matters for whether or not children will come to view God as close.

For a final example, children's understanding of God's mind does not simply reflect some noncontextual developmental "plan" according to which children would intuitively realize that God's perfect mind parts company with the minds of fallible humans. This "realization" appears to be greatly influenced by the religious sub-(cultures) in which children develop. For example, Richert and coworkers have recently found that preschool-age children raised in Muslim homes differentiate more between God's and humans' minds than do children raised in Christian (both Catholic and Protestant) and nonreligious homes (Richert, Saide, Lesage, & Shaman, 2017). Interestingly, in that study children from non-religious homes displayed the lowest differentiation, presumably because they are religiously uneducated and therefore may be more biased to think that God is entirely anthropomorphic.

Jointly, these examples illustrate the important role that social (cultural) learning plays in co-sculpting (e.g., amplifying or weakening) the expression of core cognitive dispositions (or psychological mechanisms) on religious outcomes over the course of children's development. Not taking the role of culture into account when attempting to understand culturally entrenched matters of religious and spiritual development would surely risk leading to ethnocentric portrayals, where such development might be held as "natural" in some parts of the world but "unnatural" in other ones. How such cultural co-sculpting works more precisely, however, is quite frankly a matter of speculation and differences in opinion. For example, do elements of cultural learning (merely) "fill in" the core cognitive structures with specific religious content (Kelemen, 2004), or do they play a more fundamental role in shaping the underlying structure of children's cognition (Vygotsky, 1978)? I do not attempt to answer that question here, as that would carry us away from development per se (though see Chapters 5 and 10). Whatever the case may be, the influence of culture on specific beliefs and ways of thinking with regard to God and religion probably becomes increasingly visible with the child's increasing age, from early to middle childhood. Put differently, religiousness gradually emerges from spirituality, and the transition from early to middle childhood may be a key period in that development.

Middle Childhood

Apart from a diminished crowd of unseen characters in the child's mind, again attributed by Piaget (1926/1930) to the emergence of concrete operations (i.e., thinking logically about concrete material), middle childhood (roughly from age 6 onward) is marked by an increasing focus on the outer (i.e., extrafamilial) world of peers, school, and leisure activities. Indeed, presuming that no cause of distress is present, children of these ages typically prefer to spend time with their peers rather than their parents (Zeifman & Hazan, 2016). In particular, peer relations take on a new and important role in the form of friendships, marked by trust and companionship (Hartup, 1996). Because their attachment systems are also less easily activated, attachment often appears to take on a subordinate role for the child (Bowlby, 1969/1982). However, this does not imply that attachment becomes obsolete. For example, children who fail to develop any friendships and who receive low levels of support and engagement from parents often experience a painful sense of loneliness (Cassidy & Berlin, 1999), which Weiss (1973) understands as the perceived absence of an affectional bond with an attachment figure.

Like most other developmental theorists, Bowlby had less to say about development beyond the preschool years when the goal-corrected partnership had been established. This gap in the literature has since been effectively addressed by other researchers (see, in particular, Kerns & Brumariu, 2016). In brief, although attachment undoubtedly takes on an increasingly latent role in development, the school-age child must draw on an internalized sense of competence to navigate all of the challenges associated with mastery of the outer world. Such an internalized sense of competence does not take place in a void but occurs in real-life contexts, an important one of which is attachment, both past and present (e.g., Sroufe, Carlson, & Shulman, 1993). Moreover, when the going gets tough—such as in trust-related conflicts with "friends," or late at night when the demons come out during the first sleepovers at friends' houses—even the school-age child may resort to attachment behaviors. In line with increased differentiation, such behaviors may come in many forms, such as physical (e.g., requiring hugs from a parent, sitting on a parent's lap for consolation); sensory (e.g., smelling the parent's clothing, hearing the parent's voice); and representational (e.g., thinking about the parent, remembering something supportive that the parent has said).

Along with previous experiences from interactions with caregivers, the ability of the child to navigate in relation to the wider horizon of developmental challenges facing the school-age child is an important source of self-esteem (e.g., Harter, 1999). Also, although having already begun early in childhood, many school-age children will typically find their parents engaged less in caregiving behaviors and more in "socializing" behaviors than previously in development. An authoritative parenting style, marked by a combination of warmth/acceptance, moderate control, and appropriate levels of autonomy granting, bode well for many important aspects of subsequent child development (Baumrind, 1971), although the actual processes involved are much more bi-directional and transactional (i.e., from parent to child *and* child to parent; Sameroff, 2010) than has typically been acknowledged in the socialization literature (e.g., Stattin & Kerr, 2000). Be that as it may, children of authoritative parents tend to develop high self-esteem, are relatively resilient to stress, and are inclined to agree and identify with the parent's social attitudes and behaviors (e.g., Baumrind, 1971).

Regarding the development of religious cognition, middle childhood is associated with advances in children's ideas about the afterlife and the soul. An appealing feature of many religions is that they grant (at least some) humans (and at least some "parts" of them) continued existence after death. Yet adults, whether religious or not, also understand that death means "the end," at least as far as bodily and mind-related functions are concerned. The notion of a "soul" or "spirit," however, at least holds some prospect for continuation of the self in the hereafter. Thus, the development of the notion of an afterlife and associated dualistic beliefs has been of interest to cognitive scientists of religion. Some have argued that by the end of middle childhood, children elaborate two conceptions of death: one scientific and one religious (Harris & Giménez, 2005). Children also make clearer distinctions between properties of the soul and those of the body/mind; the soul has spiritual (but not cognitive or physical) functions, it remains stable, survives death, and connects people to God (Richert & Harris, 2006).

Research has also revealed that school-age children tend to view God as less anthropomorphic than they did in early childhood. For example, 4-year-olds are somewhat more likely to say that God is like their parents than are 5- or 6-year-olds (De Roos, Iedema, & Miedema, 2003). Nonetheless, school-age children simultaneously tend to *experience* God as personally closer (i.e., more of an attachment figure; Eshleman et al., 1999; Tamminen, 1994). God's closeness is emotionally called for especially strongly in particular situations. Even in a North European (i.e., highly secularized) country such as Finland, Tamminen (1994) found that as many as 40% of 7- to 12-year-olds reported that they felt close to God particularly during loneliness and emergencies, such as when escaping or avoiding danger. It should be recalled as well that the findings reviewed above on God's closeness in a semiprojective situation (Cassibba et al., 2013; Eshleman et al, 1999; Granqvist et al., 2007) were obtained on age-mixed samples comprising not just preschool-age children but also children in middle childhood.

Finally, in middle childhood spirituality becomes increasingly religiously framed (or schematized) for children raised in religious homes. In Piagetian terms, religious ideas may then become part of the "concrete" operations that the child cognitively employs. Children raised in nonreligious homes may, however, begin to leave their unseen others behind as unbelievable relics of early childhood (preoperational) fantasies. Perhaps even more likely, though, children raised in nonreligious homes may begin to anthropomorphize nature or the cosmos without giving them more precise framing (see Chapter 8).

Adolescence and Early Adulthood

A key developmental task in adolescence and early adulthood is to develop a certain degree of autonomy vis-à-vis parents. Initially, pubertal changes tend to initiate some distancing from parents (e.g., Steinberg &

Morris, 2001), which is further strengthened by the adolescent's increasing capacity to think about relationships, including a ripening ability to evaluate the internal consistency—or lack thereof—between what parents say and do. Thus, autonomy strivings tend to take place at the instigation of the adolescent, who typically wants to take it faster and farther than his or her parents are often willing to allow (e.g., Smetana, 2002). Besides behavioral autonomy strivings, adolescents often question parental values or the values of the older generation in general (e.g., conservation values), and instead express values of their own (e.g., openness values; Knafo & Schwartz, 2001).

Moreover, adolescents' growing push for autonomy (Steinberg, 1990) typically coincides with their increasing and perhaps seemingly inappropriate dependence on peers, typically romantic partners and friends (Allen, 2008). This means that attachment functions can be met through peers while adolescents establish some autonomy in relation to their parents.

Zeifman and Hazan (e.g., 2016) have suggested that attachment formation with peers may unfold in steps analogous to attachment formation with caregivers in infancy. In other words, the transfer of attachment may begin with the transfer from parents to peers of the proximity-seeking component, then the safe haven function, and finally with the transfer of the secure base component in a step-by-step process. Although this process is typically initiated in middle childhood (transfer of the proximity component) and climaxes in adolescence (the safe haven function), it is typically not concluded until early adulthood (with the secure base component). Empirical research has now supported this stepwise model in studies of adolescents in many parts of the world, including the United States (e.g., Fraley & Davis, 1997; Zeifman & Hazan, 2016), Australia (Feeney, 2004), Germany and Sweden (Friedlmeier & Granqvist, 2006), and China (Zhang, Chan, & Teng, 2011). Degree of attachment transfer is also affected by relevant contextual conditions (such as romantic relationship status), and there appears to be some (minor) cultural differences with regard to exact timing (e.g., the secure base component is transferred a little later in an urban Chinese context).

Not surprisingly, long-term romantic partners are most often selected as the principal attachment figures of adulthood (Bowlby, 1980; Zeifman & Hazan, 2016). From an evolutionary developmental (or life-history) perspective, it seems plausible that this developmental transformation from a principal attachment to protective parents in childhood to a principal attachment to reproductive partners following pubertal maturation has been selected for (i.e., is evolutionarily adaptive). Besides surviving until adolescence, the offspring may now also pass their parents' genes on to the next generation. Moreover, in a species such as ours, where offspring are immature and dependent on high parental investment for a long segment of the life course, genetic reproduction has not sufficed, but parents may also have benefited from sticking together for mutual investment in the next generation (which is not to say they have always benefited from *sexual* monogamy). In this case, attachment may serve as an emotional "glue" that binds prospective parents together. Thus, evolution may have coopted the attachment system and put it to use in the context of adult pair bonding (e.g., Zeifman & Hazan, 2016).

As straightforward as this puberty–to–attachment–transfer process may seem from a life-history perspective, in reality it is a long and winding road. Many fall by the wayside, and others hit numerous dead ends before finally appearing to make it, only to wind up in a heart-wrenching separation and starting all over again—in some cases *ad infinitum*. Regarding the winding nature of this developmental process, there are important attachment-related individual differences to consider, which also have notable implications for religious and spiritual development (see Chapters 5 and 6).

Erik Erikson (1998), the famous developmental theorist, emphasized similar themes in his life-cycle perspective on psychosocial development. The adolescent faces the challenge of exploring and then establishing a stable sense of personal identity. However, identity formation does not require a period of storm and stress, nor complete separation from parents, or seeking a personal identity completely apart from parents. In contrast, the continued ability to use parents as secure bases for exploration appears to foster continuity of adaptation in adolescence, and this applies to identity formation as well (Lapsley, Rice, & Fitzgerald, 1990). Using Erikson's terminology, the young adult faces the challenge of establishing intimacy with age mates (e.g., reproductive partners). In Erikson's view, individuals who fail to acquire the developmental tasks of adolescence and early adulthood (identity and intimacy, respectively) run the risk of remaining directionless and confused about themselves, as well as experiencing isolation from others.

Regarding cognitive development, the capacity for formal operational thinking (Piaget, 1926/1930) brings with it new avenues of understanding. Many adolescents and adults are less dependent on concrete material and more appreciative of abstract principles and rules (e.g., hypothetical reasoning, *if–then* propositions) than previously in development. Thus, these are life periods in which they can begin to appreciate the complex weave of abstract principles that make up theologies. However, these are also life periods when they can become genuinely dumbfounded by theologies. *If* God is all good and powerful, *then* should songwriters really have to conclude: "There will always be suffering. It flows through life like water"? (Nick Cave & the Bad Seeds, *The Boat-man's Call*,[1] 1997).

Not surprisingly, adolescence and early adulthood are periods of religious and spiritual transitions. Indeed, a century of research indicates that adolescence to young adulthood is an age period that, at least for some people, is associated with notable increases in aspects of spirituality and religiousness (e.g., Argyle & Beit-Hallahmi, 1975; Hood et al., 2009). As William James (1902) observed, something about religion appeals to adolescents' sentiments. Although the cognitive components required for beliefs in and experiences in relating to unobservable agents are already in place in early childhood, it is often not until adolescence that the emotional fuel required for deep religious feelings is poured into that cognitive machinery.

On one hand, adolescence and early adulthood are the life periods most intimately associated with sudden religious conversions and other significant changes in one's relationship with God (e.g., Argyle & Beit-Hallahmi, 1975; Hood et al., 2009). On the other hand, the period of adolescence to early adulthood is also generally associated with a decline in institutional religious involvement (Benson, Donahue, & Erickson, 1989; Smith & Denton, 2009) and with apostasy/deconversion (e.g., Roof & McKinney, 1987; Streib et al., 2011). Thus, in this life period, some adolescents seem to decide, temporarily or permanently, *not* to accept the religion they grew up with.

There are probably multiple reasons for this age period being a time for religious transitions. Depending on one's theoretical persuasion, one could suggest the involvement of very different psychological processes, including links to puberty and sexuality (e.g., Coe, 1916). Formal operational thinking may also challenge one's previously anthropomorphized conceptions, such that God comes to lose some of the personal attributes that may have made for an appealing relational partner earlier in development. At the same time, religious thought may eventually become increasingly complex and differentiated (Hood et al., 2009). Also, adolescents' search for an identity may include that of a religious, or perhaps more likely a nonreligious, identity. As religion is associated with parental and other forms of "conservation" values, whereas many identity-seeking adolescents tend to endorse openness values, it is not surprising that identification with religion tends to decrease in adolescence (cf. Saroglou, 2012; Saroglou, Delpierre, & Dernelle, 2004; Smith & Denton, 2009). Finally, socialization researchers have focused on the importance of resocialization (or "secondary" socialization) processes (e.g., Hood et al., 2009; Ozorak, 1989).

Without denying that such processes may be involved, we might also consider that the co-occurrence of attachment transfer is an additional and important reason for the religious/spiritual transitions often observed during adolescence and early adulthood (Granqvist, 2012). Relinquishing one's parents as attachment figures creates a vulnerability for loneliness (Weiss, 1973). This is partly because satisfying attachments to peers may be hard to come by and even harder to maintain, potentially leaving an adolescent in a void without any satisfying attachments at all. At such a time, adolescents may turn to God as a surrogate attachment figure. Thus, attachment components may be transferred not only to peers but also to God. However, as adolescence also signifies a growing pressure of autonomy from parents and their values, attachment transfer may lead some adolescents to shy away from God and religion. The contemporary world provides plenty of "idols" to engage with, not least in the digital world, ranging from avatars to porn "stars," from drugs to playmates. None, however, is likely to provide sustainable satisfaction.

The critical theoretical question in relation to adolescence and early adulthood viewed as religious/spiritual transitional periods thus becomes one of individual differences: Why do some adolescents/young adults become increasingly "attached to God," whereas others shy away from God and religion? Answering that question would take us away from normative (typical) development, but I return to it in Chapters 5 and 6.

Middle Adulthood and Old Age

Over the course of adulthood, as with development in general (Nelson & Dannefer, 1992), the development of attachment becomes increasingly diverse. This implies that individual, cultural, and subcultural differences make it difficult to characterize typical adult attachment development. As implied already by Freud (1961a), however, two major themes stand out as important characteristics of a psychologically healthy adult life, namely, love and work. Attachment scholars tend to concur (e.g., Hazan & Shaver, 1990). Unlike Freud, however, attachment scholars do not tend to view attachment behavior in adults as manifestations of regression or unhealthy dependency. In contrast, Bowlby (1969/1982, 1973, 1980) not only claimed that the attachment system is active from cradle to grave but he also regarded attachment as healthy throughout the life cycle.

For most adults, however, the domain of love is no longer restricted to romantic pair bonds, but also includes the love of one's children (i.e., caregiving or bonding love). This is not to say that romantic love has been "fixed" or taken care of already, as any marriage counselor would hasten to add. To the contrary, navigating long-term romantic relationships is continuously challenging for many adults. This is not surprising as it requires successful integration of behavioral systems governing sex, caregiving, attachment (and more), and within self, the partner, and relationship alike (Bowlby, 1980; Hazan & Shaver, 1987; Mikulincer & Shaver, 2016; Shaver, Hazan, & Bradshaw, 1988). Indeed, navigating romantic relationships is so challenging that divorce (and similar break-ups) are on the verge of normative, at least in the Western world, where divorce is relatively less culturally stigmatized. Not surprisingly then, a large number of adults live their lives as uncommitted singles, or else have difficulty finding mates. Divorce is of course intensely attachment-activating, and the single life may lead to emotional loneliness.

Regarding love of one's children, bonding love stands out as a more emotionally profound relationship than any other in many adults' lives. The signs of immaturity with which infants come equipped (e.g., their disproportionately large heads, their characteristic facial features, those big eyes, their unmasked social smile) tend to disarm most adults, get them hooked on the infant, and activate a disposition to engage in care-giving behaviors, and to do so for a very long period of time (George & Solomon, 2008). Those 20 years are certainly not just characterized by love, but also by sleep deprivation, frustration, and worries. The com-bination of work, caregiving, and spousal investments effectively keeps many middle-aged adults overly busy, often marking this period as a delicate balancing act between work and family commitments on one hand and incapacitating exhaustion on the other.

Further increases in lifestyle diversity in late adulthood makes it dif-ficult to arrive at a normative yet nonstereotypical conceptualization of the development of the elderly (Nelson & Dannefer, 1992). Nevertheless, in addition to some physical and sensory ailments, clearly experiences of loss increase through the death of loved ones, such as spouses or close friends. Thus, a psychologically painful process of grief or mourning is very common among the elderly, in particular following the death of a spouse (Bowlby, 1980; Fraley & Shaver, 2016). As described in Chapter 1, loss of a principal attachment figure, such as a spouse, is a power-ful stressor, indeed a potentially traumatic event. Consequently, spousal bereavement is associated with depression and elevated risks for suicide (Rosenzweig, Prigerson, Miller, & Reynolds, 1997).

Research and theorizing on development and aging has shown that some older adults also have profoundly positive experiences. For example, research relating to Erikson's (1998) idea of "ego integrity" (or wisdom) indicates that some elderly report high levels of psychological well-being (e.g., James & Zarrett, 2007). Relatedly, some elders experi-ence "gerotranscendence" (Tornstam, 1997)—states of inner calm and serenity, of peace of mind when engaging in quiet reminiscence—which characterizes favorable development in the final stages of life. The notion of gerotranscendence denotes a cosmic or transcendent perspective on life, directed beyond the individual's self.

Regarding religious and spiritual development, middle adulthood is associated less with religious "drama" and more with consolidation of the religious or nonreligious approach to life that has been taken. William James (1890/1950, p. 121) noted that "Habit is . . . the enormous fly-wheel of society, its most precious conservative agent." In middle adulthood, as people are busy with mundane tasks related to caregiving and work, religiosity typically takes the form of consolidating such a habit, at least when compared to the religious/spiritual developments that occur during the other major life periods discussed in this chapter (cf. Dillon, 2007; Krause, 2006). Also, the "religious habit" may become an important component of what is to be transmitted to the next generation as part of children's social or cultural learning (cf. Hood et al., 2009; Mahoney, 2010). In that regard, religion may also become a conserving agent (cf. Saroglou, 2012); of going to church on Sunday or to the synagogue on Saturday and of socializing and forming fitness-enhancing alliances with a community of like-minded people. On the whole, religion also appears to aid in consolidating family ties and in fostering authoritative parenting (e.g., Mahoney, 2010).

As always, however, there are exceptions to the stability implied in the notion of religion as habit. One such exception is the experience of falling madly in love, with a partner or a child, which may be so transformative that it engenders the formation of religious faith or at least augments one's sense of connections beyond the self (cf. "spirituality"; e.g., Palkovitz & Palm, 1998). Another exception is the experience of marital discord and breakup. Research suggests that religiousness may increase following the separation from loved ones, but this is likely to depend on individual differences in attachment security (discussed in Chapters 5 and 6).

Aging often brings with it situations that activate the attachment system and at the same time increase "mortality salience" (e.g., Maxfield et al., 2007; illness, physical ailments, loss, loneliness). For these reasons, it is not surprising that religion and spirituality tend to gain increased importance for many elderly (Dillon, 2007; Krause, 2006), often making aging a period of spiritual and religious "reawakening." For example, the findings reported by Cicirelli (2004) and Brown and colleagues (2004), and reviewed in the previous chapter, indicate that spousal bereavement often triggers attachment-related components of religiousness, which may in turn contribute to a more favorable mourning process.

Relatedly, Bowlby (1980) noted that to proceed favorably in terms of promoting adaptation to a life without the loved one's physical accessibility, the mourning process requires that bereaved individuals eventually accommodate information regarding the permanence of the person's death into their representational world. Otherwise, the individual may remain unresolved or disorganized with respect to the loss; for example, the individual may display continued searching for the lost person. Although we have no direct evidence that increased religiousness as a response to loss leads to mental resolution, empirical research indicates that the proportion of unresolved/disorganized loss (as studied in the Adult Attachment Interview; Main et al., 2003) may be slightly lower in religious samples (Cassibba, Granqvist, Costantini, & Gatto, 2008; Cassibba et al., 2013; Granqvist, Ivarsson, et al., 2007) than in a nonclinical meta-analytic sample (Bakermans-Kranenburg & van IJzendoorn, 2009). As suggested by Cassibba and colleagues (2008), religion may promote mental resolution of loss via offering the prospect of reunion with deceased loved ones in the hereafter. In addition, the bereaved individual's attachment to God may itself serve as a surrogate bond assisting the individual in "grief work" in lieu of the inaccessibility of a lost attachment figure (Granqvist & Kirkpatrick, 2016).

Finally, religious and spiritual beliefs may offer additional interpretive benefits added to the states experienced by some elders. Elders capable of gerotranscendence, for example, may through religious and spiritual beliefs gain an increased sense of the interconnectedness of all things, of death as meaningful, and of security with God. Death may then finally lose its sting (cf. Vaillant, 2002).

CHAPTER SUMMARY AND CONCLUSIONS

I have argued in this chapter that religious and spiritual development stems from general developmental maturation, which is itself understood as contingent on specific forms of interactions between certain genetic dispositions ("experience expectancy") and repeated exposure to corresponding environmental input. More specifically, religious and spiritual development has been held to reflect plasticity-driven increases in differentiation, integration, and complexity of underlying psychological systems (or modalities), resulting in religious and spiritual diversity. Developmental spurts in those systems/modalities directly extend to religious and spiritual development. While these general conclusions are relatively straightforward, it is more difficult to determine more precisely which underlying systems and modalities are key for understanding religious and spiritual development. Beyond the attachment system, I have placed particular emphasis on certain core cognitive dispositions, while also emphasizing that domain-general principles of abstract thinking, imitation, and cultural learning must be taken into account.

In considering the life cycle, I argued that infancy through toddlerhood is a prereligious and prespiritual phase of development, which is nonetheless of unparalleled importance for what is later to emerge as religious and spiritual development. The preschool period (early childhood) was portrayed as a key developmental period in which religiously and spiritually colored ideas and experiences may begin to flourish, including a "living" representation of a God that ultimately often comes to trump other imaginary figures in children's lives. Although God is typically viewed as highly anthropomorphic in early childhood, such anthropomorphism gradually decreases over the course of middle childhood, while God is also sensed as personally closer. Furthermore, school-age children have typically become increasingly susceptible to the socializing influence of the stronger and wiser others who have cared for them, such that the spirituality of children from religious homes often becomes increasingly religiously framed. Children brought up in secular (nonreligious) homes, however, increasingly part company with their past religiously/spiritually colored ideas and experiences. Just as adolescence to early adulthood is a period of major attachment transitions (often from parents to peers), this period is often marked by religious and spiritual transitions. Adolescence to early adulthood is a religious and spiritual "juncture," characterized for some by religious awakening and for others by apostasy/deconversion. While middle adulthood is associated with "religion as habit" and cultural transmission to the next generation, attachment-related events, such as falling in and out of love, often have repercussions in the religious and spiritual arena. Finally, old age may be spiritually vitalizing both via attachment-activating life events and states of gerotranscendence.

In closing this chapter, I should acknowledge that much of my analysis of religious/spiritual development has been oriented to religions with a single human-like deity. This is because the overwhelming bulk of research has been conducted in Western and Middle Eastern countries. How religious development occurs in other places, where there is no single deity—indeed occasionally no deity at all—remains to be determined in future research.

INDIVIDUAL DIFFERENCES IN ATTACHMENT, RELIGION, AND SPIRITUALITY

In this second part of the book, I move from the foundational commonalities considered in Part I to a consideration of important particulars in the attachment–religion connection. More specifically, Part II deals with individual differences in attachment and in the attachment–religion connection.

An important component of attachment research that goes beyond the normative framework outlined by Bowlby is the idea that individual differences in attachment often qualify (or moderate) the output of the attachment system. This implies that individual differences in attachment often qualify the religious and spiritual "outcomes" discussed in prior chapters. Not surprisingly then, as with attachment research in general, religion-as-attachment research has intensely focused on individual differences in attachment and how they relate to various aspects of religion and spirituality.

In the first of three chapters, I provide an overview of theory and research concerning individual differences in attachment (Chapter 4). Next, from a developmental viewpoint, I argue that there are two general attachment-related pathways to religion/spirituality and to different modes of being religious/spiritual. I deal with theorizing and research pertaining to one of those—the "correspondence" pathway—in Chapter 5. Briefly, I contend that via social (or cultural) learning, individuals who are secure with respect to attachment often come to adopt religious or nonreligious standards that are similar to those held by their sensitive attachment figures in childhood. Also, via generalizing working models of self and others, securely attached individuals often represent God as a correspondingly sensitive (i.e., reliably security-maintaining) attachment figure. Finally, although the generalization of working models often complicates matters for individuals with an insecure attachment history, I argue in the third and final chapter (Chapter 6) of Part II that some insecure individuals may find in God a beneficial surrogate or alternative attachment figure, who helps to compensate for states of insecurity and other unsatisfactory attachments (i.e., the compensation pathway).

CHAPTER 4

Individual Differences in Attachment

This chapter contains five major sections. The first provides a brief introduction to the origin of ideas about individual differences in attachment and highlights why this aspect of attachment theory may have become so influential. In the second section, I characterize individual differences in attachment at the conceptual level. However, the principal ideas about attachment-related individual differences largely derive from, and are intertwined with, the methods used to measure such individual differences. In the third section, I therefore review some of the major measures of attachment, particularly the ones used in the attachment–religion research highlighted in subsequent chapters (Chapters 5–8). Fourth, I provide a selective review of the empirical literature on development, and psychological outcomes more generally, that have been related to individual differences in attachment. Fifth and finally, I conclude the chapter with reminders—designed to be sobering—that the topic of attachment is much larger and more foundational than that of individual differences.

HISTORICAL INTRODUCTION TO THE NOTION OF INDIVIDUAL DIFFERENCES IN ATTACHMENT

As part of her research designed to test Bowlby's attachment theory on infants in Uganda, Mary Ainsworth (1967), a North American developmental psychologist, made an important discovery: Not all infants displayed the attachment behaviors anticipated in Bowlby's theory. She did so following thousands of hours of naturalistic observations. More specifically, not all infants seemed to use the caregiver either as a safe haven when distressed or as a secure base during exploration. Nor did all infants continually seek to maintain proximity. That a majority of Ugandan infants did behave in line with Bowlby's normative theory by no means blinded Ainsworth to the fact that a substantial minority did not. What's more, whether they displayed anticipated attachment behaviors or not appeared to be closely related to their primary caregiver's characteristic styles of interacting with them during their first year of life.

Later, back on American soil, Ainsworth set out to test whether these conclusions applied to American infants as well, so she initiated her famous Baltimore study in which she observed a relatively small group of infant–mother dyads, again for thousands of observational hours (see Ainsworth et al., 1978). However, American infants generally seemed less fazed by strangers and less reactive to separations occurring in their naturalistic environments—presumably because the American infants were more accustomed to strangers and brief separations than were infants in Uganda. This made it challenging to observe infant attachment behavior in the United States. Ainsworth and colleagues' (1978) solution to the problem—the Strange Situation procedure—revolutionized child psychology, perhaps more so than any other individual study or method ever has (Dixon, 2015).

By subjecting American infants to a mildly stressful laboratory procedure—the key ingredients being a novel environment, a stranger, and a repeated separation–reunion sequence with the caregiver—Ainsworth and colleagues found a structured means to activate infants' attachment systems, predictably yielding attachment behaviors in a majority of infants. As in Uganda, a minority of the American infants studied by Ainsworth and colleagues did not display the patterns of behavior anticipated in Bowlby's normative theory, and whether or not infants displayed clear-cut attachment behaviors was again tied to their interaction history with their mothers. Furthermore, deviations from the normative scenario took similar forms as those observed in Uganda.

These now cross-culturally validated observations were exciting. However, rather than overthrowing, falsifying, or replacing Bowlby's normative theory, they simply indicated that there were more nuances (or variations) to the story of attachment than Bowlby had himself considered in constructing his theory, although Bowlby (1969/1982, 1973) had in fact also anticipated that there should be individual differences in attachment without systematizing them. We saw several examples in Chapter 1 of how Bowlby was attempting to cut nature at its joints rather than engage with every particularity of nature. That theme applies here as well. Nonetheless, now that a laboratory-based procedure had been introduced, and one that could simultaneously evoke attachment behaviors under controlled circumstances *and* yield a reliable measure of individual differences in attachment organization, chapter two of the attachment story had begun: attachment as a "research program" (Lakatos, 1980).

Empirical researchers in developmental psychology were thrilled. This was probably in part because researchers thrive on natural variation, which enables the implementation of research on topics (such as attachment) that cannot, or should not, be experimentally manipulated. (No one randomly assigns infants to caregivers of different quality.) The now classical longitudinal attachment studies ensued in Minnesota, Berkeley, New York, and Germany, followed by a next generation of studies in the United Kingdom, Netherlands, Israel, Sweden, and then virtually in all continents of the world.

Although Bowlby's original focus was on foundational commonalities in attachment, many people have now come to identify attachment theory with an important particular: the idea of variation in attachment. Indeed, the notion of attachment-related individual differences has almost come to define attachment research, especially within developmental psychology. In my view, this is both the boon and bane of contemporary attachment research. I implicitly deal with the "boon" parts in the bulk of this chapter, but I also elaborate on the "bane" parts in the concluding section.

CONCEPTUAL CHARACTERIZATION
OF INDIVIDUAL DIFFERENCES IN ATTACHMENT

Following the work of Ainsworth and colleagues (1978) and, later, Main and Solomon (1990), contemporary attachment researchers typically consider four types or categories of attachment: *secure, insecure/avoidant* (sometimes referred to as dismissing), *insecure/resistant* (sometimes referred to as ambivalent or preoccupied), and *disorganized/disoriented* (sometimes referred to as fearful and unresolved) attachment. Researchers who are not persuaded that typologies offer the best way to represent individual differences often focus instead on underlying continuous dimensions of avoidance and anxiety/resistance. Those dimensions also derive from Ainsworth and colleagues' work, which included a discriminant function analysis showing that two linear combinations of coded ratings (e.g., crying, clinging, turning away, resistance) could predict well which "type" (or region of the two-dimensional space) a particular infant would fall into.

For didactic purposes, typologies (where every individual is categorized as belonging to one category or "type") offer some advantages over the dimensional approach (where every individual is represented by two or more continuous scores). Therefore, I largely proceed here with a description of the attachment categories. However, this does not imply that categories necessarily offer the best (or truest) representation of attachment-related individual differences.[1] I personally adopt a pragmatic stance with respect to the question of categories versus dimensions, and I see clear pragmatic benefits in flexibly shifting between them. Although adopting the typological approach here, I caution that attachment classifications should be taken with a considerable grain of salt at the individual level, in part because of measurement error, in part because they rarely do full justice to single individuals. They are nonetheless quite meaningful in research at an aggregated level. In the concluding remarks, we will see why such cautioning is warranted.

Mary Main (e.g., 1990) at the University of California, Berkeley, and a former PhD student of Mary Ainsworth's, has in my view offered the most parsimonious account of attachment-related individual differences, applicable throughout the lifespan. She argues that such differences can be understood in terms of flexibility versus rigidity/breakdown of attention to attachment-related information. In the paragraphs that follow, I therefore adopt Main's interpretation as my point of departure, but I also provide additional elaborations. Although attachment matures and transforms over the lifespan, and although conceptualizations of attachment-related individual differences are dependent on what particular method is used to "measure attachment," I for the most part ignore maturation and method dependence in the conceptual sketches that follow.

Secure Attachment

Secure attachment is present in roughly 60% of people studied in general-population samples around the world (e.g., Bakermans-Kranenburg & van IJzendoorn, 2009; van IJzendoorn, Schuengel, & Bakermans-Kranenburg, 1999). Security can be characterized in terms of *flexibility* of attention vis-à-vis attachment-related information. When the attachment system of secure individuals is activated, for example, by separation from an attachment figure, their attention reliably (and often rapidly) switches to attachment, for example, to visually locating the attachment figure. Similarly, when the attachment system has been (relatively) deactivated, say, following reunion with their attachment figure after a brief separation, their attention switches to other matters, such as exploration of the environment. At the level of behavioral systems, then, secure attachment can be conceptualized in terms of balance—or a well-coordinated integration—of behavioral systems related to attachment (Ainsworth et al., 1978).

At the level of mental representations, secure attachment can be characterized in terms of positive, nondefensive representations of self, others, and perhaps the world at large (Bowlby, 1973). The secure individual represents the self as worthy of care and others as reliable (i.e., usually available and accessible) providers of care. The world at large may for the most part be represented as benign—indeed, potentially even as benevolent (see further Chapter 5)—that is, as a place to explore with confidence and freedom. Also, Bowlby's (1973) description of *singular*, or "coherent" and well-integrated working models, marked by compatibility and consistency between unconscious and conscious processes (see Chapter 1), is particularly applicable to secure attachment.

Viewed in terms of communication, security is marked by the free-flowing, open, nondefensive communication of emotions, needs, thoughts, and desires (Siegel, 1999). However, rather than the secure individual's mind being overwhelmed by affective processes, communication is often free and autonomous. For these reasons, not much interpretation is typically required to understand secure individuals. They also seem to have a relatively realistic (or truthful) understanding of themselves (Main et al., 2003). There's no subtext to uncover, no riddle to solve, no hidden plot. Readers with an affinity for the twisted or unexpected may find the psychology of security slightly boring, although it should be noted that as far as close relationships are concerned, nothing beats a secure partner (cf. Mikulincer & Shaver, 2016).

Security goes hand in hand with a positive valuing of attachment (Main et al., 2003). Because there is generally not much to be afraid of, the self isn't inherently shameful, and others are not perceived as threatening, intimacy, closeness, and even dependence can be embraced as charitable aspects of life, especially relational life (Mikulincer & Shaver, 2016).

Perhaps the most obvious way to characterize secure attachment is in terms of a solid fit to Bowlby's (1969/1982) normative (or species-typical) portrayal of attachments. Secure individuals do indeed tend to selectively maintain proximity to their attachment figures; protest against involuntary separation; nondefensively mourn the permanent loss of attachment figures (but nonetheless become functionally reorganized in due course); display attachment behaviors to their attachment figures/safe havens when the attachment system is activated; use their attachment figures/secure bases as security-enhancing while exploring other things; and implicitly assess their attachment figures as stronger and wiser when distressed, worried, and so on. Although insecurely attached individuals also display some fit to these species-typical aspects of attachment, they also exhibit defensiveness and inconsistency of various kinds.

Regarding the development of secure attachment, in Bowlby's (1973) view, singular/coherent working models naturally unfold as a function of the individual having received relatively consistent sensitive and responsive caregiving, with the infant's needs having been respected and prioritized by the caregiver. Furthermore, Bowlby and later Main (1990) portrayed the development of singular/coherent models, and thus of secure attachment, as a developmentally *primary* attachment strategy. In other words, secure attachment is understood as the strategy that virtually all infants first try out, and repeatedly so; babies cry and engage in other nondistorted signaling behaviors as if expecting their caregivers to help them resolve what's bothering them (cf. "experience-expectancy)." If their attachment behaviors are met by sensitive and responsive caregiving, the primary/secure strategy will be consolidated.

For some infants, however, the primary/secure strategy does not help bring about safety and security, so they ultimately develop secondary (or "conditional"[2]) attachment strategies (Main, 1990). This naturally brings us to insecure patterns of attachment.

Insecure/*Avoidant* Attachment

Insecure/avoidant attachment is present in roughly 15–20% of people in the general population (e.g., Bakermans-Kranenburg & van IJzendoorn, 2009; van IJzendoorn et al., 1999). This attachment pattern can be characterized in terms of attentional *rigidity* in the face of attachment-related information. When the attachment system of avoidant individuals is activated, their attention does not typically switch to attachment-related information and instead remains (defensively) focused on other things, such as toys, smartphones, or the TV (Main, 1990). Should the attachment figure approach them during attachment activation, avoidant individuals may signal their discomfort by subtly moving away, avoiding close physical contact, or pointing the attachment figure's attention in another direction. At the level of behavioral systems, then, avoidant attachment can be conceptualized in terms of imbalance. More specifically, avoidant individuals tend to (defensively) explore, at the expense of engaging in attachment (Ainsworth et al., 1978).

At the level of mental representations, avoidant attachment can be characterized in terms of an *implicit* negative model of others—as intrusive and rejecting (Bowlby, 1973). This often coincides, however, with an *explicit* positive model of others, as when overly positive descriptors of caregivers ("My dad was very loving") are left unsubstantiated or contradicted by more specific comments (Main et al., 2003). Typically, the model of self is equally contradictory. On the one hand, the self is implicitly represented as unlovable and unworthy of care (i.e., negative), thus the shying away from attachment figures (Bowlby, 1973). On the other hand, the self is explicitly represented as strong and self-sufficient (i.e., positive), and thus in no need of others' care (Main et al., 2003; Mikulincer & Shaver, 2016). Bowlby's (1973) and Main's (1990) notion of *plural* (or incoherent) working models (Chapter 1) are thus applicable here; both self and others are represented in an ultimately incoherent fashion.

Viewed in terms of communication, avoidance is marked by closed, defensive communication of emotions, needs, and desires (Siegel, 1999). Those tendencies are evoked particularly when self-threatening topics are raised, such as when relationship partners seem to expect the mutual sharing of intimate information (i.e., self-disclosure; Mikulincer & Shaver, 2016). However, avoidant individuals may be at ease in communicating about other, less personal matters. For these reasons, interpretation is often required to understand avoidant individuals—for example, why they don't want to maintain greater closeness or talk about what might be bothering them. Matters are made even worse considering that avoidant individuals do not seem to have a realistic (or truthful) understanding of themselves (Main et al., 2003), and they definitely do not enjoy "psychobabble."

Similarly, avoidance goes in tandem with negative valuing of attachment, though this is again more likely to be implicitly expressed than explicitly declared (Main et al., 2003). As there's much to be afraid of, and as both self and others are implicitly represented as flawed, intimacy, closeness, and dependence become threatening (Mikulincer & Shaver, 2016).

Regarding Bowlby's normative portrayal of attachments, avoidant individuals provide an inconsistent fit. While they do not appear interested in maintaining close, selective proximity to their attachment figures, they do tend to prefer to have the attachment figure around, though at a comfortable distance (Main, 1981). For the most part, they do not protest against separations, and some avoidant individuals even give the appearance of indifference to separation. Most strikingly, perhaps, is that avoidant individuals do not display clear-cut attachment behaviors to their attachment figures as safe havens when the attachment system is activated. Or at least they don't do so within the constraints of attachment assessment procedures (described in the section below), although they might very well engage in attachment behaviors in some other situations. Finally, avoidant individuals tend not to use their attachment figures as secure bases while exploring other things; they often appear to be sufficiently strong and wise to get by entirely on their own (Ainsworth et al., 1978).

Avoidant individuals may appear to be so independent and sturdy—and at such young ages—that it makes sense to question whether the label "insecure" applies (e.g., Kagan, 1982). According to most attachment researchers, it does, and that conclusion is probably warranted. Beyond their suspicion that avoidance reflects defensive maneuvers, this is because empirical research has shown that avoidant individuals do tend to react with physiological stress (e.g., increased heart rate and skin conductance) to attachment activation, while concealing (inhibiting or suppressing) most overt behavioral expressions of that stress (e.g., Dozier & Kobak, 1992; Sroufe & Waters, 1977b; Zalenko et al., 2005). Also, unlike secure individuals, avoidant individuals' stress responses may remain elevated even after attachment activation should have ceased, such as after reuniting with their attachment figures following a brief separation (Sroufe & Waters, 1977b).

Regarding the development of avoidant attachment, in Bowlby's view, plural/incoherent working models generally develop as a function of the individual having received reliably insensitive or markedly inconsistent caregiving (cf. "experience dependency"). Furthermore, Bowlby (1973) and Main (1990) portrayed the development of plural/incoherent working models, and thus of insecure attachment, as a developmentally *secondary* attachment strategy. In other words, when the primary/ secure strategy of proximity-seeking and open, undistorted signaling behaviors have consistently or repeatedly failed to yield safety and security, the individual may mobilize attachment-related defenses such as defensive exclusion and diversion of attention from attachment-related information. More specifically, the avoidant individual learns to inhibit behavioral manifestations of the attachment system and thus develops a *minimizing* (Main, 1990) or *deactivating* (Mikulincer & Shaver, 2016) attachment strategy. In doing so, he or she may maintain "reasonable" proximity to—and also comfortable distance from—a rejecting or intrusive attachment figure, without risking further rejection, abandonment, or even infanticide by demanding "too much." If *real* danger should arise, then the attachment figure might finally come to the individual's aid (Main, 1981).

Insecure/*Resistant* Attachment

Insecure/resistant attachment is present in roughly 5–10% of people in the general population (e.g., Bakermans-Kranenburg & van IJzendoorn, 2009; van IJzendoorn et al., 1999). This attachment pattern in many ways represents the flip side of avoidant attachment, though against a common backdrop of insecurity, rigidity of attention, behavioral imbalance, and representational incoherence. The attachment system of resistant individuals is often very easily activated, and when it is, these individuals react either with marked behavioral passivity or anger, and often with both (Ainsworth et al., 1978). Furthermore, both of these reactions tend to interfere with an agentic solution to the current problem. For example, although the resistant individual may passively signal the self's helplessness to deal with a distressing situation, when the attachment figure finally offers help, it is often angrily (perhaps resentfully) rebutted. So strong is the effect of attachment activation that it is often difficult for resistant individuals to settle and shift attention to other matters, such as exploration, even when the attachment system is expected to be (relatively) deactivated (Main, 1990). At the level of behavioral systems, then, resistant attachment is marked by an imbalance in which (unproductive) attachment trumps and interferes with exploration (Ainsworth et al., 1978).

At the level of mental representations, the resistant individual's representation of self is largely negative; the self is viewed as unlovable, unworthy of care, and unable (passive/helpless) to do anything about it (Bowlby, 1973). And yet, strong anger and separation protest reactions also signal that the self is somehow worthy of more than what the self currently gets. The model of others is also typically incoherent; on the one hand, others are represented as potential rescuers who might save the helpless self (cf. Bartholomew & Horowitz, 1991), but on the other hand, they are untrustworthy, disappointing, and unreliable.

Viewed in terms of communication, resistance is marked by dramatic and unproductive ways of communicating emotions, needs, and desires (Siegel, 1999). Those tendencies are evoked particularly when the attachment figure momentarily attends to something other than the resistant individual, which sometimes gives rise to intense jealousy and preoccupation with the attachment figure's thoughts and actions (e.g., Mikulincer & Shaver, 2016). However, resistant individuals may well be at ease in expressing seemingly unregulated emotions and affective states, which relationship partners are likely to view as cumbersome. Although resistant individuals tend to be "generous" with affective expressions, much interpretation is often required to understand these individuals; for example, why they are so untrusting and what can possibly be done to provide them with sustainable satisfaction and trust. Matters are made worse considering that many resistant (or preoccupied; see the next section, which deals with the Adult Attachment Interview [AAI]) individuals act like authoritative experts on relationships (Main et al., 2003), so they may not take lightly to receiving relational advice from their partner. Although resistant individuals often claim that they value attachment and intimacy, they tend to wind up with a markedly negative bias, for example, selectively attending to their attachment figure's shortcomings.

Regarding Bowlby's normative portrayal of attachments, resistant individuals provide an inconsistent fit, though one that differs from that of avoidant individuals. While they appear to be interested in maintaining close proximity to their attachment figures, they may also angrily rebuff contact. They tend to protest intensely against separations, and they act as though separation is nothing short of disastrous when it happens. They are likely to display attachment behaviors when the attachment system is activated, but they may resort to passive signaling rather than clear-cut, agentive behaviors. Finally, resistant individuals tend not to use their attachment figures as secure bases for exploring other things. Instead, they often remain (negatively) fixated on the attachment figure as a failing safe haven. In fact, they may demand that their attachment figure take over initiative and responsibility for exploration, for example, while sitting close by, on occasion touching a toy, but appearing for the most part to be passive.

Regarding development, resistant attachment is thought to reflect a secondary strategy of *maximizing* (negative) attention to attachment-related information (Main, 1990) or of *hyperactivating* attachment (Mikulincer & Shaver, 2016). Thus, defensive exclusion here takes the form of excluding information about safety and exploration, and attention is similarly diverted from clues of safety and exploration to negative attachment-related information. In doing so, the resistant individual's attention and behaviors may activate an otherwise inconsistently accessible and occasionally neglectful caregiver's attention to the self. It is obviously a resource-demanding strategy, however, and equally so for the other party in a relationship. Not surprisingly, then, resistant attachment is both rare in the general population and likely to crumble over time.

Disorganized/Disoriented Attachment

Disorganized/disoriented (henceforward disorganized, D) attachment is present in roughly 15% of people in the general population (e.g., Bakermans-Kranenburg & van IJzendoorn, 2009; van IJzendoorn et al., 1999). While the insecure (avoidant and resistant) patterns of attachment are thought to be organized (secondary) strategies for dealing with suboptimal caregiving, disorganized attachment is thought, in many cases, to reflect a breakdown in attention and behavior during stress (Main & Hesse, 2006; Main & Solomon, 1990).

Such a "breakdown" may take many different forms. Indeed, Main and Solomon (1990), the originators of the D classification system, list *seven* thematic indices of D behaviors. When the behavior of an infant, while in the presence of the caregiver (in the Strange Situation procedure), shows a good fit with one or several of these indices, the infant may be classified as primarily displaying disorganized attachment. Those seven indices are: (1) sequential and (2) simultaneous display of contradictory behavior patterns; (3) undirected, misdirected, incomplete, and interrupted movements and expressions; (4) stereotypies, asymmetrical and mistimed movements, and anomalous postures; (5) freezing, stilling, and slowed movements and expressions; (6) direct indices of apprehension regarding the parent; and (7) direct indices of disorganization and disorientation.

It is the intensity of the display of contradictory behavior (cf. conflict behavior in ethology; Hinde, 1966), disorientation, or fear, and the extent to which this behavior disrupts a child's underlying attachment strategy that lead to a D classification. For this reason, infants classified as primarily disorganized are also given an alternate "best-fitting" organized category (e.g., D/avoidant attachment). This convention has led to a marked decrease in primary resistant category assignments; thus, when strong resistance is present, often so is D behavior (van IJzendoorn et al., 1999).

As D behaviors take so many different forms (the underlying theme almost being disruption of form), it is nearly impossible to briefly characterize disorganization. It is therefore tempting to understand disorganization in negative terms—in terms of what it is not rather than what it is. D attachment then becomes the negation (breakdown) of the other attachment patterns (see Main & Solomon's [1990] initial "exclusion principle," p. 152). However, an infant's behavior could fail to fit one of the organized attachment patterns in many ways. For example, the infant could simply be "unattached." Thus, Main and Solomon's (1990) seven indices were established to define D behaviors in positive, operational terms. Main and Hesse (1990) have also suggested a more general way of understanding D attachment psychologically, as "fright without solution."

As described by Hesse and Main (2006), a breakdown in attention and behavior during stress may occur within the infant's relationship with caregivers because of the behavioral paradox in which infants find themselves when their caregivers are simultaneously the *source* of alarm (e.g., due to being abusive/maltreating or simply frightened, frightening, or dissociative) and the only possible *solution* to alarm (i.e., because the offspring is strongly biologically predisposed to turn to his or her stronger and wiser attachment figure to deal with cues to danger). Thus, the more alarmed the infant is, the more motivated he or she should be to turn to his or her attachment figure/the *solution* to alarm, but the closer the infant gets to the attachment figure/the *source* of alarm, the more motivated he or she should be to flee from the attachment figure. Hence, a positive feedback loop may be created, with inescapable fear as a likely psychological outcome. At the representational level, then, both self and other would be represented in a segregated (or dissociated) manner, for example, as both perpetrator and rescuer (see e.g., Liotti, 2009).

While Main and Hesse's (1990) hypothesis has been reliably supported empirically, two important qualifiers—both of which these scholars (e.g., Main, Hesse, & Hesse, 2011) also acknowledge—should be noted to prevent misapplications. First, there are other pathways to D behaviors besides a fear-inducing interaction history with caregivers (e.g., see Granqvist et al., 2016, 2017). Thus, it is not logically correct to conclude from an infant's display of D behaviors that he or she must have been maltreated or otherwise frightened by the caregiver.[3] Second, while "fright without solution" sounds ominous, I have not yet seen persuasive evidence that the lion's share of D behaviors does in fact reflect fear of the caregiver. Granted, behaviors fitting to index 6 (direct indices of apprehension) yield converging evidence, but those behaviors tend to be quite rare in normal infant populations. Also, for behaviors fitting the remaining six indices, a central role of fear remains hypothetical (see Duschinsky, 2018). Interestingly, in unpublished texts reflecting on D-related behaviors, Bowlby conjectured that such behaviors range on a continuum from relatively benign to trauma-induced and malignant (see Reisz et al., 2018). It does not seem far-fetched to propose that direct indices of apprehension may fit the latter, but that many behaviors captured by the other six D indices fall elsewhere along such a continuum.

Beyond infancy and toddlerhood, children who were judged disorganized in infancy often develop organized, though suboptimal, ways of relating to their caregivers. For example, they may engage in controlling or role-reversing behaviors, such as being punitive and caregiving (Main & Cassidy, 1988). Elements of fear may still be present, however, as conveyed in formerly disorganized children's narratives about events during fictional separations (e.g., "everybody dies"; Kaplan, 1987; Main et al., 1985).

Regarding disorganization in adulthood, and in view of the presumed centrality of fear for disorganization, disorganized attachment should not be confused with a "fearful/avoidant" adult attachment style (reviewed below). They do not refer to the same thing. Even if some elements of fear are present in both cases, fearful/avoidant attachment style refers to fear of intimacy (not of a caregiver) and consequent avoidance (Bartholomew & Horowitz, 1991). The closest conceptual counterpart of disorganized attachment in adulthood is unresolved/disorganized loss or trauma (Main et al., 2003), where presumed attentional breakdown is manifested in linguistic lapses when the unresolved person discusses some specific loss or trauma (see the next section on the AAI).

METHODS TO TAP INDIVIDUAL DIFFERENCES IN ATTACHMENT

Methods used to assess individual differences in attachment display great diversity. This is natural considering that attachment transforms over the lifespan. Such transformation has implications for what kind of data (e.g., behavioral observations, verbal utterances) and attachment targets (e.g., childhood caregivers, adult romantic partners) attachment researchers focus on. More specifically, the attachment system is relatively easily activated in infants, and its manifestations are directly visible for observers. Furthermore, infants have yet to master the vocabulary required to talk about attachment. Therefore, behavioral observations become a suitable data collection method.

Later in childhood, when the attachment system is less easily activated, its manifestations are less directly observable, and children have developed the vocabulary required to talk about attachment, the toolbox for measuring attachment expands to include representational products, most notably speech but also drawings and various role-playing enactments. In introducing such measures, Main and colleages (1985) argued for a move to the level of representation in attachment research. Thus, from childhood on, interviews and questionnaires are also useful.

By adolescence and adulthood, attachments are no longer restricted to asymmetrical relationships with "stronger and wiser" caregivers but also include symmetrical relationships with peers, especially romantic partners. Consequently, adult attachment measures may also focus on "romantic attachment," following the pioneering work of Hazan and Shaver (1987). Below, divided by developmental period, I sample some widely utilized attachment measures, with selective attention to those used in attachment–religion research.

Infancy and the Strange Situation Procedure

As we have seen, Ainsworth and colleagues' (1978) Strange Situation procedure (SSP) is "the mother of all" attachment methods. With its more than 25,000 scientific citations, it is also the most influential. Indeed, it is often held up as the "gold standard" attachment method, and it is widely used by developmental attachment researchers as an anchor against which novel attachment methods are grounded, both conceptually and empirically.

The SSP is a 20-minute, semistructured, laboratory-based behavioral procedure in which infants (and an attachment figure) undergo a mini-drama containing eight brief (usually 3-minute) episodes, organized around a repeated separation–reunion sequence. This mini-drama is designed to evoke both the attachment system (e.g., via separation in a novel environment) and the competing exploratory system (e.g., via attractive, age-appropriate toys) of participating infants (12–20 months of age). Furthermore, it is designed to be mildly, at most moderately, stressful. Besides issues of research ethics, when infants are overstressed, their capacity for behavioral organization may be temporarily jeopardized, potentially leading to unrepresentative behaviors (see Granqvist et al., 2016). Therefore, the separation episodes must be curtailed rapidly if the infants are crying intensely. Notably, when SSPs are coded and classified, the coder assigns particular weight to what happens in the two reunion episodes, when the attachment figure reappears following the brief separations. Important behaviors are infant greeting, approaching, avoiding, snubbing, whining, striking parent, throwing toys, and falling apart behaviorally, with no working strategy to get through the reunion.

Secure attachment is seen in the SSP when infants strike a balance between attachment and exploration, and thus readily shift their attention between the two in line with expectations derived from the normative tenets of attachment theory (e.g., explores the room with the attachment figure as a secure base, protests separation, seeks proximity or interaction with the attachment figure following reunion). More colloquially, SSPs with secure infants can be described as a drama with a happy ending, a good Hollywood script, or a crisis giving way to resolution—and the resolution follows upon the return of the attachment figure.

Avoidant attachment is identified via behavioral imbalance, where the infant engages in (defensive) exploration (cf. displacement behavior) at the expense of attachment, and the infant may also (usually subtly) avoid close contact with the attachment figure. Considered as a drama, nothing really seems to happen beyond appearances of everything being all right; there's no Aristotelian structure of beginning, middle (crisis), or end (resolution).

In contrast, the imbalance of resistant attachment takes the opposite expression to avoidance; the resistant infant engages (negatively) in attachment, at the expense of exploration. The infant is also behaviorally passive and may show angry behavior toward the attachment figure. Considered as a drama, it has decidedly Scandinavian ("Bergmanesque") qualities; it starts with tension, builds to crisis, and there is no resolution; both "actors" are likely to be unhappy in the end.

Disorganized attachment is intimately identified with the SSP, so much so that other concepts than "disorganized" are typically used in other attachment methods (see further below). Also, disorganized attachment is identified strictly with the seven indices developed by Main and Solomon (1990) and thought to characterize behavioral breakdown.

Considered as part of a drama, disorganized behaviors are analogous to horror (i.e., fear of caregiver) or to what some may regard as "poorly" structured scripts in which something inexplicable happens that neither the director (David Lynch, as an example) nor the audience is able to grasp.

Virtually all of the classical longitudinal studies of attachment have utilized the SSP, so in much of the empirical overview (see the next section) I reference findings based on the SSP. Regrettably, however, the SSP has not yet (to my best knowledge) been utilized in attachment–religion research. Finally, although the SSP has dominated infant attachment research, the naturalistic, behavior-based Attachment Q-Sort (Waters & Dean, 1985) has also been developmentally validated (van IJzendoorn et al., 2004).

Early to Middle Childhood and the Separation Anxiety Test

Many methods, without concerted validation efforts, have been developed to capture individual differences in attachment in early to middle childhood (for a review, see Solomon & George, 2016). In this chapter, however, I focus largely on one approach: the Adapted Separation Anxiety Test (SAT; Kaplan, 1987; see also Main et al., 1985). Though infrequently used, this method is mentioned in part because only the SAT has apparently been used in attachment–religion research and in part because many of the other methods developed for these age groups were originally spawned and inspired by the SAT.

In the SAT, which is valid for children ages 5–7 years, the participating child is presented with six pictures of parent–child separations. For example, the parents go out in the evening and leave the child at home; the parents go away for 2 weeks and give the child a gift as they leave. Each picture is followed by questions regarding what the separated child might feel and do.

Regarding security, SAT interviews are considered secure (or "resourceful") if the participating child attributes a feeling of sadness, anger, or some other form of vulnerability to the pictured child and yet is also able to provide a constructive solution for what the pictured child will do in the majority of situations. Constructive solutions are present not only when the pictured child displays attachment behaviors or in other ways tries to persuade the parents not to leave, but also when the child is involved in social play with peers or relatives and in independent, detailed play activities.

Regarding insecurity, SAT interviews are judged insecure/avoidant (or "inactive") if the participating child gives responses to the "feel questions" implying distress in the pictured child but in the absence of constructive, detailed solutions to the "do questions" (e.g., "I don't know," "Nothing," "Run away," "Just play"). Interviews are instead considered insecure/ambivalent (or "aggressive"; cf. resistant) if the pictured child is portrayed, for example, as displaying aggressive or passive-aggressive behaviors against attachment figures.

Finally, texts are judged "fearful" (cf. disorganized) if the child or pictured child seems inexplicably afraid and unable to do anything about it. Indices of fear include prolonged and repeated silences and whispering, linguistic disorganization, and catastrophic fantasies in which the parents or child dies. Such classifications are also assigned based on out-of-control behaviors in the participating child (e.g., hitting the examiner).

Kaplan's (1987) adaptation of the SAT has shown adequate developmental validity, most notably in relation to the same individual's infant SSP classification with mother in at least three samples (Grossmann et al., 2002; Jacobsen & Hofmann, 1997; Main et al., 1985). Also, SAT classifications based on the Kaplan adaptation have prospectively predicted the same individual's AAI classification (see below; Main, Hesse, & Kaplan, 2005).[4]

Adolescent and Adult Attachment

Reflecting naturally converging developmental diversification, the attachment literature branches off in two distinct directions from adolescence onward. One of these directions deals with adolescents' and adults' "state of mind" regarding attachment-related experiences with childhood caregivers. This tradition originates in developmental and clinical psychology, and more specifically in an interest in Bowlby's (1969/1982, 1973, 1980) notion of nongenomic transmission of attachment across generations (i.e., from caregivers to their children). Methodologically, pertinent research on individual differences in attachment largely clusters around the AAI (Main et al., 2003).

The second tradition deals with adolescents' and adults' long-term pair bonds with peers, usually romantic partners. This tradition originates in Bowlby's (e.g., 1980) analysis of adult pair bonds as attachments. Social and personality psychologists adopted and further expanded Bowlby's analysis (see Hazan & Shaver, 1987; Shaver et al., 1988), yielding what was to become a field-changing research program on romantic love from an attachment perspective (for a review, see Mikulincer & Shaver, 2016). Methodologically, pertinent research clusters around self-report questionnaires such as the Experiences in Close Relationships (ECR) scale (Brennan, Clark, & Shaver, 1998).

These two traditions of adult attachment theory and research have largely developed side by side, in parallel, without much cross-referencing or mutual influence. In other words, there is (quite regrettably, in my view) a major divide operating here.[5] As we shall see in the remaining chapters, however, attachment–religion research has been conducted on both sides of the divide, so I review both the AAI and the ECR in the following sections.

The Adult Attachment Interview

The AAI (George, Kaplan, & Main, 1996) is a semistructured, linguistically coded interview comprising approximately 20 questions with standardized probes, including questions about general descriptions of childhood relationships with parents, to be supported by the recall of specific episodes. Interview questions also reference what happened when the interviewee as a child was emotionally upset, ill, and in pain; possible separation, rejection, loss, and abuse events; effects of childhood experiences with parents on current personality; and possible changes in the relationship during adolescence. A final set of interview questions ask about the current, adult relationship with parents.

These interviews, which normally vary in length between 45 and 90 minutes, are recorded and then transcribed verbatim. This yields transcripts that are typically 20–40 pages long. Finally, coding requires certification (i.e., reliability). When coded according to the Main and colleagues (2003) system, interview transcripts are first scored on three types of 9-point scales: (1) probable experiences with parents, (2) organized states of mind with regard to attachment, and (3) unresolved/disorganized loss/abuse. Individuals are finally classified into one of four categories in part based on these scores (on [2] and [3]).

The discourse of participants assigned a secure/autonomous classification is characterized by coherence (i.e., collaboration and credibility). Regardless of whether their past experiences were primarily positive or negative, their transcripts provide an internally consistent picture of the participant's experiences, feelings, and viewpoints regarding attachment. Furthermore, such participants tend to value attachment and yet be relatively autonomous and objective in their descriptions. Importantly, when participants are estimated to have had markedly negative experiences with all their childhood attachment figures and yet are able to maintain a coherent discourse, they are classified into a special subcategory called "earned" secure. Earned security tends to go in tandem with sincere attempts at understanding caregivers, setting them in relevant contexts when evaluating their shortcomings, and implicitly forgiving attitudes.

The insecure/dismissing (cf. avoidant) classification is most often characterized by a structural inconsistency between positive/generalized portrayals of parents and the failure to support these portrayals with specific episodes (i.e., idealization). Failed support is either due to frequent appeals to lack of memory that serve to block discourse or to direct and unmonitored contradictions. An extreme example of direct contradiction is an interviewee having only markedly positive things to say about a particular caregiver at the general/semantic level (e.g., "very, very loving mom") but then—when asked to support that portrayal—instead recalls that the self couldn't go to that caregiver when seriously hurt because of anticipated scolding. The dismissing classification also goes hand in hand with emphases on personal normalcy, strength, independence, and invulnerability.

The discourse of participants assigned an insecure/preoccupied (cf. resistant) classification is characterized by an ongoing, mentally preoccupying anger against the parent and/or vagueness of mental processes concerning attachment. Preoccupying anger is usually present in long, detailed passages listing the perceived faults of a parent, grammatically confused statements, and repeated unlicensed citations of the parent and self in dialogue. Passivity of thought processes are present, for example, in vague expressions (e.g., "blah blah blah"), childlike speech, and self–other confusion. Preoccupied individuals may also engage in "psychobabble" and act like authoritative experts on relationships (e.g., "my mother is borderline, absolutely borderline").

Finally, interviewees who are assigned an unresolved/disorganized (U/d) classification usually demonstrate striking lapses in reasoning or discourse, specifically in response to loss (through death) or abuse. Reasoning lapses—which violate principles of Newtonian physics and/or formal logic—are present, for example, in statements implying that a dead person remains alive in the physical sense or in considerable spatial–temporal confusion surrounding a loss or abuse event. Discourse lapses are present, for example, when visual/sensory images related to the trauma intrude in discourse, in excessive details, and when the discourse becomes markedly incoherent specifically in the context of loss/abuse events. Because speakers assigned to the U/d category show lapses in reasoning or discourse specifically surrounding loss and/or abuse, this category is superimposed on one of the other three categories (e.g., unresolved/dismissing; cf. disorganized attachment in the SSP system).

The AAI is obviously a resource-intensive method. Developmental researchers and clinicians use it for a reason, though. First, the AAI has impressive psychometric properties (e.g., Hesse, 2016). This holds up not just for convergent and predictive validity (e.g., AAI classifications of parents predict their infants' attachment classifications) but also for specificity (discriminant validity). Second, compared to most other nomothetic research instruments, AAIs also yield "thick descriptions" of processes operating within single individuals. Although underutilized as such at present, the AAI and related instruments can therefore profitably be used in idiographic research as well (e.g., case studies).

The Experiences in Close Relationships Scale

Research and theorizing have suggested that a romantic partner, close friend, or some other age mate is typically the principal attachment figure in adulthood (e.g., Bowlby, 1980; Zeifman & Hazan, 2016). Consequently, much research on individual differences in adult attachment has taken interpersonal rather than parental attachment as the point of departure. Various self-report questionnaires have been devised since Hazan and Shaver's (1987) seminal work on individual differences in interpersonal attachment. The most widely used instrument is the ECR scale (Brennan et al., 1998). In line with Ainsworth and colleagues' (1978) discriminant functions, this 36-item scale yields scores on two orthogonal, continuous dimensions, derived by means of factor analyses.

The first factor is labeled Avoidance and refers to avoidance of intimacy and emotional dependency (e.g., "I get uncomfortable when someone wants to be very close to me"). In Mikulincer and Shaver's (2016) interpretation, avoidance represents a disposition for attachment-system deactivation. A 45° rotation of this factor yields a negative (vs. positive) working model of others.

The second factor is labeled Anxiety and refers specifically to anxiety or worry about an attachment figure's availability and potential abandonment (e.g., "My desire to be very close sometimes scares people away"). Anxiety represents a disposition for attachment–system hyperactivation (Mikulincer & Shaver, 2016). Following a 45-degree rotation, it yields a negative (vs. positive) model of self.

Some people wonder if and how security is represented within this system. The answer is yes, it is represented: Security can be inferred from low scores on *both* the avoidance and anxiety dimensions. This does not imply that security is only a negation of insecurity, as the originators of the ECR (Brennan et al., 1998) were aware. Indeed, they framed roughly half of the items in the secure (positive) direction. Those items are then reversed when the avoidance and anxiety dimensions are calculated.

Most attachment researchers in social and personality psychology do not use a typological approach to characterize attachment-related individual differences (Mikulincer & Shaver, 2016). This is because taxometric analyses have not shown evidence of latent taxa underlying the ECR dimensions (e.g., Fraley & Waller, 1998). Categories would therefore unnecessarily impose arbitrary cutoffs, restrict natural variation, and limit both the statistical degrees of freedom and type of statistical techniques employed in subsequent analyses. Nonetheless, categories can of course be derived from the continuous avoidance and anxiety scores.

Viewed as a category, then, secure attachment is present when both avoidance and anxiety are scored low. In keeping with the notion of behavioral balance, security is not marked by either deactivation (cf. minimizing strategy) or hyperactivation (cf. maximizing strategy) of the attachment system, but by an intermediate position. At the representational level, security is characterized by a positive model of self *and* others. Secure individuals are comfortable with closeness, intimacy, and dependence.

In the ECR system (see also Bartholomew & Horowitz, 1991), avoidant attachment is represented by two different types. The first is dismissing/avoidant attachment, characterized by high avoidance but low anxiety, or a (defensively) positive model of self but a negative model of others. Dismissing individuals shy away from intimacy and dependence, presumably because they represent others as rejecting and a threat to independence. The second avoidant category is known as fearful/avoidant attachment, characterized by high avoidance *and* high anxiety, or a negative model of both self and others. Generally, this can be viewed as the most seriously insecure attachment style, not only because it is characterized by high scores on both insecurity dimensions but also because these individuals thereby have difficulties finding any attachment strategy that works, as their attachment systems are readily both deactivated and hyperactivated. Also, they crave external rescuers due to their negative self-model, and yet they fear the consequences of intimacy and dependence because of a negative other-model.

Finally, the preoccupied (cf. resistant) attachment category is characterized by high anxiety but low avoidance, or a negative model of self but a positive (though inconsistently so) model of others. Preoccupied individuals crave external rescuers because of their negative self-models. Once found, however, those presumed rescuers tend to fall short of perfection in the long run, often leading to emotional turmoil and intensely conflictual relationships.

Despite being a relatively simple self-report measure, the ECR is a validated method for tapping individual differences in adult romantic attachment at the group level, and it has produced a large and theoretically coherent body of research, including many experimental studies using implicit and physiological measures and behavioral observations (see Mikulincer & Shaver, 2016). For example, my colleagues and I have recently found that relatively secure individuals on the ECR display lower physiological stress responses (i.e., skin conductance) when smelling their partner's body odor (vs. other odors), whereas relatively insecure adults displayed higher physiological stress when smelling their partners' odor (Granqvist et al., 2019).

Besides romantic attachment measures, some of the attachment–religion research has used attachment history paragraphs (e.g., Hazan & Shaver, 1987), which were inspired by the romantic attachment typologies and have repeatedly been found to be empirically associated with them (see Mikulincer & Shaver, 2016). More specifically, secure romantic attachment is related to memories of receiving sensitive caregiving in childhood (thus perceptions of a secure attachment history), whereas insecure romantic attachment is related to memories of receiving insensitive (rejecting, distant, fearful) or markedly inconsistent caregiving in childhood (thus perceptions of an insecure attachment history).

DEVELOPMENT AND INDIVIDUAL DIFFERENCES IN ATTACHMENT

In this section, I provide a selective review of key findings that have accrued in the large body of extant empirical research on individual differences in attachment. I first consider the origins of individual differences in childhood and then their developmental sequelae. In the interest of both brevity and reliability, my review deals primarily with meta-analytically corroborated findings and broad (rather than specific) aspects of socioemotional and cognitive functioning (for a more detailed review, see Forslund & Granqvist, 2016a). Though in principle relevant in this section, I consider research and theorizing on attachment-related individual differences in relation to social learning/socialization (Chapter 5) and the use of surrogate attachment objects (Chapter 6) in later chapters.

The Developmental Origins of Individual Differences in Attachment

As the founding figures of attachment theory and research conjectured, individual differences in attachment have most consistently been predicted by aspects of caregiving, most notably caregiver sensitivity (De Wolff & van IJzendoorn, 1997) but also caregiver mentalization (Fonagy, Steele, Steele, Moran, & Higgitt, 1991; Koren-Karie, Oppenheim, Dolev, Sher, & Etzion-Carasso, 2002; Meins, Fernyhough, Fradley, & Tuckey, 2001). Not surprisingly, caregivers of secure children have been found to be more sensitive and to engage in more mentalizing caregiving than caregivers of insecure and disorganized children. Similarly, at the representational level, sensitive caregivers and caregivers of secure children have been found to be more autonomous in their own states of mind regarding attachment (e.g., van IJzendoorn, 1995; Verhage et al.,

2016) as well as to hold more flexible and balanced representations of their children in relation to themselves (see George & Solomon, 2008).

Although research has consistently reported a sizeable "transmission gap" between parents' states of minds regarding attachment and their children's attachment classifications (i.e., observations of parental sensitivity have not fully explained the link between the two), constitutional factors alone do not provide a viable explanation for children's attachment quality (van IJzendoorn, 1995; Verhage et al., 2016). This is because the bulk of research that has used validated attachment measures has indicated that genetic heritability and infant temperament are not related to children's attachment qualities (e.g., Bakermans-Kranenburg & van IJzendoorn, 2016; Bokhorst, Bakermans-Kranenburg, Fonagy, & Schuengel, 2003; Roisman & Fraley, 2010).[6]

In line with this book's advocacy of nature–nurture interactionism, however, findings have accrued suggesting that patterns of nature–nurture interaction (gene × environment and epigenetic effects) are applicable to the origins of individual differences in attachment as well. For example, Dutch researchers Bakermans-Kranenburg and van IJzendoorn (2007, 2016) have presented evidence that infants with a particular allele on the dopamine receptor gene *DRD4* who have *also* been cared for by mothers with unresolved/disorganized loss/abuse are much more likely than other infants to develop disorganized attachment. Notably, the gene–environment interaction patterns discovered by these researchers indicate that so-called "risk genes" may be better conceptualized as "susceptibility genes," indicating a heightened susceptibility to environmental influences (cf. developmental plasticity) both for better and for worse. Children with such genetic variants do not just develop adversely under detrimental rearing conditions but also thrive more than children without susceptibility genes if they are reared in good environments (see also Belsky, 1997).

Similarly, researchers are starting to uncover epigenetic effects on adult attachment categories and dimensions, both in the domain of romantic attachment (Ein-Dor, Verbeke, Mokry, & Vrtička, 2018) and in the AAI (van IJzendoorn, Caspers, Bakermans-Kranenburg, Beach, & Philibert, 2010). However, specific gene–environment and epigenetic effects are notoriously difficult to replicate, so it remains to be seen whether they hold up in future attachment research (see e.g., Fraley et al., 2013; Lujik et al., 2011.

Broad Aspects of Socioemotional and Cognitive Functioning

Much attachment research has been organized around Bowlby's notion of internal working models of self and others as generalizing (or extending) to other situations, individuals, and relationships. Thus, via generalizing working models, individual differences in attachment should be related to social behavior and personality development more generally. Although the actual workings of working models remain hidden—they have for the most part been *inferred* from attachment measures—eye-tracking research has begun to corroborate some of Bowlby's hypotheses. For example, securely attached infants do indeed appear to attentionally expect (other) caregivers to respond sensitively to (other) distressed infants, whereas insecure infants attentionally expect caregivers to respond insensitively (Johnson, Dweck, & Chen, 2007; Johnson et al., 2010).

Regarding developmental sequelae, as attachment theory is at its core a relational theory, a particularly large body of research has examined individual differences in attachment in relation to socioemotional functioning. Meta-analyses have demonstrated significant, replicable links (though of small to moderate magnitudes) between attachment insecurity and (1) higher levels of internalizing behavior problems (e.g., anxiety, sadness, fearfulness, withdrawal; Groh, Roisman, van IJzendoorn, Bakermans-Kranenbur, & Fearon, 2012); (2) higher levels of externalizing behavior problems (e.g., aggression, conduct problems; Fearon, Bakermans-Kranenburg, van IJzendoorn, Lapsley, & Roisman, 2010); and (3) lower social competence (e.g., peer rejection/acceptance, popularity, prosociality; Groh et al., 2014). The associations with externalizing behavior problems and social competence were larger than those with internalizing problems (though internalizing problems are difficult to observe). Moreover, these meta-analyses highlighted insecure/avoidant attachment as most strongly associated with internalizing problems, and disorganized attachment as most strongly associated with externalizing problems. Associations between attachment and psychosocial adjustment were obtained using parent and teacher ratings, researchers' behavioral observations, and children's self-reports.

Beyond the socioemotional domain, because caregiver sensitivity and child attachment security are believed to facilitate nondefensive exploration, and because exploration should in turn lead to more advanced cognitive development, it follows that caregiver sensitivity and child security should be related to cognitive development as well. More specifically, parental sensitivity may impact the cognitive development of secure children by enlarging the child's epistemic space. Knowing that the caregiver can be reliably counted on in case of alarm may infuse the child with confidence to explore its surroundings and thereby learn from it more freely. Research has indeed indicated that both caregiver sensitivity and child attachment security are related—over and above parental intelligence—to more advanced child cognitive development (including higher IQ; e.g., Ainsworth & Bell, 1972; Lindberg, Fransson, Forslund, Springer, & Granqvist, 2017; Matas, Arend, & Sroufe, 1978; van IJzendoorn, Dijkstra, & Bus, 1995). These findings are particularly noteworthy when we consider that child cognitive development (IQ in particular) is substantially genetically heritable whereas attachment security is not.

As straightforward as these links between attachment security and favorable development might seem, it should be noted that we generally know little about the underlying mechanisms at work and about the influence of potential moderators (e.g., child temperament, attachment to additional caregivers, the broader ecological context; e.g., Forslund & Granqvist, 2016a). Nonetheless, a large body of published data indicates that attachment security acts as a salutogenic factor in development that may also serve as a buffer (protective factor) against other adversities. In contrast, insecure and disorganized attachment may be conceptualized as vulnerability and risk factors, respectively (e.g., Fearon et al., 2010).

CONCLUDING REMARKS: CLARIFICATIONS AND CAVEATS

As I've explained, the notion of individual differences in attachment flows relatively seamlessly from the normative tenets of attachment theory, and especially from Bowlby's descriptions of internal working models and associated defenses. Probably in part for that reason, many people, whether implicitly or explicitly, assume that attachment-related individual differences represent the "real deal" of attachment. I contend, however, that as important as natural variation is to researchers and practitioners alike, the idea of individual differences in attachment is really an amendment (or supplement or extension) to attachment theory; individual differences do *not* supersede the normative aspects of the theory. And yet, as can also be seen in the world of politics, amendments may well come to be viewed as the principal matters at stake, even to the point of blinding people to the foundational principles that, in point of fact, still remain applicable to most cases, whether it be children's attachments or a country's constitution. Regarding attachment, even though insecure and disorganized attachment may seem like a rotten deal in life—especially when dealt with as prototypes, as I have done here—most caregivers of insecure and disorganized children love their children and hope for their best outcomes, and they also feed, protect, and care for them in many other important ways. This is the case just as most insecure and disorganized children love their caregivers, protest against separation from them, mourn their loss, and so on.

It is therefore not surprising that research on developmental sequelae of attachment generally indicates that only small to moderate effect sizes can be attributed solely to individual differences in attachment. In addition, development is *complex* and thus involves many important functions and components beyond attachment, and even more so beyond individual differences in attachment. Consequently, single factors, whether risk, salutogenic, or protective, rarely explain much variation in development on their own, although they can still be important in interaction with other factors.

Besides being truthful, I make these humbling remarks about the restricted (or limited) implications of individual differences in attachment not to dismiss them from consideration but to prevent further reifications, oversimplifications, exaggerations, and misapplications (see Granqvist et al., 2017). Without pointing fingers, such reifications and exaggerations have appeared at increasing rates in the literature in recent years, especially in applied literature and particularly with regard to disorganized attachment. Furthermore, they have begun to have tragic consequences for individual children, caregivers, and families. For example, some children have been removed from their caregivers *solely* because social authorities (in Sweden), using poorly validated attachment measures, have estimated that these children have had insecure and disorganized attachments to their caregivers (see Granqvist, 2016a). Naturally, permanent or repeated removals of children from their caregivers are likely to have more seriously negative effects on child development than "merely" insecure or disorganized attachment does.[7] Indeed, Bowlby's species-typical theory was originally founded to explain the serious untoward effects of prolonged, repeated separations from caregivers (Chapter 1). Some practitioners seem not to have paid attention to foundational matters of attachment but appear instead to have been seduced by exaggerated claims about individual differences.

Contrasting with a view of attachment patterns as fixed or trait-like qualities of the mind, Main (1990) has speculated that the secondary/insecure attachment strategies never fully override the primary/secure (species-typical) strategy. Rather, secondary strategies can be thought of as defensive maneuvers or layers of information processing that tend to become somewhat habitual for the mind and yet are activated particularly in certain kinds of situations (e.g., mild stress in an unfamiliar setting) but not necessarily in others (e.g., in the child's home). Ainsworth and colleagues' (1978) early research already indicated that such subtleties need to be borne in mind to prevent misleading reifications of attachment patterns. For example, in their studies, avoidant infants in the Strange Situation tended not to display avoidant behaviors at home but in fact engaged in clingy, whiny, and dependent behaviors at home. Furthermore, if they were reexposed to the Strange Situation too soon after a first Strange Situation visit, they typically did not show avoidant behaviors but, rather, unclassifiable and D-like behaviors during the second visit (see also Granqvist et al., 2016).

These latter findings illustrate an important point that has both clinical implications and much relevance for the attachment–religion connection: The defensive/secondary strategies are fragile and thus prone to crumble when sufficiently challenged (e.g., by high levels of stress). In such situations, then, even characteristically avoidant individuals may be thrown off-guard (see also Mikulincer & Shaver, 2016). Furthermore, even though they may be likely to temporarily "break down" behaviorally if the only attachment figure available in such a stressful situation is their characteristically insensitive, rejecting attachment figure, they may well try out proximity-seeking (i.e., the primary/secure strategy) if some *other* suitable attachment figure is perceived to be available. I return to this issue when discussing God and other surrogate attachment figures in Chapter 6. In the present context, my main point is that what can appear to be a stable insecure strategy may in truth be used especially when the individual is under the constraints associated with attachment measurement procedures. In other situations, the individual's behaviors may be much more variable.

Bowlby's and Main's notions of a species-typical/primary/secure attachment strategy versus deviating/secondary/insecure strategies naturally emanates from Bowlby's understanding of the environment of evolutionary adaptedness (EEA) in the singular. Based on behavioral ecology and evolutionary psychology, scholars such as Simpson and Belsky (2016) and Kirkpatrick (2005) have argued that there is nothing primary about "security," nor is there anything secondary, let alone "defensive," about "insecurity." Rather, the argument goes, security can be seen as a facultative adaptation to some environmental circumstances (e.g., high parental investment), whereas insecurity can be seen as a facultative adaptation to other environmental circumstances (e.g., low parental investment). This latter strand of evolutionary scholar asserts that such adaptations should be understood as adaptive tactics designed for improving reproductive fitness in their respective EEAs and not (solely) as strategies designed to promote survival. Although this is not the place to discuss the pros and cons of these differing interpretations in detail, they do serve as important theoretical divides in contemporary attachment theory and research, and they have important implications for how we understand the connection between attachment-related individual differences and religion/spirituality (see Kirkpatrick, 2005, for an evolutionary psychology understanding).

I therefore state (and without implying that they are mutually exclusive in every respect) that I largely adopt the Bowlby/Main position in this book. I do so because evidence appears to indicate that virtually all newborns and very young infants signal and seek proximity in a relatively undistorted fashion as if they expected their caregivers to care about and respond to their signals, and I am aware of no evidence that runs counter to these observations. Moreover, infants do so repeatedly, as if implicitly expecting that any initial error in the caregiver's detection of the signal will be corrected over time. It's only when their implicit expectations of benevolent responses have been repeatedly disconfirmed that infants will find alternative ways of organizing their attachment behaviors. They do so then by displaying distorted (or defensive) signals to their caregivers.

Relatedly, if avoidance were merely a quantity/short-term reproductive strategy, rather than a strategy promoting protection/survival in lieu of a rejecting caregiver, why should avoidant individuals (in the AAI and related measurement systems) insist on idealizing their mothers and partners? Why pretend that everything is okay with self and others when that clearly is not the case? If there were nothing defensive about avoidance, avoidant individuals could just avoid their attachment figures and be clear about their shortcomings. As we will see in Chapter 6, religion and spirituality may become an appealing arena for insecure individuals precisely because it offers God as a perfect attachment surrogate, who resonates with lingering experience-expectancy for benevolent responses.

Finally, in this chapter I have not "picked sides" in the disagreements that have occupied the field of attachment regarding measurement of individual differences. These disagreements have been particularly heated regarding adult attachment, yielding two almost entirely parallel traditions of adult attachment theory and research (i.e., developmental/clinical research using the AAI vs. social/personality research using self-reports). I have dodged picking sides for three reasons. First, I have a deep personal antipathy against closing ranks, especially if the ranks are closed (as they have been here) around fuzzy constructs and variation (i.e., individual differences) rather than foundational matters.

Second, and consonant with this book's advocacy of methodological pluralism, there are many parts of the famous elephant for us blind men and women to explore. Although some ways of exploring might yield a better portrait of the whole animal than others, we can surely learn more from trying different approaches than from sticking to one. In particular, different attachment measures are called for in different situations, depending, for example, on research question, design, age group, access to research grant, time window for a particular study, and attachment target of interest. Along with the psychometric properties of the instruments, pragmatic considerations should settle the choice of attachment measure to use. I call on the field of attachment researchers here not to lose sight of the foundational matters of attachment that risk remaining unnoticed if too much attention is devoted to variation and its measurement. It is particularly important that young researchers are encouraged to do something more creative than to devise yet another method of measuring variation in attachment at some particular developmental period. Enough is enough as far as measures are concerned. The field of attachment can do better than be a "measurement paradigm."

Third and finally, both threads of adult attachment theory and research are in my view perfectly legitimate. Therefore, my colleagues and I have conducted attachment–religion research within both traditions and with largely converging findings. Again, readers who prefer one approach—*the* approach—will find that one represented somewhere in the following chapters. But readers who are willing to digest a plurality of approaches will be more amply rewarded.

CHAPTER SUMMARY

The idea of individual differences in attachment was spawned by Ainsworth's discoveries of variations of attachment patterning among infants, first in Uganda and then in the United States. Her Strange Situation procedure enabled developmental researchers to classify natural variations in attachment and to track their sequelae later in development. In this chapter, I have characterized the three patterns of attachment (secure, insecure/avoidant, insecure/resistant) described by Ainsworth as well as Main and Solomon's addition of a fourth, disorganized, attachment category. Beyond the Strange Situation, I have described other attachment methods that have been used in attachment–religion research (the SAT, the AAI, and the ECR). I have also considered the developmental origins of and sequelae to attachment-related individual differences. Finally, I concluded that, although a focus on individual differences and their measurement has almost come to define attachment research, the topic of attachment is more foundational than individual differences, and attachment theory is much too important to get lost in a measurement paradigm.

CHAPTER 5

The Correspondence Pathway

In this chapter I deal with secure attachment and the "correspondence" pathway to religion and spirituality. In other words, I argue that via social (or cultural) learning, individuals who are secure with respect to attachment often adopt religious or nonreligious standards that are similar to those held by their sensitive attachment figures in childhood. Also, via generalizing working models of self and others, securely attached religious individuals often represent God as a correspondingly sensitive (i.e., reliably security-maintaining) attachment figure.

The chapter contains six sections. In the first, I pay tribute to William James, who early on provided seminal ideas, especially his notion of "healthy-minded" religion. In the second section, I explain briefly how the "correspondence hypothesis" emerged and has since been revised. The third section covers theory and research on what I have called "socialized correspondence": the fact that religion, for people who are secure with respect to attachment, corresponds in important ways to their attachment figure's religious standards. In the fourth section, I examine theory and research on what Lee Kirkpatrick (1992, 2005) calls "internal working model correspondence": the fact that working models derived from attachment-related experiences are generalized to mental models of God in relation to self. In the fifth section, I consider socialized and internal working models correspondence simultaneously and integrate them in terms of ideas borrowed from gene–culture coevolution models. Finally, because the research reviewed in this chapter is somewhat heavy on empirical findings from quantitative analyses of variables assessed across persons, I provide a case study illustrating the

123

integration of socialized and internal working model correspondence within a single individual.

SECURE ATTACHMENT AND "HEALTHY-MINDED" RELIGION

In his pioneering work, published at the dawn of both psychology in general and the psychology of religion in particular, William James (1902) directed his considerable intelligence to the complex phenomenon of religion. He quickly realized that the *varieties* of religious experience (spotlighted in the title of his book) were so pervasive that any normative (i.e., general or species-typical) account would be inadequate. So, at a time when most psychologists focused exclusively on normative processes in other domains, such as visual perception or verbal memory, James focused on individual differences in religious experience (Wulff, 1991).

James advocated an early version of what has become the "prototype approach" for characterizing individual differences in religious experience. Although prototypes may not do full justice to single individuals and to more fine-grained individual differences, at a point in conceptual development where science is fumbling in the dark, prototypes serve important pragmatic functions (James was *also* one of the founding figures of pragmatism in philosophy). Moreover, James was hesitant to move beyond description to explanation at such an early phase of investigation because explanation requires that the phenomenon to be explained has first been properly described. In our eagerness to measure phenomena and set up experiments somewhat prematurely so that we can test predictions, even today's psychology researchers have a lot to learn from James.

Jointly, these Jamesian points of departure—rich description and a focus on individual differences—have been incredibly useful for the psychology of religion and spirituality. We are very fortunate to have his careful initial road-mapping. The attachment–religion framework, and especially the individual-difference components of this framework, can be viewed as a tribute to James's legacy. However, rather than being engaged mainly with description, my colleagues and I, standing on James's shoulders, are aiming for explanation and prediction.

In his elegantly written descriptive prototypes, James (1902) famously distinguished between the "once-born" religion of "healthy-minded" individuals and the "twice-born" religion of the "sick soul." Tellingly for a psychologist, James was more interested in and deeply engaged with the "sick-soul" prototype, perhaps because it applied to himself. I deal with that prototype in the next chapter. In comparison, his thoughts and descriptions pertaining to the "healthy-minded" prototype (typified, probably incorrectly, by the poet Walt Whitman) were somewhat sketchy, as if for James this prototype did not require much attention or elaboration. Nonetheless, James's sketch of "healthy-minded" religion has turned out to possess prophetic qualities.

Most of what James said converges with what my colleagues and I have found to be true about religion and spirituality in the case of secure attachment. Individuals who are secure with respect to attachment often adopt religious or nonreligious standards similar to those held by their sensitive attachment figures in childhood. Also, by generalizing their childhood working models of self and others, secure individuals often represent God as a sensitive attachment figure who loves them and cares for them. Although James did not know much about "social learning" or "generalizing working models," details of which were not discovered until long after his time, and although learning principles and the notion of mental representations branched off, within academic psychology, in completely different theoretical directions, James understood the rudiments of both. Consider, for example, the following (unbroken) citation from one of James's exemplars of the healthy-minded prototype:

> I observe, with profound regret, the religious struggles which come into many biographies, as if almost essential to the formation of the hero. I ought to speak of these, to say, that any man has an advantage, not to be estimated, who is born, as I was, into a family where the religion is simple and rational; who is trained in the theory of such a religion, so that he never knows, for an hour, what these religious or irreligious struggles are. I always knew God loved me, and I was always grateful to him for the world he placed me in. (1902, p. 82)

This is, in essence, the substance of what has been developed further in the research discussed in the present chapter. Although it is still difficult for many psychologists to fathom, religiosity and spirituality are not necessarily dramatic, deficiency-based, or marked by turmoil and crisis ("as if almost to the formation of the hero"). In fact, in most cases, religiosity and spirituality are natural results of social learning ("trained in the theory of such a religion") and the generalization of working models (e.g., "I always knew God loved me"). Furthermore, in many ways it is "an advantage" to come from such circumstances and to have such an outlook, as compared to most of the available options (see Chapter 7). No wonder that the similarly fortunate protagonist from the old Washington Phillips folk tune "I Had a Real Good Mother and Father," who's been taught by the parents "how to pray," is now "walkin' on the narrow way."

DEVELOPMENT AND REVISION
OF THE CORRESPONDENCE HYPOTHESIS

Lee Kirkpatrick (1992, 2005; Kirkpatrick & Shaver, 1990) initially derived two opposing hypotheses about how individual differences in attachment might relate to religiousness. First, based on Bowlby's (1973) notion of internal working models (IWMs) generalized across relationships, he suggested that such IWMs extend to religion, in particular to the individual's beliefs about and perceived relationship with God. This understanding of correspondence implies that individuals who are secure with respect to attachment and who possess positive IWMs of themselves and others will view God in a similar manner, that is, as a reliable safe haven and secure base with whom one can have an enduring personal relationship. Second, Kirkpatrick (1992, 2005; Kirkpatrick & Shaver, 1990) also noted that insecure individuals may develop an attachment to God or other divine figures as surrogates or replacements for unsatisfactory human attachment figures. This *compensation* hypothesis was based on Ainsworth's (1985) discussion of the use of surrogate attachments among insecure children and will be dealt with in more detail in the next chapter (Chapter 6).

Kirkpatrick also conducted some pioneering empirical studies on how individual differences in attachment relate to religion (for a review, see Kirkpatrick, 2005). In the first of these studies, Kirkpatrick and Shaver (1990) found that participants reporting an insecure (especially avoidant) attachment history with parents were generally more religious, but that this held only at low levels of parental religiousness (i.e., parental religiousness acted as a moderator, or qualifier, of the link between perceived attachment history and religiousness). These findings (along with others described in the next chapter) were interpreted as supporting the compensation hypothesis. If participants reporting a secure attachment history were religious in this study, they had typically grown up with religious caregivers. Furthermore, the religiousness of participants reporting a secure history was positively related to parental religiousness, whereas the religiousness of participants reporting an insecure attachment history was generally unrelated or negatively related to parental religiousness.

When I was a young undergraduate student at Uppsala University, I replicated Kirkpatrick and Shaver's (1990) findings in what appeared to be surprising detail—surprising because their study was conducted in the "Bible Belt" of the United States (presumably with a predominantly fundamentalist sample), whereas my study was conducted in a highly secular country, Sweden (with a largely theologically liberal Lutheran sample; see Granqvist, 1998). There was one aspect of my findings, however, that differed slightly from those of Kirkpatrick and Shaver. I found that at high levels of parental religiousness, participants reporting a secure attachment history were significantly more religious than those reporting an insecure history. Although the pattern of data in Kirkpatrick and Shaver's study generally pointed in the same direction, they found no significant differences between groups differing in attachment security at high levels of parental religiousness, presumably because of a ceiling effect. When we consider that their study was conducted in a highly religious population, conceivably with a strong cultural norm favoring religion beyond that provided by parents, such a ceiling effect is not surprising.

At high parental religiousness, then, the findings from the Swedish study supported the correspondence hypothesis. However, and as in Kirkpatrick and Shaver (1990), at low levels of parental religiousness the contrasting compensation hypothesis was supported (i.e., insecure participants outscored secure participants in religiousness). Finally, as in Kirkpatrick and Shaver, I found that offspring–parent similarity in religiousness was marked among participants reporting a secure attachment history, whereas parental religiousness was unrelated to offspring religiousness among those with an insecure history.

Following my initial study (Granqvist, 1998), I suggested that the pattern of data supporting the correspondence hypothesis did not necessarily support the idea of IWM correspondence. Instead, together with my PhD advisor, Berit Hagekull, I proposed the idea of *socialized* correspondence. In the case of secure attachment, an offspring's religion reflects partial adoption of a sensitive caregiver's religion (Granqvist & Hagekull, 1999). This interpretation, it seemed to us, was not only as consonant with the data as the original (IWM) correspondence hypothesis proposed by Kirkpatrick but also had several advantages.

First, the original formulations of the correspondence and compensation hypotheses, considered jointly, implied that virtually any empirical outcome, except for completely null results, would support attachment-theory predictions. For example, if, on the one hand, secure individuals prove to have more theistic beliefs, it is due to generalizing IWMs; if, on the other hand, insecure individuals have more theistic beliefs, it is the result of turning to God for a more satisfactory attachment surrogate. In other words, almost no empirical instance (again besides completely null results) could "falsify" attachment-based predictions. Put differently, because contrasting predictions were derived from the same theory, contrasting findings could be accommodated within the theory. Although this may appear to be a happy situation for a theory (who wants to risk falsification?), it is commonly viewed as a problem in the philosophy of science. Indeed, Karl Popper (e.g., 1962/2014) did his best to eradicate this kind of problem from science altogether by rendering falsifiability a core criterion of scientific theories, as distinct from what he called "pseudoscience" (a category in which he included psychoanalysis, Marxism, and astrology). Inspired by Popper's philosophy of science, I asked myself, who wants to risk having a theory border on pseudoscience? In comparison, I thought it was better to risk falsification. Thus, I worked on revising the hypotheses to make more specific predictions from attachment theory, and I did so by adding a moderator (qualifying) variable: parental religiosity.

Parental religiousness had repeatedly been shown to act as such a moderator, both in Kirkpatrick and Shaver's (1990) pioneering study and in my own first study (Granqvist, 1998). It should be noted, too, that many studies not explicitly based on attachment theory but, rather, on parenting styles and the general socialization literature had shown that parent–offspring similarity in religiousness is much greater if the parent–child relationship has positive qualities (e.g., authoritative rather than authoritarian parenting; for reviews, see Hood et al., 2009; Oman, 2013).

Furthermore, and as I detail in the next section, some strands of attachment research had suggested that secure children are more successfully socialized in general than other children. The conclusion from that strand of studies was that socialization does not require special techniques of discipline but that it is a natural consequence of sensitive caregiving and mutual affection between caregiver and child.

However, as my understanding of science, attachment theory, and the collected empirical literature deepened, I realized that by dropping the notion of IWM correspondence altogether, we had effectively thrown the baby out with the bath water. So, in the end I decided it was wiser to keep that notion and just add the idea of socialized correspondence to it (Granqvist & Hagekull, 2001). From then on, my colleagues and I referred to two different aspects (or levels) of correspondence, one referring to socialized correspondence and the other to IWM correspondence.

Kirkpatrick (2005) was initially hesitant to adopt the idea of socialized correspondence. In his book on evolution and the attachment–religion connection, he mentioned three reasons for this reluctance under the heading "The Inadequacy of 'Socialization' as Explanation." Specifically, Kirkpatrick noted that (1) there is a problem of infinite regress (i.e., how to account for why some initial ancestor(s) thought up religion); (2) socialization is probably false as often as it is true (e.g., children do not like broccoli even if their parents do); and (3) offspring–parent similarity can be caused by processes other than social learning such as shared biological design (e.g., shared genes). It is important to note here that Kirkpatrick was working within a particular strand of evolutionary psychology that sought to replace a causally mind-shaping role of culture with a consideration of domain-specific, evolved psychological mechanisms. It should not come as a surprise, therefore, that some evolutionary psychologists see red when a writer appeals to learning and socialization, as these are viewed as exemplars of domain-general, tabula rasa ideas associated with the "standard social science model" (e.g., Buss, 1995). This is the model that evolutionary psychologists have hoped to replace.

Nonetheless, after discussing those three caveats, Kirkpatrick (2005, p. 121) wound up acknowledging that he had "no doubt that socialization does occur, and that people do acquire religious ideas in large part via social learning from other people." He clarified, however, that he did not view socialization processes as an "*alternative* explanation" for the acquisition of religious beliefs but, rather, as "operating simultaneously and in concert with, psychological and emotional processes such as attachment" (p. 121). Although I'm obviously less resistant to attribute a causal role to culture in co-sculpting the human mind, I largely concur with Kirkpatrick in these conclusions. In the fifth section of this chapter, I consider in more detail how to understand the simultaneous operation of social learning/socialization and the generalization of IWMs, after considering each of them separately.

Kirkpatrick and I have managed to set aside our differences in explanatory emphasis by focusing on developmental *pathways* to religion (rather than explanation per se) and to different modes of being religious/spiritual (Granqvist & Kirkpatrick, 2008, 2013, 2016). In so doing, we underscore that we are dealing with developmental issues. With the correspondence pathway, then, we have stated that religion in the case of secure attachment develops from (1) generalized, positive representations of self and other (IWM correspondence) and (2) partial adoption of a sensitive caregiver's religion (socialized correspondence). In other words, if parents have been observably religious, secure offspring are expected to be religious as well, in which case their perceptions of God will more or less mirror those of a reliably sensitive attachment figure.

SOCIALIZED CORRESPONDENCE

In the three subsections that follow, I first deal with socialized correspondence at the conceptual level, drawing on theory and research that have implicated a robust link between attachment security on the one hand and social learning and socialization on the other. In the second,

I review empirical research on socialized correspondence regarding religion. In the third, I discuss the implications of socialized correspondence for the psychology of religion and for intergenerational norm transmission more generally.

Attachment Security, Socialization, and Social Learning

Beyond generalizing working models as a possible mechanism linking individual differences in attachment to various developmental outcomes (discussed in the previous chapter), the attachment literature is replete with examples hinting at the possibility of learning- and socialization-based mechanisms (for a strong advocate, see Kagan, 1984). I already touched upon one such general idea when I discussed attachment security and cognitive development in Chapter 4: Presumably, by enhancing a child's freedom to explore, security facilitates learning from the environment and thus also cognitive development (cf. Aber & Allen, 1987). However, learning- and socialization-related notions have never achieved a strong standing in the field of attachment research, probably because of their association with Bowlby's contested "cupboard theories of love" (i.e., behaviorism). (In its early years, attachment theory was competing with both behaviorism and traditional psychoanalysis.)

Nonetheless, early on, Ainsworth, Bell, and Stayton (1974) wrote an important chapter titled "Infant Mother Attachment and Social Development: 'Socialisation' as a Product of Reciprocal Responsiveness to Signals" (see also Stayton, Hogan, & Ainsworth, 1971). As the title makes clear, based on emerging findings from Ainsworth's laboratory (Stayton et al., 1971), they argued that caregiver sensitivity and infant attachment security jointly enable "socialization," which was understood as unfolding naturally from mutual affection between mother and child, in turn serving as the basis for a cooperative relationship between them. Socialization does not, in Ainsworth's understanding, require any behaviorist (or psychoanalytic) assumption of the stronger and wiser partner (caregiver) serving as an agent of external control. Thus, a sensitive and responsive caregiver does not have to set up explicit behavioral norms that the child can acquire through conditioning or reinforcement/punishment (cf. Richters & Waters, 1991).

In Ainsworth's understanding, the secure child will ultimately comply ("obey" even) with the parent's behavioral norms not because of fear of punishment or to receive exogenous reward but because of mutual love and affection. Incomplete though this portrayal is (just listen to the many sensitive caregivers who really struggle to get their strong-willed 2- to 4-year-olds to "cooperate"), this somewhat romantic idea has received ample empirical support beyond Ainsworth's own studies (e.g., Kochanska, 1995, 1997; Kochanska, Aksan, Knaack, & Rhines, 2004; Kochanska, Forman, & Coy, 1999; Londerville & Main, 1981). For example, secure children (or children with sensitive caregivers) tend to heed their caregiver's directives more in laboratory situations involving "do and don't do" than do insecure children (children with insensitive caregivers). In other words, caregiver sensitivity and child security do seem to facilitate a child's behavioral adoption of parental norms.

This is not to say that disciplinary tactics are superfluous throughout the secure child's upbringing. Secure children can be particularly strong-willed and stubborn when they find their own contrasting position to be legitimate—for example, "I hate broccoli, why do I have to eat it!? YOU don't eat what you hate!" This is a natural indicator of autonomy as well as a demonstration that the child is not afraid of his or her caregivers or of losing their affection. On central and important matters, however, secure children do tend to identify with their sensitive caregivers' norms.

Peter Fonagy's later idea of epistemic trust (e.g., Fonagy & Campbell, 2015) helps illuminate why secure children, despite their autonomy, tend to agree with their caregivers on important matters. Briefly, secure children have had many, many experiences of being respected and prioritized by their caregivers, who have also helped them resolve states of distress and competently led them through challenging situations. Over time, then, secure children naturally come to trust the good will and competence of their caregivers. So, the default position for the child becomes one of cooperation or compliance. However, as illustrated by findings reported by Corriveau and colleagues (2009), if the parent clearly says or does something that can't or shouldn't be trusted, the autonomy of secure children will typically show itself with vigor: "Dad, you're crazy! I can't do THAT." Thus, secure children do not suck up what parents say or do like sponges, nor do they show blind trust or absolute obedience. Instead, they tend to be flexible and strategic, moving between positions of default trust versus autonomy depending on the credibility of the caregiver's particular statements about the world.[1]

As noted, socialization theory and research have often been dismissed as examples of the standard social science model rejected by evolutionary psychologists. For example, David Buss (1995, p. 26) claimed that "explanations advanced as causal (e.g., 'culture,' 'learning,' and 'socialization') are at best descriptions of phenomena awaiting explanation and at worst empty names given to ignorance of actual causal processes that give the illusion of having explained something." Perhaps as a response to this kind of critique, many contemporary socialization researchers take evolution-informed considerations and principles of nature–nurture interaction seriously (e.g., transactional effects, domain-specificity, genetic constraints; for an illustration, see the socialization handbook edited by Grusec & Hastings, 2015). These advancements toward a more nuanced, nature–nurture inclusive understanding of socialization should also make the topic area fit better with attachment theory.

Studies of infants' and children's imitation have yielded findings that cohere with those on attachment and socialization. Infants and children are more likely to imitate behavioral models who display warmth, enthusiasm, sensitivity, and mutual responsiveness in interactions (Bandura & Walters, 1977; Baumrind, 1978; Hetherington & Frankie, 1967; Kochanska et al., 1999; Waxler & Yarrow, 1975). These findings indicate that security-promoting attributes in a caregiver should facilitate not only child socialization in general but also the most "primitive" form of social learning, imitation.

Critics of social learning theory have occasionally dismissed social learning as a simple tabula rasa notion (e.g., Buss, 1995; Pinker, 2003). In that spirit, Kirkpatrick (2005, p. 120) noted, quite correctly, that "children do not simply soak up parental beliefs and values like a sponge." Although such criticism has sometimes been warranted, the originators of social learning theory, Bandura and Walters (1977), clearly emphasized the selective nature of social learning. They noted, for example, that "the functional value of the behaviors displayed by different models is highly influential in determining which models will be closely observed and which will be ignored" (p. 6). They also pointed explicitly to the survival-enhancing function of children learning danger-related cues from observing more experienced members of their social group. The notion of "prepared" learning (Öhman & Mineka, 2001; Seligman, 1971) is another example of such an evolutionarily informed understanding of social learning.

In summary, sensitive caregiving and secure attachment are systematically and positively linked to socialization and social learning. Furthermore, this link can be understood within an evolutionarily informed framework and is no longer restricted to the province of behaviorism (which itself has evolved over the years). Because social learning is a very real and important phenomenon in development—indeed, it is almost ubiquitous in nature, especially among primates (Laland, 2017)—social learning has become an important part of some strands of contemporary evolutionary biology (see Chapter 10).

For these reasons, I argued in Chapter 1 that considerations of the functional consequences of attachment should not be restricted to physical protection alone. Now that cupboard theories of love (based on the idea that we love the one that feeds us) have been buried for several decades, I contend that the time is ripe to reconsider learning, and particularly social learning (including socialization), not just as a phenomenon somewhat linked to attachment but as a functional consequence of attachment. Learning from being in proximity to caregivers should aid children's survival via increased identification and management of dangers. Even more importantly for us here, learning from attachment figures should increase the child's social and cultural adaptation via intergenerational transmission of norms that are central for a given social and cultural group. Furthermore, I hold that sensitive caregiving and secure attachment are likely to facilitate these functional consequences. I return to these matters of function and adaptation in Chapter 10, where I examine attachment in the light of cultural evolution and gene–culture coevolution processes. In the present chapter, I deal with the implications of the links among sensitive caregiving, attachment security, and socialization/social learning specifically for the intergenerational transmission of religion.

Beyond respect for the pattern of findings that emerged in attachment–religion studies, I hope this section has clarified why I insisted on attending to the role of social learning and socialization to understand the link between an individual's attachment history and his or her current religiosity and spirituality. I wish to note, too, that my insistence on this stance remained adamant even though social learning and socialization had become unfashionable in psychological science.

Review of Socialized Correspondence Findings

As applied to the attachment–religion connection, the notion of socialized correspondence implies that, for people who are secure with respect to attachment, religion partially reflects correspondence with their attachment figures' religious standards, via social learning/socialization. In other words, the religious beliefs and behaviors of people who have been cared for by relatively sensitive/responsive caregivers and who are currently secure with regard to attachment can be expected to reflect their sensitive attachment figure's religious standards. In contrast, attachment-insecure individuals can be expected less often to adopt their relatively insensitive or unresponsive attachment figure's religious standards.

Parent–Offspring Similarity in Religiousness and Religious Stability

Considerable support has emerged for socialized correspondence in research conducted in several countries, regardless of whether social-psychological (questionnaire) or developmental (e.g., the Adult Attachment Interview [AAI]) attachment methods have been used. As already noted, specifically in the context of high parental religiosity, individuals reporting experiences of being sensitively cared for by parents score higher in religiousness than those reporting experiences of being less sensitively cared for. Such findings have been obtained not only in my initial study (Granqvist, 1998) but in conceptual replications based on two additional adult samples (Granqvist, 2005; Granqvist & Hagekull, 1999) and one adolescent sample (Granqvist, 2002) in Sweden, and a young adult sample in the United States (Reinert & Edwards, 2009).

In addition, people reporting experiences of being sensitively cared for by parents have been found to score higher on a scale explicitly constructed to assess religiosity as socially rooted in the parental relationship (the socialization-based religiousness scale; e.g., "I give/intend to give my children an equally religious/non-religious upbringing as my parents gave me"; Granqvist, 2002; Granqvist & Hagekull, 1999). Similarly, in the case of romantic attachment styles, secure attachment has been associated with higher scores on the socialization-based religiousness scale (Granqvist, 2002; cf. Greenwald, Mikulincer, Granqvist, & Shaver, 2018).

Moreover, converging findings were obtained in the first AAI-based study conducted on the attachment–religion connection (Granqvist, Ivarsson, et al., 2007). Importantly, in the AAI system, estimates of parental sensitivity (loving vs. rejecting or role-reversing caregiving) are assigned not by direct self-reports but by independent, "blinded" interview coders who take the coherence of participant memories into account in assigning ratings. In other words, high parental sensitivity scores require consistent episodic substantiation; mere statements such as "My parents were loving" or "I felt loved" do not suffice. Even with this more rigorous assessment, participants with parents estimated as higher in sensitivity scored higher on the socialization-based religiousness scale.

Also, the socialized correspondence idea has been strongly supported in an American study dealing with the link between maltreatment and representations of God (Reinert & Edwards, 2009). Beyond an adverse effect of maltreatment on participants' representations of God, Reinert and Edwards (2009) reported that even among those who may have suffered maltreatment, security with both mother and father facilitated parent–offspring similarity in religiousness, at least as far as more positive representations of God were concerned (e.g., perceiving God as loving). In contrast, the religiosity among participants who reported an insecure history with a particular parent was again independent of parental religiousness. The authors concluded that "even when childhood mistreatment is taken into account, . . . a secure attachment to parents provides the necessary context for socialization into religion" (p. 25).

As a corollary to the socialized correspondence thesis, if the religiosity of secure individuals and individuals cared for by relatively sensitive attachment figures is grounded in primary socialization processes, then their religiosity, once formed, should be relatively stable and typically will not undergo radical fluctuations over time. Several studies have supported this hypothesis (e.g., Granqvist, 1998, 2002; Granqvist & Hagekull, 1999, 2001; Granqvist, Ivarsson, et al., 2007). In an intriguing quasi-experimental study, Wright (2008) even documented some "immunity" to being persuaded by a "foreign" proselytizing message of ministry among secure participants raised by religious caregivers. He concluded that "securely attached individuals with religious caregivers are socialized into their caregiver's religious system and are thus unlikely to express interest in other religious organizations" (p.75).

There are two reasons for nonetheless deeming the "stability corollary" overly simplistic. The first is that religiosity is not a fixed or static "trait" that remains untouched by life or is impervious to change over the life cycle. I hope the developmental chapter (Chapter 3) made this clear. Indeed, the psychology of religion would not have drawn my interest, nor probably that of the founding figures of psychology, if religiosity were merely a trait. Second, and relatedly, it is characteristic of secure individuals to be exploratory, open, curious, and flexible (e.g., Fransson, Granqvist, Bohlin, & Hagekull, 2013; Mikulincer & Shaver, 2016; Wulff, 2006), so we should not expect them typically to have made up their minds "once and for all" about religious and spiritual matters. Thus, even if religiosity is *relatively* stable among secure individuals (compared to insecure ones, as shown in the next chapter), they can also undergo religious changes. When they do, their religious changes again tend to point to the now familiar theme of offspring–parent similarity. Two studies using Jewish Israeli samples illustrate this point (Greenwald et al., 2018; Pirutinsky, 2009).

In a recent study of both apostates and converts, Greenwald and colleagues (2018) found that those who had relatively secure (nonavoidant) romantic attachments tended to experience a religious change that went in the same general direction as their parents' religiosity/nonreligiosity during the participants' childhood; that is, they tended to become apostates if their parents had been nonreligious but to become converts if their parents had been religious. Similarly, Pirutinsky (2009) found that nonconverts and intra-Orthodox Jewish converts (i.e., those who converted within the same general tradition in which they had been brought up) scored higher on a measure of secure attachment history with parents than did converts who converted across traditions (from Orthodox to non-Orthodox Judaism or vice versa). These studies also demonstrate that socialized correspondence has been supported in Jewish (and not just Christian) contexts.

Furthermore, socialized correspondence has been supported not just in cross-sectional, retrospective, and quasi-experimental studies but also in a real-time prospective longitudinal study (Schnitker, Porter, Emmons, & Barrett, 2012). In that study of American adolescents about to undergo a Young Life Evangelical summer camp, secure attachment with parents prospectively predicted an at-camp reaffirmation of the faith in which they had been brought up.

Characteristics of Religious Change

In the studies discussed so far, socialization was for the most part not directly studied but was simply inferred from parent–offspring similarity, religious stability, or religious changes going in the same direction as parental religiousness during participants' childhoods. As evolutionary psychologists have pointed out, such inferences are potentially problematic because in principle there may be other explanations for similarity besides socialization, such as shared genes. Although there is no reason to assume that secure attachment and memories of being sensitively cared for should more readily imply shared biological design with parents than insecure attachment and memories of being insensitively cared for, the notion of socialized correspondence would benefit from more direct support. To be persuasive, studies should show that actual socialization factors are present and predictive of religious changes among relatively secure people. Fortunately, there are such studies.

More specifically, and again converging with James's (1902) characterization of the "once-born" religion of "healthy-minded" individuals, when positive increases in religiosity occur for people reporting a secure attachment history, they tend to be gradual (rather than sudden), to occur at a comparatively young age, and not to be preceded by emotional turmoil (e.g., Granqvist & Hagekull, 1999, 2001; Granqvist, Ivarsson, et al., 2007; Schnitker et al., 2012). More to the point here, numerous studies have found that these individuals tend to experience increases in religiosity specifically in a life context pointing to a positive influence of other relationships, which we (Granqvist & Hagekull, 1999) label as "themes of correspondence." These themes include the socializing influence of exposure to other people's religious beliefs and behaviors—for example, new friendships with religious peers and the parents' religious beliefs becoming influential (Granqvist, 2002; Granqvist & Hagekull, 1999, 2001; Granqvist, Ivarsson, et al., 2007; Halama, Gasparikova, & Sabo, 2013).

The recent study by Greenwald and colleagues (2018) found that, regardless of the form of religious change (i.e., apostasy or conversion), romantic attachment security (low anxiety and/or avoidance) was related to gradual changes and themes of correspondence, indicating the importance of both socialization and exploration motives. This study demonstrates that the conclusions drawn in the preceding paragraph are not restricted to attachment history with parents but also apply to romantic attachment; that they are not restricted to increases in religiosity/conversion but apply also to decreases in religiosity/apostasy; and that they are not restricted to Christians but also apply to Jews.

Social Learning of Religion: Conclusions, Qualifications, and Advice for Parents

In conclusion, strong and consistent empirical evidence has been presented in support of socialized correspondence. Experiences with sensitive attachment figures as well as being securely attached at present facilitate offspring–parent similarity in religiousness. Individuals with such experiences and such an attachment orientation also tend to experience religious changes in the direction of their parents' religiousness—or lack thereof—during childhood, and such religious changes are in turn propelled by socialization themes.

Apparently, support for socialized correspondence has so far been obtained only in studies of adolescent and adult samples. In the few child studies in which it has been tested (e.g., De Roos, 2006; Granqvist, Ljungdahl, et al., 2007), findings have shown that secure and insecure children are not yet *differentially* susceptible to adopting parental religious standards (see Richert & Granqvist, 2013). I speculate that it is not until adolescence that most individuals have attained sufficient autonomy and independence from parents for such differential susceptibility to become visible. Unlike children, adolescents and adults may then either distance themselves from the religious standards associated with insensitive caregivers or come to embrace (or perhaps re-embrace, following a period of exploration) the religious standards associated with sensitive caregivers. These conclusions also help to account for why adolescence to early adulthood is often a period marked by religious and spiritual transitions (again both increases and decreases in religiosity; see, e.g., Smith & Denton, 2009).

Although strongly implied in the preceding sections, the notion of socialized correspondence applies not just to religious standards in parents but also to nonreligious ones. Thus, if sensitive caregivers have modeled nonreligious—perhaps even antireligious—behaviors and attitudes, the findings reviewed in the sections above indicate that their secure offspring are inclined to partially adopt these nonreligious standards as well. I speculate that social correspondence may in fact be applicable to almost any form of intergenerational value transmission (including political and social norms). I return to this possibility when I consider security as a facilitator of intergenerational norm transmission and cultural evolution more generally (see Chapter 10).

Psychologists of religion and especially scholars who approach the topic from a social learning perspective have often suggested that parental religiousness is the single strongest predictor of religiousness in offspring (e.g., Batson, Schoenrade, & Ventis, 1993; Spilka, Hood, Hunsberger, & Gorsuch, 2003). I reiterate, therefore, that the statistical effect of parental religiousness is importantly moderated by the estimated quality of the offspring–parent attachment relationship. Again, whereas parent–offspring correlations for retrospectively defined secure dyads have typically been positive and substantial in terms of effect size, they have usually been nonsignificant and close to zero, occasionally even negative, for insecure dyads (e.g., Granqvist, 1998; Kirkpatrick & Shaver, 1990; Reinert & Edwards, 2009). One implication of these findings is that parents have to deserve their role as sustainable models, as Ainsworth and colleagues (1974) implied more than 40 years ago in writing about attachment and "socialization."

I therefore end by advising religious parents who wish their children to embrace their own religion that religious preaching and teaching are not enough. In fact, such preaching and teaching may ultimately fall on deaf ears unless it is combined with placing a high priority on sensitive caregiving that meets children's needs for protection and security. In the absence of formal religious training, sensitive caregiving may even suffice as long as the child has repeated opportunities to observe the caregiver engage in religious speech and behavior.

INTERNAL WORKING MODEL CORRESPONDENCE

According to Bowlby's theory, continuity of attachment patterns across time and transmission of attachment patterns across generations can largely be traced to "internal working models" (IWMs; Bowlby, 1973; Main et al., 1985). As a consequence of repeated experiences in interactions with their attachment figures, children develop beliefs and expectations (IWMs) about the availability and responsiveness of caregivers, and these models guide the children's future behavioral, emotional, and cognitive responses in other social interactions. Moreover, the models of interaction partners are linked to models of the self—beliefs about the degree to which one sees oneself as worthy of love, care, and protection.

In the previous chapter, we saw how the notion of generalizing (or extending) IWMs has functioned as the central organizing principle for most developmental research informed by attachment theory. As it flows so naturally from the normative tenets of attachment theory, it is easy to see why Kirkpatrick (1992; Kirkpatrick & Shaver, 1990) would also apply the idea of generalizing IWMs as a central organizing principle for research on the attachment–religion connection. As noted above, although I initially attempted to replace this notion with the idea of socialized correspondence (Granqvist & Hagekull, 1999), I quickly reconsidered and also came to embrace IWM correspondence (Granqvist & Hagekull, 2001; see also Granqvist & Kirkpatrick, 2008, 2013, 2016).

As noted in Chapter 1, people likely maintain both (1) IWMs of attachment figures in general and (2) IWMs specific to particular relationships. These different levels of IWMs may be envisioned as hierarchically arranged (e.g., Bretherton & Munholland, 2016) or perhaps as nodes in a larger neural attachment network (Mikulincer & Shaver, 2016). Using a topographical analogy, we might consider that the top level comprises a highly general model of self and others; that a second level might comprise models of parent–child relationships as distinct from peer relationships; and so on. We have suggested that for many individuals, IWMs of God (or perceived relationships with God) hold an important place somewhere in this hierarchy or neural network (Granqvist & Kirkpatrick, 2008, 2016).

Consideration of the interrelatedness of IWMs leads to a straightforward set of predictions, referred to as "IWM correspondence": Individual differences in religious beliefs and experience should correspond with individual differences in IWMs of self and other. Put differently, IWMs derived from attachment-based experiences are generalized to mental models of God in relation to self. Setting aside the issue of social learning, or socialization, we suggest that individuals who possess positive or "secure" generalized IWMs of themselves and their attachment figures may be expected to represent God and other deities in similar terms. Likewise, an avoidant attachment may be expected to manifest itself in the religious realm as agnosticism or atheism or in a representation of God as remote and inaccessible (religious deactivation/minimization). In addition, an anxious (or resistant) attachment may find expression in a deeply emotional, all-consuming, "clingy" relationship to God (religious hyperactivation/maximization). Finally, a disorganized (and fearful) attachment may relate to a representation of God as frightening and ominous (religious disorganization).

The notion of IWM correspondence resembles prior psychodynamic and anthropological ideas about people's representations of God, offered, for example, in object-relational studies (e.g., Rizzuto, 1979; see Chapter 9) and cross-cultural research (e.g., Lambert, Triandis, & Wolf, 1959; Rohner, 1986). The cross-cultural findings have been particularly striking seen from the lens of IWM correspondence. In cultures where parenting is typically harsh and rejecting, people tend to have a corresponding representation of God or gods as wrathful and punitive. In contrast, in cultures where parenting is typically warm and accepting, people tend to have a corresponding representation of God or gods as loving and accepting (Lambert et al., 1959; Rohner, 1986). Of course, such research by no means demonstrates causal direction because the associations can just as well run in the reverse direction (i.e., cultural ideas about God/gods foster corresponding patterns of caregiving). What is interesting about these findings, however, is that IWM correspondence is not merely a phenomenon at the individual or micro level but also at the cultural or macro level.

Review of Internal Working Model Correspondence Findings

As in attachment research in general, IWM correspondence is the one idea within the larger attachment–religion literature that has been subjected to and supported in the largest number of empirical studies, conducted now in many countries and faith traditions. As with the notion of socialized correspondence, support for IWM correspondence remains largely inferential. Such support has been largely inferred from a particular pattern of correlational links between attachment security and religious/spiritual "outcomes." In other words, no one has actually observed IWMs as such, let alone observed the actual process of IWM generalization to the religious/spiritual realm. The large research literature that supports IWM correspondence has typically used relatively simple methodologies, such as convenience (often undergraduate student) samples, cross-sectional research designs, and self-report scales to tap both attachment and religiosity. Because the literature is large while simultaneously suffering from obvious methodological shortcomings, my research review will be selective. My particular emphasis is on the early studies that spurred this line of research and on later studies that have been comparatively methodologically strong (e.g., employing experimental designs or "implicit" methodologies).

The notion of IWM correspondence has been supported in studies conducted within both adult attachment traditions (i.e., social psychology and developmental psychology) and with reference to both parent-related and romantic attachment. My review starts with correlational (cross-sectional and longitudinal) research on parent-related attachment, then on romantic attachment, and finally on experimental research.

Correlational Studies: Parent-Related Attachment

Evidence for IWM correspondence has accrued in relation to attachment history, as estimated through the AAI. The AAI study described above (Granqvist, Ivarsson, et al., 2007) revealed that coded estimates of probable experiences with sensitive parents were associated with participants' reports of a loving, as opposed to a distant, God image. Conversely, inferred experiences with rejecting and role-reversing parents were associated positively with a distant image of God and negatively with a loving image of God. Furthermore, using a Religious Attachment Interview (RAI; Granqvist & Main, 2017) modeled on the AAI as part of a 3-year prospective longitudinal follow-up, these findings have recently been shown to hold up also when using an independent interview coder's coherency-based (e.g., degree of coherence between episodic memories and general/semantic statements) ratings of God. More specifically, coded estimates of probable experiences with sensitive parents were associated with participants coherently representing God as functionally benevolent, as opposed to malevolent, in their lives (Nkara, Main, Hesse, & Granqvist, 2018). Furthermore, coherency of mind (a primary indicator of security) on the AAI was positively predictive of coherent discourse as well as benevolence of God and negatively predictive of malevolence of God on the RAI (Nkara et al., 2018).

Similar findings have been reported in an Italian AAI study (Cassibba et al., 2008). This study was particularly interesting theoretically because it contained two subsamples. The first was a highly religious group (Catholic nuns, priests, and seminarians) who lived a religious life seemingly designed to foster a principal attachment to God and to prevent competing interpersonal attachments from developing (i.e., the vow of chastity, prohibition against marriage, participation in at least six religious services daily). The second group was a comparison group of lay Catholic believers, matched for sex. The highly religious group was coded significantly higher not only on loving experiences with mothers, but also on a continuous dimension of coherent discourse. This group also contained a higher proportion of secure/autonomous classifications (80%) than the worldwide nonclinical meta-analytic distribution (< 60%; Bakermans-Kranenburg & van IJzendoorn, 2009). Finally, regardless of subsample, secure/autonomous participants reported a more loving God image than insecure/nonautonomous participants (Cassibba et al., 2008).

Links between parent-related attachment assessments and corresponding aspects of religion have also been predicted and observed in another prospective longitudinal study. In that study, participants who had reported sensitive parenting at study time-point 1 experienced an increase in religiousness over time specifically following the establishment of a new intimate relationship (i.e., themes of correspondence) in between the religiosity assessments (Granqvist & Hagekull, 2003).

Correlational Studies: Romantic Attachment

Research examining relations between romantic attachment (or adult attachment "style") and religion variables has typically supported the notion of IWM correspondence in concurrent relations between romantic attachment security and religion variables. For example, in the first study conducted in this area, Kirkpatrick and Shaver (1992) found that people with a secure romantic attachment displayed a higher personal belief in and relationship with God, as well as perceptions of God as loving, whereas people reporting avoidant romantic attachment were agnostic or atheist to a larger extent (i.e., religious deactivation/minimization). These findings have since been conceptually replicated in a large number of studies, in many countries, and across faith traditions (e.g., Bayramoglu, Harma, & Yilmaz, 2018; Beck & McDonald, 2004; Byrd & Boe, 2000; Eurelings-Bontekoe, Hekman-Van Steeg, & Verschuur, 2005; Granqvist, Mikulincer, et al., 2012, Study 1; Granqvist & Hagekull, 2003; Greenwald et al., 2018; Hall, Fujikawa, Halcrow, Hill, & Delaney, 2009; Kirkpatrick, 1998; Limke & Mayfield, 2011; Lopez, Riggs, Pollard, & Hook, 2011; McDonald, Beck, Allison, & Norsworthy, 2005; Rowatt & Kirkpatrick, 2002; TenElshof & Furrow, 2000). For example, Byrd and Boe (2000) found that participants reporting secure romantic attachment engaged more in a form of prayer that served to maintain closeness to God. As in Kirkpatrick and Shaver's initial study, this literature has also supported correspondence between romantic attachment security and security in believers' "attachment to God"—that is, a relationship with a God perceived to be warm, responsive, and caring (Rowatt & Kirkpatrick, 2002) or low scores on anxiety and avoidance with reference to one's relationship with God (Beck & McDonald, 2004). Moreover, even in prospective analyses, IWM correspondence between romantic attachment security and religious change has been supported in expected contexts, such as following the formation of a romantic relationship in between assessments of religiosity (Granqvist & Hagekull, 2003; cf. Greenwald et al., 2018).

Just as positive or secure IWMs of self and others generalize to one's relationship with God, so too may negative or insecure IWMs. Beyond initial findings linking avoidant romantic attachment to atheism and agnosticism, research suggests that insecurity dimensions of romantic attachment are linked to corresponding dimensions of insecurity in one's attachment to God (Beck & McDonald, 2004; Granqvist, Mikulincer, et al., 2012, Study 1; Kirkpatrick, 1998; Kirkpatrick & Shaver, 1992; Rowatt & Kirkpatrick, 2002). These findings harmonize with the sentiments of this poor protagonist:

I'm trying, but I've gone
Through the glass again
Just come and find me
God loves everybody, don't remind me
I took the medicine and I went missing
Just let me hear your voice, just let me listen
Graceless.

("Graceless," The National,
Trouble Will Find Me, 2013)

However, we should not necessarily expect that an insecure attachment orientation will always correspond with an insecure attachment to God. First, some generally insecure individuals may simply shy away from God because of generalizing IWMs of others as rejecting, frightening, and so on (see Chapter 8). If so, they may simply be "unattached" rather than "insecurely attached" to God. Second, because of God's unique characteristics as a noncorporeal attachment figure, some insecure individuals may be able to establish a reparative, secure relationship with God (see Chapter 6).

Finally, it should be noted that much "attachment to God" research has examined links between attachment to God and psychological outcomes beyond attachment. I return to this strand of literature when I discuss the attachment–religion connection in relation to mental health and unhealth (Chapter 7).

Experimental Studies

In the previous section, I moved quickly past a large set of cross-sectional studies that used self-report assessments to tap both attachment and religion variables. I did so not to dismiss them from consideration but because of well-known validity threats rendering it difficult, if not impossible, to disambiguate substantive findings from shared method variance. Although the prospective longitudinal studies reviewed offered tentative support for the presumed process direction, and although some of the authors of the cross-sectional studies attempted to control statistically for the influence of other variables, experimental designs are needed to fully support causal hypotheses.

I know of four sets of published attachment and religion experiments (or quasi-experiments) that enable us to address cause–effect relations more directly: Birgegard and Granqvist (2004); Cassibba and colleagues (2013); Granqvist, Ljungdahl, and colleagues (2007); Granqvist, Mikulincer, and colleagues (2012). All these studies have involved subtle attempts to activate the attachment system. The normative/main effects of attachment activation observed in these studies have already been described (see reviews in Chapters 2 and 3). However, all of the studies documenting main effects have indicated that those effects were moderated, or qualified, by perceived attachment history or current attachment security in a manner that supports the notion of IWM correspondence.

First, across the three experiments that I conducted with Andreas Birgegard on theistic believers (mostly Christians) in Sweden, an increase in the use of God to regulate distress was observed following subliminal separation primes—again targeting both God and mothers—specifically among adult believers who had reported sensitive experiences with parents (Birgegard & Granqvist, 2004). These findings strongly supported IWM correspondence. Because indirect assessments of religious distress–regulation (i.e., regression residuals from pre- to postpriming) were used in the context of *subliminal* priming, participants were unaware of attachment activation. Although we were surprised by the direction of the findings after the first experiment (at the time we expected insecure individuals to draw on God to regulate distress; see Chapter 6), the interaction pattern replicated across two additional experiments. We speculated then that these conditions of subliminality and nonconscious processes might have undermined the possibility of a compensatory use of religion in individuals who had experienced parental insensitivity, thus resulting in their withdrawal from God. Conversely, presumably via automatic activation of IWMs, individuals with more sensitive caregivers and positive IWMs could draw upon their representations of God in this situation.

Second, a later series of three experiments conducted on Jewish theistic Israelis conceptually replicated and extended these findings (Granqvist, Mikulincer, et al., 2012). In the first experiment, the observation of a heightened psychological accessibility of God concepts following subliminal threat exposures (i.e., God as an implicit safe haven) was particularly notable in participants with a relatively secure (nonavoidant) romantic attachment orientation (Study 2).[2] Thus, this experiment conceptually replicated those of Birgegard and Granqvist (2004).

Similarly, concerning implicit access to God as a secure base, the second Israeli experiment, which extended the first, showed that participants with a relatively secure romantic attachment orientation had particularly heightened cognitive access to secure-base-related concepts (e.g., "loving," "accepting") following subliminal priming with the word "God," compared with a neutral control prime (Study 3).

In the third Israeli experiment, these latter effects were extended by findings showing that relatively secure participants implicitly reacted with more positive affect (i.e., previously neutral Chinese ideograms were rated more positively) following subliminal exposure to a religion-related symbol (a picture of the Torah scroll), compared with both a neutral symbol (a picture of a book) and no symbol/picture (Study 4). Hence, not only was attention to God more heightened for individuals reporting relatively secure romantic attachment than for those reporting insecure attachment when faced with unconscious threat, but the former individuals were also more likely to implicitly associate God with secure-base constructs and to implicitly benefit more from being unconsciously exposed to God-related material.

Third, in our Swedish "felt board" study of 5- to 7-year-old children who were asked to place a God symbol at a chosen distance from a fictional child who was in attachment-activating or attachment-neutral situations (Granqvist, Ljungdahl, et al., 2007), secure children placed the God symbol closer to the fictional child when the fictional child was in attachment-activating situations. Notably, the pattern was reversed when the fictional child was in attachment-neutral situations (i.e., insecure children placed God closer). Overall, the discrepancy in God proximity between the two types of situations was much larger among secure than among insecure children. Our interpretation of this interaction was that secure children's attention shifted to God following attachment activation, whereas insecure children's attention to God did not shift as a function of attachment activation. Of note also is that this study used the adapted Separation Anxiety Test (SAT; Kaplan, 1987), which is an implicit (semiprojective) method, to measure security (for more details, see Chapter 4). The God placement procedure was similarly semiprojective; that is, the fictional child, not the study participants, was in different situations that were more or less likely to activate a child's attachment system. As in the adult experiments using subliminal priming techniques, this semiprojective procedure may have undermined a compensatory use of religion among insecure children and instead yielded automatic activation of IWMs and thus support for IWM correspondence.

Fourth and finally, Cassibba and colleagues (2013) have extended these "felt board" findings in a study using the AAI in an Italian sample. These researchers pioneered the investigation of generalizing IWMs across generations in attachment–religion research. The background to this undertaking, as reviewed in Chapter 4, was that previous research had shown that attachment security tends to be transmitted across generations from parent to child largely via nongenomic transmission mechanisms (e.g., aspects of caregiving; van IJzendoorn, 1995; Verhage et al., 2016). Although such findings have been enormously important within the field of attachment, they can to some extent be trivialized by the fact that a given parent figures in all of the pertinent assessments. A given parent's state of mind with regard to attachment is assessed on the AAI; that caregiver's caregiving is assessed with observations of sensitivity and other caregiving behaviors; and the child's attachment is assessed with respect to that particular caregiver as well. If attachment is intergenerationally transmitted and Bowlby's notion of generalizing IWMs is correct, then we should expect a caregiver's attachment representations to manifest in domains that transcend a particular parent–child relationship. Cassibba and colleagues' findings strongly supported this corollary by showing that maternal security on the AAI strongly predicted a higher degree of proximity in their children's God symbol placements vis-à-vis a fictional child. These findings are theoretically important in illustrating, perhaps for the first time, that mothers' IWMs generalize to the next generation's perceptions of the availability of another attachment figure (i.e., God) besides the mother.

In summary, beyond a large correlational literature, studies using experimental designs to subtly (or "implicitly") activate attachment or religious parameters have consistently supported IWM correspondence. In other words, attachment security is linked to a security-maintaining mental access to one's relationship with God under conditions of implicit threat (i.e., attachment activation). Theoretically, this reflects a coherent representation of the self as worthy of care and of God as a reliable safe haven and secure base.

CORRESPONDENCE REVISITED: INTEGRATION

Kirkpatrick (2015) and I (e.g., Granqvist, 2014b; Granqvist & Nkara, 2017) agree that although social learning and IWM correspondence are different (explanatory) principles, the pertinent processes in fact tend to be integrated at the individual level. In this final section, I discuss how they may be integrated.

If the child is provided care by sensitive attachment figures who simultaneously act as religious models (i.e., who are observed to pray to God and who also teach the child about God's charitable traits), then God will very likely become an "intuitively" appealing character for the child to engage with. In other words, such episodes of social (or cultural) learning will help to tweak the child's attachment system (and other cognitive modalities) to identify God as one of its targets. In this process, the child will increasingly become socially adapted to its local environment (its belief system and values). Children cared for by equally sensitive caregivers who do not act as religious models—for example, children growing up in largely "secular" parts of the world with attachment figures who are foreign to ideas about God and religion—will naturally be much less likely to identify God as a target for their attachment systems. Notably, *not* identifying God as target will make children in such contexts more socially adapted to their particular local environments.

These considerations of the importance of culture or cultural transmission point to a major shortcoming in some core cognition and evolutionary psychology proposals (see Granqvist & Nkara, 2017; Jensen, 2009). The child's representation of the world is not a solitary undertaking, but is heavily influenced by other members of the child's culture (Boyatzis, 2005; Tomasello et al., 1993; Vygotsky, 1978), especially by the testimonies of those viewed as stronger and wiser by the child and, somewhat later, by others holding a respected position in the child's culture. In other words, the child's representation of the world is built from his or her own core cognitive dispositions (e.g., generalizing working models) *in interaction with* the cultural tweaking (social learning) of those dispositions.

Two simple tools by which cultural tweaking of cognitive dispositions may be accomplished are imitation of and instruction from important models (Tomasello et al., 1993). If the model's behavior/instruction accords well with the child's cognitive dispositions (e.g., positive working models), then the child is all the more likely to imitate it and embrace it. For example, a model's testimonies about unseen others who possess some anthropomorphic attributes (e.g., a mind) should fall on more attentive ears than a model's testimonies about purely abstract entities. Thus, presumably, children also abandon certain unseen others partly because they are discouraged by important models in their lives, but they maintain or ultimately embrace others because they accord with children's cognitive dispositions *and* important models demonstrate affirmative information and behaviors.

Consistent with this integrated emphasis on cognitive dispositions and social learning, scholars within different evolutionary schools of thought have all grappled with how to make sense of cultural learning from an evolutionary perspective. These schools of thought include cultural evolution (e.g., Boyd & Richerson, 1985), (late) sociobiology (Lumsden & Wilson, 2005), some evolutionary psychology (Durham, 1991), and especially the gene–culture coevolution framework (Laland & Brown, 2011). They have proposed principles such as "social learning strategies" (e.g., biased cultural transmission), "epigenetic rules," and, more generally, "dual inheritance" (i.e., gene-based *and* culture-based). The basic idea is that given a choice between two alternatives (e.g., to represent God as loving or rejecting), people are more likely to adopt one rather than the other. Which one they adopt will depend not just on which one they have been exposed to (social learning) but also on how it harmonizes with their cognitive dispositions (e.g., their IWMs).

For example, two individuals who grow up with attachment figures who (1) express equally strong beliefs in a loving God but who

(2) display different patterns of caregiving behaviors (one is loving, the other rejecting) will be differentially biased to "copy" the attachment figure's belief expressions. The one growing up with a loving attachment figure will be more inclined to copy the attachment figure's expressions of belief in a loving God because it harmonizes with the individual's positive and coherent IWMs of others. In contrast, the one growing up with a rejecting caregiver will be less biased to represent God as loving and may in fact come to represent God as rejecting, no matter what the attachment figure professes because a loving God doesn't harmonize with the rejected individual's negative IWMs of others. Of course, the rejected individual might adopt or profess explicit beliefs in a loving God at the general, semantic or declarative level, but may nonetheless represent God as rejecting at an implicit/unconscious level (cf. the notion of incoherent representations).

This example should demonstrate that there is a *third way* of evaluating psychological sources of religious cognition, between the (1) "tabula rasa" approach implicitly advocated by some social scientists of religion (who attend only to social learning explanations) and the (2) culturally deprived understanding offered by some evolutionary psychologists and cognitive scientists of religion (who attend only to evolved mechanisms/core cognitions). Such a culturally deprived understanding would also result within the attachment–religion framework if we merely entertained generalizing IWMs and did not also attend to the role of cultural/social learning. The third way, integrated understanding, is an important theoretical addition not just to the attachment–religion connection itself but also more broadly to the psychological sciences of religion in general (see also Granqvist & Nkara, 2017).

MRS. GREEN: A CASE STUDY

The research reviewed in this chapter has largely treated socialized and IWM correspondence as separate processes, and each is studied in different variable-oriented analyses. I now offer a person-oriented approach, or case study, to illustrate how socialized and IWM correspondence may be integrated at the individual level in secure, religious people.

In this section, I present the first of three case studies[3] covered in this book (see also Chapters 6 and 8). These case studies are drawn from our Swedish AAI and religion study (Granqvist, Ivarsson et al., 2007) in which semistructured interviews were conducted on both parent-related attachment (i.e., the AAI) and, 3 years later, religious participants' representations of God in relation to self (the Religious Attachment Interview [RAI]; Granqvist & Main, 2017; Nkara et al., 2018). This latter interview was given only to participants who indicated that they had experienced a personal relationship with God at some point in their lives.

Mrs. Green is a middle-aged, working-class woman, married, with two children. She grew up in a rural setting in a Methodist home, with parents who were actively religious participants in their local church. Mrs. Green received a prototypically secure/autonomous classification on the AAI (i.e., F3 or "balanced") by two independent coders. Furthermore, her security appeared to be continuous (rather than "earned" later on), in that both parents were coded high in sensitivity (or "loving") and low on the "negative" probable experience scales of the AAI. In other words, Mrs. Green provided highly coherent discourse on the AAI. For example, in support of a positive adjective to describe her relationship with her mother as a child, she recalled that she used to become really upset and frightened when she suffered stomach flu as a child, sensing that she was about to suffocate when she vomited. Her mother then sat close behind her, stroked her forehead with a cold towel, caressed her cheeks, sang to her, and assured her, very effectively, that vomiting was not dangerous. While excusing herself for talking about "gross" events, Mrs. Green spoke fondly of these memories. She then quickly referenced how, as an adult, she had asked her dumbfounded, and somewhat disgusted, husband to act like her mother used to do. She also noted that she makes sure to treat her own children with gentle affection when they are ill, remembering how important it was for her as a child.

Mrs. Green speaks just as coherently about God on the RAI, where she also represents God as functionally benevolent, so she received a secure classification here as well (by four independent coders). She starts the religious interview by distinguishing the nonpersonal elements of faith/religion that were a natural part of her childhood from her "personal faith," when she got a more "personal relationship with God." She acknowledges that her personal relationship with God started later (elementary school age).

The "action stories" of the Bible drew her excitement as a young child, but later prayer and its experienced positive effects became influential. She carefully notes about such positive effects that "one could *interpret* them as an answer to prayer" (italics added), thus implying that other explanations may apply as well. She also notes that she learned from her religious community that one can be eternally saved by believing in God, so she acknowledges—with understated humor—that it was "well worth trying and it works great." This again implies that ideas are provisional and that her mind is autonomous enough to be open to other possibilities. Such implied metacognitive distinctions (e.g., reality can be interpreted in many ways) create a theme throughout much of this interview. This is especially suggestive of a secure, nondefensive, and autonomous mind in this particular case, because Mrs. Green is by no means trained as a theologian or philosopher of religion. Indeed, she notes about herself that she's somewhat ignorant about theology and about theoretical matters at large.

When asked to provide five adjectives or other words to describe her relationship with God, Mrs. Green chooses "forgiving," "accepting," "He wants my best," "caring," and "He lets me make my own decisions." These positive, relational, reparative, and autonomy-supporting words strongly resemble Bowlby's (1973) portrayal of a safe haven and secure base. When probed about events that can illustrate the adjective *forgiving*, Mrs. Green recalls talking behind people's back, feeling bad about it, and praying to God for forgiveness, noting that she felt better afterwards (i.e., growth-promoting prayers, another salient feature of many secure interviewees) but without necessarily implying any particular action from God.

Mrs. Green's sense of self as imperfect and still unconditionally accepted is reiterated with respect to a personal episode supporting the adjective *accepting*. She notes that God loves everybody equally, and she adds that this applies whether or not you are Christian. Thus, God's love is represented as socially inclusive, which is another hallmark of many secure interviewees. Under *He wants my best*, Mrs. Green notes that God had a plan for Mrs. Green's marriage with a "wonderful man . . . that we two of us found each other is a sign that He wants my best." The relationship focus then continues when discussing the adjective *caring*, where she endorses her friends, whom she views as another sign of God's caring. Finally, Mrs. Green notes, with respect to *He lets me make my own decisions*, that she is free to do so, and again she mentions marrying her husband. When realizing that being free might seem to contradict her earlier notion of God having a plan for her marriage, she adds, "paradoxically . . . God may control everything but it is still my own decision." This is another example of metacognitive elaboration. Throughout these first interview sections, Mrs. Green also states explicitly that her views of God have undergone developmental change. In sum, in the adjectival section of the interview, Mrs. Green discusses examples coherently in line with propositional ideas about a benevolent God to happy outcomes in her own life, and she does so while maintaining cognitive openness.

When asked about possible experiences of being separated from God, Mrs. Green says she has never experienced entirely losing contact ("slipping away"), but nonetheless she acknowledges that she has occasionally felt "farther from God." As examples she describes some episodes that, serendipitously, also express compassion with the suffering of others, which is another hallmark of security. She concludes this discussion by noting, autonomously, that she doesn't understand why God allows "all people to have such a hard time."

Similarly, asked about possible experiences of rejection by God, Mrs. Green acknowledges having felt "abandoned" while at youth camp, where she did not have the kind of strong religious experiences that many other youths "*appeared* to have" (italics added). Mrs. Green's response was to pray to God, but that failed to provide clarity. Then she adds, "I cannot get any clarity now either." When probed as to why God appeared to act that way, or not act at all, Mrs. Green gives a concise answer, "That I have no explanation for. Cannot understand." This passage is very rich; it contains honest admittance of vulnerability; clear display of attachment behavior (praying); openness to appearance–reality distinctions, and in general many signs of an open, questioning mind that doesn't gloss over uncertainty or engage in cognitive foreclosure. At a superficial level, Mrs. Green might appear to display mistrust of God. However, at a deeper level—and taking the transcript as a whole into consideration— she expresses autonomy as well as a representation of God and her relationship with God as able to harbor Mrs. Green's troubles.

About changes in her relationship with God in adolescence, Mrs. Green mentions that she was trying more personally to understand God but "nothing more revolutionary." Her discussion describes a reaffirmation and deepening of the faith she grew up with. On her current relationship with God, Mrs. Green mentions that "it's a personal relationship," with "straight talk" from herself to God, including praise when thankful and blame following perceived unjust ills (thus repeating the theme that God can be criticized). With understated humor, she adds that she doesn't perceive "the same straight answers" from God; thus she playfully repeats the word "straight" and is also at ease with God's nonconcrete character. When probed about possible sources of dissatisfaction in her current relationship with God, Mrs. Green acknowledges that she would want to feel God's presence more concretely than she does (i.e., valuing attachment), and she makes a poetic slip and addresses God directly: "to let me feel your presence." She adds that God's presence would be especially important in difficult situations. She also levels what again appears to be justified criticism against God, noting how easy it should be for God to make "His" presence known. Apart from the benevolence implied in Mrs. Green's freedom to criticize, her criticism is coherent, flowing from her semantic portrayal of God as benevolent and powerful.

About prayers, Mrs. Green says she prays as "good as daily." She notes that prayers may come true but adds spontaneously, "perhaps purely coincidentally." She asserts that the same outcome might also occur without prayer (i.e., equifinality; the same outcome can be attributed to different causes). She answers affirmatively to a probe about unanswered prayers, exemplifying with her own prayers for a friend's sick father who wound up dying in spite of Mrs. Green's prayers. Without any positive "wrap-up" or self-serving reinterpretation, she concludes that it's "hard to see any meaning in that." She goes on to express strong compassion for her friend's family and reiterates her difficulties in understanding why God lets such things happen. Probed about praying when upset, Mrs. Green answers affirmatively and mentions attempts at interpersonal reconciliation. For example, she asks for God's help to forgive her husband when she's been upset with him. Thus again, she turns to a God represented as benevolent (i.e., a God who cares about her difficulties) to help her with something else that's very important for her, her spousal attachment.

Toward the end of the interview, when asked about the influence of her own upbringing on her religious beliefs, Mrs. Green acknowledges that her parents were influential, referring, for example, to bedtime prayers. However, she also expresses missing deeper theological discussions, a theme resonating with her still.

Many additional passages could be cited to illustrate Mrs. Green's generally secure (coherent and benevolent) representation of God in relation to self and others. I end this case study by noting that, although Mrs. Green has been raised within a family with a fairly "simple" religion, characterized largely by fundamentalist beliefs, her benevolent representation of God ultimately overshadows any authoritarian aspects of God's character. For example, when asked about life after death, Mrs. Green acknowledges that she's been taught that both heaven and hell are real, and that she still believes that to be true. Then she gives a somewhat literal description of both "places." When asked who will go to heaven, she presents a list that starts out narrowly but ultimately expands to include most people, with particular emphasis on children and the mentally handicapped (i.e., compassion). When asked who will go to hell, she expresses hope that it will be "an empty place." She admits to wondering—her professed beliefs to the contrary—if maybe "everyone gets to heaven, that God after all is so forgiving even toward those who have not taken a stand for Christianity." She concludes by expressing uncertainty, explicitly acknowledging that her mind switches evaluative positions (i.e., metacognition).

CHAPTER SUMMARY

In this chapter I have attended primarily to secure attachment and the "correspondence" pathway to religion and spirituality. I introduced the core ideas about social learning and generalizing internal working models as expressed in the religious and spiritual realm by paying tribute to William James's notion of healthy-minded religion, echoed by our findings a full century later. I gave a historical description of how Kirkpatrick developed the correspondence hypothesis and how it has since been revised. I next discussed theory and research concerning "socialized correspondence"—the notion that religion for people who are secure with respect to attachment partially reflects correspondence with their attachment figure's religious standards. I also described theory and research on "internal working model correspondence." That is, working models derived from attachment-based experiences are generalized to mental models of God in relation to self. I then revisited the two aspects of correspondence, attempting to integrate them in accordance with principles from contemporary evolutionary science. Finally, I provided a case study of Mrs. Green, illustrating how social learning and generalizing working models may play out at the individual level.

CHAPTER 6

The Compensation Pathway

What do you do when you simply can't endure any more suffering? When your relationships are all in ruin? When not even the bottle, the pill, or whatever else has provided a degree of equanimity no longer provides relief? When the nights bring eternal hours of solitary tossing and turning, with a racing heart in the dark? When daytime brings out the zombie in you, when you're dragging your body around relentlessly hoping it will wear you out and you'll finally get some sleep? Add a drink, a second one, then a third, and everything becomes a little hazy. You go numb, doze off. You wake up in the early hours of the morning, with no sense of gravity, and the waking nightmare starts all over again. Ad infinitum. Or so it may seem. So, you finally cry your heart out, mentally reaching out for someone—anyone—and you find that God is there.

In this chapter, I deal with the "compensation" pathway to religion and spirituality. In other words, I argue that some individuals who have experienced parental insensitivity or who are currently insecure with regard to attachment may find in God or other religious entities a surrogate (or alternative) attachment figure, one who may aid in compensating for states of insecurity and other unsatisfactory attachments. The chapter contains five sections. In the first, I again pay tribute to William James, this time for his description of the "twice-born" religion of "sick souls," which is in many ways similar to what my colleagues and I have described as the compensation pathway. The second section addresses adults' (and adolescents') use of attachment surrogates more generally, that is, beyond God and religion. In the third section, I formalize the compensation hypothesis as it applies more specifically to religion, and I provide a review of pertinent empirical research. The fourth section contains a case study—the case of Mr. Blue. In the fifth and final section, I conclude the chapter with a discussion of whether religion-as-compensation has beneficial psychological effects.

THE RELIGION OF THE "SICK SOUL"

In his descriptive characterization of two religious prototypes and their associated religious "sentiments," William James (1902) described the "twice-born" religion of the "sick soul" as crisis-based, dramatic, and prone to major fluctuations over time, including a proclivity for sudden religious conversions occurring during periods of emotional turmoil. Key to James's analysis was his assumption that sick-souled individuals possess a divided (cf. incoherent) self that is prone to doubt, suffering (anxiety and depression), and sinfulness. When the person hits rock bottom, the only solution may be to give up on futile attempts at regulating distress—futile because they only perpetuate the distress. James held such "self-surrender" to be at the core of sudden religious conversion experiences, which through a renewed relationship with God could aid in bringing unity to a previously divided self. The self that used to feel worthless and unlovable now feels loved and accepted. The fruit of such conversions is not only attenuated suffering but also restored hope, optimism, and mastery.

However, James was not so naïve as to portray this "new morning" as necessarily permanent. In some cases, sudden religious conversion may be a tipping point setting life on a more positive and sustainable trajectory. However, doubt, suffering, and perceptions of sinfulness often strike back in due course, making it necessary for the "sick soul" to call on rigid defenses to maintain emotional equilibrium in the long run.

Like James's sketch of healthy-minded religion discussed in Chapter 5, his thicker description of the religion of "sick souls" has turned out to possess prophetic qualities. Although James did not know much about the details of "attachment figures," which were of course delineated much later, most of what he said converges with what my colleagues and I have found to be true about religion and spirituality in the context of insecure attachment. In other words, some individuals who have experienced parental insensitivity or who are currently insecure with regard to attachment may—propelled by emotional turmoil—surrender themselves to God or another religious entity who is treated as a surrogate (or alternative) attachment figure. Doing so may help them compensate for states of insecurity and for other unsatisfactory attachments. Receiving God's unconditional love may also yield a rare sense of unity.

James discussed several examples of sick-souled religion, not least among them theological pioneers such as St. Paul, Martin Luther, and John Bunyan. Luther was a particularly striking example because he thought that he, along with other humans, was so deeply sinful that he could never do anything to deserve God's grace. According to Luther, any attempt to do so is just a perpetuation of egoism (i.e., sinfulness), which God naturally sees through. Luckily, however, Christ had already set the stage for reconciling humankind with God after the Fall, so if a person is fortunate enough to believe in God, he or she may receive God's grace. From an attachment perspective, Luther obviously possessed a deeply negative model of self and of other humans but somehow a positive model of God.

Another example of the sick soul's route to religion is provided by the Russian novelist Leo Tolstoy. Consider, for example, the predicament in which he found himself prior to his conversion experience (which James viewed as the start of Tolstoy's "recovery"):

> During the whole course of this year, when I almost unceasingly kept asking myself how to end the business, whether by the rope or by the bullet, during all that time . . . my heart kept languishing with another pining emotion. I can call this by no other name than that of a thirst for God. This craving for God had nothing to do with the movement of my ideas . . . but it came from my heart. It was like a feeling of dread that made me seem like an orphan and isolated in the midst of all these things that were so foreign. And this feeling of dread was mitigated by the hope of finding the assistance of some one. (From Tolstoy's autobiographical *Confessions*, cited in James, 1902, p. 156)

It's tempting to ask how a person with a mind as great as Tolstoy's could possibly resort to something so culturally predictable as becoming an almost prototypical religious convert.[1] Notably, however, and in clear contrast with the themes of religious change that I described in the previous chapter, Tolstoy does not convey a sense of intellectual exploration here, nor of socialization. Indeed, he explicitly distinguishes his experience from "the movement of my ideas" and feels entirely alone in his misery, indeed "an orphan and isolated"—metaphors of considerable interest to attachment theorists. The "some one" he so desperately hopes for who will prevent his suicide is God, the perfect attachment figure, who remains steadily available even when all other options have been exhausted. Like Luther, Tolstoy thus has a positive model of God. Without such a model, his life would presumably have come to a sudden and tragic end.

At its core, I believe the sudden religious conversion experience reveals an affective-cognitive bias that is fundamental among more or less all human beings who have received *some* sensitive care during their immature years, namely, the lingering "experience expectancy" for benevolent responses. In some cases, that bias may be expressed only when the psychological need for benevolent responses is critical and acute. Even great minds like Tolstoy's may fall victim to such a bias.

In essence, this is the substance of what has been explored and clarified in the research discussed in the present chapter. No wonder then that the 12-step program of Alcoholics Anonymous (AA), to whom the suffering protagonist cited at the outset of this chapter may turn, take such a strikingly Jamesian ("self-surrender") approach to overcoming suffering and addiction (for example, we admitted we were powerless, we made a decision to turn our will and our lives over to the care of God; the 12 steps of Alcoholics Anonymous). Since its founding, AA has been joined by Narcotics Anonymous, Sexaholics, Pillaholics, Sex and Love Addicts, Gamblers, Overeaters, TV Show Addicts, Clutterers, Bloggers, Dual Diagnoses, Self-mutilators, Procrastinators—and the list goes on. The contemporary world certainly has a way of leading people "into temptation." The originators of the AA model realized that in order for addiction treatment to have sustainable effects, the addict must be regularly surrounded by a supportive group of peers, and the special group of peers should be beyond natural associates (such as family members) who are likely to develop co-addiction or co-dependency problems. Similarly, the positive "effects" of sudden religious conversion can probably be sustained longer if the convert finds a new social group, such as a religious community, that can provide a "holding environment" (Winnicott, 1971), helping to carry the convert through life's inevitable upheavals (cf. Greenwald et al., 2018).

For many psychologists, James's notion of the religion of the "sick soul," along with the research reviewed in the present chapter, might seem truer or deeper than that of the "healthy-minded" religion dealt with in the previous chapter. Anyone, whether a psychologist or not, who views religion first and foremost as deficiency-based, marked by turmoil, and dependent on rigid psychological defenses would probably come to that conclusion. This is not so far from Feuerbach's (1854/2004) and later Freud's (1961a, 1961b) analyses of religion as providing the (ultimately neurotic) illusion of safety and security via projective mechanisms. Readers more familiar with sociological literatures on religion may instead see resemblances with Marxist (1844/1977) thinking or later "deprivation" theory (e.g., Glock & Stark, 1965). In my view, although Feuerbach, Freud, Marx, and others indisputably offered

important insights into the functions of religion, they all pale when compared with James because they failed to realize that religion simultaneously serves multiple vital functions. (In passing, this is probably key to
the remarkable sustainability of religion.) For that reason, those thinkers
misrepresented the role of religion in many (e.g., relatively non-neurotic,
affluent, healthy) people's lives. My reason for opening these chapters
by paying tribute to James is that his understanding of religion was not
so restricted; he could appreciate that several, even incompatible, psychological approaches to religion are true; as we have seen, religion *also*
arises out of love and happiness. James's realization of the importance of
individual differences in religious experience thus remains a key insight.

Furthermore, even when religious experience is rooted in deficiency,
as emphasized in this "compensation" chapter, it does not necessarily
end with deficiency. As James realized, people's religious biographies are
often dynamic rather than static; hence, beginnings reeking of deficiency
may develop into middles and endings that are growth-promoting. With
that said, I now dig deeper into the deficiencies.

SURROGATE OBJECTS OF ATTACHMENT IN ADULTHOOD

As described in Chapter 1, Bowlby (1969/1982) noted that when an
attachment figure is unavailable to them, young children tend to seek
out concrete attachment surrogates (e.g., blankets, teddy bears). As has
been noted, such concrete objects are often supplemented with imagined, noncorporeal relational partners (e.g., imaginary companions)
from early childhood on, and these imagined interaction partners can
take on a particularly "real" existence for children who are lonely and
socially deprived.

In line with this reasoning, in Ainsworth's (1985) discussion of
potential attachment relationships after early childhood, she formulated a surrogate or "compensation" hypothesis: insecurely attached
children, she posited, may direct their unsatisfied attachment systems
toward someone other than their principal attachment figures. Although
research pertaining to this matter has been remarkably scant, Ainsworth's hypothesis has been reliably supported with respect to insecurely attached children's reliance on peers, teachers, and relatives outside the immediate family context (e.g., Booth, Rubin, & Rose-Krasnor,
1998; Elicker, Englund, & Sroufe, 1992).

In adulthood, and in line with the observation of increased differentiation in development, attachment surrogates (or substitutes) may take
many different forms. Some of them are nonanthropomorphic and therefore cannot be conceptualized as attachment figures without stretching

the attachment concept unreasonably beyond its (admittedly fuzzy) boundaries (see Chapter 2). Yet, attachment substitutes may nonetheless be relied upon to regulate attachment-related states of insecurity and stress, and their noncorporeal nature may actually be an advantage for insecure individuals who hold negative working models of self and/or other people. Although the list of potential adult attachment substitutes can be very long, for brevity I elaborate on only four examples here.

First, as implied by my earlier references to addiction problems, insecure (and especially avoidant) adults may self-medicate with various drugs that can effectively downregulate stress in general and perhaps attachment-related stress in particular (e.g., Allen, Hauser, & Borman-Spurrell, 1996; Schindler, Thomasius, Petersen, & Sack, 2009). Opioids are especially interesting from an attachment viewpoint because they can engender states that are very similar to feelings associated with attachment formation (Zeifman & Hazan, 1997), but without any "need" to be intimate with or dependent upon relational partners. No wonder then that the late singer Lou Reed, who was a heroin addict at the time, declared, "Heroin, it's my wife and it's my life" ("Heroin"; *Velvet Underground & Nico*, 1967). Conversely, attachment formation mimics the effects of opioids (e.g., "She's Like Heroin to Me"; The Gun Club, *Fire of Love*, 1981). Indeed, heroin is known by users to be capable of inducing states of felt security—for example "contentedness, well-being, and feeling carefree" and "a feeling of calm, a relief from fear and sorrow" (Julien, 2000, p. 260). Beyond being highly addictive and hazardous, the tragedy of opioids is in no small part due to their short-term effectiveness in regulating distress without depending on other people. Attempts to counter the current opioid epidemic in many societies could profitably target relational insecurities as well as chemical dependency. Central stimulants (e.g., cocaine and amphetamines) may also be temporarily effective in boosting one's sense of self-solidity and self-efficacy, which might be especially appealing for people with a fragile self.

Second, although pets may fill many functions (e.g., providing someone to care for, helping with hunting), serving as attachment substitutes appears to be one of them. I have encountered some Adult Attachment Interview (AAI) interviewees who have had adverse childhood experiences with parents and for whom a favorite pet became an important relationship partner in childhood. Unresolved loss has also been observed with regard to the death of a pet (Main et al., 2003). Similarly, Field, Orsini, Gavish, and Packman (2009) have documented especially complicated grief responses following pet loss among adults who are high in attachment-related anxiety. There is also more general experimental evidence that the presence (physical or cognitive) of a pet may function as a secure base (i.e., for generating goals) as well as a safe haven (i.e., attenuating blood pressure during challenging tasks; Zilcha-Mano, Mikulincer, & Shaver, 2012). As in much human adult attachment research, pet attachment security has been found to facilitate those effects (Zilcha-Mano, Mikulincer, & Shaver, 2011). These findings are not surprising, especially for dogs. Dogs were domesticated many thousands of years ago and have effectively coevolved with humans; they have been selectively bred to optimize relationships and communication with humans. It should also be recalled that interspecies emotional bonds are by no means restricted to human–pet relationships but also occur between members of other species (e.g., Holland, 2013). These findings illustrate both the target flexibility with which emotional bonds may develop and the pervasiveness of such bonds in nature; they are not restricted to relational partners who possess specific within-species-typical characteristics. Konrad Lorenz's early work on imprinting (e.g., 1937) on birds demonstrated this basic idea, showing that newly hatched geese would follow the first moving objects they saw, be it a person, a ball, or an airplane.

Third, there is now compelling experimental evidence that adults with a preoccupied attachment style (i.e., those who score high on attachment-related anxiety and low on avoidance) are disproportionately likely to use material objects, such as their smartphones, to regulate separation- and rejection-related threats (Keefer, Landau, Rothschild, & Sullivan, 2012). Partly with such findings in mind, Keefer, Landau, and Sullivan (2014) have even advocated an extension of attachment theory to accommodate people's reliance on material (nonanthropomorphic) security providers as "attachment figures." While I do not believe that most people's relationships to material objects are best described as attachments, it seems indisputable that some, especially insecure, people may endow their treasured material objects with substitute attachment functions. Whether this is for better or worse remains to be seen. As Keefer and colleagues (2014, p. 532) have speculated, "Non-human targets may . . . be a diversion from—or even worse, a barrier to—the psychological benefits that can only be gained from interacting with living, present human beings, warts and all."

Fourth and finally, it has been suggested that some people, beyond early childhood, develop "attachments" to places (e.g., Counted, 2018; Morgan, 2010) as substitutes for interpersonal attachments. Although I am not persuaded that most people's relationships with places are best understood as attachments (see Gruneau Brulin & Granqvist, 2018), it is true that certain specific places—not least in nature settings—can provide solace and serenity for many people. This solace may be sought in specific places rather than in human relationships, especially by people who are lonely, undergoing divorce, or are insecure with regard to attachment.

These and other attachment substitutes have something in common that should be especially attractive to insecure individuals; they can be endowed with attributes other than those expected (via negative working models) from human relationship partners. For example, in relying on these substitute attachment targets, one does not have to fear interpersonal rejection, betrayal, excessive control, or abandonment. Thus, even when one represents self and other humans as failing, he or she may achieve security and comfort from attachment substitutes. Although opioids are probably the most efficacious substitute in the short term, I speculate that pets (and especially dogs) are particularly effective in the long term. A living, social organism has the advantage over the other examples given of actually responding to its owner, of possessing warm bodies that can provide physical contact (yielding oxytocin release) when needed, of remaining loyal even when the owner falls short of perfection, and of not leading to chemical or other unhealthy forms of dependence. In this regard, it should also be interesting to follow advancements in artificial intelligence, especially robotics. The more the robots mimic biological organisms, and yet remain unconditionally supportive of their owner, the more successful they should be as potential attachment surrogates.

To prevent misapplications, I reiterate that just because an object can function as an attachment surrogate or substitute for a particular individual (i.e., *instead of* a human attachment figure), he or she does not necessarily have an "attachment" to that object (e.g., the object may not have the attributes of an attachment figure who responds in an agentic way to oneself). In some cases, such as with pets and perhaps robots, he or she might develop an attachment, but in other cases, such as with opioids and places, this is unlikely. Unlike infants, older children and especially adults have typically developed a large and varied set of strategies for regulating stress and promoting well-being that transcend the boundaries of attachments per se. Beyond those considered above, these strategies include engagement in the arts (writing, reading, music, and dance—what Freud referred to as "sublimation"), physical exercise, sexual behaviors (including masturbation), eating, watching television, playing video games, and even sleeping. Any or all of these might be viewed as attachment substitutes insofar as a person engages in them as a means of regulating distress and deriving security *instead of* turning to attachment figures. This palette illustrates the flexibility and diversity of human behavior, which clearly transcends the conceptual boundaries of attachments. Also, it should be clear that not only insecure individuals engage with attachment surrogates, although they may be particularly prone to use them at the expense of "real" attachment figures.

Finally, whether or not some specific object, organism, or activity becomes an attachment surrogate largely hinges on its cultural and cognitive accessibility. For example, if there are no opioids around, other surrogates are more likely to be sought out. This applies to God as well. Thus, in a highly secularized country, where the notion of God is more or less cognitively inaccessible, other attachment surrogates are more likely to be relied upon.

COMPENSATION AND THEISTIC RELIGION

In this section, I begin by reviewing how my colleagues and I have thought about the compensation hypothesis as applied specifically to religion and how I view it at present. I then provide a review of pertinent empirical research.

Formalization of the Compensation Pathway

According to Bowlby's control system model of attachment, the attachment system continually monitors internal states and external circumstances in relation to the question "Is the attachment figure sufficiently near, attentive, responsive, approving, etc.?" (Hazan & Shaver, 1994, p. 3). The set point of the system is variable, depending on expectancies (i.e., components of internal working models [IWMs]) concerning the attachment figure and perceived cues of environmental dangers (versus safety). According to the theory, a negative answer to the question activates a suite of potential attachment behaviors designed to restore an adequate degree of proximity. Under certain conditions, however, the individual (based on prior experience and/or current circumstances) may anticipate that efforts to achieve proximity and comfort from the primary attachment figure(s) are unlikely to be successful. If so, a search for alternative and more situation-adequate attachment figures may be initiated, which in some cases will lead to God. In the chapters dealing with normative aspects of attachment and religion (Chapters 2 and 3), I noted a number of such situations. In this chapter, and in line with Ainsworth's compensation hypothesis, we are concerned with whether individual differences in attachment history and current attachment security are associated with a compensatory use of God and religion in times of distress.

Kirkpatrick and Shaver's (1990) seminal study found support for the compensation hypothesis in results showing that study participants who reported an insecure (particularly avoidant) attachment history were much more prone than those who reported a secure history to have experienced a sudden religious conversion at some point in their lives. Also interpreted as supporting the compensation hypothesis were their findings indicating that, specifically at low levels of parental religiousness, participants reporting an insecure history were more religious than those reporting a secure attachment history. I then replicated both sets of findings in my first attachment–religion study (Granqvist, 1998).

In our efforts to specify correspondence and compensation-related processes more explicitly, we suggested that compensation refers specifically to emotional processes (hence "emotional compensation"). That is, we hypothesized that attachment-insecure individuals use religion and their perceived relationship with God primarily to downregulate states of distress (or negative affect) and thereby to obtain or maintain felt security (Granqvist & Hagekull, 1999). At the time, I thought that such an emotion-regulatory use of God and religion was more or less habitual for attachment-insecure, religious individuals. Also, I thought that specifying the emotional processes would distinguish compensation from the religious socialization processes that are principally involved among attachment-secure individuals (see Chapter 5). In hindsight, although this distinction did work at the group level, I now believe that my "chopping" was too crude to do justice to the individual level of analysis. For example, many avoidant, religious individuals probably do not habitually draw on God to regulate distress but, rather, tend to shy away from God because of their negative working models of others, including God. For another example, attachment-secure, religious individuals may gain felt security through God. Indeed, they are more likely to do so at the level of implicit processes than are attachment-insecure, religious individuals (see Chapter 5). In that regard, secure individuals may also employ their relationship with God in the service of emotion regulation. Also, emotional processes and socialization-related processes are by no means mutually exclusive.

Approaching the idea of compensation as a developmental pathway to (rather than current processes involved in) religion and spirituality has helped Kirkpatrick and me to disambiguate these matters to some extent (Granqvist & Kirkpatrick, 2008, 2013, 2016). With compensation viewed as a developmental pathway, we expect that insofar as attachment-insecure individuals develop religiosity/spirituality, they do so by using God and other religious or spiritual entities as attachment surrogates to regulate distress. Even more specifically, I now suspect that religion/spirituality in the case of insecure attachment often develops as a response to emotional turmoil that is sufficiently severe to overthrow the insecure individual's secondary (or insecure) emotion-regulation strategies. In other words, in the context of overwhelming turmoil, religion/spirituality may help to activate the insecure person's primary (proximity-seeking, secure) strategy, albeit in relation to a surrogate attachment figure (e.g., God).

As explained in Chapter 4, insecure (i.e., avoidant or resistant/anxious) attachment is believed to reflect a developmentally secondary attachment strategy stemming from defensive processes (e.g., exclusion of attachment-related information and diversion of attention) in the face of a failed primary strategy of obtaining sufficiently sensitive care from the attachment figure (Main, 1990). I also noted in Chapter 4 that attachment-insecure individuals are not necessarily insecure 24 hours a day, 7 days a week. Rather, their behavior is actually quite variable outside the constraints of attachment assessments, which are designed in part to activate and reveal their insecure strategies. The insecure/secondary strategies can therefore be viewed as defensive filters that may become somewhat habitual but that are triggered especially by certain, mildly-to-moderately attachment-activating situations. For example, the Strange Situation procedure is designed to be mildly to moderately stressful for infants. Accordingly, researchers, by default, use separation episodes that are only 3 minutes long. Should an infant react with intense crying, the separations are made even briefer. This is because infants who are "overstressed" in the Strange Situation by overly long separations often do not display their habitual attachment strategy (e.g., avoidant infants may seek proximity or become disorganized; Ainsworth et al., 1978; Granqvist et al., 2016).

My point is that secondary/insecure strategies may never fully override the primary/secure strategy, which continues to lie dormant and can be triggered by other kinds of situations. As illustrated by overextended separations in the Strange Situation, the secondary strategies are fragile and therefore prone to crumble, particularly during intense distress. I opened this chapter by noting some of the kinds of extreme emotional turmoil that may cause people, including attachment-insecure ones, to reveal that they do, after all, still carry hopes and expectations of benevolent responses. If they didn't, there would be no use in crying. The late singer–songwriter Leonard Cohen put it succinctly: "There is a crack, a crack, in everything / That's how the light gets in" ("Anthem"; *The Future,* 1994).

The use of God as a surrogate attachment figure may provide us as researchers a unique opportunity to observe these remnants of a primary/secure attachment strategy. That is, the experience of God may provide a kind of love one rarely experienced with one's parents or other primary attachment figures. I hypothesize that regulation of severe distress is at the core of this surrogate use of God and religion.

Besides using secondary/insecure strategies, people who have experienced frightening or other aberrant behaviors from attachment figures (i.e., often those with disorganized attachment) are predisposed to enter dissociative states, which can be experienced within the religious realm as "altered spiritual states." Such states could be analyzed as a form of compensation but are distinct enough to warrant their own chapter (Chapter 8). Here, I stay largely within the constraints of "ordinary" theistic religion.

Research Review

In this section, I review empirical research relating to the compensation hypothesis. Some of the arguments presented in the normative attachment and religion chapters (Chapters 2 and 3), especially those pertaining to sudden religious conversions and similar religious changes, have been found to hold specifically for individuals who are likely to have experienced parental insensitivity while growing up and for participants who are currently insecure with regard to attachment. I begin with the former case and then address the latter. My empirical review will be factual and impersonal, and it may therefore appear as hard-headed and impassionate, even cold-blooded, because it largely deals with suffering and its attempted resolution. So I take this opportunity to empathize with the predicament of gifted singer–songwriter Lloyd Cole: "You say I'm dry—a scientist. No mate for the lioness you are / Yes—I can hear you roar" (*Music in a Foreign Language,* 2004). However, my account will get more personal and somewhat emotional when I take on the case study of Mr. Blue in the next section.

Previous findings and theoretical orientations within the more general psychology of religion literature converge with the findings and interpretations that I review in this chapter. I have already touched upon William James's (1902) notion of the religion of sick souls, which probably provides the most striking example. For another example, Ullman (1982) found that an overwhelming majority of the sudden religious converts in her study had experienced intense emotional turmoil at the time of their conversions and that their conversions could be viewed as an attempt to reduce that turmoil. The findings I review should also strike a chord for readers familiar with Freud's (1961b) analysis of religion and associated experiences. In his analysis, God is understood as the result of a "helpless" person projecting his or her wishful representations of perfect caregivers onto the cosmos. But two things are new in the religion-as-compensation approach offered in this chapter. First, there is evidence linking *attachment-related individual differences* to religion-as-compensation. Second, rather than adopting a descriptive

(James, Ullman) or psychoanalytic, drive-theory (Freud) approach, I (like Bowlby) adopt an *ethological, systems-theory* approach to the matter of religion as compensation.

Parental Attachment

Many studies using self-report assessments of attachment history with parents support the compensation hypothesis (e.g., Granqvist, 1998, 2002; Granqvist & Hagekull, 1999, 2003; Granqvist & Kirkpatrick, 2004; Halama et al., 2013; Kirkpatrick & Shaver, 1990; Pirutinsky, 2009; Schnitker et al., 2012). Perhaps most notably, sudden religious conversions, the most pronounced examples of religious drama, are associated with estimates of parental insensitivity. Sudden conversions have been defined in the literature as religion becoming *much more important* for the individual at some point in his or her life, via *a sudden and intense personal experience* (Kirkpatrick & Shaver, 1990). As noted, the connection between sudden conversion and an insecure attachment history was reported in the first study of attachment and religion, conducted in the American "Bible Belt" (Kirkpatrick & Shaver, 1990). These findings were then replicated in my first attachment–religion study, conducted in Sweden (Granqvist, 1998).

Because sudden conversions are relatively rare even in largely religious samples, findings from these first two individual studies, both of which used moderate sample sizes, could easily be misleading. In short, sudden conversions could be linked to attachment history because of chance. For these reasons, Kirkpatrick and I metà-analyzed the connection between sudden conversions and perceived attachment history with parents, using all 11 studies that had been conducted before 2004 (Granqvist & Kirkpatrick, 2004). This meta-analysis featured almost 1,500 participants. The results confirmed the association: Participants reporting an insecure attachment history with mother (9.3%) or fathers (8.5%) were almost twice as likely to have experienced a sudden conversion at some point in their lives, as were participants reporting a secure attachment history with mothers (5.7%) or fathers (4.8%). These conclusions were strengthened by comparisons among sudden converts, gradual converts, and nonconverts using continuous attachment–history scales. Sudden converts scored lower than both nonconverts and gradual converts on attachment security with both mother and father, with small to moderate effect sizes (Granqvist & Kirkpatrick, 2004).

I have noted that sudden conversions often occur during emotional turmoil. As might be expected from the distress-regulating nature of sudden conversions, in our meta-analysis we found that sudden converts, compared with gradual converts, reported a relationship with God that was more likely to be used to regulate distress—focusing explicitly on attachment aspects of the relationship (e.g., God being viewed as a safe haven and secure base; Granqvist & Kirkpatrick, 2004).

Subsequent to the publication of our meta-analysis, two additional studies of Christian samples have yielded converging evidence for the association between attachment insecurity and sudden conversions (Halama et al., 2013; Schnitker et al., 2012). Halama and colleagues (2013) found in their study of Catholic converts in the Slovak Republic that sudden and intense conversion processes were linked to an insecure attachment history, especially with fathers. Schnitker and colleagues' (2012) study of American Young Life Evangelical summer campers similarly found that participants with insecure parental attachment classifications were much more likely to provide faith narratives indicating sudden and intense conversion experiences (38%) than were participants with a secure parental attachment classification (10%).

Naturally, self-reports of attachment history with parents must be regarded with caution. Not only may memories from childhood be inadequate and biased in general, but some attachment-insecure individuals may be particularly unwilling to admit that their parents were insensitive or rejecting when in fact they were (see Chapter 4). The findings from the studies reviewed above are sensitive to this validity threat. Fortunately, however, in our study using the AAI we have observed supportive evidence for a link between sudden religious changes and estimates of attachment history. In that study, we found that participants whose parents were estimated by an independent AAI coder (using coherency-based coding) to have been relatively less loving/sensitive reported more sudden and intense increases in religiousness (Granqvist, Ivarsson, et al., 2007). We have since conducted follow-up analyses of this sample, revealing strong links between probable experiences with less loving/sensitive parents and current attachment insecurity on the one hand and "religious syncretism" on the other, reflecting an unorthodox blend of theistic religiosity *and* New Age spirituality (Granqvist, Broberg, & Hagekull, 2014; see also Chapter 8). We interpret these latter findings, along with others from the same study, as suggesting that experiences of parental insensitivity and current attachment insecurity predispose a person to "desperate searching," in which the person grabs on to whatever religious/spiritual means are available to regulate distress.

Most of these studies were conducted with largely Protestant Christian samples. The notion of sudden conversions can justifiably be said to represent a Protestant "born-again" stereotype, modeled on St. Paul's famous conversion on the road to Damascus as well as on many later examples from Pietist and Evangelical faith traditions. In other words, it is legitimate to question whether sudden conversions and changes are at all representative of the religiosity of attachment-insecure individuals outside of Protestant Christianity. It should be recalled, therefore, that Halama and colleagues' (2013) study yielded converging findings on a sample of Catholic converts. Furthermore, a study of Orthodox Jewish converts has provided cross-religion evidence for the association between an insecure attachment history and "radical" conversion (Pirutinsky, 2009). Specifically, Pirutinsky (2009) found that converts who converted across major faith traditions (i.e., to or from Orthodox Judaism) reported greater insecurity with mother and father, as compared to both nonconverts and those with intra-Orthodox religious changes.

As noted earlier, the compensation hypothesis is based on the assumption that individuals who have experienced parental insensitivity may use religion, and their perceived relationship with God in particular, to regulate distress. It follows that if such individuals experience sudden religious conversions or other increases in religiousness, this should occur during life situations in which the need to regulate distress is particularly marked. Several studies support this corollary. Increases in religiousness among individuals whose parents were judged low in sensitivity (whether in the AAI or on questionnaires) have typically been precipitated by relationship problems with family and romantic partners, separation, mental and physical illness, or general crises (Granqvist & Hagekull, 1999; Granqvist, Ivarsson, et al., 2007; Halama et al., 2013). My colleagues and I have collectively referred to such life themes as "themes of compensation" (Granqvist & Hagekull, 1999).

A viable objection to the studies reviewed thus far is that in all of them religious conversions and changes were assessed retrospectively. Again, memories may be erroneous. For example, it is conceivable that study participants who have decided, for whatever reason, to invest more in their religion than they used to do may seek to legitimize their current investments by distinguishing their current, happy selves from their past, unhappy selves. One way to do this would be to emphasize the deficiencies of one's life prior to conversion. However, we have also found that the association between an insecure attachment history and religious changes occurs in prospective longitudinal studies. We have observed, for example, that self-reports of parental insensitivity predict subsequently increased religiousness—particularly an increased importance of the perceived relationship with God—following the breakup of a romantic relationship (Granqvist & Hagekull, 2003).

Current Attachment Insecurity

Paralleling the research just reviewed, an insecure romantic attachment orientation in the present can reliably predict essentially the same kinds of religious changes. For example, in an early U.S. study, Kirkpatrick (1997) found that over a 4-year period, women with an insecure (particularly anxious) attachment orientation established a new relationship with God and reported religious experiences, such as being "born again" and speaking in tongues, to a larger extent than women with a secure (nonanxious) attachment orientation. These findings were conceptually replicated in a second study by Kirkpatrick (1998), this time over a 5-month period, and in both men and women. This study utilized Bartholomew and Horowitz's (1991) four-category model of attachment patterns, based on two dimensions: positive versus negative model of self, and positive versus negative model of other. Kirkpatrick again found that increases in the image of a loving God and in a perceived personal relationship with God were predicted by an anxious/preoccupied, but also by a fearful–avoidant, romantic attachment style. Just like preoccupied attachment, fearful–avoidant attachment is characterized by a negative model of self and high attachment–anxiety.

The magnitude of the effects was modest in Kirkpatrick's (1997, 1998) studies. However, when we focused on the context of a romantic relationship breakup in yet another sample, insecure romantic attachment prospectively predicted increased religiousness somewhat more strongly (Granqvist & Hagekull, 2003). We interpreted romantic relationship breakup as a situation likely to increase the need to regulate attachment-related distress. Also, in their recent study of Israeli Jewish converts, Greenwald and colleagues (2018) reported that romantic attachment anxiety was associated with reports of more sudden religious changes and more compensation themes. This study demonstrates cross-religion validity beyond Christianity for the association between insecure romantic attachment and compensatory religious changes.

One interpretation of the findings from these romantic attachment studies is that for people who assess themselves as unworthy of love and care (i.e., who possess a negative model of self) from other humans and who are high in anxiety (i.e., whose attachment systems are hyperactivated), turning to God may be possible because of God's unique characteristics as compared with human relationship partners. Turning to God is comparatively free of risk because a noncorporeal figure's responsiveness can always be imagined as benevolent and need never be experienced as disconfirmed. Also, in many religious belief systems, God's love is unconditional, so one need not be "worthy" of love to receive it (cf. Luther, above). Alternatively, God's love may be available through particular courses of action (e.g., good deeds, prayer), which can allow an otherwise "unworthy" person to "earn" God's love and forgiveness when it is most needed.

The studies reviewed thus far might seem to suggest that individuals with insecure attachment-related experiences in the past or insecure attachment patterns at present become increasingly religious over time. However, it should be recalled that increased religiousness is expected primarily in the context of a need to regulate intense distress. Accordingly, religiousness may also decrease for such individuals (Granqvist, 2002). This might happen under conditions where the need to regulate distress through attachment surrogates is comparatively low, such as after establishing a new intimate relationship with another person (Granqvist & Hagekull, 2003). Interestingly, Greenwald and colleagues (2018) found that apostasy (i.e., leaving the religion one grew up with) converges in intriguing ways with religious conversion. In their study, anxious romantic attachment was also related to sudden apostasy, rejection of parents' religiosity, and compensation themes.

In summary, the compensation pathway has received consistent and strong empirical support. Studies indicate that experiences of parental insensitivity and current attachment insecurity, especially attachment anxiety, are linked to religious instability, including both its waxing and waning. Moreover, both its waxing and waning are predictable based on the compensation idea. These conclusions hold true for research based on both cross-sectional and longitudinal designs; for studies using both romantic attachment-style measures and developmental attachment interview methods; and for studies conducted in both Christian and Jewish populations. I conclude that the developmental pathway to religion in the case of parental insensitivity and insecure attachment is one marked by attachment system (hyper)activation, under conditions in which a perceived relationship with God helps to regulate a believer's distress when no other adequate attachment figures are perceived to be available. This conclusion also corresponds well with the general speculations about the use of attachment surrogates offered by Bowlby (1969/1982) and Ainsworth (1985). It also converges with William James's (1902) descriptive portrayal of the religion of sick souls.

Finally, although not undertaken as attachment–religion research per se, a strand of research bridging attachment theory with terror management theory (TMT) has yielded observations that are in keeping with a defensive interpretation of compensation-related processes. Briefly, TMT deals with humans' defenses against the sting of mortality awareness (e.g., Greenberg, Solomon, & Pyszczynski, 1997). According to the theory and its considerable research base, mortality reminders lead to death-thought accessibility, which in turn activates defensive strategies—for example, the defense of one's worldview (e.g., religion and political persuasions) against perceived transgressions from members of out-groups.

However, Mikulincer and Florian (2000), in an intriguing set of experiments, found that mortality reminders led to more death-thought accessibility and more severe judgments of transgressions only among adults with insecure (anxious or avoidant) attachment styles. Similarly, they observed that worldview defense following mortality reminders reduced death-thought accessibility only among attachment-insecure (avoidant) study participants. In contrast, potentially positive effects of mortality reminders—like confidence in symbolic immortality and desire for intimacy with others—were observed only among attachment-secure study participants. Considered jointly, these findings indicate that attachment-insecure individuals erect rigid worldview defenses against threats, that their defenses may have destructive effects for members of out-groups, and that they do not reap the benefits with which mortality awareness can endow a secure person. In short, rather than acknowledging their vulnerability and sharing that vulnerability with other people, attachment-insecure individuals tend to mobilize their defenses. On the basis of findings and conclusions such as these, Hart, Shaver, and Goldenberg (2005) proposed and found empirical support for a tripartite security-system model consisting of dynamically interrelated processes of attachment, self-esteem, and worldview. Particularly for attachment-insecure individuals, threats to one component of the security system (e.g., attachment) result in compensatory defensive activation of other components (e.g., worldview defense, self-enhancement). I now explore how such defenses operate in the case of Mr. Blue. Later, in Chapter 9, I return to the relation between attachment theory and TMT.

MR. BLUE: A CASE STUDY

The study participant I call Mr. Blue is approaching old age. He grew up in a nonreligious family in an urban setting. He received a college education, but his current occupation (if any) is unknown. He reports no particular religious denomination. His questionnaires were cluttered with objections to the word "religion," among many other objections. Instead, he seems to go in and out of different Christian movements and denominations, without settling on any one in particular.

Mr. Blue was coded insecure/dismissing (Ds1) on the AAI by two independent coders. Although he described both his parents in markedly positive terms at the general/semantic level ("Everything was really good," "She did everything I needed"), he had virtually no convincingly supportive memories at the episodic level. Instead, he inadvertently conveyed a childhood characterized by loneliness and emotional isolation from parents who seemed largely uninterested in their son's psychological states. Both parents were therefore coded as low on the "loving" scale, and Mr. Blue's coherence was also coded low because of the striking discrepancy between positive general descriptors and an inability to provide episodic support for them (i.e., idealization). Beyond an "organized" dismissing state of mind, Mr. Blue's AAI discourse was judged as unresolved with regard to the loss of his paternal grandmother (i.e., U/Ds1).[3]

Anyone with the least compassion would hope that Mr. Blue could find reparative security and solace in his relationship with God, which could transform his relational life in a beneficial direction. Sadly, however, on the Religious Attachment Interview (RAI), Mr. Blue was classified as fearful/insecure by four independent coders. This "match" with the AAI is in line with internal working model correspondence because Mr. Blue is fearful/insecure, not secure, in his relationship with God. What I wish to illustrate with this case study, however, is how Mr. Blue has nevertheless used and uses God as a compensatory, surrogate figure to regulate distress and to maintain felt security. In other words, compensation and IWM correspondence both apply to Mr. Blue, as is regrettably often the case for attachment-insecure individuals who fail to find "real" security through God and religion. This again resembles James's (1902) characterization of the religion of many "sick souls." It also reminds us that life is not fair. One would like for children who do not receive the care and attention they deserve undergo the transformative processes that can unfold from receiving genuine love and security later in life. Sadly, however, such is not typically the case, nor is it for Mr. Blue.

The RAI with Mr. Blue was very long, yielding a transcript of more than 40 single-spaced pages. In what follows I give only a brief summary of the interview, with emphasis on text fragments that illustrate religious compensation. I also cite the most important passages underlying the coders' decisions to assign a fearful/insecure classification to this interview. As you will see, on the whole Mr. Blue's discourse is both incoherent and markedly defensive, which is why it was judged to indicate insecurity. Although he offers a benevolent representation of God at the general/semantic level, his representation is distinctly conflicted at the episodic level. Beyond memories of God's protection and instrumental support, which are in keeping with a benevolent representation, it becomes clear as the interview progresses that God is also represented as someone who does not accept doubt, anger, or expressions of being emotionally upset, which is not in keeping with a benevolent representation. God's protection is also conditional, and when his conditions are not met, real danger lurks. In addition, Mr. Blue engages in defensive self-enhancement and doctrinal discourse in much of the interview, and occasionally he denigrates religious out-groups. Finally, he offers virtually no metacognitive elaborations (i.e., no ability to consider his beliefs from various perspectives). All of this indicates that an insecure RAI classification is warranted.

In response to the opening questions about first memories of God and religion, Mr. Blue said that he found "the real Christian teachings" (i.e., doctrinal emphasis) that he was exposed to in elementary school. These teachings inspired him, but he did not develop a personal relationship with God until "much later." When asked to provide five adjectives to describe his relationship with God, Mr. Blue gave a loud sigh, adding ironically, "That's a good question." He then revealed his true opinion as he exclaimed, "What terrible questions!"—explicitly referring to the interviewer's "interest in words." Mr. Blue thus displayed a derogatory stance toward both the questions and the interviewer. He ultimately described his relationship with God in positive, relational, and doctrinal words ("love," "omniscient," "life-giving," "gives ability," "close").

Asked for more detail regarding "love," Mr. Blue refers to two powerful spiritual experiences, both involving "baptism of the spirit." One of these occurred when he was in military service early in adulthood. He describes an experiential state in which "time in some way disappeared," he was "completely floating on a cloud," and he experienced "an enormous joy." The source of this experiential state was an event in which Mr. Blue was literally forced into a corner by fellow military personnel who put their hands on his forehead and spoke in tongues. It started out as a frightening experience, but Mr. Blue uses mostly doctrinal expressions in his ensuing elaboration of it, mentioning "salvation," "conversion," "christening," and a state of being "filled with love."

It is difficult to separate Mr. Blue's lived experience of the event used to illustrate "love" from his religious interpretations of it; they appear to be one and the same to him. When probed, he simply uses new religious expressions to describe it. This reaction resembles many dismissing interviewees on the AAI who, instead of giving an episodic description (i.e., indicating a specific, concrete memory), replace one semantic descriptor with another (e.g., "She was loving because she was caring"; Main et al., 2003). Nonetheless, the implication of Mr. Blue's discussion is that love is equivalent to powerful subjective states. His discussion contains no interpersonal or relational elements, which is remarkable given that "love" is the topic of conversation. Although a compassionate reader would hope that Mr. Blue would find a steadfast, loving relationship, sadly he or she cannot see any substance to love beyond a suggestible mind's response to a frightening ritual.

In the passages intended to illustrate "love," Mr. Blue also introduces two themes that are carried forward in the interview. The first pertains to a grandiose, narcissistic self—"I am gifted with ability." The second is about religious doubting, which for Mr. Blue "seems strange, I'll never do that." Both themes indicate a markedly self-enhancing, defensive strategy and a mind that closes itself to the inescapable uncertainties of human life.

With respect to "omniscient," Mr. Blue talks about prayers and how they cause "seemingly random things" to become "orchestrated" into the precisely right outcome. When prompted for a specific event, Mr. Blue recalls how God gave him a parking permit when he really needed one. Intermingled in that discussion are several examples of gratuitous praise ("When God gives something it usually turns out perfect"). These features again resemble dismissing speech in the AAI (e.g., positive descriptors are illustrated with practical rather than emotional support). Also, the example illustrates a markedly concrete (anthropomorphic) understanding of God's involvement in Mr. Blue's affairs. Although the nature of the event recalled would seem naturally to invite metacognitive elaboration (e.g., "There could be other explanations for the parking permit"), Mr. Blue offers no such elaborations. Instead, he takes natural uncertainty ("seemingly random things") and eliminates it, effectively closing his mind by appealing to God's orchestration.

Asked about experiences of feeling separated from God, Mr. Blue starts hesitantly but ultimately acknowledges that he has felt that way. When further probed about separation, Mr. Blue mentions "thoughts planted in your mind." He attributes those thoughts to "the prosecutor" (i.e., Satan). Mr. Blue continues, "As long as you turn the right way, as long as you turn the right way . . . " but ends with an unfinished sentence. Here Mr. Blue understands Satan as a causal agent operating from without but finding "his" way into people's minds. This sets up another theme that unfolds during the interview.

When asked about memories of being emotionally upset, Mr. Blue recalls an event in which he became "justifiably angry" with a colleague, adding, "Really scary and then I felt like this has destroyed my relationship with God." Why his justified anger felt "scary" and as though it destroyed his relationship with God might seem unclear, but not if we consider that anger risks upsetting or alienating a rejecting caregiver (Bowlby, 1973). An avoidant stance with regard to attachment is in fact believed to reflect the suppression of anger (Main, 1981). Any failure to suppress would become "scary" in such a context.

Upon further probing for memories of being emotionally upset, Mr. Blue refers to a recurrent situation in which his wife initiates discussions "that lead nowhere." Mr. Blue then derogates her subtly by saying, "She can talk a lot." He adds that he tries to "end the discussion. . . . I usually put a deaf ear, start singing, like, hymns to myself, turn to

God, like trying to get peace." When one loses peace, he says, it can go on for a long time, adding, "I have learned that there are warning signs, and then I pull back to God." Not only does Mr. Blue devalue his wife's attempts at communication with him, but he also notes how he zones out of dialogue with her, actively using religious behaviors to compose and redirect himself from her in a spousally avoidant way. This is clearly a compensatory, defensive use of God. He also reiterates how being upset is threatening (i.e., risks losing peace).

Later in the interview, Mr. Blue mentions that God has personally selected him for important things, which are not further specified. He notes about his divine mission that he "won't exactly be loved" by others for what he will say and do. Mr. Blue's grandiosity combined with the absence of metacognition lends an eerie quality to this discussion. Not surprisingly, he also alludes to fear ("fear, Godliness") and his active attempts to please God so that he can retain divine protection. Earlier in the interview, he had noted several examples of how God gave "blatantly clear" protection to him in various situations of danger.

When asked about other religions, Mr. Blue demonstrates clear dislike. For example, about hell, he says that God will send believers with the wrong faith (along with nonbelievers) there, and it's "a place of gnashing teeth." Similarly, when probed about how he would feel if his children were to develop different religious affinities than his, Mr. Blue laughs, "They won't become Muslims."

When asked about faith and his own children, Mr. Blue stresses the importance of children developing a relationship with God early in life. When they have experienced illness, Mr. Blue has therefore advised his children "that you pray, that you go to God first . . . because the later in your life you learn this, the bigger the head is which is in the way." As a caregiver, then, Mr. Blue redirects his children's attachment behavior from himself to God. This is a form of rejection and possibly of neglect as well. If generally characteristic of his caregiving stance toward his children, we would expect intergenerational transmission of dismissing/ avoidant attachment (e.g., van IJzendoorn, 1995).

Toward the end of the interview, Mr. Blue discusses how slips from the right faith can cause God's protection to cease. Satan returns to the discussion, with Mr. Blue expressing worries that the devil might do harm to his children (e.g., "The enemy could very well hurt them"). When asked how, Mr. Blue clarifies, "I'm thinking if they'd perhaps die." This discussion is what led us to assign a primary "fearful" classification to Mr. Blue's RAI.

In summary, beyond revealing fearfulness, Mr. Blue's discourse is incoherent (thus insecure). Although God is in some ways represented as benevolent, it is equally clear that God is portrayed as someone who does not accept justified anger or feelings of being upset, and whose protection is predicated on blind allegiance—a nondoubting, closed-off mind that simply praises God. Also, if God's protection ceases, one is thrown to the lions, in the form of another metaphysical entity who may do concrete and terrible things—the devil. Thus, in the end, God is malevolent, akin to a high-strung, punitive Mafia boss.[4]

Mr. Blue's fearful/insecure representation of God is clearly very different from Mrs. Green's secure representation (in Chapter 5). For Mrs. Green, God is someone who can handle anger, who can be questioned, and whose courses of action are open to alternative interpretations. The difference between these two speakers' representations of God is particularly striking considering that both of them engage with similarly literal faith traditions. Also, as far as education is concerned, Mr. Blue trumps Mrs. Green. Along with other findings from the study, this comparison of educational levels indicates that believers' representations of God stem from something other than, or in addition to, both faith traditions and education. More than anything, they are anchored in relational development.

CONCLUSIONS AND THE POSSIBILITY
OF EARNED SECURITY VIA RELIGIOUS COMPENSATION

So far in this chapter, I have shown that some individuals who have experienced parental insensitivity or who are currently attachment-insecure find in God a surrogate attachment figure. I have also shown that such a compensatory relationship with God and religion tends to originate in situations of emotional turmoil and give rise to sudden religious change. Religion may also wane in importance for such individuals in life periods marked by relative tranquility. In addition, I have argued that whether God is selected as a surrogate target for the attachment system hinges largely on the cultural–cognitive accessibility of ideas related to God and religion. When such ideas are inaccessible, for example, because of secularization, the individual is more likely to select other attachment surrogates (e.g., opiates, pets, material objects).

Key to my understanding of why attachment-insecure individuals choose God as a surrogate attachment figure is an assumption that they possess a lingering, dormant bias for benevolent responses from an attachment figure (i.e., the primary/secure attachment strategy). I have also argued that such a bias is triggered especially in situations of considerable emotional turmoil, when the individual's habitual, insecure (secondary) attachment strategy breaks down. In other words, the individual suffers terribly, and avoidance or resistance/preoccupation does not bring about relief, in fact perpetuating the suffering. Because of negative working models of self and/or others in human relationships, the potential caregiving that other humans (e.g., parents, partners, friends, therapists) could provide is not sought out.

Instead, God, or some other nonhuman figure, may be selected as a target of attachment, with the advantage of not disconfirming the individual's lingering expectations of benevolent responses. Such a target can be mentally endowed by the perceiver with whatever attributes are required to meet the suffering individual's unmet needs for security and safety. Compared with other conceivable attachment surrogates, God is perhaps ideal. The cultural evolution process that has sculpted the God of theistic religions has been a work in progress for millennia and is designed to meet such needs. Consequently, God's love is believed to be everywhere; it is endless, perfectly potent, and unconditional. To top things off, God's behaviors are so subtle—indeed invisible—that they need never disconfirm even the highest of expectations.

Earlier in this chapter, I hinted at the possibility that experiencing God's love and care, or perhaps some other component of religion/spirituality, when it is most needed might be positively transformative (reparative) for attachment-insecure individuals , not only in decreasing their suffering but potentially also in promoting "earned security" of attachment. The reason for merely hinting at this possibility is that pertinent research evidence is still at best inferential. Also, the available inferential evidence is both mixed and inconclusive. I nonetheless discuss the matter here because of its clinical and pastoral importance.

In support of the idea that earned security might be achieved via religious compensation, self-reported romantic attachment (particularly a negative self-model or a high degree of attachment anxiety) has been linked to increasing religiousness over time (longitudinal compensation), whereas self-reported secure attachment has been linked to higher religiousness at a given time (contemporaneous correspondence; see Kirkpatrick, 2005). It is possible that this discrepancy exists because over time people who are insecure with respect to romantic attachment can become secure via religion-as-compensation.

Similarly, whereas AAI coders' estimates of parental insensitivity during interviewees' childhoods were able to predict the interviewees' history of religion-as-compensation in our AAI study (Granqvist, Ivarsson, et al., 2007), classifications of the interviewees' *current* attachment organization were generally unrelated to such compensatory use of religion. Thus, participants who had used religion-as-compensation were not currently insecure beyond the level expected by chance. This discrepancy might occur because some individuals who suffered attachment-related difficulties (e.g., rejection) in the past have "earned" a certain degree of attachment security from their surrogate relationship with God.

For a third example, in Kirkpatrick and Shaver's (1992) early study, security of attachment to God was positively associated with security of adult romantic attachment, but only among respondents who described their childhood maternal attachments as insecure. Among other interpretations, these findings may suggest that for those who were insecure with mother, a secure attachment to God could develop due to religion-as-compensation, which then also might have had a positively transformative effect on romantic attachment.

Fourth, in Brown and colleagues' (2004) population-based study of spousal bereavement and religiousness, widowed individuals who were estimated to be insecure, based on a brief "face-valid" measure of attachment orientation, were more likely than those estimated to be secure to have reduced grief as a function of increased spiritual/religious beliefs. These researchers concluded that the observed pattern of results "is consistent with the possibility that insecure widowed individuals who turn to God are better able to use God as a compensatory attachment figure and regulate emotional distress compared to individuals who are relatively more secure" (p. 1172). This conclusion is in keeping with the idea of the positively transformative effects of religion-as-compensation.

Although some scholars (e.g., Noller, 1992) have pointed to the compensation hypothesis as a "deficiency" approach to religion, the aforementioned examples illustrate the possibility that what starts out as deficiency may wind up as reparative and growth-promoting. In passing, the dynamic transformations to which religion-as-compensation may contribute should make religion of interest to psychologists.

On the other hand, we have equally compelling evidence that religion-as-compensation does not generally yield "earned" attachment security or promote psychological adjustment. This is illustrated with the case of Mr. Blue who, though clearly on the religion-as-compensation path, not only has a markedly insecure state of mind on the AAI but has also failed to find real security in his perceived relationship with God, as revealed by the RAI. Thus, generalization of negative (insecure) working models at present coexist with a compensatory, albeit insecure, use of God in this case—along with many other cases who were insecure on the AAI in our study (Nkara et al., 2018).

Similarly, in their study of Jewish converts and apostates, Greenwald and colleagues (2018) found that compensatory themes, for both forms of religious change, were associated with lower well-being at present and that endorsement of such themes exacerbated a link between current attachment anxiety and distress. The latter findings indicate that highly attachment-anxious converts and apostates who experienced their religious changes during periods of high emotional turmoil continue to experience high levels of distress and low well-being. Contrarily, in that study correspondence (e.g., socialization) themes were related to higher well-being at present and weakened the link between attachment anxiety and distress. Jointly, these findings suggest that for highly attachment-anxious people, religious change, whether conversion or apostasy, may be beneficial if it takes place in the context of other positive and supportive relationships (e.g., with religious believers), but not when the religious change reflects a solitary attempt to regulate distress.

Relatedly, Miner (2009) found that a self-reported secure attachment to God does not typically compensate for perceptions of an insecure attachment history with parents on current levels of well-being and distress. Her findings showed that a group of participants who self-classified as secure with God but insecure with parents scored nearly as low in well-being and as high in distress as a group of participants who self-classified as insecure with both God and parents. Miner interpreted these findings as failing to support a "strong surrogacy model" (p. 121) and as being more in line with a notion of differentiated working models in which differential working models of parents and God presumably exert independent effects on psychological adjustment (cf. Collins & Read, 1994). Beck (2006, p. 125) has similarly concluded, with regard to religion-as-compensation for insecure attachment, that "once the relationship with God is established, prior [i.e., insecure] attachment styles may begin to exert themselves in this new . . . relationship" (brackets added). These conclusions, sad as they are, appear to be warranted, and they again bring the case of Mr. Blue back to mind.

Thus, for every hint in the literature that religion-as-compensation may promote earned attachment security and improved psychological adjustment, there are equally compelling empirical reasons to resist such conclusions as generally true. The inconclusive nature of the evidence is echoed in recent findings from our AAI–RAI study (Nkara et al., 2018). For example, on the one hand we have observed a group of participants who are insecure on the AAI but secure on the RAI, suggesting that religion-as-compensation may be successful in yielding security with God. On the other hand, we have observed at least an equal number of participants who are secure on the AAI and yet insecure on the RAI, thus suggesting that some generally secure people may fail to find security with God (see Miner, 2009, for similar self-report findings). Although our material suggests that many of these latter participants may be "autonomous doubters" rather than "truly" insecure with God,[4] these findings indicate that any favorable religion-as-compensation outcome is merely one among other equally notable exceptions to the general rule of internal working model correspondence.

In conclusion, religion-as-compensation may promote psychological adjustment, possibly including earned security of attachment, but this is by no means the default outcome. Many moderators (qualifying variables) are likely to operate, given the marked inconsistency (cf. heterogeneity) of study findings. The bulk of the evidence, along with clinical judgment, points to the importance that the attachment-insecure individual who is on the compensation path can profit from being "held" by a stable group of fellow believers, such as a religious community and pastoral carers, rather than being entirely on his or her own. This should be helpful not only in maintaining the religious or spiritual path on which the individual has embarked and in preventing regression to the "previous life" of suffering and potential "idolatry" (e.g., engagement with addictive substances and material objects), but also in showing that other humans can be trusted and relied upon. As an aside, an inclusive group of fellow believers may also profitably challenge any rigidly defensive uses of God and religion, and counter feelings of shame and sinfulness to which the insecure individual may be prone. Reparative experiences in relationships with human interaction partners are likely to add substantially in the long term to any initial, positive effects that might result from experiencing God's love and support.

With these observations and speculations in place, we are ready to tackle a larger question that has been of considerable interest to psychologists of religion, along with other academic groups: Does religion generally promote or undermine mental health? As it turns out, attachment theory and research provide a valuable platform for addressing that question.

CHAPTER SUMMARY

In this chapter I have argued that some individuals who have experienced parental insensitivity or who are currently insecure with regard to attachment may find in God a surrogate attachment figure, aiding a person in compensating for states of insecurity and other unsatisfactory attachments. I started by acknowledging the contribution of William James, who vividly described the "twice-born" religion of "sick souls," which in many ways precognized what we have much later described as the compensation pathway to religion. I then addressed adults' use of attachment surrogates more generally, noting (in line with the notion of increased differentiation in development) that adults may use a wide variety of attachment surrogates to regulate stress. These surrogates include various drugs, pets, material objects, particular places, and many more, most of which do not typically qualify as attachment "figures" in Bowlby's and Ainsworth's sense. I formalized the compensation hypothesis as it applies more specifically to religion, noting that attachment-insecure individuals may turn to God and religion when they are in turmoil severe enough to cause their insecure strategies to break down. In such states, a lingering experience-expectant bias for benevolent responses may be expressed toward God. I also provided a research review, demonstrating that the compensation pathway has been supported by a considerable body of empirical research, especially by findings on sudden religious changes occurring during stressful life situations. I provided an in-depth case study of Mr. Blue, who used God as an attachment surrogate to derive security and protection—partly from the devil who was perceived as lurking around every corner with great malevolence. Mr. Blue ultimately failed to become secure with God. I concluded the chapter with a discussion of whether religion-as-compensation may have beneficial psychological effects, noting that this is not the case by default, but only by exception. Finally, I attended to contextual (social) factors that may facilitate the transformative potential of religious compensation.

PART III

EXPANSIONS

A Wider View of Attachment and Religion/Spirituality

In the first two parts of this book, I adopted a fairly narrow perspective, focusing on how attachment, at the individual or micro-level, is linked to organized forms of religion, particularly theistic religion. In this third part, containing two chapters, I return to my promise of adopting "a wider view." First, I move beyond the attachment–religion connection per se to examine the role that this connection plays in our understanding of mental health and unhealth (Chapter 7). Second, beyond theistic religion I consider attachment in relation to less institutionally organized forms of spirituality, as expressed, for example, in the New Age movement and in mystical experiences (Chapter 8).

CHAPTER 7

Religion as Attachment in Relation to Mental Health

We undoubtedly live in an age of anxiety, depression, and fear. Already by the turn of this century, the average American child scored higher in anxiety than did the average psychiatric child patient at midcentury (Twenge, 2000).[1] To make matters worse, the same trend can be seen throughout the Western world and is evident in many other psychopathological conditions (Twenge et al., 2010). A recent World Health Organization (2018) report even indicates that mental illness is now a leading health problem globally. It pains me, not least as a father of four children, to add that things aren't looking much brighter for the near future. Beyond the ordinary stressors of life, our children will have to grapple with a worsening climate (for a review, see Burke, Sanson, & Van Hoorn, 2018), regular cyber and terror attacks, mass human migration, fear-mongering and science-refuting politicians, periodic school shootings, and major political upheavals—all of these crises dramatically and continuously amplified by the mass media. In the chilling words of songwriter Nick Cave: "I was just a boy when I sat down / To watch the news on TV / I saw some ordinary slaughter / I saw some routine atrocity" ("Nature Boy"; *Abbatoir Blues/The Lyre of Orpheus*, 2004). The conclusion seems inescapable: As far as mental health is concerned, the normal population will increasingly resemble the psychiatric populations of the past.

Two things appear paradoxical about this steady worsening of mental health. First, people around the world have, in parallel, experienced a sharp rise in material prosperity, life expectancy, and health.

So we have many reasons to celebrate being alive in this particular day and age. Second, people—in the Western world in particular—are nothing short of obsessed with "the pursuit of happiness," which has been evident in the epidemic spread of the mental health movement (Lyubomirsky, Sheldon, & Schkade, 2005). Why then don't we feel happy or at least happ*ier*?

This important question has many answers. A key one is that many Westerners, residing in increasingly individualistic societies, have lost a sense of social connection and community, including sustainable family ties (Twenge, 2000; Twenge et al., 2010). Solid relationships anchor the human mind, which is a fundamental fact about our very social species. Without being part of closely knit social groups and without enduring intimate relationships, humans tend to become anxious and despondent over time. Beyond the cultural shifts away from community and affiliation, Twenge and colleagues (2010) point to shifts away from meaning in life and toward materialism and extrinsic goals. If we add all of these societal symptoms together, we see that many of the central pillars of religion are dissolving. More than perhaps any other "institution" in society, religions have provided welcoming social communities, emphasized the importance of sustainable relationships, promoted a sense of meaning in life, and sought to counteract materialism and other extrinsic goals.

Given these usual functions of religion, it is natural to wonder whether religion facilitates mental health, and perhaps even health in general. A huge body of research has been devoted to this topic. Indeed, almost no other religion-related topic has received as much attention in the scientific literature. A Google Scholar search for "religion + health" yields more than 10,000 hits. This is similar to "religion + society," twice as high as "religion + violence" and 20 times as high as "religion + patriarchy." In fact, psychologists of religion have focused on the religion–health connection for over 50 years, at least since Gordon Allport (1950; Allport & Ross, 1967) suggested making a distinction between "intrinsic" and "extrinsic" religion.[2] Since then, scholars from many other academic disciplines—not least the medical sciences—have joined the effort.

As largely an outsider to this literature, I have felt dumbfounded by the "naïve empiricism" of most of this research and by what appears to be a collective failure within the field to make the basic distinctions required to understand why and how religion should be linked to health in the first place. For example, it does not make much scientific sense to assume that religious involvement per se causes people to survive, but a statistical association between degree of religious involvement and mortality has nonetheless been investigated in numerous studies. These studies have even been meta-analyzed (McCullough, Hoyt, Larson, Koenig, & Thoresen, 2000), and the meta-analysis has been widely cited in the literature. As might be expected, the modest favorable "effect" of religious involvement on survival is highly heterogeneous, indicating multiple powerful moderators (or qualifying variables). Naturally, then, researchers have been forced to embark on a post-hoc expedition to try to identify the linking (mediating) mechanism(s), but without much success. A reverse research process might have been more useful—one starting with the identification of some health-relevant psychological or physiological mechanism, and then identifying some aspect of religion that is strongly linked to that mechanism.

In this chapter, I focus specifically on "religion + *mental* health" rather than health generally. I do so partly because it yields a more manageable body of scientific literature (1,500 hits) and partly because the attachment-related mechanisms I discuss have a more obvious bearing on mental health. Not surprisingly, empirical research has shown that religion and mental health are also interconnected in complex ways, suggesting multiple moderators (Batson et al., 1993; Bergin, 1983; Hackney & Sanders, 2003; Salsman et al., 2015). The link is often positive but weak, although it is sometimes stronger and occasionally negative.

These inconsistencies in research findings seem to depend on a few salient sets of moderators—aspects of religion, mental health, and contexts—all of which I discuss in this chapter. Attending to important moderators will help us understand why religion and mental health are connected. Drawing on the religion-as-attachment model presented in previous chapters, I argue here that attachment-theoretical considerations provide vital insights into why these particular moderators matter (see also Granqvist, 2014b).

My aim is not to provide a detailed review of all the research on religion and mental health that has been undertaken from an attachment viewpoint. Attachment-based research on the religion–mental health connection has been limited, not so much in quantity perhaps but in quality. Rather, by attending to the moderators that make a difference for the association, my aim is to increase our scientific understanding of why religion and mental health are connected. This understanding may in turn serve as a heuristic device, helping to steer future research endeavors and clinical applications in fruitful directions.

The chapter is divided into three main sections. The first is introductory and provides important conclusions that have been drawn about the religion–mental health connection. I review the best attachment-based studies and elaborate on why I assess attachment-based research in this area as generally limited in quality. The second section deals with moderators that make a difference for the religion–mental health connection.

In the third and final section, I summarize my conclusions and provide caveats and suggestions for future research directions.

OVERVIEW OF THE TERRAIN

To make a decades-long story short, scholars who have considered the religion–mental health connection have suggested that attachment to God is a key component of religion that fosters mental health. For example, in their attempts to arrive at a causal model that accounts for the many atheoretical findings in this field of research, Koenig and colleagues (2012, p. 587) put "attachment to God" at the center of their model, identifying it as the source of religiosity/spirituality that causes people to engage in other, more specific health-promoting religious behaviors (e.g., rituals, prayer, commitment, religious coping). A review by Pargament (2002) similarly concluded that on the one hand mental health and well-being are uniquely and positively predicted by a secure relationship with God and a perceived closeness to God. On the other hand, he asserted that a tenuous (insecure, unstable) relationship with God has negative effects on mental health and well-being (see also Hill & Pargament, 2003). This latter idea converges with the literature surrounding Julie Exline's notion of spiritual struggles (including anger toward God; e.g., Exline, Yali, & Sanderson, 2000). Spiritual struggles are shown to be not only inversely related to mental health but also rooted in negative perceptions of human caregivers (Exline, Homolka, & Grubbs, 2013).

As a researcher of the attachment–religion connection, I generally believe that these scholars (Koenig, Pargament, Exline, and others) have drawn the correct conclusions. However, the empirical evidence for the vital role of attachment to God is far from conclusive. A relatively large body of research has examined associations between attachment-related matters of religion (especially dimensions of attachment to God) and aspects of mental health, drawing on samples from a variety of religious traditions.[3] Along with studies on internal working model correspondence (reviewed in Chapter 5), this topic has come to dominate attachment–religion research, which is itself a testimony to the importance researchers assign to mental health. However, and again mirroring much research on internal working model correspondence, with a few exceptions the studies have suffered from regrettable methodological limitations, rendering their conclusions somewhat ambiguous.

Specifically, most studies have employed a cross-sectional questionnaire methodology, applied it to samples from largely religious, nonclinical populations, and examined concurrent associations between self-reported attachment to God and self-reported aspects of mental health and unhealth (e.g., life satisfaction, well-being, depression, anxiety, general distress). The findings have yielded a consistent picture suggesting that perceptions of being attached to God, and especially of having a secure attachment to God, are moderately linked to mental health and, conversely, that insecure (especially anxious) attachment to God is linked to mental unhealth. Moreover, in better-controlled studies, these links have usually withstood statistical control of relevant covariates, such as romantic attachment, attachment history with parents, God image, prayer, church attendance, and personality dimensions.

Importantly, a few studies have demonstrated prospective links between attachment to God and mental health, including predicted changes in mental health (e.g., Bradshaw & Kent, 2017; Duncan, 2007; Ellison, Bradshaw, Kuyel, & Marcum, 2012). Duncan (2007), studying a relatively large sample from the nonclinical New Zealand population, found that self-reported anxious (but not avoidant) attachment to God prospectively predicted increased rates of self-reported depression, even following statistical control of attachment to others and depression at the beginning of the study. Also, Duncan found that anxious attachment to God prospectively predicted decreased well-being, again following statistical control of relevant variables, and that this predictive relation occurred specifically in a group of participants subjected to high life stress. Ellison and colleagues' (2012) prospective study of American Presbyterians showed that a secure attachment to God predicted decreased anxiety over time and also buffered against the deleterious effects of stressful life events. Similar to Duncan's study on depression, an anxious attachment to God was observed to exacerbate the deleterious effects of stress on anxiety. Ellison and colleagues (2012) concluded that attachment to God is a more robust predictor of changes in distress than many more commonly studied parameters such as ethnicity, gender, socioeconomic status, and church attendance. In an American sample of older adults studied in the specific context of a secure attachment to God, Bradshaw and Kent (2017) also found that prayer predicts increased well-being over time.

Although this extensive literature has obvious value, the data collected so far has been limited by at least four methodological problems. First, the causal direction of cross-sectional correlations between attachment to God and mental health remains open to question. Does a secure attachment to God facilitate mental health, or does mental health facilitate secure attachment to God? Or is the association perhaps bidirectional, or are both variables a consequence of some third variable? This is why I emphasized prospective longitudinal studies in the paragraph above, showing that, yes, a secure attachment to God does seem to facilitate mental health, at least as measured by self-reports. However, conflicting findings suggesting the opposite process direction have also accrued. For example, a study of Belgian religious elders residing in nursing homes showed that depression predicted increased attachment insecurity to God over time rather than the other way around (Thauvoye, Granqvist, Golovchanova, & Dezutter, 2018).

To illustrate just how pervasive the problem of process direction is for cross-sectional studies, if God functions as both a safe haven and a secure base, then encountering trouble and suffering should temporally forecast people's turning to God qua safe haven (cf. "longitudinal compensation," Kirkpatrick, 2005). Yet, contemporaneously, using God as a secure base should ameliorate distress and should thus be linked to better mental health (cf. "contemporaneous correspondence"; Kirkpatrick, 2005). There is no way to do justice to this supposedly dynamic interplay between attachment to God and mental health in cross-sectional studies. Because of competing processes, the relation between the two could be zero at a given point in time.

Second, the overreliance on self-reports to measure both attachment to God and mental health makes it impossible to rule out some combination of social desirability bias (impression management and self-deception), shared method variance, semantic overlap, and lack of sufficient self-awareness as being at least partly responsible for the obtained associations. Prior meta-analytic research comprising 65 independent studies indeed showed that religious people tend to have elevated social desirability scores, interpreted as indicating a self-enhancement strategy (Sedikides & Gebauer, 2010). For a case in point, on the questionnaires used in our study (Nkara et al., 2018), Mr. Blue (see the case study in Chapter 6) self-reported not only that he had a secure attachment to God, in contrast to what independent interview coders concluded, but also that he was doing well with regard to his mental health (e.g., low anxiety and depression). In contrast, we have good reason to suspect that he is engaging in wishful thinking here, but the self-reports employed in the literature on attachment to God and mental health remain open to criticism on these grounds. For another related example, experiencing an attachment to God, and a secure one in particular, typically overlaps substantially with being religious, so general religiousness emerges as a potential third variable. Although some of the pertinent studies have statistically controlled for other aspects of religiousness (e.g., Keefer & Brown, 2018; Rowatt & Kirkpatrick, 2002), overall this problem has not received much attention. Assessments of individual differences in attachment to God would seem to presuppose that an individual experiences an attachment to God in the first place. A persuasive demonstration that secure attachment to God facilitates mental health then presupposes that the influence of other aspects of religiousness have been ruled out.

Third, positive associations between attachment to God and mental health obtained in largely religious populations remain of questionable generalizability to populations that are less religious and especially to populations that are largely secular (nonreligious). For example, people who turn to religion despite being made secure by generous social welfare programs, for example, in secular "welfare states," might differ from those who turn to religion when faced with genuine poverty, uninsured medical costs, and the like in other and typically more religious societies.

Finally, as noted in Chapter 2, religion is especially important in times of trouble. Therefore, although mental unhealth is spreading in the general population, it may not be advisable to study the importance of neither attachment to God for mental health nor of religion more generally in samples drawn from the general population. Besides the possibility of insufficient levels of stress in some such samples, there is likely a restriction of range or variation in self-reported mental health. This would attenuate the size of the "true" contribution of attachment to God (and religion variables more generally), which is conceivably expressed most clearly when the going gets tough.

In conclusion, the methodological limitations of most published studies of attachment to God in relation to mental health make it difficult to draw clear-cut conclusions. Put differently, although attachment theory as applied to religion would suggest that secure attachment to God facilitates mental health, the existing body of empirical research does not suffice to draw that conclusion. As a research community, we should do better than this, and I am confident that adequate funding would enable us to do so. Rather than reviewing this body of research in more detail, I turn to lessons we may learn from the more general literature on the religion–mental health connection.

ATTACHMENT-RELATED MODERATORS
OF THE RELIGION–MENTAL HEALTH CONNECTION

The general literature on religion and mental health indicates that the association between the two is complex and dependent on moderators (Batson et al., 1993; Bergin, 1983; Hackney & Sanders, 2003; Park & Slattery, 2013; Salsman et al., 2015). This is almost a given when one considers the breadth of the concepts of both "religion" and "mental health." Therefore, it matters a great deal which aspects of religion we focus on. Similarly, the specific aspects of mental health that we examine matter a great deal. (Both of these qualifiers have been widely recognized; e.g., see Batson et al., 1993; Hood et al., 2009.) Last but not least, the contexts within which study participants find themselves are of great importance. Unlike the first two moderators, this third qualifier has not received the attention it deserves. I now discuss each set of qualifiers vis-à-vis attachment theoretical considerations, starting—as in a good three-course dinner—with the tastiest course as appetizer.

Aspects of Context

Research has pointed to several contexts, at both the individual, micro level and the societal, macro level, that facilitate religious beliefs and behaviors. When people and societies are faced with such contexts, God and religion become more important in order for people to achieve or maintain mental health.

Micro-Level Contexts: Emotional Turmoil, Stress, and Vulnerability

Stress and emotional turmoil are well-known facilitators of religious experiences. Moreover, the general literature on religion and health seems to show, repeatedly, that not only are people more inclined to turn to religion during stress but also that religion has its most salubrious effects during times of serious trouble. For example, the salubrious effects of "positive" religious coping (e.g., seeking spiritual support, experiencing spiritual connection) and intrinsic religiousness on mental health are typically moderated by levels of stress, such that religion confers its most beneficial effects in times of trouble. This has often been found in coping research (see meta-analysis by Ano & Vasconcelles, 2005; see also Pargament, 1997, 2002). It has also been confirmed in a meta-analysis of studies of religion and depression (Smith, McCullough, & Poll, 2003). This meta-analysis found that aspects of religion, such as those mentioned above, were negatively linked to depression, especially under conditions of high stress, whereas the main effect of religion on depression was negligible.

Research on religious conversions offers converging evidence. Not only are intense and sudden conversion experiences likely to occur during stress, but such experiences are also associated with marked attenuation of distress and increases in well-being, at least in the short run (Hood et al., 2009; Pargament, 1997). In attachment terms, stress and emotional turmoil are relevant because they are associated with heightened attachment activation, as well as the potential use of God and religion as a safe haven to deal with the situation.

An additional context in which religion and particularly a secure attachment to God might have a protective effect is when risk factors for mental unhealth such as anxiety and depression are present. This idea was supported in a short-term longitudinal study showing that distal risk factors for eating disorders (e.g., pressure to be thin, thin-ideal internalization) prospectively predicted more proximal risk factors for eating disorders (i.e., body dissatisfaction, dieting) exclusively among study participants who experienced an insecure attachment to God (Homan & Boyatzis, 2010). In other words, women who experienced a secure attachment to God, that is, women who felt loved and accepted by God, were buffered from the adverse effects of the distal risk factors. In an intriguing follow-up experiment, a secure attachment to God mitigated the adverse causal effect of exposure to ultra-thin models (i.e., a proximal factor) on women's satisfaction with their bodies (Homan, 2012).

Macro-Level Contexts: Welfare States and Cultural Normativity of Religion

The broader societal and cultural context is also important. International demographic data from countries affiliated with the Organisation for Economic Co-operation and Development (OECD) shows that, in bivariate analyses, one key variable explains a surprisingly large amount of statistical variance in population estimates of religiosity. That key variable is the proportion of the gross domestic product (GDP) that governments spend on social welfare, potentially covering costs for education, health care, social insurance, and pensions (Gill & Lundsgaarde, 2004; Scheve & Stasavage, 2006; see also Barber, 2013, for an extension of these findings to 114 countries). People are markedly less religious in welfare states, with parts of Europe, especially Scandinavia, being the most pronounced examples among the OECD nations of largely nonreligious, secular societies. In these countries, state agencies and other functions of the welfare system have taken over responsibility for many of the material and social security functions that were historically covered by religion (e.g., churches, religious communities) and the family. It is important to note that the high welfare–low religiosity link is not restricted to either demographic religiosity variables, such as frequency of church attendance, or merely to theistic beliefs. Rather, it is equally applicable to religiosity variables of considerable psychological importance, such as seeking comfort (a safe haven) from God and religion. These observations are in keeping with Norris and Inglehart's (2011) theory about "existential security"; with greater security provided by other means, people have less "need" for the security that religion otherwise provides.

Also, when something, whether a matter of religion or other, is normative in a society, it is usually also associated with favorable outcomes, such as mental health. When that same thing has a marginal role in a society, however, it is usually not linked to favorable outcomes but may even set the stage for unfavorable ones. There is a simple reason for this: normativity matching signals that a person is well adapted to cultural norms—the person "fits in." Not being well adapted to cultural norms comes with a certain cost. I can illustrate this basic idea with an example from two of my homes: the San Francisco Bay area, where this book is being composed, and Sweden, my birthplace and usual country of residence. In the San Francisco area, recreational drugs have been in common use at least since the heyday of the flower-power movement in the 1960s. Among youngsters here, occasional marijuana smoking has been associated with positive mental health outcomes, whereas complete abstinence has been linked with poorer mental health (Shedler & Block, 1990). I can assure you that most of my Swedish compatriots, residing in a country with one of the most repressive policies against "narcotics" in the free world (e.g., Goldberg, 2005), would have a hard time believing that those findings are accurate. In Swedish society, where the so-called "gateway" theory has been prevalent (e.g., marijuana consumption ulti-mately leads to heroin addiction), even a single cannabis use seems to increase the risk for poor mental health (e.g., Zammit, Allebeck, Andre-asson, Lundberg, & Lewis, 2002).

We should not be surprised, then, if religion is positively linked to mental health in societies where religion is culturally normative but not in societies where religion is on the fringe, as in Scandinavian welfare states. Lo and behold, this is what international comparative research shows. One of the best and most ambitious studies was conducted by Diener, Tay, and Myers (2011). They found that religiosity was positively linked to well-being (an aspect of mental health) in countries like the United States, where religion is culturally normative. They also found that, among the mediators tested, the link between religiosity and well-being was statistically explained by factors such as social support and meaning in life. In a global sample, however, the association between religiosity and well-being was qualified by societal circumstances. Spe-cifically, people in nations with more difficult life circumstances or low "existential security"—widespread hunger, for example—were more religious, and in those particular contexts religion was associated with social support, meaning provision, and well-being. However, in nations such as the Scandinavian countries with more favorable life conditions or high "existential security," religion was not normative, and religiosity was not related to greater well-being.

The key "normativity" findings have since been replicated and extended in a larger sample of countries by Stavrova (2015; see also Zuckerman, Li, & Diener, 2018). Interestingly, Stavrova also found that the same discrepancy can be observed within the United States. In states where religion is highly normative (e.g., the southern region), religiosity was robustly positively linked to health, but that was not the case in states where religion was less culturally normative (e.g., the West and Northeast).

In view of these conclusions, it is notable that most of the religion–health (including mental health) research conducted has been undertaken in the United States on American samples, thus inevitably causing somewhat ethnocentric conclusions. No wonder then that the religion–health associations observed often seem to have questionable relevance for many European populations (cf. la Cour, Avlund, & Schultz-Larsen, 2006; Zwingmann, Wirtz, Müller, Körber, & Murken, 2006). Perhaps more in those parts of Europe than in large parts of the United States, a broader range of meaning-making systems and support functions beyond strictly religion must be taken into consideration (Ahmadi, 2006; la Cour & Hvidt, 2010).

From an attachment viewpoint, the successful implementation of welfare politics may help to keep people relatively safe and secure from alarm, thus helping to keep their attachment systems at bay (see also Chapter 11). People need not be deeply frightened by normal stressors because there is, for the most part, a safety net to fall back on. They do not need to sign a liability release when the family goes for a pony ride, so they don't interpret a pony ride as a signal of impending danger. As time passes and welfare support continues, with each new generation becoming higher in existential security and less religiously active, religious concepts and frames of reference become increasingly inaccessible, both cognitively and affectively (cf. Gruneau Brulin et al., 2018). Secularism may even reach a point where for most people there is no "religious orienting system" (Pargament, 1997) left to speak of.

The mental health of people residing in such secular welfare states can still be maintained, of course, at least insofar as they manage to fill "the gaps" that religion in dissolution has left behind (e.g., sense of community, sustainable relationships, meaning in life). If they do not manage to fill those gaps, however, they may be susceptible to some of the ailments associated with poor mental health, such as loneliness and alienation. Sadly, "even in Sweden" (to use a notorious expression from the current American president), much research indicates a spread of mental unhealth, especially in younger segments of the population (see review by Bremberg, Hæggman, & Lager, 2006). To make matters worse, further increases in vulnerability are to be expected should Swedes' lifeline, the welfare system, start to crumble. A new religious orienting system is then likely to be created from the ashes of the old, as seems to have happened in Russia following the collapse of the Soviet Union. As at the individual level, so it is at the cultural level: Religion in society is dynamic, not static.

On the alternative side of this picture, in societies that refuse to implement welfare politics, religion can continue to be of vital importance as a source of social, emotional, and material support. Even though rates of religious involvement may be declining slightly in the United States (Pew Research Center, 2015), adherence to the foundational principles of American society (e.g., the Bill of Rights, the First Amendment, the Declaration of Independence)[4] will probably continue to certify that no large welfare state, which could interfere with the individual's relationship with God, will come into existence (on civil religion, see Bellah & Hammond, 2013). By extension, religion can continue not only to be normative in society but also to serve as a facilitator of mental health.

I should acknowledge before concluding this section that my contextual analysis has been based to some degree on a "deficiency approach" to religion—first at the individual, micro level and then at the cultural, macro level. However, this analysis should not preclude the very real possibility that religion can also aid people in secure contexts to flourish more fully (cf. Park & Slattery, 2013). Indeed, religion potentially provides additional (i.e., not just surrogate) safe havens and secure bases for protection, exploration, and growth. Similarly, religion may provide a frame of reference for understanding positive, growth-related experiences, such as those of beauty, wonder, flow, "peak experiences," and awe (e.g., van Cappellen & Sarogolou, 2012). Indeed, "negative" and "positive" psychologies in general do not so much compete as complement each other, and the same applies to psychologies of religion. My reason for confining the contextual case largely to deficiencies is that I, like William James (1902), am primarily concerned with the basic requirements for avoiding serious suffering and with the potential for humans to achieve some tranquility even in the presence of serious stressors.

Aspects of Mental Health

With respect to the aspects of mental health that make a difference for the religion–mental health association, from an attachment viewpoint the benefits of religion can be analyzed in terms of having God or some other religious entity as a safe haven and a secure base, from which one can gain felt security. Felt security is in turn expressed in the domain of mental health as freedom from worry and fear and a corresponding freedom to explore. Such a "secure attachment to God" might also protect the individual against the adverse effects of other attachment-related difficulties, such as the loss of another attachment figure (e.g., a spouse).

In addition, like a secure relationship with a psychotherapist or other attachment figure, a secure attachment to God might help to repair maladaptive internal working models (IWMs) stemming from, for example, parental insensitivity or interpersonal loss. If so, the individual should regain a sense of self as being worthy of care and a representation of others as available in times of need, along with an open, nondefensive way of processing attachment-related information.

Freedom from Worry and Fear, Freedom to Explore

Having access to a safe haven gives a person the sense of being able to turn to a stronger and wiser other when he or she is alarmed and distressed. This should be accompanied by attenuated worry and fear. Having access to a secure base promotes a person's sense of personal competence and control, which enables calm and confident exploration. Jointly, these attachment functions lead to a sense of being protected. Not coincidentally, in their now classical review of research on associations between various aspects of mental health and religious orientations, Batson and colleagues (1993) concluded that the most consistent positive links had been observed between freedom from worry and fear as well as personal competence and control, on the one hand, and intrinsic religiousness (religion as a master-motive in life) on the other.

These conclusions are based on correlational findings but they were later echoed by the conclusions we drew from our subliminal experiments on Israeli theistic Jews (Granqvist, Mikulincer, et al., 2012; see Chapter 2): We found that exposure to the word "God" heightened participants' cognitive access to positive secure-base-related concepts (e.g., loving, accepting, forgiving) but not to negative, controlling concepts (Study 3). We also found that exposure to a religious symbol (the Torah Scroll) infused previously neutral material (Chinese ideograms) with study participants' positive feelings. These findings were further extended in a separate line of experiments on American and Swedish samples, demonstrating the causal effects of God-reminders on the willingness of religious believers to take exploratory risks (e.g., camping in the wilderness), presumably due to a sense of being protected by God (Gruneau Brulin et al., 2018; Kupor et al., 2015; Chapter 2 this volume). Furthermore, in both of the Israeli studies (Granqvist, Mikulincer, et al., 2012), the experimental effects were particularly notable among attachment-secure (nonavoidant) participants (Chapter 5). Although our published findings were based on assessments of romantic attachment, unpublished results from those studies indicate that attachment to God had virtually identical effects. In other words, secure attachment to God also facilitated the positive secure-base-related effects observed. Thus, research demonstrates that having God as a mentally accessible safe haven and secure base may not only *correlate* with mental health-related outcomes such as freedom from worry and fear and a sense of personal competence and control but may also *cause* religious believers, especially attachment-secure believers, to feel safe and protected, to view their surroundings positively, and to be willing to take risks in exploring those surroundings.

Reparation of Maladaptive Working Models, Resolution of Loss

Some people who have experienced parental insensitivity during childhood, who have an insecure romantic attachment orientation at present, or who have lost an attachment figure because of death may find security in their attachment to God (see Chapters 3 and 6). Although the jury is out with regard to whether such "successful compensation" promotes mental health, for example, by offsetting or buffering the negative effects of other attachment-related adversities, we have reason to expect that in such contexts security in relation to God should at least bode better for mental health than insecurity with God.

As noted, Cassibba and colleagues (2008) have suggested that religion can prevent unresolved states of loss from developing or being sustained by offering the prospect of reunion with deceased loved ones in the hereafter. Somewhat akin to delay of gratification, the prospect of reunion can attenuate the overwhelming sting of loss, as compared with the sensed permanence of loss that may characterize many nonbelievers' experiences of bereavement. Religious believers do not for the most part fail to realize that the dead person is "fully" gone; failure to do so would in fact predispose rather than prevent unresolved states of loss, as captured in the Adult Attachment Interview (AAI; Main et al., 2003). Instead, religious believers tend to grant continued *metaphysical,* rather than physical or concrete, existence to the lost person. Beyond the prospect of eventual reunion, a bereaved person's attachment to God can serve as a surrogate bond, providing the person with the sense of a dialogical partner who assists oneself in "grief work" when the principal attachment figure is gone and therefore can no longer be of assistance (cf. Brown et al., 2004).

As concluded in Chapter 6, however, "reparation of IWMs" is by no means the default outcome of a surrogate bond with God but is instead an exception to the general rule of generalizing (insecure) working models. This sobering conclusion may also apply to generalization of the segregated models that are expressed in unresolved states (e.g., "dead/not dead;" Main et al., 2003). If so, segregated models may extend to the religious and spiritual realm (Chapter 8) rather than be repaired by one's surrogate bond with God.

An important reason for the tentative nature of my discussion here, where competing possibilities have been highlighted, is that reparation of working models is very difficult to capture empirically. It would require careful prospective longitudinal investigation, for example, studies in which participants are observed to progress, over time, from insecure to secure attachment or, as in the case of bereavement, from unresolved to resolved states, specifically as a function of some aspect of religion. Although such studies are challenging and resource-demanding, researchers seeking to make a cutting-edge contribution to the literature are encouraged nonetheless to conduct this kind of research. To be even more clinically informative, such research should test whether reparation of working models forecasts improved mental health outcomes. For example, by being helpful in preventing or overcoming unresolved loss, religious beliefs may foster not only attenuated grief (Brown et al., 2004) but also recovery from associated states of depression.

Aspects of Religion

Although religion is clearly multifaceted, it has often been treated as a unitary construct, yielding simple operational definitions (e.g., church attendance, religious involvement) in religion–health research. Fortunately, considerable progress has been made in disentangling the aspects of religion that bode well, and less well, for mental health (e.g, Pargament, 2002, 2013). These aspects largely converge with expectations based on attachment theory, which is probably why Koenig and colleagues (2012) suggested that attachment to God is part of the motivation for religious behaviors and thus part of what is driving religion–health associations.

Attachment theory deals with the nature and psychological effects of a particular form of close relationships (i.e., "attachments"); with the generalization of working models of self and others stemming from such relationships; and with how people attempt to find security when distressed. Therefore, if we seek to identify attachment-related aspects of religion and ways in which religion and mental health are related, we should look in those areas.

More specifically, we should ask how a person *represents* God in relation to self, for example, as a security-enhancing attachment figure or not (cf. Mikulincer & Shaver, 2004)? Is this a relationship he or she can rely on, with God being represented as benevolent—loving, accepting, protective, responsive (i.e., as encouraging a secure attachment to God)? Or is God represented as a distant or punitive being (fostering avoidant/dismissing attachment), as one with whom the individual becomes mentally and uncomfortably entangled (resistant/preoccupied attachment), or as arbitrary and frightening (fearful attachment)?

Also, what does one *do* to gain closeness to and guidance from God? For example, does the person pray, and if so, how (e.g., contemplative/meditative or petitionary prayer; upward, inward, or outward prayer)? What does the person do when faced with stressors, such as when he or she is emotionally upset? For example, the person might engage in religious coping behaviors and have related experiences (e.g., seek spiritual support, experience spiritual connection).

Finally, are these representations and behaviors *coherent, integrated into the individual's life, flexible, and open*? For example, does the individual's experiential (episodic) and doctrinal (semantic) representations of God "hang together," and can the individual engage in metacognitive reflections about them? Or are these representational elements incoherent, rigidly organized, and defensive, as is evident, for example, in strict adherence to doctrinally prescribed rituals in order to ward off uncertainty and doubt? Similarly, although most theistic believers hold the doctrinal view that God is loving, caring, and forgiving, many of these believers have consistent difficulty *experiencing* God in those ways, particularly when they are experiencing negative states such as anxiety, depression, shame, or guilt. Such doctrinal–experiential incoherence may be based on recurring negative relational experiences earlier in life, such as with caregivers during childhood or with members of a religious group (for a fuller discussion, see Davis, Granqvist, & Sharp's [2018] depiction of healthy vs. unhealthy forms of theistic relational spirituality).

Not coincidentally, these distinctions converge with some of the most frequently used distinctions in the contemporary psychology of religion and in the literature on the religion–mental health connection (e.g., Pargament, 2002, 2013). Scholars probably make such a fuss about these distinctions because they are demonstrably important for people's mental health. Thus, as applied to the religion–mental health connection, attachment theory is useful and central for understanding people's perceived relationships with the divine, their representations of deities, and certain religious analogues to attachment behaviors, such as forms of prayer, conversions, and religious coping (see also Chapter 9).

I have mostly highlighted the potential benefits of religion so far. But just as there are aspects of religion that can promote mental health, there are also venomous aspects that can contribute to, and in some cases directly express, mental unhealth. Were they still alive, many victims of religiously motivated acts of terror would concur. A brief list of the most notable detrimental ingredients of religion includes the polar opposites of the beneficial ingredients that I have discussed, including insecure (especially fearful) attachment to God, "negative" religious coping, and spiritual struggles. From my viewpoint as a psychologist, the venomous list also includes forms of religious literalness (or fundamentalism) that create epistemic blindfolds for their adherents, closing believers' eyes to the many enriching uncertainties of life and the world. Similarly, as true as it is that a sense of community promotes mental health, overly cohesive religious communities in which like-minded individuals create narrow corridors of opinion can be suffocating for some individuals and even worse are bound to create animosity with various outgroups. Should the former groups become powerful in society, discrimination and bigotry against minorities are bound to take place. In any event, the secure mind should thrive in a context of social diversity, not homogeny.

CHAPTER SUMMARY, CONCLUSIONS, AND ADDITIONAL FUTURE DIRECTIONS

Drawing on the religion-as-attachment model, I have argued in this chapter that attachment-theoretical considerations provide insight into why contextual factors as well as particular aspects of mental health and religion matter a great deal for the links observed between religion and mental health. I have shown that contextual factors associated with heightened attachment activation (stress, other risk factors, low social welfare, existential insecurity) typically increase the strength of the observed links between religion and mental health. Also, aspects of mental health that are most notably affected by having a safe haven to turn to, such as freedom from worry and fear, as well as a secure base to depart from, such as a sense of personal competence and control, are particularly reliably linked to religion. Finally, we have seen that the very aspects of religion that are most consistently linked to mental health are those that express attachment components, including belief in a personal, loving God with whom one experiences a close and secure relationship.

Thus, attachment theory is a promising conceptual framework that captures many of the important moderators underlying the religion–mental health association. By extension, attachment theory helps us to understand why religion and mental health are connected. However, the promise of attachment theory for contributing to the literature on religion and mental health runs even deeper. This is because the evolutionary and developmental foundations of attachment theory, unlike most other theories in the field of religion and mental health, enable us to ask the big "why" questions. Importantly, individual differences in the aspects of religion that make a difference for links with mental health (one's perceived relationship with and representation of God, positive vs. negative religious coping, etc.) naturally have developmental trajectories preceding them. Those developmental trajectories, described especially in Chapters 5 and 6, should be of interest to scholars in this field because they lead to different ways of being religious, as well as to different effects on mental health. From a developmental viewpoint, understanding the religion–mental health connection remains incomplete until we understand how and why individual differences in ways of being religious develop in the first place. As an analogy for the statistically minded, what good is a regression or structural equation model that includes only the mediator/moderator (i.e., aspects of religion and context) and outcome variables (i.e., aspects of mental health) without any real predictor (i.e., developmental) variable?

The compensation and correspondence paths to religion are particularly worthwhile in this regard and should be explored further in research on religion and mental health. For example, religious individuals who are secure with respect to attachment have typically been cared for by sensitive, religious caregivers, and they also have a secure attachment to God. These individuals should naturally be predisposed to have good mental health and should be especially well "protected" from elevated levels of suffering in the face of stressors (Granqvist et al., 2014).

In contrast, attachment-insecure individuals who have been cared for by insensitive caregivers typically have a representation of and relationship with God that varies over time and situations (i.e., the compensation path). This profile is naturally more difficult to capture in relation to mental health because of apparent inconsistencies among such individuals and seemingly conflicting research findings (see Chapter 6). Concerning inconsistencies among these individuals, the compensation profile is likely to contain some of the individuals for whom religion may be most serviceable as a source of felt security. As a case in point, although the "religious syncretists" we studied (Granqvist et al., 2014) typically had insecure states of mind as assessed with the AAI and had been cared for by insensitive caregivers, they did not report elevated levels of distress at present, presumably in part because of their experience of a personal, compensatory relationship with the divine. Over time, that relationship might aid in bringing about reparation of maladaptive working models. In contrast, the compensation profile also contains individuals who have a tenuous relationship with and shy away from God. Presumably because of generalizing working models, God is represented as distant, inconsistent, perhaps even frightening. This latter group of individuals is much less likely to be protected from suffering. On the contrary, their representations of and feelings about God and religion are an additional risk factor for mental unhealth beyond their insecurity in other relationships.

In closing, I wish to note that in spite of its considerable promise for bringing clarity to the religion–mental health connection, attachment theory cannot serve as a comprehensive theory for understanding all links between religion and mental health (cf. Kirkpatrick, 2005). There are other "therapeutic" components of religion that can only partially be understood through attachment theory. Examples are the potential provision of meaning in life (see Dewitte, Granqvist, & Dezutter, 2019), social support through affiliative relationships within one's religious community, and an ethical code for how to behave and avoid the many hazardous temptations that the contemporary world has to offer.

In the end, rather than being reducible to separate "components," perhaps the main benefit of religion, as William James speculated a century ago, is the sense of unity (or integration) that may be achieved through the many different psychological, social, and cultural functions brought together by religion, centering on believers' perceived relationships with God. In comparison with this "culture of religion," contemporary culture, which is pluralistic and media driven, often works in the opposite direction: dividing our minds and selves in many directions simultaneously, and at an ever-increasing pace, potentially leaving behind a fragmented self with a wretched mind. People have called out loudly for unity in the past, and there is no reason to assume they will not continue to do so in the future. The contemporary rise of nationalism in large parts of the world may be telling signs. History does appear to be more cyclical than linear. What this means for the future of mental health and for the religion–mental health connection remains to be seen.

CHAPTER 8

Altered Spiritual States, Dissociation, and Attachment Disorganization

As in most domains of human endeavor, the history of religion reveals that the religious domain is marked by tension. Beyond conflicts over power and resources with surrounding "worldly regimes," religion itself is filled with tension between *religion* as a collectively organized institution, with a set of behavioral mandates and specific doctrines on the one hand, and *spirituality* as an individual, subjective experience of transcendence and connection on the other. Indeed, as a result of that tension, the psychology of religion has now become the psychology of religion and spirituality (Emmons & Crumpler, 1999; Pargament, 1999).

As many scholars have noted, the distinction between religion and spirituality should not be considered strictly dichotomous because the two often go hand in hand (e.g., Hill et al., 2000). In Pargament's (1999) view, religion and spirituality are interrelated ways of approaching the same target: "the sacred." Another way to say this is that people naturally seek interpretations of their spiritual experiences, and religions provide such interpretations (e.g., viewing the target as "sacred"). If religions did not exist already, they would surely emerge naturally as a response to people trying to make collective sense of their experiences, as they have done throughout history.[1]

Nonetheless, tensions between "the religious" and "the spiritual" are real. "The flames they followed Joan of Arc / As she was riding through the dark" ("Joan of Arc"; Leonard Cohen, *Songs of Love and Hate*, 1971). If the flames had not consumed her, Joan of Arc would have acknowledged these tensions, as would the many mystics in history who were executed because authorities judged their spiritual experiences as clashing with dominant religious doctrines. Incidentally, this is an example of a real cost paid for failing to conform to cultural (religious) norms. The tension between the spiritual and the religious is an important part of history, including women's history and the history of patriarchal oppression in particular.

Gnosticism ("having knowledge") and Esoterism ("belonging to an inner circle") are two concepts used to denote the countercultural movements that have emerged in association with unconventional spiritual experiences and have offered interpretations of them that fell outside or on the fringes of mainstream religion. I use the latter, more timeless concept, esoterism, in this chapter. The Western version of esoterism (Hanegraff, 1996), also known as the "mystery tradition" (Morris, 2006), refers to a wide range of loosely related ideas and movements that share two features: (1) they are not part of the orthodoxy of institutional, theistic religion and (2) they are not built on the foundations of Enlightenment philosophy (i.e., rationalism and empiricism). When viewed in that framework, esoterism is understood negatively, that is, in terms of what it is not rather than what it is. Given a more "positive" definition, esoterism emphasizes an enchanted worldview in which secret rituals and people's inner lives—their subjective, personal experiences and altered spiritual states in particular—are thought to yield higher knowledge about the world and cosmos than can be achieved by relying on religious doctrines, rationality, or empirical methods.

The list of esoteric movements and ideas is long (e.g., Kabbalah, Neo-Platonism, Theosophy, Roisicrucianism, Spiritism, Occultism, Hermetism, Modern Paganism, Wicca). I discuss two examples in more detail in this chapter because they have been subjected to attachment-based research: the New Age movement and Mysticism. The New Age movement is of interest for two reasons, and Mysticism is of interest for one of these reasons. (1) Both New Age spirituality and mystical experiences go hand in hand with "altered" spiritual states, and such altered states can be understood from an attachment–theory viewpoint. (2) The New Age movement is a key example of the transformed spiritual landscape that was bound to arise as individualist, liberal, consumerist cultures were undergoing "secularization." In that regard, tackling New Age spirituality functions as a bridge to my consideration of secularism (dealt with in Part V, Chapter 11).

My colleagues and I have always had research interests that go beyond theistic religion and the idea of God as an attachment figure. Early on, we also considered attachment in relation to more idiosyncratic spiritual dispositions (e.g., Granqvist & Hagekull, 2001). More than a decade ago, we observed that attachment disorganization was positively linked to New Age spirituality (Granqvist, Ivarsson, et al., 2007). Without knowing how to make sense of the association, we speculated that it may be "mediated by a propensity to enter dissociative/absorbing mental states" (p. 598). Going beyond New Age spirituality, we further hypothesized "that disorganization [would also be] overrepresented in members of traditional religions who undergo mind-altering experiences (e.g., mystical or 'trance' states), and that dissociation-absorption also mediates this presumed link" (Granqvist, Ivarsson, et al., 2007, p. 598). In this chapter, I consider why we made those predictions and how they have panned out.

More specifically, I argue that attachment disorganization leads to a proclivity for altered spiritual states. This is because attachment-disorganized individuals have a general propensity for dissociative mental processes, and such processes are part and parcel of what causes these individuals to experience altered spiritual states and that draws them to groups of like-minded individuals. First, I give a theoretical and empirical review of each part of the proposed mediational chain, starting with a section on attachment disorganization (the predictor) and dissociative processes (the mediator). Second, I consider how altered spiritual states (the outcome) can be viewed as expressions of dissociation and why they may have attachment disorganization as a developmental precursor. Third, in a case study section, I illustrate altered spiritual states using transcript excerpts from our pool of Religious Attachment Interviews (RAIs). Fourth and finally, I conclude the chapter by discussing extensions of the proposed mediational model to additional forms of altered spiritual states. I also discuss psychopathology in light of the proposed model and note important caveats.

ATTACHMENT DISORGANIZATION AND DISSOCIATION

In this section, I first consider attachment disorganization and then dissociation. This discussion is followed by a review of theoretical and empirical links between the two.

Attachment Disorganization

Attachment disorganization reflects a breakdown in attachment-related patterning during stress (Main & Solomon, 1990; see also Chapter 4), which may be present in both young children ("disorganized attachment," studied with the Strange Situation procedure) and adults ("unresolved/ disorganized" loss/abuse, studied with the Adult Attachment Interview

[AAI]).[2] Disorganized attachment in infants is identified by behavioral expressions, when displayed in the presence of a caregiver, such as prolonged freezing or stilling with a trancelike facial expression; display of opposing behaviours; and direct indices of apprehension of the caregiver (Main & Solomon, 1990; Chapter 4 this volume). Infants who display such behaviors in relation to their primary caregiver in the Strange Situation and who are also abused in childhood have been found to be more likely to develop unresolved states of mind with respect to abuse later in life (again, as measured in with the AAI; Weinfield et al., 2004).

Unresolved/disorganized states regarding loss or abuse are revealed in various forms of linguistic breakdowns—for example, in speech implying that a relationship partner lost through death would have input on the speaker's present-day life (i.e., as though the dead person were physically alive); by excessive details and invasion of the trauma into other (irrelevant) topics; and by psychologically confused statements implying that the traumatic event can be undone through mind manipulations (see Hesse, 2016). Such "linguistic trips" tend to occur specifically in relation to the individual's trauma-related narration. Besides being predicted by disorganized attachment in childhood and childhood experiences of abuse, unresolved states in parents have repeatedly been found to predict disorganized attachment in their infant children (van IJzendoorn, 1995; Verhage et al., 2016). Thus, beyond some continuity within an individual's lifespan, attachment disorganization tends to be transmitted across generations and largely by nongenetic transmission mechanisms (Chapter 4).

Attachment disorganization can be understood to reflect "segregated" mental processes (used as an antonym to "integrated") processes (Bowlby, 1973, 1980; Reisz et al., 2018). Such segregation is seen in mutually incompatible behaviors (e.g., "escape/approach") and mental representations (e.g., "dead/not dead"). Although segregated processes may have many causes, they can result from inescapable fear or trauma that overloads an individual's defensive repertoire so that organized responses—Main's (1990) primary/secure and secondary/insecure attachment strategies—break down. An important cause for this happening within a child's relationship with caregivers is the behavioral paradox children find themselves in when their caregivers are simultaneously the *source* of alarm (e.g., due to being abusive, frightening, or dissociative) and the only possible *solution* to alarm (i.e., because children are biologically predisposed to turn to an attachment figure when alarmed; e.g., Hesse & Main, 2006). As noted in Chapter 4, such a dilemma can create a positive feedback loop, with disorganized behaviors as a behavioral outcome and unsolvable fear as a psychological outcome (e.g., Hesse & Main, 2006).

Readers who are well versed in the psychoanalytic literature may see strong resemblances between the idea of segregated processes underlying attachment disorganization and the psychoanalytic defense mechanism of "dissociation" (though the concept of dissociation dates back to Janet's [1907] studies of trauma and hysteria). The resemblances are so strong that we have reason to suspect that these concepts refer to the same things. However, an important reason for Bowlby's adoption of the notion of segregated processes (from the ethological control systems literature) rather than dissociation (from psychoanalysis) was that segregated processes are not necessarily defensive. They can be defensive, of course, such as when an infant assumes a self-protective huddled position (an example of "anomalous posture"; Main & Solomon, 1990) under a chair during reunion with an abusive caregiver. But segregated processes can also indicate system collapse or breakdown rather than defense, such as when a child displays markedly incompatible, chaotic behaviors (Liotti, 2009).

Dissociation

Following liberation from its heritage as a psychoanalytic defense mechanism, dissociation is now more commonly used than segregated processes even in the attachment research literature. In what follows, I therefore refer to dissociation. "Dissociation" (an antonym to "association") refers to "a disruption of and/or discontinuity in the normal integrating of consciousness, memory, identity, emotion, perception, body representation, motor control, and behavior" (American Psychiatric Association, 2013, p. 291). Such disruptions and discontinuities are quite common, for example, when a person is asleep or has ingested psychedelic drugs. Sleep is a particularly good example because it is highly normative (species-typical) and is thus readily recognizable for everyone. For many hours every night, most people are unaware of what goes on around them. Their sensory organs (ears, noses, etc.) do not generally register incoming stimuli, at least not to the point of making the stimuli consciously accessible. During dream sleep, people do have sensations of things happening, but those things typically take place only in their own minds (i.e., as hallucinations). And when they finally wake up, they typically cannot remember much of anything from the preceding hours of sleep.

To make the concept of dissociation clinically useful, however, psychiatrists have felt compelled to clarify that dissociation refers to states of waking consciousness, when no drugs have been taken—that is, when a person can be expected to be in a "normal," integrated state of consciousness. In what follows, I adhere to this psychiatric convention.

Dissociation is clearly a multifaceted phenomenon. Several scholars have suggested a distinction between dissociation as "detachment"[3] and as "compartmentalization" (Cardeña, 1994; for a review, see Brown, 2006). In detached states, the individual experiences an altered state of consciousness characterized by a sense of detachment from certain aspects of everyday experience. The detachment can be in relation to one's own body (e.g., an out-of-body experience), to the sense of self (depersonalization), or to the surrounding world (derealization). Individuals experiencing detachment may report feeling "spaced out," "unreal," as though they are "in a dream" or "a fog." This brings the qualities and characters of filmmaker David Lynch's cinematic productions to mind (e.g., the *Twin Peaks* series). Compartmentalization, on the other hand, refers to a deficit in one's ability to deliberately control normally controllable processes or actions such as bringing normally accessible information to mind (resulting in selective amnesia) or to control one's body movements.

Both kinds of dissociation are sometimes aspects of serious psychiatric conditions, for example, the dissociative disorders, posttraumatic stress disorder, emotionally unstable (formerly borderline) personality disorder, and acute psychotic states marked by "positive" symptoms (i.e., hallucinations or delusions). However, there is a facet (or dimension) of dissociation that is more normally distributed in the general population: absorption. When studying samples from a normal, nonclinical population, absorption is the aspect of dissociation that is usually most worthwhile to investigate.

"Absorption," as a psychological construct, was named and conceptualized by Tellegen and Atkinson (1974). It refers to individual differences in "the disposition for having episodes of 'total' attention that fully engage one's representational (i.e., perceptual, enactive, imaginative, and ideational) resources" (p. 268). Such a disposition is commonly measured in psychological research with Tellegen and Atkinson's self-report Absorption Scale, including items such as "Sometimes I feel as if my mind could envelop the whole world" and "If I wish, I can imagine (or daydream) some things so vividly that they hold my attention as a good movie or story does." In other words, a high absorption disposition signifies that the individual is prone to having his or her attentional system fully absorbed by whatever mental processes are under execution at any given moment. That processing can be of something internal (e.g., imagination or daydreaming) or of some external stimulus (e.g., mental immersion in nature scenery). In either case, the individual loses track of surrounding stimuli beyond the object of absorption. For this reason, and because absorption is empirically associated with both other forms of dissociation and psychopathology, many scholars—including me—view absorption as a facet, albeit a mild one, of dissociation (e.g., Granqvist, Reijman, & Cardeña, 2011; Waller, Putnam, & Carlson, 1996; for a contrary position, see Dell, 2009). By subsuming absorption under the dissociation construct, I thus adopt an inclusive use of dissociation.

Naturally, states of absorption in and of themselves represent alterations in conscious experience, and as a personality disposition, absorption also predicts alterations in consciousness (Glicksohn, & Avnon, 1997; Pekala, Wenger, & Levine, 1985). More specifically, absorption is well established as a personality predictor of suggestibility and of hypnotizability in particular (e.g., Cardeña & Terhune, 2014; Cortes et al., 2018; Eisen & Carlson, 1998; Glisky, Tataryn, Tobias, Kihlstrom, & McConkey, 1991; Granqvist et al., 2005; Roche & McConkey, 1990). As an illustration, high absorption scorers more easily enter hypnotic states (Cardeña & Terhune, 2014). They have also been found to be more prone to misremember events specifically following misleading suggestions from an experimenter (Eisen & Carlson, 1999). Moreover, my colleagues and I have found in several studies that a spiritual priming and sensory deprivation setting leads high absorption scorers to report mystical experiences and anomalous somatosensory states (Cortes et al., 2018; Granqvist et al., 2005; Maij & van Elk, 2018; van Elk, 2014).

Links between Attachment Disorganization and Dissociation

The late Italian psychologist Giovanni Liotti (1992) hypothesized that infants with disorganized attachments should be prone to later episodes of dissociation because of repeated experiences in which the attachment figure has been represented in an incompatible fashion—both as alarming (perpetrator) and as the solution (rescuer) to alarm. Moreover, Liotti (2006) noted that some disorganized infants may in fact already be experiencing an altered state of consciousness in conjunction with their display of disorganized behaviors. He drew parallels to the "trance" states that can develop when multiple representations of incompatible information are produced using the so called confusion technique of hypnotic induction.[4] Disorganized attachment thus comprises two aspects of dissociation: "an unusual quality of conscious experience (i.e., a trance-like state) and the simultaneous multiple representations of aspects of reality normally construed as unitary" (Liotti, 2006, p. 58).

Main and Morgan (1996) have similarly noted that many concrete disorganized behaviors can be understood to reflect (proto-) dissociative states, such as multiple, segregated executors (Hilgard, 1977/1986). For example, a child in the Strange Situation who approaches the attachment figure upon reunion with one part of the body (e.g., left arm) while moving away with another part (e.g., right arm) acts as though the two body parts have different goals or are directed by incompatible execu-tors. Similarly, and presuming age-appropriate motor control, a toddler who smilingly hits the attachment figure hard in the face is showing a facial expression that suggests happiness but a motor behavior indicative of anger; thus, again, we have two dissociated (segregated) expressions.

Main and colleagues (2003) have also proposed that unresolved speech surrounding loss or abuse may result not just from segregated representations (e.g., "dead/not dead") but also from the individual being absorbed by trauma-related memories to such an extent that it prevents the usual monitoring of his or her discourse. This can result in unusual attention to detail, eulogistic ("funeral") speech, or visual-sensory intrusions of a traumatic event.

If these conceptual links between attachment disorganization and dissociated processes are correct, we should expect empirical research to verify that disorganization and dissociation are related. In fact, Liotti's (1992) hypothesis has been supported in two long-term lon-gitudinal studies showing that, as infants with disorganized attach-ment develop, they report a higher occurrence of dissociative states and behaviors throughout much of childhood and adolescence (Carlson, 1998; Lyons-Ruth, 2003; see also Ogawa, Sroufe, Weinfield, Carlson, & Egeland, 1997). Notably, the link between attachment disorganiza-tion and dissociation is not limited to infant disorganized attachment or to serious forms of dissociation but is present also among adults and in relation to absorption. Hesse and van IJzendoorn (1999) found direct evidence that unresolved adults score higher on the absorption scale. In that study, unresolved loss/abuse was particularly strongly linked to the item, "At times I feel the presence of someone who is not physi-cally there." That "someone" can presumably be a person lost to death, but it could also be a spiritual entity. Hesse and van IJzendoorn's find-ings have been directly replicated in at least two studies (Granqvist, Fransson, & Hagekull, 2009; Granqvist, Hagekull, & Ivarsson, 2012; Gribneau, 2006), and additional studies have supported a link between unresolved states and other aspects of dissociation (e.g., Marcusson-Clavertz, Gušić, Bengtsson, Jacobsen, & Cardeña, 2017; Thomson & Jaque, 2012, 2014).

Finally, dissociation (including absorption) is clearly determined by factors beyond attachment disorganization, probably including genes (Finkel & McGue, 1997; Pieper, Out, Bakermans-Kranenburg, & van IJzendoorn, 2011; but see Waller & Ross, 1997). It is therefore important to note that environmental determinants of attachment disorganization are also predisposing factors for dissociation. For example, the death of an important family member within a period of 2 years prior to or after a birth predisposes a person to both unresolved states and absorption (Bahm, Duschinsky, & Hesse, 2016; Hesse & van IJzendoorn, 1998).

(This is presumably because the loss has had disorganizing effects on the person's attachment figures). For another example, experiences of trauma have been highlighted as an important background factor in the development not just of attachment disorganization but also dissociation (Bruck & Melnyk, 2004; Eisen & Carlson, 1998). In sum, there is substantial theoretical and empirical evidence for a link between attachment disorganization and dissociation.

ALTERED SPIRITUAL STATES, DISSOCIATION, AND ATTACHMENT DISORGANIZATION

This section contains two major parts. In the first, I consider New Age spirituality and associated altered states (see also Granqvist et al., 2009). The second subsection considers mystical experiences (see also Granqvist et al., 2012). Although New Age spirituality and mystical experiences are empirically related (Granqvist et al., 2005; Thomson & Jaque, 2014), they are conceptually distinct, each with its own history. I deal with them separately here, both to serve didactic purposes and to do each tradition justice.

New Age Spirituality

The "New Age" movement is probably the most influential expression of esoterism in the contemporary Western world. When I refer to New Age as a "movement," I do not have a tight-knit, organized community in mind, like a New Religious movement (e.g., Scientology, Hare Krishna, the Unification Church), although several attachment studies have yielded support for the compensation hypothesis (Chapter 6) among members of New Religious movements (e.g., Buxant & Saroglou, 2008; Buxant, Saroglou, Casalfiore, & Christians, 2007; Murken & Namini, 2007). Rather, when I speak of New Age spirituality, I refer to a wide range of beliefs and activities that typically combine occultism, astrology, parapsychology, alternative (holistic, complementary) medicine, certain outgrowths of humanist psychology, and modifications of Eastern thinking imported into a Western context (Farias & Granqvist, 2007). New Agers have also been referred to as "free-lance spiritual seekers" (Buxant, Sarogolou, & Tesser, 2010).

The Subjective Spiritual Turn

At its inception, the New Age movement was viewed as "countercultural" by the hippies and other beatnik descendants of 1960s California

(Heelas, 1996; naturally, there were many predecessors, such as the New England transcendentalists and the Russian esoterists). Since the 1960s, much has changed. If we zoom out from its specific moment of birth and consider this movement on a larger time scale, we can see that it has emerged quite naturally in our culture's moves from big collective enterprises organized around official institutions (churches, science) to increasing pluralism and individualism, where the self is ultimately in charge of defining "truth," meaning, and value. The New Age movement can be considered an extreme—and almost inevitable—example or expression of this "subjective turn" in spirituality, but the New Age movement may also have further reinforced the turn. This movement helped unleash the spirit and the self from their bondage to religious doctrines (Heelas, 1996).

The subjective, spiritual shift should not be viewed as a definitive turn toward complete secularism, however. Rather, the transition reflects a transformation of the spiritual landscape, which allows it to exist more comfortably within contemporary cultures with their pluralism, consumerism, and individualism. Nonetheless, the subjective spiritual shift has emerged most rapidly in individualistic countries that are also marked by a high pace of secularization, especially the Scandinavian countries, the United Kingdom, France, and the Netherlands (e.g., Houtman & Aupers, 2007). This conclusion converges with more general findings from the World Values Survey (2018) showing that the transition from traditional values to self-expression values has gone further in these parts of the world than elsewhere, Sweden being the most extreme example. I should qualify this for American readers by acknowledging the immense diversity of the United States. For example, in coastal California, self-expression values and the New Age movement are now more or less culturally normative, but that is not true of Alabama or of the South in general.

Convergences and Divergences Between the New Age Movement and Religion

The New Age movement diverges from religion in some respects but resembles it in others. For psychology, an important difference between institutionalized religion and the New Age movement is that religion has a noncorporeal attachment figure (i.e., a theistic God) at its doctrinal center. Although the religious believer can gain felt security and other charitable qualities from centering the self on a cosmic attachment figure, it is also quite "costly" to invest in attachment relationships. Moreover, it may be questionable to do so if one represents the attachment figure as demanding, controlling, punitive, frightening, or authoritarian. In contrast to religion, the New Age movement does not typically provide an attachment figure at its doctrinal "center." If there is any doctrinal center to speak of, it is the unreserved "celebration of the self," as noted by distinguished sociologist and anthropologist Paul Heelas (1996). In the New Age movement, the individual is often viewed as possessing many of the attributes traditionally ascribed to the deity (i.e., there is an immanence focus on the "god within" rather than a transcendence emphasis). Also, the individual is free, even encouraged, to pick any ingredient suitable to oneself from the diverse set of spiritual dishes comprising the New Age smorgasboard. There are no demands but plenty of offerings, and all offerings are available to those who can afford them.

Another notable difference from religion is that the New Age movement is not societally institutionalized. This movement is loosely organized as an informal network associated with certain "eclectic" bookstores, alternative medicine centers, and "personal development" institutes. One home of the movement is the Esalen Institute (in Big Sur, California), founded in 1962, whose website offers "a world-wide network of seekers who look beyond dogma to explore deeper spiritual possibilities" (*www.esalen.org*).

With respect to resemblances with religion, the New Age movement offers certain texts (e.g., *A Course in Miracles*) that are viewed as especially enlightening and revealing of normally hidden truths about the world, cosmos, and self; certain healing and empowering rituals (e.g., liberating dance) and treatments (e.g., Reiki healing); special places with special meaning (c.g., Sedona, Stonehenge), and so on. Also, New Age spirituality is not negatively related to theistic religiousness. For example, at the individual level, New Age beliefs and experiences (e.g., in relation to extratheistic paranormal phenomena) are more or less empirically unrelated to traditional religiousness and associated beliefs (e.g., Granqvist & Larsson, 2006; Rice, 2003). For this reason, when I refer to "New Agers" (people who score high on New Age spirituality), it should be understood that some of those people are also religious by more traditional standards, whereas others are not.

Hospitality to New Age spirituality can sometimes be seen at the institutional level. At least in some cultural contexts, where the complex of secularism and self-expression values have become culturally normative, the New Age movement has even permeated traditional religious institutions. In such contexts, traditional religion is on the defensive and must adapt to survive. From a cultural evolution standpoint, death or adaptation is at stake. Consequently, the Swedish (formerly state) church, which was Lutheran, now regularly offers events and retreats devoted to Qigong, yoga, mindfulness, and several other practices that would seem to suggest that the "workshop catalogue" is offered by a New Age retreat center rather than a Lutheran church (Granqvist et al., 2014).

The New Age Orientation Scale

As a young PhD student investigating attachment–religion links in Swedish samples at the turn of the new millennium, I felt divided about my efforts. The attachment–religion topic drew my attention, but the church pews were mostly empty and had been for several decades, an early illustration of which can be found in Ingmar Bergman's film *Winterlights* (1963). Granted, many Swedes did go to church in conjunction with certain rites of passage, and most maintained nominal membership in the state church, but this appeared to be more out of cultural habit than spiritual enthusiasm. The state church ultimately (semi-)separated from the state in the year 2000, leading to further predictable drops in church participation among the largely state-loyal Swedish population (see Chapter 11). Sweden would have been a "spiritual freezer" had it not been for the spread of the New Age movement, which climaxed at the turn of the millennium (e.g., Thurfjell, 2015). To avoid becoming an incarnation of Mr. Jones in Bob Dylan's song[5]—who knew that something was happening but not what it was—I worked on a questionnaire to enable us to study New Age spirituality. This effort yielded the 22-item New Age Orientation Scale (NAOS; Granqvist & Hagekull, 2001).

The NAOS was designed to cover the conceptual diversity and heterogeneity of New Age spirituality while emphasizing its underlying principles (subjectivism, holism, syncretism, immanence, nondogmatism, personal development and spiritual focus, etc.). Sample items include: "The position of the stars at birth affects how one will live one's life or how one's personality develops"; "Spirituality to me is above all about realizing my true nature or becoming one with the cosmos"; and "Compared to most religious and nonreligious people, I am probably somewhat of a spiritual seeker with an unusually open mind." Several senior psychometric advisers and New Age scholars warned us that we would not achieve an internally consistent scale and that it might fragment into almost as many dimensions as items. Much to everyone's surprise, including our own, the studies conducted to date indicate that scale scores form one homogeneous factor (Granqvist & Hagekull, 2001) that is highly internally consistent (Cronbach alphas: .82–.97; e.g., Farias, Claridge, & Lalljee, 2005; Granqvist & Hagekull, 2001; Granqvist et al., 2005, 2007; Mörck, 2011; Rogers & Loewri, 2016; Swami, Stieger, Pietschnig, Nader, & Voracek, 2012; Swami et al., 2013, 2016). The scale has been evaluated in diverse countries, notably Sweden, Germany, the United Kingdom, and the United States, drawn from both New Age settings and the general population. Although the New Age movement is diverse at the conceptual level and many New Agers emphasize the importance of formulating "their own" philosophy of life, other New Agers apparently form "their own" philosophies of life in essentially the same manner.

Links between New Age Spirituality and Dissociation

The New Age movement is replete with activities, experiences, and beliefs suggesting that propensities for dissociation in general and absorption in particular are common. For example, one treatment practice within the movement is regression (or reincarnation) therapy, in which the client, having experienced a traumatic event that can allegedly explain his or her current difficulties, is hypnotized to reexperience a previous incarnation. The popularity of this hypnosis-based practice (Singer & Nievod, 2003) suggests that many New Agers have heightened hypnotic susceptibility. Other treatments suggesting generally heightened suggestibility among New Agers can be found in Reiki healing, Crystal therapy, and homeopathy. None of these remedies, to my knowledge, has been persuasively demonstrated to "beat" placebo treatment, and yet all are eagerly sought out within the New Age movement.[6]

Beyond alternative treatments, there are many examples of the role that dissociative processes play in New Age spirituality, such as trance states in conjunction with shamanistic drum trips or liberating dance. Out-of-body experiences are another example referenced in dissociation questionnaires (Bernstein & Putnam 1986) and may or may not signal pathological dissociation (Cardeña & Alvarado, 2014; Irwin, 2000; Waller et al., 1996). Jointly, these examples illustrate that many New Agers may be personally disposed to experience an unusual degree of dissociation. It is also notable that such states are often encouraged, produced, and subjected to affirmative metaphysical interpretations within the realm of many New Age practices (Farias & Granqvist, 2007).

With respect to empirical findings, much evidence supports a link between New Age spirituality and dissociation. Following an experimenter's deceptive suggestion of hidden patterns in a visual display of randomly distributed dots, Farias and colleagues (2005) found that participants scoring high in New Age spirituality were more inclined than others to "detect" such patterns. Also, like absorption, New Age spirituality is predictive of mystical experiences and various somatosensory states in an experimental setting that includes spiritual priming plus sensory deprivation (Granqvist et al., 2005; cf. Andersen, Schjoedt, Nielbo, & Sorensen, 2014). Both findings indicate heightened suggestibility among New Agers. Moreover, numerous studies have linked paranormal experiences/beliefs to a proclivity for dissociation (Irwin, 1994; Nadon & Kihlstrom, 1987; Sar, Alioğlu, & Akyüz, 2014). Finally, my colleagues and I have provided direct evidence for a strong association between New Age spirituality and absorption (Granqvist et al., 2009).

Attachment Disorganization as a Precursor of New Age Spirituality

We should now be able to expect that attachment disorganization is one developmental precursor of New Age spirituality. Beyond our direct finding of a link between unresolved states and New Age spirituality (Granqvist et al., 2007), several sources of evidence support such a link. For example, Main, van IJzendoorn, and Hesse (1993) found that unresolved loss/abuse is linked to "anomalous beliefs," comprising many of the central themes of New Age spirituality, such as belief in the paranormal, astrology, spiritualism, contact with the dead, ideas of possession (for a replication, see Sagi-Schwartz, van IJzendoorn, Joels, & Scharf, 2002). George and Solomon (1996) have also found that some mothers of disorganized children attribute supernatural powers to their offspring (e.g., psychic power, special connection with the dead). Moreover, of relevance to attachment disorganization, there is a robust link between paranormal experiences/beliefs and past experiences of abuse and trauma (e.g., Irwin, 1992; Reinert & Smith, 1997; Ring & Rosing, 1990; Sagi-Schwartz et al., 2003).

In sum, considerable research evidence indicates that attachment disorganization is a predisposing factor for both dissociation (including absorption) and New Age spirituality, and that dissociative processes characterize certain aspects of New Age spirituality. These findings are in line with the mediational model proposed at the outset of this chapter. However, to be fully supported, such a model requires that the link between attachment disorganization (the predictor) and New Age spirituality (the outcome) is observed *because* dissociation acts as the linking (mediating) variable.

Testing the Mediational Model

In a longitudinal follow-up of our AAI study (Granqvist et al., 2007), conducted 3 years after the first assessment, we readministered the New Age orientation scale along with the absorption scale to enable testing of the mediational model. Results supported the model (Granqvist et al., 2009). First, unresolved loss/abuse at the first assessment predicted New Age spirituality three years later. The relation between the two was small to moderate. Also, both unresolved loss/abuse and New Age spirituality were linked to absorption. Finally, when both unresolved loss/abuse and absorption were included in the same regression analysis, only absorption displayed a significant association with New Age spirituality, indicating that the link between unresolved states and such spirituality was accounted for (mediated) by absorption. Finally, formal statistical testing of mediation verified the mediational effect. These findings have since been conceptually replicated in a sample of performing artists (Thomson & Jaque, 2014).

Mystical Experiences

In mystical states, the perceived boundaries between self and the surrounding world evaporate. Beyond that, mystical experiences are often perceived as ineffable. Nevertheless, the literature has suggested several distinctions between different forms of mystical experience. Stace (1960) proposed an influential distinction between introvertive and extrovertive mysticism. Introvertive states refer to a pure, content-free consciousness, where perceptual objects "disappear," often resulting in an experience of "no-thing-ness." Extrovertive states are characterized by a sense of all objects being unified into a perception of totality or oneness with all things. This unity is often described as "God" by religious mystics, but mystical experiences do not require religious interpretations. Viewed through secular cognitive lenses, they may be interpreted as unity with "nature" (nature mysticism), with "the cosmos," or with "ultimate reality" not otherwise specified. Regardless of type and interpretation, mystical experiences are naturally characterized by markedly altered states.

Almost a century ago, Leuba (1925, p. ix), a psychologist of religion, noted:

> Experiences named "mystical" have played a conspicuous role at almost every level of culture; and yet, despite the vast literature devoted to them, the subject has remained . . . as dark as it is fascinating. . . . Mysticism has suffered as much at the hands of its admirers as at the hands of its materialistic enemies. If the latter have been unable to see anything else than aberrations and abnormalities, the former have gone to the other and equally fatal extreme; no descriptive adjective short of "sublime," "infinite," "divine" has seemed to them at all sufficient.

Although considerable time has elapsed, not much has changed since Leuba (1925) made these perspicacious remarks. Skeptics (e.g., Dawkins, 2006; Persinger, 2002) have evaluated mystical experiences as "aberrations and abnormalities," whereas believers (e.g., Newberg, D'Aquili, & Rause, 2002; Newberg & Waldman, 2010; see also James, 1902) have seen them as the work of "the divine" or "the Real." Mysticism is indeed a topic on which even great minds have been observed to get lost.[7] In keeping with my adherence to ontological agnosticism, I conclude that the unity experienced as part of a mystical state may or may not be the unity of reality.

The Empirical Study of Mystical Experiences

A variety of methods has been used to study mysticism. In psychology, empirical research has often used Ralph Hood's (1975) Mysticism Scale, containing 30 continuously scored items. To maintain openness to nonreligious interpretations, none of the items makes direct reference to God or deities. Sample items include the following: "I have had an experience in which ultimate reality was revealed to me," and "I have had an experience in which I realized the oneness of myself with all things." Research reveals that mystical experiences are relatively common in the general population. Averaging across samples, nations, and methods, Hood and colleagues (2009) estimate their lifetime prevalence to be roughly 35%. Thus, mystical experiences are not abnormalities in the statistical sense. Also, as demonstrated in Hood and colleagues' review, mystical experiences are linked to religiosity, affluence, higher education, and psychological health and thus are not aberrations in a functional sense either.

Mystical experiences have multiple causes. Research indicates a diverse set of triggers, such as religious priming, psychedelic drugs, prayer, meditation, solitude (especially in nature settings), sensory deprivation, sex, music, and unexpected stress (for a review, see Hood et al., 2009; for drug effects, see Griffiths, Richards, Johnson, McCann, & Jesse, 2006). Thus, no single determinant should be expected to explain the lion's share of variance in lifetime occurrence of mystical experiences. Nonetheless, unexpected stress is of special interest from an attachment perspective because it should activate the attachment system. Also, unexpected stress should function like the implementation of the confusion technique. For example, following a bright summer morning, the mountain hiker comes to expect a sunny day in solitude, a peaceful hike surrounded by majestic views and green trees. Suddenly there is heavy rain, thunder and lightning, skeleton trees, and wild animals in the distance. Such an alarming shift of scenery is intensely attention-alerting and humbling. When the scenery eventually calms down and the sun reappears, it may seem as if nature—or the forces that control nature—orchestrated a show for one's own eyes only.

Mystical Experiences and Absorption

Mystical experiences are absorbed states. As Hood and colleagues (2009) noted, "the wide diversity of triggers or conditions facilitating mystical experiences . . . may have in common the fact that an individual fascinated by any given trigger experiences a momentary loss of sense of self, being 'absorbed' or 'fascinated' by his or her object of perception" (pp. 354–355). Extrovertive mysticism in particular is prototypical for a state of "total attention." Consequently, personal familiarity with mystical experiences is directly referenced in one item on the absorption scale, and several additional absorption items refer to states that may or may not occur during a mystical experience (Granqvist et al., 2012). However, whereas mystical experiences are characterized by mind expansion, or a widening of attention, and by a subjective sense of fully perceiving all there is, some absorbed states are marked by a narrowing of attention. Trauma-induced "tunnel" states (i.e., a narrow, continued focus of attention), which can follow natural disasters, exemplifies this latter kind of absorption (Cardeña & Spiegel, 1993).

Not surprisingly, then, empirical research indicates that mystical experiences are moderately to strongly linked with absorption (Cortes et al., 2018; Granqvist et al., 2005; Spanos & Moretti, 1988; cf. Luhrmann, 2005; Luhrmann, Nusbaum, & Thisted, 2010). However, mystical experiences do not appear to be associated with other, more strongly pathology-related aspects of dissociation (Kroll, Fiszdon, & Crosby, 1996). This is expected because mystical states are experienced as unusually "real," whereas pathology-related states of dissociation are often experienced as "unreal" (e.g., derealization).

Attachment Disorganization as a Precursor of Mystical Experiences

Why then should we expect attachment disorganization to predispose a person to have mystical experiences, when mystical experiences are not linked to pathological forms of dissociation? My colleagues and I (Granqvist et al., 2007) made such a seemingly "risky" prediction (e.g., Popper, 1962/2014) because attachment disorganization had been related to absorption and mystical experiences represent highly absorbed states. In other words, no direct link between attachment disorganization and mystical experiences had been indicated.

However, Geels (2003) had suggested that parental loss is an important theme in the psychological study of mystics. Also, Rudolf Otto's (1925) classical characterization of the trembling terror ("tremendum") associated with some mystical experiences suggested to us a behavioral or experiential paradox that resembled Hesse and Main's (e.g., 2006) hypothesized pathway to disorganized attachment. Like an infant who loses his or her behavioral organization and enters a dissociated state when trapped in an approach–avoidance conflict with an alarming attachment figure, an adult experiencing a mystical state of the kind described by Otto is similarly both intensely fascinated with and simultaneously fearful of "the Holy" attachment figure (i.e., God). Because God is represented as terrifying, there should be no approach. Yet, because God is also represented as fascinating, in addition to omnipresent and omnipotent, there should be no escape. Such a religious analogue to an approach–avoidance conflict might trigger a dissociated "mystical" state, where one's usual sense of self is dissolved and experienced as unified with God. This speculation stems from reasoning by analogy, but it has testable consequences. Some forms of mystical experience (those marked by "tremendum") should be particularly likely to occur for individuals (1) who have repeatedly experienced approach–avoidance conflicts; (2) who possess segregated working models of others as, for example, both frightening and loving; and (3) who have developed a propensity to enter absorbed states when faced with stress.

Testing the Mediational Model

In the longitudinal follow-up of our AAI study (Granqvist et al., 2007), we included Hood's Mysticism Scale to enable a direct test of the hypothesized mediational model. Our findings supported the model (Granqvist et al., 2012). First, unresolved loss/abuse at the first assessment predicted lifetime occurrence of mystical experiences, as reported 3 years later. The relation between the two was small to moderate. Mystical experiences were also strongly linked to absorption and remained so after we omitted items from the absorption scale that risked tapping into mystical experiences. (This was done to rule out semantic overlap as an alternative interpretation of the association.)

Second, when both unresolved loss/abuse and absorption were included in the same regression analysis, only absorption displayed a significant association with mystical experiences. This indicated that the link between unresolved states and mystical experiences was mediated by absorption. Formal statistical testing of mediation verified the mediational effect. These findings have since been conceptually replicated (Thomson & Jaque, 2014).

Third, the mediational model was supported across subdimensions of the Mysticism Scale, that is, across extrovertive and introvertive states, and for mystical experiences interpreted with a religious frame of reference. Fourth, we found more consistent support for the proposed mediational model than for alternative models—for example, when New

Age spirituality was studied as mediator instead of absorption. Finally, supporting the specificity of the model, unresolved states were not linked to conventional aspects of religiousness (such as religious involvement), which were also unrelated to absorption.

Despite finding support for the mediational model when using the Mysticism Scale, it should be noted that this scale is somewhat biased in a "positive" direction. Specifically, it does not tap into mystical experiences associated with Otto's (1925) "tremendum" (fear), which may not be uncommon in the context of mystical experiences (cf. Griffiths et al., 2011). I speculate that this bias served to attenuate the strength of the relations observed between unresolved loss/abuse and mystical experiences in our study.

MRS. AND MR. RAINBOW: CASE STUDIES

I have demonstrated that attachment disorganization is linked to mystical experiences and New Age spirituality because these latter phenomena go hand in hand with altered (or absorbed) spiritual states. But what are these "altered spiritual states" actually like? For people who have themselves experienced such states, they are straightforward to recognize, but for those who have not, they may seem odd, "out there," or hard to pin down and recognize. For such readers, it may be useful to consider descriptions coming straight from the experiencers. Also, it is one thing to analyze study participants' differential responses to close-ended questionnaire items and quite another to listen to study participants' own open-ended descriptions of their experiences. Unlike the former approach, the latter can yield "thick" descriptions that more readily do justice to the individual's experience.

Our open-ended RAI provides many occasions for interviewees to describe and elaborate on their spiritual experiences and associated "local" beliefs surrounding them. In this section, I provide excerpts from four interviewees to illustrate altered spiritual states and associated beliefs. Rather than providing in-depth case studies of how these persons represent God across the full interviews, I mostly attend to the experiential states themselves and the beliefs surrounding them.

There are three common denominators among these cases that should be noted before we proceed. First, on their preceding AAI, the discourse of all four cases was judged to be primarily unresolved with respect to loss and/or abuse. This was not a prerequisite for my selection of cases used to illustrate altered spiritual states, but the most illustrative experiences simply "happened to" come from interviewees judged unresolved on the AAI, which is itself telling of an association between unresolved and altered spiritual states. Second, the altered states ahead of us clearly push or transcend the boundaries of ordinary religious doctrine; they are unique, idiosyncratic experiences that are more in keeping with the esoteric tradition than with patriarchal religion. It is probably no coincidence, then, that most of these cases happen to be women. Notably, Mr. Blue also experienced altered states (see Chapter 6), as did some other males in the study, but their descriptions were generally more restricted than those produced by female participants. In passing, women are generally no more likely than men to be unresolved on the AAI (van IJzendoorn, 1995; Verhage et al., 2016). Finally, part of what is unique about altered spiritual states (as with trauma-related states) is that they have notable sensory and visceral qualities (cf. Luhrmann, 2005; Luhrmann et al., 2010), which can be unsettling for some readers.

Ms. Purple

Ms. Purple has repeatedly suffered physical and sexual abuse from several men, including close relatives, beginning in adolescence. Not surprisingly, her discourse on the AAI was judged unresolved with regard to several abusive events and the loss of a family member. Ms. Purple was raised by parents (both judged markedly rejecting or role-reversing on the AAI) who practiced religion in her childhood. She reports early memories of being "scared of God" and notes how God in her mind became a disciplinarian "extension of a parent." She cannot recall having faith in God in childhood, adding "I don't remember nearly anything from my childhood . . . it's very fragmented really" (cf. compartmentalization).

Asked what it was about religion, if anything, that first appealed to her, Ms. Purple recalls a terrifying experience (i.e., *not* an appealing one) in early adolescence. She was on a missionary, evangelical church boat. The preacher was ranting about sin and the need to repent to be saved by God. Ms. Purple suffered a severe anxiety attack, with recurrent states of anxiety around the same theme for years to come. She continuously worried about whether she could be saved, and this anxiety affected "everything that had to do with religion."

As the interview progresses, Ms. Purple clarifies that as an adult she has developed a form of spirituality in which God is understood to be within (i.e., immanence). This has helped her overcome some anxiety problems, she says. Ms. Purple notes that she's "one of those nature–religiosity types." She believes in Buddhism, Shamanistic ideas, and Nordic mythologies, and says that "God is Cosmos and energy . . . and not this punitive male figure." With that said, she nonetheless describes how "God has started to present small animals on the road for me." She

notes how this started one night with her stopping for a road-killed animal, which was still "warm" (i.e., sensory quality). She passed a gas station, borrowed a shovel, dug a grave in a dark forest, and had a funeral
ceremony for this little animal. It continued with God placing additional
dead animals on the road for Ms. Purple. The next one in line "was pregnant, also still warm." Ms. Purple put the dead animal in her car and
buried it beside the first one. She now declares that she has a "cemetery"
in which at least five animals rest. Ms. Purple's description of these events
was prompted by the adjective "love" used to characterize her relationship with God. She describes how her funeral ceremonies represent love
on her part and how she is able to help "the souls of these animals make
the transition . . . to help them across." Ms. Purple contends that "when
they are still warm, their souls are alive." She concludes the discussion by
clarifying that this is a religious experience of love, adding, "I see these
animals, and when I die they'll sit and welcome me."

Beyond the sensory qualities suggested by reference to "warm,"
"pregnant," "dark forest," and "seeing" these animals, the events
recounted do not refer to altered states per se but simply a religious experience of love surrounded by an idiosyncratic belief system, according
to which God places dead animals on the road so that Ms. Purple can
practice love. God's agentic qualities here are notably at odds with Ms.
Purple's prior reference to God as merely immanent, possibly indicating
an incoherent (segregated) representation of God.

Asked about fear and worry, Ms. Purple returns to her teenage expe
rience of "fright," after which she had "20 years" of "anxiety towards
all kinds of religion." Ms. Purple says she did not "have an active relationship at all during those years," but "the seed" of a relationship with
God remained, and she locates it anatomically: "On the left side, here it
is." This anatomical location of her relationship with God gives immanence a new and quite literal dimension, and it again suggests a highly
idiosyncratic belief system.

The RAI also includes a question about experiences of feeling
threatened by God or other religious entities. When asked that question,
Ms. Purple's speech collapses, "ff vvvv . . . eemmmmmm ffffff." She
winds up saying that God was not ever threatening, although her mom
kept her in line by appealing to her fear of God. Asked about her current
relationship with God, Ms. Purple says: "It's like a close friend." She
expresses happiness about having grown out of fear, and yet she adds,
"It sometimes comes back." When it does, Ms. Purple says to herself,
"Hello, this is not now, this was this *is* then" (present tense lapse italicized). She ends by describing how she goes a "bit nuts" hearing a particular song that she heard on the boat as a teenager that anxiety-stricken
day; so she has to "shut it off." It appears that Ms. Purple is trying hard

to distinguish her own representation of God from the God that her parents offered her, but sadly she does not seem to succeed; fear is still present and actively disorganizing. If a person's representation of God is formed by integrating the God offered by the person's culture (including family members) with the person's generalized working models, we can see why it is difficult for Ms. Purple to shake off a representation of God as threatening and frightening (cf. Rizzuto, 1979).

Ms. Purple repeatedly states that the acts of abuse she's endured were "meant" to happen. She attributes intentionality to God and the cosmos, and says the abuse experiences made her into what she is now, "a helper." At the same time, she also expresses being upset that God allowed abuse to happen to her, and she sensed no reassuring presence of God during the frightful events. Nonetheless, Ms. Purple represents God as someone who intends for her to experience severely traumatizing events so that she will be able to help others. Although the theme of holy female martyrdom has a long and troubling history, extending from the holy books, through Dostoyevsky's *Crime and Punishment* to the contemporary movies of Lars von Trier, it does not help women overcome the unresolved states inflicted on them by male perpetrators.

At the very end of the interview, Ms. Purple acknowledges the negative effects of the religion she was exposed to during her upbringing. She also describes recent conversations with her aging mother, in which Ms. Purple initiated discussions with her about a "form of religion that is much more benevolent." Her mother had not known much about such a religion, but they have started to talk about it. With the abusive male presence now gone from their lives, there is hope for Ms. Purple and her mother.

Ms. Pink

Unlike Ms. Purple, Ms. Pink grew up with good parents and was not abused. Her primary unresolved/disorganized classification on the AAI with respect to the loss of a relative was assigned based on a score that just reached the threshold for that category. Ms. Pink was assigned a secondary secure/autonomous classification on the AAI.

Early in her RAI, Ms. Pink says, "I have had one of these spiritual experiences in my life, which was clear beyond the inexplicable." She notes that it has happened only once, almost 10 years prior to her RAI, and that "it's fading, which is a sorrow." However, Ms. Pink adds that she has not completely "separated from" the experience, which has had a lasting influence. This is often the case with mystical experiences, even if they are induced by psychedelic drugs (Griffiths et al., 2011, 2018; Schmid & Liechti, 2018). Ms. Pink reports that her experience occurred when a grandmother, with whom she had not had an especially close relationship, was dying. The grandmother had been ill for some time, but her death was not imminent:

> "I woke up in the middle of the night . . . and feeling that I should pray for her to die and I felt it was God or something who called on me to do so because . . . she had a hard time. . . . Suddenly I saw how my grandmother, from having been a thin old woman— she somehow looked like a small bird when she lay there in bed— became this middle-aged stylish woman she was when I was young. It was clear, she wore a red suit and heavy black shoes and held a beige handbag, and she walked along a paved path with grass on both sides, and then a Jesus character stood at the front, with open arms like you see in pictures, with this white ankle-length clothing and sort of welcomed her at the front. And she looked proud and somewhat triumphant when she walked along that road. Then I fell asleep and . . . in the morning, my mum calls and I tell her I know that you are calling to tell me my grandmother has died, and in fact she had died during the night, and so it was a very strong experience for me.

Ms. Pink's night-time precognition experience was remarkably concrete and sensory in quality. It is clear that she is not referring to a dream, for she woke up before the experience and fell asleep after it. Later in the interview, she refers back to this experience saying, "I feel immensely grateful to God for getting this . . . present that I could be a part of it and help." Ms. Pink explains that she is referring to God receiving her prayers so that she could help her grandmother "feel safe when she was about to enter the other side." Ms. Pink also expresses gratitude that her experience enabled her to "truly meet" her grandmother once while alive. Asked whether this experience has impacted her view of God, Ms. Pink answers in the affirmative, noting that this was "quite a radical experience in my life . . . which made God a lot more real to me, and my relationship with God somehow turned physically serious . . . it meant a lot." Later in the interview, when probed about after-life beliefs, Ms. Pink refers back to the experience, saying that "this must have been God's way of trying to pass something on to me."

In sum, Ms. Pink's transformative precognition experience of her grandmother's death clearly represented an altered state occurring somewhere between sleep and wakefulness. The experience was subjected to a theistic religious interpretation, where Ms. Pink was not only called upon by God to pray for her grandmother but was also causal in helping her make the transition to the other side. This experience continues to feel undeniably real to Ms. Pink. Though the experience was dissociative (markedly imaginal; Cardeña, 1994), it contained no pathology-related components of derealization or fear. In Hilgard's (1977/1986) terms, it can be viewed as a "reaggregating" rather than "disaggregating" example of dissociation. This may itself be telling of Ms. Pink's underlying secure/autonomous state regarding attachment.

Mr. Orange

Mr. Orange was judged unresolved on the AAI with respect to the loss of a grandparent who had acted like a substitute mother to him. Unlike Ms. Pink, Mr. Orange's secondary classification was insecure/preoccupied, and his attachment history with parents was much less favorable. Mr. Orange was not raised in a religious home but nonetheless experienced God "in nature" as a child. As though he were an incarnation of bird-tending St. Francis, "I made my own altar under the trees at home, in the garden . . . and there I could sit for hours."

Asked about personal tragedies, Mr. Orange refers to a markedly stressful part of his life, noting: "seriously ill," "difficult time," "many tragedies in my family," "roughed up physically and worn out." To make matters worse, in that context Mr. Orange experienced an unexplained loss, the loss that also caused his speech to break down in the AAI.

When recovering from this period of turmoil, Mr. Orange studied "the archangels" because someone had suggested it. Like Ms. Pink, one night he woke up:

> "I felt a very strong presence from something—and there was like a rain of light in the entire room. It was—like when one shoots fireworks, and this came down like rain in some kind of—dome shape. . . . There were big balls of light all over the room . . . I know I was lying with my eyes shut and opened them several times to see if it had disappeared, but it was still there."

Mr. Orange thus describes a dissociative state (hallucinations of a dome-shaped rain of light), and his experience follows on intense stress, unexplained loss of an attachment figure, and spiritual priming (i.e., reading about archangels). As with Ms. Pink, Mr. Orange's experience was positive ("unbelievable energy") and not in any way frightening.

Beyond this altered state, Mr. Orange refers to having experienced "some of my previous lives during meditation," which he associates with his "reincarnation beliefs."[8] He also expresses the belief, common within New Age circles, that a person somehow chooses his or her parents and yet nonetheless declares that those who are more spiritually developed are somehow assigned to harsher childhoods. In addition, Mr. Orange holds supposedly Christian (Lutheran) beliefs. In sum, the belief systems associated with Mr. Orange's altered states are not only idiosyncratic but also syncretistic and segregated.

Finally, Mr. Orange openly acknowledges the protective and defensive nature of his spirituality. He notes, "If I hadn't had this faith in God, then I wouldn't be alive today . . . had I been an atheist, then I would not have been able to endure life."

Ms. Turquoise

Ms. Turquoise provided a fascinating set of interviews. Although she was judged unresolved (like Ms. Pink, she just barely reached the threshold) with respect to the loss of a relative, her AAI was on the whole notably coherent and balanced, which was surprising because she had experienced attachment adversities with her mother. Ms. Turquoise's RAI was consistent on both scores. On the one hand, she reported notable altered spiritual states. On the other, her discourse was highly coherent. She consistently represented God as a benevolent, reparative, and growth-promoting attachment figure and cited numerous examples from her life where the sensed presence of God helped her to feel comforted and to overcome fear and trauma.

Ms. Turquoise did not grow up in a religious family but nonetheless attended Sunday school, where she felt estranged from the way God was presented. However, she has had spiritual experiences for almost as long as she can remember, but she did not interpret them within a religious frame of reference ("God") until much later, well into adulthood.

When asked to provide five words to describe her relationship with God, she gives five words that refer to her first influential spiritual experience, in early childhood: "light," "round," "soft," "peace," and "blood." This experience occurred in the context of a serious car accident, which left two relatives severely injured (and permanently debilitated) but Ms. Turquoise almost untouched. This is how she describes that experience, starting with "light":

> "I was walking in a ball of light, a bit like walking in a balloon that's filled with light. . . . I crawled out of the car, no one knew that I was there. . . . I walked into the forest and this was in mid-December, late at night, so it was dark in the forest, and I didn't have shoes on, and I went around in this forest. . . . Many years later in a retreat this comes back. I walked in a ball that was filled with light and then I saw my feet that didn't have shoes, so it was dark outside but I saw the ground and I wasn't scared. It was also a taste of

blood because I bit my tongue so that it was a special taste that was associated with that experience and precisely that light balloon. . . . I never understood throughout my childhood what that was, but during the retreat I woke up in the night and felt that, the taste, and then some night after that this came back, this feeling of walking in this light-balloon and then it was clear to me what it was about."

Like Mr. Orange's experience, Ms. Turquoise's experience is marked by light, this time in the form of a round balloon pattern. The taste of blood, the repeated "dark," and the sight of her feet add additional sensory qualities to her memory. Asked about "soft," Ms. Turquoise continues:

> "Because everything was soft where I walked, there were no stumps, there were no stones, I was walking in the forest and I had no shoes on but just wool socks and still everything was so soft it was like I was walking in cotton in some way. It must evidently have hurt my body because I had bruises absolutely everywhere later, but no injuries."

Following additional probing, Ms. Turquoise reports that she felt no pain ("no, nothing"), just "peace," "light," "stillness," and "security." She adds, "I walked there like really for an hour and a half," which is a considerable bout of time for a young child who has just experienced a terrifying accident. Further probes and answers indicate that this accident did happen and that Ms. Turquoise was indeed on her own in the forest for an extended period of time. Of course, whether her adult memory of how the experience felt is veridical with her childhood experience is impossible to determine, but it is clear that Ms. Turquois's memory describes a partly dissociative state. Nobody of sound mind who has walked a dark Swedish winter forest at night, lost in the forest, all alone, and with no shoes on, would describe the experience as soft, light, peaceful, and cotton-like. Her mind state clearly deviates from what one would expect in that situation.

Reminded that I was asking about her relationship with God, Ms. Turquoise clarifies that she felt "protected" and "guided" during the traumatic event. As an adult, she now attributes those feelings to God carrying her through the event. When asked for a few additional words to characterize her relationship with God at present, Ms. Turquoise uses the term "all-encompassing," which she exemplifies as being on a train and sensing God "in the train tracks and the steel plate," "in stones," "in absolutely everything." With such an uncompromising pantheistic sense, Ms. Turquoise clearly pushes the boundaries of formalized theistic belief systems.

Beyond her trauma-inflicted altered state in childhood, Ms. Turquoise recounts multiple spiritual experiences later in life, including premonitions ("I have sometimes known what will happen just before it has happened") and "a divine experience." She describes the divine experience in some detail. She was lying on the floor in a retreat room, on her own, first noting that her "bodily functions were weakening . . . and so I stopped breathing." She continues:

> "I felt I wasn't there in that room, I was in another environment. . . . I was taking part in a very deep community. I think that I understood why the church altar is only a half circle and where the other half is."

Ms. Turquoise reports that the community with which she was mentally congregating was one of "dead people." On another occasion, lying on a church floor with a woman "with great mental ailments," Ms. Turquoise had another profound experience. She held the other woman; "much guilt and shame came out of her," she noted, adding that "it was like a labor that this woman was doing." To Ms. Turquoise it felt like they were there for 5 minutes, but in truth they were there for several hours. Beyond the time lapse she experienced, Ms. Turquoise "felt in my stomach it sort of contracted itself a bit like when one gives birth," indicating that "labor" is understood not just as metaphorical.

Experiences like these might seem frightening, but they were not frightening to Ms. Turquoise, who felt "safe" and "guided" by God through them all. Asked if and how religion has affected her, Ms. Turquoise acknowledges that it has affected her "very much." She's "much less scared of people now than before," she says, which she again attributes to her relationship with God, providing her with a sense of "deep acceptance" of who she is as a person, "and that foundation gave me a security that I could meet other people."

In sum, Ms. Turquoise possesses a coherent representation of a benevolent God *and* simultaneously describes multiple altered spiritual states. Notably, metacognitive elaborations are absent in much of her interview, which is striking because the interview is internally consistent and at the same time many of Ms. Turquoise's (dissociative) spiritual states are so extreme. One might normally expect a coherent speaker recalling such experiences to provide elaborations—for example, "another way to describe my experience is as a trauma reaction." It should be recalled, however, that whereas some pathology-related dissociative states are experienced as unreal and troubling (e.g., derealization), many spiritual/mystical experiences are felt to be unusually real, and on top of that they tend to be personally transformative. Sensing that one is in direct connection with ultimate reality is a powerful experience. Therefore, difficult as it might be, we need to recognize that metacognitive elaboration may be especially hard to produce around such experiences.

My understanding of Ms. Turquoise is that her early untoward experiences, first with her mother and then the car accident, made her prone to dissociative states. For some reason—whether through reparative extraparental relationships, "constitutional" resilience, and/or massive production of endorphins—Ms. Turquoise was able to experience "dissociative calm" rather than overwhelming fear in conjunction with the car accident. Relatedly, she has been able to retain the sense that her core self is good and protected, without getting rigidly defensive (avoidant, preoccupied). Ms. Turquoise's developmental trajectory takes her through multiple dissociative experiences, which are always attributed to a benevolent God that is somehow "talking to her," and so it is that Ms. Turquoise achieves a sense of reassurance where others would be frightened. On the whole, the case of Ms. Turquoise is almost a perfect illustration of successfully using God as an attachment surrogate. Ms. Turquoise could just as well have wound up as chronically fearful, mentally disintegrated, and psychotic, yet she is none of those. God is clearly her solution to fear and is by no means a source of fear.

CONCLUSIONS: ALTERED SPIRITUAL STATES ARE NOT NECESSARILY "PATHOLOGICAL"

The central argument for which I have provided empirical evidence in this chapter is that attachment disorganization predisposes a person to altered spiritual states, via a general proclivity among attachment-disorganized individuals to experience dissociative alterations in consciousness. In this concluding section, I elaborate on the conclusions that can and, perhaps more importantly, cannot be drawn from this argument and its associated empirical evidence. First, the fact that attachment disorganization predisposes a person to altered spiritual states does not mean that such disorganization is the only cause or developmental trajectory leading to altered states. It would be illogical, therefore, to conclude that someone who has experienced an altered spiritual state must be or has been disorganized. In fact, my colleagues and I neither expected nor observed a strong relationship between the two. Our AAI study indicated small to moderate associations between unresolved loss/abuse on the one hand and both New Age spirituality and mystical experiences on the other, statistically explaining roughly 5% of the variation in the outcomes (Granqvist et al., 2009, 2012). Many important pathways to altered spiritual states are thus likely to be independent of attachment disorganization, as is also evident in some of their correlates (e.g., gender, education level; Farias & Granqvist, 2007; Hood et al., 2009). Considering that both New Age spirituality and mysticism are first and foremost part of a historically and societally shaped esoteric movement, it could be viewed as surprising that a developmental, psychological factor makes any contribution at all.

Within the larger framework of attachment-related individual differences, it is similarly notable that people who are "organized" with regard to attachment may also experience altered spiritual states, even if they are somewhat less likely to do so than attachment-disorganized individuals. For example, our AAI study indicated that almost 50% of our mostly religious/spiritual study participants with an organized classification on the AAI reported some mystical experience, compared with 75% of those with an unresolved classification (Granqvist et al., 2012). With respect to New Age spirituality, we have also observed that, like unresolved individuals, preoccupied individuals tend to outscore secure and dismissing ones (Granqvist et al., 2007). Preoccupied individuals may be drawn to the New Age movement for reasons other than altered states, however. For example, the New Age movement provides both "encounter" groups, in which participants can release preoccupying anger against "toxic" parents, and "self-help" literatures that can be consulted to regain self-worth and self-esteem. (For converging attachment self-report studies, see Buxant et al., 2010; Saroglou, Kempeneers, & Seynhaeve, 2003.)

I realize that the theoretical model proposed here and the supportive empirical evidence I have reviewed may appear discouraging for individuals who have experienced personally meaningful, potentially life-changing spiritual experiences. Relatedly, although I have attempted to be appropriately nuanced (see especially the case of Ms. Turquoise), my analysis may appear to "pathologize" altered spiritual states because I have viewed them as absorbed/dissociative states and have also linked them to attachment disorganization, which is a risk factor for maladaptive development. However, appearances should always be treated with caution, and in this case that warning strongly applies. First, whether absorption is a true example of dissociation is debatable (e.g., Dell, 2009). Granted, I hold that it is, but I have also clarified that it is a mild example of dissociation and is not strongly related to psychopathology (cf. Waller & Ross, 1997). As an analogy, and psychiatric conventions aside, I have pointed out that mind states during ordinary sleep are dissociative but far from pathological. Second, as noted, mystical experiences do not appear to be associated with pathological dissociation or with psychopathology in general (Granqvist et al., 2012; Hood et al., 2009; Kroll et al., 1996; Wulff, 2014).

Furthermore, the fact that attachment disorganization is a general risk factor for maladaptive development does not imply that everything related to such disorganization is inevitably maladaptive. To be clear: I do not view altered spiritual states as necessarily maladaptive. There is a need for psychologists, and attachment researchers in particular, to begin studying whether attachment disorganization might actually confer some advantages, to some individuals, in some contexts. Almost 30 years have passed since the field of attachment started engaging with attachment disorganization (Main & Solomon, 1990), and yet as far as I am aware, a "negative" focus has permeated each and every treatise on the matter. This is especially peculiar considering that rates of attachment disorganization are so high in the normal population around the world (roughly 15–20%; van IJzendoorn et al., 1999; Verhage et al., 2016). Why is disorganization so prevalent if there is nothing to be said for its potential functionality? And why are disorganized responses so easily induced (Granqvist et al., 2016)? (See similar questions about anxious and avoidant attachment in Ein-dor, Mikulincer, Doron, & Shaver, 2010.)

In the context of religion and spirituality, a disorganization-related propensity for alterations in consciousness may be advantageous in that it promotes "unity" experiences (e.g., mystical experience). Such experiences may in turn be conducive to adaptive life transformations, for example, following intense turmoil and other unsuccessful attempts at self-regulation (e.g., through opioids). Thus, rather than representing pathology, mystical experiences may enable some individuals to stay off the path leading to psychopathology. Notably, this line of reasoning echoes James's (1902) century-old ideas about self-surrender at the peak of the sudden religious conversion experiences of some "sick souls," which may often be succeeded by a unification of their previously divided selves.

Outside the context of religion, altered spiritual states (e.g., nature mysticism, unification with the cosmos, psychedelic trips) may also be emotionally profound and personally meaningful experiences with long-lasting positive consequences (Griffiths et al., 2006, 2008, 2011, 2018). However, I speculate that in the presence of attributions to an all-loving, all-nurturing attachment figure (God) as the source of the unity experienced, and in the presence of a "holding" social group (such as a religious or spiritual community), mystical experiences are even more likely to be beneficially life-altering and self-reparative.

Naturally, a self-reparative function of altered spiritual states does not rule out the possibility that such experiences may have destructive effects on some individuals in some contexts. Like the effects of psychedelic drugs (Griffiths et al., 2006), mystical experiences may involve a pervasive state of anxiety and fright. "The horror! The horror!" as Colonel Kurtz whispers while dying and gazing into the heart of darkness (Conrad, 1899/2014). Such destructive effects may be particularly likely for troubled individuals who have suffered abuse from attachment figures and consequently possess working models of others as frightening. The case study of Ms. Purple supports this idea, indicating that it was hard to shake off a representation of God as frightening. Beyond primary unresolved status on the AAI, she had an underlying insecure classification. In contrast, an underlying secure state of mind (see Ms. Pink and Ms. Turquoise) may be conducive to altered states experienced singularly as comforting and reparative.

Regarding future research, we need studies based on long-term prospective longitudinal designs, preferably starting in infancy, with observations of disorganized attachment and intervening life events leading up to the experience of altered spiritual states later in development. Such studies would enable inferences concerning causal direction to be established much more clearly than we were able to do in the short-term longitudinal study we conducted to test the mediational model (Granqvist et al., 2009, 2012; see also Thomson & Jaque, 2014).

Beyond mystical experiences and New Age spirituality, religions and spiritual communities may foster other experiences associated with alterations in consciousness to which the mediational model discussed in this chapter may or may not apply. Research should be conducted, for example, on glossolalia ("speaking in tongues"), healing, and baptism of the spirit during Pentecostal services (Luhrmann, 2005; Luhrmann et al., 2010); trance experiences in conjunction with chanting; the sense of being in contact with the deceased during spiritualist sessions; and feelings of being possessed by spiritual entities (Schaffler, Cardeña, Reijman, & Haluza, 2016). Although such states may be normative and highly cherished within the confines of a specific religious/spiritual community, or within some cultural setting (such as Haitian voodoo culture), the members who most readily enter them may nonetheless tend to be disorganized (like Mr. Blue, Chapter 6). Other, attachment-organized members may have to struggle more to "receive the holy spirit" (like Mrs. Green, Chapter 5).

CHAPTER SUMMARY

In this, chapter, I moved beyond theistic religiousness and the idea of God as attachment figure to examine spiritual expressions in esoteric movements. More specifically, I argued that attachment disorganization leads to a proclivity for altered spiritual states, via a general propensity for dissociative mental processes. I provided a theoretical and empirical review of each part of the proposed mediational model, and I presented empirical evidence indicating that the model is applicable to New Age spirituality and mystical experiences. In a case study section, I gave "thick descriptions" of altered spiritual states using transcript excerpts from four study participants interviewed with the RAI. I concluded the chapter by discussing psychopathology in light of the proposed model as well as possible extensions to other altered spiritual states.

PART IV

POINTS OF CONVERGENCE AND DIVERGENCE

Although Part III made clear that attachment-related processes and relationships have wide implications for theistic religion and for nontheistic expressions of spirituality, attachment theory itself has reasonably well-defined conceptual boundaries (see Chapter 1). Therefore, the theory cannot serve as a comprehensive (or exhaustive) psychology of religion and spirituality. Attachment theory is an important *midlevel* theory within a larger psychological science of religion and spirituality. Thus, other theories and perspectives are required if we wish to attain a fuller psychological grasp of religion and spirituality.

In this part of the book, Part IV, I consider how attachment theory stands in relation to other theories and perspectives within the psychological sciences of religion and spirituality. Chapter 9 deals with attachment theory in relation to other theories and conceptual approaches within mainstream psychology of religion as well as psychoanalytic understandings of religion. But much of the recent progress in the psychological study of religion has been undertaken not within psychology's mainstream or within psychoanalysis but, rather, within evolutionary and cognitive science, and (to some extent) neuroscience. Therefore, in Chapter 10, I address how the attachment–religion connection fits within a larger evolutionary, cognitive neuroscience of religion. As you will see, not only does this connection fit very well, but it may also serve as a fruitful heuristic template for improvements of other theories within that larger literature.

CHAPTER 9

Attachment Theory
and the Psychology
and Psychoanalysis of Religion

Many of the foundational ideas expressed in this book are hardly new. For example, many decades prior to Bowlby's attachment theory, Feuerbach (1854) and Freud (e.g., 1913/2013, 1961a, 1961b) asserted that people's representations of God reflect projective mechanisms; that is, these representations are constructed from people's self- and parent-related mental representations. Although Feuerbach and Freud had limited systematic empirical evidence for their assertions, later research has provided compelling evidence to support them (e.g., Epley, Converse, Delbose, Monteleone, & Cacioppo, 2009). Outside the confines of psychoanalysis, multiple frameworks within psychology have pointed to important psychological functions of religion, whether based on theories of coping (Pargament, 1997), terror management (e.g., Vail et al., 2010), self-regulation and self-control (McCullough & Willoughby, 2009), attribution (Spilka, Shaver, & Kirkpatrick, 1985), or meaning-making (e.g., Paloutzian & Park, 2013).

Why, then, is the attachment–religion approach needed? For two principal reasons. First, attachment theory provides a valuable developmental anchor for many other psychological approaches to religion and spirituality in adulthood. I deal with these in the first major section of this chapter. Second, attachment theory has a number of scientific strengths compared to psychoanalytic theories. I delineate these in the second major section of this chapter.

ATTACHMENT AND OTHER THEORIES
IN THE PSYCHOLOGY OF RELIGION

In this section, I discuss theories of religion that have some overlap with attachment theory—specifically, religious coping theory, terror management theory, and theories concerning self-regulation/self-control, meaning-making, and attribution. All of these provide valuable companions to the attachment–religion approach.

Religious Coping and Attachment

The development of the concept of religious coping is revealing with respect to the bias of mainstream psychologists against matters of religion (see the Prologue and Epilogue of this book). In the 1980s and 1990s, several influential coping studies (e.g., Bjorck & Cohen, 1993; Folkman & Lazarus, 1985; McCrae & Costa, 1986), using open-ended questions about what people do when faced with stressors, revealed the prevalence of religious responses, such as "pray to God," "ask the Lord for guidance." In some studies, religious responses were more prevalent than any other class of responses. There was a real problem in making sense of such responses in view of the coping dimensions that were under consideration at the time. Religious responses were ultimately not labeled "problem-focused" because in the minds of the researchers, they seemed to escape the problem rather than deal with it. For lack of a better fit, they were instead placed under the rubrics "emotion-focused" and "avoidance" coping (see Carver, Scheier, & Weintraub, 1989; Pargament, 1997).

Since then, Pargament (e.g., 1997) has programmatically developed theory and research pertaining specifically to religious coping. Based on general appraisal and coping theory (e.g., Lazarus & Folkman, 1984), Pargament argues that people possess a religious orienting system (cf. religious schema; McIntosh, 1995) that can potentially be activated by "stress" (i.e., various situations that tax an individual's available resources) and aid them in coping with it, thus potentiating adjustment. For example, some 90% of Americans turned to religion for solace or support following the 9/11 terrorist attacks (Schuster et al., 2001), an event that, ironically, was itself religiously motivated (e.g., Jones, 2008; Juergensmeyer, 2017). Whether religious coping promotes or hinders adjustment hinges partly on the individual's particular coping responses. Accordingly, Pargament, Smith, Koenig, and Perez (1998) have identified "positive" and "negative" religious coping styles.

Positive religious coping is characterized by dimensions such as religious forgiveness, search for spiritual support (reassurance and love from God), collaborative coping (in which the person senses that he or she solves problems together with God), spiritual connection, and benevolent religious reappraisals (when a person reinterprets seemingly negative events in positive terms, such as deepening his or her relationship with God). Not surprisingly, positive religious coping tends to benefit people undergoing stressful life events and is associated with lower levels of depression, anxiety, and hopelessness (e.g., Ano & Vasconcelles, 2005; Pargament, 1997; Smith et al., 2003).

In contrast, negative religious coping is represented by spiritual discontent and struggles and perception of God as punishing (e.g., "God gave me this disease") or demonic reappraisal of the stressful event (e.g., "evil forces at work"; Pargament et al., 1998). Negative religious coping is associated with maladjustment to stress and with higher levels of depression and anxiety (Ano & Vasconcelles, 2005; Pargament, 1997).

Although Pargament (1997) has suggested that religious coping often acts as a mediating variable linking stress to adjustment (positive coping) or maladjustment (negative coping), religious coping strategies can also be viewed as outcomes of adjustment to stress in their own right. To illustrate, some people are more able to sense a "spiritual connection" than others, who may in turn have a proclivity to sense evil forces at work. Relatedly, religious coping responses are likely to reflect the individual's initial levels of psychological adjustment and maladjustment even prior to a stressful event. As Pargament also acknowledged, the particular religious coping responses employed are presumably nested within developmental trajectories already in motion.

A person's attachment history and experiences of religious modeling from caregivers and others are likely of key importance. Accordingly, in one of my own studies, I found that, among individuals from nonreligious homes, people with a perceived insecure attachment history who were on the religion-as-compensation pathway (see Chapter 6) were especially inclined to use religious coping when faced with stress (Granqvist, 2005). That study showed that strength of religious coping (regardless of type) statistically mediated (explained) the relation between an insecure attachment history and a generally compensatory use of God and religion. In other words, religious believers with an insecure attachment history use religion as a compensatory means to cope with stressful life events. Also, unpublished findings from our Adult Attachment Interview (AAI) religion study (Granqvist, Ivarsson, et al., 2007) have shown that secure/autonomous attachment discourse and probable experiences with loving parents are related to positive religious coping.

Beyond parent-related attachment, romantic attachment-related avoidance has been linked to low scores on positive religious coping dimensions, and romantic attachment anxiety has been linked to high scores on negative religious coping (Pollard, Riggs, & Hook, 2014; see also Schottenbauer et al., 2006). Similarly, studies by Pargament and others have shown that attachment to God predicts religious coping. For example, Belavich and Pargament (2002) found that secure attachment to God was predictive of positive religious coping with a loved one undergoing surgery, which in turn predicted the individual's postsurgery adjustment (see also Kelley & Chan, 2012). Also, within an extensive artillery of predictive measures, Ano and Pargament (2013) found that anxious attachment to God, along with neuroticism and a more negative appraisal of a stressful situation, predicted unique variance in spiritual struggles (a facet of negative religious coping; see also Cooper, Bruce, Harman, & Boccaccini, 2009; Davis et al., 2008).

Positive religious coping has even been thought to presuppose, or at least involve, a secure relationship with God, whereas negative religious coping has been seen to involve an insecure relationship with God (Paloutzian, 2017; Pargament, 2002; Pargament, Feuille, & Burdzy, 2011). If this is true, there may be a certain measure of conceptual overlap between attachment to God and religious coping, which should be teased apart in future research.

As this brief review illustrates, the attachment–religion approach generally makes a good partner with religious coping theory and research. Coping research has often documented how religious individuals turn to God as a highly personal relational partner in times of stress, particularly stress related to threats (e.g., danger) and loss (e.g., death of a loved one; Bjorck & Cohen, 1993; McCrae, 1984). These are the very types of situations that should activate the individual's attachment system. Also, such use of God as a coping response seems to work over and above the effects of "secular coping" and affiliative relationships in the religious group and elsewhere (e.g., Rokach & Brock, 1998; Schottenbauer et al., 2006).

Although by no means replacing coping theory itself, attachment theory provides an important explanation of why religious coping is used particularly in some situations (i.e., situations that are attachment-relevant) and of why God is perceived to be so helpful in these situations (i.e., God is used as an attachment figure). Attachment theory also provides complementary explanations of religious coping of a more distal type, both because of its grounding in evolutionary considerations and because of the ability of attachment dispositions to predict the religious coping strategies that are described, but not explained or predicted, within coping theory itself.

By the same token, coping theory complements attachment theory in important ways. First, not all varieties of religious coping can be conceived of as attachment responses. For example, seeking support within one's spiritual community, containing mostly affiliative relationships, is an important facet of religious coping. Thus, the affiliative behavioral system is likely to be more central for such seeking than the attachment system (cf. Kirkpatrick, 2005). Second, even though attachment dispositions predict religious coping, this does not mean that religious coping is unimportant for subsequent adjustment. To the contrary, some dimensions of religious coping that are conceptually independent of attachment (such as seeking affiliative social support) are important resources for getting through major stressful experiences (e.g., Belavich & Pargament, 2002; Schottenbauer et al., 2006).

Terror Management Theory and Attachment

Terror management theory (TMT; e.g., Greenberg et al., 1997) applied to religion highlights religion's important psychological role in providing a sense of both real and symbolic immortality: "Don't fear the reaper" (Blue Öyster Cult, *Agents of Fortune,* 1976). According to proponents of TMT (e.g., Soenke, Landau, & Greenberg, 2013; Vail et al., 2010), unlike other animals, humans are aware that they will die, and this awareness is sufficiently terrifying to be defensively suppressed and for people to seek further relief in the form of culturally imbued immortality messages. Much work has already been done in spelling out the common ground as well as the divergence between this theory and attachment theory (e.g., Cox et al., 2008; Kirkpatrick, 2005; Mikulincer & Florian, 2000; Mikulincer & Shaver, 2016; Weise et al., 2008).

For example, Mikulincer and colleagues have shown that attachment styles often moderate TMT-related effects. In other words, certain terror management processes are characteristic of some individuals, but not all, and attachment theory may help to explain this. To illustrate, Mikulincer and Florian (2000) found that, among adults with insecure attachment styles, reminders of mortality lead to more death-thought accessibility and more severe judgments of cultural transgressions. Also, defending one's own worldview (e.g., one's religion) following mortality reminders reduced death-thought accessibility exclusively among attachment-insecure study participants. Potentially positive effects of mortality reminders (e.g., symbolic immortality, desire for intimacy) were observed specifically among attachment-secure participants. As highlighted by Hart and colleagues (2005), threats to one source of security (e.g., attachment) may result in compensatory, defensive activation of other security components (e.g., worldview defense, self-enhancement) among attachment-insecure individuals. These and similar findings indicate that it is first and foremost attachment-insecure individuals who

erect rigid worldview defenses, which may also have destructive effects
for members of out-groups who are targets of discrimination and hostility.

Similarly, following mortality-salience induction (asking a person
to think about death), research on political preferences has shown that
attachment-insecure participants increase their support for a conservative presidential candidate, whereas more attachment-secure participants increase their support for a liberal candidate (Weise et al., 2008).
In another experiment, Weise and colleagues (2008) found that a secure-
relationship prime, given after a mortality-salience induction, caused a
less violent response to the problem of terrorism than did a neutral-rela-
tionship prime.

On the whole, TMT and the attachment–religion framework are
mutually enriching. Both focus on psychologically protective and defensive functions of religion, and they generally do so in ways that are complementary rather than competitive, even if adult attachment styles qualify terror management processes in such a way as to indicate that not all
such processes are normative (species-typical; cf. Mikulincer & Shaver,
2016). The frameworks are largely complementary because they focus
on different facets of self-protective mental processes that religion taps
into. Attachment theory deals with specific, natural clues to danger (and
safety), which reflect recurrent adaptive problems that humans and other
primates have faced over the course of evolution, such as predators, pain,
and separation from and loss of attachment figures. The attachment
system evolved as a solution to such basic threats and is consequently
triggered by these threats (Bowlby, 1969/1982). In contrast, TMT deals
with mental processes resulting from people's cognitive awareness that
they will die, and such processes are conceivably triggered by any self-
threatening stimuli that increase mortality salience. Thus, attachment
theory delineates more basic processes, which develop early in ontogeny.
Many of these basic processes are shared with other animals (especially
primates), whereas TMT delineates "higher," more uniquely human,
later-developing existential processes. Importantly, however, both TMT
and attachment theory are built on the idea that threats of pain, disintegration, and, ultimately, death automatically trigger self-protective
responses. Attachment theory focuses on turning to attachment figures
for safety, whereas TMT focuses on boosting self-esteem in relation to
cultural standards. In both cases, the ultimate threat is death, although
infants and young children are unaware of this threat. The reaction to
threats of harm is enough, for both infants and adults, to trigger self-
protective maneuvers and defenses. With age, children may begin to
realize that the ultimate version of what they are afraid of is death (or
the permanent separation from loved ones).

Just as the attachment–religion framework may serve as a developmental anchor for religious coping theory and research (reviewed above), it may do the same for terror management theory and research. More specifically, attachment-insecure individuals whose basic needs for protection and security have been rebuffed or inconsistently met by caregivers are more likely to erect rigid worldview defenses under threat. In contrast, attachment-secure individuals, who have had continuous, reliable experiences of safety and security with their caregivers, are more likely to reap the protective and growth-promoting benefits of terror management (e.g., symbolic immortality and intimacy with others).

Of course, TMT and attachment theory can yield overlapping predictions, so it may be difficult to disentangle empirical support for one from support for the other in a given instance. This is the case, for example, when processing of any particular stimulus (say, the word "danger" or "death") should be expected to activate both the attachment system and terror management processes (cf. Granqvist et al., 2012).

From his evolutionary psychology standpoint, Kirkpatrick (1999b, 2005) has criticized TMT for implying a teleological, domain-general (i.e., avoid *all* situations that may lead to death), and forward-looking (i.e., I *will* die) psychological mechanism. Within much evolutionary psychology dealing with humans' "adapt*ed* minds," psychological mechanisms are believed to reflect past selection pressures (in that sense they are "backward-looking") and to be domain-specific (e.g., Barkow et al., 1992; Tooby & Cosmides, 1990). Although the evolutionary psychology stance may often be correct, at least for basic adaptive mechanisms, much theorizing and research within evolutionary science also point to humans' (and other animals') "adapt*ing* minds." In other words, our minds and the adaptive mechanisms (systems, modules, etc.) they comprise are generally sufficiently flexible to adapt to current ecological and cultural circumstances. I elaborate on these matters in the next chapter. For present purposes, my point is that additional kinds of mental processes, which take advantage of culture-derived material, may be set in motion as a result of the cognitive capacities that make us realize that we are mortal—processes that defend us from the pain of this realization. That is to say, TMT processes may be culture-informed "build-ons" to the more basic mechanisms, like attachment, that are emphasized in much evolutionary psychology. And surely, evolutionary psychologists would not deny that humans are cognitively aware that they will die, even if this is not how the more basic mechanisms of the mind have evolved and still operate. Thus, the critical question is whether mortality awareness plays a causal role or whether it is merely epiphenomenal. Empirical research on mortality salience clearly supports the causal role stance.

Self-Regulation, Self-Control, the Supernatural Watcher, and Attachment

Across many of the world's faith traditions, religiosity has been reliably associated with a host of correlates, many of them desirable, such as longevity of life (McCullough et al., 2000); better marital functioning (Mahoney et al., 1999); higher academic achievement (Jeynes, 2002); adherence to behavioral health and safety regimes (Wallace & Forman, 1998); prosocial behaviors (Sarogolou, Pichon, Trompette, Verschueren, & Dernelle, 2005; Shariff et al., 2015); and abstinence from drug use, addiction problems, and delinquency (Baier, & Wright, 2001). Although degree of cultural normativity of religion is likely a moderator of these and many other religion associations (cf. Stavrova, 2015), some of these associations are relatively robust and nontrivial in terms of effect sizes (e.g., McCullough et al., 2000). Why does religiosity have such a diverse list of mostly desirable correlates?

Maybe because religion fosters self-control and self-regulation? This reason has been suggested by McCullough and his colleagues (McCullough & Carter, 2013; McCullough & Willoughby, 2009). Drawing on cybernetically inspired general theories of self-regulation and self-control (e.g., Vohs & Baumeister, 2011), McCullough and Carter (2013) define self-regulation as "the processes by which a system uses information about its present state to change that state toward greater conformity with a desired end state or goal" (p. 123). Self-regulation need not be deliberative, volitional, or consciously strategic; it can just as well be automatic or unconscious. The concept of self-control is used for "situations in which people *work to* override a prepotent response" (p. 123; emphasis added), exemplified by emotions and motivations, such as battling a craving for alcohol. Other strands of psychological literature have suggested highly overlapping concepts such as the superego (Freud, e.g., 1961a, 1961b), emotion regulation (e.g., Gross, 1998), ego resiliency and control (Block & Block, 2014), delay of gratification (Mischel, Shoda, & Rodriguez, 1989), effortful control (Rothbart, 2007), executive functioning (Barkley, 1997), conscientiousness and agreeableness (McCrae & Costa, 1997), and low psychoticism (Eysenck, Eysenck, & Barrett, 1985).

How religions foster self-regulation and self-control may be relatively straightforward. McCullough and Carter (2013) argue that religions comprise ethical rules (e.g., obey God) and a watching, powerful God, which should cause religious individuals to develop proclivities for self-regulation and self-control, as a means of amassing sufficient willpower to control their behaviors and actions. By what other means than the threat of punishment from a powerful God could Abraham possibly have been persuaded to comply with God's command and exercise the self-control required to kill his beloved son? On that note, Bob Dylan interprets God as saying, "You can do what you want, Abe, but the next time you see me comin', you better run." The song continues: "Well, Abe said, "Where d'you want this killin' done?" God said, "Out on Highway 61" (*Highway 61 Revisited*, 1965).

Why, in functional, evolutionary terms, religions would foster self-regulation and self-control is a bit more intricate. Like Norenzayan (2013) and colleagues (2016; Shariff & Norenzayan, 2007; see also Laurin, 2017), McCullough and Carter argue for a gene–culture coevolution explanation. In their view, "Big God" religions comprising a powerful and morally concerned supernatural watcher evolved culturally in the wake of the agricultural revolution, an associated increased population size, and consequently a need for large-scale cooperation among nonkin. These cultural changes have conceivably also yielded a selection pressure for self-regulation and self-control.

Whatever the correct evolutionary explanation turns out to be, much research, most of which is correlational, has supported the proposed link between religiosity on the one hand and constructs related to self-regulation and self-control on the other. For example, in a meta-analysis of religiosity and Big Five personality dimensions, Saroglou (2010) showed that religiosity is reliably (but modestly) linked with conscientiousness and agreeableness across multiple contexts. In terms of the three-factor model of personality (focused on extraversion, neuroticism, and psychoticism), religiosity is negatively associated with psychoticism (e.g., impulsivity, the opposite of self-regulation and self-control; Saroglou, 2002). In a review of the literature pertaining more specifically to religiosity and self-control, McCullough and Willoughby (2009) similarly cited support for a positive link between the two in 11 out of 12 conducted studies, with small to moderate effect sizes.

Religiosity is a highly multifaceted phenomenon, so we should not expect all conceivable variants of it to be positively linked with self-regulation and self-control. For example, research based on Allport and Ross's (1967) classical distinction between intrinsic and extrinsic religiosity indicates that an intrinsic religious motivation—such as Abraham's in the Bible story—is positively related to self-control, whereas an extrinsic religious motivation appears to be negatively associated with self-control (e.g., Vitell et al., 2009).

This correlational literature has not demonstrated support for McCullough and colleagues' (e.g., 2009, 2013) hypothesis of causal direction—from religion to self-regulation and self-control. It seems equally likely that causality can run in the reverse direction—from self-regulation and self-control to religiosity—or that a third variable may explain their association, or that the association is bi-directional. Indeed, Saroglou's (2010) meta-analysis, along with some prospective longitudinal studies (see McCullough & Willoughby, 2009), have provided more consistent evidence that personality traits temporally forecast religiosity rather than the other way around. Whatever the true nature of the association is in most instances, research has indicated that religion-related experimental manipulations can cause changes in self-regulation and self-control. For example, religious primes have been shown to make people slower to recognize temptation-related words (e.g., related to substance use, forbidden sex; Fishbach, Friedman, & Kruglanski, 2003); more inclined to resist temptations (Laurin, Kay, & Fitzsimons, 2012); and better at maintaining effortful attention in a word-search task (Toburen & Meier, 2010).

What about the role of attachment theory and research then? As with religious coping and terror management processes, the attachment–religion framework has the potential to serve as a much-needed developmental anchor for this literature. First, research indicates that attachment relationships, and secure attachment in particular, facilitate the development of self-regulation and self-control. For example, in the classical Minnesota study of individual development and adaptation, attachment security with mothers during children's second year of life prospectively predicted their ego resiliency and control (e.g., successful motor inhibition) at ages 4–5 years (Arend, Gove, & Sroufe, 1979). Similarly, secure attachment in the first years of life temporally forecasts higher abilities to delay gratification at age 6 years (Jacobsen, Huss, Fendrich, Kruesi, & Ziegenhain, 1997). In a more recent study, infant attachment security prospectively predicted higher executive functioning (e.g., working memory) among 2- to 3-year-olds, over and above the effects of several conceivable confounds (Bernier, Carlson, Deschênes, & Matte-Gagné, 2012). Also, attachment relationships, and again attachment security in particular, have long been viewed as foundational contexts for the child's development of emotion regulation skills (e.g., Cassidy, 1994; on adult attachment, see Mikulincer & Shaver, 2016). Such components of early mental functioning do not just conceptually overlap with self-regulation and self-control, but are key building blocks in development for what will later manifest as self-regulation and self-control (e.g., Mischel et al., 1989; Rothbart, 2007). The fact that attachment contributes to these building blocks suggests that attachment might also play a developmental role in associations between religion and self-regulation/self-control.

Second, attachment relationships, especially secure attachment, facilitate the offspring's adoption of parental norms and perhaps cultural norm transmission more generally (see Chapters 5 and 10). If sensitive parents model and teach religiously inspired behavioral norms relating to self-regulation and self-control, then we have good reason to expect that their secure offspring will comply, not just because of their disposition for self-regulation and self-control but also because sensitive caregiving/secure attachment facilitates successful social learning in general from caregivers. In other words, religiosity, self-regulation, and self-control may be related partly because they are nested within a larger context of sensitive caregiving, secure attachment, and social learning. This is not to say that we should expect religiosity and self-regulation/self-control to be unrelated or negatively related among attachment-insecure individuals. In line with the compensation hypothesis, some attachment-insecure individuals may well "need" religion more than their secure counterparts specifically to develop the self-regulation and self-control skills required to manage life's many challenges and resist its many temptations.

Third, because God is typically conceived as an "ideal" attachment figure, who is not just watchful but also benevolent and protective, religious people should be naturally inclined to "cooperate" (or comply) with God's perceived requests. For example, they should resist temptations, which requires cultivating self-regulation and self-control. Especially for attachment-secure individuals who have a more coherently benevolent representation of God, such a cooperative stance should arise partly from (perceived) "mutual responsiveness" (Ainsworth et al., 1974) in their relationship with God rather than merely from a sense of being watched by an authoritarian, sulphurous, hellfire-threatening God (cf. Johnson, Cohen, & Okun, 2016; Laurin, 2017). Indeed, most attachment-secure individuals are unlikely to represent God as authoritarian in the first place (e.g., Granqvist et al., 2012). Instead of or in addition to activating God-fearing processes, God may function as a prosocial behavioral model for them (cf. Thomas à Kempis's "Imitatio Christi" ideal), and they may feel intrinsically motivated to act in accordance with that model (cf. Johnson et al., 2016). Also, their sense of being protected and worthy of God's love and care should provide them with a sense of confidence and mastery, adding further to their proclivities for self-regulation and self-control beyond what their early developmental experiences have endowed them with. Luckily, too, through positive generalizing working models, God won't be perceived to call them down Highway 61, so most of their self-regulation and self-control will continue to have desirable consequences for them and their surroundings.

Meaning-Making, Attribution, and Attachment

Beyond coping and terror management, highly interrelated processes of meaning-making and attributions are central facets of human intentionality that are also expressed in religion and spirituality. Regarding meaning, Park, Edmondson, and Hale-Smith (2013) have argued that humans have a "deeply rooted need for a functional meaning system" (p. 157); that this need is particularly acute when humans are faced by stress; and that it underlies people's embrace of religion. Accordingly, religious meaning-making, such as appraising a critical outcome in life as an expression of God's will, occurs particularly when humans are under conditions of high stress. Ray Paloutzian (2017) has even suggested that meaning-making offers the prospect of an overarching framework that can organize the whole of the psychology of religion and spirituality. Whichever more basic processes are involved, he argues, humans strive to make sense of their experiences, and religion appeals partly because it helps people with that sense-making.[1]

Religion undoubtedly helps people derive a sense of meaning in life. The term "meaning in life" might seem overly aspirational and somewhat pretentious. Shouldn't humans be content if they can satisfy their basic needs related to survival, reproduction, and security? However, meaning "in" life should not be confused with meaning "of" life. While the latter often implies some objective, higher, or even metaphysical, religious meaning, experiencing meaning "in" life simply means to have the subjective sense that one's life is reasonably (1) coherent/comprehensible, (2) purposeful, and (3) significant (i.e., that it matters and is worth living; George & Park, 2016; Martela & Steger, 2016). These elements are surely important for all humans, even for agnostics and atheists who question the possibility of reaching some higher, metaphysical meaning. Without such meaning, a person would risk debilitating states of confusion (life being sensed as incoherent/incomprehensible), lack of direction and agency (life as purposeless), or depression (life as insignificant). While research shows that *searching* for meaning of life can be uncomfortable (Steger, 2009), actually sensing meaning in life is related to greater well-being and better mental and physical health (for a review, see Park et al., 2013).

The experience of meaning in life supposedly arises when our current experiences and evaluation of our lives are in line with our "meaning system"—a complex network of global beliefs and goals (Park & George, 2018). To illustrate just how fundamental meaning-related processes can be, the meaning maintenance model (MMM; Proulx, 2013; Proulx & Inzlicht, 2012; Proulx, Markman, & Lindberg, 2013) postulates that when the network of representations in a meaning system is reliable—hence, informative with regard to the way things are and will be—a subjective sense of meaning will arise, informing the individual that things are making sense (i.e., things are coherent and comprehensible; Heintzelman & King, 2014). Similarly, it has been suggested that "stability and coherence in our conceptual systems" is a "fundamental need" for humans (Janoff-Bulman, 1989, p. 115) and that human meaning-making works by simply connecting events in our environment and constructing mental representations of the connections (Heine, Proulx, & Vohs, 2006).

Although humans may be strongly predisposed to make meaning in these ways, the skills needed to do so are not innate but develop as a function of species-typical experiences (Steger, Hicks, Krueger, & Bouchard, 2011). Park and colleagues (2013) argue that meaning systems are "formed through normative developmental processes as well as idiosyncratic life experiences" (p.158). Furthermore, meaning systems "serve as the filter[s] through which people attend to and perceive stimuli; organize their behavior; conceptualize themselves, others and interpersonal relationships; remember their past; and anticipate their future" (p. 158). Thus described, meaning systems are in many ways similar to Bowlby's (1969/1982, 1973, 1980) and others' (Main et al., 1985) depiction of internal working models (IWMs; see Chapters 1 and 5), although meaning systems may be somewhat more intentional (e.g., subjectively accessible) and domain-general, and IWMs more automatic (e.g., nonconscious) and domain-specific. Whether these constructs refer to genuinely different processes or are merely two labels for partially identical processes, their resemblances were sufficiently striking for my colleagues and me to start contemplating the relations between attachment- and meaning-related processes (see Dewitte et al., 2019).

From a review of the pertinent literatures, we concluded that attachment-related processes may be a vital factor in the development and maintenance of meaning throughout life. Responding to Mikulincer and Shaver's (2016) call for scholarly attention to the "optimistic, hopeful, constructive, and actualization-oriented tone of attachment theory" (p. 45), we argued that one of the ways by which attachment in general and attachment security in particular foster a strong and healthy psychological foundation is through their role in the construction of meaning (Dewitte et al., 2019). Also, Mikulincer and Shaver (2013) have reviewed a broad range of research indirectly supporting the idea that attachment can contribute to a sense of meaning in life through different psychological processes such as having a sense of purpose and direction in life, a unique personal identity, and an individualized faith.

Our review can be summarized in two central propositions (Dewitte et al., 2019). First, early attachment experiences (repeated interaction sequences with caregivers) provide a foundation for recognizing patterns and acquiring a sense of order, control, and coherence—for example, "I scream, Mom hugs me," "I scream, Dad looks at the phone." If such interaction sequences are sufficiently reliable, the child will gain a sense of order and coherence from them. For better and worse, they also have important implications for the child's behavioral and cognitive dispositions (e.g., Mom can be relied upon when needed, Dad cannot). As is typical in development, the construction of meaning starts at a basic level, in children's fundamental cognitive acquisitions, such as face recognition, self–other differentiation, and detection of cause–effect contingencies. In particular, interactions with normally sensitive attachment figures stimulate the child's mentalization capacities and exploration of the inner and outer environment, enabling the formation of positive representations of self, others, and the world. From such acquisitions, children ultimately develop broader ideas about how the world works and how they fit into it; in other words, they develop meaning systems. Because attachment-secure individuals tend to find close interpersonal relationships comprehensible, purposeful, and significant, intimate relationships are typically inherently meaningful for them, and thus their meaning systems are often relationally oriented. A life lived in close relationships with parents, romantic partners, and perhaps deities is typically an inherently meaningful life for them.

In recent years, some empirical studies on the relationship between adult attachment style and meaning in life have emerged. This literature has shown that attachment-secure adults score higher on *presence* of meaning in life than attachment-insecure (especially anxious) individuals (Bodner, Bergman, & Cohen-Fridel, 2014; Reizer, Dahan, & Shaver, 2013). In contrast, with regard to an active *search* for meaning of life, the same studies showed that attachment-anxious individuals outscored secure (and dismissing) ones. Based on these results, anxiousness, or negative models of the self, seem to be related to a higher search for meaning without finding what one is looking for. Although attachment-avoidance would seem to bode better for sensing meaning in life, it is worth noting that the meaning systems of avoidant (dismissing) adults are likely to be defensively self-enhancing and not relationally oriented (cf. Mikulincer & Shaver, 2016).

Our second proposition was that attachment relationships, and attachment security in particular, serve as an enduring and powerful resource for handling threats to and disruptions of meaning (Dewitte et al., 2019). According to the MMM, the aversive feeling that results from a disruption to meaning systems will motivate compensation efforts in order to reduce aversive arousal and restore a sense of meaning. When confronted with disruptions to meaning (e.g., a wildfire consuming one's home, the premature death of a loved one), secure attachment should provide a coherent set of representations to fall back on and from which the person can ultimately regain a sense of order and meaning under challenging circumstances. More specifically, we proposed that attachment-secure individuals should be more confident in handling the ambiguity and confusion resulting from meaning disruptions and more flexible in opening up their cognitive structures to new information (cf. accommodation). In contrast, attachment-insecure individuals should be more easily overwhelmed by the threat of uncertainty and should deal with this by guarding their mental representations against discrepant information (cf. assimilation). Overall, empirical studies clearly indicate a link between attachment security (both as dispositional attachment style and as a momentarily boosted sense of security) and openness to information-challenging meaning representations (for a review, see Mikulincer & Shaver, 2016). In sum, by promoting cognitive openness and tolerance of ambiguity, secure attachment should facilitate flexible and realistic adjustment of meaning representations when encountering discrepant information (Dewitte et al., 2019).

What about the role of religion in relation to attachment and meaning-making? Not much empirical research has been carried out on this topic. However, in a pioneering longitudinal study, Davis, Kimball, Aten, Hamilton, and colleagues (2019) recently examined religious believers' meaning-making and religious attachment responses to a natural disaster (the Louisiana flood). Both 1 month and 6 months after the flood, results revealed that most survivors engaged in religious meaning-making in which they drew on benevolent God representations and theodicies to appraise the cause and purpose of the disaster, and they also turned to God as a safe haven to get through the stressful events. These responses contributed to the making of positive religious meanings; for example, renewed beliefs and experiences of God's benevolence and providence. This study did not examine the role of attachment security in earlier "secular" attachments or in attachment to God.

In light of the review above and other findings pertaining to the attachment–religion connection, attachment-secure individuals who have been raised by sensitive caregivers in religious homes should usually sense meaning in life and should have highly functional meaning-related responses to threats and disruptions to their religious meaning systems (e.g., a desire to learn more about other religions). Contrarily, attachment-insecure individuals should generally have to struggle more to find meaning and should be prone to less functional meaning-making responses when their religious meaning systems are challenged (e.g., becoming confused, refusing to accommodate their meaning systems, denigrating religious out-groups).

With regard to attribution theory, although this theory was proposed as a framework for the psychology of religion several decades ago (Proudfoot & Shaver, 1975; Spilka et al., 1985), research into this matter has not been vigorously pursued (e.g., Barrett & Zahl, 2013; Hill

& Gibson, 2008), probably in part because the highly related theories of coping, terror management, and meaning-making have since gained momentum. Nonetheless, part of what makes religion psychologically unique is related to attributions. For example, whether a person understands an experience (e.g., an intense state of bliss and unity) as being the product of one's own brain–mind processes (e.g., I must be getting manic) or as resulting from God's presence makes a huge impact on the psychological implications of that experience. In the former case, it may be taken to imply that one should seek medical help. In the latter, it may be a life-transforming experience, providing a "new morning." Attachment theory makes a good partner for attribution theory to the extent that attachment may help delineate developmental pathways leading to dispositions for certain forms of attributions rather than other ones. For example, attachment-secure individuals should be more inclined than insecure individuals to attribute positive experiences to a loving God who cares about oneself and to attribute terrifying experiences to impersonal causes (e.g., nature, brain states).

ATTACHMENT AND THE PSYCHOANALYSIS OF RELIGION

The merits of a scientific theory are to be judged in terms of the range of phenomena it embraces, the internal consistency of its structure, the precision of the predictions it can make and the practicability of testing them.
—BOWLBY (1969/1982, p. 173)

Much of Bowlby's contribution to science can be understood as an attempt to reform and update psychoanalytic theory, and to make it compatible with the biological sciences and empirical scientific principles more generally. The quotation above, taken from Bowlby's first volume in his attachment-and-loss series, is illustrative. Although psychoanalysis, in Bowlby's assessment, fared reasonably well on the first two considerations (wide range of phenomena embraced and internal consistency), it has always done poorly on the third consideration (precision of predictions), and it does notoriously badly on the fourth (practicability of testing them).

I came to the psychology of religion as a late adolescent, after having immersed myself in Freud's writings on culture and religion (1961a, 1961b). I knew almost nothing about science at the time, but Freud's passionate pessimism about culture and religion appealed deeply to my adolescent, aesthetic sentiments. However, after a few undergraduate semesters in religious studies, psychology, and philosophy, it seemed clear to me that Freud's approach to religion had major problems. Later psychoanalytic approaches, although constructed partly to correct Freud's analysis where it had erred, were not necessarily much better. The psychoanalytic terminologies and assumptions now seemed to me hopelessly imprecise. It appeared impossible or highly impractical to test the predictions that might, in some instances, be derived from psychoanalytic theorizing. Even when such predictions had been supported by empirical research, there was the potential for alternative frameworks to account for the findings.

In contrast, Bowlby's attachment theory and the empirical research program it had garnered seemed to me much more promising for the psychology of religion. It could retain many of the true insights of psychoanalysis, accommodate much of the alleged empirical support for the psychoanalytic approach to religion, and yield novel, testable predictions, which were fairly straightforward to test. Lee Kirkpatrick and Phillip Shaver's (e.g., 1990, 1992) pioneering correlational research on the attachment–religion connection supported this hunch. I began to pursue the possibilities, obtaining many supportive results. For example, like Kirkpatrick and Shaver (1990), I found that an insecure attachment history was associated with sudden religious conversions precipitated by crisis (see Chapters 5 and 6). My colleagues and I also started doing experimental research, testing "risky" predictions (Popper, 1962/2014) based on attachment theory. The results from those studies were also supportive. For example, attachment-activating primes ("Mother is gone") caused an increase in theistic believers' motivation to experience closeness to God (Birgegard & Granqvist, 2004). I then thought the time was ripe to do with the psychoanalytic approaches to religion what Bowlby had already done with psychoanalysis in general: to critique and replace those approaches with attachment theory (Granqvist, 2006b).

In the next section, I describe some of the key psychoanalytic theories of religion. I then revisit my published critique of them, along with the exchange that followed this critique. Finally, I conclude by noting that I am no longer aiming to replace psychoanalysis but, in the service of methodological pluralism, am seeking rapprochement. As the devil ages, he grows wiser.

Key Psychoanalytic Approaches to Religion

This section describes some of the best-known psychoanalytic conceptualizations of religion, those of Freud, Erikson, Rizzuto, and Jones. This is by no means an exhaustive list of psychoanalytic theorists' views on religion (the interested reader is also referred to, among others, Corveleyn, Luyten, & Dezutter, 2013; Guntrip, 1969; Jung, 1938; McDargh, 1983; Meissner, 1984; Pruyser, 1968; and Wulff, 1991). In making explicit the functional and structural connections between child–parent relationships on the one hand and people's representations of and perceived relationships with God on the other, it nonetheless serves our purposes reasonably well.

Freud: Primal Murder, the Exalted Father, and the Grand Illusion

Freud offered the pioneering psychoanalytic account of religion, consisting of both phylogenetic and ontogenetic analyses. In *Totem and Taboo* (1913/2013), Freud presented his view of what happened at the beginning of civilization. Men supposedly lived in hordes under the domination of a single, powerful, violent, and jealous father who had privileged sexual access to females. The brothers, who had been driven out by the primeval father, joined together and killed him. Following the murderous act, each brother identified with the father and acquired some of his strengths, while the act of killing itself was repressed. To resolve the guilt and longing for the dead father, a totem animal was formed as the dead father's substitute, and the parricide was continually repeated through ritual totem sacrifices. The totemic representation of the father, along with the guilt and longing, was inherited by all sons and daughters as a latent memory trace, a repressed object representation. In Freud's analysis, this is the phylogenetic material out of which God is subsequently carved. However, an intermediate stimulus was necessary to accomplish the "return of the repressed" representation. This was provided by Moses' presentation of the monotheistic God, evoking overwhelming feelings still to date, emanating from recognition of the ancestral representation (Freud, 1939/2010).

With respect to the ontogenetic origins of people's representations of God, the inherited memory traces of the ancestral father supposedly merge with the oedipal son's ambivalent representation of his own father (Freud, 1961b). Thus, the memory traces are reawakened and the child is made "to fit into the phylogenetic pattern" (Rizzuto, 1979, p. 22). Following the libidinal energy transformations associated with the son's identification with the earthly father and the formation of the superego, this merged representation becomes exalted and projected onto the cosmos; that is, the child forms a representation of God. Freud claimed that, as a substitute for the longing for the father, the superego contains the material from which religions are built. Also important is Freud's assertion that the male individual's relationship with God depends on his experiences with his earthly father; his relationship with God "oscillates and changes along with that relation" (1913/2013, p. 147). Once the representation of God has been formed, God may be used in various challenging situations. According to Freud, this represents regression to the developmental stage of identification with the earthly father and the formation of the superego. In other words, it represents an infantile wish for parental protection in the face of one's own helplessness. In Freud's view (1961b), the mature individual should resist such a temptation because religious doctrines are understood as illusions, effectively comparable to delusions. Freud explicitly argued that religion should be replaced with science because "scientific work is the only road that can lead us to a knowledge of reality outside of ourselves" (p. 31).

Erikson: Basic Trust

Erik Erikson devoted little attention to the phylogenetic origins of religion, but he was more elaborate than Freud in specifying which personal experiences with parents (mother, in particular) in ontogeny are linked to the individual's subsequent development of faith.

Taking his own stage theory of psychosocial development as the point of departure, Erikson (1959, 1963) claimed that experiences with mother that help an infant to favorably resolve the first crisis of life, to achieve basic trust (cf. secure attachment) rather than mistrust (cf. insecure attachment), is the cornerstone of faith and hope in adult life. Like Freud, Erikson linked the adult's use of myths and rituals to regression as a defense mechanism, but unlike Freud, he understood this as a form of regression that serves important mental survival functions and, hence, potentiates mental progression (cf. regression in the service of the ego). Religion becomes a symbolic, collective arena in which the individual may be helped to resolve the trust versus mistrust crisis.

According to Erikson, three factors in the child's life determine the development of the child's God image, each being a characteristic of the child's relationship with the mother: (1) the affective tone of the relationship, (2) the presence or absence of mutual recognition, and (3) the experience of being abandoned by the mother. Erikson describes the affective tone, in favorable circumstances, as a kind of sanctified presence, leaving behind a reminiscence whose adult religious counterpart is a feeling of God's invisible presence. As regards mutual recognition, the central task for the infant is to establish a sense of being "seen" by and being able to "see" the other face to face and to feel accepted as an individual during these encounters. An analogy in religious life is to feel accepted and loved by a benevolent and caring God. In Erikson's theory, this mutual recognition is the foundation for a later sense of identity. However, there is a flip side of developing differentiation between self and mother—the sense of feeling abandoned by her. It is through this conflict between developing one's own self (underlying identity formation) and at the same time feeling abandoned in doing so that religion helps the individual to manage. In establishing a personal relationship with the deity, the individual may reestablish the security associated with "the paradise lost."

Erikson did not make an organized effort in any one particular writing to develop a unified theory of religion. Instead, his thoughts were scattered across books and papers without being fully formalized. Others (e.g., Fowler & Dell, 2006; Oser, 1991) have used Erikson's theory to derive more formalized, stage accounts of developing faith.

Rizzuto: God as a Transitional Object

Ana-Maria Rizzuto (1979, 1991) has formulated the most systematic, concerted psychoanalytic account of the development of God representations, particularly emphasizing the process of forming a "living" God representation. As an object-relationist, Rizzuto took a child's formation of object representations of self and parents (of both sexes) as the starting point in her analysis, departing from Winnicott's (1953) notion of an illusory, yet psychologically real, "transitional space," which is intermediate to the child's inner subjective and outer objective worlds.

Rizzuto argued that God is a special kind of object representation, created by an individual in the "psychic space" that encompasses transitional objects such as blankets and toys (see Chapter 3). God is special for two reasons. First, unlike most other transitional objects, God is created out of representational material whose sources are the representations of "primary objects" (i.e., human caregivers). Second, God does not follow the usual course of other transitional objects (i.e., does not fade in importance). Rather, the process of creating and finding God never ceases in an individual's life but "follows epigenetic and developmental laws that can be studied systematically" (Rizzuto, 1979, p. 179).

As an object representation, God can be used or rejected but never fully repressed. In "protecting the minimum amount of relatedness to primary objects and a baseline of self-respect," the usefulness of the object God is "at the service of gaining leverage with oneself, with others, and with life itself" (Rizzuto, 1979, p. 179). God serves the function of obtaining/maintaining psychic equilibrium, which is particularly important in critical moments (e.g., the death of a loved one, times of intense joy).

Rizzuto (1979) argued that an individual's representation of God has not only private origins, as delineated above, but also public ones. The public origins are due to God being a culturally sanctioned creation that is taken seriously by adults in general and one's parents in particular. The combination of these private and public origins creates an idiosyncratic representation of God in each individual's life, regardless of whether or not the individual consciously embraces the representation as belief in God. Rizzuto also claimed that one's sense of self is affected by God's representational traits. In favorable circumstances, God "remains a potentially available representation for the continuous process of psychic integration" (p. 180).

Rizzuto also described the developmental processes underlying the formation of the God representation. This formation can be divided into three stages, ranging from a "prestage" (ages 0 to 2–3 years) in which mirroring experiences with human caregivers are important, via the formation of a living God (2–3 to 5–7 years), containing the particular idiosyncratic blend of private and public material described above, to the final stage in which God becomes the representational object of a religion.

Favorable experiences with human caregivers are associated with favorable development of the self and God representations. For instance, Rizzuto (1979) claimed that the young infant, in the first period of his or her "narcissistic" relation to caregivers, needs to be seen as "an appealing, wonderful, and powerful child reflected in the maternal eye" (p. 185). When this mirroring evolves normally, the child slowly begins to separate his or her own representation from that of the primary object (i.e., caregiver), which involves the creation of the child's first transitional objects and representations. If the mirroring evolves differently, however, the individual may "remain fixated to a narcissistic need for psychic mirroring" (p. 186), perhaps even compensating "by feeling 'like God' " (p. 188).

Jones: Relational Psychoanalysis and the Postmodern Turn

The psychoanalytic perspective offered by Jim Jones (1991), a distinguished scholar of religion, was not so much a specific analysis. Rather, he outlined the implications that general developments in psychoanalytic theorizing on transference (e.g., Kohut, 1971; Stern, 1985) should have for the study of religion. The Freudian account of transference as the inevitable repetition of instinctually motivated behaviors (i.e., following Freud's drive theory and the idea of the primacy of instinct) should be replaced by an emphasis on the inevitability of relationships and of transference revealing internalized patterns of interaction. In this context, while objects and relationships are connected, Jones criticized Rizzuto's (1979) account for putting too much emphasis on the internalized *object* God at the expense of the internalized *relationship* with God.

Jones took Kohut's (1971) notion of the selfobject, as one pole of an interaction, as his point of departure, noting that different patterns of interaction lead different people to develop different selfobjects. It is the self, or the core sense of who we are, rather than instinctual conflict, that is reflected in transference, including transference that occurs in the context of the individual's relationship with the sacred. Jones elaborated:

> The child who feels secure grounds that security in a caring God [continuity]; the child who feels guilty and terrible grounds that sense of self by reference to a wrathful God [continuity]; the child who feels estranged envisions a distant deity [continuity] or dreams of a compensatory, warm, and tender selfobject God [discontinuity]. (p. 63, brackets added)

With this as background, Jones listed three interrelated areas of investigation that are central to the contemporary psychoanalysis of religion. First is the analysis of how religion as a relationship reflects those internalized relationships that constitute the self, starting with the internalized relationships and investigating how the individual's relationship with God is made from them. Second is the study of how an individual's relationship with God discloses his or her primary transferential patterns, starting with the person's description of the relation to the sacred and using it as "a vehicle for gaining insight into her larger relational world" (p. 66). Third, Jones suggested studying the connection between a new sense of self and its relation to a changed image of God.

In sum, as Jones (1991) understands it, the individual's religious beliefs, experiences, and practices build on the deep structure of his or her internalized relationships. In particular, the "affective bond with the sacred" was understood as enactment (or reenactment) of "transferential patterns present throughout a person's life" (p. 65).

In my view, Jones's (1991) approach in many ways served the psychoanalytic study of religion well, moving some of its assumptions and emphases closer to where a modern, empirically oriented relational psychology would take it. Unlike previous psychoanalysts of religion, Jones explicitly demarcated it from (sexual) drive approaches. He argued for a shift in emphasis from the individual's representation of the object God to a focus on the affective relational bond with the sacred; and, like Bowlby (1969/1982), he assumed that the child's developmentally acquired representations reflect real-life experiences, which are transferred within his or her affectional bond with God. However, Jones also argued for a postmodern turn in the psychoanalysis of religion, a topic to which I return in the sections that follow.

The Critique

A dozen years ago, the *International Journal for the Psychology of Religion* (IJPR) published a target article in which I evaluated the psychoanalysis of religion largely in critical terms and argued for its replacement with an attachment–theory approach (Granqvist, 2006b). Such a replacement, I claimed, held the prospect of integrating a relational approach to religion with mainstream psychology as well as with evolutionary science. Many of the reservations I raised against psychoanalysis were already widely known, so in that regard I was mainly "kicking a dead horse." Nonetheless, responses were published by two major authorities in the field, Ana-Maria Rizzuto (2006) and David Wulff (2006), a well-known scholar and intellectual historian of the psychology of religion (e.g., Wulff, 1991). Naturally, I got to write the final rejoinder (Granqvist, 2006b). Later, other additions or commentaries to this exchange appeared (in particular, see Luyten & Corveleyn, 2007; see also Barrett & Zahl, 2013; Gaztambide, 2008; Hewitt, 2008, 2014; Hood et al., 2009; Paloutzian, 2017). My critique of the psychoanalysis of religion encompassed multiple reservations, which can be grouped into metatheoretical, theoretical, methodological, and empirical reservations.

Metatheoretical Reservations

Many of the psychoanalytic ideas on religion are imprecise and almost impossible to falsify. For instance, although Freud (1913/2013, p. 147) asserted that the male individual's relationship with God "oscillates and changes along" with his relationship with the earthly father, he never specified which kinds of experiences with the father resulted in which kinds of experiences in relation to God. Similarly, Rizzuto (1979) argued that through defensive maneuvers, an individual's God representation can yield any conceivable position vis-à-vis the person's other representations (i.e., continuity, discontinuity, a combination). Because she did not specify the conditions under which each outcome was expected, Rizzuto's analysis became foolproof; Popper (1962) would characterize it as pseudoscientific (i.e., nonfalsifiable). However, in suggesting that basic trust is the cornerstone of faith and that the God relationship should be viewed through a transferential lens, Erikson and Jones fared better in terms of refutability. Both essentially predicted continuity between representations of self, others, and God, so that a person with favorable experiences with parents develops faith and a corresponding God relationship (cf. internal working model correspondence, Chapter 5).

Similarly, the drive framework of psychoanalysis does not fit with the motivational models (e.g., control systems) of contemporary evolutionary/biological sciences. Although some of the more recent psychoanalytic approaches do not stem from a drive approach, they seem to lack a motivational account altogether. By the same token, whereas Freud's phylogenetic considerations reeked of Lamarckian ideas (e.g., the inheritance of latent memory traces), post-Freudian psychoanalysis offered no phylo-genetic considerations whatsoever, thus violating Tinbergen's (1963) and Mayr's (1961) requirement that a scientific theory should provide not just proximal but also ultimate explanations (see Chapter 10).

Finally, I was particularly bothered by the postmodern turn sug-gested by Jones (1991). Rather than aiming to improve precision or to move psychoanalysis into the realm of other empirical sciences, as some psychoanalysts had done (e.g., Wallerstein, 1986; see also Luy-ten & Corveleyn, 2007), Jones appeared to aim for the exact opposite. To illustrate: "Especially in the interpersonal sphere (although quantum mechanics suggests this is also true of the physical world) there is no reality apart from our relation to it. . . . With the myth of objective real-ity refuted, analyzing the transference shifts from uncovering reality to interpreting it" (p. 23). Hence, the psychoanalysis of religion had come full circle, from the contention that religion is illusory (Freud) to the dec-laration that objective reality is a myth (Jones). I do not agree with either Freud or Jones that this is the path to take for an empirical psychology of religion.

Theoretical Reservations

The psychoanalytic approaches to religion assumed the existence of broad stages of psychosexual or psychosocial development. However, except in the cases of some biological and motor developments, the notion of discrete stages of development has long since fallen out of favor in devel-opmental psychology, largely because such distinct stages do not appear to exist (sensitive phases for environmental stimulation, which do exist, are another matter; cf. Luyten & Corveleyn, 2007). It is more common to think of development taking different pathways, partly depending on early experiences, like railroad tracks branching off from a central station, or branches and twigs branching off from a common tree trunk (Bowlby, 1973; Waddington, 1957). Also, closely tied to the notion of stages of development is the psychoanalytic assumption that when development unfolds unfavorably, the individual remains "fixated," as is evident in employing particular defense mechanisms. The emphasis on stages, fixa-tion, and associated defense mechanisms resulted in different identifica-tions of key developmental periods for religious development across the psychoanalytic theories of religion. Freud emphasized the oedipal period, and most later psychoanalysts highlighted different pre-oedipal periods. However, the assumption of one key period for religious and spiritual development is misleading and unnecessary. Similarly, any postulate of defense mechanisms should be recast along theoretical lines that do not presuppose developmental stages or fixation (see Bowlby, 1969/1982).

Another serious problem common to the psychoanalytic theories of religion is that their implications for religion as a whole are limited. Although Freud dealt with many aspects of religion (rituals, experiences, representations, etc.), Rizzuto delved mainly into representations, whereas Erikson was exclusively concerned with faith and Jones was primarily focused on the individual's relationship with God. A sound psychological theory of religion should have wider implications, particularly given that different aspects of religion tend to be highly empirically related to one another.

In addition, it is well known that one's image of both mother and father are related to one's image of God, and also that God images typically encompass both maternal and paternal attributes (see Chapter 2). However, the psychoanalytic perspectives largely failed to make sense of the influence of one parent—most notably Freud of the mother and Erikson of the father.

Freud's emphasis on the mature adult as autonomous and independent, as opposed to the child's and the religious individual's "dependency," has fallen out of favor among most psychologists, who, rather, view humans as interdependent throughout the lifespan (Bowlby, 1973; Kohut, 1971; Stern, 1985). Freud's emphasis on independence may have blinded him to non-neurotic (i.e., more secure) forms of religiosity (cf. Hewitt, 2008). A shortcoming of Rizzuto's analysis is that object-relations theory is not a framework well suited for understanding the public origins of religious representations, which she nonetheless believed to mesh with the private origins of those representations. Instead, other theories, with a clearer relation to principles of social learning and socialization, are needed (for the case of attachment, see Chapters 5 and 10).

Methodological Reservations

My critique listed multiple methodological problems common to the psychoanalytic approaches to religion (later echoed by Luyten & Corveleyn, 2007). First, one of these problems pertains to the difficulty of operationalizing the central psychoanalytic concepts, such as defense mechanisms (but see Luyten & Corveleyn, 2007), basic trust and mistrust, transitional space and object, and transference. Moreover, the psychoanalytic literature on religion presented no indication of how individual differences and relational experiences should be operationalized. This lack of operational definitions and procedures impacts unfavorably on the practicability of testing whatever prediction might be derived from a theory.

Second, virtually all empirical psychoanalytic work on religion had used idiographic case study designs, relying on a few, potentially unrepresentative cases or biographies, usually drawn from clinical contexts. There is of course nothing inherently wrong with idiographic research in psychology. To the contrary, it can yield thick descriptions of pertinent phenomena as well as insights that are hard to come by with other methods, and it is particularly worthwhile for generating hypotheses and for studying unique cases (e.g., Erikson, 1958). However, a reader trained in scientific methods naturally asks whether unstudied cases fit the schemes (cf. external validity), whether alternative interpretations of the studied cases can be ruled out (cf. internal validity), and by which criteria the researcher or clinician has determined that a true understanding has been achieved (e.g., that a given person's representations of God and parents are in fact related). The psychoanalysts of religion all seemed happily unaware of objections like these.

Third, the methodology of the psychoanalytic approaches to religion was idiosyncratic. No standardized method, such as the AAI, was used across cases and studies. Replication attempts were therefore made difficult.

Fourth and finally, within a given case study, the psychoanalyst observer may have generalized backward from the person's inferred current God representation and relation to his or her past representations and experiences (cf. Bowlby, 1969/1982; Kirkpatrick, 1995). If so, it is not surprising that they appeared to be related.

Empirical Reservations

Besides the idiographic research conducted by the psychoanalytic theorists themselves, a large literature addressing similar issues and employing a nomothetic scientific approach existed. For example, correlational and comparative research within psychology and anthropology had revealed relations among parental, self, and God imagery, largely along the lines of Erikson's notion of basic trust yielding faith, Rizzuto's hypothesis of representational continuity, and Jones's transference analysis. For example, cultures practicing caregiving marked by warmth rather than rejection had deities marked by benevolence rather than distance (e.g., Rohner, 1986). However, such findings were compatible with many other theories beyond psychoanalysis, such as attachment theory and parental acceptance–rejection theory (Rohner, 1986). In other words, although results from nomothetic research seemed to support some of the psychoanalytic predictions, the findings should not exclusively be seen as part of the psychoanalytic "data base" (cf. Grünbaum, 1984), because those same observations could be predicted from other theories.

The Exchange and Its Aftermath: Conclusions

The commentaries provided by Rizzuto (2006) and Wulff (2006) were as topically diverse as my original critique, and so was my rejoinder to the commentaries (Granqvist, 2006a). After referencing this exchange and the many conflictual positions involved, Paloutzian (2017, p. 90) succinctly concluded that "additional intellectual work is needed to resolve these issues." That is what I hope to do here. For heuristic purposes, I largely restrict my considerations to the major points on which I believe the commentators were right.

Both commentators highlighted the need for self-reflexivity (Wulff) and humility (Rizzuto) in our psychological attempts to understand religion, and they emphasized the legitimacy of a humanities (idiographic) approach in psychoanalysis. Regarding attachment research and its use of methods such as the AAI, Wulff (2006) noted that it "could provide informal occasions for new insights and realizations" (p. 30). He went on to urge attachment–religion research "to engage with the hermeneutical tradition more seriously" (p. 34). Similarly, in response to my suggested replacement of psychoanalysis with an attachment approach to religion, Rizzuto asked rhetorically, "Why don't we allow depth psychology [psychoanalysis] to continue offering new insights following its own methodology of clinical work, case studies, and theoretical inferences?" (p. 26; brackets added). The same themes were echoed in some of the later commentaries (e.g., Hood et al., 2009; Luyten & Corveleyn, 2007).

Wulff (2006) asserted that we shouldn't be too "attached" to any one theoretical framework, whether it be attachment, evolution, or any other framework. Furthermore, we all agreed, as Bowlby had originally suggested, that attachment theory is an object-relations theory and thus part of psychodynamic psychology broadly understood—the British independent school to be more precise (which is better referred to as "psychodynamic" rather than "psychoanalytic"). However, I emphasized, and still do, that attachment theory is such a special kind of object-relations theory that it is easy to see why attachment researchers would squirm like worms on a hook when categorized as psychoanalysts, and also why attachment theory was long treated as heretical within the psychoanalytic community (Granqvist, 2006a, 2006b). Unlike most of psychoanalysis and object-relations theories, attachment theory is firmly rooted in evolutionary and cognitive science; is comparatively conceptually precise; has inspired systematic empirical research using psychometrically validated instruments; and has yielded novel predictions about religion (Paloutzian, 2017). These predictions have been supported and further refined by incorporating feedback from nomothetic empirical research. In sum, the attachment approach has made an unsurpassed empirical contribution to the psychodynamic literature on religion and spirituality.

Because I emphasized matters of empirical science in my critique, Wulff (2006) mistakenly assumed that I was advocating a "positivist" framework (similarly, see Luyten & Corveleyn, 2007). However, attachment theory concerns itself with hidden realities and explanatory principles such as *internal* working models, behavioral *systems,* and *past* evolutionary selection pressures. Therefore, as an attachment researcher, I do not (and cannot) advocate positivism, at least not as conventionally understood in the philosophy of science where it is not confused with nomothetic research or attention to psychometric matters. In hindsight, it is nonetheless plain to see why the commentators were led astray by my empirical science critique, which was unnecessarily polarizing and effectively hid my actual stance.[2] As readers of this book will be aware, my actual stance is one of celebrating methodological pluralism, as illustrated also by the multiple case studies presented (Chapters 5, 6, and 8). I maintain that attachment theory and some attachment measures (like the AAI and the Religious Attachment Interview) invites such a celebration. In fact, one of the unique strengths of the attachment–religion framework is that it enables us to move flexibly between nomothetic and idiographic approaches, without getting stuck with either.

Furthermore, although I clearly had genuine cause to question the psychoanalysis of religion, the way the exchange played out reflects the tension that was present at the time between postmodernist and more modernist ways of understanding science and perhaps sometimes reality too. This was, after all, occurring at the end of the "science war," which climaxed with Sokal and Bricmont (1998; see also Turner, 2003). Jones (1991) contributed to pulling psychoanalysis into the postmodernist camp, whereas attachment theory and research rested squarely within the modernist camp. Academics within the modernist scientific mainstream (e.g., experimental psychologists engaging in hypothesis testing) often felt that their approaches were under attack from postmodern scholars on a semi-ideological mission who had set out considerably less rigorous standards for their own scientific conduct. Conversely, postmodern scholars often felt that academics within the scientific mainstream were defensive concerning the power games and socially constructed elements that contribute to every collective human undertaking, science included.

As a very young person at the time (I was still in my 20s when the critique was drafted; Granqvist, 2002), I was eager to join the troops of the Enlightenment in its defense against attack. However, I have come to reconsider this stance; enlightenment is better served by keeping an open mind and by entertaining—if just for a minute—that the perceived attack, which spontaneously arouses one's defenses, may contain at least a grain of truth (cf. Luyten & Corveleyn, 2007). That may be the case even if the "attacker" has arrived at it by nonempirical methods and even if he or she expresses it in ways that could be more careful (e.g., referring to the social construction of science or "knowledge" rather than of reality).

Now that the science war is over and both sides have won, it seems that much of the heat in our attachment versus psychoanalysis exchange was overblown and unnecessary. To be clear, I think it is fine if some psychoanalysts of religion take an idiographic, socially constructive, or perhaps hermeneutical approach, while other psychoanalysts and psychologists adopt a nomothetic, hypothesis-testing approach to increase our joint understanding of psychological processes underlying religion and spirituality. If they converge in their conclusions, then we have a more complete picture, embracing both individual and general psychological processes, than if we only held one of the two to be kosher. If their conclusions don't converge, the field may open up to fruitful distinctions that are worthy of future research endeavors. Similarly, a critical, self-reflexive approach to our own scientific undertakings—their (often) tacit assumptions, their cultural embeddedness, their constraints and limitations—are likely to facilitate further enlightenment.

In the end, I am less optimistic that attachment theory will replace the psychoanalysis of religion than I was back when the exchange took place. This is because of attachment theory's conceptual boundaries, its rudimentary defense mechanisms, and the attachment research habit of "cross-tabulating" people into types (secure vs. insecure and organized vs. disorganized), despite the fact that no individual is reducible to a type. Although these features have indisputably contributed to attachment theory's prosperity as an empirical research program, the attachment framework remains somewhat schematic and impoverished as applied at the individual level. In contrast, psychoanalysis, with its emphasis on psychological life as inherently conflictual and complex, is much better equipped to make sense of, for example, conflicts and defenses operating even among attachment-secure people. They, too, have been observed to participate in religiously inspired atrocities, file for divorce, and struggle with forbidden lusts. Thus, I end this discussion by answering Rizzuto's (2006) question affirmatively: Yes, let's allow psychoanalysis to continue offering what may become new insights. In doing so, however, I advise psychoanalytic researchers employing idiographic approaches to take advantage of the improvements that have been made in qualitative methodologies (e.g., Corveleyn et al., 2013; Lilliengren, 2014; Luyten & Corveleyn, 2007; von Below, 2017).

CHAPTER SUMMARY, CONCLUSIONS, AND DIRECTIONS

Because attachment theory is a midlevel theory, other theories and perspectives are required to attain a comprehensive psychological understanding of religion and spirituality. In this chapter, I first discussed attachment theory in relation to other theories and approaches within mainstream psychology, specifically pertaining to coping, terror management, self-regulation and self-control, meaning-making, and attribution. In all cases, I illustrated how attachment theory may serve as a valuable developmental anchor for these other midlevel psychological approaches to religion and spirituality. I then discussed attachment theory vis-à-vis the psychoanalysis of religion, focusing on Freud, Erikson, Rizzuto, and Jones. I concluded that, although attachment theory has a number of important scientific strengths compared to psychoanalytic theories, rather than entirely replacing psychoanalysis, attachment theory and psychoanalysis provide complementary approaches to religion and spirituality. Whereas the psychoanalysis of religion may yield valuable insights into unique cases and processes at the individual level, the attachment–religion approach has its most notable merits as a group-based empirical research program. As such, it has made an unparalleled empirical contribution to the psychodynamic study of religion.

Beyond the psychological phenomena I have dealt with in this chapter, many other phenomena within religious and spiritual life may (or may not) be meaningfully related to attachment. For example, concerning prayer, the most practiced form of religiosity throughout the world's different faith traditions, research could profit from distinctions based on attachment theory. Some important forms of prayer are clearly attachment-related (e.g., seeking closeness to God, seeking help and guidance from God), others are related to caregiving (e.g., praying for the ill and the poor), whereas yet others are neither (e.g., praying for a new Mercedez or for success). Again, attachment theory may aid in identifying developmental pathways associated with such dimensions of prayer. Perhaps, for example, some insecure (e.g., dismissing avoidant) individuals are especially prone to engage in nonattachment- and noncaregiving-related forms of prayer.

Because I have emphasized attachment as a developmental anchor for the links between religion on the one hand and coping, self-regulation, and the like, on the other, I wish to clarify that other developmental factors besides attachment are very likely to play a role as well. For example, heritable influences on temperament and executive functioning are indisputable; they affect self-regulation and self-control and could conceivably assert an influence on religion over and above attachment or in interaction with it. I close this chapter by calling for well-designed, large-scale, long-term, multisite longitudinal studies in which children and their families (ideally from diverse religious contexts) are followed from the first years of children's lives until much later and in which attachment, temperament, and the other key constructs discussed in this chapter are tracked and related to subsequent religious and spiritual development. If the psychology of religion and spirituality needs an important but ambitious project, this is it.

CHAPTER 10

Attachment and the Evolutionary Cognitive Neuroscience of Religion

Nowadays, science books, and especially the trade bestsellers, are dangerously seductive. They are almost like deviously well-designed addictive drug trips: After you've had one transformative "infotainment" experience, you want another. Nowhere is this truer than in books dealing with the whole of evolution, culture, religion, and the human mind. Without pointing fingers, I don't know how many books I have read in these areas in which the author or authors—offering *the* new perspective—argue that past treatises on the topic got the connections all wrong, whereas the one under consideration is "changing the entire playing field."

Each new perspective seems breathtaking: Humans are mental slaves to ancestral conditions; genes are selfish replicators; memes do the same enslaving as genes, only much more rapidly and efficiently; culture is entirely redrawing the story of evolution; evolutionary theory is dangerously deterministic and political, and the true emancipatory project requires that we free humanity from it; religious experience and cognition emanate naturally from a brain hardwired to experience God (thanks to the God module, the God spot, the spiritual gene, etc.). The reader is taken on a ride that is more thrilling than truthful, as the author creates strawmen out of past and present academic colleagues and their work. For example, evolutionary psychological perspectives are often contrasted with a mythical "standard social scientific model" (in the singular). But by no means did all or most social scientists subscribe to a view of the human mind as a blank slate equipped only with a domain-general information processor. Claiming that they did is at best poor scholarship, and at worst a devious maneuver designed to market one's own "field-changing" scientific undertaking.

I, for one, have had it with this strand of literature, so I am determined not to contribute to it. Therefore, I do not intend to offer *the* new transformative perspective on evolution, culture, religion, and the human mind. I do not argue that attachment is all there is to religion and spirituality, nor that the attachment framework is flawless or even that it offers a singular, tight narrative. As a matter of fact, I have pointed to the dangers of accepting a simplified (reified) understanding of attachment, and I have suggested that some of Bowlby's core proposals should be critically reexamined. I have not done so to make the theory (even) catchier but rather to make it richer and more truthful, that is in closer alignment with reality.

Almost without exception, the scientific "eureka" stories from which I seek to distinguish the scientific story I am telling in this book are *hardliners*. Hardlining, in either the natural or scholarly sense and often in both senses, is precisely their mistake. Nature does not draw distinct, categorical lines, and prior scientific literature is almost never so well organized or singular that it can be completely dismissed. Therefore, let me paraphrase some proposals in the form of 10 couplets in which each proposal supports rather than undermines the other proposal within the same couplet:

1. The human mind is a product of evolution, *and* the human mind is a product of culture and society.
2. The human mind comprises domain-specific mechanisms (modules, systems, etc.), *and* the human mind comprises domain-general information-processing skills.
3. Evolved psychology co-shapes culture, *and* culture co-shapes evolved psychology.
4. Evolved psychology is plastic and flexible, *and* evolved psychology constrains the mind.
5. Evolved psychology develops, *and* its developmental degrees of freedom are limited.
6. Environments (nurture) affect genes and gene expression, *and* genes (nature) affect environments.
7. Religion is natural (biological, maturational), *and* religion is cultural (socially learned, institutional).
8. Religion may be a set of evolutionary by-products (gene selection), *and* religion may have affected (cultural or gene–culture) (co-)evolution.

9. Culture is part of the environment (nurture), *and* culture differs from the (physical) environment.
10. Scientific disagreements are often real (e.g., reflecting genuinely differing appraisals of nature), *and* scientific disagreements are often fictitious (e.g., stemming from vested interests, differential emphases, and/or linguistic confusion).

Almost no knowledgeable student of science, evolution, culture, religion, or human development would seriously dispute any of these proposals if you sat down with them to have an honest, nondefensive conversation.[1] Yet each proposal appears to say almost the opposite of its couplet partner. We can see why the human mind, which is so prone to binary categorizations, might be tempted to make do with one proposal rather than attempt to include its apparent opposite. The former approach would sell more books and be easier on a reader's mind. But this is how fundamentalism and closed-mindedness operate. In science, we should do better.

In this chapter, I examine how attachment fits with and adds to other principles and theories in the evolutionary, cognitive, and neuroscientific approaches to religion, with the prospect of yielding a suitably rich and complex understanding of religion and spirituality. Despite these modest aspirations, I show why it is necessary to (re-)consider the functional consequences of the attachment system to include social/cultural learning, which is an important phenomenon in much of contemporary evolutionary science. Also, I spell out the implications of this adjustment for our understanding of the attachment–religion connection in terms of a larger gene–culture coevolutionary model. I begin with evolution and then move to cognitive science and neuroscience.

ATTACHMENT AND EVOLUTION

In this section, I first provide a brief historical overview of evolutionary science as it pertains to humans and then, in a second subsection, discuss how attachment theory fits within that context. In a third and final subsection, I address implications of this discussion for the evolutionary science of religion.

A Brief Historical Overview of Evolutionary Science: Human Minds and Behaviors

For an outsider who has peeked into evolutionary science and its history out of general intellectual curiosity, this science appears to have developed in a fairly neat, linear sequence of phases. But in recent decades things have begun to develop in many directions simultaneously. The result appears to be not only a lack of consensus on central assumptions and focal issues but also an enriching diversity of largely complementary principles and perspectives on evolution, cognition, and culture. A singular canon has yielded multiple canons.

First, Darwin's (1859) and Wallace's notion of evolution via natural and sexual selection, proposed in the 19th century, effectively outcompeted both religious (e.g., creationist) and Lamarckian (i.e., the inheritance of acquired characteristics) ideas about the origin of species. Then in the early-mid 20th century came the "modern synthesis" in which Mendelian inheritance was coupled with Darwinian theory, and genes (rather than species or individuals) came to be understood as the sole hereditary unit on which evolution acted (Huxley, 1942). Next, in the mid-late 20th century, there was a move to "inclusive fitness" theory, in which principles of kin selection (i.e., the passing on of genetically related individuals' genes) were added to natural and sexual selection theory (e.g., Hamilton, 1964). The net effect of this important move, which later spawned the sociobiological "selfish-gene" perspective (Dawkins, 1976), was that fitness came to be understood more broadly than before. In addition, reproduction of genes (sexual selection) came to be emphasized even more, whereas individual survival (natural selection) moved further into the periphery.

From its grand but controversial entrance in the 1970s, sociobiological theory (Wilson, 1975) quickly became discredited for offering "just so" stories, the charge being that virtually every observed present behavior was interpreted as an adaptation to some current, local circumstances (e.g., Gould & Lewontin, 1979). Borrowing ideas from ethology (e.g., a simplified version of Bowlby's notion of the environment of evolutionary adaptedness), the evolutionary psychology movement, distinct from sociobiology, emerged in the 1980s and 1990s (e.g., Buss, 1995; Tooby & Cosmides, 1990). With its sole emphasis on the mind's adaptation to *past* rather than current environments, an emphasis that was especially pronounced in the so-called Santa Barbara school surrounding Tooby and Cosmides, this evolutionary psychology movement can be understood as a reaction to sociobiology and its critics.

To many contemporary biologists, however, it was clear that the behaviors of organisms are not adapted just to past environments but also to current local conditions. A discipline known as behavioral ecology, including life-history theory, emerged from ethology and sociobiology to make this important point (e.g., Davies et al., 2012). The key idea in behavioral ecology is that many organisms—humans in particular—are *flexible* by design, which naturally reflects the variable environments and associated selection pressures of their ancestral pasts. Aspects of current local conditions, which forecast future survival and reproductive success, importantly co-shape behavior over and above the effects of past ancestral environments, thus effectively adapting behavior to fit current and forecasted local conditions.

In parallel with these developments, which emphasized the causal role of current ecological conditions on behavior, many biologists became increasingly interested in the role of culture. This interest grew largely out of observations that many species display notable cultural differences in habits and behavior (e.g., in tool use by crows and primates), which may happen despite virtually identical DNA and ecological conditions (e.g., Boyd & Richerson, 1988). Moreover, explaining such cultural differences and the ways in which they persist over time requires postulating some form of cultural transmission mechanism (e.g., cultural/social learning strategies, teaching) wherein cultural habits are transmitted from one generation to another. Thus, besides genetic inheritance, cultural inheritance is required.

These observations and conclusions about culture spawned two different theoretical schools of thought in evolutionary science. The first one, initially known as "memetics," began with a focus on culture per se and on how culturally acquired ideas spread among human minds, with not much weight assigned to the possibility that cultural transmission is constrained by our evolved psychology (e.g., Blackmore, 2000; Dawkins, 1976). In this approach, the focus had shifted from genetic evolution to cultural evolution (Laland & Brown, 2011). Given the pervasive, rapid, and additive (even multiplicative) nature of human cultures, which have transformed human societies from hunter–gatherer groups carrying sticks and rocks to the postindustrial, globalized world whose members carry smartphones, the move to an emphasis on cultural evolution was clearly warranted. Furthermore, much of the change and development, entirely unparalleled in other species, has come after the agricultural revolution (starting some 12,000 years ago), indicating that it is recent on an evolutionary time scale. Certainly, genetic changes, which are much slower, cannot be the primary cause of cultural evolution.

In a sense, ideas about cultural evolution can be viewed as a reinvention of evolutionary psychologists' favorite punching bag: the standard social scientific model of a "tabula rasa," domain-general mind, open to whatever inscriptions any given culture might provide. In fact, you may now encounter intellectual arguments between cultural evolutionary biologists, on one side, who argue for a strong causal role of culture on human minds and behaviors, and evolutionary psychologists, on the other side, who scratch their heads and reply, "No, our adapted mind is the cause of culture, and culture is merely epiphenomenal" (i.e., caused but not causal; cf. Barkow et al., 1992).

In line with my advocacy of nature–nurture interactionism—such interactions being understood as pivotal at every level, from past to present, from cell to species, from mind to culture—both sides paint an incomplete picture of the human mind as produced mainly by biological evolution or mainly by cultural evolution. Today, evolutionary science includes "dual inheritance" theories as part of a "gene–culture coevolution" school of thought (e.g., Boyd & Richerson, 2008; Henrich, 2016; Laland, 2017; Richerson & Boyd, 2005). Although related to cultural evolutionary theorizing, gene–culture coevolution models differ in assigning weight to both cultural *and* genetic evolution, and some acknowledge constraints on cultural evolution based on our genetically evolved psychology (e.g., the idea of *biased* cultural transmission).

In this line of thinking, genes and cultures are viewed as coevolving, and our increasingly complicated culture is viewed as creating new kinds of selection pressures, favoring increased flexibility of functioning (e.g., Laland, 2017; Richerson & Boyd, 2005). Here is one empirical example: Although adults in virtually all mammalian species lack genes (or alleles) that would allow them to digest lactose (the sugar in mammalian milk), following the agricultural revolution and the domestication of animals, alleles supporting the digestion of lactose ("lactase persistence") by adult humans have rapidly spread among some adult populations, especially Scandinavians. Tishkoff and colleagues (2007) report findings indicating a selective genetic sweep enabling lactase persistence some 7,000 years ago.

Similarly, in contemporary evolutionary theory and research, epigenetics and an evolutionary developmental ("evo devo") biological framework have taken issue with the long-standing chasm between evolution (phylogeny) and development (ontogeny) in evolutionary biology (e.g., Carroll, 2005). Evo devo research and theorizing have shown that genes (DNA) do not just cause behaviors and evoke environmental responses, but environmental factors (nurture) can activate some genes at the expense of others. Development is, therefore, truly a function of nature–nurture interactions, down to the most basic genetic level.

Whether we approach humans' adaptation to current local conditions via the lenses of behavioral ecology, cultural evolution, or gene–culture coevolution, it seems safe to conclude that understanding human cultures has become a central task of evolutionary science. It seems equally clear that humans are not stuck with a mind merely adapted to ancestral environments but one that is open to cultural learning.

The Place of Attachment in Evolutionary Science

Although attachment theory is quite compatible with the emerging views of biological and cultural evolution, being rooted in both primate biology and parental influences, some updating of the theory is required to bring it fully in line with the literature on cultural evolution and gene–culture coevolution.

Attachment, Ethology, and More

Attachment theory naturally grew first and foremost out of Darwinian theory as distilled within ethology. However, at the time when Bowlby was writing, ethologists had not decided to theoretically favor adaptation to the selection pressures of past environments over adaptation to the selection pressures of current environments, or to favor the evolution of mechanisms over the evolution of behaviors. In fact, most of ethology embraced all of these at the same time by departing from the assumption that all current behavior can be explained in ways that are complementary from an evolutionary standpoint, even though the explanations refer to very different time scales. Thus, Tinbergen (1963), building on Huxley (1942), urged ethological researchers to ask four questions to explain a given behavior, pertaining to its (1) function (or adaptation), (2) phylogeny (or evolution), (3) mechanism (or causation), and (4) ontogeny (or development). The first two questions pertain largely to what Mayr (1961) called "ultimate" explanations, and the remaining two to Mayr's "proximate" explanations.

To illustrate, what causes calluses on the skin following intense guitar practice? The answer might go something like this: During the course of evolution and faced with lethal bodily wounds, animals developed an adaptive "callous mechanism," whose function was to repair bodily wounds. This mechanism promoted survival and reproduction (in a word, fitness), presenting a case of ultimate causation. The mechanism is activated by the repeated friction of the guitar strings on the skin, a friction that is severe enough to otherwise cause bodily wounds (proximal explanation). With an example like this one, we can see that nature (i.e., the callous mechanism) and nurture (i.e., friction from guitar strings) provide complementary—not alternative—explanations. It is equally obvious that evolutionary considerations apply to both past and current environments.

While the example of a callous mechanism is didactically useful and applicable to certain simple mechanisms, it is also misleading. It applies to a situation in which there is a precise one-to-one correspondence between the ultimate and proximal explanations (see also Laland,

Sterelny, Odling-Smee, Hoppitt, & Uller, 2011). The stimulus (nurture) maps precisely onto a specific mechanism (nature), the output (calluses) is equally adaptive in ancestral and current environments, and the mechanism does not require much development (e.g., ecological, cultural co-sculpting) to deliver its outcome. The mechanism exists and is functional more or less from birth. Like a deer that takes its first autonomous steps shortly after delivery, the callous mechanism does not require complex cultural learning or guidance. These conditions are far neater than those that face us in understanding the developing human mind and most human behaviors, including religious and spiritual developments.

In hindsight, Bowlby's theory appears to have more in common with behavioral ecology than it does with either sociobiology or evolutionary psychology alone. This is because, like behavioral ecologists, Bowlby considered both (1) past selection pressures important in designing the attachment system and its set goal and (2) behavioral adaptation to a child's current local conditions (e.g., caregiving). Nevertheless, some refocusing from survival to reproductive considerations was required to make attachment theory fit comfortably within the family of behavioral ecology theories (e.g., Simpson & Belsky, 2016).

By drawing on Waddington's (e.g., 1942) canalization idea and advocating nature–nurture interactionism, Bowlby also created a theory that fits conceptually within contemporary "evo devo" biology and its associated epigenetic framework. The attachment system is a strong, genetically based propensity to develop selective attachments, but certain environmental factors (most notably the presence of caregivers who actively and repeatedly interact with the child) are required to activate the genes underlying the developing attachment system. Only then does it produce what it was designed (i.e., evolved) for.

Attachment and Cultural Transmission: Expanding the Evolutionary Toolbox

Bowlby (1969/1982) was ultimately mistaken in suggesting that the attachment system served only one evolutionary function; protection via physical proximity to a caregiver. Although he did so for good reasons at the time—reasons that helped to keep attachment theory within the confines of the ethological principles of his day—the time is now ripe to complement Bowlby's theory. Contemporary evolutionary literature shows that ethology's time has almost expired. This change is most noticeable within academia, where most biology departments that once had positions in ethology have replaced them with positions for cultural evolutionists or behavioral ecologists. They have done so in response to what has been learned about the intriguing flexibilities, environmental variabilities, and cultural embeddedness of animal behavior. Ironically, even the pioneering ethologists themselves, such as Lorenz and Tinbergen, noted that the problem with their own concept of "fixed action patterns" was that actions are rarely fixed, nor are they always displayed in neat patterns (Hinde, personal communication, April 2002; see also Schleidt, 1974). In a nutshell, this is precisely what cultural evolutionists and behavioral ecologists have gone on to study and learn from.

In particular, young animals in many species—ranging from some cognitively primitive species of fish and social insects through birds and mammals to cognitively advanced primates—learn certain behaviors from observing what the stronger and wiser others in their physical vicinities are doing. This is how some birds learned to open milk bottles in the British countryside (Laland, 2017), a skill that was not only culturally transmitted but that also migrated and ultimately forced milk corporations to seal their bottles differently. This is why some chimpanzee troops crack nuts in certain ways, whereas other troops employ different techniques. These, and many more, animal behaviors were not instinctual and did not represent simple fixed action patterns; they represented effective inventions, which were then culturally transmitted via social learning (Laland, 2017).

It turns out then that social learning is not a skill requiring advanced cognition but is almost ubiquitous in nature (e.g., Boyd, 2017). However, the more advanced (i.e., abstract, inventive) the cognitive capacities are in a species, the more skilled, faithful, and strategic the species tends to be at social learning (i.e., mimicking the particular behaviors that lead to increased ecological and cultural fit; Laland, 2017). Furthermore, the longer the period of developmental immaturity, the more plastic is the brain, and the more likely is the offspring to stay in physical proximity to their caregivers and others, and to observe and learn from them.

However, there is not yet an integrating developmental framework within which these well-established findings of cultural transmission can be understood. This is a remarkable gap in the cultural evolution literature. The attachment researcher is tempted to ask: Why haven't cultural evolutionists taken advantage of attachment theory? Attachment theory is, after all, a theory about physical closeness between immature offspring and their stronger and wiser caregivers, and it is a theory that applies especially strongly to cognitively advanced and slowly developing species. I suspect that the answer is that, to the extent that cultural evolutionists are familiar with attachment theory, they view this theory as predicated on a somewhat outdated ethological framework (see, e.g., Laland & Brown, 2011). Naturally, they may be as eager to wash their hands of ethology as Bowlby was to wash his hands of behaviorism and psychoanalysis.

It is equally tempting to ask why attachment theorists and researchers have not generally attended to cultural transmission but instead have made do with Bowlby's original ethological declaration (for notable exceptions, see Fonagy & Allison, 2014; Fonagy & Campbell, 2015; Grossmann & Grossmann, 2005). Knowing the field of attachment quite well, I suspect that this is out of orthodoxy or courtesy to Bowlby. Yet Bowlby himself never displayed such attributes, nor are they profitable in the development of science. If Bowlby were alive today, he would probably adjust his theory to take cultural transmission (learning) into account, and he would most certainly not turn a blind eye to that important literature. As an indication of such movement, in his very last, now largely forgotten, publication, he wrote: "The goal of attachment behaviour is to maintain certain degrees of proximity to, *or of communication with,* the discriminated attachment figure(s)" (Bowlby, 1991, p. 306; emphasis added), thus ultimately adding communication to proximity/protection.

Because much of attachment theory and research in recent decades has dealt with intergenerational transmission (i.e., of attachment and caregiving patterns), it is remarkable that the attachment field as a whole has not had a "Eureka" moment pertaining to cultural learning as a more fundamental process of intergenerational transmission. Perhaps there is more than relationship patterns that get transmitted across generations, as facilitated by attachment, and perhaps transmission of relationship patterns is not fully mediated by relational representations (i.e., working models of the child and parent, respectively). The child might also learn how to behave in relationships from directly observing how a parent behaves. For example, if a parent displays nurturant or rejecting behaviors to the child and others, then the child might learn such behaviors via observational learning and not just via the more complex route of working models of other (parent) and self. By also considering the small strand of social learning research demonstrating that attachment, especially secure attachment, has a facilitating effect on socialization and imitation (see Chapter 5), attachment theorists' failure to adjust attachment theory to take social learning into account is all the more remarkable.

I propose, then, that social learning is an additional functional consequence of the attachment system. This functional consequence by no means replaces but rests side by side with protection and presumably gains increased importance beyond infancy. Thus, through physical proximity to stronger and wiser attachment figures, the developing person gains not just protection but also learns culturally and ecologically important information—for example, about "unnatural" clues to danger and about how to act socially with other members of his or her culture. Whereas protection functions primarily to increase chances for survival and reproduction, social learning also promotes cultural adaptation, transmission, and ultimately cultural evolution. More incisively, attachment relationships are foundational contexts for cultural transmission and evolution, and sensitive caregiving and secure attachment facilitate cultural transmission even further (see Granqvist, in press, for a more elaborated discussion).

Attachment theory, being an ethological behavioral systems theory at its core, does not fit comfortably within a "pure" cultural evolution framework (e.g., memetics; Blackmore, 1999; Dawkins, 1976). This is because such a framework has no place for domain specificity or for constraints on cultural transmission because of evolved psychological biases. In contrast, gene–culture coevolution models, which often acknowledge domain specificity and genetically based constraints on cultural transmission, resonate much better with attachment theory. Clearly, the theme of attachment is itself part of the evolved psychology that biases cultural transmission. In Chapter 5, I explained how attachment and related working models of self and other serve to bias the cultural transmission of religious ideas and behaviors from parent to offspring. The adjustments I have suggested to attachment theory can be understood, then, as an updating of the theory to make it cohere with gene–culture coevolution models.

Attachment, Evolution, and the Psychological Sciences of Religion

Moving to evolution and religion, I address religion from a gene–culture coevolution standpoint, using the attachment–religion connection as an illustration. I also encourage evolutionary scholars of religion to move beyond the adaptation versus by-product debate to immerse themselves in the nature–nurture interactions that yield religious and spiritual development.

Religion and Gene–Culture Coevolution: The Attachment–Religion Connection

Drawing on the gene–culture coevolution framework as applied to religion and the attachment–religion connection, we can see that humans inherit religion via dual inheritance mechanisms. First, as part of genetic evolution, humans have developed an attachment system and with it a proclivity to form strong affectional bonds. Experiences with caregivers within such relationships during ontogeny are sufficiently powerful for humans that they cannot help but develop generalizing cognitive–affective biases (working models) that imbue others and the world at large with attributes such as benevolence or malevolence. Because of the generalizing nature of such working models in combination with humans' capacity for abstract thinking, they are naturally receptive to the "ontologically intuitive" idea of noncorporeal attachment figures, such as God and other spiritual entities, that cultures may or may not provide.

Second, as part of cultural evolution, developing humans are confronted with cultures (including caregivers) that often do offer ideas (i.e., information) about God and other religious entities, and that information often coheres with their cognitive–affective biases (generalizing working models) developed as a function of their relational experiences. The cultural information often coheres with their cognitive–affective biases because both are nested within genetic evolution. Such is the case for a person who has been sensitively cared for by religious caregivers within a larger "holding" religious community and culture. It would be difficult for such an individual not to sense that the world is a benevolent place governed by a benevolent attachment figure (i.e., God). Thus, religion coevolves from both genetic and cultural evolution, and it would be misleading to select one as *the* explanatory candidate over the other (e.g., Granqvist & Nkara, 2017; Jensen, 2009; Legare & Harris, 2016; Richert & Smith, 2010).

Religion as Adaptation versus By-product: Time to Move On

A gene–culture coevolution understanding of religion (e.g., Hinde, 2009; Legare & Harris, 2016; Norenzayan, 2013; Norenzayan et al., 2016) suggests that the much-debated question of religion as a set of evolutionary adaptations versus by-products ceases to be meaningful (e.g., Boyer, 2001; Kirkpatrick, 2005, 2006; Pyysiäinen & Hauser, 2010; D. S. Wilson, 2002). Inspired by an evolutionary psychology approach (e.g., Kirkpatrick, 2005), I previously joined the camp arguing that religion is a by-product of evolved psychology (e.g., the attachment system; Granqvist, 2006c). Since then, I have "evolved" conceptually, and now I strongly urge the field to move beyond the adaptation versus by-product debate. I think the debate has come to a dead end for the psychological sciences of religion in part because of ambiguities concerning which aspects of religion—by no means a neat or unitary phenomenon—are selected for discussion. Moreover, it is no longer clear what time window we should impose when determining if something is an adaptation, let alone whether to privilege gene-level or group-level selection. Again, there is no longer a singular evolutionary canon on these matters. For example, certain aspects of religion (such as religious attachment behaviors, e.g., praying for protection or guidance) may have been by-products rather than adaptations as far as past genetic selection pressures are concerned (i.e., adaptation in most evolutionary psychologists' sense; e.g., Kirkpatrick, 2005, 2006). However, those same aspects of religion may well increase a person's reproductive chances and adaptation to current cultural conditions, for example, by yielding a good fit with cultural norms, which makes a person gain higher social status and attractiveness to potential mates. In addition, cultures that adopt certain religious norms (e.g., about Big Gods) may gain advantages over other cultures, such as group cohesion, cooperation, and efficiency following rapid expansion of cultural group size (Norenzayan et al., 2016; D. S. Wilson, 2002). Being part of such a culture may then facilitate gene survival and reproduction (cf. group selection). Indeed, genetic evolution is still ongoing. Also, as memetics illustrate, evolution is not restricted to reproduction of genes but may also be validly approached as reproduction of cultural information.

My point here is not to argue in favor of any one of these specific possibilities and focal points suggested by others but simply to illustrate that the initial, seemingly simple question of religion as evolutionary adaptation versus by-product branches off and becomes almost impossible to answer once we realize that the mind is not merely adapted to past environments but also adapts to present ones and that evolution does not act only on genes but also on information. To make matters even more complicated, how minds collectively form cultures may affect future genetic adaptation. An additional reason the field should move beyond the adaptation versus by-product debate is that we have markedly limited empirical access to past selection pressures, so questions about these pressures are notoriously difficult to answer empirically.

Nature–Nurture Interaction in Development: Pay Attention, Not Lip Service

Evolutionary sciences of religion should instead examine how evolved dispositions (e.g., the attachment system) interact with experiential (including cultural) input to yield both commonalities and diversity in religious and spiritual development (cf. Geertz, 2010; Jensen, 2009; Turner, Maryanski, Petersen, & Geertz, 2018). Understanding religious and spiritual development requires studying how genetic predispositions (or biases) are co-sculpted by experience. In the Prologue, I suggested an analogy between development and sculpturing, where a raw material (clay) is sculpted to take a variety of shapes and functions. I distinguished this analogy from another common one: the unfolding of a ready-made table cloth (cf. a nativist understanding of maturation).

Religious and spiritual development is much more in keeping with the sculpturing analogy, unlike simpler phenomena such as calluses.

Although a strict evolutionary-psychology (Santa Barbara school) approach to religion is not suitable as the field's comprehensive framework, *developmental* evolutionary psychology continues to show promise, precisely by attending closely to development (Granqvist & Nkara, 2017). Beyond the issues already discussed, a serious problem with much evolutionary psychology is that, although it sets itself out paradigmatically as a nature–nurture interaction framework, in practice evolutionary psychologists have generally only paid lip service to the role of nurture in co-sculpting evolved human genetic dispositions.

To illustrate, although David Buss has explicitly asserted that nurture can provide "calibrating" input into evolved psychological mechanisms (e.g., Barker, 2006), neither he nor most other evolutionary psychologists have typically attended to such input (for exceptions, see Kirkpatrick, 2005; Öhman & Mineka, 2001). For example, in Buss's (1989) classical study of sex differences in mate preference across 37 cultures, which was designed to test hypotheses derived from sexual selection and parental investment theory, he elected not to test the moderating effects of culture (i.e., a proxy for nurture), even though his findings clearly indicated the presence of such effects. Thus, he gave biased attention to the underlying mechanisms (nature) at the expense of cultural and social input (nurture) co-shaping the development of those mechanisms. Buss himself acknowledged this in the ensuing discussion of this work, where he also noted that psychological mechanisms are flexible by design. Indeed, much in line with my emphasis in this book, Buss (p. 42) called for "an identification of important features of the environment (including structural, cultural, and resource features) that interact with given parameters of the psychological mechanisms to produce overt behavior." Even more than in understanding sex differences in mate preferences, a complete evolutionary understanding of religion and spirituality requires serious attention to how elements of culture co-shape evolved psychological dispositions to produce commonalities and diversity in religious and spiritual development.

A major shortcoming of evolutionary approaches to religion and spirituality in general (i.e., not restricted to evolutionary psychology per se) is that they do not attend seriously to developmentally derived individual and cultural differences in religion and spirituality. Instead, they remain overly focused on species-typical characteristics that might seem to make religious/spiritual output "natural" for the human mind (e.g., Atran, 2002; Barrett, 2012; Bering, 2006; Bloom, 2007; Boyer, 2001). In this book, however, I have shown that what appears to be simply "natural" actually hides an intricate pattern of nature–nurture interactions in individual development. I believe most evolutionary accounts of religion would profit from paying attention to and learning from nature–nurture interactions in development. I am hopeful that the attachment–religion framework presented in this book can be inspirational for such theoretical developments.

ATTACHMENT, COGNITIVE SCIENCE, AND NEUROSCIENCE OF RELIGION

Much of the cognitive science of religion (CSR) is nested within evolutionary science, so what I have said in the preceding sections largely applies to CSR as well (see also Chapter 3). The cognitive science approaches have made immensely useful contributions to the psychological sciences of religion (for an overview, see Barrett, 2011), and they are largely compatible with the attachment framework. Our evolved psychological dispositions lead humans to develop cognitive–affective biases for attachment, anthropomorphism, agency detection, mentalization, and intentional reasoning. Such biases are fundamental for the developing human mind, and they all serve to make God and associated religious ideas "cognitively intuitive."

That CSR approaches and attachment theory are so aligned is not surprising. Their intellectual lineages can be traced partly to the same roots in the history of science, namely, cybernetics and the early literature on artificial intelligence. Bowlby inherited many of his foundational concepts and assumptions from that strand of literature, including the control-systems approach and the idea of internal working models (Chapter 1). Had the other researchers within the emerging cognitive science movement been as interested in babies and relationships as they were in technology and mechanical devices, attachment theory could have become an integrated part of cognitive science, including its later application to religion. Instead, it was developmental psychologists, especially Mary Ainsworth, Alan Sroufe, and their students, who took attachment theory to heart. The elaboration of the theory branched off in a somewhat different direction, with a focus on individual differences, measurement procedures, psychometrics, and socioemotional development. Nonetheless, both cognitive scientists and attachment researchers ultimately reached out, via separate routes, to religion, and they did so in ways that are largely compatible but with notable differences in emphasis. In the following section, I discuss three general topic areas related to convergences and divergences between the attachment–religion connection and CSR.

Mentalization, Affect, and Defense

There is a rich tradition of theorizing and research on mentalization and associated clinical treatments, which has contributed to realigning attachment theory with the clinical, psychodynamic literature (e.g., Fonagy et al., 2004; Fonagy & Target, 1997). Peter Fonagy, Mary Target, and their colleagues have demonstrated that caregivers who are able to keep their children's minds in mind and who adequately reflect upon their children's mental functioning and intentional stances promote not just the development of secure child attachment but also children's early acquisition of mentalizing skills (e.g., Fonagy et al., 1991). Furthermore, mentalizing skills promote flexibility and cooperation within attachment-caregiving relationships and in other social relationships, and difficulties in mentalizing are associated with some forms of psychopathology (Fonagy et al., 2004).

Given the importance of mentalization within much theorizing and research in CSR (e.g., Barrett, 2011), one would have thought that CSR theorists and researchers would have drawn on the mentalization literature in clinical psychology, with the potential of gaining a rich developmental and experiential foundation for their theorizing, and bridging it to attachment theory and research. Unfortunately, they have not. Indeed, they seem to be entirely unaware of the clinical mentalization literature, as is evident in the absence of cross-referencing to it. How could this be? The emphasis on mentalization within clinical psychology is by no means a peripheral movement but, rather, is one of the most central and important developments in recent psychodynamic psychology (as an illustration, Fonagy et al.'s [2004] handbook has more than 6,000 citations).

The chief reason may be that CSR researchers remain negatively biased toward anything remotely psychodynamic within psychology. This suspicion reflects personal experience: When interacting with fellow CSR and neuroscience researchers, I have been asked on numerous occasions why I insist on working with attachment theory, which they typically represent as a "neo-Freudian" psychodynamic theory. My attempts to explain that attachment theory—if it represents any singular paradigm—is at heart an ethological theory, designed to bridge the chasm between cognitive science and psychodynamic psychology, falls on deaf ears. I always leave those conversations with a lingering sense of being the odd man out who thinks there's anything in psychodynamic psychology worth bridging to. Those who read the previous chapter of this book (or Granqvist, 2006b) featuring a critical examination of psychodynamic approaches to religion should see the great irony in that.

Accordingly, considerations of affect and associated psychological defenses, which are the provinces of psychodynamic psychology, have been conspicuously absent in cognitive science. Not even Bowlby's attempts to make defenses appear mechanistic (i.e., defensive exclusion of information, diversion of attention, segregated systems) seem to have succeeded in getting cognitive scientists to care about them. The same absence is also the case in CSR approaches to religion and spirituality. Yet, it is not merely that religious concepts are cognitively intuitive that gives religion its flesh and blood or pulls humans to religion. Until CSR models find a way of incorporating the motivational roles of affect and defense, their understanding of religion and spirituality will remain incomplete. Also, until they do, CSR and attachment theory will continue to rest side by side, accounting for different components of religion and spirituality. In other words, because attachment and CSR models do not converge in some of their central assumptions, they cannot be neatly integrated, but they can nonetheless complement one another and yield a fuller psychological account of religion than either approach alone enables. For example, attachment sheds light on the relational, experiential, and affective components of believers' representations of God in relation to themselves, whereas CSR helps account for the more propositional and intellectual qualities of God representations (e.g., God's properties and attributes; see also Davis, Granqvist, & Sharp, 2018; Richert & Granqvist, 2013).

Predictive Processing

As part of the move from a highly modular, nativist view of the mind, characteristic of some past evolutionary psychology approaches (e.g., Barkow et al., 1992; Tooby & Cosmides, 1990), the pendulum is currently swinging among younger CSR and neuroscience researchers to consider the mind as a domain-general, flexible, developmentally and culturally anchored Bayesian prediction machine (e.g., Andersen, 2019; van Elk & Aleman, 2017). For example, a person will "detect" (perceive) supernatural agency insofar as he or she has previously encountered culturally acquired supernatural concepts and a given situation is sufficiently ambiguous to pull forth an expectation for supernatural agency (Andersen, 2019). This development and its depiction of the mind as a prediction machine are in many ways fruitful because the mind does learn from experience (cf. priors), is continuously updated and flexible, and forecasts future events to yield expectancy verification, at least when sensory conditions are opaque and causal attributions ambiguous. In addition, this approach is potentially highly compatible with the attachment–religion framework (Granqvist & Nkara, 2019).

Indeed, going back in the history of cognitive science itself, Craik (1943; see also Young, 1964) offered elaborate ideas concerning mental representations, based on the assumption that experiences build and update internal working models (IWMs). Craik also claimed these ideas to be important for forecasting future events. Craik's IWMs were, as we have seen, a key component of attachment theory from its outset (Bowlby, e.g., 1969/1982). In fact, Bowlby explicitly noted the predictive nature of IWMs: "The use to which a model in the brain is put is to transmit, store and manipulate information that helps in *making predictions* as to how what is here termed set-goals can be achieved" (1969/1982, p. 80, italics added). Bowlby's underlying idea was that our flexibility, adaptability, and complexity as a species are contingent on our ability to make small-scale mental predictions, which can guide our behavior in future situations that are, to varying degrees, similar to ones we have already encountered.

However, in providing an alternative model to overly fixed (evolutionarily ultimate) modular accounts (e.g., a dedicated hyperactive agency detection device; Barrett, 2004), a predictive coding framework runs the risk of reacting against them in ways that are not beneficial. For example, it could repeat the mistake of tabula rasa memetics, that of ignoring humans' evolved propensities, which do serve to constrain their minds. Many of those propensities concern motivation, affect, and defense, and unless these are incorporated as priors into Bayesian models of religious cognition and perception, the predictive coding framework may go down in history as another incomplete CSR model applied to religion. Thus, the future utility of the predictive processing framework hinges on how researchers set the priors in their models. In this regard, it will be essential to learn from the nature–nurture interactions that ultimately steer religious and spiritual development.

Embodied Cognition

Although cognition resides largely in the brain, it is important to remember that cognition is also embodied; actions and movements are not just governed by the brain but also have cognitive and neural repercussions (e.g., Lakoff & Johnson, 1999; Siegel, 1999; M. Wilson, 2002). At first glance, the idea of embodied cognition may seem to have limited relevance for religion and spirituality because supernatural entities would seem to be highly cerebral inventions. For example, they can't be touched, smelled, heard, or seen. However, this has not prevented many religions from using images and symbols to make supernatural entities concrete, and religious believers do have embodied experiences interacting with those images and symbols (e.g., Geertz, 2010; Watts, 2013). Also, religious rituals are replete with examples of prescribed movements (e.g., folding of hands, raising of arms, bowing down), which are often undertaken in the company of fellow believers, adding further to the embodied nature of ritual. Similarly, religious experiences are often expressed using embodied metaphors such as being "touched," "carried," "held," and "leaning on God's everlasting arms." In sum, religion is both cerebral and embodied.

The embodied qualities of religious rituals and experiences naturally resonate with experiences in attachment and other forms of close interpersonal relationships. Indeed, there are intriguing phenotypical resemblances between the two. Nowhere is this more evident than in the raising of arms, which is what infants do, in a pick-up gesture, to alert the caregiver of the infant's desire to be picked up and held. This is also what believers do to signal devotion and a desire for communion with the divine. Embodied cognition in the context of religion and spirituality is an underexplored area of research where CSR and attachment could meet without having to run into touchy issues pertaining to psychological defenses and the like. In view of the common misunderstandings of attachment theory as first and foremost a "neo-Freudian" theory, I wish to clarify here that, from an attachment viewpoint, there is nothing regressive or immature about embodied cognition. In contrast, our attachment systems are active and our minds relational from cradle to grave (Bowlby, 1973). No wonder, then, that we display embodied, relational behaviors in relation to God and that we often interpret religious experience in embodied, interpersonal terms. Thus, attachment-related motivation is part and parcel of the embodied nature of religious rituals and experiences.

Neuroscience of Religion

Notwithstanding the embodied nature of religious rituals and experiences, the brain is a grand mediator of human psychology, including the psychology of religion and spirituality. For that reason, the neuroscience of religion has spurred considerable interest over the years, seen not least in the possibility that our brains are "hardwired for God," comprising a "God spot," "God module," and the like (e.g., Persinger, 1987, 2002; Ramachandran, Blakeslee, & Shah, 1998). Unfortunately, this interest has not been matched by either a corresponding quality nor quantity of empirical research. For every 100 popular magazine articles and conceptual treatises, there has probably been less than one high-quality empirical study. Furthermore, much of the public and theoretical interest in the neuroscience of religion has been naïve and misguided. We have seen how multiple scholars have almost gone out of their way to draw invalid ontological conclusions about the brain and God, whether of God as a ghost in the brain or of brain activation as a clue to God being "real." This confusion has climaxed within the field of "neurotheology" (see Granqvist, 2006c). Despite popular assertions to the contrary, the neuroscientific study of religious cognition and experience gives *no* clue as to whether God is "real," simply because observing brain activation does not yield any privileged access to ultimate reality (e.g., there is no brain circuit associated with "false" as opposed to "veridical" perception of ultimate reality).

Because religious cognition, behavior, and experience involve virtually all behavioral and psychological modalities—motor movements, motivation, memory, self-control, perception, dual cognitive processes, emotions and affects, and speech, to name a few—virtually the whole brain, and perhaps especially the temporoparietal and prefrontal regions, are involved in religious cognition, behavior, and experience (e.g., McNamara, 2009). However, this yields no direct evidence that the brain causes religious outcomes. Whether the brain or something else is studied, we cannot infer cause–effect relations from correlations, and we know from the embodied cognition literature that our actions and body movements, though produced by the brain, also feed back and affect brain activation.

In other words, neuroscience provides no secret shortcut to understand religion or spirituality on its own terms. Nor is any specific module in the brain dedicated to experience God, just as no specific brain module is dedicated to engaging with attachment. Even though Bowlby (1969/1982) referred to the attachment system as a neurally based system, it is sufficiently widespread across the brain to suggest that attachment is a neural "function," not to be confused with any specific, narrowly conceived structure or module (Granqvist, 2006c). To be serviceable, neuroscientific studies of religion and spirituality should build upon the knowledge that has been amassed in the psychological, evolutionary, and CSR approaches to religion. When they do, they can be enlightening specifically about *the neural* mechanisms associated with religious cognition, behavior, and experience, which can then provide valuable feedback for our psychological and evolutionary understanding of religion and spirituality. Next, I give three examples of neuroscience of religion approaches that are particularly relevant from an attachment viewpoint: temporal lobe activation and the sensed presence of a sentient being, oxytocin and spiritual experiences, and the mentalizing brain and interpersonal communication with God.

Temporal Lobe Activation and the Sensed Presence of a Sentient Being

Key to the attachment–religion connection is the idea that people sometimes sense the comforting presence of religious attachment figures such as God, gods, or other spiritual entities. In many cases, that "presence" should probably be understood as metaphorical, but in other cases it seems to be meant literally (see Chapter 8 for examples). Given that the brain is a grand mediator of experience, it would be fascinating if researchers could manipulate people's brains to produce religious experiences, including the sensed presence of God. That may seem like science fiction, but late Canadian psychology researcher Michael Persinger (e.g., 2002; Hill & Persinger, 2003; Persinger & Murphy, 2016) in fact claimed that he could do this with some 50–80% of people from the general population.

Persinger (e.g., 2002) held that sensed presence and other anomalous experiences are caused by certain patterns of naturally occurring geomagnetic activity, in turn affecting temporal lobe brain activity. Persinger (e.g., 2002) and his colleagues (e.g., Hill & Persinger, 2003) also created an electromagnetic "God helmet," which can allegedly reproduce the key magnetic wave pattern using very weak (and thus unhazardous) magnetic fields. Consequently, when attached to the temporal lobes under conditions of sensory deprivation, those magnetic fields can allegedly cause the brain to produce sensed presence and other anomalous experiences, somewhat akin to the limbic discharge and mystical experience associated with temporal lobe epileptic seizures (e.g., Dewhurst & Beard, 1970; McNamara, 2009). Persinger and colleagues published numerous experimental papers to support their claims, and some of the higher-quality studies contained control groups (i.e., God helmet on but with only "sham-fields" activated; e.g., Cook & Persinger, 2001; for a recent review, see Persinger & Murphy, 2016). These studies have been covered in the media, including prestigious outlets such as *BBC News* and *Discovery*.[2]

I have always been intrigued by epileptic mystics and artists, such as the great Russian author Dostoyevsky, and singers/musicians like Ian Curtis (of Joy Division) and Neil Young (nicknamed "Shakey"). My colleagues and I were sufficiently curious about the Persinger team's claims and findings that we sought to replicate and extend them (see Granqvist et al., 2005). Our ultimate aim was to study the neural correlates of experimentally induced sensed presence experiences using a brain-scanning device (positron emission tomography [PET]). However, because PET scanning is expensive, we first sought to ascertain that we could reproduce the Persinger team's experimental effects, while simultaneously overcoming some of the methodological limitations of the original experiments. Members of our group visited Persinger's team, learned from them, and were graciously offered a portable magnetic field device for purposes of conducting our replication and extension studies.

We undertook this replication and extension project with enthusiasm. Some of us even hoped we would discover the neural causes of the "God delusion." Others among us remained somewhat on the dry side, yet cautiously optimistic that we would embark upon something scientifically important. One reason for not getting carried away was the long-standing scientific deed of ontological agnosticism. Another reason for caution was that the limitations of the original experiments were sizable. The Persinger team had not employed experimental double-blinding (i.e., requiring that both study participants and experimenters interacting with them are blind to participants' experimental condition assignments), implying that differential interaction with participants across conditions and participant suggestibility were viable alternative explanations to magnetic field effects (see Persinger & Murphy's [2016] attempted rebuttal of this criticism). The scientific literature is replete with examples of how violations to double-blindness can cause various treatments to appear effective, but as soon as the experimental design is tightened and made double-blind, the effects disappear.

Unfortunately, our team failed to replicate the Persinger team's findings, despite using a properly powered (in view of the previous experiments' large effect sizes) experiment (Granqvist et al., 2005; $N = 89$; see also the ensuing exchange in Larsson, Larhammar, Fredrikson, & Granqvist, 2005; Persinger & Koren, 2005). Whereas we observed no effects of magnetic field conditions, a number of our participants (approximately 30%) across both experimental conditions had seemingly spontaneous sensed presence, mystical, and other forms of anomalous experience, and these experiences were substantially predicted by indices of suggestibility such as absorption (see Chapter 8). We suggested that spiritual priming (from answering various preexperimental religiosity and spirituality questionnaires) in combination with a sci-fi gizmo (the helmet)—whether or not it was plugged in—under the condition of sensory deprivation caused highly suggestible participants to have anomalous experiences.

These findings have since been replicated and extended by various other research teams, who have gone on to study the roles of sensory deprivation, absorption, and expectancies without focusing on brain activation per se (e.g., Andersen et al., 2014; Maij & van Elk, 2018; Maij, van Elk, & Schjoedt, 2017; van Elk, 2014). Personally, however, I remain curious about how our brains enable us to sense the comforting presence of an invisible attachment figure. I encourage other researchers to answer that question.

Oxytocin and Spiritual Experiences

Spirituality can be understood as a panhuman proclivity for self-transcendence, where the self is experienced as fundamentally related or interconnected with the divine, with nature, with the world itself, with other living beings, or simply with deeper (and usually hidden) layers of the self (Hill & Pargament, 2003). This proclivity has been extensively explored throughout human history, including experiments with plants, psychedelic drugs, and religious rites. Many people conceptualize the transcendent "object" of spirituality in anthropomorphic terms as a noncorporeal attachment figure, providing a sensed presence and yielding felt security for the individual. Given this strong relational theme of spirituality, it is reasonable to ask whether hormones associated with feelings of closeness, interpersonal trust, and love are implicated in spirituality. Oxytocin (OT) is a viable candidate hormone.

OT is a neurohormone—specifically, a pituitary gland peptide hormone and neurotransmitter—with a wide range of physiological effects. Initially considered a hormone of lactation and maternal labor, it has more recently been extensively studied with respect to its psychological effects, especially in the context of attachment and bonding (e.g., Buchheim et al., 2009). Oxytocin release is triggered by projections from the hypothalamus, where it is synthesized, and is then secreted by the pituitary gland into the bloodstream (Gimpl & Fahrenholz, 2001). It is thought to play a key role in various socioemotional abilities beyond attachment and bonding (for reviews, see Bartz, Zaki, Bolger, & Ochsner, 2011; van IJzendoorn & Bakermans-Kranenburg, 2012).

Although it is easy to imagine a role for OT in spirituality, the link between OT and spirituality is not well understood. Surprisingly, only a few studies have examined the connection. In a correlational study, Kelsch and colleagues (2013) assayed plasma oxytocin levels in HIV-positive individuals, some of whom had reported spiritual transformations. They found that higher endogenous OT levels were associated with higher spirituality, and OT levels were twice as high in individuals who had described spiritually transformative experiences relative to those who had not. However, OT levels may have been affected by antiretroviral medications. In another correlational study, Holbrook, Hahn-Holbrook, and Holt-Lunstad (2015) examined endogenous OT levels through saliva samples in a nonclinical population of American Christians. Consistent with Kelsch and colleagues' study, they found a positive relation between self-reported spirituality and endogenous OT levels.

A few years back, my colleagues and I started planning an experiment in which we aimed to test a causal role of exogenously delivered OT on spiritual experiences in a sample that had been genotyped for OT-related genetic (allelic) variations. The reason for using such a genotyped sample is that exogenous-OT effects may differ depending on dispositional parameters such as OT-related genotype (e.g., Bakermans-Kranenburg & van IJzendoorn, 2014; Szymanska, Schneider,

Chateau-Smith, Nezelof, & Vulliez-Coady, 2017), much in line with the nature–nurture interaction framework advocated in this book. I conceived of this project as a sequel to our sensed presence study, described above, in which we would replace the magnetic field conditions with OT conditions. Thus, besides experimental assignment to OT versus placebo treatment conditions, the project would entail spiritual priming via answering preexperimental spirituality questionnaires and then a sensory deprivation setting following the OT versus placebo treatment. We figured that, jointly, these design features should suffice to cause spiritual experiences such as a sensed presence or mystical experiences, and perhaps OT would amplify the effects or yield more interpersonal interpretations of the experiences. Because our previous sensed presence experiment, along with other studies, had shown absorption to predict the outcomes, we added absorption as a predictor. This enabled us to study whether exogenous OT had spirituality-enhancing effects over and above or in interaction with absorption.

By the time we geared up to conduct the study, a graduate student of mine (Mikael Skragge) found out that we had been "beaten to the chase" by an American research team that had just published a highly similar experiment on an OT-genotyped sample (van Cappellen, Way, Isgett, & Fredrickson, 2016). Van Cappellen and colleagues (2016) studied 83 midlife male participants, randomly assigned to receive a single dose of intranasal OT spray or placebo spray (sugar–salt solution), following which they completed a trait–spirituality measure (the Spiritual Transcendence Scale; Piedmont, 1999). Their results showed that OT did indeed lead to an increase in participants' self-reported spirituality, or at least it did when religious affiliation was statistically controlled. Their findings showed that OT facilitated spirituality among those who were religiously unaffiliated but not among those who were affiliated. Furthermore, their OT effects were qualified by OT-related genotypes, such that exogenous OT caused increased spirituality only among carriers of certain OT-related alleles.

Given these correlational and experimental links between OT on the one hand and spirituality on the other, we thought we had solid reasons to expect that exogenous OT would promote trait spirituality in our study as well, and perhaps also the occurrence of mystical experiences and sensed presence during sensory deprivation. Thus, we ultimately designed our own experiment to conceptually replicate that of van Cappellen and colleagues (2016) but with the additional aim of causing spiritual experiences *in vivo* (i.e., not just causing increased trait spirituality). Our study was conducted on a largely nonreligious sample in Sweden, whereas van Cappellen and colleagues' study was conducted on a largely religious sample in the United States. To ensure reasonable statistical power in view of the strength of findings reported in van Cappellen and colleagues' study (roughly 20% explained variance in the outcomes), we recruited an even larger sample than theirs (N = 116), and we included female in addition to male participants. Despite these efforts, we observed no main effects of exogenous OT, nor any interactions with OT-related genes, on any of our outcomes (trait spirituality, mystical experiences, sensed presence; see Cortes et al., 2018). Complementary Bayesian analyses of our study findings indicated much more persuasive support for the null hypothesis (i.e., no effect) than for the alternative hypothesis.

As in our previous sensed presence experiment (Granqvist et al., 2005), however, some participants did have spiritual experiences, and absorption was again found to play a role in predicting which participants did. Specifically, high absorption predicted mystical experiences, sensed presence, and trait spirituality. On closer examination, however, absorption interacted significantly with OT treatment and only predicted the outcomes in the placebo condition. Following exogenous OT administration, absorption ceased to be predictive; in other words, following OT administration, low absorption scorers became as likely to have spiritual experiences as high absorption scorers. Another, more causal, way to describe this interaction is to say that OT (relative to placebo) caused increased spiritual experiences among low-absorption scorers, thus resembling van Cappellen and colleagues' (2016) findings on religiously unaffiliated participants. Equally notable, however, OT caused *decreased* spiritual experiences among high-absorption scorers.

We concluded that the neurohormone OT may facilitate spirituality among people who are not "naturally" spiritually (or religiously) inclined (i.e., low-absorption scorers), by opening their minds to sense a connection with something beyond their regular sense of self. We also speculated that OT may have a "stabilizing" effect on the minds of high-absorption scorers, somewhat akin to the (paradoxically) calming effects of low doses of amphetamine on hyperactive individuals (see Cortes et al., 2018). Needless to say, given the failed overall replication of van Cappellen and colleagues' (2016) main findings, along with the inherent difficulty in replicating statistical interaction patterns (e.g., Open Science Collaboration, 2015), these conclusions and speculations should be viewed as tentative and hypotheses-generating rather than definitive. Nonetheless, on the whole, OT does show promise as a neural mechanism linked to both attachment and spirituality.

The Mentalizing Brain and Interpersonal Communication with God

As noted above, attachment-related experiences and maturation facilitate the development of mentalizing skills. Also, various mentalizing capacities have been posited within the CSR literature as key evolved domains underlying religion and spirituality. Just as children come to understand that their caregivers and others have minds of their own that, via intentional stances (wishes, intentions, desires, etc.), steer their behavior, so too do religious believers typically appreciate that God has a mind that steers God's actions. Indeed, communicating with God—for example, in private prayer and in some religious coping—often entails trying to get in touch with and affect God's mind (e.g., "if You only relieve the pain I'm in, I promise I will spread your love and stop goofing around"). For these reasons, we should expect that private prayers and other forms of religious communicative behaviors should recruit areas of the brain that are associated with mentalization (or "social cognition").

This is precisely what was hypothesized in one of the best-designed and most persuasive brain-imaging studies on religion (Schjoedt, Stød-kilde-Jørgensen, Geertz, & Roepstorff, 2009; for another high-quality study, on executive function and mystical experience, see Cristofori et al., 2016). Uffe Schjoedt, a Danish religion scholar, and his colleagues (2009) predicted that a private, improvised prayer (as compared with the recital of a formal prayer or a secular control condition) would recruit the three classical "theory-of-mind" areas of the brain: the anterior medial prefrontal cortex, the temporopolar region, and the temporo-parietal junction (Gallagher & Frith, 2003). Their prediction was supported, with impressive specificity, in observations of functional magnetic resonance imaging of 20 Danish Christians engaged in these three different tasks. Schjoedt and colleagues concluded that religious people, who consider God to be "real" and capable of reciprocating requests, recruit brain areas related to social cognition when they pray. They also argued, based on their own and others' findings, that praying to God is much like other intersubjective experiences, comparable to "normal" forms of interpersonal interaction. These findings are what we would expect based on the attachment–religion and attachment–mentalization connections.

What made the Schjoedt and colleagues (2009) study so impressive was not merely its design and the specificity of its findings but also—and equally importantly—the great care they took to ascertain that the participants engaged in subjectively meaningful and ecologically valid forms of prayer. In fact, I think this is an excellent example of the way neuroscience of religion research should proceed in the future, building on cross-disciplinary expertise across religious studies and neuroscience, and using study designs set up to test theoretically derived ideas pertaining to a specific form of religious behavior, experience, or cognition. As with all studies, however, this study had some limitations, not least of which was the small number of participants; such limitations call for future replications and extensions. Future research could also profitably test causal hypotheses suggested by Schjoedt and colleagues' study findings. For example, does experimental activation (e.g., via transcranial stimulation) of the brain's theory of mind regions—in appropriate contexts—cause religious believers to be increasingly prone to engage in prayer or sense intersubjective communication with God? This line of inquiry has great potential to uncover the neural mechanisms associated with the attachment–religion connection.

CHAPTER SUMMARY AND CONCLUSIONS

Much of the recent progress in the psychological study of religion has been undertaken not within psychology's mainstream but, rather, within its sister disciplines—evolutionary and cognitive science and (to some extent) neuroscience. As applied to religion, these disciplines are highly interrelated in that evolutionary science has dealt with the psychological (including cognitive) mechanisms expressed in religion; cognitive science has sought to understand the cognitive underpinnings of religion; and neuroscience has examined the neural components of those evolutionary/cognitive mechanisms. In this chapter, I have illustrated how attachment theory is part of this effort. I have even argued that the placement of attachment theory and research within mainstream psychology is largely a historical coincidence, resulting from the receptiveness of some skilled developmental psychologists to Bowlby's ideas. These psychologists adopted the theory, contributed to it, and made it a major part of psychology. However, attachment theory, originating in ethology, was among the first fully developed theories within what was later to become evolutionary approaches to human psychology. Similarly, as evidenced in Bowlby's use of a cybernetic model and his borrowing of the IWM construct, attachment theory grew in the same soil that later produced cognitive science. Consequently, attachment theory as applied to religion is part of the greater evolutionary–cognitive–neuroscience mixture that provides our understanding of how basic, evolved properties of the human brain and mind interact with culturally acquired ideas to produce what we know as religious and spiritual outcomes.

Attachment theory has some unique strengths compared to the other available theories in these fields, not least of which are a rigorous analysis of the evolution and set goal of the attachment system, close attention to how the system is co-sculpted by nurture, how it develops and transforms in ontogeny, and a complementary focus on normative aspects and individual differences. These unique features can be used as a heuristic template for theory improvements and developments within other branches of the evolutionary, cognitive, neurosciences of religion. Notwithstanding these strengths of attachment theory, Bowlby's notion of protection as the singular functional outcome of the attachment system is no longer serviceable because social/cultural learning is another functional outcome of this system. This theoretical adjustment updates attachment theory and enables it to become a developmental anchor for gene–culture coevolution models.

Much of the evolutionary–cognitive science of religion has paid insufficient attention to the role of culture as containing important "calibrators" (e.g., religious models) of the evolved psychology expressed in religion. Culture clearly pays a causal role here (cf. Hinde, 2009) and one that is more fundamental than merely adding content details (Kelemen, 2004) to an otherwise ready-made mind. In other words, and reflecting nature–nurture interactionism, religious and spiritual development reflects the continuous, bi-directional influences among underspecified genetic predispositions, the surrounding environment (its micro- and macro-features), and the developing person.

Much of the evolutionary psychology approach to religion has been unnecessarily narrow (e.g., focusing mostly on domain-specificity, gene-level selection, reproductive fitness, the adapted mind). A more comprehensive understanding of religion, in both its generality and important particulars, requires, perhaps more than almost any other phenomenon, a complete consideration of all available tools within the evolutionary toolbox, including domain-general properties of the mind (e.g., imitation, memory formation), interactions among domain-specific mechanisms, multilevel selection considerations, and gene–culture coevolutionary processes (Laland & Brown, 2011).

By the same token, much evolutionary writing on religion has concerned whether or not religion is best understood as adaptive (or a set of adaptations) or as a by-product of evolution. I would like to move beyond that focus to consider how culturally acquired input interacts with our evolved psychological dispositions to yield commonalities and diversity in religious and spiritual development (cf. Richert & Smith, 2010).

I noted some divergences between attachment theory and other evolutionary–cognitive science approaches, particularly divergences relating to the roles of affect and defensive processes, which are central to attachment but downplayed in many other evolutionary–cognitive approaches to religion. These divergences may seem to make the approaches incompatible, but that is not necessarily the case. Rather, the roles of affect and defensive processes are much more central to the "hot" outcomes and phenomena that are usually studied from an attachment viewpoint (e.g., the affective valence of God as a relational partner) than to those studied in other evolutionary–cognitive approaches (e.g., people's understandings of agency, God's properties and capacities). This does not render the theories incompatible; the theories simply deal with different parts of religion and spirituality.

In discussing attachment in relation to the cognitive science of religion, I highlighted how an attachment approach is compatible with a focus on embodied (rather than merely cerebral) religious cognition and how attachment–religion research can help set priors to predictive processing models applied to religion. Finally, in discussing the neuroscience of religion, I highlighted the compatibility between attachment theory and a neuroscientific focus on sensed presence, oxytocin, and mentalization as expressed in religion and spirituality.

PART V

BEYOND ATTACHMENT, RELIGION, AND SPIRITUALITY

The Psychology of Secularism

So far, I have been viewing religion in relation to attachment-related security, but other sources of security also affect religion. Security can be obtained in multiple ways, some of which do not have the same structure or content as the attachment–religion way. In this final part of the book, comprising only one large chapter, I consider a wholly "secular" way of gaining security–the welfare state—reflecting a societal rather than dyadic or religious source of security. One of the central findings in this area is that when security is provided by effective welfare policies, many people find it less necessary to seek security in conventional religion.

In this chapter, I dispense with the usually sharp distinction between religion and the secular, and it is a great relief to finally do so. The distinction is more convenient than real, as illustrated by the historical irony that "the secular" is an inherently Christian idea (e.g., Taylor, 2007). What's worse, the distinction between them creates arbitrary boundary conditions where nature itself offers none, and those boundary conditions then function as shackles for the mind. Psychological processes that apply to religion and spirituality also tend to apply to many of the things we usually consider secular. With regard to communal human life and from a strictly functional point of view, whether gods, spirits, or other metaphysical entities are called upon may not be as central a matter it is often thought to be when we are drawing distinctions between religion (where metaphysical entities are called upon) and the secular (where such entities are not called upon). Nonetheless, humans' communal, cooperative life tends to be organized around "mythologies"—abstract, symbolic ideas involving concepts such as insurance policies, ideologies, monetary systems, and social contracts. Harari (2014) grants all of these phenomena the status of mythologies (or fictions) because they are not "real" in any physical sense. Nor do they have any privileged reality status *in and of themselves*. Humans in large groups tend to act as though the fictions are real, however—as though money is "the real deal," as though there are some unquestionable "human rights," as though some particular political ideology identifies a true "universal" value. That humans are fundamentally mistaken about the reality status of these and similar concepts makes them functionally real. Hence, the fictions become very influential in human cultures and societies, and they of course trickle down and have delusionary effects on almost every individual's mind.

In Chapter 11, I focus on one such "secular" fiction: the idea of the universal welfare system in democratically socialist countries. Thanks to a generous but costly insurance policy, such a system is designed to grant people in a society basic material and other forms of security. Over time, the implementation of welfare politics tends to undermine the security-providing role of religion and God-related fictions in people's lives and minds. In providing people with a sense of security and undermining their "need" for religion, I argue that macro-level welfare systems have important implications for the psychology of "secularism" as well as for understanding human dependency in adulthood.

CHAPTER 11

God versus the Welfare State

Religion may be a cross-cultural and historical universal, but there is nevertheless huge variability in how central religion is to people across the world, at least as religion is conventionally defined and understood. In other words, although religion may fit with certain intuitive ontologies, in turn resulting from environmentally sculpted genetic predispositions (psychological systems or mechanisms), the nuances of how those ontologies are expressed and the extent to which they actually become central in people's lives are quite variable across nations and cultures. Considering the tiny genetic differences that exist among humans from different cultures and continents (e.g., Serre & Pääbo, 2004), this implies that important contextual, macro-level determinants need to be taken into consideration when studying religiosity. These determinants are best understood as cultural/historical in origin and must be assumed to feed back into the psychological systems (mechanisms) that presumably produce "religious" outcomes. Provided that certain cultural/historical factors are present, however, the mind may instead produce "secular" outcomes.

To begin with an extreme example, mainland China is a place where institutionalized religion is far from normative. China has long been dominated by the secular philosophy of Confucianism, followed more recently by the suppressive powers of state communism. Only some 20% of its population reports an affiliation with an institutional religion (Daoism, Buddhism, Christianity, and/or Islam), although a small majority of the population subscribes to folk beliefs or engages in associated practices (e.g., ancestor and local deity worship, fortune telling, feng shui; Yang & Hu, 2012). At the other extreme are countries in which religion is highly normative: for example, theocracies in the Middle East, such as Saudi Arabia, where Islam is not only mandatory but permeates all aspects of society, including the judicial system. As declared in the Saudi Basic Law of Governance (1992), "its constitution is Almighty God's Book." As a consequence of this powerful social pressure, it is difficult to obtain valid statistics on individual religiosity, but it seems safe to assume that religiosity levels are very high, if for no other reason than to maintain personal safety from oppression.

Major international variation in population estimates of religiosity and secularism is not restricted to atheistically versus religiously oriented dictatorships. It can also be observed in what Westerners usually consider the "free world." Following the structural decline of religion in much of the Western world, secularism has increasingly become culturally normative. Consequently, the study of secularism is rapidly emerging as an important topic within the behavioral sciences of religion (e.g., Zuckerman, 2009; Zuckerman & Shook, 2017), although it has yet to establish a common theoretical framework from which secularism can be understood. In this chapter, I aim to contribute to such a framework.

When I refer to "secularism," I do not intend to advocate a strong version of the now outdated "secularization thesis" (e.g., Durkheim, 1915/2008; Freud, 1961a, 1961b; Marx, 1844/1977)—the largely "scientistic" (e.g., Stenmark, 2017) belief that modernity and rationality will ultimately undermine the role of religion in society and in people's lives. On one hand, the decline of collective religion is an indisputable fact in most of the Western world, which does speak in favor of the secularization thesis (Zuckerman & Shook, 2017). It is largely this structural, societal decline that I have in mind when I refer to secularism. On the other hand, as discussed in Chapter 8, there has been a rise and spread of subjective spirituality and associated esoteric beliefs, showing that we are not the fully faithful children of secular Enlightenment philosophy (with its creeds of rationalism, empiricism, and universalism) that previous generations of intellectuals hoped and more or less assumed we would be at this point. This speaks against the secularization thesis. On the whole, the changes are better described as a subjective, spiritual transformation of the religious landscape than as a complete turn to some absolute form of secularism (cf. Berger, 1999; Heelas, Woodhead, Seel, & Szerszynski, 2005).

Humans in all cultures create and share collective fictions that provide them with security and control, or at least the *sense* of security and control. This is accomplished, not least, by creating and adhering to various forms of "insurance policies." The fiction may revolve around an unobserved, anthropomorphized, cosmic attachment figure (such as a theistic God) who is understood to protect certain people in the here and now and to grant them eternal security in the hereafter, provided that they meet certain conditions (e.g., faith or deeds). Naturally, the religious community may also have to chip in to provide additional material and social aid when the divine fails to act or is acting in "mysterious ways." However, the fiction may just as well revolve around a secular "social contract," in which individuals are granted earthly security by adhering, for example, to a national government's insurance policy, which is financing its welfare system. If the individual agrees to pay an artifactual premium (i.e., tax money) to the state, then the state offers generous security-related insurance in exchange, which may cover, for example, education, health care, unemployment benefits, parental leave, and pensions. It is this latter security artifact—the welfare system—that will concern us in this chapter. I argue that a particular way of organizing welfare systems, as an alliance between the individual and the state (Berggren & Trägårdh, 2015), is an especially effective means of providing a sense of earthly security, thereby yielding, as an unintended consequence, a high rate of secularism in the population. As an additional benefit, perhaps this trade-off can be accomplished without much use of force; thus, no bloodshed is required. However, anyone determined to persuade other primates to agree to a social contract revolving around a welfare system would have to shed blood. This is because other primates typically do not believe in artifacts, so they would not trade a piece of paper ("money") for some future security prospect.

This chapter contains four main sections. In the first, I review theory and research, largely from political science and international economics, pertaining to the idea of religion and welfare systems as providing competing, or alternative, insurance policies. I also note the implications of this analysis for the psychology of religion and secularism. In the second section, I explain how a welfare state can be organized so as to provide a sustainable sense of security and without a high degree of religiosity in the population as a consequence. Within that section, I draw particular attention to an individually based, universal welfare system. I also discuss "state individualism" and its key attachment-related corollary, "the Swedish theory of love" (Berggren & Trägårdh, 2015). Third, using Sweden as a case study, I briefly explain why and how one of the world's most successful welfare states developed, starting with the Protestant Reformation, through the king's or queen's nearly almighty power to the strong state and its welfare functions, and ultimately to welfare nationalism. Fourth and finally, I call for a new discipline ("welfare psychology"), consider initial empirical findings, and spell out some key research questions that this new field should address.

Needless to say, I am navigating controversial, heavily politicized territory here. The Swedish welfare system inflicts my compatriot Swedes with a rare, poorly hidden sense of national pride. Yet, I intend to examine it with the dispassionate attitude of a cultural anthropologist, giving attention not just to how Swedes prefer to present their treasured system to the world, but also to the many skeletons hidden in its closets.

RELIGION AND WELFARE SYSTEMS
PROVIDE COMPETING "INSURANCE POLICIES"

Available statistics from the World Values Survey, spanning from 1980 to the present, indicate that population variability in estimates of religiosity is far from random. Among countries in the Organisation for Economic Co-operation and Development (OECD), the strongest predictor of degree of religiosity versus secularism is simple: the proportion of the gross national product (GNP) that governments spend on welfare functions including health insurance, schools, and pensions (e.g., Gill & Lundsgarde, 2004; Scheve & Stasavage, 2006). The more governments spend on welfare, the less religious are their populations. These findings have recently been extended beyond OECD countries to a total of 114 nations (Barber, 2013; see also Zuckerman et al., 2018). In a real sense, then, a welfare system seems capable of replacing "God" and religion.

The Negative Link between Welfare Systems
and Religion Is Robust and Pervasive

This negative link does not apply only to demographic or formal aspects of religiosity, such as frequency of religious attendance, belief in God, or degree of religious involvement. It applies equally strongly to psychologically meaningful aspects of religiosity such as the importance of God in people's lives and their seeking of comfort in religion. In other words, the more governments spend on welfare, the less important is God in people's lives and the less they seek comfort in religion (Gill & Lundsgarde, 2004; Scheve & Stasavage, 2006).

Proportion of welfare spending statistically explains an unusually sizeable chunk of the large international variation in population estimates of religiosity. The link is huge by conventional standards in developmental, social, and personality psychology as well as the behavioral sciences of religion. Moreover, the negative link between welfare spending and religiosity remains robust and significant even when researchers do their best to "kill it" by controlling for potential confounds such as religious pluralism, affluence, urbanization, equality, and age (e.g., Barber, 2013; Gill & Lundsgard, 2004; Scheve & Stasavage, 2006). From their extensive analyses of the World Values Survey and other international data sets, Norris and Inglehart (2011) have provided converging findings and conclusions. Countries marked by "existential security" (a key feature of which is an efficient welfare system) have witnessed a rapid secularization process, whereas populations under existential insecurity (low welfare) retain high rates of religiosity (cf. Barber, 2013).

We can learn a great deal from studying bivariate extremes in the association between welfare spending and religiosity. Among the OECD countries, on one extreme (high welfare, low religiosity), we find Sweden,[1] followed by other Scandinavian countries, and then additional western European nations such as France (e.g., Zuckerman, 2009). In the Swedish context, a graduate student and I have found that not only do Swedish adults in general refrain from seeking comfort and security in religion, but they do so even when they are subjected to a major life stressor (Granqvist & Moström, 2014). More specifically, we found that parents whose children suffered from a serious, potentially lethal heart condition were equally likely to be atheists and agnostics and equally unlikely to pray to God or "something else" as were parents of healthy children. Contrary to the old saying that there are no atheists in foxholes, we concluded that there are plenty of atheists in distressing situations, at least in the Swedish welfare state. On the other extreme (low welfare, high religiosity), we find the United States, followed by some southern European countries, especially Greece. As we have seen in the previous chapters, people in such nations are likely to seek comfort and security in religion, and the proclivity to do so is associated with better mental health. Given that Sweden and the United States provide sharp contrasts in these regards within the free world, in this chapter I make many comparisons between these two countries and populations.

That Sweden and the United States should be each other's international opposites may seem counterintuitive; they are both relatively wealthy, high-tech Western democracies, marked by successful entrepreneurship and individualism. Also, pitting Sweden against the United States is like comparing a cherry with a watermelon, or perhaps David with Goliath. With only 10 million citizens, Sweden has the population of Michigan, which is merely one out of 50 U.S. states and not among the top five in population size. Counterintuitive or not, Swedes and Americans are vastly different both in rates of religiosity and in demands/expectations of their respective governments to engage in welfare spending. Also, Sweden and the United States are both sovereign nations with much control over welfare spending.

Beyond the negative link between welfare spending and religiosity at the population level, Scheve and Stasavage (2006) have demonstrated converging support at the individual level. Regardless of nation, individuals who support increased welfare spending (on health, age, and unemployment benefits) are less religious than those who support decreased welfare spending. This difference again withstands statistical control for confounds (e.g., income, sex, age, education, employment status, social support). In other words, not only are people residing in welfare states less religious than people not residing in welfare states; even within a particular country, individual support for welfare spending goes hand in hand with lower religiosity. In American political parlance, this might seem to translate to liberals (to the left on the political spectrum) simply being less religious and more supportive of welfare spending than conservatives (to the right on the political spectrum).[2] However, Scheve and Stasavage found that the negative association between support for welfare spending and religiosity remained surprisingly undiminished even after controlling statistically for a measure of left–right partisanship. If anything, the association was strengthened, clearly indicating that there is much more substance to the negative association between religiosity and preferences for welfare politics than can be explained by simple political persuasions.

The Idea of Equivalence: Competing Insurance Systems

What, then, explains this robust and pervasive negative association? Political and other social scientists, from Marx (1844/1977) and deprivation theorists (Glock & Stark, 1965) onward, have argued that welfare states and religion may serve as competing "insurance systems." In the studies referenced above, Gill and Lundsgaarde (2004) argued that welfare systems and religions compete in providing material benefits. Scheve and Stasavage (2006) favored a more psychological interpretation; welfare systems and religion compete in insuring people against adverse life events. The psychological literature contains no dearth of suggestions pertaining to specific protective and defensive processes involved in religion that might also benefit from welfare systems, such as overcoming helplessness (Freud, 1961b), providing attachment-related felt security (e.g., this book; Kirkpatrick, 2005), facilitating coping resources (Pargament, 1997), aiding terror management (e.g., Vail et al., 2010), and promoting self-regulation (McCullough & Willoughby, 2009) and a sense of control (Kay, Gaucher, Napier, Callan, & Laurin, 2008). I do not emphasize here the relative importance of any one specific process at the expense of the others because I think it would be mistaken reductionism to focus on merely one when the whole comprises multiple contributing parts. As an analogy, there is no use in having an elephant's trunk compete against its ears, its head against its tail, its rear legs against its front legs, and so on. The elephant is made up of all those parts, just as religion and effective welfare politics serve multiple psychological, social, and material functions. My key point of departure is to assume equivalence between welfare systems and religion. Both religion and welfare systems can provide potentially effective insurance policies across multiple domains. Interestingly, however, they do appear to compete with, rather than complement, one another. At least this is the case in general practice, although it is not necessarily so in principle. At times, some social democrats advocate welfare systems on Christian grounds, and churches sometimes advocate generous welfare spending by governments.

Common Roots in the Cultural Spread of Enlightenment Philosophy?

Readers trained in scientific methodology should have objections to the simple, straightforward findings and conclusions I have presented thus far. In particular, what is cause and what is effect between welfare spending/support and religiosity? I have implied that welfare spending, via increased security, leads to decreased religiosity, but couldn't it be the other way around—declining religiosity leading to higher demand for welfare provision and security? The answer is: Yes, in principle, it could. Strictly speaking, we cannot confidently infer causality from correlational findings, even when confounds have been controlled, trends over time have been analyzed, and results have nonetheless supported the proposed process direction. However, a reversed causal interpretation would not only beg the question of why religiosity decreased in the pertinent populations to begin with but would also be anachronistic. It is a historical fact that many of the analyzed populations, being God-fearing and church-going folks, were highly religious in the early 20th century when the welfare systems started to enter the historical scene. It remains possible, however, that bidirectional influences drive the historical changes in a process that is mutually reinforcing. It is also possible, indeed likely, that both changes in welfare spending and religiosity originate in some common, more foundational historical process that was already in motion prior to implementation of welfare systems.

For example, the cultural spread of Enlightenment philosophy through science and education might be proposed as the grand historical cause of secularism, enabling the welfare system and undermining religion in a "single" brushstroke. In particular, the cultural spread of Enlightenment philosophy may have contributed to a stronger and more efficient public demand for "secular-rational" insurance policies to replace the "illusory" security (Freud, 1961b) or "opium" (Marx, 1844/1977) provided by religion, ultimately yielding the welfare system. However, although both welfare systems and the decline of religion may be nested in a common enlightenment process, this does not render spurious the negative link between the two that has been observed in change processes during recent decades. Rather, the welfare system may have become a key weapon within the modern enlightenment artillery that causes further drops in religiosity, which can then in turn lead to further expansions and reformations of the welfare system in a mutually reinforcing process. As elaborated below, however, we should set the historical clock for key events much earlier than the Enlightenment period, while humbly recognizing that there is no unmoved mover behind historical events (i.e., no absolute beginning of history).

Welfare Spending on Education Is a Key Factor Behind Secularism

A welfare system is complex, comprising multiple, nested welfare functions (e.g., a pension plan, health care insurance, unemployment benefits, "free" education). In line with the strong negative link between religiosity and the proportion of GNP that governments spend on the welfare system as a whole, the sum total of the welfare system may be what undermines religion over time. However, different welfare functions (or components) may also have differential weights in undermining religion. When subjecting welfare spending to an analysis at the component level, Franck and Iannacone (2014), based on a well-designed set of time-series analyses spanning multiple decades, found that government spending on education appears to have played a key role in decreasing church attendance across 10 traditionally Christian countries. So powerful was government school funding that it washed away the effects of all other welfare components when entered simultaneously in a regression analysis. Also, the effect of government spending on schools withstood statistical control of affluence, urbanization, and educational attainment, the last-named of which was unrelated to church attendance. In addition, a model of reversed causality (i.e., decreased church attendance creating a demand for public school funding) provided a less persuasive fit with the data. Presumably, then, it is the source of school funding (state vs. private) that appears to matter for changes in church attendance, more than the other way around, and the extent of schooling appears to be largely irrelevant.

I suspect, however, that the content of education is a key confound lurking behind the source of school funding. When the state funds schools, educational content tends to align with Enlightenment philosophy, or "secular-rational" values (Norris & Inglehart, 2011). For example, in U.S. public schools, teaching creationism and intelligent design is viewed as legally unconstitutional (e.g., Moore, Jensen, & Hatch, 2003).

When private actors (e.g., families and religious denominations) provide direct school funding, educational content is likely to vary more. For example, instead of teaching evolution by natural selection and other principles of evolutionary biology, the biology curriculum in Evangelical Christian schools may indeed include religious concepts such as creationism and intelligent design.

In any event, presuming that Franck and Iannacone's (2014) findings regarding church attendance generalize to other aspects of religion, not all components of welfare systems appear to be equally conducive to secularism. State funding of "free" education in a tradition of secular–rationalist values appears to be the crown jewel, adding substantially to the general security enabled by other components of a welfare system.

No wonder, then, that the Christian right in the United States is doing its best to battle any state that attempts to increase school funding and determine their educational content. Franck and Iannacone (2014) perspicaciously assert that "schools are instruments of indoctrination, both religious and secular; competing interests battle endlessly over every aspect of education" (p. 386). In line with the international trend toward increased secularism in the Western world, they conclude, "No institution wields more power in modern nations than the centralized state" (p. 386). Those who have fully digested the undeniable virtues of science are likely to think that this is a good thing. However, those who have experienced the virtues of religion may well disagree, while nonetheless profiting from the products of science in their daily lives.

Implications for the Psychology of Religion and Secularism

The idea of welfare systems and religion as providing competing insurance policies should have implications for research in the psychology of religion because this discipline is concerned with all determinants of an individual's religiosity. In general, researchers in psychology rarely give due attention to the influence of variation in societal parameters on people's minds, although such variation is relevant as part of the macrosystems in which individuals develop (e.g., Bronfenbrenner, 1979). Societal arrangements matter a great deal for children's developmental contexts. To be nurtured and grow up within a welfare state, nested within secular–rational values and high existential security, is clearly a different developmental context than to be nurtured and grow up within a religious context, nested within traditional values and (often) existential insecurity. Psychologists should begin to address the implications of such developmental contexts for children's development in general, and psychologists of religion should study their implications for the development of religiosity and spirituality in particular (see also Chapter 3).

Naturally, the idea of competing insurance policies also has implications for how we understand and research the flipside of the psychology of religion—the psychology of secularism. Contemporary Europe, and especially the Scandinavian populations, again represent the best examples available in the free world. Assuming that the welfare state provides an alternative insurance system to religion, the welfare state may function like a religion as far as psychological processes and outcomes are concerned. Given that only limited research is available at present, in what follows I sketch the structural organization and historical development of a particular welfare system ("the Swedish model"—or "Nordic model," to pay due respect) that has been demonstrably effective in both providing security and promoting secularism.

HOW TO ORGANIZE A WELFARE STATE
TO ENABLE SECURITY AND PROMOTE SECULARISM

A welfare state presupposes in the first instance a strong state, that is, a state that controls a relatively large proportion of the population's GNP, typically enabled by collecting plenty of tax money. However, multiple strong states are not best characterized as welfare states. For example, a regime may devote a large chunk of the population's GNP to surveillance of its population (e.g., the former East Germany), to the military/defense complex (e.g., Israel), or to its political leaders (e.g., pre–"Arab spring" Tunisia). To qualify as a "welfare" state, the strong state must, in the second instance, devote a large chunk of its resources to welfare functions rather than to other state functions.

Two Tasks of a "Universal" Welfare State: The Case of Sweden

Welfare states typically engage in two general security-promoting tasks: (1) providing insurance to citizens and (2) redistributing income among them. By this definition the United States, with its immense economic inequality and opposition to state intervention, does not qualify as a welfare state (e.g., Piketty, 2013).[3] Sweden and its social democrats have been champions of both tasks, so I provide examples from this particular country and political movement. Beyond insurance, I illustrate how Swedish state legislation provides additional protection.

The Insurance Function (and Protective Legislation)

The first task of a welfare state is to provide an extensive insurance program that can potentially cover (or at least subsidize) citizens' costs for, or loss of income due to, health care, education, unemployment, parental leave, other living expenses (e.g., accommodation, food), pensions, and the like. The Swedish welfare system embraces its citizens literally from cradle to grave.

Not only is Swedish health care essentially "free," but it ranks fairly high from an international perspective, in terms of both quality and efficiency (e.g., Tandon, Murray, Lauer, & Evans, 2000). With respect to efficiency, the average unit of health care carries about half the cost in Sweden as compared with the United States (Kamal, Box, McDermott, Ramírez, & Sawyer, 2019). This difference is presumably due partly to the expensive legal expertise that American hospitals rely on, faced as they are with the United States' epidemic "suing culture."

In addition, Swedish education is entirely "free," from kindergarten to the very highest educational levels. Thus, Swedish university students pay no tuition. In passing, not all Swedish students are aware of this benefit; some have been observed claiming they must take loans to cover their studies, thus confusing their "studies" with their "living expenses." Moreover, student loans for living expenses are provided by a state agency, with generous conditions.

Swedes also receive comparatively generous benefits when they are faced with unemployment, social disruption, or aging-related adversities. For example, individuals who decide to divorce may receive a housing allowance from the welfare state to compensate for the drop in family income. Also, the living conditions of the elderly—largely a function of the welfare system's resources—also ranks high compared with international standards (Foley, 2018). This enables Swedish families and workers to get on with their lives without "having to" concern themselves too much with their elderly relatives. Because the elderly may still require some limited time investment from their adult children, however, the left party in Sweden recently proposed that workers with parents in elder care be granted welfare compensation for the time they spend with their elders.

Following each child's birth, the welfare state grants Swedish parents, whether rich or poor, a monthly "child allowance," which is paid until the child is 18 years of age. In addition, families are granted an astounding "parent insurance" that covers paid parental leave (80–90% of full-time work income) for 16 months, with the equality proviso that both parents (presuming two-parent families) care for the child for at least 3 months (known as "daddy months"). From the developing infant's perspective, this typically entails being continuously cared for by parents during the first to second year of life, presumably helping Swedish infants to develop representations of their attachment figures as available and accessible. Furthermore, Swedish families have the right to save and spread out some of the money provided by the welfare system until the child is 8–12 years old. Despite this opportunity, Swedish parents do not generally stay at home with their young beyond the paid months covered by the welfare state (see also Daun, 1996). Most Swedish toddlers start full-time day care by 12–15 months, so any expectations they might have had of the attachment figures' availability and accessibility may be suddenly thwarted. In fact, Sweden has among the highest rates of 0- to 2-year-olds enrolled in full-time day care across the OECD countries (OECD, 2016).

The early full-time enrolment of Swedish children in day care presumably occurs because of another privilege associated with the welfare system; it covers more than 90% of day care costs. As of 2019, Swedish parents, even in high-income families, pay a maximum of US $150 per month for a child in full-time day care/preschool. Thus, it is more economically feasible for Swedish parents to return to full-time work than to continue caring for their young, so they typically opt for the former alternative.

"Vacation reimbursement" is another illustration of the nearly all-encompassing nature of the Swedish welfare system. Swedish employers are not only legally obliged to grant their employees 4–6 weeks of annual vacation, but employers must also give employees a temporary 13% "raise in salary" when the employees take vacation. Employees' vacation-related traveling, eating, drinking, and accommodation are not free, so the state requires employers to chip in. Finally, the Swedish welfare system helps to cover funeral costs, thus literally transcending death and embracing Swedes even when they have gone to "meet their maker." In Sweden, there is obviously less cause for singer–songwriter Lucinda Williams's words of caution: "Don't buy a fancy funeral / It's not worth it in the end / Goodbyes can still be beautiful / Without the money that you'll spend" ("Fancy Funeral"; *West*, 2007). In sum, the welfare state has Swedes covered to their teeth; oh yes, dental care is also "free" for children and subsidized for adults.

Beyond the insurance provided by the welfare system, the Swedish state's sense of protective responsibilities toward its citizens is reflected in other legislative matters. Being an adult in Sweden means being prohibited from making some potentially bad but autonomous decisions for oneself and one's family. Examples abound, but I give only three here to preserve space. First, the state is so protective of adult Swedes that it prohibits commercial stores from selling regular beer and wine to them. The state has a monopoly because otherwise Swedes might be unable to control their drinking (which is probably true—just ask the Danes!).

Second, the state forbids schools and preschools to receive any donations from Swedish parents or to have parents provide lunch boxes for their children, even though the schools are more or less chronically underfunded (because they are funded almost exclusively with tax money). This is out of equality-related concerns for the potentially poor, although the Swedish population is actually among the richest and most economically homogeneous in the world. Where the state cannot regulate parents' initiative in every detail, consensus-oriented Swedish parents tend to step in and take that responsibility themselves. For example, they have been observed to develop communal policies to prevent individual families from giving snacks and drinks to school staff who educate and take care of their children. The concern is again that there might, at least in principle, be families who cannot afford such gifts and who may then feel inferior.

Third, to prevent any Swede from engaging with "narcotic" substances, the Swedish state provides some of the most repressive zero-tolerance policies against narcotics in the free world. To be on the safe side, it also teaches the gateway theory of drugs, where even the use of "light drugs" (an expression that does not please the Swedish state) is forecasted to result in heroin addiction, overdose, and ultimate death.

Although the sum total of such "gracious" state treatment of its citizens may, in some readers' assessments, indicate that the state belittles its citizens and violates their autonomy, Swedish adults are indisputably kept safe and secure. Most adult Swedes do not seem to mind these potential violations of autonomy; in free elections, they have continuously voted for ever-expanding welfare insurance and protective legislative initiatives. Apparently, most Swedes agree with Otis Redding: "I want security, yeah, and I want it at any cost" ("Security," *Pain in My Heart*, 1964).

The Redistributive Function

The second task of a welfare state is to redistribute financial resources from relatively affluent to relatively less affluent citizens, which is enabled by progressive taxation and targeted insurance functions (e.g., social and unemployment benefits). It is in some ways misleading to consider the redistribution (or "solidarity") function as a welfare state's "second" task. This is because in principle and in rhetoric—if not in practice, as we shall see—redistribution was much more fundamental to the idea of a welfare system than was its insurance component. If insurance were its principal function, everyone who is sufficiently well off in a society could just as well pay their own insurance costs and not require much state intervention for their own or their family's security (except, perhaps, to protect themselves from criminals, many of whom may be poor). Furthermore, they could select their insurance policies with greater freedom, flexibility, and relevance to their own needs than a general state insurance could provide, although in all fairness they would also have to devote much time and thought to making rational choices vis-à-vis the commercial insurance offerings on the market. Naturally, many people prefer to attend to other matters.

Political thinkers and associated movements to the left, whether associated with communism, socialism, or social democracy, initially aimed first and foremost to achieve redistribution of wealth. However, communists failed miserably with that aim and with much bloodshed as a consequence. This was partly because of the revolutionary and dictatorial means they used in pitting social classes against each other. Stealing from the rich and giving to the poor never panned out well in the long run. The rich fought the dictatorial programs, and the poor were often confused with those who supported the dictatorships, effectively resulting in nepotism, not redistribution.

The social democrats, with their decidedly reformist (rather than revolutionary) and democratic (rather than dictatorial) political program, arrived in a much more cunning disguise. Like socialists and communists, they aimed for redistribution from wealthy owners to less wealthy workers (i.e., initially their own voters), but they realized that in order to succeed with that aim they needed to get the relatively affluent and powerful segments of the population on board, without bloodshed. In early-20th-century Sweden, this necessitated bipartisan consensus, more specifically with communists to their left and social liberals to their right (support from conservatives was not needed). The social democrats succeeded in gaining bipartisan consensus, thereby achieving not only the implementation of welfare politics but also sustainable political power. And there has been no need to sing the revolutionary blues in Sweden, nor in Scandinavia as a whole.

The social democrats' recipe for success was the idea of a "universal" welfare state. The universal welfare system, designed by the most skilled of social engineers, sought not just to accomplish redistribution (i.e., their original aim), but also to devise a general insurance program that could be marketed as beneficial for most or all, even for owners of large industries. This aim struck a chord with social liberals who accepted the ideas of a social safety net and limited redistribution politics.

The social democrats were amply rewarded by achieving and maintaining political power over the course of many decades. Since 1936, they have ruled Sweden roughly 80% of the time with their own majority, or in alliance with other parties, or as a minority government. Although extremely important in shaping the Swedish welfare state, earlier historical events had effectively paved the way for a strong Swedish state. In that regard, then, social democracy was a movement waiting to happen.

I return to the earlier historical events in a later section and also trace the fate of social democracy to the present.

Redistribution versus Insurance—or Redistribution Equals Insurance?

It is reasonable to wonder how many societal resources could possibly remain for redistributive ends following the generous welfare benefits provided to all citizens within an expansive universal welfare system, such as the Swedish one. Not much, one might assume, so the idea of accepting refugees, who may require initial aid (i.e., redistribution), currently appears unacceptable to many contemporary Swedes, especially white male laborers. Pitting redistribution against insurance, I speculate that successful welfare systems inevitably tilt toward the insurance component, however much solidarity (redistribution) was at stake in their original designs. Over the course of time and succeeding generations, "what you can do for the system" (i.e., obligations) gradually tilts toward "what the system can do for you" (i.e., rights). This is because sustaining political power in a democratic society requires that the political program continue to be popular even after people have been helped to make it out of poverty. With Sweden as the prime example, there is no end to how much security people can ask for in a politically reformist welfare society that continually works on system improvements to please the voters.

It also appears inescapable to conclude that segments of the population that have traditionally benefited from the redistributive function of the welfare system continue to feel entitled to that function and may not want to share it with others, such as new refugees. As the welfare system marches on over time and succeeding generations, increasing segments of the population may feel entitled to its redistributive function. In fact, research indicates that an increasing proportion of Swedish adults are not even morally at odds with requesting state benefits to which they are in fact *not* entitled. Even on a self-report measure, this is now the case for roughly 40% of the adult Swedish population, a figure that has doubled since the 1980s. With a figure of more than 70% among young adults at present, welfare ethics are disappearing, especially in the younger generations (Dousa, 2018; see also Statens Offentliga Utredningar [SOU], 2007). This dissolving welfare ethic coupled with demanding increased security for the self suggests that welfare systems are fragile. They may in fact collapse unless people realize that their rights must be balanced against their obligations. "You can't always get what you want . . . / You get what you need," as summarized by the Rolling Stones (from the album *Let It Bleed,* 1969).

Before concluding this section, I wish to point out that pitting insurance against redistribution, as I have done in the preceding sections, is potentially misleading. As distinguished political philosopher John Rawls (1971/2009) emphasized, we should all carry a "veil of ignorance" to our view of how life and society will ultimately unfold. Therefore, aiming for political reforms that benefit those in society's most vulnerable positions implies not just redistribution but also insurance. Nations employing universal welfare politics (again, insurance + redistribution) appear to develop higher levels of equality than nations whose welfare systems are targeted exclusively toward redistribution (Korpi & Palme, 1998). This is presumably because when taxpayers receive benefits for the premiums they pay, they are willing to accept higher taxation rates, which ultimately yields more resources to redistribute than if whatever they pay is redistributed to others from the outset. In that regard, a well-balanced universal welfare state functions as a clever solution to an advanced game theory exercise (e.g., the prisoner's dilemma), where a good solution for others is a good-enough solution for oneself. Moreover, reasonable levels of equality within societies bring many additional benefits.

The Devil's Organizational Scheme: Individualistic Welfare Systems

Every modern society comprises at least three fundamental units: the individual, the family, and the state. Beyond these units, societies of course comprise religious institutions, markets, labor unions, political parties, and seemingly spontaneous civil engagements, or what many Americans refer to as "the community." However, I keep things as simple as possible, largely restricting my consideration to the individual–family–state triad. Also, the importance and functions of some of those additional societal units are dependent on how the individual–family–state triad is organized. For example, religious institutions tend to be comparatively strong in societies where the family is important, unlike the situation in societies where the family is not so important.

Individually Based versus Family-Based Welfare Systems

For a welfare state to work smoothly, the state needs an ally who is both willing to pay the high premiums (i.e., taxes) associated with the costs of the welfare functions and to grant the state a certain measure of authority over how people live their lives (Berggren & Trägårdh, 2015). The second requirement, in particular, is probably why many Americans disapprove of the idea of a welfare state and one reason why some Europeans are so tempted to cross the pond and live the life of a "freeborn."

As noted, however, in democratic societies the state also needs to please the premium payers in order to be granted this authority, or else it will be overthrown.

Depending on how the insurance system is designed, the state's ally can be either individuals (i.e., an individually based insurance system) or families (i.e., a family-based insurance system). However, the ally cannot be both individuals and families. A practical problem with a state's simultaneous alliance with both individuals and families is that the insurance system becomes structurally complicated. Another problem is that individuals and families could grow so strong that they would be able to overthrow the authority of the state. It is more strategic for the state to keep one of the units—whether individuals or families—in line.

The Nordic welfare model, characteristic especially of Sweden and Denmark but in many ways also of Norway, Finland, and Iceland—typifies an individualistic welfare system, which keeps families at bay. It dates back to the early half of the 20th century but has been continuously reformed ever since. That it is an individualistic system means, in practice, that individuals are responsible for paying welfare premiums, regardless of their potential spouse's resources, and individuals are also the recipients of welfare benefits, again (almost) regardless of their potential spouse's resources. An important reason for this arrangement was that it undermined financial dependence within families, and a related—less idealistic one—was that it prompted women to work outside the home, thus facilitating dual-earner families and rapid economic growth in society. In any event, this arrangement was believed to be emancipatory for women, who no longer needed to rely on a spouse's resources to get by. Although it might seem to selectively serve women's interests, women previously had to tolerate male oppression because of material dependence, so the time was ripe for society to help release women from such dependence.[4]

Interestingly, individualistic welfare systems tend to be central to reformed (especially Lutheran) European countries, in other words the very countries marked by the highest pace and rates of secularization. So, if the devil were to design a welfare system, he would make it individually based. Thus, in what follows I largely discuss the individually based system. In contrast, to the extent that they employ welfare politics, southern European countries and Germany tend to employ family-based systems. In practice, this means either that families pay premiums and receive benefits or that individuals are differentially taxed depending on family. For example, unmarried Germans are taxed at a higher rate than their married counterparts. Such family-based welfare systems tend to be central to Catholic countries in Europe. These countries have thus not undergone secularization to the same extent as the Protestant countries.

State Individualism and the Swedish Theory of Love

A dozen years back, two Swedish historians, Henrik Berggren and Lars Trägårdh (2015), published a book with the provocative title, *Is the Swede a Human Being?* (see Ekman, 2006). The book has not, to my knowledge, been translated into English, but it became an immediate classic within Sweden, and for good reason. Much of my structural analysis of the Swedish welfare state is built on Berggren and Trägårdh's notion of an individually based welfare system, or what they refer to as "state individualism." In their analysis, the individually based welfare arrangement expresses a Swedish "national character" with deeper historical roots. More specifically, they argue that Swedes have a long lineage of autonomy-striving, of valuing solitude and of pursuing independence from other human beings. In the welfare state, they have found their ally, which has helped to free them from relational dependence. One likely reason for the success of Berggren and Trägårdh's book is that it helped many Swedish readers appreciate that they may not be the state-engineered collectivists that some previous treatises of Swedish culture had indicated (cf. Daun, 1991). In fact, Swedes are just as individualistic as Americans, though in decidedly different ways. Whereas American individuals tend to team up with their families and keep the state at bay, Swedish individuals team up with the state and keep their families at bay.

People from most non-Nordic countries may find it hard to understand how the most wonderful asset—the family—could possibly deserve to be kept at bay. I addressed this issue in the previous section, noting that families are breeding grounds for financial dependence. Also, it is not that Swedes necessarily shun families or relationships in general. Granted, with a comparatively high rate (40%) of single households, many Swedes and other Nordic populations do appear to shun family life (Chamie, 2017). But more fundamentally, they do not want to have to depend on whatever family they may establish. Berggren and Trägårdh (2006) clarify this with what they call "the Swedish theory of love"—the romantic idea that love is not about dependence but about volitional relationships with other autonomous humans. In other words, many Swedes don't financially need a partner, but they couple up with one because of love.

Nonetheless, state individualism rests on the implicit assumption that relational partners and other family members are less reliable security providers than the welfare state. Using attachment parlance, we can describe the arrangement as expressing a culturally normative positive representation of a nonrelational institution (i.e., the welfare state), coupled with a negative representation of relational partners (i.e., other individuals). With his famous dictum, "Hell is other people," the French existentialist Jean Paul Sartre (1944/1989) probably expressed this stance more bluntly than almost anyone else (although he referred to others' "look" at oneself rather than to interpersonal dependence per se). Canonical Scandinavian authors and playwrights such as August Strindberg (Swedish), Henrik Ibsen (Norwegian), and many others are not far behind, and without them the world might not have generated a similar lineage of later American playwrights, including Eugene O'Neill, Tennessee Williams, and Edward Albee. The common denominator in their dramas appears to be that there is no end to the sufferings of relational life and of family life in particular.

In essence, within a state individualist arrangement, the state becomes the individual's ally and wedge against the family, so the individual—armed to his or her teeth–can drive a hard bargain against the rest of the family. It should not be surprising, then, if Scandinavian families display high conflict levels. Also, separation and divorce are not necessarily seen as anything to mourn. This is because the family is understood as a dependency-creating, conservative agent in society that suppresses the individual and makes the individual unable or unwilling to pursue his or her own interests and agendas. Thus, in progressive Sweden, divorce has been reinterpreted from being a negative (e.g., marital failure) to a positive outcome, at least for women (Wennstam & Sveland, 2011). The implication that the individual is much more dependent on the state than on his or her family remains largely unspoken, for the state is understood as the liberator, not the oppressor. The state is a liberator because it frees the individual from the interpersonal dependencies that would otherwise be required for security (e.g., reliance on the spouse or on the kindness of strangers).

Also, because Swedes tend to shun dependence, they typically do not want to use that word in reference to their relationship to the treasured welfare system. This mindset is echoed in Berggren and Trägårdh's (2015) book, in which Swedes are portrayed as autonomous, with the welfare state granting them that autonomy. However, the nearly all-encompassing insurance and protective legislation I described previously suggest that "autonomy" should be among the last words that come to mind to characterize adult Swedes' mindsets: They are anything but autonomous in relation to the state. Rather, not unlike young, needy children, they request much assistance, supervision, and guidance from their "stronger and wiser" state (see also Petersson, 2012). In my generalizing assessment, then, Swedes may be autonomous individualists in their intimate relationships but not in relation to the state. Unless attachment was predicated on interpersonal relationships, one could even entertain the idea that perhaps the welfare system functions as an attachment "figure" for adults residing in individually based, universal welfare states like Sweden, at least in the metaphorical sense of providing a safe haven and secure base. In the concluding section, I describe how my colleagues and I have begun to test this idea.

Welfare Studies: Equality, Gender Egalitarianism, Social Mobility, Trust, Consensus

A consideration of the efficiency of individualistic welfare systems gives additional clues as to why welfare states promote secularism. Research on welfare systems is an important part of the social sciences, political science in particular. Much of the pertinent research has demonstrated that welfare systems, especially the individualistic ones, are related to a host of societal and individual desirables, as summarized in Norris and Inglehart's (2011) notion of "existential security." These include relatively low-income spread (i.e., economic equality). Although some beg to differ that equality is desirable in society—for example, based on the fact that societal resources are not a "zero-sum game" or on the idea that equality undermines economic growth (e.g., Li & Zou, 1998)—when resources are highly unevenly spread in the population, society is nonetheless faced with challenges.

In part, this is because most humans are creatures of social comparison. People who find themselves considerably below the population median (even when that median is very high) tend to perceive themselves as poor. Such "relative poverty" (e.g., Foster, 1998) is indeed a risk factor in development (e.g., Wilkinson, 1997). As an example, a child growing up in a rich country (say Norway) with parents who can't afford to buy any toys except plastic, toxic ones and who is surrounded by children whose parents can afford to buy ecological toys, is likely to have a more adverse developmental trajectory, relatively speaking, than a third world child who, unlike his or her neighboring children in poverty, has been fortunate enough to get the job of manufacturing the toxic plastic toys. Being considerably below the population median is taxing, just as it is rewarding to be above it. This is one reason why research consistently shows that equality is important in sustaining cohesion, peace, and trust in society, and in preventing high crime rates, polarization, and alienation (Piketty, 2013; Wilkinson & Pickett, 2010).

Another equality-related outcome prompted by individually based welfare systems is gender egalitarianism, which benefits the vast majority of the population. Women are not reduced to a fetus-carrying, child-bearing, and child-caring role but can also prosper from the satisfaction of engaging in an independent work life. It should also be noted that gender egalitarianism can liberate males from their traditional role as family "breadwinners," enabling them to engage in other important tasks, such as caring for their children. That is not only conducive to males' adult development, but the child also profits from having an additional safe haven to turn to and a secure base to depart from.

Ironically, in view of the "American Dream," individualistic welfare states go hand in hand with "social mobility," that is, the prospect that the younger generation will reach a higher position in society than their parents have. Denmark and Sweden top this list, whereas the United States, with all its "self-made" men and women, has a mediocre position (e.g., Beller & Hout, 2006; Breen & Jonsson, 2005). In addition, individualistic welfare states have high democratic participation rates. In other words, people care enough about politics to vote, typically attracting some 80–90% of potential voters, as compared with roughly half of the adult population in the United States (Pew Research Center, 2018).

Furthermore, people in individualistic welfare states display comparatively high trust (cf. faith), in one another as well as in the official agencies/institutions of society (e.g., Rothstein, & Uslaner, 2005). Such trust functions as a psychological glue that holds society—if not family relationships—together. That trust presumably reflects the idea that the agencies generally deserve to be trusted; they typically do a comparatively efficient and reliable job in providing services to citizens (e.g., Barr, 2012). Granted, following increased pluralism, trust rates may be declining in Scandinavian countries, but the rates remain high (e.g., Statens Offentliga Utredningar, 2007). We may witness an increasingly conditional form of trust and a gradual move from a somewhat "blind trust." If so, there is cause for celebration because unconditional trust may be dangerous in society, for example, blinding people to corruption and incompetence.

Another important finding in the political science literature is that individualistic welfare states foster resiliency in the face of economic hardship (e.g., unemployment; Rothstein, 1998). This is presumably because the state offers a safety net (e.g., reasonable unemployment benefits) to lean on when the going may get tough. Moreover, common concerns about the strongly negative effects of high taxation rates on economic growth do not necessarily apply (Piketty, 2013; Rothstein, 1998). While this topic is a major political divider on the left–right dimension, individualistic welfare states are among the richest countries on earth, and yet for multiple decades they have experienced the world's highest taxation rates. National economists are scratching their heads about this anomaly, or else are looking the other way, and so would Adam Smith and Milton Friedman were they still alive.

In addition, welfare state populations appear to be *comparatively* happy[5] and to achieve high rankings on the United Nations' (UN)

Human Development Index, which comprises life expectancy, educational level, and GNP/capita (UN, 2016, 2018). Finally, although a strong state might seem to indicate a certain measure of totalitarianism, individualistic welfare states are ranked high on indices of freedom, including free elections and free press (e.g., Freedom House, 2018). Any totalitarianism present in societies such as the Swedish one seems largely self-inflicted; Swedes are widely known to aim for consensus and to keep their corridors of expressed opinions relatively narrow. Anyone in doubt about this should ask the Danes (see also Booth, 2015, for amusing examples). In other words, these are free people (in the political sense) who, when they come together, tend to reach consensus. That must sound utterly strange for Americans and southern Europeans, but it is nonetheless true. Nowhere is this consensus culture more pervasive than in their embrace of the individualistic welfare system. As a matter of fact, there is currently no political opposition to insurance-based welfare politics in Sweden, even though the Swedish parliament houses as many as eight parties.

By and large then, individualistic welfare states are undeniably a success story. A secular social contract—the individually based welfare system—can provide "real" security in society and in people's lives. No wonder that people in such nations perceive less need for the "illusory" (Freud, 1961b) security provided by God/religion. And no wonder that political scientists from Sweden have found their favorite topic in welfare studies; seeing Sweden among the other Scandinavian countries heading international lists gives a rare sense of national pride. Carrying deep personal antipathies against nationalism myself, including its covert forms, I may act as a party pooper at Sweden's national celebration in the historical exposé that follows, which deals with the not so flattering historical factors that have enabled the Swedish welfare state.

FROM REFORMATION THROUGH THE STRONG STATE TO WELFARE NATIONALISM

In this section, I provide a brief historical overview of the historical factors that enabled welfare politics and secularism to be established in Sweden, starting with the Reformation, extending to the strong Swedish state and the social democrats, and concluding with the spread of welfare nationalism. Parts of the overview apply largely to the other Scandinavian countries (Denmark and Norway) as well. The Fall, a British postpunk band, appears to have captured the pertinent historical processes quite succinctly: "Reformation / Arbeit mit uns / Arbeit mit uns" (from the album *Reformation Post TLC, 2007*).

The Reformation and the Almighty King

The kings of northern Europe were quite hospitable to Martin Luther's theology and for good reason. This was most certainly the case for Swedish king Gustav Vasa (1496–1560), who deserves to be remembered not least for his Machiavellian methods and political genius. In a single stroke, he reformed the Church (from Catholic to Lutheran), enabling him to overtake the Church's power and resources, successfully putting down the mighty Swedish peasants' repeated revolts, and creating an even mightier state. The king, controlling both the earthly and religious institutions of society, became nearly almighty.

Luther's work on two kingdoms naturally served regents nearly unlimited power on a silver platter. Briefly, God was believed to rule the whole world, but to use different kingdoms for doing so, the first being a secular government (or worldly regiment), ruled by law, and the second being the heavenly kingdom, ruled by grace or the gospel. Luther asserted that people, liberated from the corrupt Catholic Church, still needed to be controlled, or else they and society would fall out of order and into anarchy. In the heavenly kingdom, all people are free and equal in the eyes of God but in the worldly regiment, there must be a strict hierarchy; people will always have to obey the earthly king, and social disarray or revolution is always evil (but see Whitford, 2004, for Luther's later position). In any event, overtaking the Church was a relatively straightforward matter for Gustav Vasa. Swedes, a tradition-ally heathen population, were latecomers to Catholic Christianity, and Sweden was very far from Rome (Thurfjell, 2015).

Succeeding generations of kings and queens exercised almighty power to their own advantage. Using a "good-cop, bad-cop" kind of arrangement, the Church was dedicated to the task of controlling the Swedish population: Did they know their Luther? Did they go to Church on Sundays? Did they abstain from liquor, song, and dance? Though actually foreign to Luther's *sola fide* (by faith alone) theology, as well as to Luther as a person—the hedonist wine–song–and–dance man that he was—the Church's demands on the population to live a pious religious life is referred to as "Lutheran orthodoxy" (Thurfjell, 2015). This bas-tard version of Lutheran theology, consolidated during the 16th–17th centuries, ultimately spawned pietism and various "law-abiding" reli-gious awakening movements in later centuries, and thus largely shaped Christianity in post-Reformation Sweden/Scandinavia.

When contemporary Swedes reflect back on the long historical era dominated by Christianity, they see almost nothing but control and oppression—a Marxist's nightmare image of religion (Thurfjell, 2015). So much so, I think, that it amounts to something akin to a collectively unresolved trauma (see Ms. Purple in Chapter 8 for an example). Accustomed to thinking of the secular state as liberator, they fail to appreciate the secular regents' wicked power over the Church and all of its affairs. That power and influence has continued to the present day, even beyond the alleged "separation" of church and state. The Swedish Church—the "People's Church"—is still governed by the state, in the form of political elections and politically assigned decision makers who, in principle, can decide about all Church matters, whether economy, policy, or liturgy.

The Strong State

Fast-forwarding to the democratic era (the 20th century), it is no wonder that the Swedish population had had it with religion—the bad cop. It's no wonder, too, that they were longing for redistributed resources from the royal affiliates (i.e., aristocracy). If another good and strong cop showed itself—the redistributing and insuring state envisioned by social democrats—then it's easy to see why Swedes would go for that option. Thus, they elected the democratic counterpart of an enlightened king, or the secular version of Luther's two-kingdom idea, which states that all individuals are free insofar as they respect and have faith in the authority of the state (Svensson, 2008).

With the social democrats in control, the welfare system blossomed rapidly during the 20th century. Many Swedish academics were keen to help. For example, adopting Benito Mussolini's concept of "the People's Home," the highly influential couple Alva and Gunnar Myrdal, along with other social democrats, envisioned the Swedish society as one big family (Berman, 2006). To steer the Swedish population in the direction of equality, gender egalitarianism, and an extended family with all of society, a number of progressive reforms were implemented. This movement blossomed during the 1960s–1970s, when one radical family reform after the other was implemented. The common denominator among these reforms was a move from traditional family dependence to progressive liberation of the individual; the state had found its ally (Berggren & Trägårdh, 2015).

As part of this move, children were also "liberated" from family dependence. For example, they were granted more or less free access to day care, and mothers were given the societal benefit of returning to the workforce as productive members. Whether children wanted early day care placement is difficult to know, for they weren't the ones voting for it. As another example, Sweden was the first country to pass a law against corporeal punishment of children (1979), known in Sweden as "physical abuse." For a final example, to ascertain that Swedish children did not have to grow up with "imbeciles," a widespread (world-leading) sterilization program was implemented on various minorities, not least of which were *Samis* (the indigenous population) and intellectually disabled women (continuing until 1976; Runcis, 1998). In some countries, such practices were known as eugenics, but in Sweden, they were widely believed to represent rational social engineering. When children's health and development were perceived as being hampered, state agencies also interfered and placed children in foster care at rates not seen in most other countries in the free world (Runcis, 2007).

It may appear risky for a state to take individuals' rights so lightly, especially when the system relies on an alliance with individuals. However, the violation of individual rights has always been selective, so the powerful segments of the electorate have been able to remain in the dark. In particular, the state has been keen to serve the Swedish laborers and the middle class, which comprises the vast majority of the electorate. Those segments have typically retained a positive, benevolent representation of the Swedish state, including its welfare functions. Naturally, that has sufficed for the strong state to continue.

From Social Democracy to Welfare Nationalism

Although social democracy has almost come to define the individualistic welfare state, like any political party, the social democrats have had to fight and compromise to maintain popularity. Now it seems clear from political developments across Europe, including Sweden, that the heyday of social democracy is in the past. This is apparently not the case for welfare politics, however. In Sweden, the social democrats are still the largest party, but in the latest election (held in September 2018) they garnered only 28% of the votes and, according to the latest averaged poll (November 2019), they have decreased further to 24%—their lowest endorsement in more than a century. The social democrats are currently not much larger in size than the nationalists (the "Sweden democrats," of neo-Nazi origin; 18% in the election, 23% in the latest averaged poll) or the conservatives (the "Moderates"; 20% in the election, 18% in the latest averaged poll). Considering that the social democrats in Sweden have always had their hands in the same pockets as labor unions—indeed, the social democrats even started the labor unions—it is particularly remarkable that laborers have abandoned the social democrats en masse, largely for the Sweden democrats. Social democracy has helped Swedish workers achieve among the highest-paying, safest working conditions and the most generous welfare benefits worldwide. A lesson learned is that political preferences rarely express gratitude. Regardless of occupation, Sweden democrat is in fact currently the most popular party among males.

How, then, did the moderates (conservatives) and Sweden democrats (nationalists) manage to challenge social democracy? The answer is straightforward: By adopting welfare rhetoric—a recipe for success in Sweden—they cunningly denied social democrats their "monopoly" on welfare politics. Thus, while social democrats are on the losing end, welfare politics prevail, though increasingly steered toward the insurance rather than the redistributive function of the welfare state.

More specifically, by rebranding themselves the "new moderates"—which entailed abandoning the welfare criticism of their past, adopting an insurance-leaning version of welfare politics, and both promising and delivering considerable tax cuts for employees—the Moderate party gained and retained access to leadership for 8 years (2006–2014). Swedish workers kept most of their welfare insurance but now also had more cash in their hands. The Sweden democrats' recipe for success is their public mourning of days long gone when Sweden and its People's Home appeared to be even more secure and ethnically homogeneous and when Swedes did not have to adapt to the perils of pluralism or competition on an open labor market.

Naturally, the rapid rise and spread of nationalism has sent shock waves through the Swedish political establishment, as it has throughout Europe and the United States. So successful have the Sweden democrats been that social democrats and moderates have felt compelled to adapt, and they have done so partly by adopting the sworn enemy's rhetoric. Thus, the three largest political parties in Sweden now portray immigration as a threat to the welfare system, and they do so despite a continuing economic boom even after having accepted large numbers of refugees (until 2015). Popularity among voters aside, the immigration-as-threat analysis is factually misleading because, like many parts of the Western world, Sweden has an aging population and an undersupply of manufacturing and service workers in many sectors of society. In other words, Sweden needs to import more—not fewer—workers.

I believe that the rapid spread of "welfare nationalism" also illustrates that the welfare system is ultimately not first and foremost about solidarity, in any altruistic (agape) sense of the word, although there has been no shortage of Swedes adopting the moral high ground, or of praise for Sweden as a model of conscience to the world. Their welfare system is principally about insuring themselves within the confines of their nation-state. That the same applies to many Western countries at present does not make it less true for Sweden.

The rise of nationalism may appear to be an entirely "new animal" in Swedish welfare politics, but this is another case of appearances being somewhat misleading. From its very outset, the Swedish welfare state built its success partly on a treacherous arrangement: a secret alliance with Nazi Germany. While neighboring Nordic populations were suffering under Nazi occupation during the Second World War, Sweden was secretly trading with the Nazis (exporting iron ore, in particular), and allowed the Nazis to pass on Swedish railways. The Nazis required plenty of steel at the time, so the Swedish iron industry blossomed. In Karlbom's (1965) estimate, Swedish ore provided the raw material for some 40% of Nazi German guns, and Sweden delivered far more than any other country. The fruit of the trade helped finance the Swedish welfare system, while the war raged on and many Nordic neighbors were denied refuge in the People's Home. To the world, Sweden appealed to its neutrality policy, while the Swedish government—in deference to commands from the German Nazis—censored the press and effectively silenced most intellectual opposition. The relentless resistance that was nonetheless expressed by a few liberal intellectuals, such as Torgny Segerstedt (an editor in chief and historian of religion) and Vilhelm Moberg (a fictional and historical writer) was therefore all the more laudable. These exceptions notwithstanding, Sweden wore "Swastika eyes" (Primal Scream, *XTRMNTR*, 2004).

Similarly, Sweden is currently among the countries with the most extensive weapons manufacturing and export program. It is consistently on the "top 15" list of per capita weapons exported, even topping the list in 2011 (Svenska Freds, 2019). Swedish weapons exports include extensive sales to dictatorships such as Saudi Arabia, the United Arab Emirates, Qatar, and Oman. The money gained in this way helps to finance the welfare system.

Sweden has been praised internationally partly because of its supposedly humane immigration policy. Yet much of the Swedish immigration policy has traditionally been motivated by a need for more workers, a side benefit being additional voters for the social democrats. This is better described as a win–win situation than as an expression of humanitarian values. Granted, among Western countries, Sweden has accepted one of the highest numbers of refugees per capita (especially from the 1990s through 2015). However, that is currently being superseded by the spread of welfare nationalism. Accordingly, Sweden's current finance minister (a social democrat) has argued that rates of child poverty have increased as a result of the influx of refugees. Because it is important to maintain equality in Sweden, this contributes to the need for a (continued) restrictive immigration policy (Schück, 2018). In other words, child poverty may tear the rich, egalitarian Sweden apart, so better to keep poor families and children outside of the nation-state's boundaries.

In this section, I have deliberately drawn attention to the dark corners of modern Swedish history and contemporary Sweden. I have done so to shed light on the ghosts in the welfare nursery, to provide nuance to the rosy colors painted by welfare research, and to counteract the many idealized understandings of Sweden and Swedes that inflict progressives around the world. The Swedish state has violated individual rights and humanitarian considerations to such an extent that it calls for adjustments to the world's mental representations of Sweden. Yet there should be no doubt that building an all-encompassing, universal welfare state and keeping the citizens safe and sound have been expensive undertakings, perhaps necessitating that the Swedish state get its hands dirty from time to time, or else its authority would have been challenged or rejected. An increasingly secure and rich welfare population makes increasing demands on its state. Also, most societies carry skeletons in their closets, so moral regrets may not be more inevitable for Sweden than for many other countries. Nonetheless, an open society, continued enlightenment, and political reformism benefit from knowledge about a society's dark corners, not from maintaining biased attention to its charitable qualities. And so far, with respect to our main concern here, the blemishes on the welfare state's history have not proved a deterrence to replacement of religious security with political and economic security.

WELFARE PSYCHOLOGY

Although welfare research has been an important part of the macro-level social sciences, the same cannot be said for psychology. Indeed, psychological research on welfare systems is almost absent, and experimental, psychological research on welfare systems has been entirely absent. Given the well-documented strong negative links between individualistic welfare systems and religion as well as religion's role in psychological processes and outcomes, the absence of psychological research on welfare systems is remarkable. In particular, we do not know whether welfare systems like religion and the family affect attachment (e.g., provide a source of psychological security), inspire people to act altruistically, or affect individuals' mental health. Next, I review preliminary research, pose questions for future studies, and call for a new discipline to address the questions: welfare psychology.

Attachment and Psychological Security

This book has described how aspects of religion (particularly one's perceived attachment to God) as well as aspects of the family (particularly one's spouse or adult attachment figure) are important sources of an adult's psychological security. For example, when one's attachment system is activated, whether implicitly or explicitly, one's mind and behavior may seek either God or one's spouse, and most people experience relief from such seeking. In individualistic welfare states, where God appears absent in people's minds and their potential spouse is represented as a threat to independence, what do people do when their attachment systems are activated? For example, do they mentally and behaviorally seek impersonal functions of the welfare system, as would be expected if the welfare system functions as a safe haven? And do they use the welfare system as a secure base for exploration?

Together with a PhD student, Joel Gruneau Brulin, and colleagues, I have attempted to answer these questions (see Gruneau Brulin et al., 2018) using conceptual replications of two prior experiments (Granqvist, Mikulincer, et al., 2012; Kupor et al., 2015). Briefly, in one of the previous experiments, using a lexical decision task, we found that Israeli theistic Jews gained increased cognitive access to the concept of God following subliminal threat primes, indicating that God may function as a safe haven even at unconscious levels (Granqvist, Mikulincer, et al., 2012). In the other experiment, Kupor and colleagues (2015) found that U.S. study participants (many of whom were probably religious) who had been primed with God, as opposed to those given a neutral prime, were more willing to take exploratory, recreational risks, presumably reflecting a sense of being protected by God as a secure base. Our corresponding welfare experiments added welfare-related material to the experimental designs and were executed both on Swedish (high-welfare, low-religion) and U.S. (low-welfare, high-religion) samples. This enabled us to test whether the welfare system functions as a safe haven/secure base, particularly for Swedes.

First, in our replication of Granqvist, Mikulincer, and colleagues' (2012) study, neither Swedish ($N = 90$) nor U.S. ($N = 106$) study participants had increased cognitive access to welfare-related concepts (e.g., health care, subsidy) following threat primes (i.e., failure and separation), whether the primes were subliminal or supraliminal. Thus, the welfare system does not appear to function cognitively as a safe haven, not "even in Sweden." The only major positive findings observed in these studies were that, regardless of priming condition, U.S. participants had faster cognitive access to God-related concepts than to welfare and neutral concepts, which were equally accessible, whereas the pattern was reversed for Swedish participants. In other words, Swedes had slower cognitive access to God-related concepts than to welfare and neutral concepts, which were again equally accessible. Comparing across nations/samples, U.S. participants had considerably faster access to God-related concepts, but there was no difference across nations on welfare (or neutral) concepts.

We concluded that people residing in a religious U.S. context have more readily accessible religious schemas, whereas people residing in a welfare state do not have superior access to welfare schemas. Presumably, this difference arises because religion revolves around a perceived personal relationship with an anthropomorphic figure (i.e., God), along with other cognitively intuitive ontologies, thus readily lending religious cognition much like other relationships and social categories render social cognition. In comparison, welfare systems are comparatively abstract and nonrelational inventions by the standards of the human mind. Not even Swedes, for whom they are omnipresent, seem able to schematize them. This is presumably in part because the welfare system does not fit the mental model of interpersonal others, such as that of an attachment figure, for which the mind has been designed. Hence, although the welfare system can provide much of the security needed for a comfortable life, it does so without being represented as a person. Humans simply did not evolve with a biological preparedness to represent a protective, kind, or lovable welfare system. As a case in point, people do not fall in love with the state. Naturally, this cognitive–affective nonintuitiveness may pose an additional challenge for welfare systems. For example, despite their vast generosity, welfare systems may not arouse any sense of gratitude, simply because there is no relational partner or other personal agent cognitively assessed as responsible for whatever benefit the individual has been granted. A political leader like Mao Zedong or the iconic Olof Palme of Swedish social democracy can, however, arguably function as the requisite personification.

Second, and similarly, in our conceptual replication of Kupor and colleagues' (2015) study, welfare priming did not lead to increased willingness to take exploratory risks, among either Swedes (N = 158) or Americans (N = 264). Thus, the welfare system does not appear to function cognitively as much of a secure base either. In fact, and contrary to our prediction, welfare priming (like religious priming) led to a *lower* proclivity to take risks specifically in the Swedish sample. In contrast, among highly religious participants (drawn mostly from the U.S. sample), religious priming did facilitate a willingness to take risks.

Jointly, these initial welfare–cognition experiments indicate that the welfare system does not yield attachment-related felt security, not even when the cultural context (i.e., Sweden) for such a function would appear to be optimal. In that regard, the welfare system does not display psychological equivalence with either religion or the family. Thus, the question remains: In individualistic welfare states, what do adult individuals do when their attachment systems are activated? Do they just "suck it up," go visit some nature scene, engage with materialism (e.g., shopping, turning to their smartphones), focus attention inwardly (i.e., on themselves), sublimate (e.g., engage in the arts), take medicine, or march on with work? Whatever means they use, do they experience relief from doing so? And when in development does the transition occur from turning to personal attachment figures to turning to some other object, activity, or the self? How do individual differences in attachment figure here: Do they predict who does what, or are such individual differences also affected by a society's move away from religion and the family and toward welfare systems?

I don't know the answers to these questions at present, but given the importance of religious and spousal attachment relationships for security provision in most other adult populations, these are important questions for future research to address. Answers to such questions are also important for understanding the psychological implications of secularism in general and welfare systems in particular. Last but not least, the answers to these questions may shed light on the theoretical possibility that macro-level features of society and culture may, at some point in development, adjust the attachment system so that its target or set goal changes from relational others/attachment figures to other targets.

Other Psychological Outcomes: Altruism and Mental Health

With respect to altruism, we know that aspects of religion (e.g., imperatives such as "love thy neighbor . . . ") as well as aspects of the family (e.g., prosocial models) may be important in encouraging altruistic (or helpful) behaviors. Indeed, many of the virtues connected with religion have to do with inspiring, unselfish acts of kindness, such as those associated with Mahatma Gandhi, Martin Luther King Jr., the occasional Christian who hid Jews from the Nazis, or the Moroccan Muslim who feels that Allah resides in every stranger. Naturally, this implies that neither religion nor the family is always a promoter of altruism. Examples to the contrary abound: religion-inspired wars, acts of terror, persecution, and antisocial models within the family. Yet available systematic research (including experimental religious priming studies) do indicate that, on the whole, religion tends to foster altruistic behaviors, at least within the in-group, although perhaps not toward members of out-groups (e.g., Saroglou et al., 2005; Shariff et al., 2016). However, the jury is still out as to why. Ara Norenzayan (2013) and his colleagues (e.g., Norenzayan et al., 2016; Shariff & Norenzayan, 2007) have suggested that it is the feeling of being watched by God that makes religion promote altruistic behavior, at least toward in-group members (see also Chapters 9 and 10). Their findings also suggest that being watched by some other agent, such as law enforcement officers, may have a similar effect.

Whatever the true mechanism(s) may be in the religion–altruism link, in the wake of increasing secularism, do welfare systems promote or counteract altruism? On the pro-altruism side, the redistribution policy of welfare states may act as a solidarity model. Perhaps the individual is grateful, after all, for the "welfare checks" he or she has been able to collect and therefore seeks to be supportive to others. Or perhaps the sheer pervasiveness of state functions gives the individual a sense of the state's omnipresence (cf. an Orwellian state) and thus of being watched? On the contrasting side, perhaps the high taxes individuals pay (cf. letters of indulgence within Catholicism) undermine their sense of moral agency and responsibility—for example, by making them feel that they have already paid their fair share and that the state or someone else should provide any additional needed help. Or, as discussed earlier, maybe the individual in welfare systems is prone to strategically conceive of and express the self as the worthy recipient of resources (what the system can do for me) rather than the provider of help to others (what I can do for the system). Although answers to such questions are exceedingly important, virtually no research has yet addressed them. In particular, experimental research is entirely absent.

Regarding mental health and unhealth, I have described the roles of religion (Chapter 7) and attachment-related matters within the family (Chapter 4) in relation to mental health. The evidence is reasonably clear that religion, and especially a perceived, personal relationship with a loving God, is related to important aspects of better mental health and that it may counteract suffering during particularly stressful times. The same of course holds for being part of a family and having sustainable, close interpersonal relationships. Yet, as I have noted, macro-level qualifiers must be considered in the links between religion and mental health, such as welfare systems and the cultural normativity of religion. Thus, a question arises as to whether welfare systems promote or reduce mental health.

On the positive side, such systems have a safety net that usually keeps people safe and secure from the worst forms of alarm; for example, people usually do not suffer from poverty, and serious medical conditions and mental health problems may be treated "free of charge" using tax money collected by the welfare state. On the negative side, the fall of religion may lead to existential and meaning-making crises, and the fall of the family may in addition lead to a decrease in informal support networks. A spread of mental health problems related to anxiety, depression, and exhaustion might suggest that the negative alternative is more likely, but, as we have seen, such problems are also on the rise in other societies besides welfare states (see Twenge, 2000). Needless to say, rigorous, cross-cultural research is needed to tease apart and compare the effects of religion and welfare systems on mental health outcomes.

Call for a New Discipline

I call for a new discipline--the psychology of welfare systems—to help answer these important questions raised by the cultural transition from religion to secularism in large parts of the Western world. This discipline will require skills and cooperative research across several social sciences, including psychology, political science, sociology, economics, and the behavioral sciences of religion.

CHAPTER SUMMARY

In this chapter, I have reviewed theory and research pertaining to the idea that religion and welfare systems provide competing but functionally equivalent insurance policies, and I have also noted the implications for the psychology of religion and secularism. I have provided an explanation of how a welfare state can promote a sense of security and ultimately contribute to a high rate of secularism in a population. I drew particular attention to an individually based, universal welfare system, comprising both insurance and redistribution functions. I noted that however much redistribution (solidarity) was at stake in their original designs, over time and succeeding generations successful welfare systems will, almost out of necessity, gradually tilt from redistribution toward insurance. Using Sweden as the prime example, I discussed "state individualism" (i.e., the alliance between state and individual against families) and "the Swedish theory of love" (i.e., a union, based not on dependence but on love between two "autonomous" partners). I gave a brief historical account of why and how Sweden's welfare state developed, starting with the Protestant Reformation and Martin Luther's associated two-kingdom idea, through the regents' nearly almighty power, over to the strong state and its granting of welfare functions, and finally to welfare nationalism. At the same time, I showed how successfully cunning and strategic the Swedish state has been in collecting the extra resources required to maintain the exceedingly generous welfare system. Fourth and finally, I called for a new discipline ("welfare psychology"), considered initial empirical findings, and spelled out some key research questions that this field should address.

Epilogue

There are two well-known rules for polite conversation: Don't discuss politics and don't discuss religion. In my conversation with readers of this book, I have broken both rules. And if there were a third rule, it might be not to discuss the emotional undercurrents of one's close interpersonal relationships. I have broken that one too. May my discourtesy be forgiven! And may the rules for polite conversation be scrutinized in their own right. These rules naturally reflect the topics' touchiness; they are frequently the source of strong disagreements. Voicing them runs the risk of creating tension at a cocktail or holiday party. Their touchiness is, in turn, revealing. How we stand when it comes to religion, politics, and close interpersonal relationships is not first and foremost a matter of the impersonal, rational, conscious, and "mature" human mind, but equally about the personal, emotional, unconscious, and (some might say) "immature" human mind. Politics, religion, and close interpersonal relationships are topics of strong feelings and affective reactions, only some of which may be contained and monitored by conscious processes. That is why they risk not just creating tension and conflict at a cocktail party, but turning the party into a full-fledged Scandinavian drama, into a Strindberg or Ibsen play, an Ingmar Bergman film. That is also why they should not be avoided in psychology but instead form key subjects for discussion; their related psychological underpinnings are too important and interesting to be left out. These underpinnings would not be dealt with adequately if the topics were restricted to their traditional key narrators—religion to religious scholars and theologians; politics to political scientists and politicians; and close interpersonal relationships to poets, novelists, songwriters, and social psychologists.

THIS IS THE END, THIS IS THE BEGINNING

While writing this book, I have continuously had the troubling sense of scrutinizing the world of humans at the end of their history, or at least at a position past the tipping point of the civilized Western world. Luckily, I am no stranger to metacognition; many authors have been mistaken on the matter of apocalypse (or millennialism) before me, and I remain somewhat hopeful that I am mistaken as well, so that future authors arise who can repeat the mistake. It's just that outside my window, the world seems to be moving toward some kind of war—again. Nationalism has risen from the ashes of its well-attested atrocious history, and universalist humanitarian values seem to be going down the drain. Refugees are left to die in the cold, cold seas, and the richest populations on earth say they can't afford to help. Mental unhealth is spreading epidemically throughout the Western world, liberal democracies are dissolving, and climate threats are moving past their boiling points. Only dictators have cause for celebration. All of this, all of its ugly detail, is continuously trumpeted by the media. Streaming services perpetuate the bad news in fictional form with *Twin Peaks: The Return, The Handmaid's Tale,* and *The Walking Dead,* to mention just a few of the astounding artistic creations fed by a world in turmoil.

It hasn't exactly helped the blues that I've written large parts of this book in a building (Tolman Hall, at UC Berkeley) that is vulnerable to earthquakes and sitting atop the notorious San Andreas Fault. The building occasionally trembles, and there's a fear that its parts will slide in all directions. And it's beginning to move. Removal men are clearing out everything from adjacent rooms, and they will soon enter what I have come to think of as my writing cave (which is actually my dear friend Mary Main's office). In several respects, I sense being among the last few rats remaining on a sinking ship.

Although this preapocalyptic vibe may have affected some of my writing, I have nonetheless endeavored to write the book in an open, constructive, and heuristically forward-looking manner. I have tried to tear down unnecessary walls, just as the construction workers do in adjacent buildings even as I write. And it turns out that many walls are doomed to go. I've aimed to raise the roof higher and to push the sky away to help future generations of researchers continue to build this thing—the attachment–religion connection. I've tried to avoid taking wrong turns, steering away from dead-end streets. What I have provided is not a neat, close-ended package, brought to closure and then finally wrapped up in some Final Synthesis. In my humble opinion, that's what you do with cheap gifts, but it's not how science works, nor how my own mind operates. Science unceasingly, restlessly moves forward, profiting from open roads in the plural, not from a closed alleyway in the singular.

Yet, for me, personally, this is the end. "I'm leaving the table, I'm out of the game" (Leonard Cohen, *You Want It Darker,* 2016). This book has been my farewell song to the attachment–religion connection, and I call on other scholars, researchers, and students to take it from here. However, if religion would make a return even in my neck of the woods, following the major upheavals surrounding and ahead of us, I may as well. Because welfare psychology remains in infancy, I will try to follow this offspring beyond its immature years. Ditto with the idea of attachment as a framework to understand the intergenerational transmission of culture and the implications of attachment for gene–culture coevolution more generally. Among the topics loosely related to the attachment–religion connection, that's what I will do after retiring from working on this connection itself. This book is only the beginning.

Finally, and as my last attempt to counter the blues, let me emphasize that in this day and age of the *anthropocene,* humans have their own destiny and that of most other living organisms in their own hands. If we develop global communal policies and make decisions based on science, humanitarianism, and ecological considerations—as we should, in view of enlightenment values—we have the power to switch ecological and welfare conditions around in a sustainable direction (e.g., Sterner et al., 2019).

WHY ARE PSYCHOLOGISTS BIASED AGAINST RELIGION?

A major wall that my colleagues and I have always aimed to remove with our work on the attachment–religion connection is the wall separating the academic study of religion from mainstream psychology. Although I have continuously preached about that wall to my mainstream psychology compatriots and although my coworkers and I have published widely in mainstream psychology outlets to help remove it, I am not satisfied with how this mission has panned out. To this day it remains the case that psychologists of religion, many of whom are theologians and religious scholars by education, have shown much more openness to and interest in the attachment–religion connection than have mainstream psychologists. That has always surprised me because I anticipated that scholars of religion would feel estranged from the application of a Darwinian theoretical descendant to religion, and, perhaps to make matters worse, an application largely using quantitative (cf. "positivist," "reductionist") analyses. I thought mainstream psychologists would be much more hospitable to this line of thought and inquiry, but my expectations were quickly disconfirmed. In particular, attachment researchers, and socioemotional developmental psychologists in general—my own breed, in other words—appear to be almost hopelessly deaf and blind to the application of attachment theory to religion and spirituality, as well as to the many deep and interesting things we have learned about the human proclivity to form attachments from that application. Being stubborn, I offer part of this epilogue as my final attempt to tear down what appears to be a barrier akin to the Great Wall of China. I do so by considering why research psychologists have been biased against religion in general. In other words, the final straw I reach for is my hope that understanding *why* may aid in removing heaps of stones and bricks from the great wall.

To begin with, there is no reason to assume that psychologists, compared with biologists, chemists, physicists, or other academic groups, should be inherently more skeptical about religion's metaphysical postulates (including the assumption that there are gods and spirits). Although psychologists have been teased for their "physics envy" (e.g., Leahey, 1991), other natural scientists are even more keen on reducing nature. Thus, other explanations must be sought. As elsewhere in the social sciences and humanities, causes come in the plural and they are difficult to establish with confidence, so the discussion here is largely speculative.

One reason for psychology's neglect of religion may be the overlaps between its key topics of interest and those of religious professionals: emotional experiences; ways of coping with threats, losses, and deaths; ways of making meaning of life's experiences (and coping with the occasional loss of meaning). The proportion of psychologists who are themselves not religious is only slightly lower than the proportion of physicists, chemists, and biologists who are not religious (Bergin & Jensen, 1990; Delaney, Miller, & Bisonó, 2013), but scientists in those latter fields (except perhaps for evolutionary biologists) can pursue their research without coming into conflict with religious interpretations. Consequently, they can more easily move between the two "nonoverlapping magisteria" (Gould, 2011) of science and religion in their lives and minds. In contrast, psychologists may feel a need to close their minds to one of them.

Related to this difference is the inherent "competition" between religious professionals (e.g., clergy) and psychological professionals as helping professionals dealing with personal distress, antisocial behavior, and mental and physical illnesses. One of religion's major tasks has always been to understand and help people deal with suffering. Pastoral counseling and care has played a central role throughout the history of Christianity. Similarly, one of psychology's major tasks is to understand and remedy human suffering, and it is partly for this reason that the field has been financially supported by government research grants. The ascendance of the mental health movement has required that a sufficient number of influential people and institutions be persuaded to approach matters of suffering (or mental and physical illness) using assumptions and approaches associated with scientific psychology. If psychologists' explanations seem in danger of supplanting religious ones, it is natural for religious professionals to fight back. Psychologists can try to avoid or minimize this conflict by ignoring religion, while still perhaps maintaining openness to spirituality.

Psychologists' neglect of religion and spirituality may also stem partly from a common but ultimately prejudicial assumption that one's area of academic interest equates with one's personal convictions. Hence, studying religion or spirituality might be perceived as synonymous with being religious or spiritual. Thus, an atheist, agnostic, or religiously unaffiliated psychologist might not want to study religion/spirituality out of fear of being mistaken as a religious/spiritual person. It is notable, however, that this principle does not seem to apply to other areas of psychological study. For example, not all experts on autism are themselves autistic, nor are all experts on passionate love themselves passionately in love. So why should this principle apply to the psychological study of religion and spirituality?

Psychologists' bias against religion may also be due in part to their overexposure to the "dark side" of religion, at least in view of the secular–liberal beliefs and values that most mental health professionals hold. That they hold such values should not come as a surprise. Indeed, liberalism came about in the wake of Renaissance humanism and, later, the Enlightenment period and its associated strong pushes to distinguish the secular worldview of science from a religious worldview. This liberalism became an important part of the historical movement that spawned psychology as a science in the first place. It did so by sanctioning the individual and the self as worthy topics of interest and by simultaneously liberating the individual from the shackles of tradition (including religious traditions) that had prevented the realization of individual liberties (cf. Rose, 1998).

From a secular–liberal viewpoint, the dark side of religion includes values and approaches associated with conservatism, fundamentalism, dogmatism, moralism, in-group favoritism (or exclusivism), authoritarianism, and guilt and shame induction for experiencing and expressing inherently natural human impulses, especially sexual impulses. As viewed from a psychological standpoint, the dark side of religion also encompasses a corresponding representation of the deity (or deities)—God as controlling, punitive, vindictive, and frightening. Scholars influenced by psychoanalytic psychology view such representations as expressions of primitive defenses, among them splitting, projection, regression, and identification with the aggressor.

However, mental health professionals' overexposure to the dark side of religion comes with their own professional territory: human suffering. Clinicians are always selectively confronted by people in trouble and by humanity's shadow side. Curiously, this rarely leads mental health professionals to form generalizing conclusions about *humanity* as faulty, maybe because they have witnessed humanity's "positive" side in many other situations, outside of work as well as within the healing processes that are an integral part of their profession. Because they have little representative knowledge of religion, it is easy to see why overexposure to its dark side could lead them to conclude, erroneously, that *religion* itself is faulty. Religion would then become a cause of humanity's troubles and shadowy side: religion as perpetrator, humanity as its victim. It should be recalled, therefore, that religion is one of the human species' unique and more or less constant companions. Wherever humans collectively rear their heads, religion seems to come along in one form or the other, something that does not happen when other animals collectively rear their heads. A reification of religion on the part of mental health professionals may aid them in retaining the hopeful prospect that, after all, humanity itself is not at fault. Need I remind readers, then, that it is humans (not religions or gods) who have created the mess that we and many other species currently find ourselves in? Although some of the mess might result from religious conservatism interfering with secular–rational political decisions, humans have created some of the most atrocious political agendas the world has ever witnessed—the eugenics movement, nazism, communism, strands of fascism. These horrors rest not on the shoulders of religion but on the basis of humans' understanding of the Enlightenment, science, and secular values—indeed, in direct opposition to and persecution of religion. Needless to say, a negative characterization of religion may also serve to alienate religious people from the legitimate insights that the mental health movement offers.

Of course, it is important *not* to wear blindfolds to the "dark side" of religion or to the historical, social, and psychological processes among humans that brings it about. Some of this book has focused on this side. We have seen, for example, how certain forms of religion can reinforce fear, close minds, and interfere with progressive, emancipatory political decisions. Thus, readers with liberal or progressive political persuasions may continue to be troubled by the conservatism that, all else equal, does seem to go hand in hand with religion on the whole (e.g., Saroglou, Delpierre, & Dernelle, 2004). Naturally, though, readers with conservative persuasions are unlikely to view this as a bad thing.

While being aware of the dark side of religion and spirituality, it is equally important not to ignore the psychologically "bright" aspects of religion and spirituality. Key among those, as has been emphasized in this book, is religion's explicit emphasis on the fundamental *relationality* of the human mind (or "soul" or "spirit"). This is in fact a more central component of religion and spirituality than any conservative, antihumanistic tendencies associated with religion. As we have seen, religion's emphasis on the relationality of the human mind fits squarely with our contemporary scientific understanding of how the mind is constituted and how it operates. Thus, there is important common ground here between "religionists" and psychologists. Another bright aspect of religion, viewed from a psychological perspective, is that religion offers the potential of relational repair (dealt with in Chapters 6 and 7). For example, people who have not felt loved and cared by their human relationship partners may, via religion, come to experience a self-transformative sense of "being held" by God and a religious community. On the whole, the "narrow road" may be a much more beneficial path for such individuals to take than continuing to engage with "idols" (e.g., opiates, alcohol) to regulate states of insecurity and distress. It is important for psychologists not to miss these promises while attending selectively to the dark side of religion.

With these matters out of the way and with the rest of this book as a backdrop, I hope to have demonstrated that psychologists can tackle religion head on, without being fearful or wary. There are real intellectual gains to be made from studying religion, not least because wide terrains—wholly/holy uncharted territory—still remain open. Just roll away the stones.

SUMMARY AND REITERATION

In the first part of this book, I dealt with the *species-typical* (normative) components of attachment and the attachment–religion/spirituality connection, as well as with how this connection emerges and transforms over the course of human development. In Chapter 1, attachment theory was traced back to Bowlby's early work as a child psychoanalyst, its principal concepts were defined, and its ethological, psychobiological assumptions were delineated. I concluded that Bowlby was unnecessarily narrow in some of his evolutionary assumptions. In particular, attachment has had functional consequences beyond protection and survival, such as facilitating cultural learning and transmission. I also highlighted how Bowlby's thinking on representations and defenses aimed to bridge the chasm that existed, and continues to exist, between cognitive science and psychoanalysis. Finally, I addressed the maturation of attachment during the first few years of life and discussed "surrogate" attachments from a developmental perspective.

In Chapter 2, I reviewed evidence that God is socially and mentally constructed and used as a noncorporeal attachment figure, showing that believers' perceived personal relationships with God tend to meet most of the defining characteristics of attachment relationships (e.g., proximity seeking, safe haven, secure base, viewing God as stronger and wiser). However, I also discussed the obvious differences between God and other attachment figures (e.g., God is noncorporeal, God's actual responsiveness is ambiguous). Nonetheless, I concluded that "attachment to God" belongs in the larger family of attachment relationships, forming a special subclass of "noncorporeal" attachments. I also discussed nontheistic religions such as Buddhism in relation to attachment-based considerations.

In the third chapter, lifespan religious and spiritual development were examined in relation to general developmental maturation. Developmental maturation is contingent on specific forms of interactions between underspecified genetic dispositions and repeated exposure to environmental (including cultural) input. I argued that religious and spiritual development reflects plasticity-driven increases in the differentiation, integration, and complexity of underlying psychological systems (e.g., the attachment system), resulting in religious and spiritual diversity. Developmental spurts in those systems directly extend to religious and spiritual development. Beyond the attachment system, I discussed certain core cognitive dispositions (e.g., mentalization), but I also emphasized that domain-general principles of abstract thinking, imitation, and cultural learning must be taken into account to fully understand religious and spiritual development.

I concluded that although infancy through toddlerhood is best viewed as a prereligious/-spiritual phase of development, this period is nonetheless of unparalleled importance for religious and spiritual development. The preschool period was portrayed as a key developmental period in which religious and spiritual ideas and experiences may begin to flourish and when God may ultimately come to trump other imaginary figures in children's lives. School-age children typically become increasingly susceptible to the socializing influence of the stronger and wiser others who have cared for them. Consequently, the spirituality of children from religious homes often becomes increasingly religiously framed, whereas children brought up in secular (nonreligious) homes increasingly part company with their past religious/spiritual proclivities. Adolescence to early adulthood is a period of major attachment transitions, often marked by religious and spiritual transformations as well, characterized for some by religious awakening and for others by apostasy. Middle adulthood is associated with "religion as habit" and cultural transmission of religion to the next generation, but attachment-related events, such as falling in and out of love, may have repercussions in the religious and spiritual arena. Old age may be spiritually vitalizing via attachment-activating life events and states of gerotranscendence.

Part II dealt with *individual differences* in attachment and in the attachment–religion connection. The notion of individual differences in attachment was spawned by Ainsworth's discoveries of natural variations in attachment patterning among infants. Her Strange Situation procedure enabled developmental researchers to classify such variations. I characterized Ainsworth's three patterns of attachment (secure, insecure/avoidant, insecure/resistant) as well as Main and Solomon's addition of a fourth, disorganized, category. Beyond the Strange Situation, I described other attachment methods used in attachment–religion research. I also considered the developmental origins of and sequelae to attachment-related individual differences. Although a focus on individual differences and their measurement has almost come to define attachment research, I stressed that the topic of attachment is much more foundational than a consideration of individual differences (Chapter 4).

From a developmental viewpoint, there are two general attachment-related pathways to religion/spirituality and to different modes of being religious/spiritual. First, via social (or cultural) learning, individuals who are secure with respect to attachment often come to adopt religious or nonreligious standards that are similar to those held by their sensitive attachment figures in childhood ("socialized correspondence"). Also, via generalizing working models of self and others, attachment-secure individuals often represent God as a correspondingly sensitive (i.e., reliably security-maintaining) attachment figure ("internal working model correspondence"). I introduced the core ideas about social learning and generalizing working models as expressed in religion by drawing parallels to William James's notion of healthy-minded religion. I reviewed theory and provided an extensive review of the large body of empirical evidence supporting both socialized and working model correspondence. I also integrated these facets of correspondence, asserting that the attachment-secure individual's representation of God is typically built from his or her generalizing working models *in interaction with* the cultural tweaking (often accomplished via social learning) of those models. Finally, I provided an illustrative case study of Mrs. Green, who possessed a genuinely secure (benevolent and coherent) representation of God in relation to self and others, as identified using a Religious Attachment Interview (RAI; Chapter 5).

Second, although the generalization of working models complicates matters for individuals with an insecure attachment history, some attachment-insecure individuals may find in God a beneficial surrogate attachment figure, who may partially compensate for states of insecurity and other unsatisfactory attachments (i.e., the compensation pathway). William James, who characterized the "twice-born" religion of "sick souls," in many ways forecasted this pathway to religion. In Chapter 6, I addressed adults' use of attachment surrogates more generally, noting that adults may use a wide variety of attachment surrogates to regulate stress, including drugs, pets, material objects, places, and many more, most of which do not qualify as attachment "figures." Regarding religion, attachment-insecure individuals may turn to God and religion when in turmoil severe enough to cause their insecure strategies to break down. In such states, a lingering experience-expectant bias for benevolent responses may be expressed toward God. I provided a research review, demonstrating that the compensation pathway to religion has been supported by a considerable body of empirical research, especially by findings regarding sudden religious changes during stressful life situations. I provided an in-depth case study of Mr. Blue, who used God as an attachment surrogate to derive security but ultimately failed to become secure with God. I discussed whether religion-as-compensation may have beneficial psychological effects, concluding that this is not the case by default but by exception, and I attended to social factors that may facilitate the transformative potential of religious compensation.

In Part III, I moved *beyond the attachment–religion connection per se*. First, I examined the role that this connection may play in our understanding of mental health and unhealth. I argued that attachment-theoretical considerations provide insight into why contextual factors as well as particular aspects of mental health and religion matter a great deal for the links observed between religion and mental health. Contextual factors associated with heightened attachment activation (stress, other risk factors, low social welfare, existential insecurity) typically increase the strength of the observed links between religion and mental health. Also, aspects of mental health that are most notably affected by having a safe haven to turn to and a secure base to depart from are particularly reliably linked to religion. Finally, the aspects of religion that are most consistently linked to mental health are those that express attachment components, including belief in a personal, loving God with whom one experiences a close and secure relationship. Thus, attachment theory helps us to understand why religion and mental health are connected (Chapter 7).

Second, in Part III, beyond theistic religion, I considered attachment in relation to less institutionally organized, more esoteric forms of spirituality. More specifically, I argued that attachment disorganization leads to a proclivity for altered spiritual states via a general propensity for dissociative mental processes. I provided a theoretical and empirical review of each part of the proposed model, presenting empirical evidence indicating that the model is applicable to New Age spirituality and mystical experiences. I also gave "thick descriptions" of altered spiritual states, using transcript excerpts from four study participants interviewed with the RAI. Finally, I discussed psychopathology and possible extensions to other altered spiritual states in light of the proposed model (Chapter 8).

Because attachment theory is a midlevel theory, with relatively well-defined conceptual boundaries, other theories and perspectives are required to attain a fuller psychological grasp of religion and spirituality. In Part IV, I dealt with *points of convergence and divergence* between attachment theory and other prominent frameworks within the psychological sciences of religion. I started with attachment theory in relation to other theories and approaches within mainstream psychology, specifically coping, terror management, self-regulation and self-control, meaning-making, and attribution theories of religion. In all cases, I illustrated how attachment theory may provide a valuable developmental anchor for these other midlevel psychological approaches to religion and spirituality. Next, I discussed attachment theory vis-à-vis psychoanalytic understanding of religion (Freud, Erikson, Rizzuto, and Jones). Although attachment theory has a number of notable scientific strengths compared to psychoanalytic theories, rather than entirely replacing psychoanalysis I argued that attachment theory and psychoanalysis provide complementary approaches to religion. Specifically, whereas the psychoanalysis of religion may yield valuable insights into unique cases and processes at the individual level, the attachment–religion approach has its most notable merits as a group-based empirical research program (Chapter 9).

In Chapter 10, I illustrated that the attachment approach is an integral part of a larger evolutionary, cognitive neuroscience of religion dealing with how the basic, evolved properties of the human brain and mind interact with culturally acquired ideas to produce what we know as religious and spiritual outcomes. I delineated how some of the unique strengths of attachment theory and research can be used as a heuristic template for theory improvements and developments within other branches of the evolutionary, cognitive neuroscience of religion. I reiterated that an adjustment of attachment theory—viewing social/cultural learning as another functional outcome of the attachment system beyond protection and survival—importantly updates the theory and enables it to become a developmental anchor for gene–culture coevolution models.

Regarding cognitive science, I highlighted how the attachment approach converges with a focus on embodied religious cognition, and I discussed how attachment–religion research can aid in setting priors to predictive processing models applied to religion. Finally, in discussing the neuroscience of religion, I highlighted the compatibility between attachment theory on the one hand and a neuroscientific focus on sensed presence, oxytocin, and mentalization as expressed in religion and spirituality on the other hand.

Finally, in Part V (Chapter 11), I moved beyond attachment, religion, and spirituality to considering *the psychology of secularism,* arguing that there are other sources of security besides attachment and religion. I considered a wholly secular matter, reviewing theory and research on religion and welfare systems as comprising competing but functionally equivalent insurance policies. This idea has important implications for the psychology of religion and secularism. I illustrated how a welfare state can promote a sense of security and ultimately contribute to high secularism in a population, and I drew particular attention to an individually based, universal welfare system comprising both insurance and redistribution functions. Using contemporary Sweden as the prime example, I gave a brief historical account of why and how Sweden's welfare state developed, from the Protestant Reformation through the regents' nearly supreme power, over to the strong state and its granting of welfare functions, and finally to welfare nationalism. I called for "welfare psychology" as a new discipline, considered initial empirical findings, and spelled out key research questions that this field should address, pertaining to psychological security, altruism, mental health, and more.

In sum, I have touched upon a great variety of attachment- and religion-related themes and literatures in this book. So, what's the take-home message? Well, I can't give you just one but, like the Good Book, I give you 10. Note, however, that my list contains science-based propositions, not norm-based commandments.

I. Religion and spirituality capitalize on the attachment system, as expressed in many religious believers' noncorporeal attachments to God and other spiritual entities.

II. Religious and spiritual developments stem from general developmental maturation, in turn reflecting specific forms of interactions between underspecified genetic dispositions and repeated exposure to environmental/cultural input.

III. Religion and spirituality reflect the generalization of attachment-related mental representations, such that attachment-secure, unlike attachment-insecure, believers tend to represent

God coherently as a security-maintaining relational figure (internal working model correspondence).

IV. Caregiving quality and attachment security influence a child's receptivity to parental values in general and to religious standards in particular (socialized correspondence), which also facilitates cultural transmission and (perhaps) evolution.

V. Religion provides surrogate attachment figures (e.g., God) that may be used to regulate distress and gain felt security when an insecure attachment strategy has been sufficiently challenged (i.e., compensation).

VI. Attachment theory helps to explain why and how religion and mental health are related; specifically, attachment-related contextual factors and aspects of mental health and religion are central to the association.

VII. Attachment disorganization is linked to esoteric, altered spiritual states, via a proclivity for absorption/dissociation (evidenced in research on New Age spirituality and mystical experiences).

VIII. The attachment approach has made an unsurpassed empirical contribution to the psychodynamic literature on religion and spirituality, and it provides a valuable developmental anchor for many other key psychological approaches to religion and spirituality in adulthood.

IX. The attachment approach is an integral part of a larger evolutionary, cognitive neuroscience of religion dealing with how the evolved properties of the human mind interact with culturally acquired ideas to produce religious and spiritual outcomes.

X. Macro-level arrangements facilitating financial and economic security (such as societal welfare systems) counteract dependency in adult attachment relationships, undermine religion, and promote secularism.

Playlist

The world of song has greatly influenced my appreciation of the attachment–religion connection and the writing of this book. Here's a "soundtrack" to the book, available on both Spotify and YouTube under the book's title:

Washington Phillips—"I Had a Real Good Mother and Father"
Townes van Zandt—"I'll Be Here in the Morning"
Joy Division—"Atmosphere"
Emmylou Harris—"Every Grain of Sand"
Nick Cave and the Bad Seeds—"Lime-Tree Arbour"
Kris Kristofferson—"Help Me Make It through the Night"
Cesaria Evora—"Sodade"
Gram Parsons and Emmylou Harris—"In My Hour of Darkness"
Lana del Rey—"Blue Velvet"
Sister Rosetta Tharpe—"Precious Lord, Take My Hand"
Mavis Staples—"Ain't No Doubt about It"
Cowboy Junkies—"Angel Mine"
The National—"Graceless"
Bob Dylan—"Moonshiner"
The Triffids—"Lonely Stretch"
Lloyd Cole—"For Cryin' Out Loud"
Mary Gauthier—"Mama Here, Mama Gone"
Nick Cave and the Bad Seeds—"Brompton Oratory"
Swamp Dogg—"Sam Stone"
Bob Dylan—"Not Dark Yet"
American Music Club—"Sick of Food"

The Velvet Underground—"Heroin"
The Gun Club—"She's Like Heroin to me"
Lana del Rey—"Gods and Monsters"
Bob Dylan—"Where Are You Tonight? (Journey through Dark Heat)"
Gillian Welch—"Orphan Girl"
Nina Simone—"I Shall Be Released"
The War on Drugs—"Thinking of a Place"
When in Rome—"The Promise"
Leonard Cohen—"Anthem"
Lloyd Cole—"Music in a Foreign Language"
The Triffids—"Bury Me Deep in Love"
Nick Cave and the Bad Seeds—"Nature Boy"
Jim Ford—"Big Mouth USA"
Robert Forster—"Frisco Depot"
Leonard Cohen—"Joan of Arc"
Neil Young—"Like a Hurricane"
The Cure—"A Forest"
Mazzy Star—"Fade into You"
Bob Dylan—"Ballad of a Thin Man"
Lucinda Williams—"Fancy Funeral"
Blue Öyster Cult—"Don't Fear the Reaper"
Bob Dylan—"Highway 61 Revisited"
Father John Misty—"The Comedy of Man"
Otis Redding—"Security"
Thåström—"Ner Mot Terminalen"
The Pogues—"The Body of an American"
The Jesus & Mary Chain—"Just Like Honey"
The Rolling Stones—"You Can't Always Get What You Want"
The Fall—"Reformation!"
Primal Scream—"Swastika Eyes"
Deutsche Amerikanische Freundschaft (DAF)—"Der Mussolini"
Leonard Cohen—"The Future"
Nick Cave and the Bad Seeds—"Are You the One That I've Been
    Waiting For?"
Marianne Faithfull—"Gypsy Fairie Queen"
Leonard Cohen—"Leaving the Table"
Nina Simone—"Sinnerman"
Palace Brothers—"I Had a Real Good Mother and Father"

Notes

PROLOGUE

1. I am indebted to Frances Nkara (a doctoral student at UC Berkeley) for this analogy.

CHAPTER 1

1. By present-day standards—whatever their worth in future judgments—Harlow's research was highly unethical in view of animal rights considerations. Although Bowlby was clearly influenced by Harlow's work, and Harlow by Bowlby's (van der Horst, LeRoy, & van der Veer, 2008), Bowlby was vocally critical of the crude treatment of the infant monkeys in Harlow's laboratory. During one of Bowlby's lab visits, he is even on record as saying, "Why are you trying to produce psychopathology in monkeys? You already have more psychopathological monkeys in the laboratory than have ever been seen on the face of the earth" (Harlow & Suomi, 1970, p. 8; see also discussion in Singer, 1975).

CHAPTER 2

1. It is important to note that other religious figures might fill this relationship role in addition to or instead of "God." In some Christian traditions (especially Evangelical ones), it is Jesus with whom one maintains an active day-to-day relationship, while "God, the Father" is represented as a more distant background figure. In Catholicism, Mary typically represents the "maternal functions" related to attachment (Wenegrat, 1989). Outside of Christianity,

the worlds of different groups of believers are populated by a variety of gods and other deities, many of whom might function as noncorporeal attachment figures (see Kirkpatrick, 1994, for a discussion). Throughout this chapter I refer to "attachment to God," but it should be understood that in some cases another religious figure, or merely one or some of God's personages, may fill this role.

2. It is debatable whether Ainsworth's use of an "individual," as a requisite for an attachment figure, should be understood as merely "discriminated object" (R. Duschinsky, personal communication, September 2019) or as "discriminated person" (my interpretation). Ainsworth's (1985) surrounding discussion makes it hard to tell. More importantly, however, I think discriminated person is a better criterion, so I adopt it here. One important reason is that the attachment system presumably evolved because it potentiated infants' proximity specifically to discriminated, expectably protective persons (mostly caregivers), not their proximity to discriminated objects more generally. See also the discussion of surrogate objects in Chapters 3 and 6.

3. In a private conversation with Mary Main, Ainsworth had reportedly expressed great enthusiasm for the attachment–religion idea and for its articulation in Lee Kirkpatrick's (1999b) chapter in the first volume of the *Handbook of Attachment* (M. Main, personal communication, 2001).

4. I have previously tried out "symbolic" (see also Mikulincer & Shaver, 2016) but not to my satisfaction because symbolic implies a one-to-one correspondence with something else for which the symbol stands in. And I don't mean to suggest that attachment to God is merely a symbol for something else. I have also previously tried "attachment-like," but the "-like" part is merely vague. And I have tried "imaginary" and "illusory," which are concepts with a credible track record in the object-relations school of psychoanalysis (e.g., Winnicott, 1971) but nonetheless easy to misunderstand for people who are unaware (see Slife & Reber, 2009) that, in the object-relational sense of those words, they do not imply that the referent is nonexistent. I have also considered but ruled out "abstract," "bodyless," and "disembodied": Even though God is abstract, God is also anthropomorphized and made into something at least somewhat concrete and bodily, and without necessarily having had body parts chopped off ("disembodied"). Finally, I have tried "supernatural" but discarded that option as well because it doesn't do much to open up for other potential candidate members beyond God (and related manifestations, e.g., spirits), and it unnecessarily closes the door to potential nonsupernatural candidate members (e.g., imaginary companions).

CHAPTER 3

1. This album as a whole (along with some other songs from this songwriter) is a truly remarkable feat in view of the attachment–religion connection under elaboration here. God and other targets of love, protection, sorrow, and

longing are often commingled, building a theme of religion juxtaposed with attachment. The singer aims to characterize a feeling known as "saudade" in Portuguese, "an inexplicable longing for something that's gone and cannot be retrieved" (interview in *Melody Maker,* March 17, 1990). Consider, for example, the psalm-like "Brompton Oratory" and its reversed separation–reunion sequence: "Up those stone steps I climb / Hail this joyful day's return / . . . Outside I sit on the stone steps / With nothing much to do / Forlorn and exhausted, baby / By the absence of you."

CHAPTER 4

1. Readers who have already familiarized themselves with my fuzzy-boundary evaluation of "attachment relationships" and "attachment figures"—which are clearly more foundational matters of attachment categorization than the categorization of individual differences—should not be surprised that I find attachment categories (as applied to individual differences) to have even fuzzier boundaries. Thus, the attachment categories I describe should be viewed as prototypes, not essentialist categories.

2. The term "conditional" is misleading if it is taken to imply that the contrast— secure attachment—would somehow be "unconditional." Though probably a developmentally primary strategy, maintaining secure attachment is clearly "conditional" (i.e., on caregiver sensitivity/responsiveness). For this reason, I instead use "primary" versus "secondary" strategies in reference to secure versus organized insecure patterns.

3. In philosophy, such a logical error is known as an "error of the consequent." From cognitive psychology, it can be understood as a "single-cause bias" (Granqvist et al., 2016).

4. Other useful attachment methods developed for these age groups are the Manchester Child Attachment Story Task (Green, Stanley, Smith, & Gold-wyn, 2000), Friends and Family Interview (Steele & Steele, 2005), Child Attachment Interview (Target, Fonagy, & Shmueli-Goetz, 2003), and, for ease of administration, the (self-report) Security Scale (Kerns, Klepac, & Cole, 1996).

5. While regrettable, this divide can be at least partly understood as a natural consequence of the AAI and the self-reports being (virtually) empirically unrelated (Roisman et al., 2007; although see Shaver, Belsky, & Brennan, 2000). Readers interested in finding intermediates between these two types of attachment assessments may be interested in the secure-base script (Waters & Waters, 2006).

6. One notable exception to this conclusion is that newborn temperamental dysregulation has predicted several subtypes of disorganized (D) attachment (e.g., Padrón, Carlson, & Sroufe, 2014; Spangler, Johann, Ronai, & Zimmermann, 2009). Interestingly, however, the findings reported by Padrón

and colleagues (2014) indicate that temperamental dysregulation does *not* predict apprehension of the caregiver. Main effects of candidate genes for D attachment have also been suggested (e.g., Lakatos et al., 2000) but have not withstood replication attempts (Luijk et al., 2011).

7. I hasten to add that I do not intend to gloss over the negative effects of untoward caregiving or forms of insecure attachment on child development. As detailed in our consensus statement (Granqvist et al., 2017), clinical attachment researchers have developed a number of supportive, evidence-based caregiving interventions that can and should be implemented to help caregivers and children when need be. Also, there are clearly instances in which child removal is fully justified and indeed even imperative. Such is the case, for example, when maltreatment ensues despite the implementation of evidence-based interventions and other reasonable forms of support.

CHAPTER 5

1. On this note, as part of playful interaction with young children, I recommend that caregivers once in a while tell them "lies." For example, if a picture book shows a cow, by all means assert, "This is a horse." Not only is this funny for young children but it should also aid in sharpening their minds and developing their potential for autonomy vis-à-vis natural authorities. Nothing has done so much damage in human history as *blind* trust, so caregivers who give their children a playful head start in critical thinking have the potential to serve humanity. Yet, blind *mis*trust hasn't exactly served humankind/society either, so do make sure not to lie to young children on important matters, when they need honesty and sincerity.

2. These findings have since failed to replicate in two samples—a largely secular Swedish sample and a highly theistic U.S. sample (see Gruneau Brulin et al., 2018). Failed replications are common in experimental research, especially in social psychology, and interaction effects are particularly difficult to replicate (Open Science Collaboration, 2015). That results "failed" to replicate in the secular Swedish sample is not surprising (indeed, we had predicted that) because attachment–religion effects would seem to presuppose theistic beliefs and a perceived relationship with God, and (relatedly) religious priming methodology is typically effective only with religious participants (Shariff, Willard, Andersen, & Norenzayan, 2015). That results failed to replicate in the U.S. sample was, however, more surprising. Notably, there was no main-effect of threat to begin with, thus "nothing" for attachment security to moderate (or qualify). Although undetected methodological problems are a possibility, I speculate that one reason for the absent main effect of threat was the low threat baseline in the U.S. sample studied, especially as compared to the situation in Israel (Gruneau Brulin et al., 2018; see also Granqvist, Mikulincer, et al., 2012).

3. To prevent identification of these cases, I have added fictional biographical information. Their real names have also been replaced with fictional names.

CHAPTER 6

1. Incidentally, many fans of Bob Dylan wondered the same thing when he, renowned for his rebellious nonconformism, suddenly appeared as a "born-again" Christian. However, considering his Jewish background, he was more or less acting in line with his nonconforming character. Also, in hindsight it is plain to see that his conversion did not appear out of the blue. Consider, for example, how he finishes his preconversion album *Street Legal* (1978) with a song called "Where Are You Tonight? (Journey through Dark Heat)":

   > There's a new day at dawn and I've finally arrived
   > If I'm there in the morning, baby, you'll know I've survived
   > I can't believe it, I can't believe I'm alive
   > But without you it just doesn't seem right
   > Oh, where are you tonight?

2. I largely set aside the unresolved/disorganized components of Mr. Blue's representations as I am concerned here with compensatory (i.e., organized) strategies.

3. Mr. Blue appears to employ "splitting," a primitive defense, in his distinctions between God (good object) and devil (bad object). Although such splitting may have been theologically reinforced by the denominations with which Mr. Blue affiliated over the years, it seems unlikely that his use of splitting is merely the result of religious socialization. First, that would beg the question of why Mr. Blue sought out those affiliations in the first place (again, he was not born into them). Second, Mr. Blue has changed affiliations multiple times when he has felt that a denomination strayed from "true faith." Hence, it seems likely that religious splitting represents true faith for Mr. Blue.

4. Via generalizing working models, these AAI-secure participants seem to have had positive, biased expectations that God should be benevolent, but they have not observed persuasive manifestations of God's actual benevolence in their own lives or in the lives of others. Instead, they have witnessed much unjust suffering, about which they tend to be markedly compassionate, and they have come to doubt that a benevolent God would let that happen. In the end, many of these individuals appear to have simply "given up" on God, and they do not typically experience a personal relationship with God at present. For the latter reason, the RAI system is probably not applicable, so the insecure classification is likely misleading in these cases. We have called these individuals "autonomous doubters," with reference to Thomas "the doubter" in the New Testament, because even when they have been raised by sensitive, religious caregivers, they have come to different conclusions on their own. In that regard, they resemble secure children who are autonomous enough to call their parents' bluff when the parents give epistemically misleading cues (e.g., Corriveau et al. 2009; see also Chapter 5).

CHAPTER 7

1. Although self-report biases might explain some of the sharp increase in mental unhealth, sadly, much of it remains real. It probably has now become more socially acceptable to admit suffering than it was in the past. However, such increased acceptance is itself an indication that unhappiness has become almost normative.

2 In his motivational theory, Allport argued that, whereas intrinsic or "mature" religion (i.e., religion as an end, a master motive in life) promotes mental health, extrinsic or "immature" religion (i.e., religion as an instrumental means for other ends) undermines mental health. This claim may seem counterintuitive because the high-extrinsic scorer might use religion as an active attempt to achieve mental health (e.g., well-being, social connectedness). Allport's distinction became so influential as to distort the psychology of religion into (1) an almost singular focus on intrinsic versus extrinsic religion and (2) the best way to measure the two forms of religiosity with self-reports—a focus that regrettably lasted roughly 40 years. In hindsight, however, the distinction appears naïve and misguided. In brief, even though high-intrinsic scorers may be under the conscious impression that their religion is an end onto itself, that is not how motivation works. Nothing in nature is merely an end onto itself; rather, everything is instrumental (or extrinsic) for something else. Even "love," the most cherished of emotions, is instrumental to survival and reproduction (e.g., parental investment). Without its instrumental function, it is doubtful that we would be capable of even experiencing love. An important lesson is that self-reports may not do full justice to motivation.

3. These studies include Beck (2006); Beck and McDonald (2004); Bradshaw, Ellison, and Flannelly (2008); Bradshaw, Ellison, and Marcum (2010); Bradshaw and Kent (2017); Davis (2010); Davis, Hook, and Worthington (2008); Duncan (2007); Ellison et al. (2014); Ellison, Bradshaw, Kuyel, and Marcum (2012); Eurelings et al. (2005); Granqvist et al. (2014); Greenwald, Mikulincer, Granqvist, and Shaver (2018); Homan (2012); Homan and Boyatzis (2010); Keefer and Brown (2018); Kelley and Chan (2012); Keshavarz, Sheikh, Jahanbakhshi, Karimian, & Ghahvehchi-Hosseini (2016); Kirkpatrick and Shaver (1992); Limke and Mayfield (2011); Miner (2009); Miner, Dowson, and Malone (2014); Pirutinsky, Rosmarin, and Kirkpatrick (2019); Proctor, McLean, Miner, Dowson, and Devenish (2012); Reiner, Anderson, Hall, and Hall (2010); Rowatt and Kirkpatrick (2002); Sim and Loh (2003); Sim and Yow (2011); Thauvoye et al. (2018); Zahl and Gibson (2012).

4. In its opening statement, the Declaration of Independence refers to the "Laws of Nature and of Nature's God," which are usually interpreted as standing above and in judgment of state laws. Bellah (1976) argues that this document gives priority to the individual's relationship with God over his or her relationship to the state. This is exemplified in the Declaration itself by the citizens' declared right to form a new government if the state should violate individual rights. In Bellah's (p. 167) interpretation, "It is of the essence of the American civil religion that it 'challenges institutional authority.'"

The inherently liberal idea of separating church and state (found in the First Amendment to the U.S. Constitution), along with the particular form of civil religion that has developed in the population, appear to have had a markedly paradoxical effect on U.S. politics. On the one hand, and unlike the situation in large parts of Europe at the time, church and state were effectively separated, and many freedoms were consequently granted. Also, to prevent the state from interfering in the individual's relationship with God, the U.S. government is typically not allowed to expand to cover areas of life that clearly bear upon religious life, such as social security and family-related matters. Consequently, a "universal" welfare state (see Chapter 11) still meets fierce resistance in the United States, with the recent Tea Party movement as a telling example. On the other hand, however, because "the wall of separation between Church & State" (Jefferson, 1802) has been used to prevent a universal welfare state from being realized, the American population has maintained high levels of religiousness, which are then of course reflected in political elections and decisions. In recent years, religiously influenced policies on stem cell research, gay marriage, abortion, science priorities and education, and so on have almost become norms in U.S. politics. In conclusion, the liberal principle of independence between church and state has paradoxically yielded a practice of conservative intermingling of civil religion and politics.

CHAPTER 8

1. That said, I do not intend to support any strong perennialist position on "core" spiritual experiences, understood to denote that such experiences are entirely untouched by culturally influenced interpretations (e.g., Gellman, 2004). As true as it is that people's experiences yield interpretations, which can ultimately become cultural norms, culturally entrenched interpretations should also affect experience. This "transactional" view of the interplay among experience, interpretation, and culture is in keeping with my position on nature–nurture interactions permeating virtually everything in development.

2. For lack of a better word, I use "attachment disorganization" as a generic term to refer both to disorganized attachment in infancy/the early years of life and unresolved states regarding loss and abuse in adulthood. It should be noted, however, that unresolved states do not necessarily result from a disorganized attachment history, nor do they necessarily indicate attachment disorganization in any specific relationship at present. For example, unresolved states might result from the loss of a grandparent who was not an attachment figure, or from sexual or physical abuse by a stranger, even in a person who had a largely secure attachment history. My reason for including unresolved states under attachment disorganization is that they are nonetheless part of the "nomological network" (e.g., Cronbach & Meehl, 1955) surrounding disorganized attachment. Thus, they are linked, both conceptually and empirically, to disorganized attachment (see Hesse, 2016).

3. The use of detachment to denote a type of dissociation should not be confused with Bowlby's (1973) use of detachment in the protest–despair–detachment cycle following separation/loss, where it refers to the process of a child acting defensively "unattached."

4. The aim of the confusion technique is to induce bewilderment via, in the words of its originator, "the sudden and inexplicable introduction of an irrelevant idea" (Erickson, 1964, p. 184). This can be accomplished in many ways, for example, with wordplays. One amusing example is found in the opening lines of a tragicomical Tom Waits song titled "Hell Broke Luce" (not "loose"), about a war-traumatized soldier: "I had a good home but I left / I had a good home but I left, right, left" (from the album *Bad as Me*, 2011). Mr Waits's wordplay may not induce sufficient confusion, however, so instead consider listening (rather than reading) and trying to follow this instruction: "Write right right, not wright or write" (Erickson, 1964, p. 183). The momentary state of bewilderment that results from successful implementation of the confusion technique might facilitate hypnotic induction.

5. "Ballad of a Thin Man" (*Highway 61 Revisited*, 1965).

6. This is not to say that placebo effects are not "real." Not only can placebo effects (say, from sugar pills) be substantial, but they can also mimic those of evidence-based treatments, even at the physiological and neural levels (e.g., Faria et al., 2012; Stewart-Williams & Podd, 2004). Moreover, effects from successful "evidence-based" treatments (say, from efficacious medications) refer to average effects in certain samples drawn from certain populations, but they are not necessarily more real at the individual level than "placebo" effects; no individual is a group average. We can learn much more from placebo—for example about the importance of people's trust, faith, and suggestibility—than we do from simply treating it as a neutral control condition in randomized controlled trials.

7. Dawkins's scientific track record is nothing short of astounding; he is the father of both "the selfish gene" move in evolutionary biology and of memetics, which, in modified form, spawned the literature on cultural evolution. Even James (1902) lost his agnostic caution when dealing with mystical states, for example, in granting them the epistemic status of "superior points of view" (p. 429) and as pointing toward optimism about the existence of a supernatural world. James clearly approached supernatural embracement, but it should be noted that he did so in the context of radical pragmatism. In James's view, when ontological matters relating to experience cannot be answered via empirical or rational means, pragmatic considerations should settle the matters (e.g., "Their significance must be tested . . . by the value of their fruits" [p. ix]). In view of the celebration of James's contributions that I have offered in this book, note that I disagree with James here. I deny that any conclusions about supernatural ontology can be drawn from mystical experiences and also that pragmatism is an advisable "stand-in" to determine questions of ontology. In my view, it's better for psychologists of religion simply to leave them unanswered. I also think James's exclusive focus

on religion as what "individual men in their solitude" (p. 31) experience is somewhat regrettable partly because religion is often experienced in the company of others and partly because it blinded later psychologists of religion to the cultural determinants of what individuals experience (see Chapters 5 and 11).

8. Although it appears common within the decidedly Western, consumerist New Age movement to think that one can experience previous lives, via some special technique that can be bought and sold, this idea is at odds with most reincarnation beliefs expressed within their Eastern traditions of origin (but see, e.g., Stevenson, 2000). This is merely one of many examples of how the New Age movement unwittingly "appropriates" other religious/spiritual traditions (e.g., Dein, 2005; York, 2001).

CHAPTER 9

1. I respectfully disagree that meaning-making should serve as *the* overarching framework for the psychology of religion and spirituality. It is true, as Paolutzian and many others have argued, that cognitively higher, existential matters pertaining to meaning cannot be entirely reduced to their more basic constituent parts (e.g., attachment). However, those basic parts would surely get lost if meaning-making models were used as the overarching, research-guiding framework. Many people do all sorts of religious things without really knowing why or deriving much meaning from their behaviors. For example, they may robotically repeat the Lord's Prayer and sing hymns as part of religious services without reflecting on what the words actually mean. After the fact, they may second-guess why they behaved in a particular manner and what they got out of it. Listening to the meanings people make can be illuminating in various ways, but it will not necessarily help us understand *why* they behaved in particular ways or *why* they make certain meanings out of it. No doubt, the meaning-making framework is important in the psychology of religion and spirituality, but it is better treated as a midlevel theory, dealing with, for example, intentionality and justifications. An overarching framework should also be capable of explanation.

2. All commentators agreed that self-reflexivity is important in science and that the different approaches researchers adopt may reflect differential socialization into different academic cultures. Even more specifically, Luyten and Corveleyn (2007) invited a self-reflective answer to why Bowlby and Popper should be favored over Freud and Polanyi. While much of this book helps answer this question, I take this opportunity to state that my critique and the ensuing rejoinder were written while I was in an academic environment (in Sweden) that was marked by (post-)behaviorist persuasions and much psychoanalysis- and humanities-bashing. Cracking an innocent joke at the expense of behaviorism—"What did the behaviorist say after sex? 'It was good for you, but how was it for me?'"—was met by Swedish faces that looked even more like stone than they usually do. In this environment, I

probably felt a need to justify the "solid-science basis" underlying my own work on the attachment–religion connection. Therefore, my psychoanalysis critique and rejoinder probably came out as more polarized and venomous than they might otherwise have been.

CHAPTER 10

1. In fact, even songwriters can get it right: "The comedy of man starts like this: Our brains are way too big for our mothers' hips. And so Nature, she divines this alternative: We emerged half-formed and hope that whoever greets us on the other end is kind enough to fill us in. And, babies, that's pretty much how it's been ever since" (Father John Misty, *Comedy of Man,* 2017).

2. Media outlets loved the God helmet story so much that they even covered our failed replication study (*Nature News, The Economist, Die Zeit,* and multiple other outlets and channels). Because it is highly unusual for media to take the responsibility to cover the "sobering news" of failed replications, it is tempting to think that something other than error detection was on the journalists' minds. Indeed, the God and brain couplet is too sexy not to cover, whatever its form. Sure enough, despite not having even studied the brain directly, nor finding any evidence that the magnetic fields caused experiences of a sensed presence, I sat through dozens of interviews in which journalists couldn't stop asking questions pertaining mostly to whether God is in the brain and if so, where? I always responded, "Sure he is, almost everywhere," and I reminded journalists that maybe they should also ask whether God might be outside of the brain. Some felt that was a good additional question and posed it back to me. "I don't know," was my standard answer. They then hung up. I had finally had it when Norway Television sought to arrange an event in which I would be interviewed about "God in the brain" in prime time. Being ever suspicious of media dramaturgy, where the idea is to pitch a reductionist natural scientist against some religious person, I asked if someone else would be interviewed in the same show, and if so, who? "Yes," the reporter said. "A pastor who believes that God is real." *I* then hung up and didn't take any more calls on God and the brain.

CHAPTER 11

1. On a personal note, the scatterplots provided in the referenced studies added substantially to my divided feelings about studying the attachment–religion connection in Sweden. There I was, in the most extreme secular population of the free world, studying religion of all things. It didn't exactly help that my discipline was psychology. If even the American Psychological Association asserts that American psychology is biased against the psychological study of religion, just imagine what a corresponding Swedish psychological organization would say. (In truth, they say nothing because religion isn't on

their radar, except as a big question mark following the influx of religious immigrants.) To make matters worse, almost no senior colleague understood why I studied religion: "Whatever talent that guy has is going down the drain." Then one day, pondering whether to submit a grant application, I came out of the hole I had found myself in. I had what I like to think of as a "Eureka moment," though it may have been insanity (we may live to tell). My idea was to take what we had on attachment—religion in religious samples and test whether we see the same links on attachment–welfare systems in secular samples. This simple idea of testing the psychological equivalence between welfare systems and religion seemed like a viable hypothesis. To top things off, maybe Swedish psychology colleagues and granting agencies would be equally enthusiastic about this move? They were not. No grants came from Sweden to test this idea either. Known to my colleagues as an attachment researcher, I moved even further from studying "real" attachments. Studying God was enough of a departure already, and now I was contemplating studying security provision from a nonpersonal societal arrangement. Yet, as a master of rationalizing defenses, my colleagues' lack of enthusiasm became my confirmation: Who would've thought that Swedes would like the comparison of their treasured welfare system with religion to begin with? So, I plowed ahead, looking for grants elsewhere. Thank you to the John Templeton Foundation in the United States for providing funding!

2. This contrast reflects a somewhat anachronistic understanding of liberalism as the advocacy of a strong state: "liberal" spending of governmental resources. With such an understanding, liberalism can rightly be viewed as a leftist ideology. For most Europeans, such as myself, however, liberalism is understood to denote uncompromising individualism, expressed as strong advocacy of individual liberties in stark opposition to the idea of a strong state (cf. libertarianism). A moderate and less neoliberal version is found in the common advocacy of "social liberalism" (originating in, e.g., Mill, 1859/1966), where individual liberties and responsibilities are upheld but are balanced against the perceived need for a moderately strong state. In any event, on a left–right scale, most liberals are in the center in Europe, not on the left. To their left, they find Marxists, "progressives," and social democrats. To their right, they find conservatives. And scattered elsewhere, they typically find nationalists. Liberals in parliamentary democracies may strike alliances to the left, to the right, or with nationalists. Whichever way they go, they come out tarnished in the end: "I had a good home but I left / I had a good home but I left, right, left" ("Hell Broke Luce"; Tom Waits, *Bad As Me,* 2011).

3. While most Americans may view that assertion as a compliment to their system, most Europeans may regard it as a critical remark. Therefore, I wish to clarify that I intend neither; my intentions are merely descriptive.

4. In the event that some (male) readers object to the description of male oppression, may I suggest you attend to the testimonies of the recent "#MeToo movement"? I'm not saying all men have oppressed all women, nor that

women don't oppress. What I am saying is that some structures facilitate oppression of women, whereas others help prevent it.

5. Note the italicized qualifier. No one who has met many Swedes or Finns is likely to describe them as happy in some blissful or spiritual sense. (Accordingly, when my family and I were back on Swedish soil after a prolonged stay in California, where I drafted this book, one of my daughters asked, "Dad, why does everyone look so sad?") Three qualifiers are needed. First, "comparatively happy" might be better described as "somewhat less miserable." Second, differences among nations in "happiness" are modest. Third, measures of happiness are often impure (e.g., the UN's happiness assessment includes trust, income, and health), and that impurity may lead to confounding happiness with welfare systems.

References

Aber, J. L., & Allen, J. P. (1987). Effects of maltreatment on young children's socio-emotional development: An attachment theory perspective. *Developmental Psychology, 23*, 406–414.

Ahmadi, F. (2006). Culture, religion and spirituality in coping: The example of cancer patients in Sweden. In *Acta Universitatis Upsaliensis, Studia Sociologica Upsaliensia, No. 53*. Uppsala, Sweden: Uppsala University.

Ainsworth, M. D. S. (1967). *Infancy in Uganda: Infant care and the growth of love.* Baltimore: Johns Hopkins University Press.

Ainsworth, M. D. S. (1985). Attachments across the life span. *Bulletin of the New York Academy of Medicine, 61*, 792–812.

Ainsworth, M. D. S., & Bell, S. M. (1970). Attachment, exploration, and separation: Illustrated by the behavior of one-year-olds in a Strange Situation. *Child Development, 41*, 49–67.

Ainsworth, M. D. S., & Bell, S. M. (1972). *Mother–infant interaction and the development of competence.* Washington, DC: U.S. Department of Health, Education and Welfare, Office of Education.

Ainsworth, M. D. S., Bell, S. M., & Stayton, D. J. (1974). Infant–mother attachment and social development: "Socialization" as a product of reciprocal responsiveness to signals. In M. P. M. Richards (Ed.), *The integration of a child into a social world* (pp. 99–137). Cambridge, UK: Cambridge University Press.

Ainsworth, M. D. S., Blehar, M. C., Waters, E., & Wall, S. (1978). *Patterns of attachment: A psychological study of the Strange Situation.* Hillsdale, NJ: Erlbaum.

Ainsworth, M. D., & Marvin, R. S. (1995). On the shaping of attachment theory and research: An interview with Mary D. S. Ainsworth (Fall 1994). *Monographs of the Society for Research in Child Development, 60*(2–3), 3–21.

Allen, J. P. (2008). The attachment system in adolescence. In J. Cassidy & P. R. Shaver (Eds.), *Handbook of attachment: Theory, research, and clinical applications* (2nd ed., pp. 419–435). New York: Guilford Press.

Allen, J. P., Hauser, S. T., & Borman-Spurrell, E. (1996). Attachment theory as a framework for understanding sequelae of severe adolescent psychopathology:

An 11-year follow-up study. *Journal of Consulting and Clinical Psychology, 64*(2), 254.

Allport, G. W. (1950). *The individual and his religion.* New York: Macmillan.

Allport, G. W., & Ross, J. M. (1967). Personal religious orientation and prejudice. *Journal of Personality and Social Psychology, 5,* 432–443.

Altizer, T. J., Hamilton, W., & Hamilton, W. (1966). *Radical theology and the death of God.* New York: Bobbs-Merrill.

American Psychiatric Association. (2013). *Diagnostic and statistical manual of mental disorders* (5th ed.). Arlington, VA: Author.

American Psychological Association Council of Representatives. (2007, August 16). *Resolution on religious, religion-based and/or religion-derived prejudice.* Washington, DC: Author.

Andersen, M. (2019). The Bayesian observer and supernatural agents. *Religion, Brain and Behavior, 9*(1), 99–104.

Andersen, M., Schjoedt, U., Nielbo, K. L., & Sørensen, J. (2014). Mystical experience in the lab. *Method and Theory in the Study of Religion, 26,* 217–245.

Ano, G. G., & Pargament, K. I. (2013). Predictors of spiritual struggles: An exploratory study. *Mental Health, Religion and Culture, 16,* 419–434.

Ano, G. G., & Vasconcelles, E. B. (2005). Religious coping and psychological adjustment to stress: A meta-analysis. *Journal of Clinical Psychology, 61,* 461–480.

Arend, R., Gove, F. L., & Sroufe, L. A. (1979). Continuity of individual adaptation from infancy to kindergarten: A predictive study of ego-resiliency and curiosity in preschoolers. *Child Development, 50,* 950–959.

Argyle, M., & Beit-Hallahmi, B. (1975). *The social psychology of religion.* London: Routledge & Kegan Paul.

Atran, S. (2004). *In gods we trust: The evolutionary landscape of religion.* New York: Oxford University Press.

Bahm, N. I. G., Duschinsky, R., & Hesse, E. (2016). Parental loss of family members within two years of offspring birth predicts elevated absorption scores in college. *Attachment and Human Development, 18,* 429–442.

Baier, C. J., & Wright, B. R. (2001). "If you love me, keep my commandments": A meta-analysis of the effect of religion on crime. *Journal of Research in Crime and Delinquency, 38,* 3–21.

Baillargeon, R., & DeVos, J. (1991). Object permanence in young infants: Further evidence.*Child Development, 62,* 1227–1246.

Bakermans-Kranenburg, M. J., & van IJzendoorn, M. H. (2007). Research review: Genetic vulnerability or differential susceptibility in child development: The case of attachment. *Journal of Child Psychology and Psychiatry, 48,* 1160–1173.

Bakermans-Kranenburg, M. J., & van IJzendoorn, M. H. (2009). The first 10.000 Adult Attachment Interviews: Distributions of attachment representations in clinical and non-clinical groups. *Attachment and Human Development, 11,* 223–263.

Bakermans-Kranenburg, M. J., & van IJzendoorn, M. H. (2014). A sociability gene?: Meta-analysis of oxytocin receptor genotype effects in humans. *Psychiatric Genetics, 24,* 45–51.

Bakermans-Kranenburg, M. J., & van IJzendoorn, M. H. (2016). Attachment, parenting, and genetics. In J. Cassidy & P. R. Shaver (Eds.), *Handbook of attachment: Theory, research, and clinical applications* (3rd ed., pp. 155–179). New York: Guilford Press.

Bandura, A., & Walters, R. H. (1977). *Social learning theory* (Vol. 1). Englewood Cliffs, NJ: Prentice-Hall.

Barber, N. (2013). Country religiosity declines as material security increases. *Cross-Cultural Research, 47*, 42–50.

Barker, L. (2006). Teaching evolutionary psychology: An interview with David M. Buss. *Teaching of Psychology, 33*, 69–76.

Barkley, R. A. (1997). Behavioral inhibition, sustained attention, and executive functions: Constructing a unifying theory of ADHD. *Psychological Bulletin, 121*, 65–94.

Barkow, J. H., Cosmides, L., & Tooby, J. (Eds.). (1992). *The adapted mind: Evolutionary psychology and the generation of culture*. New York: Oxford University Press.

Barr, N. (2012). *Economics of the welfare state*. Oxford, UK: Oxford University Press.

Barr, R., Muentener, P., & Garcia, A. (2007). Age-related changes in deferred imitation from television by 6- to 18-month-olds. *Developmental Science, 10*, 910–921.

Barrett, J. L. (1999). Theological correctness: Cognitive constraint and the study of religion. *Method and Theory in the Study of Religion, 11*, 325–339.

Barrett, J. L. (2004). *Why would anyone believe in God?* Lanham, MD: AltaMira Press.

Barrett, J. L. (2011). Cognitive science of religion: Looking back, looking forward. *Journal for the Scientific Study of Religion, 50*, 229–239.

Barrett, J. L. (2012). *Born believers: The science of children's religious belief*. New York: Free Press.

Barrett, J. L., Richert, R. A., & Driesenga, A. (2001). God's beliefs versus mother's: The development of nonhuman agent concepts. *Child Development, 72*, 50–65.

Barrett, J. L., & Zahl, B. P. (2013). Cognition, evolution, and religion. In K. Pargament (Ed.), *APA handbook of psychology, religion, and spirituality: Vol. 1. Context, theory, and research* (pp. 221–237). Washington, DC: American Psychological Association.

Bartholomew, K., & Horowitz, L. M. (1991). Attachment styles in young adults: A test of a four-category model. *Journal of Personality and Social Psychology, 61*, 226–244.

Bartz, J. A., Tchalova, K., & Fenerci, C. (2016). Reminders of social connection can attenuate anthropomorphism: A replication and extension of Epley, Akalis, Waytz, and Cacioppo (2008). *Psychological Science, 27*, 1644–1650.

Bartz, J. A., Zaki, J., Bolger, N., & Ochsner, K. (2011). Social effects of oxytocin in humans: Context and person matter. *Trends in Cognitive Sciences, 15*, 301–330.

Bateson, P. P. G., & Hinde, R. A. (Eds.). (1976). *Growing points in ethology*. New York: Cambridge University Press.

Batson, C. D. (1997). An agenda item for psychology of religion: Getting respect. In B. Spilka & D. N. McIntosh (Eds.), *The psychology of religion; Theoretical approaches* (pp. 3–8). Boulder, CO: Westview Press.

Batson, C. D., Schoenrade, P., & Ventis, W. L. (1993). *Religion and the individual: A social psychological perspective*. New York: Oxford University Press.

Baumrind, D. (1971). Current patterns of parental authority. *Developmental Psychology Monographs, 4*(1, Pt. 2), 1–103.

Baumrind, D. (1978). Parental disciplinary patterns and social competence in children. *Youth and Society, 9*, 239–267.

Bayramoglu, Y., Harma, M., & Yilmaz, O. (2018). The relationship between attachment to God, prosociality, and image of God. *Archive for the Psychology of Religion, 40*, 202–224.

Beck, R. (2006). God as a secure base: Attachment to God and theological exploration. *Journal of Psychology and Theology, 34,* 125–132.

Beck, R., & McDonald, A. (2004). Attachment to God: The Attachment to God
Inventory, tests of working model correspondence, and an exploration of faith
group differences. *Journal of Psychology and Theology, 32,* 92–103.

Belavich, T. G., & Pargament, K. I. (2002). The role of attachment in predicting spiritual coping with a loved one in surgery. *Journal of Adult Development, 9,* 13–29.

Bellah, R. N. (1976). Comment on "Bellah and the New Orthodoxy." *Sociology of
Religion, 37,* 167–168.

Bellah, R. N., & Hammond, P. E. (2013). *Varieties of civil religion.* Eugene, OR:
Wipf & Stock.

Beller, E., & Hout, M. (2006). Intergenerational social mobility: The United States
in comparative perspective. *The Future of Children, 16,* 19–36.

Belsky, J. (1997). Theory testing, effect-size evaluation, and differential susceptibility to rearing influence: The case of mothering and attachment. *Child Development, 68,* 598–600.

Belsky, J. (2007). Childhood experiences and reproductive strategies. In R. Dunbar
& L. Barrett (Eds.), *Oxford handbook of evolutionary psychology* (pp. 237–
254). Oxford, UK: Oxford University Press.

Belsky, J., Houts, R. M., & Fearon, R. P. (2010). Infant attachment security and the
timing of puberty: Testing an evolutionary hypothesis. *Psychological Science,
21,* 1195–1201.

Benson, P. L., Donahue, M. J., & Erickson, J. A. (1989). Adolescence and religion:
A review of the literature from 1970 to 1986. *Research in the Social Scientific
Study of Religion, 1,* 153–181.

Berger, P. L. (1999). The desecularization of the world: A global overview. In P. L.
Berger (Ed.), *The desecularization of the world: Resurgent religion and world
politics* (pp. 1–18). Grand Rapids, MI: William B. Eerdmans.

Berggren, H., & Trägårdh, L. (2015). *Är svensken människa?: Gemenskap och
oberoende i det moderna Sverige* (2nd ed., rev.) [Is the Swede a human being?:
Communion and independence in modern Sweden]. Stockholm: Norstedts.

Bergin, A. E. (1983). Religiosity and mental health: A critical reevaluation and meta-
analysis. *Professional Psychology: Research and Practice, 14,* 170–184.

Bergin, A. E., & Jensen, J. P. (1990). Religiosity of psychotherapists: A national survey. *Psychotherapy: Theory, Research, Practice, Training, 27,* 3–7.

Bering, J. M. (2006). The folk psychology of souls. *Behavioral and Brain Sciences,
29,* 453–498.

Berman, S. (2006). *The primacy of politics: Social democracy and the making of
Europe's twentieth century.* New York: Cambridge University Press.

Bernier, A., Carlson, S. M., Deschênes, M., & Matte-Gagné, C. (2012). Social factors in the development of early executive functioning: A closer look at the
caregiving environment. *Developmental Science, 15,* 12–24.

Bernstein, E. M., & Putnam, F. W. (1986). Development, reliability, and validity of
a dissociation scale. *Journal of Nervous and Mental Disease, 174,* 727–735.

Birgegard, A., & Granqvist, P. (2004). The correspondence between attachment to
parents and God: Three experiments using subliminal separation cues. *Personality and Social Psychology Bulletin, 30,* 1122–1135.

Bjorck, J. P., & Cohen, L. H. (1993). Coping with threats, losses, and challenges.
Journal of Social and Clinical Psychology, 12, 56–72.

Bjorklund, D. F. (1997). The role of immaturity in human development. *Psychological Bulletin, 122,* 153–169.

Bjorklund, D. F., Blasi, C. H., & Ellis, B.J. (2005). Evolutionary developmental psychology. In D. Buss (Ed.), *The handbook of evolutionary psychology* (pp. 828–850). New York: Wiley.

Blackmore, S. (1999). *The meme machine.* New York: Oxford University Press.

Block, J., & Block, J. H. (2014). The role of ego-control and ego-resiliency in the organization of behavior. In W. A. Collins (Ed.), *Development of cognition, affect, and social relations* (Minnesota Symposia on Child Psychology, Vol. 13, pp. 39–102). New York: Psychology Press.

Bloom, P. (2007). Religion is natural. *Developmental Science, 10,* 147–151.

Bodner, E., Bergman, Y., & Cohen-Fridel, S. (2014). Do attachment styles affect the presence and search for meaning in life? *Journal of Happiness Studies, 15,* 1041–1059.

Bokhorst, C. L., Bakermans-Kranenburg, M. J., Fonagy, P., & Schuengel, C. (2003). The importance of shared environment in mother–infant attachment security: A behavioral genetic study. *Child Development, 74,* 1769–1782.

Bonne, O., Canetti, L., Bachar, E., De-Nour, A. K., & Shalev, A. (1999). Childhood imaginary companionship and mental health in adolescence. *Child Psychiatry and Human Development, 29,* 277–286.

Booth, C. L., Rubin, K. H., & Rose-Krasnor, L. (1998). Perceptions of emotional support from mother and friend in middle childhood: Links with social–emotional adaptation and preschool attachment security. *Child Development, 69,* 427–442.

Booth, M. (2015). *The almost nearly perfect people: Behind the myth of the Scandinavian utopia.* London: Random House.

Bosworth, D. A. (2013a). The tears of God in the book of Jeremiah. *Biblica, 94,* 25–46.

Bosworth, D. A. (2013b). Weeping in the Psalms. *Vetus Testamentum, 63,* 36–46.

Bosworth, D. A. (2015a). Ancient prayers and the psychology of religion: Deities as parental figures. *Journal of Biblical Literature, 134,* 681–700.

Bosworth, D. A. (2015b). Weeping in recognition scenes in Genesis and *The Odyssey. The Catholic Biblical Quarterly, 77,* 619–639.

Bowlby, J. (1944). Forty-four juvenile thieves: Their characters and home-life (I and II). *International Journal of Psycho-Analysis, 25,* 19–52, 107–127.

Bowlby, J. (1951). *Maternal care and mental health.* Geneva, Switzerland: World Health Organization.

Bowlby, J. (1953). *Child care and the growth of love.* London: Pelican Books.

Bowlby, J. (1973). *Attachment and loss: Vol. 2. Separation: Anxiety and anger.* New York: Basic Books.

Bowlby, J. (1980). *Attachment and loss: Vol. 3. Loss.* New York: Basic Books.

Bowlby, J. (1982). *Attachment and loss: Vol. 1. Attachment.* New York: Basic Books. (Original work published 1969)

Bowlby, J. (1988). *A secure base: Clinical applications of attachment theory.* London: Routledge.

Bowlby, J. (1991). Ethological light on psychoanalytical problems. In P. Bateson (Ed.), *The development and integration of behaviour: Essays in honour of Robert Hinde* (pp. 301–313). Cambridge, UK: Cambridge University Press.

Bowlby, J. (1992). *Charles Darwin: A new life.* New York: Norton.

Boyatzis, C. J. (2005). Religious and spiritual development in childhood. In R. F. Paloutzian & C. L. Park (Eds.), *Handbook of the psychology of religion and spirituality* (pp. 123–143). New York: Guilford Press.

Boyatzis, C. J. (2017). Progress on nature and nurture: Commentary on Granqvist and Nkara's "Nature meets nurture in religious and spiritual development." *British Journal of Developmental Psychology, 35,* 156–161.

Boyd, R. (2017). *A different kind of animal: How culture transformed our species.* Princeton, NJ: Princeton University Press.

Boyd, R., & Richerson, P. J. (1988). *Culture and the evolutionary process.* Chicago: University of Chicago Press.

Boyd, R., & Richerson, P. J. (2008). Gene–culture coevolution and the evolution of social institutions. In C. Engel & W. Singer (Eds.), *Better than conscious?: Decision making, the human mind, and implications for institutions* (pp. 305–314). Cambridge, MA: MIT Press.

Boyer, P. (2001). *Religion explained: The evolutionary origins of religious thought.* New York: Basic Books.

Bradshaw, M., Ellison, C. G., & Flannelly, K. J. (2008). Prayer, God imagery, and symptoms of psychopathology. *Journal for the Scientific Study of Religion, 47,* 644–659.

Bradshaw, M., Ellison, C. G., & Marcum, J. P. (2010). Attachment to God, images of God, and psychological distress in a nationwide sample of Presbyterians. *International Journal for the Psychology of Religion, 20,* 130–147.

Bradshaw, M., & Kent, B. V. (2017). Prayer, attachment to God, and changes in psychological well-being in later life. *Journal of Aging and Health, 30,* 667–691.

Breen, R., & Jonsson, J. O. (2005). Inequality of opportunity in comparative perspective: Recent research on educational attainment and social mobility. *Annual Review of Sociology, 31,* 223–243.

Bremberg, S., Hæggman, U., & Lager, A. (2006). *Ungdomar, stress och psykisk ohälsa– analyser och förslag till åtgärder.* Stockholm, Sweden: Socialdepartementet.

Brennan, K. A., Clark, C. L., & Shaver, P. R. (1998). Self-report measurement of adult attachment: An integrative overview. In J. A. Simpson & W. S. Rholes (Eds.), *Attachment theory and close relationships* (pp. 46–76). New York: Guilford Press.

Bretherton, I. (1987). New perspectives on attachment relations: Security, communication, and internal working models. In J. D. Osofsky (Ed.), *Handbook of infant development* (2nd ed., pp. 1061–1100). New York: Wiley.

Bretherton, I., & Munholland, K. A. (2016). The internal working model construct in light of contemporary neuroimaging research. In J. Cassidy & P. R. Shaver (Eds.), *Handbook of attachment: Theory, research, and clinical applications* (3rd ed., pp. 63–88). New York: Guilford Press.

Broen, W. E., Jr. (1957). A factor-analytic study of religious attitudes. *Journal of Abnormal and Social Psychology, 54,* 176–179.

Bronfenbrenner, U. (1979). *The ecology of human development.* Cambridge, MA: Harvard University Press.

Bronfenbrenner, U., & Ceci, S. J. (1994). Nature–nuture reconceptualized in developmental perspective: A bioecological model. *Psychological Review, 101,* 568–586.

Brown, D. E. (1991). *Human universals.* New York: McGraw-Hill.

Brown, R. J. (2006). Different types of dissociation have different psychological mechanisms. *Journal of Trauma and Dissociation, 7,* 7–28.

Brown, S. L., Nesse, R. M., House, J. S., & Utz, R. L. (2004). Religion and emotional compensation: Results from a prospective study of widowhood. *Personality and Social Psychology Bulletin, 30,* 1165–1174.

Bruck, M., & Melnyk, L. (2004). Individual differences in children's suggestibility: A review and synthesis. *Applied Cognitive Psychology, 18,* 947–996.

Buchheim, A., Heinrichs, M., George, C., Pokorny, D., Koops, E., Henningsen, P., . . . Gündel, H. (2009). Oxytocin enhances the experience of attachment security. *Psychoneuroendocrinology, 34,* 1417–1422.

Buller, D. J. (2005). *Adapting minds: Evolutionary psychology and the persistent quest for human nature.* Cambridge, MA: MIT Press.

Burke, S. E., Sanson, A. V., & Van Hoorn, J. (2018). The psychological effects of climate change on children. *Current Psychiatry Reports, 20*(5), 35.

Buss, D. M. (1995). Evolutionary psychology: A new paradigm for psychological science. *Psychological Inquiry, 6,* 1–30.

Buxant, C., & Saroglou, V. (2008). Joining and leaving a new religious movement: A study of ex-members' mental health. *Mental Health, Religion, and Culture, 11,* 251–271.

Buxant, C., Saroglou, V., Casalfiore, S., & Christians, L.-L. (2007). Cognitive and emotional characteristics of New Religious Movement members: New questions and data on the mental health issue. *Mental Health, Religion, and Culture, 10,* 219–238.

Buxant, C., Saroglou, V., & Tesser, M. (2010). Free-lance spiritual seekers: Self-growth or compensatory motives? *Mental Health, Religion, and Culture, 13,* 209–222.

Byrd, K. R., & Boe, A. D. (2000). The correspondence between attachment dimensions and prayer in college students. *International Journal for the Psychology of Religion, 11,* 9–24.

Campos, J. J., & Stenberg, C. (1981). Perception, appraisal, and emotion: The onset of social referencing. In M. E. Lamb & L. R. Sherrod (Eds.), *Infant social cognition: Empirical and theoretical considerations* (pp. 273–314). Hillsdale, NJ: Erlbaum.

Camras, L. A., Meng, Z., Ujiie, T., Dharamsi, S., Miyake, K., Oster, H., . . . Campos, J. (2002). Observing emotion in infants: Facial expression, body behavior, and rater judgments of responses to an expectancy-violating event. *Emotion, 2,* 179–193.

Cardeña, E. (1994). The domain of dissociation. In S. J. Lynne & J. W. Rhue (Eds.), *Dissociation: Clinical and theoretical perspectives* (pp. 15–31). New York: Guilford Press.

Cardeña, E., & Alvarado, C. S. (2014). Anomalous self and identity experiences. In E. Cardeña, S. J. Lynn, & S. Krippner (Eds.), *Dissociation, trauma, memory, and hypnosis series: Varieties of anomalous experience: Examining the scientific evidence* (pp. 175–212). Washington, DC: American Psychological Association.

Cardeña, E., & Spiegel, D. (1993). Dissociative reactions to the San Francisco Bay Area earthquake of 1989. *American Journal of Psychiatry, 150,* 474–478.

Cardeña, E., & Terhune, D. B. (2014). Hypnotizability, personality traits, and the propensity to experience alterations of consciousness. *Psychology of Consciousness: Theory, Research, and Practice, 1,* 292–307.

Carlson, E. A. (1998). A prospective longitudinal study of attachment disorganization/disorientation. *Child Development, 69,* 1107–1128.

Carlson, E. A., Yates, T. M., & Sroufe, L. A. (2009). Dissociation and development of the self. In P. Dell & J. A. O'Neil (Eds.), *Dissociation and the dissociative disorders: DSM V and beyond* (pp. 39–52). New York: Routledge.

Carroll, S. B. (2005). *Endless forms most beautiful: The new science of evo devo and the making of the animal kingdom.* New York: Norton.

Carver, C. S., Scheier, M. F., & Weintraub, J. K. (1989). Assessing coping strategies: A theoretically based approach. *Journal of Personality and Social Psychology, 56,* 267–283.

Cassibba, R., Granqvist, P., & Costantini, A. (2013). Mothers' attachment security predicts their children's sense of God's closeness. *Attachment and Human Development, 15,* 51–64.

Cassibba, R., Granqvist, P., Costantini, A., & Gatto, S. (2008). Attachment and God representations among lay Catholics, priests, and religious: A matched comparison study based on the Adult Attachment Interview. *Developmental Psychology, 44,* 1753–1763.

Cassibba, R., Papagna, S., Calabrese, M. T., Costantino, E., Paterno, L., & Granqvist, P. (2014). The role of attachment to God in secular and religious/spiritual ways of coping with a serious disease. *Mental Health, Religion, and Culture, 17,* 252–261.

Cassidy, J. (1994). Emotion regulation: Influences of attachment relationships. *Monographs of the Society for Research in Child Development, 59*(2–3), 228–249.

Cassidy, J. (2016). The nature of the child's ties. In J. Cassidy & P. R. Shaver (Eds.), *Handbook of attachment: Theory, research, and clinical applications* (3rd ed., pp. 3–24). New York: Guilford Press.

Cassidy, J., & Berlin, L. J. (1999). Understanding the origins of childhood loneliness: Contributions of attachment theory. In K. J. Rotenberg & S. Hymel (Eds.), *Loneliness in childhood and adolescence* (pp. 34–55). Cambridge, UK: Cambridge University Press.

Cassidy, J., & Shaver, P. R. (Eds.). (2016). *Handbook of attachment: Theory, research, and clinical applications* (3rd ed.). New York: Guilford Press.

Cavalli-Sforza, L. L., & Feldman, M. W. (1981). *Cultural transmission and evolution: A quantitative approach.* Princeton, NJ: Princeton University Press.

Chamie, J. (2017, February 22). The rise of one-person households. Retrieved May 24, 2019, from *www.ipsnews.net/2017/02/the-rise-of-one-person-households.*

Chödrön, P. (2008). *Comfortable with uncertainty: 108 teachings on cultivating fearlessness and compassion.* Boston: Shambhala.

Cicirelli, V. G. (2004). God as the ultimate AF for older adults. *Attachment and Human Development, 6,* 371–388.

Clark, E. T. (1929). *The psychology of religious awakening.* Oxford, UK: Macmillan.

Coe, G. A. (1916). *Psychology of religion.* Chicago: University of Chicago Press.

Collins, N. L., & Read, S. J. (1994). Cognitive representations of attachment: The structure and function of working models. In D. Perlman & K. Bartholomew (Eds.), *Advances in personal relationships* (Vol. 5, pp. 53–90). London: Jessica Kingsley.

Conrad, J. (2014). *The heart of darkness.* New York: Global Classics. (Original work published 1899)

Cook, C. M., & Persinger, M. A. (2001). Geophysical variables and behavior: XCII. Experimental elicitation of the experience of a sentient being by right hemispheric, weak magnetic fields: Interaction with temporal lobe sensitivity. *Perceptual and Motor Skills, 92,* 447–448.

Cooper, L. B., Bruce, A. J., Harman, M. J., & Boccaccini, M. T. (2009). Differentiated styles of attachment to God and varying religious coping efforts. *Journal of Psychology and Theology, 37,* 134–141.

Corriveau, K. H., Harris, P. L., Meins, E., Fernyhough, C., Arnott, B., Elliott, L., . . . De Rosnay, M. (2009). Young children's trust in their mother's claims: Longitudinal links with attachment security in infancy. *Child Development, 80,* 750–761.

Cortes, D. S., Skragge, M., Döllinger, L., Laukka, P., Fischer, H., . . . Granqvist, P. (2018). Mixed support for a causal link between single dose intranasal oxytocin and spiritual experiences: Opposing effects depending on individual proclivities for absorption. *Social Cognitive and Affective Neuroscience, 13,* 921–932.

Corveleyn, J., Luyten, P., & Dezutter, J. (2013). Psychodynamic psychology and religion. In R. F. Paloutzian & C. Park (Eds.), *Handbook of the psychology of religion and spirituality* (2nd ed., pp. 94–117). New York: Guilford Press.

Counted, V. (2018). The Circle of Place Spirituality (CoPS): Towards an attachment and exploration motivational systems approach in the psychology of religion. *Research in the Social Scientific Study of Religion, 29,* 149–178.

Cox, C. R., Arndt, J., Pyszczynski, T., Greenberg, J., Abdollahi, A., & Solomon, S. (2008). Terror management and adults' attachment to their parents: The safe haven remains. *Journal of Personality and Social Psychology, 94,* 696–717.

Craik, K. (1943). *The nature of explanation.* London: Cambridge University Press.

Cristofori, I., Bulbulia, J., Shaver, J. H., Wilson, M., Krueger, F., & Grafman, J. (2016). Neural correlates of mystical experience. *Neuropsychologia, 80,* 212–220.

Cronbach, L. J., & Meehl, P. E. (1955). Construct validity in psychological tests. *Psychological Bulletin, 52,* 281–302.

Darwin, C. (1859). *On the origin of species by means of natural selection.* London: John Murray.

Daun, Å. (1991). Individualism and collectivity among Swedes. *Ethnos, 56,* 165–172.

Daun, Å. (1996). *Swedish mentality.* University Park, PA: Penn State Press.

Davies, N. B., Krebs, J. R., & West, S. A. (2012). *An introduction to behavioural ecology.* Hoboken, NJ: Wiley.

Davis, D. E., Hook, J. N., & Worthington, E. L., Jr. (2008). Relational spirituality and forgiveness: The roles of attachment to God, religious coping, and viewing the transgression as a desecration. *Journal of Psychology and Christianity, 27,* 293–301.

Davis, E. B. (2010). *Authenticity, inauthenticity, attachment, and God-image tendencies among adult Evangelical Protestant Christians.* Doctoral dissertation, Regent University, Virginia Beach, VA.

Davis, E. B., Granqvist, P., & Sharp, C. (2018). Theistic relational spirituality: Development, dynamics, health, and transformation. *Psychology of Religion and Spirituality.* [Epub ahead of print]

Davis, E. B., Kimball, C. N., Aten, J. D., Andrews, B., van Tongeren, D. R., Hook, J. N., . . . Park, C. L. (2019). Religious meaning making and attachment in a disaster context: A longitudinal qualitative study of flood survivors. *Journal of Positive Psychology, 14*(5), 659–671.

Davis, E. B., Kimball, C. N., Aten, J. D., Hamilton, C., Andrews, B., Lemke, A., . . . Chung, J. (2019). Faith in the wake of disaster: A longitudinal qualitative study of religious attachment following a catastrophic flood. *Psychological Trauma: Theory, Research, Practice, and Policy.* [Epub ahead of print]

Dawkins, R. (1976). *The selfish gene.* New York: Oxford University Press.

Dawkins, R. (2006). *The God delusion.* London: Random House.

De Roos, S. A. (2006). Young children's God concepts: Influences of attachment and religious socialization in a family and school context. *Religious Education, 101,* 84–103.

De Roos, S. A., Iedema, J., & Miedema, S. (2003). Effects of mothers' and schools' religious denomination on preschool children's God concepts. *Journal of Beliefs and Values, 24,* 165–181.

De Wolff, M. S., & van IJzendoorn, M. H. (1997). Sensitivity and attachment: A meta-analysis on parental antecedents of infant attachment. *Child Development, 68,* 571–591.

Dein, S. (2005). Spirituality, psychiatry and participation: A cultural analysis. *Transcultural Psychiatry, 42,* 526–544.

Delaney, H. D., Miller, W. R., & Bisonó, A. M. (2013). Religiosity and spirituality among psychologists: A survey of clinician members of the American Psychological Association. *Spirituality in Clinical Practice, 1*(S), 95–106.

Dell, P. F. (2009). Understanding dissociation. In P. F. Dell & J. A. O'Neil (Eds.), *Dissociation and the dissociative disorders: DSM-V and beyond* (pp. 709–825). New York: Routledge.

Dewhurst, K., & Beard, A. W. (1970). Sudden religious conversions in temporal lobe epilepsy. *British Journal of Psychiatry, 117,* 497–507.

Dewitte, L., Granqvist, P., & Dezutter, J. (2019). Meaning through attachment: An integrative framework. *Psychological Reports, 122*(6), 2242–2265.

Dickie, J. R., Charland, K., & Poll, E. (2005). *Attachment and children's concepts of God.* Unpublished manuscript, Hope College, Hope, MI.

Diener, E., Tay, L., & Myers, D. G. (2011). The religion paradox: If religion makes people happy, why are so many dropping out? *Journal of Personality and Social Psychology, 101,* 1278–1290.

Dillon, M. (2007). Age, generation, and cohort in American religion and spirituality. In J. A. Beckford & N. J. Demerath, III (Eds.), *The SAGE handbook of the sociology of religion* (pp. 526–546). London: SAGE.

Dixon, N. F. (1971). *Subliminal perception: The nature of a controversy.* New York: McGraw-Hill.

Dixon, W. E. (2015). *Twenty studies that revolutionized child psychology* (2nd ed.). London: Pearson.

Dousa, B. (2018). *Snöflingorna faller över Husby* [The snowflakes are falling over Husby]. Stockholm, Sweden: Timbro.

Dozier, M., & Kobak, R. R. (1992). Psychophysiology in attachment interviews: Converging evidence for deactivating strategies. *Child Development, 63,* 1473–1480.

Dozier, M., Stovall, K. C., Albus, K. E., & Bates, B. (2001). Attachment for infants in foster care: The role of caregiver state of mind. *Child Development, 72,* 1467–1477.

Duncan, P. (2007). *Christians' attachment to God and mental health.* Unpublished master's thesis, University of Auckland, New Zealand.

Durham, W. H. (1991). *Coevolution: Genes, culture, and human diversity.* Stanford, CA: Stanford University Press.

Durkheim, E. (2008). *The elementary forms of the religious life.* Mineola, NY: Dover. (Original work published 1915)

Duschinsky, R. (2018). Disorganization, fear and attachment: Working towards clarification. *Infant Mental Health Journal, 39,* 17–29.

Duschinsky, R. (2020). *Cornerstones of attachment research.* New York: Oxford University Press.

Ein-Dor, T., Mikulincer, M., Doron, G., & Shaver, P. R. (2010). The attachment paradox: How can so many of us (the insecure ones) have no adaptive advantages? *Perspectives on Psychological Science, 5,* 123–141.

Ein-Dor, T., Verbeke, W. J., Mokry, M., & Vrtička, P. (2018). Epigenetic modification of the oxytocin and glucocorticoid receptor genes is linked to attachment avoidance in young adults. *Attachment and Human Development, 20*(4), 439–454.

Eisen, M. L., & Carlson, E. B. (1998). Individual differences in suggestibility: Examining the influence of dissociation, absorption, and a history of childhood abuse. *Applied Cognitive Psychology, 12,* S47–S61.

Ekman, I. (2006, November 13). Like Garbo, Swedes just want to be alone. *New York Times.* Retrieved from *www.nytimes.com/2006/11/13/world/europe/13iht-swedes.3512334.html?_r=0.*

Elicker, J., Englund, M., & Stroufe, L. A. (1992). Predicting peer competence and peer relationships from early parent–child interactions. In R. D. Parke & G. W. Ladd (Eds.), *Family–peer relationships: Modes of linkage* (pp. 77–106). Hillsdale, NJ: Erlbaum.

Ellison, C. G., Bradshaw, M., Flannelly, K. J., & Galek, K. C. (2014). Prayer, attachment to God, and symptoms of anxiety-related disorders among US adults. *Sociology of Religion, 75,* 208–233.

Ellison, C. G., Bradshaw, M., Kuyel, N., & Marcum, J. P. (2012). Attachment to God, stressful life events, and changes in psychological distress. *Review of Religious Research, 53,* 493–511.

Emmons, R. A., & Crumpler, C. A. (1999). Religion and spirituality?: The roles of sanctification and the concept of God. *International Journal for the Psychology of Religion, 9,* 17–24.

Epley, N., Converse, B. A., Delbosc, A., Monteleone, G. A., & Cacioppo, J. T. (2009). Believers' estimates of God's beliefs are more egocentric than estimates of other people's beliefs. *Proceedings of the National Academy of Sciences of the USA, 106,* 21533–21538.

Epley, N., Waytz, A., & Cacioppo, J. T. (2007). On seeing human: A three-factor theory of anthropomorphism. *Psychological Review, 114,* 864–886.

Erickson, M. H. (1964). The confusion technique in hypnosis. *American Journal of Clinical Hypnosis, 6,* 183–207.

Erikson, E. H. (1958). *Young man Luther: A study in psychoanalysis and history.* London: Faber & Faber.

Erikson, E. H. (1959). *Identity and the life cycle* (Monograph, *Psychological Issues,* Vol. 1). New York: International Universities Press.

Erikson, E. H. (1963). *Childhood and society* (2nd ed.). New York: Norton.

Erikson, E. H. (1998). *The life cycle completed: Extended version with new chapters on the ninth stage by Joan M. Erikson.* New York: Norton.

Eshleman, A. K., Dickie, J. R., Merasco, D. M., Shepard, A., & Johnson, M. (1999). Mother God, father God: Children's perceptions of God's distance. *International Journal for the Psychology of Religion, 9,* 139–146.

Eurelings-Bontekoe, E. H., Hekman-Van Steeg, J., & Verschuur, M. J. (2005). The association between personality, attachment, psychological distress, church denomination and the God concept among a non-clinical sample. *Mental Health, Religion and Culture, 8,* 141–154.

Evans, E. M. (2001). Cognitive and contextual factors in the emergence of diverse belief systems: Creation versus evolution. *Cognitive Psychology, 42,* 217–266.

Exline, J. J., Homolka, S. J., & Grubbs, J. B. (2013). Negative views of parents and struggles with God: An exploration of two mediators. *Journal of Psychology and Theology, 41,* 200–212.

Exline, J. J., Yali, A. M., & Sanderson, W. C. (2000). Guilt, discord, and alienation: The role of religious strain in depression and suicidality. *Journal of Clinical Psychology, 56,* 1481–1496.

Eysenck, S. B., Eysenck, H. J., & Barrett, P. (1985). A revised version of the psychoticism scale. *Personality and Individual Differences, 6,* 21–29.

Faria, V., Appel, L., Åhs, F., Linnman, C., Pissiota, A., Frans, Ö., . . . Wahlstedt,

K. (2012). Amygdala subregions tied to SSRI and placebo response in patients with social anxiety disorder. *Neuropsychopharmacology, 37,* 2222–2232.

Farias, M., Claridge, G., & Lalljee, M. (2005). Personality and cognitive predictors of New Age practices and beliefs. *Personality and Individual Differences, 39,* 979–989.

Farias, M., & Granqvist, P. (2007). The psychology of the New Age. In D. Kemp (Ed.), *Handbook of New Age* (pp. 123–150). Leiden, the Netherlands: Brill.

Fearon, R. P., Bakermans-Kranenburg, M. J., van IJzendoorn, M. H., Lapsley, A. M., & Roisman, G. I. (2010). The significance of insecure attachment and disorganization in the development of children's externalizing behavior: A meta-analytic study. *Child Development, 8,* 435–456.

Feeney, J. A. (2004). Transfer of attachment from parents to romantic partners: Effects of individual and relationship variables. *Journal of Family Studies, 10,* 220–238.

Ferm, V. (1945). *The encyclopedia of religion.* Secaucus, NJ: Poplar.

Feuerbach, L. (2004). *The essence of Christianity.* New York: Barnes & Noble. (Original work published 1854)

Field, N. P., Orsini, L., Gavish, R., & Packman, W. (2009). Role of attachment in response to pet loss. *Death Studies, 33,* 334–355.

Finkel, D., & McGue, M. (1997). Sex differences and nonadditivity in heritability of the Multidimensional Personality Questionnaire Scales. *Journal of Personality and Social Psychology, 72,* 929–938.

Fishbach, A., Friedman, R. S., & Kruglanski, A. W. (2003). Leading us not into temptation: Momentary allurements elicit overriding goal activation. *Journal of Personality and Social Psychology, 84,* 296–309.

Foley, K. E. (2018, September 17). The best countries to live in when you are old. *Quartz.* Retrieved from *https://qz.com/1391824/norway-sweden-us-the-best-countries-for-the-elderly.*

Folkman, S., & Lazarus, R. S. (1985). If it changes it must be a process: Study of emotion and coping during three stages of a college examination. *Journal of Personality and Social Psychology, 48,* 150–170.

Fonagy, P., & Allison, E. (2014). The role of mentalizing and epistemic trust in the therapeutic relationship. *Psychotherapy, 51*(3), 372.

Fonagy, P., & Campbell, C. (2015). Bad blood revisited: Attachment and psychoanalysis, 2015. *British Journal of Psychotherapy, 31,* 229–250.

Fonagy, P., Gergely, G., & Jurist, E. L. (Eds.). (2004). *Affect regulation, mentalization and the development of the self.* London: Karnac Books.

Fonagy, P., Steele, M., Steele, H., Moran, G. S., & Higgitt, A. C. (1991). The capacity for understanding mental states: The reflective self in parent and child and its significance for security of attachment. *Infant Mental Health Journal, 12,* 201–218.

Fonagy, P., & Target, M. (1997). Attachment and reflective function: Their role in self-organization. *Development and Psychopathology, 9,* 679–700.

Forslund, T., & Granqvist, P. (2016a). Consequences of attachment quality and organization. In T. K. Shackelford & V. A. Weekes-Shackelford (Eds.), *Encyclopedia of evolutionary psychological science.* Cham, Switzerland: Springer.

Forslund, T., & Granqvist, P. (2016b). The evolutionary foundations of the attachment system and its functions. In T. K. Shackelford & V. A. Weekes-Shackelford (Eds.), *Encyclopedia of evolutionary psychological science.* Cham, Switzerland: Springer.

Foster, J. E. (1998). Absolute versus relative poverty. *American Economic Review, 88,* 335–341.

Foster, R. J. (1992). *Prayer: Finding the heart's true home.* San Francisco: Harper.

Fowler, J. W., & Dell, M. L. (2006). Stages of faith from infancy through adolescence: Reflections on three decades of faith development theory. In P. L. Benson, E. C. Roehlkepartain, P. E. King, & L. Wageners (Eds.), *The handbook of spiritual development in childhood and adolescence* (pp. 34–45). Thousand Oaks, CA: SAGE.

Fraley, R. C. (2002). Attachment stability from infancy to adulthood: Meta-analysis and dynamic modeling of developmental mechanisms. *Personality and Social Psychology Review, 6*(2), 123–151.

Fraley, R. C., & Davis, K. E. (1997). Attachment formation and transfer in young adults' close friendships and romantic relationships. *Personal Relationships, 4,* 131–144.

Fraley, R. C., Roisman, G. I., Booth-LaForce, C., Owen, M. T., & Holland, A. S. (2013). Interpersonal and genetic origins of adult attachment styles: A longitudinal study from infancy to early adulthood. *Journal of Personality and Social Psychology, 104*(5), 817.

Fraley, R. C., & Shaver, P. R. (2016). Attachment, loss, and grief: Bowlby's views, new developments, and current controversies. In J. Cassidy & P. R. Shaver (Eds.), *Handbook of attachment: Theory, research, and clinical applications* (3rd ed., pp. 40–62). New York: Guilford Press.

Fraley, R. C., Vicary, A. M., Brumbaugh, C. C., & Roisman, G. I. (2011). Patterns of stability in adult attachment: An empirical test of two models of continuity and change. *Journal of Personality and Social Psychology, 101*(5), 974–992.

Fraley, R. C., & Waller, N. G. (1998). Adult attachment patterns: A test of the typological model. In J. A. Simpson & W. S. Rholes (Eds.), *Attachment theory and close relationships* (pp. 77–114). New York: Guilford Press.

Franck, R., & Iannaccone, L. R. (2014). Religious decline in the 20th century West: Testing alternative explanations. *Public Choice, 159,* 385–414.

Fransson, M., Granqvist, P., Bohlin, G., & Hagekull, B. (2013). Interlinkages between attachment and the Five-Factor Model of personality in middle childhood and young adulthood: A longitudinal approach. *Attachment and Human Development, 15,* 219–239.

Freedom House. (2018). About freedom in the world. Retrieved May 30, 2018, from *http://freedomhouse.org/report-types/freedom-world.*

Freud, A., & Burlingham, D. (1943). *War and children.* New York: Medical War Books.

Freud, S. (1961a). *Civilization and its discontents* (J. Strachey, Trans.). New York: Norton. (Original work published 1930)

Freud, S. (1961b). *The future of an illusion* (J. Strachey, Trans.). New York: Norton. (Original work published 1927)

Freud, S. (2010). *Moses and monotheism.* New York: Vintage Books. (Original work published 1939)

Freud, S. (2013). *Totem and taboo: Some points of agreement between the mental lives of savages and neurotics.* London: Routledge. (Original work published 1913)

Friedlmeier, W., & Granqvist, P. (2006). Attachment transfer among German and Swedish adolescents: A prospective longitudinal study. *Personal Relationships, 13,* 261–279.

Furnham, A., & Brown, L. B. (1992). Theodicy: A neglected aspect of the psychology of religion. *International Journal for the Psychology of Religion, 2*(1), 37–45.

Galanter, M. (1979). The "Moonies": A psychological study of conversion and membership in a contemporary religious sect. *American Journal of Psychiatry, 136,* 165–170.

Gallagher, H. L., & Frith, C. D. (2003). Functional imaging of "theory of mind." *Trends in Cognitive Sciences, 7,* 77–83.

Gallup, G., Jr., & Jones, S. (1989). *One hundred questions and answers: Religion in America.* Princeton, NJ: Princeton Religious Research Center.

Gaztambide, D. J. (2008). Relocating, reanalyzing, and redefining miracles: A psychodynamic exploration of the miraculous. *Miracles: God, Science and Psychology in the Paranormal, 2,* 27–49.

Geels, A. (2003). Transforming moments—A psychological perspective on religious visions: Contemporary and historical cases. *International Series in the Psychology of Religion, 13,* 235–262.

Geertz, A. W. (2010). Brain, body and culture: A biocultural theory of religion. *Method and Theory in the Study of Religion, 22,* 304–321.

Gellman, J. (2004). Mysticism. In *Stanford encyclopedia of philosophy.* Retrieved May 1, 2018, from *https://stanford.library.sydney.edu.au/entries/mysticism.*

George, C., Kaplan, N., & Main, M. (1996). *The Adult Attachment Interview.* Unpublished manuscript, University of California, Berkeley, CA.

George, C., & Solomon, J. (1996). Representational models of telationships: Links between caregiving and attachment. *Infant Mental Health Journal, 17,* 198–216.

George, C., & Solomon, J. (2008). The caregiving system: A behavioral systems approach to parenting. In J. Cassidy & P. R. Shaver (Eds.), *Handbook of attachment: Theory, research, and clinical applications* (2nd ed., pp. 833–856). New York: Guilford Press.

George, L. S., & Park, C. L. (2016). Meaning in life as comprehension, purpose, and mattering: Toward integration and new research questions. *Review of General Psychology, 20*(3), 205–220.

Ghobary Bonab, B., Miner, M., & Proctor, M. T. (2013). Attachment to God in Islamic spirituality. *Journal of Muslim Mental Health, 7*(2), 77–104.

Gibbs, H. W., & Achterberg-Lawlis, J. (1978). Spiritual values and death anxiety: Implications for counseling with terminal cancer patients. *Journal of Counseling Psychology, 25,* 563–569.

Gill, A., & Lundsgaarde, E. (2004). State welfare spending and religiosity: A cross-national analysis. *Rationality and Society, 16,* 399–436.

Gimpl, G., & Fahrenholz, F. (2001). The oxytocin receptor system: Structure, function, and regulation. *Physiological Reviews, 81,* 629–683.

Glicksohn, J., & Avnon, M. (1997). Explorations in virtual reality: Absorption, cognition and altered state of consciousness. *Imagination, Cognition and Personality, 17,* 141–151.

Glisky, M. L., Tataryn, D. J., Tobias, B. A., Kihlstrom, J. F., & McConkey, K. M. (1991). Absorption, openness to experience, and hypnotizability. *Journal of Personality and Social Psychology, 60,* 263–272.

Glock, C. Y., & Stark, R. (1965). *Religion and society in tension.* Chicago: Rand McNally.

Godin, A., & Hallez, M. (1965). Parental images and divine paternity. In A. Godin (Ed.), *From religious experience to a religious attitude* (pp. 65–96). Chicago: Loyola University.

Goldberg, T. (2005). Will Swedish and Dutch drug policy converge?: The role of theory. *International Journal of Social Welfare, 14,* 44–54.

Gopnik, A. (1996). The post-Piaget era. *Psychological Science, 7,* 221–225.

Gorsuch, R. L. (1968). The conceptualization of God as seen in adjective ratings. *Journal for the Scientific Study of Religion, 7*, 56–64.

Gorsuch, R. L. (1984). Measurement: The boon and bane of investigating religion. *American Psychologist, 39*, 228–236.

Gould, S. J., & Lewontin, R. C. (1979). The spandrels of San Marco and the Panglossian paradigm: A critique of the adaptationist programme. *Proceedings of the Royal Society of London B, 205*, 581–598.

Granqvist, P. (1998). Religiousness and perceived childhood attachment: On the question of compensation or correspondence. *Journal for the Scientific Study of Religion, 37*, 350–367.

Granqvist, P. (2002). Attachment and religiosity in adolescence: Cross-sectional and longitudinal evaluations. *Personality and Social Psychology Bulletin, 28*, 260–270.

Granqvist, P. (2003). Attachment theory and religious conversions: A review and a resolution of the classic and contemporary paradigm chasm. *Review of Religious Research, 45*, 172–187.

Granqvist, P. (2005). Building a bridge between attachment and religious coping: Tests of moderators and mediators. *Mental Health, Religion, and Culture, 8*, 35–47.

Granqvist, P. (2006a). In the interest of intellectual humility: A rejoinder to Rizzuto and Wulff. *International Journal for the Psychology of Religion, 16*, 37–49.

Granqvist, P. (2006b). On the relation between secular and divine relationships: An emerging attachment perspective and a critique of the depth approaches. *International Journal for the Psychology of Religion, 16*, 1–18.

Granqvist, P. (2006c). Religion as a by-product of evolved psychology: The case of attachment, and implications for brain and religion research. In P. McNamara & E. Harris (Eds.), *Where God and science meet: How brain and evolutionary studies alter our understanding of religion* (pp. 105–150). Westport, CT: Greenwood.

Granqvist, P. (2012). Attachment and religious development in adolescence: The implications of culture. In G. Trommsdorff & X. Chen (Eds.), *Values, religion, and culture in adolescent development* (pp. 315–340). New York: Cambridge University Press.

Granqvist, P. (2014a). Mental health and religion from an attachment viewpoint: Overview with implications for future research. *Mental Health, Religion, and Culture, 17*, 777–793.

Granqvist, P. (2014b). Religion and cognitive, emotional, and social development. In V. Saroglou (Ed.), *Religion, personality, and social psychology* (pp. 283–312). New York: Psychology Press.

Granqvist, P. (2016a). Attachment, emotion, and religion. In M. Fuller, D. Evers, A. Runehov, & K.-W. Saether (Eds.), *Issues in science and theology: Do emotions shape the world?* (pp. 9–26). Cham, Switzerland: Springer.

Granqvist, P. (2016b). Observations of disorganized behaviours yield no magic wand: Response to Shemmings. *Attachment and Human Development, 18*, 529–533.

Granqvist, P. (in press). Attachment, culture, and gene-culture co-evolution: Expanding the evolutionary tool-box. *Attachment and Human Development*.

Granqvist, P., Broberg, A. G., & Hagekull, B. (2014). Attachment, religiousness, and distress among the religious and spiritual: Links between religious syncretism and compensation. *Mental Health, Religion, and Culture, 17*, 726–740.

Granqvist, P., & Dickie, J. R. (2006). Attachment theory and spiritual development in childhood and adolescence. In P. L. Benson, E. C. Roehlkepartain, P. E.

King, & L. Wageners (Eds.), *The handbook of spiritual development in child-hood and adolescence* (pp. 197–210). Thousand Oaks, CA: SAGE.

Granqvist, P., Fransson, M., & Hagekull, B. (2009). Disorganized attachment, absorption, and New Age spirituality—A mediational model. *Attachment and Human Development, 11,* 385–403.

Granqvist, P., Fredrikson, M., Unge, P., Hagenfeldt, A., Valind, S., Larhammar, D., & Larsson, M. (2005). Sensed presence and mystical experiences are predicted by suggestibility, not by the application of weak complex transcranial magnetic fields. *Neuroscience Letters, 379,* 1–6.

Granqvist, P., & Hagekull, B. (1999). Religiousness and perceived childhood attachment: Profiling socialized correspondence and emotional compensation. *Journal for the Scientific Study of Religion, 38,* 254–273.

Granqvist, P., & Hagekull, B. (2001). Seeking security in the new age: On attachment and emotional compensation. *Journal for the Scientific Study of Religion, 40,* 529–547.

Granqvist, P., & Hagekull, B. (2003). Longitudinal predictions of religious change in adolescence: Contributions from the interaction of attachment and relationship status. *Journal of Social and Personal Relationships, 20,* 793–817.

Granqvist, P., Hagekull, B., & Ivarsson, T. (2012). Disorganized attachment promotes mystical experiences via a propensity for alterations in consciousness (Absorption). *International Journal for the Psychology of Religion, 22,* 180–197.

Granqvist, P., Hesse, E., Fransson, M., Main, M., Hagekull, B., & Bohlin, G. (2016). Prior participation in the strange situation and overstress jointly facilitate disorganized behaviours: Implications for theory, research and practice. *Attachment and Human Development, 18,* 235–249.

Granqvist, P., Ivarsson, T., Broberg, A. G., & Hagekull, B. (2007). Examining relations between attachment, religiosity, and New Age spirituality using the Adult Attachment Interview. *Developmental Psychology, 43,* 590–601.

Granqvist, P., & Kirkpatrick, L. A. (2004). Religious conversion and perceived childhood attachment: A meta-analysis. *International Journal for the Psychology of Religion, 14,* 223–250.

Granqvist, P., & Kirkpatrick, L. A. (2008). Attachment and religious representations and behavior. In J. Cassidy & P. R. Shaver (Eds.), *Handbook of attachment: Theory, research, and clinical applications* (2nd ed., pp. 906–933). New York: Guilford Press.

Granqvist, P., & Kirkpatrick, L. A. (2013). Religion, spirituality, and attachment. In K. Pargament (Ed.), *APA handbook for the psychology of religion and spirituality: Vol 1. Context, theory, and research* (pp. 129–155). Washington DC: American Psychological Association.

Granqvist, P., & Kirkpatrick, L. A. (2016). Attachment and religious representations and behavior. In J. Cassidy & P. R. Shaver (Eds.), *Handbook of attachment: Theory, research, and clinical applications* (3rd ed., pp. 856–878). New York: Guilford Press.

Granqvist, P., & Larsson, M. (2006). Contribution of religiousness in the prediction and interpretation of mystical experiences: Activation of religious schemas. *Journal of Psychology, 140,* 319–327.

Granqvist, P., Ljungdahl, C., & Dickie, J. R. (2007). God is nowhere, God is now here: Attachment activation, security of attachment, and perceived closeness to God among 5–7-year-old children from religious and non-religious homes. *Attachment and Human Development, 9,* 55–71.

Granqvist, P., & Main, M. (2017). *The Religious Attachment Interview: Coding and Classification System.* Unpublished manuscript, Stockholm University, Sweden/University of California, Berkeley.

Granqvist, P., Mikulincer, M., Gewirtz, V., & Shaver, P. R. (2012). Experimental findings on God as an AF: Normative processes and moderating effects of internal working models. *Journal of Personality and Social Psychology, 103,* 804–818.

Granqvist, P., Mikulincer, M., & Shaver, P. R. (2010). Religion as attachment: Normative processes and individual differences. *Personality and Social Psychology Review, 14,* 49–59.

Granqvist, P., & Moström, J. (2014). There are plenty of atheists in foxholes–in Sweden. *Archive for the Psychology of Religion, 36,* 199–213.

Granqvist, P., & Nkara, F. (2017). Nature meets nurture in religious and spiritual development. *British Journal of Developmental Psychology, 36,* 142–155.

Granqvist, P., & Nkara, F. (2019). Predictive coding in the psychological sciences of religion: On flexibility, parsimony, and comprehensiveness. *Religion, Brain, and Behavior, 9,* 86–89.

Granqvist, P., Reijman, S., & Cardeña, E. (2011). Altered consciousness and human development. In E. Cardeña & M. Winkelman (Eds.), *Altering consciousness: A multidisciplinary perspective* (pp. 211–234). Santa Barbara, CA: ABC-CLIO.

Granqvist, P., Sroufe, L. A., Dozier, M., Hesse, E., Steele, M., van IJzendoorn, M. H., . . . Duschinsky, R. (2017). Disorganized attachment in infancy: A review of the phenomenon and its implications for clinicians and policy-makers. *Attachment and Human Development, 19,* 534–558.

Granqvist, P., Vestbrant, K., Döllinger, L., Olsson, M. J., Liuzza, M. T., Blomkvist, A., & Lundström, J. (2019). The scent of security: Odor of romantic partner alters subjective discomfort and autonomic stress responses in an adult attachment-dependent manner. *Physiology and Behavior, 198,* 144–150.

Greeley, A. M. (1981). *The religious imagination.* New York: Sadlier.

Greeley, A. M. (1990). *The Catholic myth: The behavior and beliefs of American Catholics.* New York: Scribner.

Green, J., Stanley, C., Smith, V., & Goldwyn, R. (2000). A new method of evaluating attachment representations in young school-age children: The Manchester Child Attachment Story Task. *Attachment and Human Development, 2,* 48–70.

Greenberg, J., Solomon, S., & Pyszczynski, T. (1997). Terror management theory of self-esteem and cultural worldviews: Empirical assessments and conceptual refinements. In M. P. Zanna (Ed.), *Advances in experimental social psychology* (Vol. 29, pp. 61–139). New York: Academic Press.

Greenough, W. T., Black, J. E., & Wallace, C. S. (1987). Experience and brain development. *Development, 58,* 539–559.

Greenwald, Y., Mikulincer, M., Granqvist, P., & Shaver, P. R. (2018). Apostasy and conversion: Attachment orientations an individual difference in the process of religious change. *Psychology of Religion and Spirituality.* [Epub ahead of print]

Gribneau, N. I. (2006). *Event-related potentials to cemetery images distinguish electroencephalogram recordings for women unresolved for loss on the Adult Attachment Interview.* Unpublished doctoral dissertation, University of California, Berkeley, CA.

Griffiths, R. R., Johnson, M. W., Richards, W. A., Richards, B. D., Jesse, R., MacLean, K. A., . . . Klinedinst, M. A. (2018). Psilocybin-occasioned mystical-type experience in combination with meditation and other spiritual practices produces enduring positive changes in psychological functioning and in trait measures of prosocial attitudes and behaviors. *Journal of Psychopharmacology, 32,* 49–69.

Griffiths, R. R., Johnson, M. W., Richards, W. A., Richards, B. D., McCann, U., & Jesse, R. (2011). Psilocybin occasioned mystical-type experiences: Immediate and persisting dose-related effects. *Psychopharmacology, 218,* 649–665.

Griffiths, R. R., Richards, W. A., Johnson, M. W., McCann, U., & Jesse, R. (2008). Mystical-type experiences occasioned by psilocybin mediate the attribution of personal meaning and spiritual significance 14 months later. *Journal of Psychopharmacology, 22,* 621–632.

Griffiths, R. R., Richards, W. A., McCann, U., & Jesse, R. (2006). Psilocybin can occasion mystical-type experiences having substantial and sustained personal meaning and spiritual significance. *Psychopharmacology, 187,* 268–283.

Groh, A. M., Fearon, R. P., Bakermans-Kranenburg, M. J., van IJzendoorn, M. H., Steele, R. D., & Roisman, G. I. (2014). The significance of attachment security for children's social competence with peers: A meta-analytic study. *Attachment and Human Development, 16,* 103–136.

Groh, A. M., Roisman, G. I., van IJzendoorn, M. H., Bakermans-Kranenburg, M. J., & Fearon, R. P. (2012). The significance of insecure and disorganized attachment for children's internalizing symptoms: A meta-analytic study. *Child Development, 83,* 591–610.

Gross, J. J. (1998). The emerging field of emotion regulation: an integrative review. *Review of General Psychology, 2,* 271–299.

Grossmann, K. E., & Grossmann, K. (2005). Universality of human social attachment as an adaptive process. In C. S. Carter, L. Ahnert, K. E. Grossmann, S. B. Hrdy, M. E. Lamb, S. W. Porges, & N. Sachser (Eds.), *Attachment and bonding: A new synthesis* (Dahlem Workshop Report 92, pp. 199–229). Cambridge, MA: MIT Press.

Grossmann, K., Grossmann, K. E., Fremmer-Bombik, E., Kindler, H., Scheurer-Englisch, H., & Zimmermann, P. (2002). The uniqueness of the child–father attachment relationship: Fathers' sensitive and challenging play as a pivotal variable in a 16-year longitudinal study. *Social Development, 11,* 307–331.

Grünbaum, A. (1984). *The foundations of psychoanalysis.* Berkeley: University of California Press.

Gruneau Brulin, J., & Granqvist, P. (2018). The place of place within the attachment-religion framework: A commentary on the circle of place spirituality. *Research in the Social Scientific Study of Religion, 29,* 175–185.

Gruneau Brulin, J., Hill, P. C., Laurin, K., Mikulincer, M., & Granqvist, P. (2018). Religion vs. the welfare state—the importance of cultural context for religious schematicity and priming. *Psychology of Religion and Spirituality, 10*(3), 276–287.

Grusec, J. E., & Hastings, P. D. (Eds.). (2015). *Handbook of socialization: Theory and research* (2nd ed.). New York: Guilford Press.

Gullestad, S. E. (2001). Attachment theory and psychoanalysis: Controversial issues. *Scandinavian Psychoanalytic Review, 24,* 3–16.

Guntrip, H. (1969). Religion in relation to personal integration. *British Journal of Medical Psychology, 42,* 323–333.

Hackney, C. H., & Sanders, G. S. (2003). Religiosity and mental health: A meta-analysis of recent studies. *Journal for the Scientific Study of Religion, 42,* 43–55.

Halama, P, Gasparikova, M., & Sabo, M. (2013). Relationship between attachment styles and dimensions of the religious conversion process. *Studia Psychologica, 55,* 195–207.

Hall, L. (2017). *Swinburne's hell and Hick's universalism: Are we free to reject God?* New York: Routledge.

Hall, T. W., Fujikawa, A., Halcrow, S. R., Hill, P. C., & Delaney, H. (2009). Attachment to God and implicit spirituality: Clarifying correspondence and compensation models. *Journal of Psychology & Theology, 37,* 227–242.

Hamilton, W. D. (1964). The genetical evolution of social behaviour: I and II. *Journal of Theoretical Biology, 7,* 1–52.

Hanegraaff, W. J. (1996). *New age religion and western culture: Esotericism in the mirror of secular thought* (Vol. 72). New York: SUNY Press.

Harari, Y. N. (2014). *Sapiens: A brief history of humankind.* New York: Random House.

Harlow, H. F. (1958). The nature of love. *American Psychologist, 13,* 673–685.

Harlow, H. F., & Suomi, S. J. (1970). Induced psychopathology in monkeys. *Engineering and Science, 33,* 8–14.

Harris, J. R. (2011). *The nurture assumption: Why children turn out the way they do.* New York: Simon & Schuster.

Harris, P. L., & Giménez, M. (2005). Children's acceptance of conflicting testimony: The case of death. *Journal of Cognition and Culture, 5,* 143–164.

Hart, J., Shaver, P. R., & Goldenberg, J. L. (2005). Attachment, self-esteem, worldviews, and terror management: Evidence for a tripartite security system. *Journal of Personality and Social Psychology, 88,* 999–1013.

Harter, S. (1999). *The construction of self: A developmental perspective.* New York: Guilford Press.

Hartup, W. W. (1996). The company they keep: Friendships and their developmental significance. *Child Development, 67,* 1–13.

Hatano, G., & Inagaki, K. (1994). Young children's naive theory of biology. *Cognition, 50,* 171–188.

Hazan, C., & Shaver, P. (1987). Romantic love conceptualized as an attachment process. *Journal of Personality and Social Psychology, 52,* 511–524.

Hazan, C., & Shaver, P. R. (1990). Love and work: An attachment-theoretical perspective. *Journal of Personality and Social Psychology, 59,* 270–280.

Hazan, C., & Shaver, P. (1994). Attachment as an organizational framework for research on close relationships. *Psychological Inquiry, 5,* 1–22.

Heelas, P. (1996). *The New Age movement: The celebration of the self and the sacralisation of modernity.* Oxford, UK: Blackwell.

Heelas, P., Woodhead, L., Seel, B., & Szerszynski, B. (2005). *The spiritual revolution: Why religion is giving way to spirituality.* Oxford, UK: Blackwell.

Heiler, F. (1932). *Prayer: A study in the history and psychology of religion* (Vol. 16). New York: Oxford University Press.

Heine, S. J., Proulx, T., & Vohs, K. (2006). The meaning maintenance model: On the coherence of social motivations. *Personality and Social Psychology Review, 10,* 88–110.

Heintzelman, S. J., & King, L. A. (2014). Life is pretty meaningful. *American Psychologist, 69,* 561–574.

Heller, D. (1986). *The children's God.* Chicago: University of Chicago Press.

Henrich, J. (2016). *The secret of our success: How culture is driving human evolution, domesticating our species, and making us smarter.* Princeton, NJ: Princeton University Press.

Henrich, J., Heine, S. J., & Norenzayan, A. (2010). The weirdest people in the world? *Behavioral and Brain Sciences, 33,* 61–83.

Hesse, E. (2016). The Adult Attachment Interview: Protocol, method of analysis, and empirical studies: 1985–2015. In J. Cassidy & P. R. Shaver (Eds.),

Handbook of attachment: Theory, research, and clinical applications (3rd ed., pp. 553–597). New York: Guilford Press.

Hesse, E., & Main, M. (2006). Frightened, threatening and dissociative behavior in low-risk samples: Description, discussion and interpretations. *Development and Psychopathology, 18,* 309–343.

Hesse, E., & van IJzendoorn, M. H. (1998). Parental loss of close family members and propensities towards absorption in offspring. *Developmental Science, 1,* 299–305.

Hesse, E., & van IJzendoorn, M. H. (1999). Propensities towards absorption are related to lapses in the monitoring of reasoning or discourse during the Adult Attachment Interview: A preliminary investigation. *Attachment and Human Development, 1,* 67–91.

Hetherington, E., & Frankie, G. (1967). Effects of parental dominance, warmth, and conflict on imitation in children. *Journal of Personality and Social Psychology, 6,* 119–125.

Hewitt, M. A. (2008). Attachment theory, religious beliefs, and the limits of reason. *Pastoral Psychology, 57,* 65–75.

Hewitt, M. A. (2014). *Freud on religion.* London: Routledge.

Hidalgo, M. C., & Hernandez, B. (2001). Place attachment: Conceptual and empirical questions. *Journal of Environmental Psychology, 21,* 273–281.

Hilgard, E. R. (1986). *Divided consciousness: Multiple controls in human thought and action.* New York: Wiley. (Original work published 1977)

Hill, D. R., & Persinger, M. A. (2003). Application of transcerebral, weak (1 microT) complex magnetic fields and mystical experiences: Are they generated by field-induced dimethyltryptamine release from the pineal organ? *Perceptual and Motor Skills, 97*(3, Suppl.), 1049–1050.

Hill, P. C. (2005). Measurement in the psychology of religion and spirituality: Current status and evaluation. In R. F. Paloutzian & C. L. Park (Eds.), *Handbook of the psychology of religion and spirituality* (pp. 43–61). New York: Guilford Press.

Hill, P. C., & Gibson, N. J. (2008). Whither the roots?: Achieving conceptual depth in psychology of religion. *Archive for the Psychology of Religion, 30,* 19–35.

Hill, P. C., & Pargament, K. I. (2003). Advances in the conceptualization and measurement of religion and spirituality: Implications for physical and mental health research. *American Psychologist, 58*(1), 64–74.

Hill, P. C., Pargament, K. I., Hood, R. W., McCullough, M. E., Jr., Swyers, J. P., Larson, D. B., & Zinnbauer, B. J. (2000). Conceptualizing religion and spirituality: Points of commonality, points of departure. *Journal for the Theory of Social Behaviour, 30*(1), 51–77.

Hinde, R. A. (1966). *Animal behavior: A synthesis of ethology and comparative psychology.* New York: McGraw-Hill.

Hinde, R. A. (2009). *Why gods persist: A scientific approach to religion.* London: Routledge.

Hoff, E. V. (2005). Imaginary companions, creativity, and self-image in middle childhood. *Creativity Research Journal, 17,* 167–180.

Holbrook, C., Hahn-Holbrook, J., & Holt-Lunstad, J. (2015). Self-reported spirituality correlates with endogenous oxytocin. *Psychology of Religion and Spirituality, 7,* 46–50.

Holland, J. S. (2013). *Unlikely loves: 43 heartwarming true stories from the animal kingdom.* New York: Workman.

Homan, K. J. (2012). Attachment to God mitigates negative effect of media exposure on women's body image. *Psychology of Religion and Spirituality, 4,* 324–331.

Homan, K. J., & Boyatzis, C. J. (2010). The protective role of attachment to God against eating disorder risk factors: Concurrent and prospective evidence. *Eating Disorders: The Journal of Treatment and Prevention, 18*, 239–258.

Hong, K. M., & Townes, B. D. (1976). Infants' attachment to inanimate objects: A cross-cultural study. *Journal of the American Academy of Child Psychiatry, 15*(1), 49–61.

Hood, R. W., Jr. (1975). The construction and preliminary validation of a measure of reported mystical experience. *Journal for the Scientific Study of Religion, 21*, 29–41.

Hood, R. W., Jr., Hill, P. C., & Spilka, B. (2009). *The psychology of religion: An empirical approach* (4th ed.). New York: Guilford Press.

Hood, R. W., Jr., Spilka, B., Hunsberger, B., & Gorsuch, R. (1996). *The psychology of religion: An empirical approach* (2nd ed.). New York: Guilford Press.

Houtman, D., & Aupers, S. (2007). The spiritual turn and the decline of tradition: The spread of post-Christian spirituality in 14 Western countries, 1981–2000. *Journal for the Scientific Study of Religion, 46*, 305–320.

Hrdy, S. B. (1999). *Mother nature: A history of mothers, infants and natural selection.* New York: Pantheon.

Hrdy, S. B. (2011). *Mothers and others.* Cambridge, MA: Harvard University Press.

Huxley, J. (1942). *Evolution: The modern synthesis.* London: George Allen & Unwin.

Iacoboni, M., & Dapretto, M. (2006). The mirror neuron system and the consequences of its dysfunction. *Nature Reviews Neuroscience, 7*, 942–951.

Irwin, H. J. (1992). Origins and functions of paranormal belief: The role of childhood trauma and interpersonal control. *Journal of the American Society for Psychical Research, 86*, 199–208.

Irwin, H. J. (1993). Belief in the paranormal: A review of the empirical literature. *Journal of the American Society for Psychical Research, 87*, 1–39.

Irwin, H. J. (1994). Paranormal belief and proneness to dissociation. *Psychological Reports, 75*, 1344–1346.

Irwin, H. J. (2000). The disembodied self: An empirical study of dissociation and the out-of-body experience. *Journal of Parapsychology, 64*, 261–277.

Irwin, H. J. (2009). *The psychology of paranormal belief: A researcher's handbook.* Hatfield, UK: University of Hertfordshire Press.

Jacobsen, T., & Hofmann, V. (1997). Children's attachment representations: Longitudinal relations to school behaviour and academic competency in middle childhood and adolescence. *Developmental Psychology, 33*, 703–710.

Jacobsen, T., Huss, M., Fendrich, M., Kruesi, M. J., & Ziegenhain, U. (1997). Children's ability to delay gratification: Longitudinal relations to mother–child attachment. *Journal of Genetic Psychology, 158*, 411–426.

James, J. B., & Zarett, N. (2007). Ego integrity in the lives of older women. *Journal of Adult Development, 13*, 61–75.

James, W. (1902). *The varieties of religious experience.* New York: Longmans, Green.

James, W. (1950). *The principles of psychology* (2 vols.). New York: Dover. (Original work published 1890)

James-Roberts, I. S., & Halil, T. (1991). Infant crying patterns in the first year: Normal community and clinical findings. *Journal of Child Psychology and Psychiatry, 32*, 951–968.

Janet, P. (1907). *The major symptoms of hysteria.* New York: Macmillan.

Janoff-Bulman, R. (1989). Assumptive worlds and the stress of traumatic events: Applications of the schema construct. *Social Cognition, 7*, 113–136.

Jefferson, T. (1802, January 1). Jefferson's letter to the Danbury Baptists. Retrieved July 31, 2019, from *www.loc.gov/loc/leib/9806/danpre.html*.

Jensen, J. S. (2009). Religion as the unintended product of brain functions in the "standard cognitive science of religion model": On Pascal Boyer, *Religion Explained* (2001) and Ilkka Pyysiäinen, *How Religion Works* (2003). In M. Stausberg (Ed.), *Contemporary theories of religion* (pp. 129–155). London: Routledge.

Jeynes, W. H. (2002). A meta-analysis of the effects of attending religious schools and religiosity on Black and Hispanic academic achievement. *Education and Urban Society, 35,* 27–49.

Jipson, J. L., & Gelman, S. A. (2007). Robots and rodents: Children's inferences about living and non-living kinds. *Child Development, 78,* 1675–1688.

Johnson, K. A., Cohen, A. B., & Okun, M. A. (2016). God is watching you . . . but also watching over you: The influence of benevolent God representations on secular volunteerism among Christians. *Psychology of Religion and Spirituality, 8,* 363–375.

Johnson, P. E. (1945). *Psychology of religion.* New York: Abingdon-Cokesbury.

Johnson, S. C., Dweck, C. S., & Chen, F. S. (2007). Evidence for infants' internal working models of attachment. *Psychological Science, 18,* 501–502.

Johnson, S. C., Dweck, C. S., Chen, F. S., Stern, H. L., Ok, S. J., & Barth, M. (2010). At the intersection of social and cognitive development: Internal working models of attachment in infancy. *Cognitive Science, 34,* 807–825.

Jones, J. W. (1991). *Contemporary psychoanalysis and religion: Transference and transcendence.* New Haven, CT: Yale University Press.

Jones, J. W. (2008). *Blood that cries out from the earth: The psychology of religious terrorism.* New York: Oxford University Press.

Juergensmeyer, M. (2017). *Terror in the mind of God: The global rise of religious violence* (4th ed.). Berkeley: University of California Press.

Julien, R. M. (2000). *A primer of drug action: A concise nontechnical guide to the actions, uses, and side effects of psychoactive drugs* (9th ed.). New York: Worth.

Jung, C. G. (1938). *Psychology and religion.* New Haven, CT: Yale University Press.

Kagan, J. (1982). *Psychological research on the human infant: An evaluative summary.* New York: W. T. Grant Foundation.

Kagan, J. (1984). *The nature of the child.* New York: Basic Books.

Kamal, R., Cox, C., McDermott, D., Ramirez, M., & Sawyer, B. (2019). U.S. health system is performing better, though still lagging behind other countries (Brief, Peterson–Kaiser Health System Tracker). Retrieved May 24, 2019, from *www.healthsystemtracker.org/brief/u-s-health-system-is-performing-better-though-still-lagging-behind-other-countries*.

Kaplan, N. (1987). *Individual differences in 6-years olds' thoughts about separation: Predicted from attachment to mother at age 1.* Unpublished doctoral dissertation, University of California, Berkeley, CA.

Karen, R. (1994). *Becoming attached: Unfolding the mystery of the infant–mother bond and its impact on later life.* New York: Warner Books.

Karlbom, R. (1965). Sweden's iron ore exports to Germany, 1933–1944. *Scandinavian Economic History Review, 13,* 65–93.

Kaufman, G. D. (1981). *The theological imagination: Constructing the concept of God.* Philadelphia: Westminster.

Kay, A. C., Gaucher, D., Napier, J. L., Callan, M. J., & Laurin, K. (2008). God and the government: Testing a compensatory control mechanism for the support of external systems. *Journal of Personality and Social Psychology, 95,* 18–35.

Keefer, L. A., & Brown, F. L. (2018). Attachment to God uniquely predicts variation in well-being outcomes. *Archive for the Psychology of Religion, 40*, 225–257.

Keefer, L. A., Landau, M. J., Rothschild, Z. K., & Sullivan, D. (2012). Attachment to objects as compensation for close others' perceived unreliability. *Journal of Experimental Social Psychology, 48*, 912–917.

Keefer, L. A., Landau, M. J., & Sullivan, D. (2014). Non-human support: Broadening the scope of attachment theory. *Social and Personality Psychology Compass, 8*(9), 524–535.

Kelemen, D. (1999). Why are rocks pointy?: Children's preference for teleological explanations of the natural world. *Developmental Psychology, 35*, 1440–1452.

Kelemen, D. (2004). Are children "intuitive theists"?: Reasoning about purpose and design in nature. *Psychological Science, 15*, 295–301.

Kelley, M. M., & Chan, K. T. (2012). Assessing the role of attachment to God, meaning, and religious coping as mediators in the grief experience. *Death Studies, 36*, 199–227.

Kelsch, C. B., Ironson, G., Szeto, A., Kremer, H., Schneiderman, N., & Mendez, A. J. (2013). The relationship of spirituality, benefit finding, and other psychosocial variables to the hormone oxytocin in HIV/AIDS. In R. Piedmont & A. Village (Eds.), *Research in the social scientific study of religion* (Vol. 24, pp. 137–162). Leiden, the Netherlands: Brill.

Kerns, K. A., & Brumariu, L. E. (2016). Attachment in middle childhood. In J. Cassidy & P. R. Shaver (Eds.), *Handbook of attachment: Theory, research, and clinical applications* (3rd ed., pp. 349–365). New York: Guilford Press.

Kerns, K. A., Klepac, L., & Cole, A. (1996). Peer relationships and preadolescents' perceptions of security in the child–mother relationship. *Developmental Psychology, 32*, 457.

Keshavarz, H., Sheikh, M., Jahanbakhshi, Z., Karimian, A., & Ghahvehchi-Hosseini, F. (2016). Relationships between attachment to God and marital satisfaction, and mental health in parents of children with special needs. *International Journal of Behavioral Sciences, 10*, 84–88.

Kimball, C. N., Cook, K. V., Boyatzis, C. J., & Leonard, K. C. (2013). Meaning making in emerging adults' faith narratives: Identity, attachment, and religious orientation. *Journal of Psychology and Christianity, 32*, 221.

Kirkpatrick, L. A. (1992). An attachment-theory approach psychology of religion. *International Journal for the Psychology of Religion, 2*, 3–28.

Kirkpatrick, L. A. (1994). The role of attachment in religious belief and behavior. In K. Bartholomew & D. Perlman (Eds.), *Advances in personal relationships: Vol. 5. Attachment processes in adulthood* (pp. 239–265). London: Jessica Kingsley.

Kirkpatrick, L. A. (1995). Attachment theory and religious experience. In R. W. Hood, Jr. (Ed.), *Handbook of religious experience* (pp. 446–475). Birmingham, AL: Religious Education Press.

Kirkpatrick, L. A. (1997). A longitudinal study of changes in religious belief and behavior as a function of individual differences in adult attachment style. *Journal for the Scientific Study of Religion, 36*, 207–217.

Kirkpatrick, L. A. (1998). God as a substitute AF: A longitudinal study of adult attachment style and religious change in college students. *Personality and Social Psychology Bulletin, 24*, 961–973.

Kirkpatrick, L. A. (1999a). Attachment and religious representations and behavior. In J. Cassidy & P. R. Shaver (Eds.), *Handbook of attachment: Theory, research, and clinical applications* (pp. 803–822). New York: Guilford Press.

Kirkpatrick, L. A. (1999b). Toward an evolutionary psychology of religion. *Journal of Personality, 67,* 921–952.

Kirkpatrick, L. A. (2005). *Attachment, evolution, and the psychology of religion.* New York: Guilford Press.

Kirkpatrick, L. A. (2006). Religion is not an adaptation. In P. McNamara (Ed.), *Where God and science meet: How brain and evolutionary studies alter our understanding of religion* (Vol. 1, pp. 159–179). Westport, CT: Praeger.

Kirkpatrick, L. A., & Shaver, P. R. (1990). Attachment theory and religion: Childhood attachments, religious beliefs, and conversion. *Journal for the Scientific Study of Religion, 29,* 315–334.

Kirkpatrick, L. A., & Shaver, P. R. (1992). An attachment theoretical approach to romantic love and religious belief. *Personality and Social Psychology Bulletin, 18,* 266–275.

Knafo, A., & Schwartz, S. H. (2001). Value socialization in families of Israeli-born and Soviet-born adolescents in Israel. *Journal of Cross-Cultural Psychology, 32,* 213–228.

Kochanska, G. (1995). Children's temperament, mothers' discipline, and security of attachment: Multiple pathways to emerging internalization. *Child Development, 66,* 597–615.

Kochanska, G. (1997). Multiple pathways to conscience for children with different temperaments: From toddlerhood to age 5. *Developmental Psychology, 33,* 228–240.

Kochanska, G., Aksan, N., Knaack, A., & Rhines, H. M. (2004). Maternal parenting and children's conscience: Early security as moderator. *Child Development, 75,* 1229–1242.

Kochanska, G., Forman, D. R., & Coy, K. C. (1999). Implications of the mother–child relationship in infancy for socialization in the second year of life. *Infant Behavior and Development, 22,* 249–265.

Koenig, H. G., King, D. E., & Carson, V. B. (2012). *Handbook of religion and health* (2nd ed.). New York: Oxford University Press.

Kohut, H. (1971). *The analysis of the self.* New York: International Universities Press.

Koren-Karie, N., Oppenheim, D., Dolev, S., Sher, E., & Etzion-Carasso, A. (2002). Mothers' insightfulness regarding their infants' internal experience: Relations with maternal sensitivity and infant attachment. *Developmental Psychology, 38,* 534.

Korpi, W., & Palme, J. (1998). The paradox of redistribution and strategies of equality: Welfare state institutions, inequality, and poverty in the Western countries. *American Sociological Review, 63,* 661–687.

Krause, N. (2006). Religion and health in late life. In J. E. Birren & K. W. Schaie (Eds.), *Handbook of the psychology of aging* (6th ed., pp. 499–518). San Diego, CA: Academic Press.

Kroll, J., Fiszdon, J., & Crosby, R. D. (1996). Childhood abuse and three measures of altered states of consciousness (dissociation, absorption and mysticism) in a female outpatient sample. *Journal of Personality Disorders, 10,* 345–354.

Kupor, D. M., Laurin, K., & Levav, J. (2015). Anticipating divine protection?: Reminders of God can increase nonmoral risk taking. *Psychological Science, 26,* 374–384.

la Cour, P., Avlund, K., & Schultz-Larsen, K. (2006). Religion and survival in a secular region: A twenty year follow-up of 734 Danish adults born in 1914. *Social Science and Medicine, 62,* 157–164.

la Cour, P., & Hvidt, N. C. (2010). Research on meaning-making and health in secular society: Secular, spiritual and religious existential orientations. *Social Science and Medicine, 71,* 1292–1299.

Lakatos, I. (1980). *The methodology of scientific research programmes: Vol. 1. Philosophical papers.* New York: Cambridge University Press.

Lakatos, K., Toth, I., Nemoda, Z., Ney, K., Sasvari-Szekely, M., & Gervai, J. (2000). Dopamine D4 receptor (DRD4) gene polymorphism is associated with attachment disorganization in infants. *Molecular Psychiatry, 5,* 633–637.

Lakoff, G., & Johnson, M. (1999). *Philosophy in the flesh* (Vol. 4). New York: Basic Books.

Laland, K. N. (2017). *Darwin's unfinished symphony: How culture made the human mind.* Princeton, NJ: Princeton University Press.

Laland, K. N., & Brown, G. R. (2011). *Sense and nonsense: Evolutionary perspectives on human behavior.* New York: Oxford University Press.

Laland, K. N., Sterelny, K., Odling-Smee, J., Hoppitt, W., & Uller, T. (2011). Cause and effect in biology revisited: Is Mayr's proximate–ultimate dichotomy still useful? *Science, 334,* 1512–1516.

Lambert, W. W., Triandis, L. M., & Wolf, M. (1959). Some correlates of beliefs in the malevolence and benevolence of supernatural beings: A cross-societal study. *Journal of Abnormal and Social Psychology, 58,* 162–169.

Lapsley, D. K., Rice, K. G., & Fitzgerald, D. P. (1990). Adolescent attachment, identity, and adjustment to college: Implications for the continuity of adaptation hypothesis. *Journal of Counseling and Development, 68,* 561–565.

Larsson, M., Larhammar, D., Fredrikson, M., & Granqvist, P. (2005). Letter to the editor. *Neuroscience Letters, 380,* 348–350.

Laurin, K. (2017). Belief in God: A cultural adaptation with important side effects. *Current Directions in Psychological Science, 26,* 458–463.

Laurin, K., Kay, A. C., & Fitzsimons, G. M. (2012). Divergent effects of activating thoughts of God on self-regulation. *Journal of Personality and Social Psychology, 102,* 4–21.

Lazarus, R. S., & Folkman, S. (1984). *Stress, appraisal, and coping.* New York: Springer.

Leahey, T. H. (1991). *A history of modern psychology.* Englewood Cliffs, NJ: Prentice Hall.

Legare, C. H., Evans, E. M., Rosengren, K. S., & Harris, P. L. (2012). The coexistence of natural and supernatural explanations across cultures and development. *Child Development, 83,* 779–793.

Legare, C. H., & Harris, P. L. (2016). The ontogeny of cultural learning. *Child Development, 87,* 633–642.

Leuba, J. H. (1925). *The psychology of religious mysticism.* New York: Harcourt, Brace.

Li, H., & Zou, H. F. (1998). Income inequality is not harmful for growth: Theory and evidence. *Review of Development Economics, 2,* 318–334.

Lilliengren, P. (2014). *Exploring therapeutic action in psychoanalytic psychotherapy: Attachment to therapist and change.* Doctoral dissertation, Department of Psychology, Stockholm University, Stockholm, Sweden.

Limke, A., & Mayfield, P. B. (2011). Attachment to God: Differentiating the contributions of fathers and mothers using the experiences in parental relationships scale. *Journal of Psychology and Theology, 39*(2), 122–129.

Lindberg, L., Fransson, M., Forslund, T., Springer, L., & Granqvist, P. (2017). Maternal sensitivity among mothers with mild intellectual disabilities is related to experiences of maltreatment and predictive of child attachment: A matched comparison study. *Journal of Applied Research in Intellectual Disabilities, 30,* 445–455.

Liotti, G. (1992). Disorganized/disoriented attachment in the etiology of the dissociative disorders. *Dissociation, 5,* 196–204.

Liotti, G. (2006). A model of dissociation based on attachment theory and research. *Journal of Trauma and Dissociation, 7,* 55–73.

Liotti, G. (2009). Attachment and dissociation. In P. F. Dell & J. A. O'Neil (Eds.), *Dissociation and the dissociative disorders: DSM-V and beyond* (pp. 53–66). New York: Routledge.

Londerville, S., & Main, M. (1981). Security of attachment, compliance, and maternal training methods in the second year of life. *Developmental Psychology, 17,* 289–299.

Lopez, J. L., Riggs, S. A., Pollard, S. E., & Hook, J. N. (2011). Religious commitment, adult attachment, and marital adjustment in newly married couples. *Journal of Family Psychology, 25,* 301–309.

Lorenz, K. (1937). Imprinting. *Auk, 54*(1), 245–273.

Loveland, G. G. (1968). The effects of bereavement on certain religious attitudes. *Sociological Symposium, 1,* 17–27.

Luhrmann, T. M. (2005). The art of hearing God: Absorption, dissociation, and contemporary American spirituality. *Spiritus: A Journal of Christian Spirituality, 5,* 133–157.

Luhrmann, T. M., Nusbaum, H., & Thisted, R. (2010). The absorption hypothesis: Learning to hear God in evangelical Christianity. *American Anthropologist, 112,* 66–78.

Luijk, M. P., Roisman, G. I., Haltigan, J. D., Tiemeier, H., Booth-LaForce, C., van IJzendoorn, M. H., . . . Verhulst, F. C. (2011). Dopaminergic, serotonergic, and oxytonergic candidate genes associated with infant attachment security and disorganization?: In search of main and interaction effects. *Journal of Child Psychology and Psychiatry, 52,* 1295–1307.

Lumsden, C. J., & Wilson, E. O. (2005). *Genes, mind, and culture: The coevolutionary process.* Cambridge, MA: Harvard University Press.

Luyten, P., & Corveleyn, J. (2007). Attachment and religion: The need to leave our secure base: A comment on the discussion between Granqvist, Rizzuto, and Wulff. *International Journal for the Psychology of Religion, 17,* 81–97.

Lyons-Ruth, K. (2003). Dissociation and the parent–infant dialogue: A longitudinal perspective from attachment research. *Journal of the American Psychoanalytic Association, 51,* 883–911.

Lyubomirsky, S., Sheldon, K. M., & Schkade, D. (2005). Pursuing happiness: The architecture of sustainable change. *Review of General Psychology, 9,* 111–131.

Mahoney, A. (2010). Religion in families, 1999–2009: A relational spirituality framework. *Journal of Marriage and Family, 72,* 805–827.

Mahoney, A., Pargament, K. I., Jewell, T., Swank, A. B., Scott, E., Emery, E., & Rye, M. (1999). Marriage and the spiritual realm: The role of proximal and distal religious constructs in marital functioning. *Journal of Family Psychology, 13,* 321–338.

Maij, D. L., & van Elk, M. (2018). Getting absorbed in experimentally induced extraordinary experiences: Effects of placebo brain stimulation on agency detection. *Consciousness and Cognition, 66,* 1–16.

Maij, D. L., van Elk, M., & Schjoedt, U. (2017). The role of alcohol in expectancy-driven mystical experiences: A pre-registered field study using placebo brain stimulation. *Religion, Brain and Behavior, 9*(2), 1–18.

Main, M. (1981). Avoidance in the service of attachment: A working paper. In K.

Immelmann, G. Barlow, L. Petrinovic, & M. Main (Eds.), *Behavioral development: The Bielefeld Interdisciplinary Project* (pp. 651–693). New York: Cambridge University Press.

Main, M. (1990). Cross-cultural studies of attachment organization: Recent studies, changing methodologies, and the concept of conditional strategies. *Human Development, 33*(1), 48–61.

Main, M. (1991). Metacognitive knowledge, metacognitive monitoring, and singular (coherent) vs. multiple (incoherent) models of attachment: Findings and directions for future research. In C. M. Parkes, J. Stevenson-Hinde, & P. Marris (Eds.), *Attachment across the life cycle* (pp. 127–159). London: Tavistock/Routledge.

Main, M., & Cassidy, J. (1988). Categories of response to reunion with the parent at age 6: Predictable from infant attachment classifications and stable over a 1-month period. *Developmental Psychology, 24*, 415–426.

Main, M., Goldwyn, R., & Hesse, E. (2003). *Adult attachment scoring and classification system.* Unpublished manuscript, University of California at Berkeley, Berkeley, CA.

Main, M., & Hesse, E. (1990). Parents' unresolved traumatic experiences are related to infant disorganized attachment status: Is frightened and/or frightening parental behavior the linking mechanism? In M. T. Greenberg, D. Cicchetti, & E. M. Cummings (Eds.), *Attachment in the preschool years: Theory, research, and intervention* (pp. 161–182). Chicago: University of Chicago Press.

Main, M., Hesse, E., & Hesse, S. (2011). Attachment theory and research: Overview with suggested applications to child custody. *Family Court Review, 49*, 426–463.

Main, M., Hesse, E., & Kaplan, N. (2005). Predictability of attachment behavior and representational models at 1, 6, and 19 years of age: The Berkeley Longitudinal Study. In K. E. Grossmann, K. Grossmann, & E. Waters (Eds.), *Attachment from infancy to adulthood* (pp. 245–304). New York: Guilford Press.

Main, M., Kaplan, N., & Cassidy, J. (1985). Security in infancy, childhood, and adulthood: A move to the level of representation. In I. Bretherton & E. Waters (Eds.), Growing points of attachment theory and research. *Monographs of the Society for Research in Child Development, 50*(1–2, Serial No. 209), 66–104.

Main, M., & Morgan, H. (1996). Disorganization and disorientation in infant Strange Situation behavior: Phenotypic resemblance to dissociative states. In L. Michelson & W. Ray (Eds.), *Handbook of dissociation: Theoretical, empirical, and clinical perspectives* (pp. 107–138). New York: Plenum Press.

Main, M., & Solomon J. (1990). Procedures for identifying infants as disorganised/disoriented during the Ainsworth Strange Situation. In M. T. Greenberg, D. Cicchetti, & E. M. Cummings (Eds.), *Attachment in the preschool years* (pp. 121–160). Chicago: University of Chicago Press.

Main, M., van IJzendoorn, M. H., & Hesse, E. (1993). *Unresolved/unclassifiable responses to the Adult Attachment Interview: Predictable from unresolved states and anomalous beliefs in the Berkeley–Leiden Adult Attachment Questionnaire.* Unpublished manuscript.

Marcusson-Clavertz, D., Gušić, S., Bengtsson, H., Jacobsen, H., & Cardeña, E. (2017). The relation of dissociation and mind wandering to unresolved/disorganized attachment: An experience sampling study. *Attachment and Human Development, 19*, 170–190.

Martela, F., & Steger, M. F. (2016). The three meanings of meaning in life: Distinguishing coherence, purpose, and significance. *Journal of Positive Psychology, 11*(5), 531–545.

Marx, K. (1977). *Critique of Hegel's "Philosophy of right."* Cambridge, MA: Cambridge University Press. (Original work published 1844)

Matas, L., Arend, R. A., & Sroufe, L. A. (1978). Continuity of adaptation in the second year: The relationship between quality of attachment and later competence. *Child Development, 49*(3), 547–556.

Mattlin, J. A., Wethington, E., & Kessler, R. C. (1990). Situational determinants of coping and coping effectiveness. *Journal of Health and Social Behavior, 31,* 103–122.

Maxfield, M., Pyszczynski, T., Kluck, B., Cox, C. R., Greenberg, J., Solomon, S., & Weise, D. (2007). Age-related differences in responses to thoughts of one's own death: Mortality salience and judgments of moral transgressions. *Psychology and Aging, 22,* 341–353.

Mayr, E. (1961). Cause and effect in biology. *Science, 134,* 1501–1506.

McCrae, R. R. (1984). Situational determinants of coping responses: Loss, threat, and challenge. *Journal of Personality and Social Psychology, 46,* 919–928.

McCrae, R. R., & Costa, P. T., Jr. (1997). Personality trait structure as a human universal. *American Psychologist, 52,* 509–516.

McCullough, M. E., & Carter, E. C. (2013). Religion, self-control, and self-regulation: How and why are they related? In K. Pargament (Ed.), *APA handbook of psychology, religion, and spirituality: Vol. 1. Context, theory, and research* (pp. 123–138). Washington, DC: American Psychological Association.

McCullough, M. E., Hoyt, W. T., Larson, D. B., Koenig, H. G., & Thoresen, C. (2000). Religious involvement and mortality: A meta-analytic review. *Health Psychology, 19,* 211–222.

McCullough, M. E., & Willoughby, B. L. (2009). Religion, self-regulation, and self-control: Associations, explanations, and implications. *Psychological Bulletin, 135,* 69–94.

McDargh, J. (1983). *Object relations theory and the psychology of religion.* Lanham, MD: University Press of America.

McDonald, A., Beck, R., Allison, S., & Norsworthy, L. (2005). Attachment to God and Parents: Testing the Correspondence vs. Compensation Hypotheses. *Journal of Psychology and Christianity, 24,* 21–28.

McIntosh, D. N. (1995). Religion-as-schema, with implications for the relation between religion and coping. *International Journal for the Psychology of Religion, 5,* 1–16.

McNamara, P. (2009). *The neuroscience of religious experience.* New York: Cambridge University Press.

Meins, E., Fernyhough, C., Fradley, E., & Tuckey, M. (2001). Rethinking maternal sensitivity: Mothers' comments on infants' mental processes predict security of attachment at 12 months. *Journal of Child Psychology and Psychiatry and Allied Disciplines, 42,* 637–648.

Meissner, W. W. (1984). *Psychoanalysis and religious experience.* New Haven, CT: Yale University Press.

Mikulincer, M., & Florian, V. (2000). Exploring individual differences in reactions to mortality salience: Does attachment style regulate terror management mechanisms? *Journal of Personality and Social Psychology, 79,* 260–273.

Mikulincer, M., Hirschberger, G., Nachmias, O., & Gillath, O. (2001). The affective component of the secure base schema: Affective priming with representations of attachment security. *Journal of Personality and Social Psychology, 81,* 305–321.

Mikulincer, M., & Shaver, P. R. (2004). Security-based self-representations in adulthood: Contents and processes. In W. S. Rholes & J. A. Simpson (Eds.), *Adult attachment: Theory, research, and clinical implications* (pp. 159–195). New York: Guilford Press.

Mikulincer, M., & Shaver, P. R. (2013). Attachment orientations and meaning in life. In J. A. Hicks & C. Routledge (Eds.), *The experience of meaning in life: Classical perspectives, emerging themes, and controversies* (pp. 287–304). Dordrecht, the Netherlands: Springer.

Mikulincer, M., & Shaver, P. R. (2016). *Attachment in adulthood: Structure, dynamics, and change* (2nd ed.). New York: Guilford Press.

Mill, J. S. (1966). On liberty. In J. M. Robson (Ed.), *A selection of his works* (pp. 1–147). London: Palgrave. (Original work published 1859)

Miller, G. A., Galanter, E., & Pribram, K. H. (1960). *Plans and the structure of behavior.* New York: Holt, Rinehart & Winston.

Miller, L. (2015). *The spiritual child: The new science on parenting for health and lifelong learning.* New York: Macmillan.

Miner, M. (2009). The impact of child–parent attachment, attachment to God and religious orientation on psychological adjustment. *Journal of Psychology and Theology, 37,* 114–124.

Miner, M., Dowson, M., & Malone, K. (2014). Attachment to God, psychological need satisfaction, and psychological well-being among Christians. *Journal of Psychology and Theology, 42,* 326–342.

Miner, M., Ghobary, B., Dowson, M., & Proctor, M. T. (2014). Spiritual attachment in Islam and Christianity: Similarities and differences. *Mental Health, Religion and Culture, 17,* 79–93.

Mischel, W., Shoda, Y., & Rodriguez, M. I. (1989). Delay of gratification in children. *Science, 244,* 933–938.

Moore, R., Jensen, M., & Hatch, J. (2003). Twenty questions: What have the courts said about the teaching of evolution and creationism in public schools? *AIBS Bulletin, 53,* 766–771.

Mörck, R. C. (2011). *Do students and spiritualists differ regarding their health locus of control?* Master's thesis, Department of Psychology, University of Gothenburg, Gothenburg, Sweden.

Morgan, P. (2010). Towards a developmental theory of place attachment. *Journal of Environmental Psychology, 30,* 11–22.

Morris, B. (2006). *Religion and anthropology: A critical introduction.* Cambridge, MA: Cambridge University Press.

Murken, S., & Namini, S. (2007). Childhood familial experiences as antecedents of adult membership in New Religious Movements: A literature review. *Nova Religio, 10,* 17–37.

Nadon, R., & Kihlstrom, J. F. (1987). Hypnosis, psi, and the psychology of anomalous experience. *Behavioral and Brain Sciences, 10,* 597–599.

Nelson, E. A., & Dannefer, D. (1992). Aged heterogeneity: Fact or fiction?: The fate and diversity in gerontological research. *The Geronotologist, 32,* 17–23.

Nelson, M. O. (1971). The concept of God and feelings toward parents. *Journal of Individual Psychology, 27,* 46–49.

Nelson, M. O., & Jones, E. M. (1957). An application of the Q-technique to the study of religious concepts. *Psychological Reports, 3,* 293–297.

Newberg, A., D'Aquili, E., & Rause, V. (2002). *Why God won't go away: Brain science and the biology of belief.* New York: Ballantine Books.

Newberg, A., & Waldman, M. R. (2010). *How God changes your brain: Breakthrough findings from a leading neuroscientist.* New York: Ballantine Books.

Nickerson, R. S. (1998). Confirmation bias: A ubiquitous phenomenon in many guises. *Review of General Psychology, 2,* 175–220.

Nkara, F., Main, M., Hesse, E., & Granqvist, P. (2018). *Attachment to deities in light of attachment to parents: The Religious Attachment Interview.* Manuscript in preparation.

Noller, P. (1992). Religion conceptualized as an attachment process: Another deficiency approach to the psychology of religion? *International Journal for the Psychology of Religion, 2,* 29–36.

Norenzayan, A. (2013). *Big Gods: How religion transformed cooperation and conflict.* Princeton, NJ: Princeton University Press.

Norenzayan, A., Shariff, A. F., Gervais, W. M., Willard, A. K., McNamara, R. A., Slingerland, E., & Henrich, J. (2016). The cultural evolution of prosocial religions. *Behavioral and Brain Sciences, 39,* e1.

Norman, D. A. (1976). *Memory and attention.* New York: Wiley.

Norris, P., & Inglehart, R. (2011). *Sacred and secular: Religion and politics worldwide.* New York: Cambridge University Press.

O'Brien, M. E. (1982). *Journal of Religion and Health, 21*(1), 68–80.

Ogawa, J. R., Sroufe, L. A., Weinfield, N. S., Carlson, E., & Egeland, B. (1997). Development and the fragmented self: Longitudinal study of dissociative symptomatology in a nonclinical sample. *Development and Psychopathology, 9,* 855–879.

Öhman, A., & Mineka, S. (2001). Fears, phobias, and preparedness: Toward an evolved module of fear and fear learning. *Psychological Review, 108,* 483–522.

Oman, D. (2013). Spiritual modeling and the social learning of spirituality and religion. In K. Pargament (Ed.), *APA handbook of psychology, religion, and spirituality: Vol. 1. Context, theory, and research* (pp. 187–204). Washington, DC: American Psychological Association.

Open Science Collaboration. (2015). Estimating the reproducibility of psychological science. *Science, 349,* aac4716.

Organisation for Economic Co-operation and Development. (2016). Enrollment in childcare and pre-school. Retrieved May 31, 2018, from *www.oecd.org/els/soc/PF3_2_Enrolment_childcare_preschool.pdf.*

Oser, F. K. (1991). The development of religious judgment. *New Directions for Child and Adolescent Development, 1991,* 5–25.

Otto, R. (1925). *The idea of the holy.* London: Oxford University Press.

Overall, N., Fletcher, G. J. O., & Friesen, M. (2003). Mapping the intimate relationship mind: Comparisons between three models of attachment representations. *Personality and Social Psychology Bulletin, 29,* 1479–1493.

Overton, W. F. (2013). A new paradigm for developmental science: Relationism and relational-developmental systems. *Applied Developmental Science, 17,* 94–107.

Ozorak, E. W. (1989). Social and cognitive influences on the development of religious beliefs and commitment in adolescence. *Journal for the Scientific Study of Religion, 28,* 448–463.

Padrón, E., Carlson, E. A., & Sroufe, L. A. (2014). Frightened versus not frightened disorganized infant attachment. *American Journal of Orthopsychiatry, 84,* 201–208.

Palkovitz, R., & Palm, G. (1998). Fatherhood and faith in formation: The developmental effects of fathering on religiosity, morals, and values. *Journal of Men's Studies, 7,* 33–51.

Paloutzian, R. F. (2017). *Invitation to the psychology of religion* (3rd ed.). New York: Guilford Press.

Paloutzian, R. F., & Kirkpatrick, L. A. (Eds.). (1995). Religious influences on personal and societal well-being [Special issue]. *Journal of Social Issues, 51*(2).

Paloutzian, R. F., & Park, C. (Eds.). (2013). *Handbook of the psychology of religion and spirituality* (2nd ed.). New York: Guilford Press.

Pargament, K. (1997). *The psychology of religion and coping.* New York: Guilford Press.

Pargament, K. I. (1999). The psychology of religion and spirituality?: Yes and no. *International Journal for the Psychology of Religion, 9*(1), 3–16.

Pargament, K. (2002). The bitter and the sweet: An evaluation of the costs and benefits of religiousness. *Psychological Inquiry, 13,* 168–181.

Pargament, K. (Ed.) (2013). *APA handbook for the psychology of religion and spirituality* (Vols. 1–2). Washington DC: American Psychological Association.

Pargament, K., Feuille, M., & Burdzy, D. (2011). The Brief RCOPE: Current psychometric status of a short measure of religious coping. *Religions, 2,* 51–76.

Pargament, K. I., Smith, B. W., Koenig, H. G., & Perez, L. (1998). Patterns of positive and negative religious coping with major life stressors. *Journal for the Scientific Study of Religion, 37,* 710–724.

Park, C. L., Edmondson, D., & Hale-Smith, A. (2013). Why religion?: Meaning as motivation. In K. I. Pargament (Ed.-in-Chief), *APA handbook of psychology, religion, and spirituality: Vol. 1. Context, theory, and research* (pp. 157–172). Washington, DC: American Psychological Association.

Park, C. L., & George, L. S. (2018). Lab- and field-based approaches to meaning threats and restoration: Convergences and divergences. *Review of General Psychology, 22,* 73.

Park, C. L., & Slattery, J. M. (2013). Religion, spirituality, and mental health. In R. F. Paloutzian & C. L. Park (Eds.), *Handbook of the psychology of religion and spirituality* (pp. 540–559). New York: Guilford Press.

Parkes, C. M. (1972). *Bereavement: Studies of grief in adult life.* New York: International Universities Press.

Pekala, R. J., Wenger, C. F., & Levine, R. L. (1985). Individual differences in phenomenological experience: States of consciousness as a function of absorption. *Journal of Personality and Social Psychology, 48,* 125–132.

Persinger, M. A. (1987). *Neuropsychological bases of God beliefs.* New York: Praeger.

Persinger, M. A. (2002). Experimental simulation of the God experience: Implications for religious beliefs and the future of the human species. In R. Joseph (Ed.), *Neurotheology* (pp. 267–284). San Jose, CA: University Press.

Persinger, M. A., & Koren, S. A. (2005). Letter to the editor. *Neuroscience Letters, 380,* 346–347.

Persinger, M. A., & Murphy, T. R. (2016). Validating new technologies to treat depression, pain and the feeling of sentient beings: A reply to "Neuroscience for the Soul." *Neuroscience and Medicine, 7,* 27–44.

Petersson, O. (2012). Maktutredningen och statsindividualismen. Retrieved May 30, 2018, from *www.olofpetersson.se/_arkiv/skrifter/timbro120925.pdf.*

Pew Research Center. (2015). U.S. public becoming less religious. Retrieved April 30, 2018, from *www.pewforum.org/2015/11/03/u-s-public-becoming-less-religious.*

Pew Research Center. (2018). U.S. trails most developed countries in voter turnout. Retrieved May 30, 2018, from *www.pewresearch.org/fact-tank/2018/05/21/u-s-voter-turnout-trails-most-developed-countries.*

Piaget, J. (1930). *The child's conception of the world.* New York: Harcourt, Brace, & World. (Original work published 1926)

Piaget, J. (2013). *The construction of reality in the child* (Vol. 82). New York: Routledge. (Original work published 1954)

Piedmont, R. L. (1999). Does spirituality represent the sixth factor of personality?: Spiritual transcendence and the five-factor model. *Journal of Personality, 67,* 985–1013.

Pieper, S., Out, D., Bakermans-Kranenburg, M. J., & van IJzendoorn, M. H. (2011). Behavioral and molecular genetics of dissociation: The role of the serotonin transporter gene promoter polymorphism (5-HTTLPR). *Journal of Traumatic Stress, 24*(4), 373–380.

Piketty, T. (2013). *Capital in the 21st century.* Cambridge, MA: Harvard University Press.

Pinker, S. (2003). *The blank slate: The modern denial of human nature.* New York: Penguin.

Pirutinsky, S. (2009). Conversion and attachment insecurity among Orthodox Jews. *International Journal for the Psychology of Religion, 19,* 200–206.

Pirutinsky, S., Rosmarin, D. H., & Kirkpatrick, L. A. (2019). Is attachment to God a unique predictor of mental health?: Test in a Jewish sample. *International Journal for the Psychology of Religion, 29*(3), 1–11.

Pollard, S. E., Riggs, S. A., & Hook, J. N. (2014). Mutual influences in adult romantic attachment, religious coping, and marital adjustment. *Journal of Family Psychology, 28,* 615–624.

Poloma, M. M., & Gallup, G. H., Jr. (1991). *Varieties of prayer: A survey report.* Philadelphia: Trinity Press International.

Popper, K. (2014). *Conjectures and refutations: The growth of scientific knowledge.* New York: Basic Books. (Original work published 1962)

Proctor, M. T., McLean, L., Miner, M., Dowson, M., & Devenish, S. (2012). Exploring the psycho-spiritual construct "Attachment to God": The contribution of Australian researchers. *Critical Issues,* pp. 157–167.

Proudfoot, W., & Shaver, P. (1975). Attribution theory and the psychology of religion. *Journal for the Scientific Study of Religion, 14,* 317–330.

Proulx, T. (2013). Beyond mortality and the self: Meaning makes a comeback. In K. D. Markman, T. Proulx , & M. J. Lindberg (Eds.), *The psychology of meaning.* Washington, DC: American Psychological Association.

Proulx, T., & Inzlicht, M. (2012). The five "A"s of meaning maintenance: Finding meaning in the theories of sense-making. *Psychological Inquiry, 23,* 317–335.

Proulx, T., Markman, K. D., & Lindberg, M. J. (2013). Introduction: The new science of meaning. In K. D. Markman, T. Proulx, & M. J. Lindberg (Eds.), *The psychology of meaning.* Washington, DC: American Psychological Association.

Pruyser, P. W. (1968). *A dynamic psychology of religion.* New York: Harper & Row.

Pyysiäinen, I., & Hauser, M. (2010). The origins of religion: Evolved adaptation or by-product? *Trends in Cognitive Sciences, 14,* 104–109.

Ramachandran, V. S., Blakeslee, S., & Shah, N. (1998). *Phantoms in the brain: Probing the mysteries of the human mind.* New York: William Morrow.

Rawls, J. (2009). *A theory of justice: Revised edition.* Cambridge, MA: Harvard University Press. (Original work published 1971)

Reed, B. (1978). *The dynamics of religion: Process and movement in Christian churches.* London: Darton, Longman & Todd.

Reiner, S. R., Anderson, T. L., Hall, M. E. L., & Hall, T. W. (2010). Adult attachment, God attachment and gender in relation to perceived stress. *Journal of Psychology and Theology, 38,* 175–185.

Reinert, D. F., & Edwards, C. E. (2009). Attachment theory, childhood mistreatment, and religiosity. *Psychology of Religion and Spirituality, 1,* 25–34.

Reinert, D. F., & Smith, C. E. (1997). Childhood sexual abuse and female spiritual development. *Counseling and Values, 41,* 235–245.

Reisz, S., Duschinsky, R., & Siegel, D. J. (2018). Disorganized attachment and defense: Exploring John Bowlby's unpublished reflections. *Attachment and Human Development, 20,* 107–134.

Reizer, A., Dahan, D., & Shaver, P. R. (2013). The contributions of attachment and caregiving orientations to living a meaningful life. *Psychology, 4,* 1039–1045.

Rice, T. W. (2003). Believe it or not: Religious and other paranormal beliefs in the United States. *Journal for the Scientific Study of Religion, 42,* 95–106.

Richerson, P. J., & Boyd, R. (2005). *Not by genes alone: How culture transformed human evolution.* Chicago: Chicago University Press.

Richert, R., & Granqvist, P. (2013). Religious and spiritual development in childhood. In R. F. Paloutzian & C. Park (Eds.), *Handbook of the psychology of religion and spirituality* (2nd ed., pp. 165–182). New York: Guilford Press.

Richert, R. A., & Harris, P. L. (2006). The ghost in my body: Children's developing concept of the soul. *Journal of Cognition and Culture, 6,* 409–427.

Richert, R. A., Saide, A. R., Lesage, K. A., & Shaman, N. J. (2017). The role of religious context in children's differentiation between God's mind and human minds. *British Journal of Developmental Psychology, 35,* 37–59.

Richert, R. A., & Smith, E. I. (2010). The role of religious concepts in the evolution of human cognition. In U. Frey (Ed.), *The nature of God: Evolution and religion* (pp. 93–110). Antwerp, Belgium: Tectum.

Richters, J. E., & Waters, E. (1991). Attachment and socialization: The positive side of social influence. In M. Lewis & S. Feinman (Eds.), *Genesis of behavior: Vol. 6. Social influences and socialization in infancy* (pp. 185–213). New York: Plenum Press.

Ring, K., & Rosing, C. J. (1990). The Omega Project: An empirical study of the NDE-prone personality. *Journal of Near-Death Studies, 8,* 211–239.

Rizzuto, A. M. (1979). *The birth of the living God: A psychoanalytical study.* Chicago: University of Chicago Press.

Rizzuto, A. M. (1991). Religious development: A psychoanalytic view. In F. K. Oser & W. G. Scarlett (Eds.), *Religious development in childhood and adolescence* (pp. 47–60). San Francisco: Jossey-Bass.

Rizzuto, A. M. (2006). Discussion of Granqvist's article "On the relation between secular and divine relationships: An emerging attachment perspective and a critique of the 'depth' approaches." *International Journal for the Psychology of Religion, 16,* 19–28.

Robertson, J. (Ed.). (1963). *Hospitals and children: A parent's eye view: A review of letters from parents to the observer and the BBC.* New York: International Universities Press.

Rochat, P., & Hespos, S. J. (1997). Differential rooting responses by neonates: Evidence for an early sense of self. *Early Development and Parenting, 6,* 105–112.

Roche, S. M., & McConkey, K. M. (1990). Absorption: Nature, assessment, and correlates. *Journal of Personality and Social Psychology, 59,* 91–101.

Rogers, P., & Lowrie, E. (2016). Varieties of childhood maltreatment as predictors of adult paranormality and New Age Orientation. *Personality and individual differences, 92,* 37–45.

Rohner, R. P. (1986). *The warmth dimension: Foundations of parental acceptance-rejection theory.* Newbury Park, CA: SAGE.

Roisman, G. I., & Fraley, R. C. (2008). A behavior-genetic study of parenting quality, infant attachment security, and their covariation in a nationally representative sample. *Developmental Psychology, 44,* 831–839.

Roisman, G. I., Holland, A., Fortuna, K., Fraley, R. C., Clausell, E., & Clarke, A. (2007). The Adult Attachment Interview and self-reports of attachment style: An empirical rapprochement. *Journal of Personality and Social Psychology, 92,* 678–697.

Roisman, G., Sroufe, L. A., Madsen, S., & Collins, W. A. (2001). The coherence of dyadic behavior across parent–child and romantic relationships as mediated by the internalized representation of experience. *Attachment and Human Development, 3,* 156–172.

Rokach, A., & Brock, H. (1998). Coping with loneliness. *Journal of Psychology, 132,* 107–127.

Roof, W. C., & McKinney, W. (1987). *American mainline religion: Its changing shape and future.* New Brunswick, NJ: Rutgers University Press.

Rosch, E. (1987). Wittgenstein and categorization research in cognitive psychology. In M. Chapman & R. A. Dixon (Eds.), *Meaning and the growth of understanding* (pp. 151–166). Berlin: Springer.

Rosch, E. (1988). Principles of categorization. In A. Collins & E. E. Smith (Eds.), *Readings in cognitive science: A perspecitve from psychology and artificial intelligence* (pp. 312–322). San Francisco: Morgan Kaufmann.

Rosch, E., & Mervis, C. B. (1975). Family resemblances: Studies in the internal structure of categories. *Cognitive Psychology, 7,* 573–605.

Rose, N. (1998). *Inventing our selves: Psychology, power, and personhood.* New York: Cambridge University Press.

Rosenzweig, A., Prigerson, H., Miller, M. D., & Reynolds, C. F. (1997). Bereavement and late-life depression: Grief and its complications in the elderly. *Annual Review of Medicine, 48,* 421–428.

Rothbart, M. K. (2007). Temperament, development, and personality. *Current Directions in Psychological Science, 16,* 207–212.

Rothstein, B. (1998). *Just institutions matter: The moral and political logic of the universal welfare state.* New York: Cambridge University Press.

Rothstein, B., & Uslaner, E. M. (2005). All for all: Equality, corruption, and social trust. *World Politics, 58,* 41–72.

Rowatt, W. C., & Kirkpatrick, L. A. (2002). Two dimensions of attachment to God and their relation to affect, religiosity, and personality constructs. *Journal for the Scientific Study of Religion, 41,* 637–651.

Runcis, M. (1998). Sterilisation in the Swedish welfare state: A gender issue? In B. M. Felder & P. J. Weindling (Eds.), *Baltic eugenics: Bio-politics, race and nation in interwar Estonia, Latvia, and Lithuania, 1918–1940* (pp. 76–85). Leiden, the Netherlands: Brill.

Runcis, M. (2007). *Makten över barnen: Tvångsomhändertagande av barn i Sverige 1928–1968* [Power over the children: Forced removal of children in Sweden 1928–1968]. Stockholm, Sweden: Atlas.

Sagi-Schwartz, A., van IJzendoorn, M. H., Grossmann, K. E., Joels, T., Grossmann, K., Scharf, M., . . . Alkalay, S. (2003). Attachment and traumatic stress in female Holocaust child survivors and their daughters. *American Journal of Psychiatry, 160,* 1086–1092.

Sagi-Schwartz, A., van IJzendoorn, M. H., Joels, T., & Scharf, M. (2002). Disorganized reasoning in Holocaust survivors. *American Journal of Orthopsychiatry, 72,* 194–203.

Salsman, J. M., Pustejovsky, J. E., Jim, H. S., Munoz, A. R., Merluzzi, T. V., George, L., . . . Fitchett, G. (2015). A meta-analytic approach to examining the correlation between religion/spirituality and mental health in cancer. *Cancer, 121,* 3769–3778.

Sameroff, A. (2010). A unified theory of development: A dialectic integration of nature and nurture. *Child Development, 81,* 6–22.

Sar, V., Alioğlu, F., & Akyüz, G. (2014). Experiences of possession and paranormal phenomena among women in the general population: Are they related to traumatic stress and dissociation? *Journal of Trauma and Dissociation, 15*(3), 303–318.

Saroglou, V. (2002). Religion and the five factors of personality: A meta-analytic review. *Personality and Individual Differences, 32,* 15–25.

Saroglou, V. (2010). Religiousness as a cultural adaptation of basic traits: A five-factor model perspective. *Personality and Social Psychology Review, 14,* 108–125.

Saroglou, V. (2012). Adolescents' social development and the role of religion: Coherence at the detriment of openness. In G. Trommsdorff & X. Chen (Eds.), *Values, religion, and culture in adolescent development* (pp. 391–423). New York: Cambridge University Press.

Saroglou, V., Delpierre, V., & Dernelle, R. (2004). Values and religiosity: A meta-analysis of studies using Schwartz's model. *Personality and Individual Differences, 37,* 721–734.

Saroglou, V., Kempeneers, A., & Seynhaeve, I. (2003). Need for closure and adult attachment: Dimensions as predictors of religion and reading interests. In P. Roelofsma, J. Corveleyn, & J. van Saane (Eds.), *One hundred years of psychology and religion* (pp. 139–154). Amsterdam, the Netherlands: VU University Press.

Saroglou, V., Pichon, I., Trompette, L., Verschueren, M., & Dernelle, R. (2005). Prosocial behavior and religion: New evidence based on projective measures and peer ratings. *Journal for the Scientific Study of Religion, 44,* 323–348.

Sartre, J. P. (1989). *No exit.* New York: Vintage International. (Original work published 1944)

Saudi Arabia, "The Basic Law of Governance" (1992). Retrieved May 15, 2018, from *www.saudiembassy.net/about/countryinformation/laws/The_Basic_Law_of_Governance.aspx.*

Schaffler, Y., Cardena, E., Reijman, S., & Haluza, D. (2016). Traumatic experience andsomatoform dissociation among spirit possession practitioners in the Dominican Republic. *Culture, Medicine, and Psychiatry, 40,* 74–99.

Scheve, K., & Stasavage, D. (2006). Religion and preferences for social insurance. *Quarterly Journal of Political Science, 1,* 255–286.

Schindler, A., Thomasius, R., Petersen, K., & Sack, P. M. (2009). Heroin as an attachment substitute?: Differences in attachment representations between opioid, ecstasy and cannabis abusers. *Attachment and Human Development, 11,* 307–330.

Schjoedt, U., Stødkilde-Jørgensen, H., Geertz, A. W., & Roepstorff, A. (2009). Highly religious participants recruit areas of social cognition in personal prayer. *Social Cognitive and Affective Neuroscience, 4,* 199–207.

Schleidt, W. M. (1974). How "fixed" is the fixed action pattern? *Ethology, 36*(1–5), 184–211.

Schmid, Y., & Liechti, M. E. (2018). Long-lasting subjective effects of LSD in normal subjects. *Psychopharmacology, 235,* 535–545.

Schnitker, S. A., Porter, T. J., Emmons, R. A., & Barrett, J. L. (2012). Attachment predicts adolescent conversions at Young Life religious summer camps. *International Journal for the Psychology of Religion, 22,* 216–230.

Schottenbauer, M. A., Klimes-Dougan, B., Rodriguez, B. F., Arnkoff, D. B., Glass,

C. R., & LaSalle, V. H. (2006). Attachment and affective resolution following a stressful event: General and religious coping as possible mediators. *Mental Health, Religion and Culture, 9,* 448–471.

Schück, J. (2018, May 30). Finansministern: Barnfattigdom skäl för stramare flyktingpolitik [The finance minister: Child poverty reason for more restrictive refugee politics]. *Dagens Nyheter.* Retrieved October 2, 2019, from *www.dn.se/ekonomi/finansministern-barnfattigdom-skal-for-stramare-flyktingpolitik.*

Schuster, M. A., Stein, B. D., Jaycox, L. H., Collins, R. L., Marshall, G. N., Elliott, M. N., . . . Berry, S. H. (2001). A national survey of stress reactions after the September 11, 2001, terrorist attacks. *New England Journal of Medicine, 345,* 1507–1512.

Sears, R. R., Maccoby, E. E., & Levin, H. (1976). *Patterns of child rearing.* Palo Alto, CA: Stanford University Press. (Original work published 1957)

Sedikides, C., & Gebauer, J. E. (2010). Religiosity as self-enhancement: A meta-analysis of the relation between socially desirable responding and religiosity. *Personality and Social Psychology Review, 14,* 17–36.

Seligman, M. E. (1971). Phobias and preparedness. *Behavior Therapy, 2,* 307–320.

Serre, D., & Pääbo, S. (2004). Evidence for gradients of human genetic diversity within andamong continents. *Genome Research, 14,* 1679–1685.

Shariff, A. F., & Norenzayan, A. (2007). God is watching you: Priming God concepts increases prosocial behavior in an anonymous economic game. *Psychological Science, 18,* 803–809.

Shariff, A. F., Willard, A. K., Andersen, T., & Norenzayan, A. (2015). Religious priming: A meta-analysis with a focus on prosociality. *Personality and Social Psychology Review, 20,* 27–48.

Shaver, P. R., Belsky, J. A. Y., & Brennan, K. A. (2000). The Adult Attachment Interview and self-reports of romantic attachment: Associations across domains and methods. *Personal Relationships, 7,* 25–43.

Shaver, P. R., Hazan, C., & Bradshaw, D. (1988). The integration of three behavioral systems. In R. J. Sternberg & M. L. Barnes (Eds.), *The psychology of love* (pp. 68–99). Binghamton, NY: Vail-Ballou Press.

Shaver, P. R., Murdaya, U., & Fraley, R. C. (2001). Structure of the Indonesian emotion lexicon. *Asian Journal of Social Psychology, 4,* 201–224.

Shaver, P., Schwartz, J., Kirson, D., & O'Connor, C. (1987). Emotion knowledge: Further exploration of a prototype approach. *Journal of Personality and Social Psychology, 52,* 1061–1086.

Shedler, J., & Block, J. (1990). Adolescent drug use and psychological health: A longitudinal inquiry. *American Psychologist, 45,* 612–630.

Shtulman, A. (2008). Variation in the anthropomorphization of supernatural beings and its implications for cognitive theories of religion. *Journal of Experimental Psychology: Learning, Memory, and Cognition, 34,* 1123–1138.

Sibley, C. G., & Bulbulia, J. (2012). Faith after an earthquake: A longitudinal study of religion and perceived health before and after the 2011 Christchurch New Zealand earthquake. *PLOS ONE, 7*(12), e49648.

Siegel, D. J. (1999). *The developing mind.* New York: Guilford Press.

Silverman, G. S., Johnson, K. A., & Cohen, A. B. (2016). To believe or not to believe, that is not the question: The complexity of Jewish beliefs about God. *Psychology of Religion and Spirituality, 8*(2), 119.

Sim, T. N., & Loh, B. S. M. (2003). Attachment to God: Measurement and dynamics. *Journal of Social and Personal Relationships, 20,* 373–389.

Sim, T. N., & Yow, A. S. (2011). God attachment, mother attachment, and father attachment in early and middle adolescence. *Journal of Religion and Health, 50*(2), 264–278.

Simpson, J. A., & Belsky, J. (2016). Attachment theory within a modern evolutionary framework. In J. Cassidy & P. R. Shaver, *Handbook of attachment: Theory, research, and clinical applications* (3rd ed., pp. 91–116). New York: Guilford Press.

Singer, M. T., & Nievod, A. (2003). New age therapies. In S. O. Lilienfeld, S. J. Lynn, & J. M. Lohr (Eds.), *Science and pseudoscience in clinical psychology* (pp. 176–204). New York: Guilford Press.

Singer, P. (1975). *Animal liberation: A new ethic for our treatment of animals.* New York: New York Review.

Slife, B. D., & Reber, J. S. (2009). Is there a pervasive implicit bias against theism inpsychology? *Journal of Theoretical and Philosophical Psychology, 29,* 63–79.

Smetana, J. G. (2002). Culture, autonomy, and personal jurisdiction in adolescent–parent relationships. In R. V. Kail & H. W. Reese (Eds.), *Advances in child development and behavior* (Vol. 29, pp. 51–87). San Diego, CA: Academic Press.

Smith, C., & Denton, M. L. (2009). *Soul searching: The religious and spiritual lives of American teenagers.* New York: Oxford University Press,

Smith, E. I., & Richert, R. A. (2011, April). *The creation of belief: Chinese children's use of evolution to explain the origin of species.* Poster presented at the biennial meeting of the Society for Research in Child Development, Montreal, ON, Canada.

Smith, T. B., McCullough, M. E., & Poll, J. (2003). Religiousness and depression: Evidence for a main-effect and the moderating influence of stressful life-events. *Psychological Bulletin, 129,* 614–636.

Soenke, M., Landau, M. J., & Greenberg, J. (2013). Sacred armor: Religion's role as a buffer against the anxieties of life and the fear of death. In K. I. Pargament (Ed.-in-Chief), *APA handbook of psychology, religion, and spirituality: Vol. 1. Context, theory, and research* (pp. 105–122). Washington, DC: American Psychological Association.

Sokal, A. D., & Bricmont, J. (1998). *Intellectual impostures: postmodern philosophers' abuse of science* (pp. xiii–xiii). London: Profile Books.

Solomon, J., & George, C. (2016). The measurement of attachment security and related constructs in infancy and early childhood. In J. Cassidy & P. R. Shaver (Eds.), *Handbook of attachment: Theory, research, and clinical applications* (3rd ed., pp. 366–396). New York: Guilford Press.

Sorce, J. F., Emde, R. N., Campos, J. J., & Klinnert, M. D. (1985). Maternal emotional signaling: Its effect on the visual cliff behavior of 1-year-olds. *Developmental Psychology, 21,* 195–200.

Spangler, G., Johann, M., Ronai, Z., & Zimmermann, P. (2009). Genetic and environmental influence on attachment disorganization. *Journal of Child Psychology and Psychiatry, 50,* 952–961.

Spanos, N. P., & Moretti, P. (1988). Correlates of mystical and diabolical experiences in a sample of female university students. *Journal for the Scientific Study of Religion, 27,* 106–116.

Spilka, B., Armatas, P., & Nussbaum, J. (1964). The concept of God: A factor-analytic approach. *Review of Religious Research, 6,* 28–36.

Spilka, B., Hood, R. W., Jr., Hunsberger, B., & Gorsuch, R. (2003). *The psychology of religion: An empirical approach* (3rd ed.). New York: Guilford Press.

Spilka, B., & Ladd, K. L. (2012). *The psychology of prayer: A scientific approach.* New York: Guilford Press.

Spilka, B., Shaver, P., & Kirkpatrick, L. A. (1985). A general attribution theory for the psychology of religion. *Journal for the Scientific Study of Religion, 24,* 1–20.

Sroufe, L. A., Carlson, E., & Shulman, S. (1993). Individuals in relationships: Development from infancy through adolescence. In D. C. Funder, R. D. Parke, C. Tomlinson-Keasey, & K. Widaman (Eds.), *Studying lives through time: Personality and development* (pp. 315–342). Washington, DC: American Psychological Association.

Sroufe, L. A., & Waters, E. (1977a). Attachment as an organizational construct. *Child Development, 48,* 1184–1199.

Sroufe, L. A., & Waters, E. (1977b). Heart rate as a convergent measure in clinical and developmental research. *Merrill–Palmer Quarterly of Behavior and Development, 23,* 3–27.

St. John of the Cross. (1990). *Dark night of the soul.* New York: Doubleday.

Stace, W. T. (1960). *Mysticism and philosophy.* Philadelphia: J. B. Lippincott.

Starbuck, E. D. (1899). *The psychology of religion.* New York: Scribner.

Statens Offentliga Utredningar. (2007). *Vem fuskar och varför?: Om attityder till bidragsfusk i Sverige [Who cheats and why?: On attitudes to welfare cheating in Sweden].* Stockholm: Author.

Stattin, H., & Kerr, M. (2000). Parental monitoring: A reinterpretation. *Child Development, 71,* 1072–1085.

Stavrova, O. (2015). Religion, self-rated health, and mortality: Whether religiosity delays death depends on the cultural context. *Social Psychological and Personality Science, 6,* 911–922.

Stayton, D. J., Hogan, R., & Ainsworth, M. D. S. (1971). Infant obedience and maternal behavior: The origins of socialization reconsidered. *Child Development, 42,* 1057–1069.

Steele, H., & Steele, M. (2005). *The construct of coherence as an indicator of attachment security in middle childhood: The friends and family interview.* Unpublished manuscript, New School, New York.

Steger, M. F. (2009). Meaning in life. In S. J. Lopez & C. R. Snyder (Eds.), *Oxford handbook of positive psychology* (pp. 679–687). New York: Oxford University Press.

Steger, M. F., Hicks, B. M., Krueger, R. F., & Bouchard, T. J. (2011). Genetic and environmental influences and covariance among meaning in life, religiousness, and spirituality. *Journal of Positive Psychology, 6,* 181–191.

Steinberg, L. (1990). Interdependency in the family: Autonomy, conflict, and harmony in the parent–adolescent relationship. In S. Feldman & G. Elliott (Eds.), *At the threshold: The developing adolescent* (pp. 225–276). Cambridge, MA: Harvard University Press.

Steinberg, L. D., & Morris, A. S. (2001). Adolescent development. *Annual Review of Psychology, 52,* 83–110.

Stenberg, G. (2003). Effects of maternal inattentiveness on infant social referencing. *Infant and Child Development, 12,* 399–419.

Stenmark, M. (2017). *Scientism: Science, ethics and religion.* New York: Routledge.

Stern, D. (1985). *The interpersonal world of the infant.* New York: Basic Books.

Sterner, T., Barbier, E. B., Bateman, I., van den Bijgaart, I., Crépin, A. S., Edenhofer, O., . . . Lange, A. (2019). Policy design for the Anthropocene. *Nature Sustainability, 2,* 14–21.

Stevenson, I. (2000). *Children who remember previous lives: A question of reincarnation* (rev. ed.). Jefferson, NC: McFarland.

Stewart-Williams, S., & Podd, J. (2004). The placebo effect: Dissolving the expectancy versus conditioning debate. *Psychological Bulletin, 130*, 324–340.

Stouffer, S. A. (1949). *The American soldier: Vol. 2. Combat and its aftermath.* Princeton, NJ: Princeton University Press.

Stovall, K. C., & Dozier, M. (2000). The development of attachment in new relationships: Single subject analyses for 10 foster infants. *Development and Psychopathology, 12*, 133–156.

Streib, H. (2001). Faith development theory revisited: The religious styles perspective. *International Journal for the Psychology of Religion, 11*, 143–158.

Streib, H., Silver, C. F., Csöff, R. M., Keller, B., & Hood, R. W. (2011). *Deconversion: Qualitative and quantitative results from cross-cultural research in Germany and the United States of America* (Vol. 5). Göttingen, Germany: Vandenhoeck & Ruprecht.

Strickland, F. L. (1924). *Psychology of religious experience: Studies in the psychological interpretation of religious faith.* Nashville, TN: Abingdon Press.

Strunk, O. (1959). Perceived relationships between parental and deity concepts. *Psychological Newsletter, 10*, 222–226.

Suomi, S. J. (1995). The influence of attachment theory on ethological studies of biobehavioral development in nonhuman primates. In S. Goldberg, R. Muir, & J. Kerr (Eds.), *Attachment theory: Social, developmental and clinical perspectives* (pp. 185–202). Hillsdale, NJ: Routledge.

Suomi, S. J. (2008). Attachment in rhesus monkeys. In J. Cassidy & P. R. Shaver (Eds.), *Handbook of attachment: Theory, research, and clinical applications.* (2nd ed., pp. 173–191). New York: Guilford Press.

Svenska Freds. (2019). Snabba fakta om fapenexport [Quick facts about arms exports]. Retrieved October 2, 2019, from *www.svenskafreds.se/vad-vi-gor/vapenexport/snabba-fakta-om-vapenexport.*

Svensson, P. (2008). *Frihet, jämlikhet, reformation!: 500 år med Luther [Freedom, equality, reformation!: 500 years with Luther].* Stockholm: Weylers förlag.

Swami, V., Pietschnig, J., Tran, U. S., Nader, I. N. G. O., Stieger, S., & Voracek, M. (2013). Lunar lies: The impact of informational framing and individual differences in shaping conspiracist beliefs about the moon landings. *Applied Cognitive Psychology, 27*, 71–80.

Swami, V., Stieger, S., Pietschnig, J., Nader, I. W., & Voracek, M. (2012). Using more than 10% of our brains: Examining belief in science-related myths from an individual differences perspective. *Learning and Individual Differences, 22*, 404–408.

Swami, V., Tran, U. S., Stieger, S., Pietschnig, J., Nader, I. W., & Voracek, M. (2016). Who believes in the giant skeleton myth?: An examination of individual difference correlates. *SAGE Open.* Retrieved October 10, 2019, from https://journals.sagepub.com/doi/full/10.1177/2158244015623592.

Szymanska, M., Schneider, M., Chateau-Smith, C., Nezelof, S., & Vulliez-Coady, L. (2017). Psychophysiological effects of oxytocin on parent–child interactions: A literature review on oxytocin and parent–child interactions. *Psychiatry and Clinical Neurosciences, 71*, 690–705.

Tamayo, A., & Desjardins, L. (1976). Belief systems and conceptual images of parents and God. *Journal of Psychology, 92*, 131–140.

Tamminen, K. (1994). Religious experiences in childhood and adolescence: A viewpoint of religious development between the ages of 7 and 20. *International Journal for the Psychology of Religion, 4*, 61–85.

Tandon, A., Murray, C. J., Lauer, J. A., & Evans, D. B. (2000). *Measuring overall health system performance for 191 countries.* Geneva, Switzerland: World Health Organization.

Target, M., Fonagy, P., & Shmueli-Goetz, Y. (2003). Attachment representations in school-age children: The development of the Child Attachment Interview (CAI). *Journal of Child Psychotherapy, 29,* 171–186.

Taylor, C. (2007). *A secular age.* Cambridge, MA: Harvard University Press.

Taylor, M. (2001). *Imaginary companions and the children who create them.* New York: Oxford University Press.

Tellegen, A., & Atkinson, G. (1974). Openness to absorbing and self-altering experiences ("absorption"), a trait related to hypnotic susceptibility. *Journal of Abnormal Psychology, 83,* 268–277.

TenElshof, J. K., & Furrow, J. L. (2000). The role of secure attachment in predicting spiritual maturity of students at a conservative seminary. *Journal of Psychology and Theology, 28,* 99–108.

Thauvoye, E., Granqvist, P., Golovchanova, N., & Dezutter, J. (2018). Attachment to God, depression and loss in late life: A longitudinal study. *Mental Health, Religion and Culture, 21,* 825–837.

Thomson, P., & Jaque, S. V. (2012). Dissociation and the Adult Attachment Interview in artists and performing artists. *Attachment and Human Development, 14,* 145–160.

Thomson, P., & Jaque, S. V. (2014). Unresolved mourning, supernatural beliefs, and dissociation: A mediation analysis. *Attachment and Human Development, 16,* 499–514.

Thouless, R. H. (1923). *An introduction to the psychology of religion.* New York: Macmillan.

Thurfjell, D. (2015). *Det gudlösa folket: De postkristna svenskarna och religionen [The godless people: The post Christian Swedes and religion].* Stockholm, Sweden: Molin & Sorgenfrei.

Tinbergen, N. (1951). *The study of instinct.* New York: Oxford University Press.

Tinbergen, N. (1963). On aims and methods of ethology. *Zeitschrift für Tierpsychologie, 20,* 410–433.

Tishkoff, S. A., Reed, F. A., Ranciaro, A., Voight, B. F., Babbitt, C. C., Silverman, J. S., . . . Ibrahim, M. (2007). Convergent adaptation of human lactase persistence in Africa and Europe. *Nature Genetics, 39,* 31–40.

Toburen, T., & Meier, B. P. (2010). Priming God-related concepts increases anxiety and task persistence. *Journal of Social and Clinical Psychology, 29,* 127–143.

Tomasello, M., Kruger, A. C., & Ratner, H. H. (1993). Cultural learning. *Behavioral and Brain Sciences, 16,* 495–552.

Tooby, J., & Cosmides, L. (1990). The past explains the present: Emotional adaptations and the structure of ancestral environments. *Ethology and Sociobiology, 11*(4–5), 375–424.

Tornstam, L. (1997). Gero-transcendence: A reformulation of disengagement theory. *Aging, 1,* 55–63.

Trier, K. K., & Shupe, A. (1991). Prayer, religiosity, and healing in the heartland, USA: A research note. *Review of Religious Research, 32,* 351–358.

Trivers, R. L. (1974). Parent–offspring conflict. *American Zoologist, 14,* 249–264.

Turner, J. H., Maryanski, A., Petersen, A. K., & Geertz, A. W. (2018). *The emergence and evolution of religion: By means of natural selection.* New York: Routledge.

Turner, S. (2003). The third science war. *Social Studies of Science, 33,* 581–611.

Twenge, J. M. (2000). The age of anxiety?: The birth cohort change in anxiety and neuroticism, 1952–1993. *Journal of Personality and Social Psychology, 79,* 1007–1021.

Twenge, J. M., Gentile, B., DeWall, C. N., Ma, D., Lacefield, K., & Schurtz, D. R. (2010). Birth cohort increases in psychopathology among young Americans, 1938–2007: A cross-temporal meta-analysis of the MMPI. *Clinical Psychology Review, 30,* 145–154.

Ullman, C. (1982). Change of mind, change of heart: Some cognitive and emotional antecedents of religious conversion. *Journal of Personality and Social Psychology, 42,* 183–192.

Ullman, C. (1989). *The transformed self.* Boston: Springer.

United Nations. (2016). Human development for everyone. Retrieved May 30, 2018, from *http://hdr.undp.org/sites/default/files/HDR2016_EN_Overview_Web.pdf.*

United Nations. (2018). World happiness report. Retrieved May 30, 2018, from *https://s3.amazonaws.com/happiness-report/2018/WHR_web.pdf.*

Vail, K. E., Rothschild, Z. K., Weise, D. R., Solomon, S., Pyszczynski, T., & Greenberg, J. (2010). A terror management analysis of the psychological functions of religion. *Personality and Social Psychology Review, 14,* 84–94.

Vaillant, G. E. (2002). *Aging well.* Boston: Little, Brown.

van Cappellen, P., & Saroglou, V. (2012). Awe activates religious and spiritual feelings and behavioral intentions. *Psychology of Religion and Spirituality, 4,* 223–236.

van Cappellen, P., Way, B. M., Isgett, S. F., & Fredrickson, B. L. (2016). Effects of oxytocin administration on spirituality and emotional responses to meditation. *Social and Affective Neuroscience, 11,* 1579–1587.

van der Horst, F. C., LeRoy, H. A., & van der Veer, R. (2008). "When strangers meet": John Bowlby and Harry Harlow on attachment behavior. *Integrative Psychological and Behavioral Science, 42,* 370–388.

van der Horst, F. C., van der Veer, R., & van IJzendoorn, M. H. (2007). John Bowlby and ethology: An annotated interview with Robert Hinde. *Attachment and Human Development, 9,* 321–335.

van Elk, M. (2014). An EEG study on the effects of induced spiritual experiences on somatosensory processing and sensory suppression. *Journal for the Cognitive Science of Religion, 2,* 97–133.

van Elk, M., & Aleman, A. (2017). Brain mechanisms in religion and spirituality: An integrative predictive processing framework. *Neuroscience and Biobehavioral Reviews, 73,* 359–378.

van IJzendoorn, M. H. (1995). Adult attachment representations, parental responsiveness, and infant attachment: A meta-analysis on the predictive validity of the Adult Attachment Interview. *Psychological Bulletin, 117,* 387–403.

van IJzendoorn, M. H., & Bakermans-Kranenburg, M. J. (2012). A sniff of trust: Meta-analysis of the effects of intranasal oxytocin on face recognition, trust to in-group, and trust to out-group. *Psychoneuroendocrinology, 37,* 438–443.

van IJzendoorn, M. H., Bard, K. A., Bakermans-Kranenburg, M. J., & Ivan, K. (2008). Enhancement of attachment and cognitive development of young nursery-reared chimpanzees in responsiveversus standard care. *Developmental Psychobiology, 51,* 173–185.

van IJzendoorn, M. H., Caspers, K., Bakermans-Kranenburg, M. J., Beach, S. R., & Philibert, R. (2010). Methylation matters: Interaction between methylation density and serotonin transporter genotype predicts unresolved loss or trauma. *Biological Psychiatry, 68,* 405–407.

van IJzendoorn, M. H., Dijkstra, J., & Bus, A. G. (1995). Attachment, intelligence, and language—A metaanalysis. *Social Development 4*, 115–128.

van IJzendoorn, M. H., Goossens, F. A., Tavecchio, L. W. C., Vergeer, M. M., & Hubbard, F. O. A. (1983). Attachment to soft objects: Its relationship with attachment to the mother and with thumbsucking. *Child Psychiatry and Human Development, 14*, 97–105.

van IJzendoorn, M. H., & Juffer, F. (2006). The Emanuel Miller Memorial Lecture 2006: Adoption as intervention: Meta-analytic evidence for massive catch-up and plasticity in physical, socio-emotional, and cognitive development. *Journal of Child Psychology and Psychiatry, 47*, 1228–1245.

van IJzendoorn, M. H., Schuengel, C., & Bakermans-Kranenburg, M. J. (1999). Disorganized attachment in early childhood: Meta-analysis of precursors, concomitants, and sequelae. *Development and Psychopathology, 11*, 225–250.

van IJzendoorn, M. H., Vereijken, C. M., Bakermans-Kranenburg, M. J., & Marianne Riksen-Walraven, J. (2004). Assessing attachment security with the attachment Q sort: Meta-analytic evidence for the validity of the observer AQS. *Child Development, 75*(4), 1188–1213.

Vergote, A., & Tamayo, A. (Eds.). (1981). *The parental figures and the representation of God*. The Hague, the Netherlands: Mouton.

Verhage, M. L., Schuengel, C., Madigan, S., Fearon, R. M., Oosterman, M., Cassibba, R., . . . van IJzendoorn, M. H. (2016). Narrowing the transmission gap: A synthesis of three decades of research on intergenerational transmission of attachment. *Psychological Bulletin, 142*, 337–366.

Vitell, S. J., Bing, M. N., Davison, H. K., Ammeter, A. P., Garner, B. L., & Novicevic, M. M. (2009). Religiosity and moral identity: The mediating role of self-control. *Journal of Business Ethics, 88*, 601–613.

Vohs, K. D., & Baumeister, R. F. (Eds.). (2011). *Handbook of self-regulation: Research, theory, and applications* (2nd ed.). New York: Guilford Press.

von Below, C. (2017). *When psychotherapy does not help: . . . . and when it does: Lessons from young adults' experiences of psychoanalytic psychotherapy.* Doctoral dissertation, Department of Psychology, Stockholm University, Stockholm, Sweden.

Vygotsky, L. S. (1978). *Mind in society: The development of higher psychological processes*. Cambridge, MA: Harvard University Press.

Waddington, C. H. (1942). Canalization of development and the inheritance of acquired characters. *Nature, 150*, 563–565.

Waddington, C. H. (1957). *The strategy of the genes*. London: George Allen & Unwin.

Wallace, J. M., Jr., & Forman, T. A. (1998). Religion's role in promoting health and reducing risk among American youth. *Health Education and Behavior, 25*, 721–741.

Waller, N. G., Putnam, F. W., & Carlson, E. B. (1996). Types of dissociation and dissociative types: A taxometric analysis of dissociative experiences. *Psychological Methods, 1*, 300–321.

Waller, N. G., & Ross, C. A. (1997). The prevalence and biometric structure of pathological dissociation in the general population: Taxometric and behavior genetic findings. *Journal of Abnormal Psychology, 106*, 499–510.

Wallerstein, R. S. (1986). Psychoanalysis as a science: A response to the new challenges. *Psychoanalytic Quarterly, 55*, 414–451.

Walter, S. (2013). *"Det var en plågsam stund, en stund af indre smärta": En psykobiografi över Lina Sandells sorgebearbetning mellan åren 1858–1861 ["It was a painful moment, a moment of inner pain": A psychobiography on Lina Sandell's mourning process during the years 1855–1866].* Skellefteå, Sweden: Artos & Norma bokförlag.

Waters, E., & Deane, K. E. (1985). Defining and assessing individual differences in attachment relationships: Q-methodology and the organization of behavior in infancy and early childhood. *Monographs of the Society for Research in Child Development, 50,* 41–65.

Waters, H. S., & Waters, E. (2006). The attachment working models concept: Among other things, we build script-like representations of secure base experiences. *Attachment and Human Development, 8,* 185–197.

Watts, F. (2013). Embodied cognition and religion. *Zygon, 48,* 745–758.

Waxler, C. Z., & Yarrow, M. R. (1975). An observational study of maternal models. *Developmental Psychology, 11,* 485–494.

Weinfield, N. S., Whaley, G. J., & Egeland, B. (2004). Continuity, discontinuity, and coherence in attachment from infancy to late adolescence: Sequelae of organization and disorganization. *Attachment and Human Development, 6,* 73–97.

Weise, D. R., Pyszczynski, T., Cox, C. R., Arndt, J., Greenberg, J., Solomon, S., & Kosloff, S. (2008). Interpersonal politics: The role of terror management and attachment processes in shaping political preferences. *Psychological Science, 19,* 448–455.

Weiss, R. S. (1973). *Loneliness: The experience of emotional and social isolation.* Cambridge, MA: MIT Press.

Weiss, R. S. (1982). Attachment in adult life. In C. M. Parkes & J. Stevenson-Hinde (Eds.), *The place of attachment in human behavior* (pp. 171–184). New York: Basic Books.

Wellman, H. M. (1985). The child's theory of mind: The development of conceptions of cognition. In S. R. Yussen (Ed.), *The growth of reflection* (pp. 169–206). Orlando, FL: Academic Press.

Wellman, H., Cross, D., & Watson, J. (2001). Meta-analysis of theory of mind development: The truth about false-belief. *Child Development, 72,* 655–684.

Wellman, H. M., & Gelman, S. A. (1992). Cognitive development: Foundational theories of core domains. *Annual Review of Psychology, 43,* 337–375.

Wenegrat, B. (1989). *The divine archetype: The socio-biology and psychology of religion.* Lexington, MA: Lexington Books.

Wennstam, K., & Sveland, M. (2011). *Happy, Happy: En bok om skilsmässa [Happy, happy: A book about divorce].* Stockholm, Sweden: Atlas.

Wheeler, S. C., & Petty, R. E. (2001). The effects of stereotype activation on behavior: A review of possible mechanisms. *Psychological Bulletin, 127,* 797–826.

Whitford, D. M. (2004). Cura religionis or Two Kingdoms: The late Luther on religion and the state in the lectures on genesis. *Church History, 73,* 41–62.

Wilkinson, R. G. (1997). Socioeconomic determinants of health: Health inequalities: Relative or absolute material standards? *British Medical Journal, 314,* 591–599.

Wilkinson, R., & Pickett, K. (2010). *The spirit level: Why more equal societies almost always do better.* London: Bloomsbury.

Wilson, D. S. (2002). *Darwin's cathedral: Evolution, religion, and the nature of society.* Chicago: University of Chicago Press.

Wilson, E. O. (1975). *Sociobiology: The new synthesis.* Cambridge, MA: Harvard University Press.

Wilson, M. (2002). Six views of embodied cognition. *Psychonomic Bulletin and Review, 9,* 625–636.

Winnicott, D. W. (1953). Transitional objects and transitional phenomena—A study of the first not-me possession. *International Journal of Psychoanalysis, 34,* 89–97.

Winnicott, D. W. (1971). *Playing and reality.* New York: Routledge.

Wittgenstein, L. (1999). *Philosophical investigations* (G. E. M. Anscombe, Trans.). New York: Macmillan. (Original work published 1953)

Woolley, J. D. (1997). Thinking about fantasy: Are children fundamentally different thinkers and believers from adults? *Child Development, 68,* 991–1011.

World Health Organization. (2018, April 9). Mental disorders. Retrieved May 6, 2019, from *www.who.int/news-room/fact-sheets/detail/mental-disorders.*

World Values Survey. (2019, September 10). Migrant voices: How migrants view Sweden and their subjective integration. Retrieved October 16, 2019, from *www.worldvaluessurvey.org/WVSEventsShow.jsp?ID=403.*

Wright, P. J. (2008). Prediciting reaction to a message of ministry: An audience analysis. *Journal for the Scientific Study of Religion, 47,* 63–81.

Wright, R. (1987). *Leaving cults: The dynamics of defection.* Washington, DC: Society for the Scientific Study of Religion.

Wulff, D. M. (1991). *Psychology of religion: Classic and contemporary views.* New York: Wiley.

Wulff, D. M. (2006). How attached should we be to attachment theory? *International Journal for the Psychology of Religion, 16,* 29–36.

Wulff, D. M. (2014). Mystical experiences. In E. Cardeña, S. J. Lynn, & S. Krippner (Eds.), *Varieties of anomalous experience: Examining the scientific evidence* (pp. 369–408). Washington, DC: American Psychological Association.

Yang, F., & Hu, A. (2012). Mapping Chinese folk religion in mainland China and Taiwan. *Journal for the Scientific Study of Religion, 51,* 505–521.

York, M. (2001). New Age commodification and appropriation of spirituality. *Journal of Contemporary Religion, 16,* 361–372.

Young, J. Z. (1964). *A model of the brain.* London: Oxford University Press.

Zahl, B. P., & Gibson, N. J. (2012). God representations, attachment to God, and satisfaction with life: A comparison of doctrinal and experiential representations of God in Christian young adults. *International Journal for the Psychology of Religion, 22,* 216–230.

Zammit, S., Allebeck, P., Andreasson, S., Lundberg, I., & Lewis, G. (2002). Self reported cannabis use as a risk factor for schizophrenia in Swedish conscripts of 1969: Historical cohort study. *British Medical Journal, 325,* 1199.

Zeanah, C. H., Smyke, A. T., Koga, S. F., & Carlson, E. (2005). Attachment in institutionalized and community children in Romania. *Child Development, 76,* 1015–1028.

Zeifman, D., & Hazan, C. (1997). Attachment: The bond in pair-bonds. In J. A. Simpson & D. T. Kenrick (Hrsg.), *Evolutionary social psychology* (pp. 237–263). Mahwah, NJ: Erlbaum.

Zeifman, D., & Hazan, C. (2016). Pair-bonds as attachments: Mounting evidence in support of Bowlby's hypothesis. In J. Cassidy & P. R. Shaver (Eds.), *Handbook of attachment: Theory, research, and clinical applications* (3rd ed., pp. 416–434). New York: Guilford Press.

Zelenko, M., Kraemer, H., Huffman, L., Gschwendt, M., Pageler, N., & Steiner, H. (2005). Heart rate correlates of attachment status in young mothers and their infants. *Journal of the American Academy of Child and Adolescent Psychiatry, 44,* 470–476.

Zhang, H., Chan, D. K., & Teng, F. (2011). Transfer of attachment functions and adjustment among young adults in China. *Journal of Social Psychology, 151,* 257–273.

Zilcha-Mano, S., Mikulincer, M., & Shaver, P. R. (2011). An attachment perspective on human–pet relationships: Conceptualization and assessment of pet attachment orientations. *Journal of Research in Personality, 45,* 345–357.

Zilcha-Mano, S., Mikulincer, M., & Shaver, P. R. (2012). Pets as safe havens and secure bases: The moderating role of pet attachment orientations. *Journal of Research in Personality, 46,* 571–580.

Zuckerman, M., Li, C., & Diener, E. (2018). Religion as an exchange system: The interchangeability of God and government in a provider role. *Personality and Social Psychology Bulletin, 44*(8), 1201–1213.

Zuckerman, P. (2009). Why are Danes and Swedes so irreligious. *Nordic Journal of Religion and Society, 22,* 55–69.

Zuckerman, P., & Shook, J. R. (Eds.). (2017). *The Oxford handbook of secularism.* New York: Oxford University Press.

Zwingmann, C., Wirtz, M., Müller, C., Körber, J., & Murken, S. (2006). Positive and negative religious coping in German breast cancer patients. *Journal of Behavioral Medicine, 29,* 533–547.

Index